small studios

PAGEONE

small studios

PAGE ONE

small studios

PAGE ONE

small studios

PAGE ONE

Preface

Less is more.

Small Studios? Big Companies?

Q & A with designers

Piet Gerards (The Netherlands)
Catherine Griffiths (New Zealand)
Stefan Sagmeister (USA)
Bernard Stein (Germany)
Henry Steiner (Hong Kong)
Niklaus Troxler (Switzerland)

Piet Gerards started his studio Piet Gerards/AAP (Anarcho Artistieke Producties) in Heerlen, in the south of Holland, around 1980. He was one of the central figures in a group of inspired activists who organised policital-cultural activites and published posters and magazines. Gerards developed himself as a self-taught man from activist and silk-screen printer to gallery owner, publisher and ultimately graphic designer. Because of his engagement and interest in art history his interests lay in modernism and historical avant-garde. Experimenting in that sense for three decennia he developed a wholly own approach, in which aesthetic ideals and subservience keep each other balanced. In the nineties the studio came into being where Gerards works with various co-designers. The main acitivity of the studio has become book design, especially in the area of architecture and art. But under the Huis Clos imprint, exceptional books are published frequently. Piet Gerards also organises, together with staff and collegues, various projects on art and culture. Like the recent exchange project between art academies (graphic design) in Holland and the National University of Art in Bucharest. Since 2006 Piet Gerards Ontwerpers is located in Amsterdam.

Piet Gerards/005

Catherine Griffiths (New Zealand)

Typography and Design is a design practice where there exists a passion for typography, and more recently, the visual arts. Sole practitioner, Catherine Griffiths, has remained independent, becoming internationally recognized for her typography projects in the landscape. Since opening her own studio in 1995, projects have included a mix of exhibition and book design, arts-related projects, corporate branding and design, and working with typography in public spaces, architecture and landscape. Catherine participates regularly on discussion and judging panels including the 2007 D&AD Global Awards for typography, and as a guest speaker at design conferences – New Zealand, Australia, Finland (ATypI Helsinki), the UK (Fast Type, Slow Type), and the Alaska Design Forum's 2008 lecture series. Physically, the studio has slowly metamorphosed from a fully-equipped, purpose-designed space to one of minimalism and simplicity (a single table) centering on an extensive design and photography book collection shared with husband and photographer Bruce Connew. The objective is to be flexible and able to transmit to an even smaller space – a canal boat in Paris for pockets of time. Finally, the hunger for space will win out and result in two separate studios planned to be built in amongst native Kanuka trees on an exquisite piece of land, west of Auckland. There, new work will come out of the pockets of time in those other places.

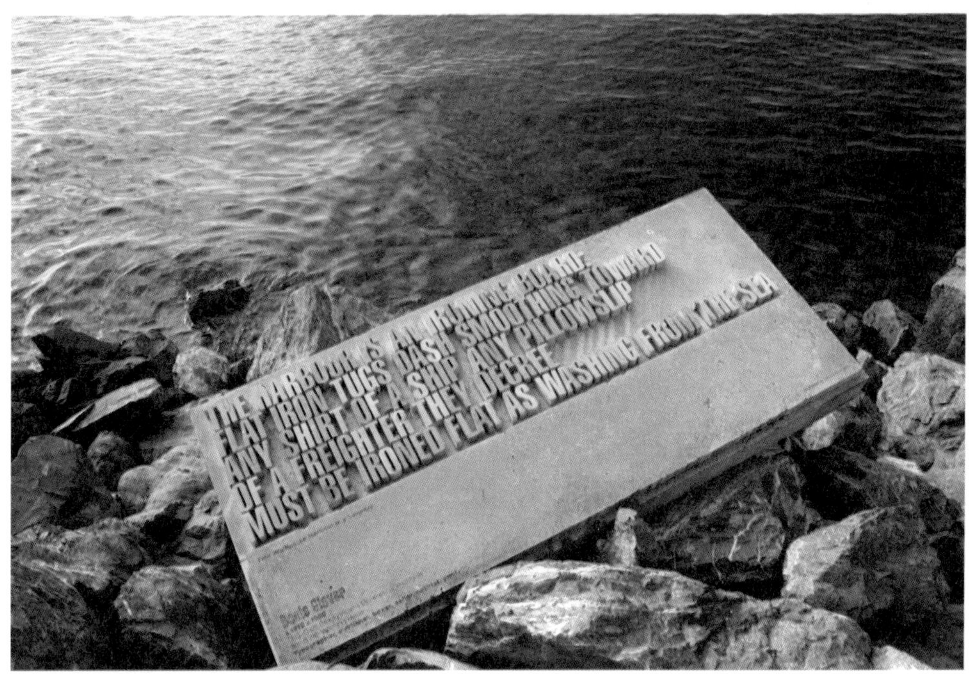
THE HARBOUR IS AN IRONING BOARD.
FLAT IRON TUGS DASH SMOOTHING TOWARD
ANY SHIRT OF A SHIP ANY PILLOWSLIP
OF A FREIGHTER THEY DECREE
MOST BE IRONED FLAT AS WASHING FROM THE SEA

Stefan Sagmeister (USA)

A native of Austria, he received his MFA in graphic design from the University of Applied Arts in Vienna and, as a Fulbright Scholar, a master's degree from Pratt Institute in New York. He formed the New York-based Sagmeister Inc. in 1993 and has since then designed graphics and packaging for the Rolling Stones, Talking Heads and Lou Reed. Having been nominated five times for the Grammies, he finally won one for the Talking Heads boxed set. He also earned many international design awards. In 2001, a best-selling monograph about his work, titled "Sagmeister, Made you Look", was published by Booth-Clibborn editions. Solo shows on Sagmeister Inc's work have been mounted in Zurich, Vienna, New York, Berlin, Tokyo, Osaka, Prague, Cologne and Seoul. Stefan has always worked hard to keep the studio small (currently it consists of himself, Matthias Ernstberger and one intern). He lectures extensively on all continents.

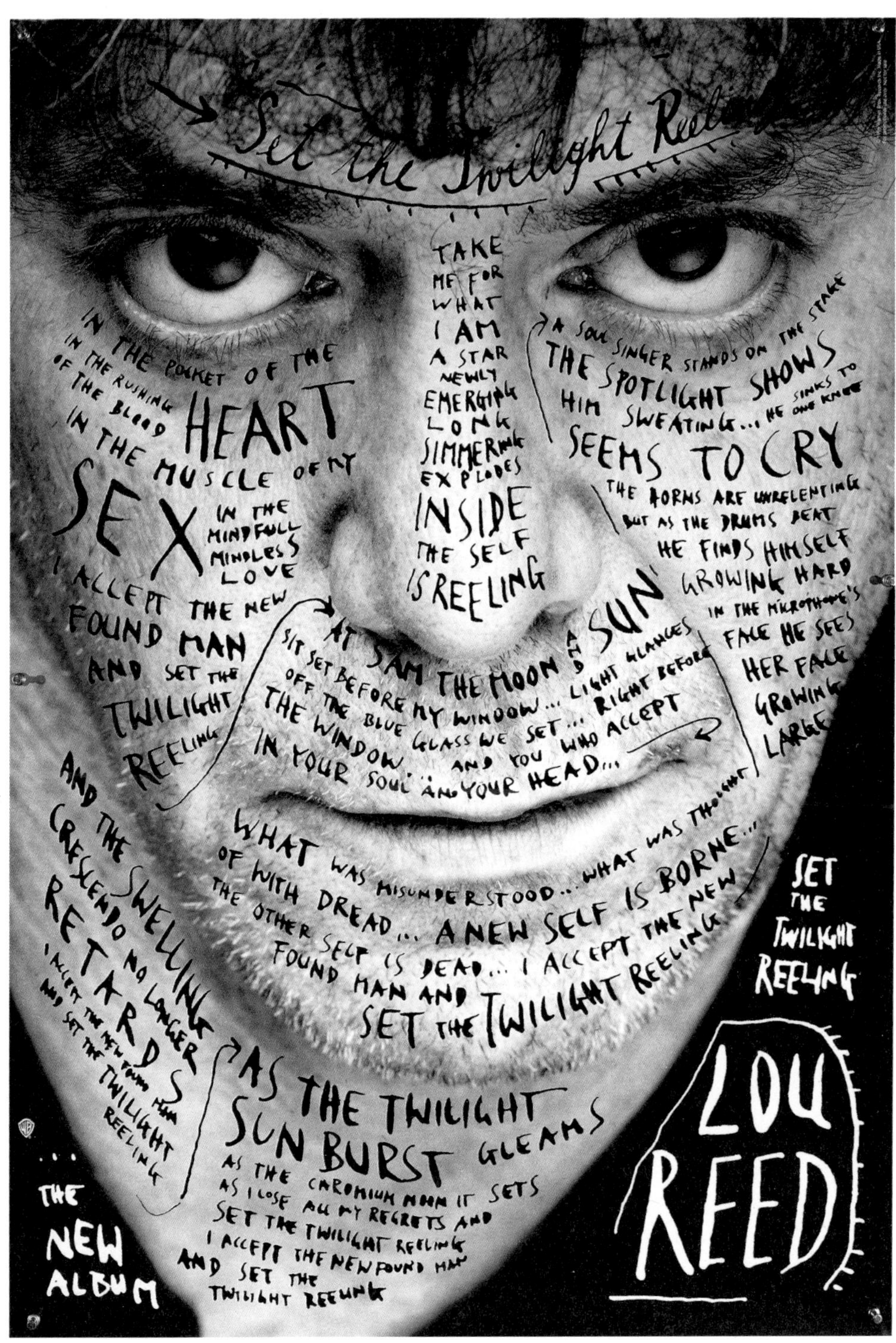
Set the Twilight Reeling
TAKE ME FOR WHAT I AM A STAR NEWLY EMERGING LONG SIMMERING EXPLODES INSIDE THE SELF IS REELING
IN THE POCKET OF THE HEART IN THE RUSHING OF THE BLOOD IN THE MUSCLE OF MY SEX IN THE MINDFULL MINDLESS LOVE
I ACCEPT THE NEW FOUND MAN AND SET THE TWILIGHT REELING
A SOUL SINGER STANDS ON THE STAGE THE SPOTLIGHT SHOWS HIM SWEATING... HE SINKS TO HIS ONE KNEE SEEMS TO CRY
THE HORNS ARE UNRELENTING BUT AS THE DRUMS BEAT HE FINDS HIMSELF GROWING HARD
IN THE MICROPHONE'S FACE HE SEES HER FACE GROWING LARGE
AT 5AM THE MOON AND SUN SIT SET BEFORE MY WINDOW... LIGHT GLANCES OFF THE BLUE GLASS WE SET... RIGHT BEFORE THE WINDOW AND YOU WHO ACCEPT IN YOUR SOUL AND YOUR HEAD...
WHAT WAS MISUNDERSTOOD... WHAT WAS THOUGHT OF WITH DREAD... A NEW SELF IS BORNE... THE OTHER SELF IS DEAD... I ACCEPT THE NEW FOUND MAN AND SET THE TWILIGHT REELING
AND THE SWELLING CRESCENDO NO LONGER RETARDS
I ACCEPT THE NEW FOUND MAN AND SET THE TWILIGHT REELING
AS THE TWILIGHT SUN BURST GLEAMS AS THE CHROMIUM MOON IT SETS AS I LOSE ALL MY REGRETS AND SET THE TWILIGHT REELING I ACCEPT THE NEWFOUND MAN AND SET THE TWILIGHT REELING
SET THE TWILIGHT REELING
... THE NEW ALBUM
LOU REED

Photo by Ulf Erdmann Ziegler

Bernard Stein was born in Berlin in 1949. He attended at the University of Applied Arts (UdK) in Berlin as a student of Prof. Helmut Lortz. In 1978, he founded the design studio Ott+Stein in Berlin, co-directing it until 2004. Since 1997, he has been a member of AGI. In 1998, he was a co-editor of the typography lexicon "TYPO * wann, wer, wie?", and became Professor for Visual Communications at the Academy of Arts in Kassel. Since 2002, he has been Curator and Adviser – between 2004 and 2006, he was Creative Director and Co-Executive of MetaDesign Berlin. He is an arts counselor of the German Treasury Department and the founder of the "Archiv für Historische Abbildungspraxis" (Archive of Historic Imagery) in Berlin.

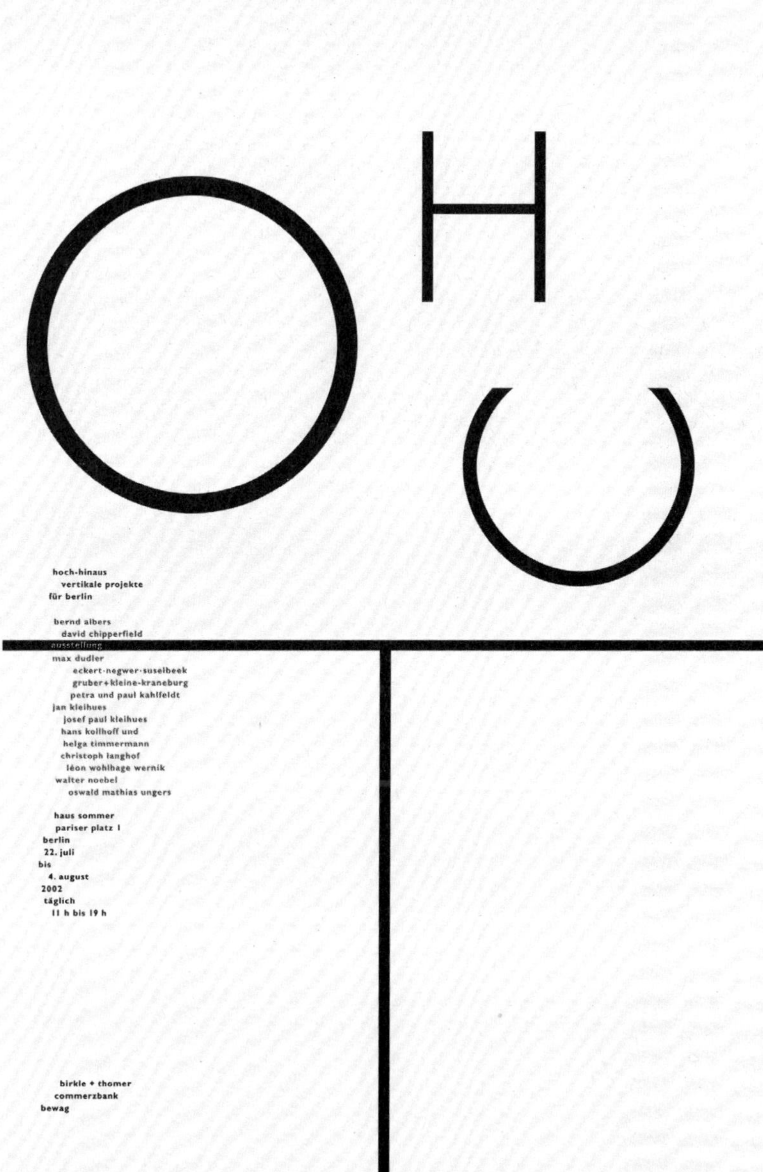

hoch-hinaus
vertikale projekte
für berlin
bernd albers
david chipperfield
ausstellung
max dudler
eckert-negwer-suselbeek
gruber+kleine-kraneburg
petra und paul kahlfeldt
jan kleihues
josef paul kleihues
hans kollhoff und
helga timmermann
christoph langhof
léon wohlhage wernik
walter noebel
oswald mathias ungers
haus sommer
pariser platz 1
berlin
22. juli
bis
4. august
2002
täglich
11 h bis 19 h
birkle + thomer
commerzbank
bewag

In collaboration with Nicolaus Ott

Henry Steiner (Hong Kong)

Henry Steiner is known as "the father of Hong Kong design," and Steiner&Co. is one of the world's leading design firms, concentrating on branding and corporate identity for clients such as HSBC, CiticPacific, Ssangyong, Unilever and The Hong Kong Jockey Club. Steiner was Hong Kong Designer of the Year in 1990 and was cited by Next magazine as among the 100 most influential people in Hong Kong's history. He was also named a World Master by Idea magazine and one of Icograda's Masters of the 20th century. He is a member and past president of Alliance Graphique Internationale. Steiner was educated at Hunter College (BFA), Yale University (MFA), and the Sorbonne on a Fulbright Fellowship. His "Cross-Cultural Design: Communicating in the Global Marketplace" was published in 1995. "Henry Steiner: Design Life", in Chinese, appeared in 1999.

Photo by Melk Imboden

20
香港渣打銀行
Standard
Chartered Bank
AC000013
港幣貳拾圓
50
香港渣打銀行
Standard
Chartered Bank
AC000013
ESTABLISHED IN HONG KONG 1859
PROMISES TO PAY THE BEARER ON DEMAND
100
香港渣打銀行
Standard
Chartered Bank
AC000013
500
香港渣打銀行
Standard
Chartered Bank
AC000013
1000
香港渣打銀行
Standard
Chartered Bank
AC000013
ESTABLISHED IN HONG KONG 1859
PROMISES TO PAY THE BEARER ON DEMAND
AT ITS OFFICE IN HONG KONG
港幣壹仟圓
One Thousand
HONG KONG DOLLARS
BY ORDER OF THE COURT OF DIRECTORS
CHIEF FINANCIAL OFFICER
DIRECTOR
HONG KONG 1 JULY 2003

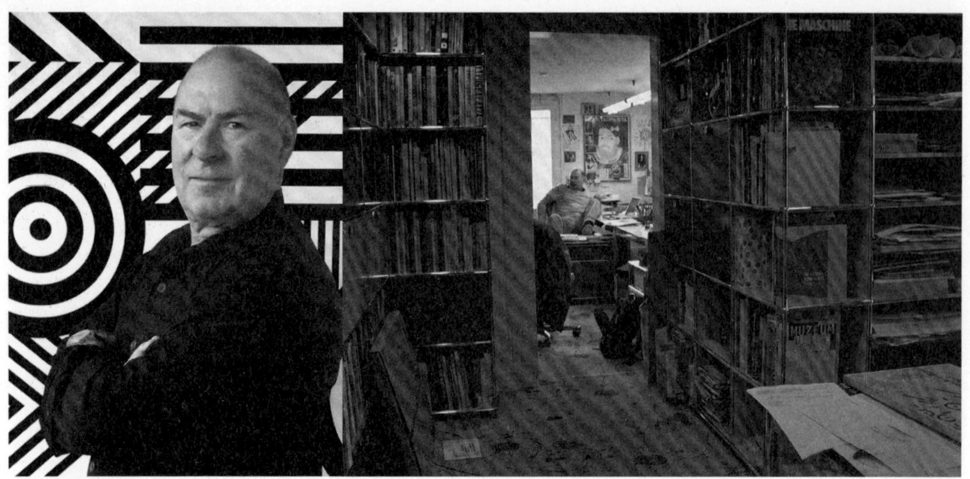

Niklaus Troxler (Switzerland)

Born in Willisau, Switzerland 1947. From 1963 to 1967, he worked as a typographer's apprentice. He studied Graphic Design Education at the Art School of Lucerne from 1967 to 1971. In 1973 he founded his own Graphic Design Studio in Switzerland. Since 1998, he has been a professor at the State Academy of Art and Design in Stuttgart, Germany. His posters are in many important collections such as the Museum of Modern Art New York, the Museum for Art and Craft Hamburg, the Toyama Museum of Modern Art Japan, the Ogaki Poster Museum Japan, the Poster Museum Essen, the Stadedeljk Museum Amsterdam, and the Zurich Poster Collection. Troxler has won numerous important poster and design awards: Hong Kong, Hangzhou, Toyama, Brno, Chaumont, Lahti, Helsinki, Colorado, Trnava, Mexico, Taiwan, awards from Art Directors Clubs of Switzerland and New York, Type Directors Club New York, Tokyo Type Directors Club, and Red Dot Communication Awards Essen among many others.

The New York Times

"All the News That's Fit to Print"

VOL. CLV . . . No. 53,3.. NEW YORK, SUNDAY, OCTOBER 23, 2005 $3.50

American marines on patrol in downtown Ramadi on Thursday with a robot used to detonate the homemade bombs used by Iraqi insurgents.

COLLEGES OPPOSE CALL TO UPGRADE ONLINE SYSTEMS

SAY COST WOULD BE HUGE

The Change Is Needed for Internet Surveillance, Government Argues

By SAM DILLON and STEPHEN LABATON

When Even Health Insurance Is No Safeguard

By JOHN LELAND

Arnold and Sharon Dorsett with their children, Dana, Zachery and Jessica. Though they had insurance, the Dorsetts had to file for bankruptcy because of Zachery's health costs.

Unseen Enemy Is at Its Fiercest In a Sunni City

By SABRINA TAVERNISE

COAST OF MEXICO TAKES THRASHING AS STORM STALLS

MANY ARE LEFT AT RESORTS

Hurricane Wilma Delayed on Path to Florida; Evacuations Begin

By ROBERT D. McFADDEN

Thousands of Demolitions Near, New Orleans Braces for New Pain

Monica Agrawal, a hairdresser, was hired to determine which of New Orleans's houses might be

Leak Case Renews Questions on War's Rationale

By RICHARD W. STEVENSON and DOUGLAS JEHL

INSIDE

No Charges Seen at C.I.A. In Most Prisoner Deaths

Who'll Wear Evita's Mantle?

Skiing and Religion Collide

Thirteen Indian tribes in Arizona are suing to block a plan that calls

28. Jan. 06

20.30

Small Studios? Big Companies?

Q & A with designers

Piet Gerards = **PG**

Catherine Griffiths = **CG**

Stefan Sagmeister = **SS**

Bernard Stein = **BS**

Henry Steiner = **HS**

Niklaus Troxler = **NT**

Who do you think will dominate the design market in the future, small studios or big companies? Are they able to coexist?

PG: Especially customers from the cultural sector prefer a more personal contact with the designer. This offers them the possibility to influence the result of the works more easily and to control the budget. A trustful relationship between the customer and the designer can develop. With a big design company this could be more difficult. A big company, on the other hand, is more adapted to longtime projects, companies, complex corporate identities and websites.

CG: World domination by small studios – of course! Really, I feel there will forever be a place for both – and probably everything in between – the world is vast, complex and bewildering. Both are so different, so what one may offer over the other would never replace or dominate, so I don't think it's so much a matter of domination ... each has its place.

SS: Yes, both will continue to do work, in the case of large branding projects I could even see a successful collaboration between the two worlds, where the strategic work could be developed by the large studio, the conceptual and design work by the small studio, and the implementation by the large one again. This could prove to be advantageous for clients, audiences and the studios themselves, as all could benefit from it.

BS: My feeling is that both will share the design market with every workable size in between about evenly. Not only that, but they will develop into each other, I think.

HS: Like Yin and Yang, designers come in two flavors: those committed to the project and those driven by the next paycheck. Edgy creativity usually comes from the hand of the former. The latter is likely to deliver dependable, familiar solutions; what one large branding firm has dubbed "CA" (for commercially acceptable). Of course, not all clients want challenging designs. Most will prefer the safer CA approach. The camouflage of the herd is what they crave, rather than distinction. Hiring a seemingly risk averse and reassuringly large company for their design requirements is the consequence. And if that big firm had produced fine work from time to time in the past, is the same team still residing in their bull pen? Were their best efforts achieved locally or in some far flung capital, whose office would have no involvement in the new project? Fortunately, knowledgeable clients understand that individuality will drive their businesses, so they demand the best from their design consultants.

NT: There will always be big companies and small studios. But I think the smaller studios will have more importance and effect in future. Some customers ask for a more personal design expression and they give preference to small studios or a specific designer with a special expression. For full service jobs, customers might prefer bigger companies.

Today, it is difficult for young designers to find their place. How did you feel about it at the time when you founded your studio?

PG: Engagement is the key word of 30 years design-work. I was predominantly able to do what I was interested in and to give myself the challenges. Because I handled the production myself (silkscreen, publishing) I was able to develop autonomously without feeling the pressure of the market. A half-time job as a teacher made me partially independent, financially. I could find inspiration less in the own field (which I hardly knew at the beginning) than in the fine arts, literature, movies and music. Design academies should provide more technical contents as well as a much wider cultural input.

CG: I made two beginnings – the first in 1987 when I graduated. I struggled to find a position, because I didn't have "experience". But to have "experience", I needed to find a position! That was perplexing in a tiny city where the total number of graduates looking for work was around 20. I mean, how else do you start? That's when I realized I was on my own. It made me even more determined, as failures can do. In my anger, I realized I must be innovative, that I must find my own voice. With two friends from design school, young women in their early twenties, I set up a studio space with next to no money – we were a little unusual at the time in New Zealand. For a year, we worked very hard, approaching clients directly, and many late nights. We learned plenty, making mistakes and making successes. But I wanted more than my hometown. I landed in London with my portfolio, and for three years worked from tiny design houses to one of the largest studios around – I was thrown in the deep end, and kept stashing away the experience. My second beginning was in 1995, back in my hometown,

Wellington. I was a senior designer, with a particular approach and philosophy, at a medium-sized design house, until finally I became frustrated and impatient with egos and petty office politics. I quit, unexpectedly, and with no plan. Within a month, in that deliciously serendipitous way (this is how my life seems to travel), I found myself renting a beautiful 1930s studio space – tall windows, glass doors – all this to myself, separate within a large studio of architects. I took out a bank loan, and turned around to find a handful of my previous employer's best clients following me. I was shocked. That was a moment of affirmation – I followed my instincts for the right reasons, against conservative common sense, to find myself gloriously alone, surrounded by work. I can recall making a conscious decision at that time to always work independently, never to have employees or business partners. I realized so clearly that I needed to work in a way that comes naturally, where my ideas retain their integrity and strengthen along the way. That's when I learned, as a designer, to stand my ground with clients. I needed to be hired and respected for what I did well.

SS: I just opened and resolved from the very beginning to stay small. I tried to keep the cost overhead low so we could remain financially independent from our clients.

BS: Together with my partner I did not find it hard to open up a studio. It seemed like the proper thing to do in order to find out if this was right for us.

HS: When I joined Brownjohn, Chermayeff and Geismar in 1957 as their second employee, the principals outnumbered the staff. Mine was a favored position, because the other assistant had to sweep up the studio at day's end. The work coming from them in those days continues to appear in design books. I stopped in on Ivan and Tom in Manhattan last year. Their space is somewhat larger than the one room where we all worked but the number of staff has grown little. Another design great working in this tradition is George Tscherny whom I visited in 1965. I admired his brilliant work for years and wanted to meet him to gain some insight on his working methods. His studio was in the basement of a brownstone on East 72nd Street. Actually, he owned and lived in the building. Like most New York brownstones, one could either climb the large staircase from the sidewalk to the front entrance or take a few steps down from the street to a door under the main stairs into the basement. These basements can be pleasant, as was his, with access to a backyard garden that also provided daylight and privacy.

NT: Young designers should think about what they want to do specifically. I think the time for allrounders is more or less over – the market looks for specialists. Of course, it's always good to have more than one specialty. The personal character is important, let's say the market has to recognize a designer's specific kind of design.

Has it become more difficult to establish a studio on the basis of one's own financial funds since then?

CG: You see, I am not so afraid to take risks. Now, after 13 independent years, I can work, mostly, as I wish, if I am prepared to accept an uncertain money supply. My overheads are low, so why be forced to make work you'd rather not!

SS: And while many things are unrecognizably different since we opened our studio, I don't think that particular situation – with the exception of sharply increased real estate cost – has changed much in New York over the past 15 years.

BS: For establishing a studio, I regard the financial funding not as an important question. To be truly interested in what you do, for me, seems to be of main concern.

NT: I think a designer should be able to create his own pictures – let's say, the designer should also be a good drawer. But fact is today that only a few designers can draw and create their own images. Image creators should stay small, should express their talent in their work. And that is – in my opinion – only possible in small studios.

With how many designers did you found your studio, and how many work together with you today? How did your studio / your company develop with regard to the size of your bureau (in m)?

PG: Since the nineties the studio has the following scale: two till four (co)designers, which work relatively independent on their projects. The studio is relatively small, but technical developments make it possible that techniques which were quite complicated before (composing, lithograph, montage) can be done now at a compact working place.

CG: After graduation, three of us began our first design studio, as you have read above, which lasted a year. My second design studio has been and remains me alone – perfect! The work spaces have mostly been a dedicated single room, the biggest at 30m2 in the house we had designed, and the smallest, now the table on the canal barge, no more than 1m2, and that is shared with Bruce! Is that possible?!! Of course! We use whatever other space we need to lay out projects, pin them up – and because Bruce and I share space now, the idea of "studio" has changed somewhat, given our different disciplines. We dream of building separate studios perched amongst the native trees of our land at Karekare ("The Piano" film; "Crowded House" music video) near Auckland in New Zealand, but who knows what will happen.

SS: I purposefully bought a small space (60m2) so that we could not grow. We started as two designers, and are now three designers. As the economy in NYC was mostly bustling and booming over the last 15 years, it would have been possible (with some hard work – I am sure) to grow the place to almost any size desired during that time. We certainly had the clients, knew the designers, the real estate and the systems. My mentor Tibor Kalman's line when I started was: The most difficult thing when running a design studio is to figure out how not to grow. Everything else is easy. I figured it out.

BS: 2 in 1978, 30 in between, 2 now; 48m in 1978, 440m in between, 96m now.

HS: By the time of this visit, I had established Graphic Communication Ltd in a hotel room of the new Hong Kong Hilton. With two assistants and a secretary, as well as a growing family, I was feeling just a bit nervous about how to structure my young business in a place literally halfway around the world. Hence the appointment with George. By the mid nineties I was agonizing over a decision to change my own firm's name. Graphic Communication Ltd had been a solid, original, even visionary title three decades earlier, when design was more about commercial art than communicating ideas. But now it had imitators and my – now much larger – staff urged a change. The clincher was when a potential client complained that on a visit to Hong Kong he couldn't find my number in the telephone directory. Of course he was looking under S, not G. So I launched Steiner&Co. with some trepidation but no eventual regrets, except for not having done it sooner. Since the name change I have decided to narrow my focus and corporate description to brand creation and strategy. My support staff is now smaller, thanks in part to the computer, which replaces most manual labor from the pre-digital epoch, and partly due to the greater availability of skilled freelancers in Hong Kong and the rest of the globe. Again following Tscherny's example, I own my office space.

NT: Just by myself! After working as an Art Director in a big design company in Paris, I wanted to start my own business, to be independent. I had an office of about 25m2, which was quit big for a one-man-studio.

It is often asserted that big companies represent a standardized design while small studios stick to their own style and prioritize creativity. What is your idea about that?

PG: Not only big but also small studios should take attention not to represent a standardized design. The danger to replicate yourself always exists. Additionally, the client is coming to us just because of our style. The only solution is to handle the briefing consequently. You should always ask yourself: what is it, what is it about, what are the expectations? This helps not to fall to easy for designing too freely and losing the sentence. Economic and technical aims are rarely a restriction to us.

CG: Maybe there's truth to that, sure – the large guys can take risks, but always within the need to ensure turnover of work to sustain larger overheads – there are people's livelihoods at stake. But I have seen distinctive styles coming out of large design houses, as so with smaller design studios where there is a very strong voice. I'm sure there are large studios that nurture individuality; they must, to survive in a creative industry. I think it's a philosophical culture that determines the approach, and that applies whether large or small – I have seen formulaic design depart both large and small studios.

SS: Large companies by and large have to be generalist because their vast financial needs require them to take on clients from all over the spectrum, while a small studio can be more individualistic and can afford to have a more subjective point of view, be it regarding content or form.

BS: In my view, good design matches its purpose, bad design doesn't. That is why I think standardized design is very good in standardized situations and creative design when an innovative approach might be interesting.

HS: How can these clients identify the strong design firms? If there is a person's name on the door of a studio, a useful rule of thumb is to ask whether he or she is still alive and practicing there. If instead there's a generic name, has the head designer achieved recognition on the basis of past work?

For example, I can choose any design project on my website, point at my nose (Asian style) and say in all honesty: "I did this."

NT: Absolutely – too many hands prevent good design. A group arrives always at compromises. It's a great advantage to work alone on a design project! Let's say – young designers should know about this fact. They should try to reach an outstanding and ownstanding expression in their design. Otherwise they play in a large field where all the bigger studios are at home.

Small studios often have clients from the cultural sector – big companies often concentrate on the commercial field. Does that have an impact on their creativity? Are small studios more creative and imaginative due to their focus on cultural clients?

PG: In my experience, in the Netherlands big clients also find their way for specific requests to specialized small studios.

CG: I don't accept this premise. Both large and small studios can produce creative and imaginative work. Some do and, for whatever reason, many don't, large and small. My experience suggests there is not a split of commercial and cultural clients, government and private, between large and small design studios, quite the contrary. There has always been a mixture, and one that is continually evolving. Individual personalities within the large and small design studios affect the client base – it is a relationship. Perhaps, if you are small, young and hungry with little to lose, then it's simpler to be crazier, to take greater creative risks – it's not so black and white.

SS: There is not a single large design company in the world that I respect. No, sorry, I am wrong, IDEO does good work, and Landor manages to pull of a successful project every once in a while. But there is problem with this: Very large clients want to work with large design consultancies, it gives them a level of service and security that smaller places like mine have more difficulties to convey. This leads to the sad fact that many of the most talented designers work for smallish projects in the cultural realm, while the work that really influences the look of this world, the gigantic branding programs for the multinationals are conceived by marketing people who could not care less about issues of culture. This is as much the fault of clients (who find the pseudo-scientific reasoning of the consultancies comforting), as it is of designers (who are not willing to deal with the far more complex approval and implementation process). I have the highest admiration for the person or group who can pull off a large project in good quality. It's BY FAR the hardest thing to do.

BS: From my experience, these two questions have nothing to do with creativity, but everything with structure. To be able to cope with each other, structures should be similar. The director of a theatre, an architect or an author, an artist or a gallerist as well as the head of a company who still decides by him- or herself will be able to work best with a single designer or a small studio – the structures match. The same holds true for the opposite. A company or institution with departments and different levels of decision-making will wish for the equivalent in the design area.

HS: For the last four decades of his career, my mentor Paul Rand worked from his home in rural Connecticut in a studio with one assistant. During this period he created the brands for ABC, Westinghouse, UPS, Cummins Diesel, IBM... How does one designer with one assistant handle the massive workload of creating and implementing the visual output of a giant like IBM? Paul supervised the setting up of a large studio and design staff within IBM, which he visited monthly, assigning, critiquing, inspiring. This pattern was replicated by him in other countries and for other clients, with resultant work of distinct integrity and quality.

NT: Many designers think it would be easier to design for cultural affairs. But we must know that the challenge is much bigger in these fields. I know small studios who are just designing in the corporate design or in the exhibition design. Some others prefer the cultural stuff. It's always a question of the preferences you have. Of course, you cannot earn that much money in cultural fields as you can in more business-oriented sectors. But the great challenge in the cultural design helps to develop your design on a high level.

In big companies, the employees are often organized in separated working spheres, while designers in small studios are very often allrounders. What kind of influence does this fact have on the design? How is your studio /your company structured?

CG: Being independent, I have to look after all aspects of the design process, so the hierarchical structure is very horizontal! My preferred process is to have the input work out-sourced, leaving me to craft and detail the finished object.

SS: That small companies can do a job much more efficient, with less misunderstandings, wrong briefs, endless meetings and constant heartaches. 5, 50, 200 and 10,000 employees, the simple rule of thumb stemming from my having worked in design and advertising companies employing 3 experience: the more, – the worse.

BS: In my view, the design from a big company tends to be more rational and communicative, whereas a small studio allows a more complex and subjective approach. Around everything in which I am deeply interested.

NT: I don't think designers in small studios have to be allrounders – they can be outstanding specialists. It was always important to me that I design my projects myself – from the start to the end. My assistants also work that way: they do their projects themselves. My role is a kind of director – or correctioner.

Working overtime is the order of the day in small studios. Does that mean that there is more passion involved in comparison to big companies with regular work hours, or is this just caused by pressure of time?

PG: With overtime you often get over-worked.

CG: Well, first of all, long hours do occur in the larger studios too – I know that for sure! I think it is a matter of choice – when I was younger, I did all-nighters regularly for all the reasons you mention – passion, pressure, pay! But now, a late night is rare, and only if essential. I try to work more intensively through the day – but it all depends on the project.

SS: Yes, I find passion all the time among small companies and am truly surprised when it occurs in a larger one, so many people I encounter in the bigger consultancies seem to have given up a long time ago. Students tend to get a job with them. Also, my worst!

BS: To equate overtime with passion seems to me rather funny. The time you invest should compare to the intensity and quality you want – how you spread the time has more to do with your stamina and your need for rest.

NT: To have enough free time and leisure time was always important to me. You can get blind if you are always looking and thinking on your design projects. You need inputs – and inputs you can get at cinemas, concerts, pleasure time...

Was your studio successful straight from the start or did the number of your contract jobs increase only slowly? Would you mind telling us about the financial profit of your first project?

PG: I started alone and the the design work was more of a sideline than the core activity. Through publishing activities and the initiation in an art center I profiled myself and was able to build up my own studio without noteworthy promotion. My first project was the Dutch edition of the Polish futuristic poem "Europe" of Anatol Stern with the original design of Mieczyslaw Sczcuka. Because I handled the production totally on my own (montage, silkscreen, technical preparation) the costs were extraordinary low and I could even keep a small amount which I invested in a folder and a second edition. The positive reaction to the first editions brought me up to new clients which gave me the motivation to work further on.

CG: My first project was for free – does that count? In my second studio (in 1995), I did very well straight off – high quality commercial clients (university, arts council, city council, commercial) followed me, so I was able to continue working hard. The surprise was that a good portion of the charge-out rate ended up in my pocket – the same hard work and creativity for greater reward.

SS: We started with one client in place and gained two more in the first couple of months. But I had opened the studio to pursue design for music and it took us almost a year before we had completed our first music client.

BS: Over a period of two years our work had increased to the point that we always had more work than we could finish. My first project was a DIN A1 poster for an architectural exhibition for one thousand Deutsche Mark.

NT: I started quite well. I already had a layout job for another year. I had to design a magazine with 24 pages every week. That was my great help to start my business. On the other hand I had my management for the Jazz concerts. I did not invest a lot of money in my first studio. My equipment was quite simple: a table, scissors, pencils, brushes, color... and a lot of paper. There was no other technical equipment. Later, I bought a repro camera, a photocopier... and so on. I started with my first Macintosh in 1994, quite late.

Did you have to invest a lot of initiative or did you have to work without profit to increase the recognition of your studio's name in the beginning? Could you give us an example of the efforts you made?

CG: Because the transition from employment to self-employment was so smooth, I had the luxury of an already established reputation with my clients, and was able to follow my pattern, my way of working, without distraction. I also insisted on working with clients, not for them, and with decision-makers, the higher up the chain of command, the better. There were times where I had to stand firm, not be bullied, which earned me respect – sometimes. I lost clients and I have fired clients – I have always been prepared to let clients go, rather than reconfigure my principles. Of course, it sometimes altered cash-flow more than I would have wished! As a designer, I operate in a quite instinctive way – it may not sound terribly strategic, but I've discovered over time that following my own instincts is where my value lies, where unexpected things are allowed to occur – nudging, shaping, adjusting, reinventing ...

SS: Sure. The first music client was HP Zinker, a band where I was friends with the singer. We put 220 design hours into the project and got paid $ 1800.00, the equivalent of $ 8.00 per hour. As the cleaning personnel made $12.00/hour, this was not going to work in the long run. But the CD packaging was nominated for a Grammy and got us a real foot in the door with the record labels.

BS: When we started, we made a mailing to 352 separate cultural and institutional facilities with a very professional approach – not one replied. Friends, word to mouth and staying in one place over a fair time helped a lot.

Today, it is very hard for young designers to find an adequate job after the end of their studies. Therefore, many of them try to establish studios of their own. Is this situation familiar to you or were there more job offerings at the time you started your career?

SS: Sounds familiar and I started working freelance, mostly direct with clients. This proved to be a fantastic learning ground, as it's basically the same as running a very tiny design studio.

NT: I had no other chance than to earn enough money to save my life. Of course, I had to work hard. I did not get any guarantees from outside and I also didn't want to ask for bank credits in that time.

What, in your opinion, does have the biggest negative influence on the existence of a small studio or a big company?

CG: Such a negative question! Small studio – the negative things are insignificant, hardly worth mentioning. Time and resources can always be found, and if you need to bounce ideas off someone, those whose opinions you respect are always there for you. Large company – the list is quite long... where do I begin? Alas, I am not an expert on larger studios; really the question does not interest me. However, certainly from experience and more lately through conversation, there is much general pressure, which can be traced to maintaining turnover against overheads. Creatives become managers, with little or no time to creatively express themselves. Certainly, any design house system that stands between designer and client, between the possibility of a good relationship, often creates lesser work. Sometimes, a designer needs to be protected from a client and their unreasonable demands. In my small studio, whenever that has been the case, the client has been sacked!

SS: For a small studio: the fact that big companies get all the big jobs for the big companies: That everybody thinks all the good work is done by the small studios. I just returned from Semi-Permanent in New Zealand, a very well run design conference with 1600 attendees and 12 speakers. There was not a single big company represented.

BS: Bad design work over a long time period.

HS: Before finding my vocation as a graphic designer at Yale, I studied painting with, among others of the New York School of Abstract Expressionism, William Baziotes. He was a charming raconteur, down to earth, a treasure trove of anecdotes. He measured no more than 170 cm tall and once intimated that most great artists were about his height. We seldom consider how tall or how stout were the painters, writers and composers in our personal pantheons. Important designs come from important designers: size is immaterial.

NT: The greatest benefit of working with a small studio or even alone is independence. You can get quite great pressure when you have to run a big company. You always have to look for enough work for all the employees. It costs you too much concentration on the business. In a small studio you feel much more free. You do what you want to do. The business is maybe not that big – but there are always enough jobs to do. And you do it in your own way – in your personal style.

100 Small Studios

2xGoldstein

team:
Andrew Goldstein
Jeffrey Goldstein
contact:
Kriegsstr. 89
76133 Karlsruhe, Germany
T +49 721 2016757
M +49 175 1662709
F +49 721 2016758
mail@2xgoldstein.de
www.2xgoldstein.de

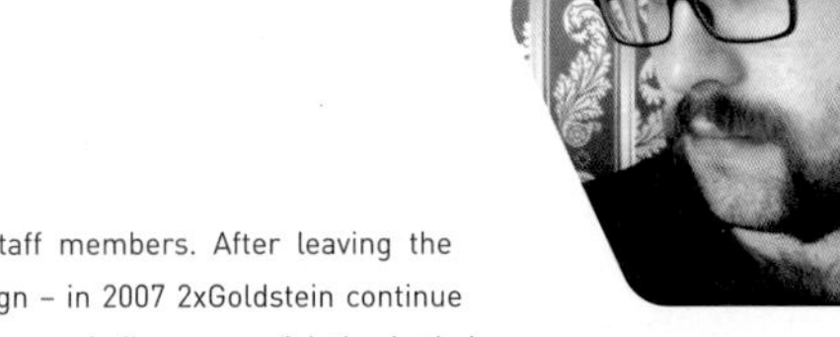

2xGoldstein consists of 2x family members respectively staff members. After leaving the academic shelter – the Karlsruhe University of Arts and Design – in 2007 2xGoldstein continue their collaboration which exists since the day they met. Both have a similar scope of duties in their everyday life as designers. Normally, one of them attends to a project full-time and the other one does the ordered preliminary work for the project if necessary. 2xGoldstein work for the so-called cultural sector which is hard to characterize. Among other things 2xGoldstein design the annual report for the university they studied at. Every year they are in charge of the INMM conference of new music and music education in Darmstadt as well as the complete appearance of the literature day of the Adam Seide Archiv in Karlsruhe. After designing a book about the photographer Arnold Zwahlen for the well-known Swiss publishing house Benteli Verlag Bern, they are now finalizing a book about the Panorama photographer Willy P. Burkhardt together with their formerly professor Melchior Imboden, a well-known Swiss designer. At the moment, they are designing the corporate identity and the Internet presence of the DOKUBLOG, a radio drama project of the German cultural radio station SWR2, the Südwest-Rundfunk.

Interview with 2xGoldstein

1. What led to the formation of your studio?

Our personality and further more adjustment of our work.

2. How many staff people does your studio have and what are their main working fields?

Are we a family or a business? We are 2x family members, respectively staff members. Both of us have the similar scope of duties. Normally, one of us attends to a project full-time and the other one does the ordered preliminary work for the project, if necessary.

3. How does a regular working day at your studio look like, how is the day structured?

It starts in the morning and ends in the evening. The hours of work are fluently portioned out the day, the week, the year. This is possible because we work where we live.

4. How much leisure time do you have during a year?

We live where we work. As we just started in May 2007 it is hard to answer by now.

5. Which business areas do your clients mainly come from? Is the number of your clients increasing or rather declining?

Roughly speaking we work for the so-called cultural sector. The number of clients is strictly increasing because as aforementioned 2xGoldstein just the left the academic shelter in May 2007.

6. Do you have a specific corporate philosophy or maybe a mission statement like other companies, which is reflected in the way you steer the studio's course?

PLUS ULTRA – for an excess of substance in design. For further information please look up PLUS ULTRA from 2xGoldstein at www.ausnahmeverlag.de

7. What, from your point of view, makes the difference between a small studio and a big company?

The same as small studios are notional and sometimes more mobile and independent in creative belongings, they can also reject something which is against their ideas more easily because the circle of liable and particularly dependent persons is smaller. In a small studio every member can put into practice that, even though design is a service (corporate design), the designer can be more than simply a service provider ("corporated" designer).

8. What kind of advantages and disadvantages does a small studio have compared to a big company?

At first sight there are no ostensible disadvantages. One may say that it is a disadvantage that in a small studio the designer has to take care of everything himself. But this should rather be taken as a challenge than as a handicap.

9. What is your idea about the future of small studios? Do you think that small studios do not have any other choice but to expand in order to survive in these times of globalization?

We think the answers to questions 7 and 8 give an impression of where the future of a small studio lies. If anything, the often quoted trend "times of globalization" is helpful for both types of studios. The preservation of small studios lies in their reliable reputation and is not connected to any trend or temporary fashion.

10. Please describe and elaborate on the goals or plans that you have for your studio for the next five years?

One great goal will be that our design copes with verbalized pretensions both in practice and in theory, and to devise these pretensions. Last but not least, to keep it a family business.

Ilona Herreiner – book – Ilona Herreiner – 2007

The village photographer Arnold Zwahlen – book – benteli verlag – 2006

Litarature in the blue salon – poster – blauer salon – 2007

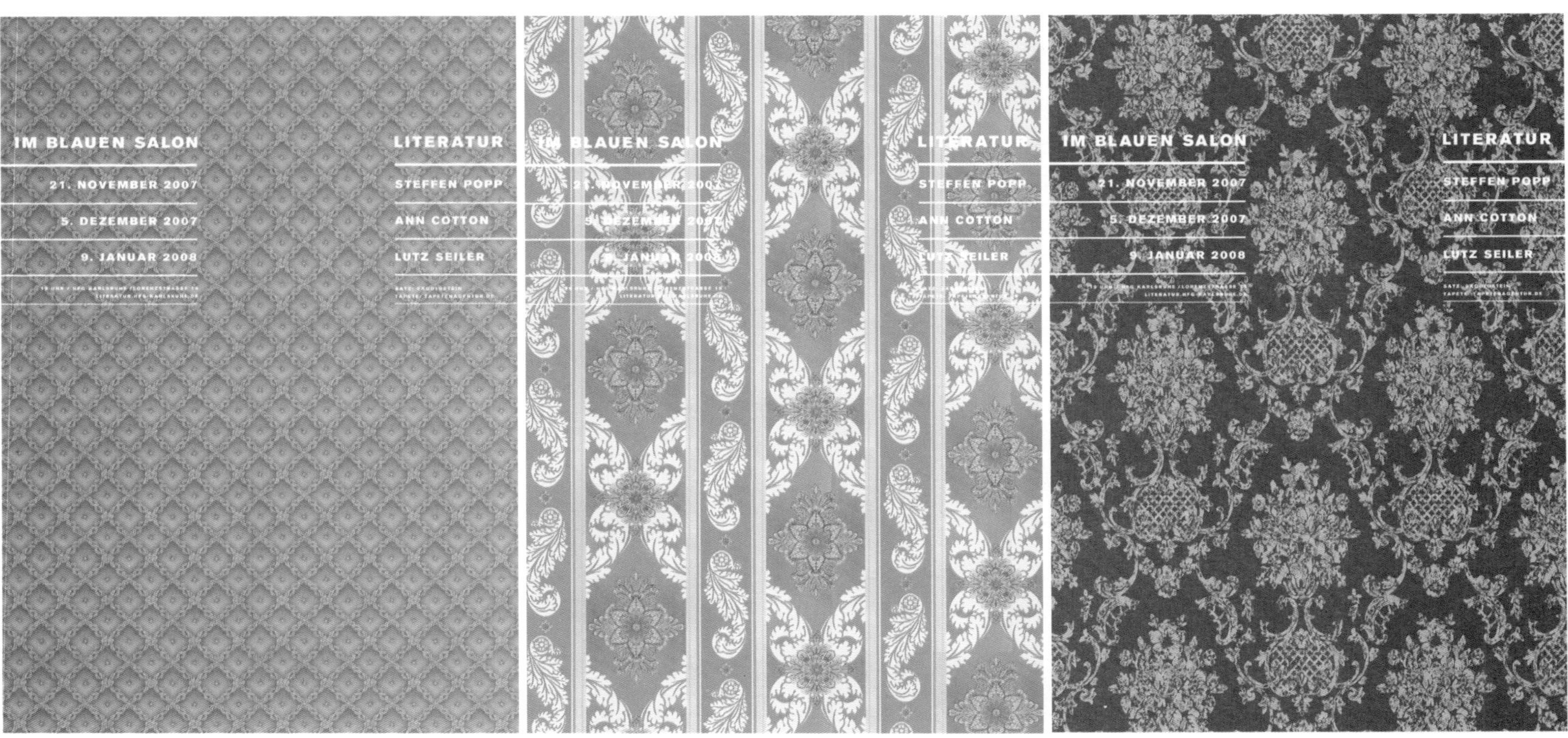

Adam Seide literature day – poster – Adam Seide – 2007

Designer portraits Melchior Imboden – poster – kunstzone – 2007

"Nabi

team:
Sung Min Park
Bo Bae Kim
Chang Gun Kim
Se Young Lee
contact:
1f, Hyehwa Castle,
8-10 Hyehwa-dong,
Chongro-gu
110-530 Seoul
Korea
T + 82 2 7428742
F + 82 2 7423742
nabiooo@empal.com

"Nabi means butterfly. Founder Se Young Lee has worked as creative director at the influential design company "Ahn Graphics" based in Seoul, Korea. He became independent and founded "Nabi in November 2006. Since then, he has been participating in more than hundred projects. Se Young Lee has also been a member of AGI. Like the butterfly effect, he wishes to influence design history by the results of small creativity from the works of the studio "Nabi". He has deep interest in the visual culture of traditional Korea which he has been trying to conceive in terms of modernism. The identity of Korea design will be altered by his work.

Interview with "Nabi

1. What led to the formation of your studio?

I worked for 10 years in one of the oldest and most influential design firms in Korea, "Ahn Graphics". Based on those experiences, I have established a firm called "Nabi (meaning = butterfly) in November 2006. Currently, the company is composed only of designers.

2. How many staff people does your studio have and what are their main working fields?

There are four members including myself: I am the president and creative director, plus there are one art director and two designers. Works other than design like planning, copy writing or shootings are performed by freelancers.

3. How does a regular working day at your studio look like, how is the day structured?

The working starts at 9 am and regularly finishes at 7 pm. But like any other design studio we often rather work for 12 hours, from 9 to 9.

4. How much leisure time do you have during a year?

Most companies in Korea have a five working day system. Sometimes, however, we need to work on Sundays, and we have about 7 free days every year during the summer that everyone enjoys.

5. Which business areas do your clients mainly come from? Is the number of your clients increasing or rather declining?

Corporate C.I., various promotional materials like brochures or annual reports (e.g. for universities), book design for publishers, design for exhibitions hosted by public organizations like museums and art galleries, package designs. The number of clients is increasing gradually since we started to realize projects two years ago.

6. Do you have a specific corporate philosophy or maybe a mission statement like other companies, which is reflected in the way you steer the studio's course?

Korea has developed an outstanding traditional visual culture through five thousand years of history, representing distinct forms of design. Today, we are exploring those designs again from the perspective of the creative mind. The identity of Korean design will be further strengthened through the studio Nabi.

7. What, from your point of view, makes the difference between a small studio and a big company?

The important thing is that in big companies projects are realized by internal staff members while small studios undertake jobs through networking with freelancers.

8. What kind of advantages and disadvantages does a small studio have compared to a big company?

Advantages: Jobs are done efficiently. Cost saving is easy. Communication is smooth. Free and clear identity. Disadvantages: It is difficult to realize package jobs and large projects.

9. What is your idea about the future of small studios? Do you think that small studios do not have any other choice but to expand in order to survive in these times of globalization?

It is not that I insist on a small-sized studio but the size clearly involves limits in terms of efficient management. I believe that a number of around 10 staff members is ideal for jobs, operational efficiency and displaying identity. Global competitiveness is the result of individual competency in the end, not the problem of organization and size.

10. Please describe and elaborate on the goals or plans that you have for your studio for the next five years?

The goal is to firmly establish Studio Nabi not only in Korea but also globally with around 10 staff members. Business conditions for design studios in Korea are difficult currently. The goal is to establish a successful design studio through an efficient management system and increasing efficiency of profitability.

Character expressions – poster – vidak – 2004

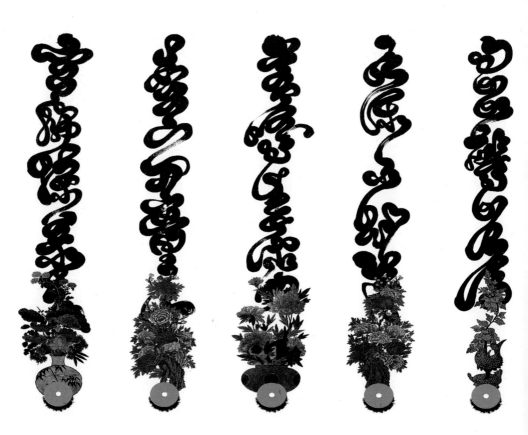

Character tree – poster – dic color square gallery – 2005

Character tree – poster – artist group Jindallae – 2004

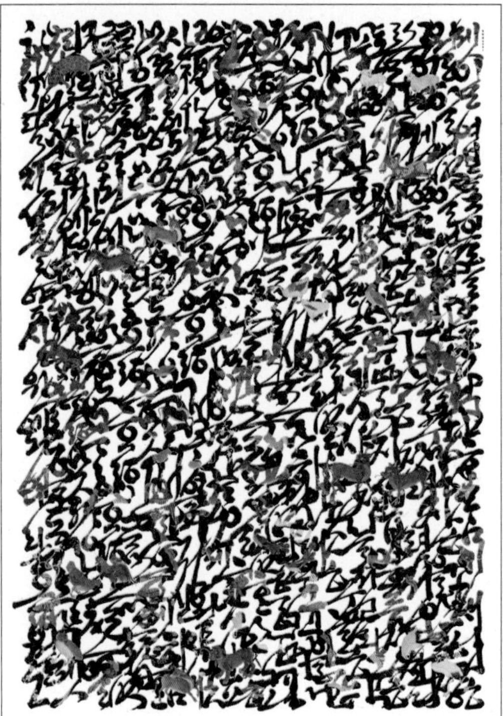

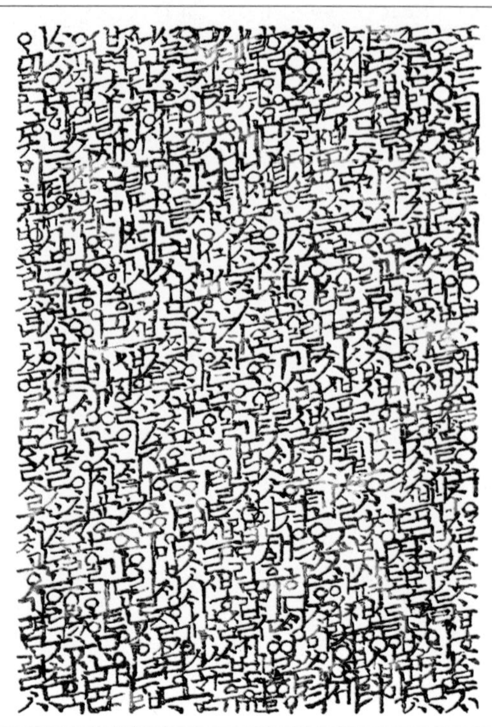

Hangeul – poster – gallery DDD (Osaka) – 2002

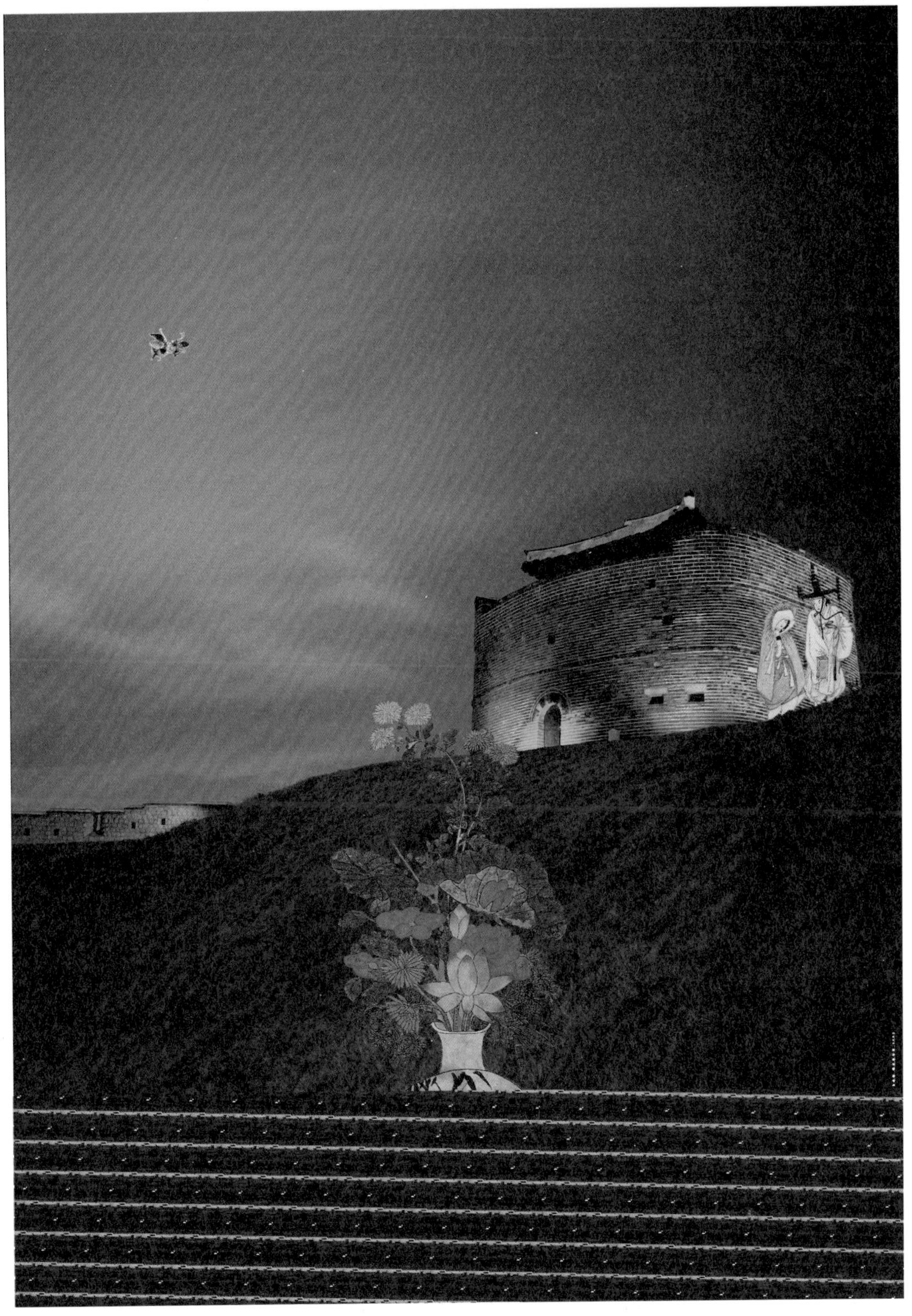

Image Korea – poster – Seoul art center – 2003

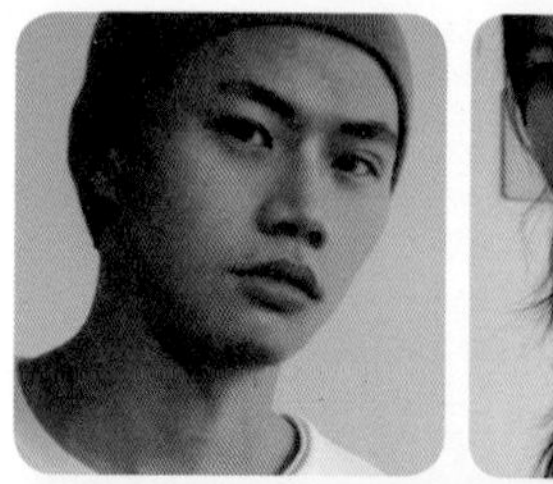

Aaron Nieh Workshop

team:
Aaron Nieh
Yung-mei Nieh
contact:
3F, No.145, Sec. 2, Anhe Rd.
106 Taipei, Taiwan
T + 886 2 27358735
F + 886 2 27321550
somekidding@mac.com

Interview with Aaron Nieh Workshop

1. What led to the formation of your studio?

Design for music albums, book art, and the other graphic arts.

2. How many staff people does your studio have and what are their main working fields?

We are two people. Both of us partake of all the work.

3. How does a regular working day at your studio look like, how is the day structured?

We begin our day working with radio or i-pod music around noon. Working busily, picking up phones and smoking all the afternoon. After supper we start working hard again. Sometimes we go out at night, having fun by shopping, visiting night markets and bars when work makes us crazy.

4. How much leisure time do you have during a year?

1 to 3 months. But we leave work anytime just when we are getting tired.

5. Which business areas do your clients mainly come from? Is the number of your clients increasing or rather declining?

Mass media, entertainment companies, records companies and publishing houses. We're glad to have more new friends (clients) every year.

6. Do you have a specific corporate philosophy or maybe a mission statement like other companies, which is reflected in the way you steer the studio's course?

Careful and adventurous, believe in yourself.

7. What, from your point of view, makes the difference between a small studio and a big company?

We (and our customers) have good taste, sensitive senses and talents. We hate commercial, normal, common artwork. That's the difference between small and big studios.

8. What kind of advantages and disadvantages does a small studio have compared to a big company?

The advantage is that more and more clients trust small studios to deliver more private, quick, specific and styled works than a big company. The disadvantage is that in a large studio things and duties can be organized more easily than in a small one.

9. What is your idea about the future of small studios?

Inversely, I think small studios are more important and chicer in times of boring globalization.

10. Please describe and elaborate on the goals or plans that you have for your studio for the next five years?

Just feeling free and happy to do anything we want, taking care of our health!

Aaron Nieh Workshop is controlled by Nieh, Yung-chen (1977). He was involved in the most important artworks on Chinese music albums and books for 7 years since his graduation from Commercial Design Dept. of Taiwan University of Science & Technology. To be honest, tax saving was the main reason why he decided to register his own studio after having been a freelancer (who had no concept of money) for several years.

Mayday campaign/all about music play – book – kadokawa group publishing co., ltd. – 2005

Scares on memory – poster – public tv service/Taiwan/director Mickey Chen – 2005

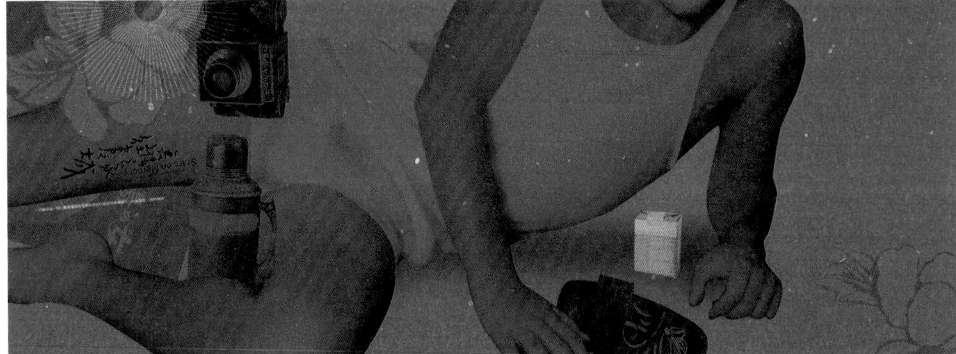

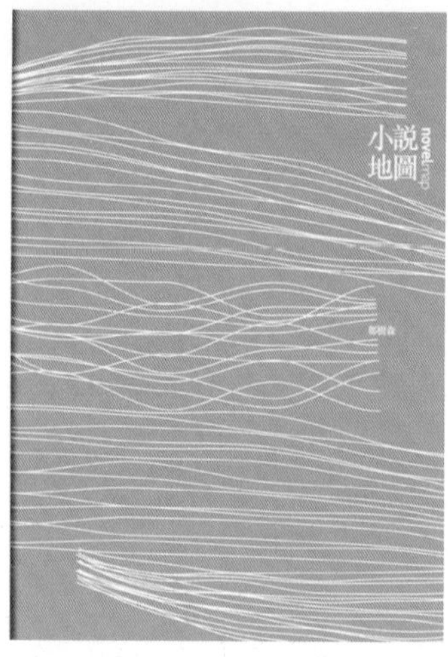

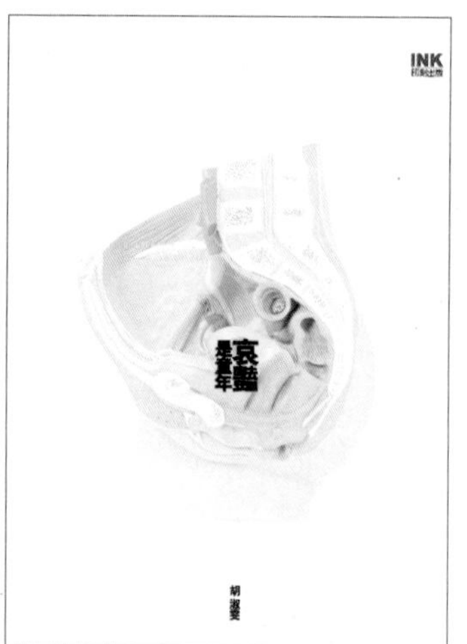

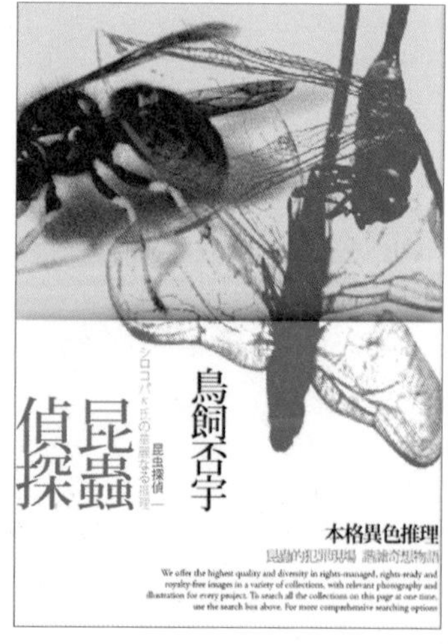

Cover design of books/all about music play – book – INK publishing co., ltd. – 2006/2007

Gary Chaw/grid blue – cd package – rock records co., ltd. – 2005

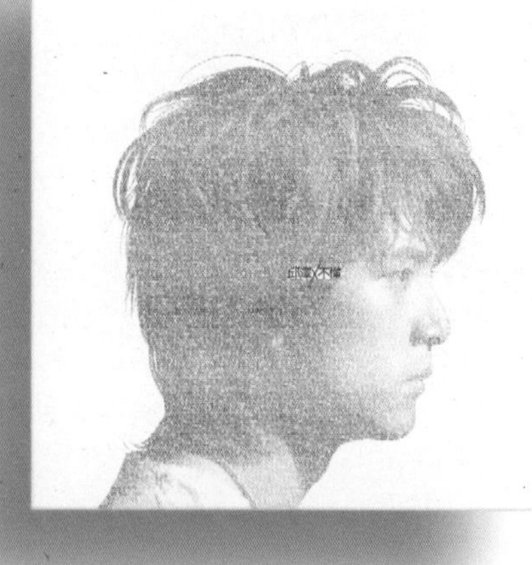

Roy Chiu/incomprehension – cd package – skyhigh entertainment co., ltd. – 2003

and is :
comfort
myself

and is :
early childhood

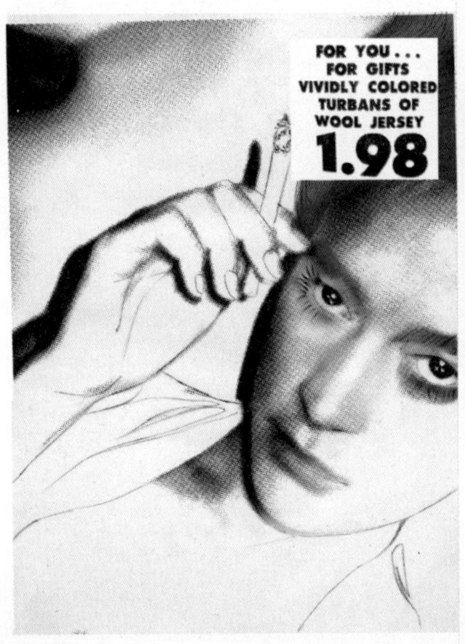
FOR YOU...
FOR GIFTS
VIVIDLY COLORED
TURBANS OF
WOOL JERSEY
1.98

a deal
a disguise

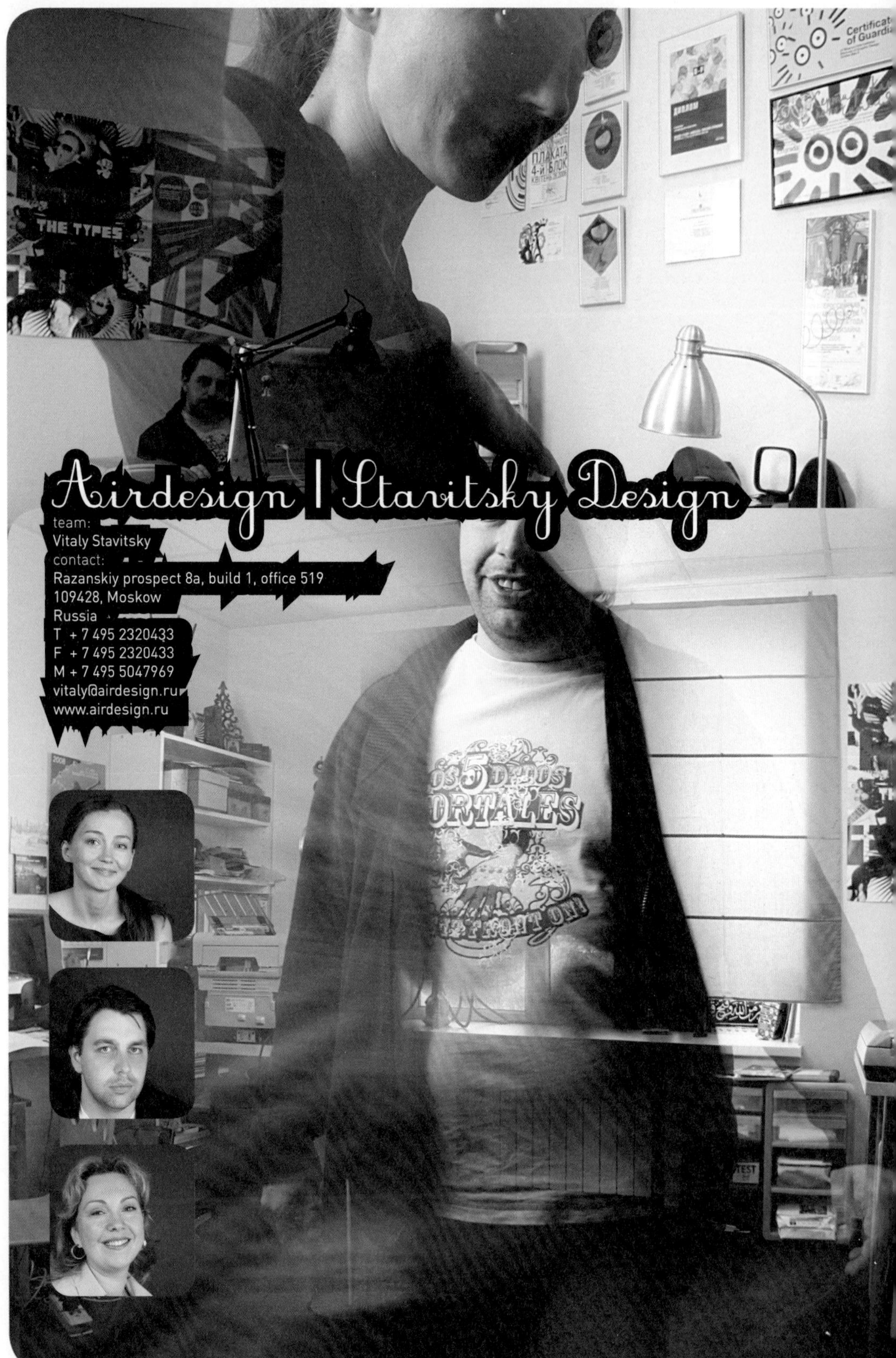

Airdesign | Stavitsky Design

team:
Vitaly Stavitsky

contact:
Razanskiy prospect 8a, build 1, office 519
109428, Moskow
Russia
T + 7 495 2320433
F + 7 495 2320433
M + 7 495 5047969
vitaly@airdesign.ru
www.airdesign.ru

Airdesign | Stavitsky Design was established in 2000 by Vitaly Stavitsky. At the moment, there are 3 people working in the studio, 2 designers and a manager. Our studio is in the list of 10 best brand agencies in Russia in the rating of ACAR (association of communicative agency of Russia). Our clients are perfectly aware that by hiring us they will obtain the best result in the shortest time, and that we are ready to work on their project for 24 hours without weekends or holidays. This is probably the most important advantage of a small studio. For the last 4 years, our studio was the Guardian of the Moscow International biennale Golden Bee. Yes, we are a small studio, we are 3, but nevertheless our materials are published in the most important international publication and magazines such as GRAPHIS POSTERS (USA) or Design for Special Events by Rockport. Our works are presented in different exhibition and concourses like the Tehran International Poster Biennale of Iran, the Moscow International Biennale of Graphic Design, Good Design (Chicago), the Tokyo Type Directors Club and International poster and graphic design of Chaumont. We have won more than 20 Russian and international awards for design and advertising, and one piece of our work is presented in the Chicago Athenaeum (museum of architecture and design).

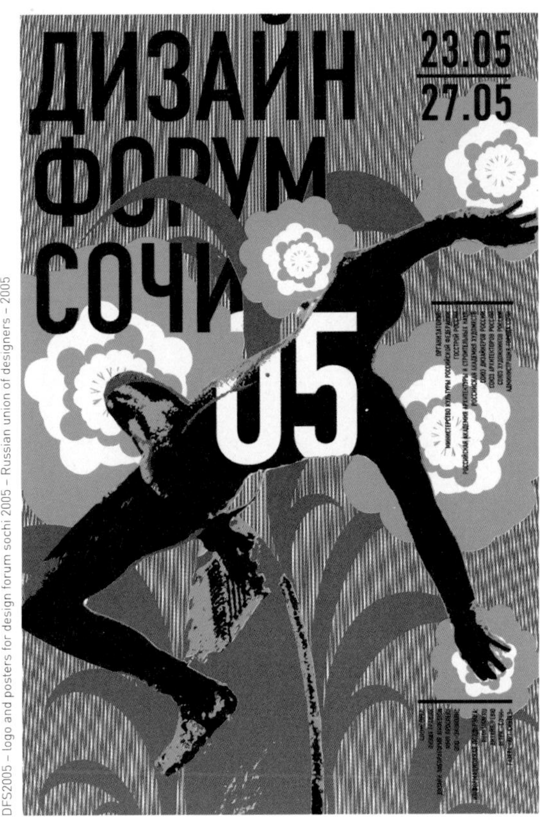

DFS2005 – logo and posters for design forum sochi 2005 – Russian union of designers – 2005

Design2006 – logo and poster for exhibition design 2006 – Russian union of designers – 2006

Interview with Vitaly Stravitsky

1. What led to the formation of your studio?

Ambitions.

2. How many staff people does your studio have and what are their main working fields?

We have 2 designers responsible for the creative part of the business and 1 manager whose main work is to acquire clients and accompany them until the end of a project.

3. How does a regular working day at your studio look like, how is the day structured?

Being constantly in contact with our client on one hand and our suppliers on the other.

4. How much leisure time do you have during a year?

Usually some time at the end of the spring and some time during the summer.

5. Which business areas do your clients mainly come from?

Mostly from the field of cosmetics, banks and other financial structures, public organizations.

Is the number of your clients increasing or rather declining?

It remains at the same level.

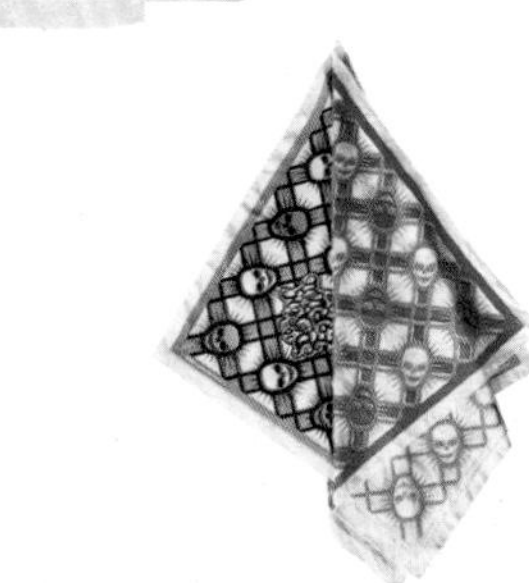

Design forum sochi 2007 – brand identity – Russian union of designers – 2007

Desam_catalog – catalog of sport dresses – photographer - Vladimir Barinov – desam – 2005

ASDR5 – poster for assembly of union of designers Russia – Russian union of designers – 2007

15 years of Russian union of designers annual report – Russian union of designers – 2007

РЕЗОЛЮЦИЯ
ПЕРВОЙ
АССАМБЛЕИ
СОЮЗА
ДИЗАЙНЕРОВ
РОССИИ

1

РЕГИОНАЛЬНЫЕ
ОТДЕЛЕНИЯ
СОЮЗА
ДИЗАЙНЕРОВ
РОССИИ

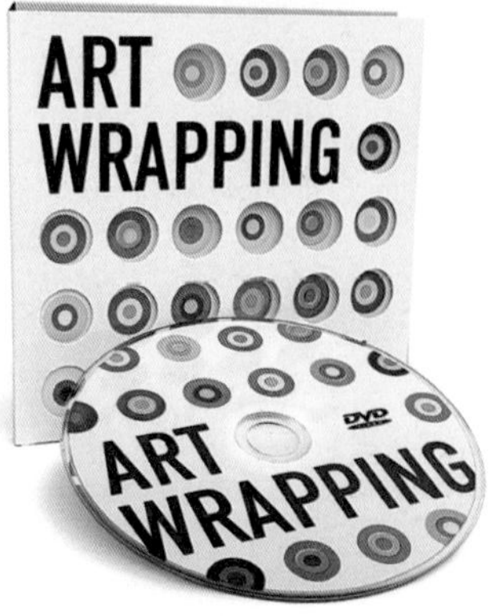

ArtWrapping – packaging for DVD – the school of modern wrapping – 2005

Airdesign2003 – calendar – airdesign – 2002

ДИЗАЙН/07
XV ВСЕРОССИЙСКАЯ
ВЫСТАВКА-КОНКУРС
ЛУЧШАЯ РАБОТА ГОДА
В ОБЛАСТИ ДИЗАЙНА
МОСКВА
КРЫМСКИЙ ВАЛ / 10
ЦДХ / ЗАЛЫ: 8, 9
21/12
24/12
ОРГАНИЗАТОР ВЫСТАВКИ: СОЮЗ ДИЗАЙНЕРОВ РОССИИ

Design2007 – poster – Russian union of designers – 2007

Paper collection catalog – booklet – arjo wiggins – 2005

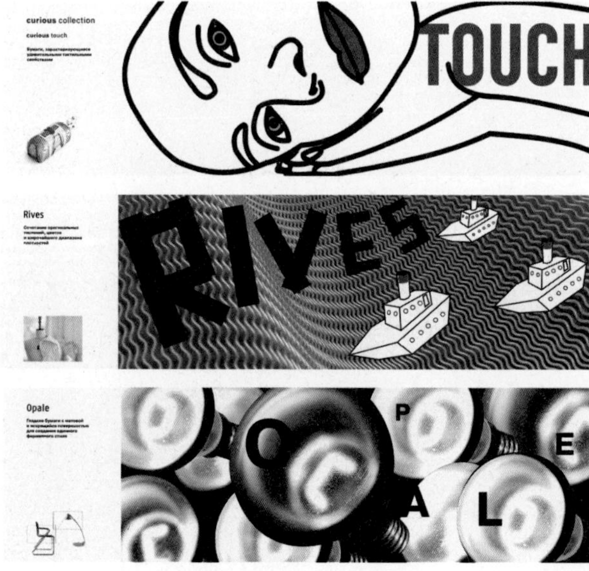

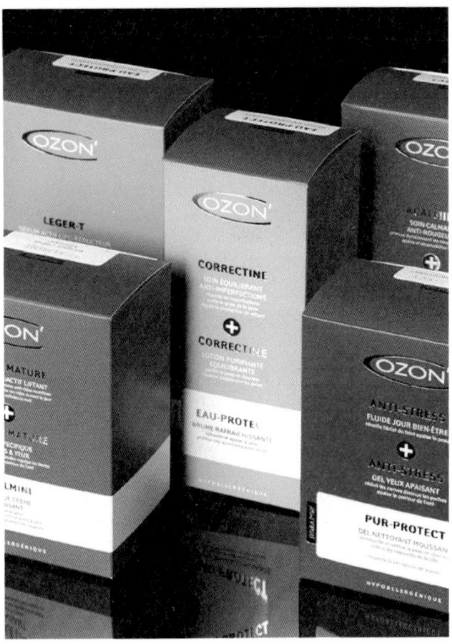

OZON' – packaging for brand promotion – ozon'c – 2008

6. Do you have a specific corporate philosophy or maybe a mission statement like other companies, which is reflected in the way you steer the studio's course?

Design will save the world. :)

7. What, from your point of view, makes the difference between a small studio and a big company?

The time we spend for each client, the warm atmosphere between studio and client.

8. What kind of advantages and disadvantages does a small studio have compared to a big company?

Advantages: We work 24 hours a day, always available for our clients, we are much more flexible than big companies.

9. What is your idea about the future of small studios? Do you think that small studios do not have any other choice but to expand in order to survive in these times of globalization?

As in the field of trade there are people that prefer to go to big malls while others prefer small boutiques.

10. Please describe and elaborate on the goals or plans that you have for your studio for the next five years?

To become known over the frontiers of Russia, to open a studio somewhere in Europe.

The types – poster – garage rock group the types – 2007

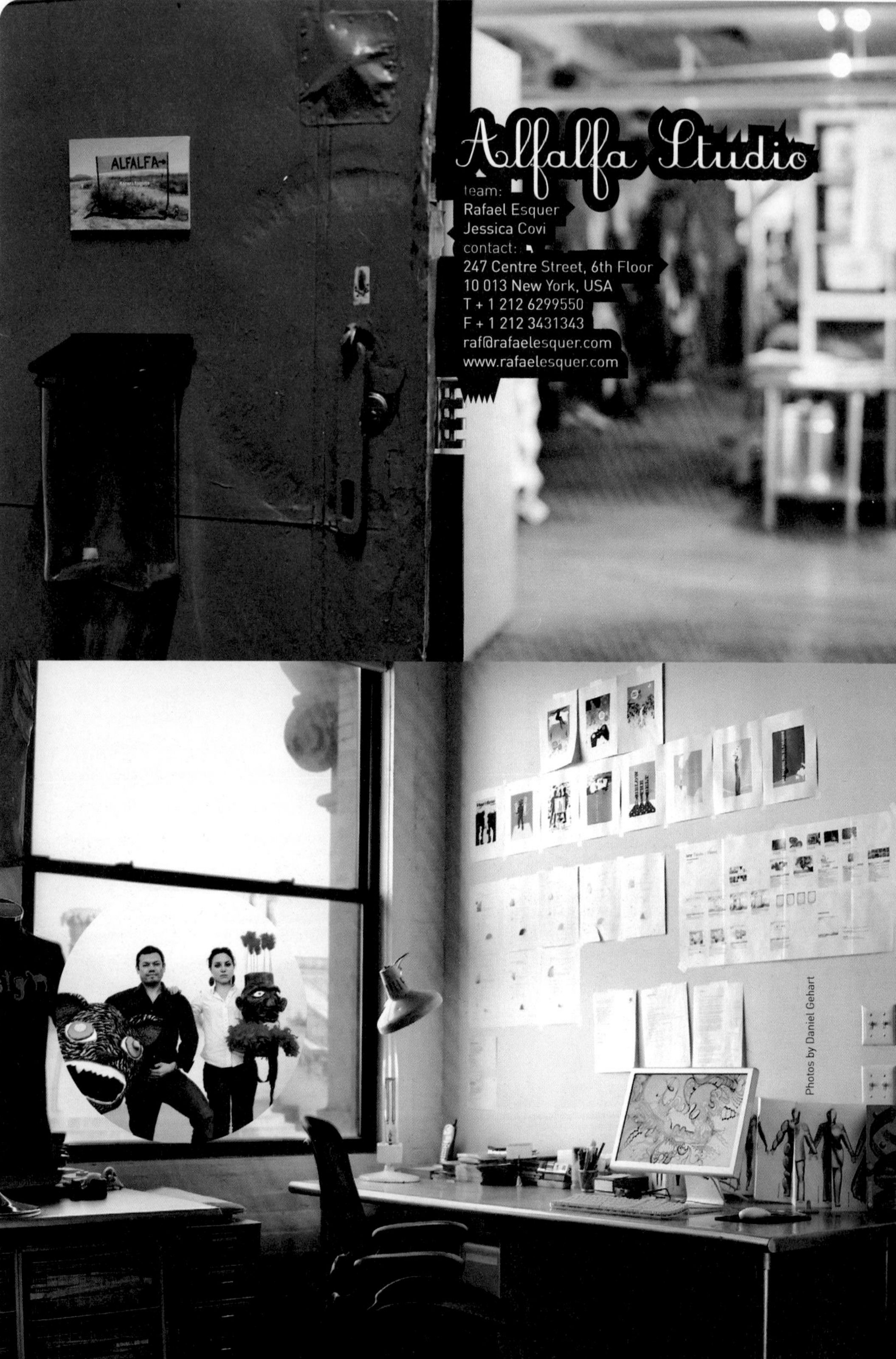

Alfalfa Studio

team:
Rafael Esquer
Jessica Covi
contact:
247 Centre Street, 6th Floor
10 013 New York, USA
T + 1 212 6299550
F + 1 212 3431343
raf@rafaelesquer.com
www.rafaelesquer.com

Photos by Daniel Gehart

Alfalfa Studio opened its doors in New York in 2004 and is devoted to interdisciplinary projects. A native of the Sonora desert of Mexico, Rafael Esquer has made New York City his home for a decade. As Creative Director at @radical.media, his group's work in communication design received the National Design Award in 2004 from the Cooper-Hewitt National Design Museum. Clients have included The New York Times Magazine, Nike, Björk, AIGA, Tommy Boy Records, Target, IBM, International Flavors & Fragrances, Scholastic, The Robin Hood Foundation, Elle Magazine and MTV. Widely published, Esquer's work has won numerous national and international design awards, and some of his pieces are contained in the collection of the Olympic Museum in Lausanne, Switzerland, the AIGA Design Archives at the Denver Art Museum, the poster collection of the Library of Congress in Washington, D.C. and the Poster Museum in Wilanów, Poland. Rafael received his BFA with distinction in graphic design from Art Center College of Design. He frequently serves as juror and speaker at national and international design events. Make the idea clear and simple, but the design surprising and beautiful – in his experience, integrity should be one of the highest values in graphic design, as in the world in general. A designer with integrity is original and designs with responsibility. He seek to bring integrity to his work by approaching every project as if it were his first and last. He does not follow formulas or rules but searches instead for a unique solution to the design problem at hand. He begins with a white canvas, so to speak, as if the project were a painting. But his canvas is always stretched by his personal journeys through many worlds: language, love, literature, film, fine art, pop culture, music, science, politics, travelling, and dreams. What keeps him excited about going to work every day is the challenge of adding another drop of integrity to the world through simplicity, surprise and beauty.

Amphibian stage productions – branding – amphibian stage productions – 2006

AIGA global membership campaign – print – AIGA – 2006

Interview with Alfalfa Studio

1. What led to the formation of your studio?

For more than 7 years I was in charge of the design group of an international, multi-disciplinary creative firm as their creative director, there were many appealing things about that position: stable salary, infrastructure, higher-profile projects lined up at the door. Everything I thought I wanted was there. And then, one lucky day, I was fired. It really took me by surprise. After the initial shock, I took a long, well-deserved vacation to mull over my options. Several job offers came along, but I was wary. So I kept a freelance practice working out of my apartment. Soon after, I was designing for big and small independent companies: MTV, The New York Times Magazine, Amphibian Productions and Talene Reilly were some of my first clients. And in the fall of 2004 Alfalfa studio was born. I founded Alfalfa because I wanted to surround myself with nice people, so when that's not the case, I quickly say goodbye. Life is too short.

2. How many staff people does your studio have and what are their main working fields?

Two. Both are multi-tasking graphic designers. We are always ready to take on any design challenge in print, web, dimensional, motion, you name it. The studio could not get along without the creative energy of our interns who come from across the country and around the world.

3. How does a regular working day at your studio look like, how is the day structured?

It's hard to describe a typical working day as every day seems to be different. It usually starts by answering emails and planning the day. At some days we have client meetings, presentations, or work on proposals. Most days we do research, sketch ideas, design, and plan future projects. We like to always be thinking of what kind of project we'd like to create for ourselves. Being independent gives you more control over your destiny.

4. How much leisure time do you have during a year?

Leisure time is important. Even though running a business is demanding, we always manage to have at least 5 weeks of vacation a year. Very un-American of us!

5. Which business areas do your clients mainly come from? Is the number of your clients increasing or rather declining?

The studio's clients come from entertainment, art and culture, luxury, sports, music and fashion. The client roster is incrementally increasing.

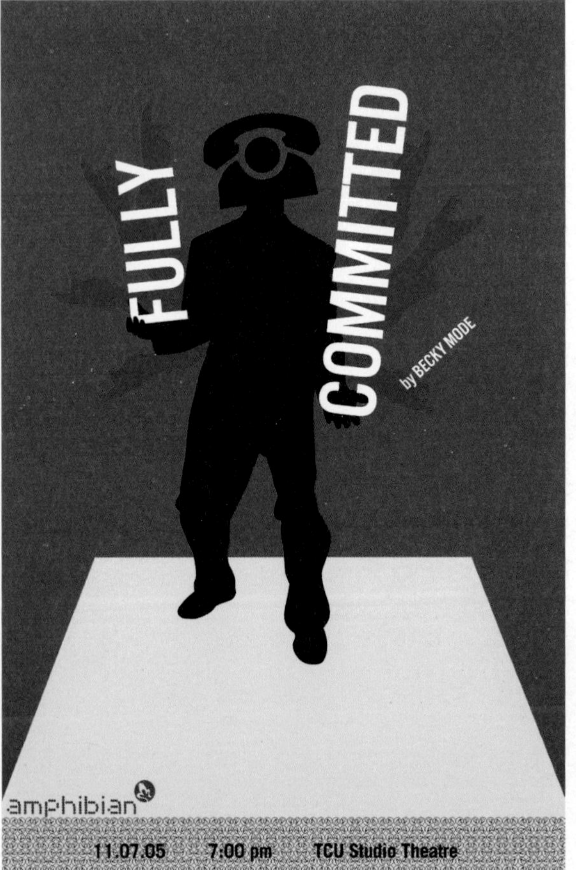

Amphibian theater poster – poster – amphibian stage productions – 2006

6. Do you have a specific corporate philosophy or maybe a mission statement like other companies, which is reflected in the way you steer the studio's course?

Make the idea clear and simple, but the design surprising and beautiful.

7. What, from your point of view, makes the difference between a small studio and a big company?

A small studio can give more personal attention and service since most of the creative work is done by the principals. Alfalfa studio's clients know exactly who is doing the work. I feel that it's more like the old-fashioned way of doing business: based on mutual trust and respect. You get to really know your clients and their business.

8. What kind of advantages and disadvantages does a small studio have compared to a big company?

Many advantages and many disadvantages: The biggest disadvantage to that being small is the lack of infrastructure: it makes it much more challenging to complete big projects. But now, with current technologies, the need for high overhead is diminishing, and even small studios can assemble a global team composed of the very best in their fields. The advantage over big companies is that every project always has a great possibility of being fresh and innovative because you can bring together new, different people. Small places foster creative collaboration. Most big companies cover their design needs internally, which makes it harder to stay fresh.

ICARUS
BY EDWIN SÁNCHEZ
amphibian
08.19.06
8:00 pm
TCU Hayes Theatre

9. What is your idea about the future of small studios? Do you think that small studios do not have any other choice but to expand in order to survive in these times of globalization?

I feel small studios are always on the edge of the abyss, playing a perpetual balancing act. Each assignment brings an adrenaline rush. You take more risks and think of creative solutions. As the old saying goes "necessity is the mother of invention." No question, she's a real Mother! In my view, the most interesting work being produced today – not only in graphic design but in film, literature, music, publishing or theatre – comes from independent places. The short history of graphic design has taught us that the fate of small studios is anything but longevity. Some grow, some disappear. Very few stay around as they are. But some are indeed making a lasting impression and will influence many generations to come, studios such as Tibor Kalman's M & Company, or Octavo, Tomato, Graphic Thought Facility, Sagmeister Inc. and Irma Boom Office just to name a few.

10. Please describe and elaborate on the goals or plans that you have for your studio for the next five years?

In my professional experience I recognize that there's a lack of minority representation in the design community (at least in the US). My immediate goal, in 2008, is to establish a scholarship to help minority art students continue their design education. To raise funds, Alfalfa studio launched alfalfa-seeds.com, a place online that seems to be the perfect canvas to continue experimenting with the new ideas, images, materials. The first venture is a line of stylish, fun, young and hip graphic tees. My perpetual goal is to keep the independent spirit alive and continue approaching every project as if it were my first and last. I'd love to be able to, 25 years from now, look back at the work we are producing and be proud of it. Keep playing, keep experimenting, keep making work that, in my opinion, is relevant, strange, challenging, fun, poetic, memorable, simple, surprising and beautiful.

Made in NY – logo – New York city – 2004

Forever now – banner – times square alliance, AIGA New York chapter and worldstudio foundation – 2006

Esquer urban forest – bag – times square alliance, AIGA New York chapter and worldstudio foundation – 2006

Ambulatory museum plan – print – galeria Ramis Barquet – 2007

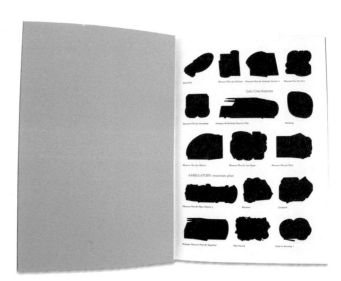

Amen

team:
Michaela Mansch
Claudio Prisco
contact:
Klenzestr. 99
80469 Munich, Germany
T + 49 89 20206501
F + 49 89 20206502
amen@soseies.com
www.soseies.com

Amen consists of Michaela Mansch and Claudio Prisco's. Michaela Mansch specializes in corporate design. She loves colours, materials and typography. Before founding AMEN she worked as an associate director in various theatres in Germany. She acquired a Master of Arts diploma. During her studies of drama, fine arts and psychology in Munich she specialized in stage design.

Claudio Prisco's main focus is based in design development. Before he formed AMEN he worked in several advertising agencies. He studied in the Art Center College of Design in Montreux and Los Angeles and has a Bachelor of fine Arts diploma.

Formstelle – business card – formstelle, design of room & object – 2006

Interview with Amen

1. What led to the formation of your studio?

Two souls united in one idea: AMEN.

2. How many staff people does your studio have and what are their main working fields?

There's two of us running the studio and two employees who help us to complete our work.

3. How does a regular working day at your studio look like, how is the day structured?

Coffee, telephone, emails, telephone, coffee, creation, lunch, coffee, telephone, meeting with clients, music, telephone, chocolate, emails, creation...

4. How much leisure time do you have during the year?

About 30 days.

5. Which business areas do your clients mainly come from? Is the number of your clients increasing or rather declining?

Our clients come from different fields as: hotels, fabrics, fine arts, film industry, galleries, gastronomy, retail. The number of our clients is increasing.

6. Do you have a specific philosophy or maybe a mission statement like other companies, which is reflected in the way you steer the studio's course?

The idea of AMEN is to give the viewers a feeling like they had just seen a good movie. AMEN wants to win the contemplator through design, wants to amuse him, to reveille a prickle and lift his spirits. AMEN wants to set the mind in motion, wants to excite, to instigate and to seduce. AMEN is a designing bureau that deals with graphic arts, advertising and design, but also likes to explore the limits of product design and art. AMEN wants to give products, needs or ideas a soul, to revive them. AMEN doesn't just decorate. It transforms matters into shapes, colours, materials and text, so they can easily be read off in all their complexity. The idea is our discipline. AMEN looks for the glamour in the ordinary, for the poetry in the well-known. AMEN inspires an outstanding view on the common, seduces to new perceptions. AMEN believes in more than pure thinking. AMEN accepts intuition and thus connects modernity, vitality and creativity. AMEN is international. AMEN stands for design that glows. AMEN means: So be it.

7. What from your point of view makes the difference between a small studio and a big company?

Quality doesn't depend on size.

8. What kind of advantages and disadvantages does a small studio have compared to a big company?

Advantage: a little bit more freedom – Disadvantage: restriction regarding the amount of clients.

9. What is your idea about the future of small studios? Do you think that small studios do not have any other choice but to expand in order to survive in these times of globalization?

No, you don't need to expand. Excellent quality and good networking is more important than ever to be successful for a small studio.

10. Please describe and elaborate on the goals or plans that you have for your studio for the next five years?

To reformate, to reanimate, to restyle, to redraft, to rediscover.

Artinvestor – magazine – artpartners GmbH – 2004/2007

Jungle – business card – Alexander Klezok – 2007

QF Hotel – poster – qf hotel Dresden – 2006

ERLEBE DAS FEST

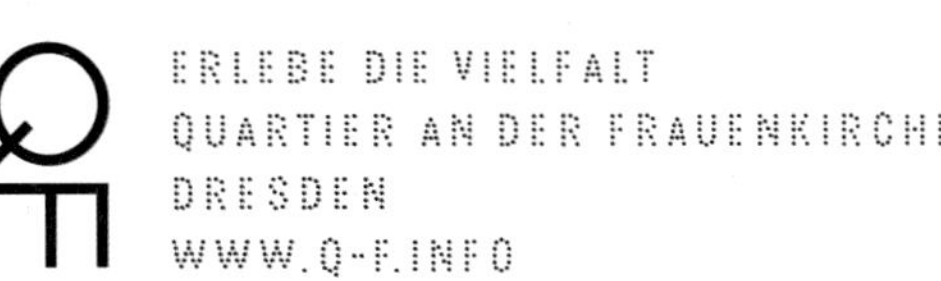

Kaleidoskop – advertisement – qf hotel Dresden – 2008

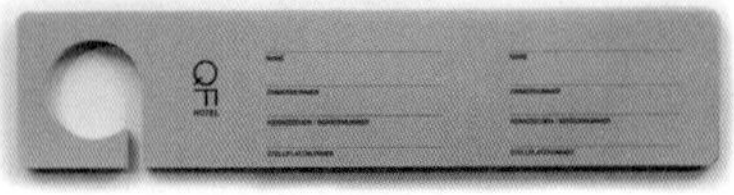

QF Hotel – ci – qf hotel Dresden – 2006

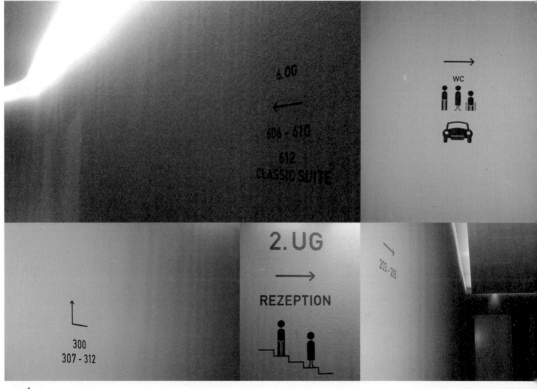

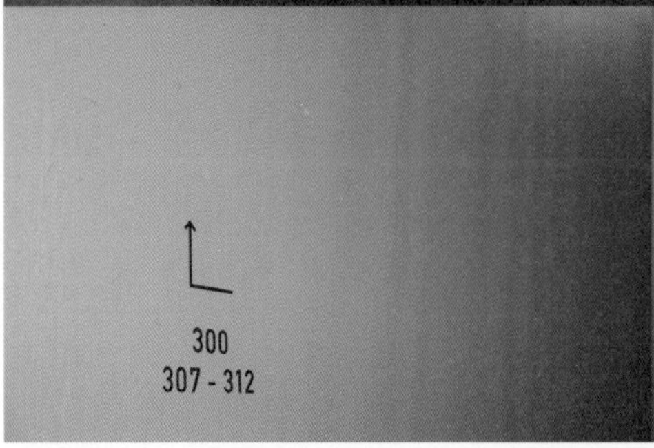

Becker – booklet – Becker fabrics – 2007

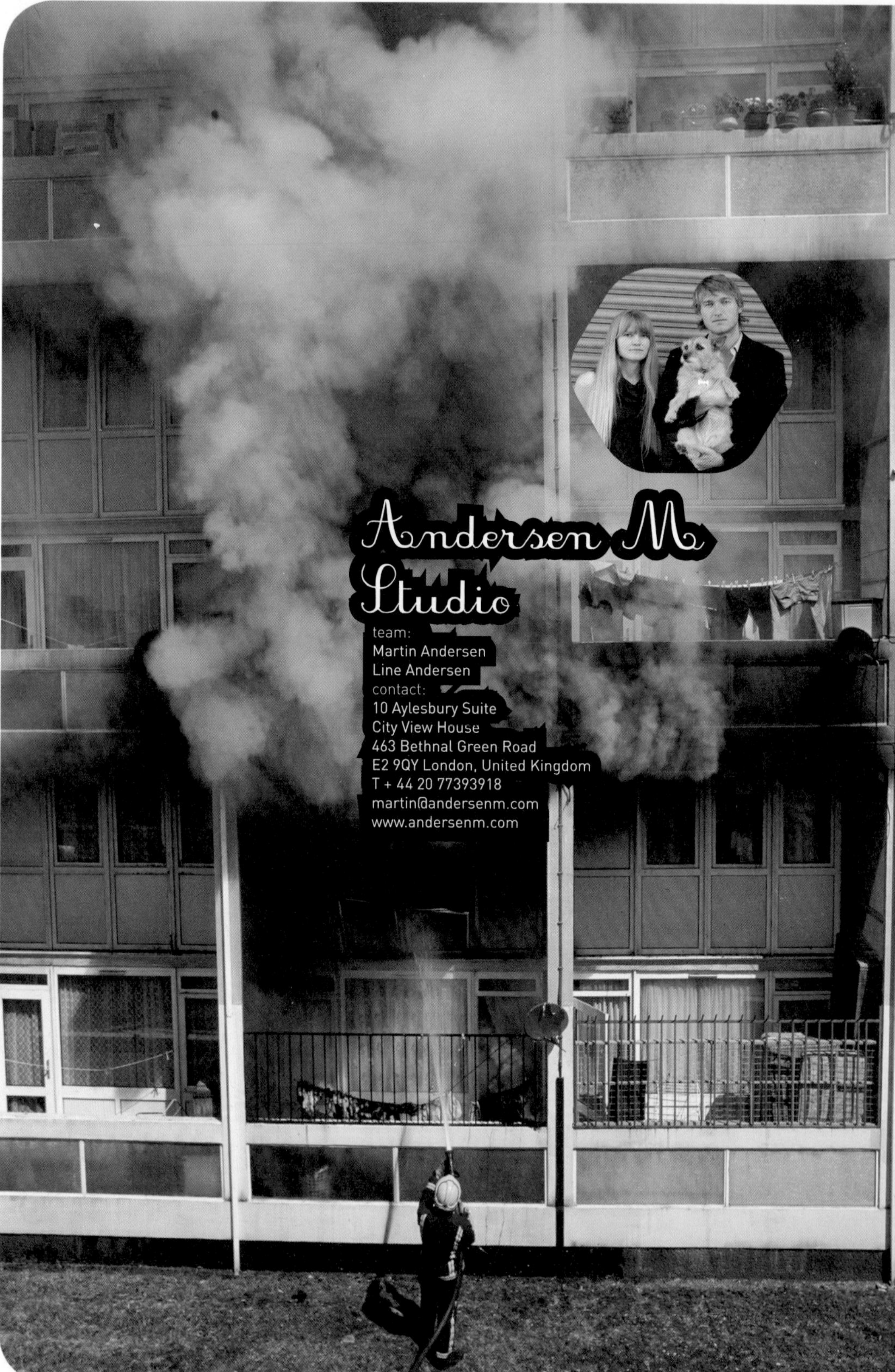
Andersen M
Studio
team:
Martin Andersen
Line Andersen
contact:
10 Aylesbury Suite
City View House
463 Bethnal Green Road
E2 9QY London, United Kingdom
T + 44 20 77393918
martin@andersenm.com
www.andersenm.com

Enjoy your parrot 1 till 3 – cd album – self published – 2005

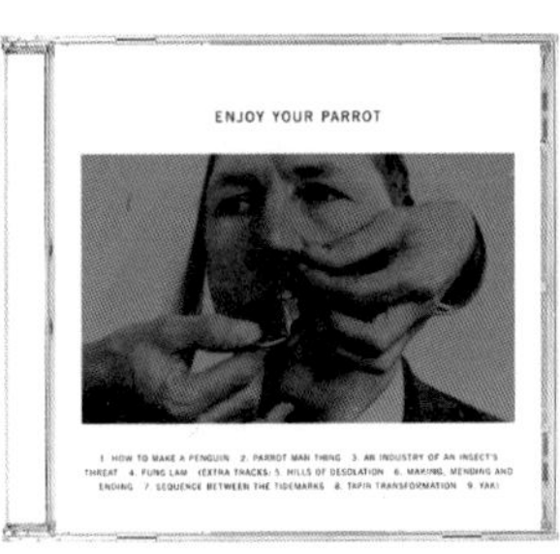

Enjoy your parrot 4 – cd album – self published – 2005

Hest/hest 2 – cd album – self published – 2007

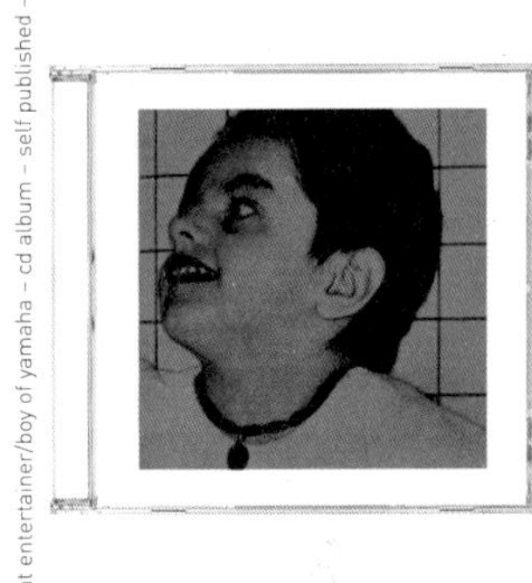

16/beat entertainer/boy of yamaha – cd album – self published – 2007

Anderson M Studio is an independent creative studio in London, UK. It was formed by graphic designer, photographer and musician Martin Andersen (MA, RCA) in 2001. Last year, Line Andersen (MA, CSM), his sister, joined to form the partnership that is now a creative multi-disciplinary studio. The studio works in the areas of graphic design, art direction, photography, illustration, music and animation. Their client list include amongst many: Cartier, American Express, Magnum, Reuters, Accenture, Southbank Centre, Martini, Channel 4, Thames & Hudson. Their work has been exhibited internationally and has been published in numerous international publications.

July skies – cd album – make mine music – 2004/2008

Roger Eno, Kate St. John – cd album – all saints records – 2006

Hugo Largo – cd album – all saints records – 2005

Interview with Anderson M Studio

1. What led to the formation of your studio?

Martin graduated from the Royal College of Art, London in 1998. He worked for 2 years with Vaughan Oliver/v23 before setting up Andersen M Studio. It was a desire to continue and evolve the freedom Martin had as a designer and photographer working for Vaughan Oliver/v23 (1998–2000). We are both close, have a good companionship, are good at different creative fields and wanted to test how far we could go by ourselves. None of us has ever had any interest in working for a bigger company (just being another cogwheel in a big machine). We are both ambitious and want to put our signature on the work we do.

Reuters, the state of the world – book – thames & hudson/reuters – 2006

2. How many staff people does your studio have and what are their main working fields?

Andersen M Studio consists of the partnership between siblings Martin (MA, RCA) and Line Andersen (MA, CSM). Martin mainly works with typography, photography, art direction and music. Line works with animation, illustration, art direction and identity design, but the fields are often shared and collaborated on. Depending on project the studio also has a variety of designers who work for the studio on a freelance basis.

3. How does a regular working day at your studio look like, how is the day structured?

Chaotic – normally we start at 10:00 and work until around 19:00. Each day is different depending on the project (design, illustration, photography, music and animation), but most days are started of with a meeting, going through the tasks of the day. Some days go without sleep, some are more relaxing.

4. How much leisure time do you have during a year?

It can be difficult to pinpoint what is work and what is leisure, which is nice. We take about 5 weeks of holidays every year.

5. Which business areas do your clients mainly come from? Is the number of your clients increasing or rather declining?

Widespread – we create work for individual artists, publishing houses, advertising companies, fashion, the music industry, cultural institutions, art galleries and museums, TV stations, arts and music festivals. Luckily, our clients have increased every year both in numbers, but also in fields, and we are now in the lucky position to be able to turn down work.

6. Do you have a specific corporate philosophy or maybe a mission statement like other companies, which is reflected in the way you steer the studio's course?

We want to keep evolving as individuals, but also as a partnership. We want to explore different avenues of creative possibilities. Our personal work and ideas keeps feeding into our commercial work and vice versa. We don't see ourselves as traditional designers knocking out layout upon layout in Helvetica.

7. What, from your point of view, makes the difference between a small studio and a big company?

As soon as you have a Coke vending machine, table football, a secretary... You must be big.

8. What kind of advantages and disadvantages does a small studio have compared to a big company?

That totally depends on each individual company. From our point of view our advantage is that we have a much closer relationship with our clients than most big companies. We are commissioned because we have individuality, something bigger companies rarely have, we are given time and freedom to express and have a bigger share of the money. Our disadvantage is that we work in isolation and therefore don't have many "interesting" colleagues. The bigger companies rely on having a lot of trusted designers who are willing to work long hours for hardly any cash, while their bosses takes the icing of the cake. Their work is often very time-limited, stressful and very rarely creatively interesting. But having said that we guess it all depends on what makes you tick as a creative person.

9. What is your idea about the future of small studios? Do you think that small studios do not have any other choice but to expand in order to survive in these times of globalization?

We think the really good small studios will survive and that the not so good ones will close down. The same goes for the bigger studios. There will always be big clients who want to work with small studios and vice versa.

10. Please describe and elaborate on the goals or plans that you have for your studio for the next five years?

More interesting commercial projects. We would also like to make a film, publish a book, release more records and just keep learning and feeling inspired. As long as we feel like we have something to express and give, we will keep going.

Magnum Ireland – book –thames & hudson – 2006

Piano Magic/disaffected – cd – piano magic – 2007

Piano Magic/incurable – cd – important records – 2007

Cartier – book – thames & hudson/cartier – 2007

Southbank centre classical season 2007/2008 – catalogue – southbank centre – 2007

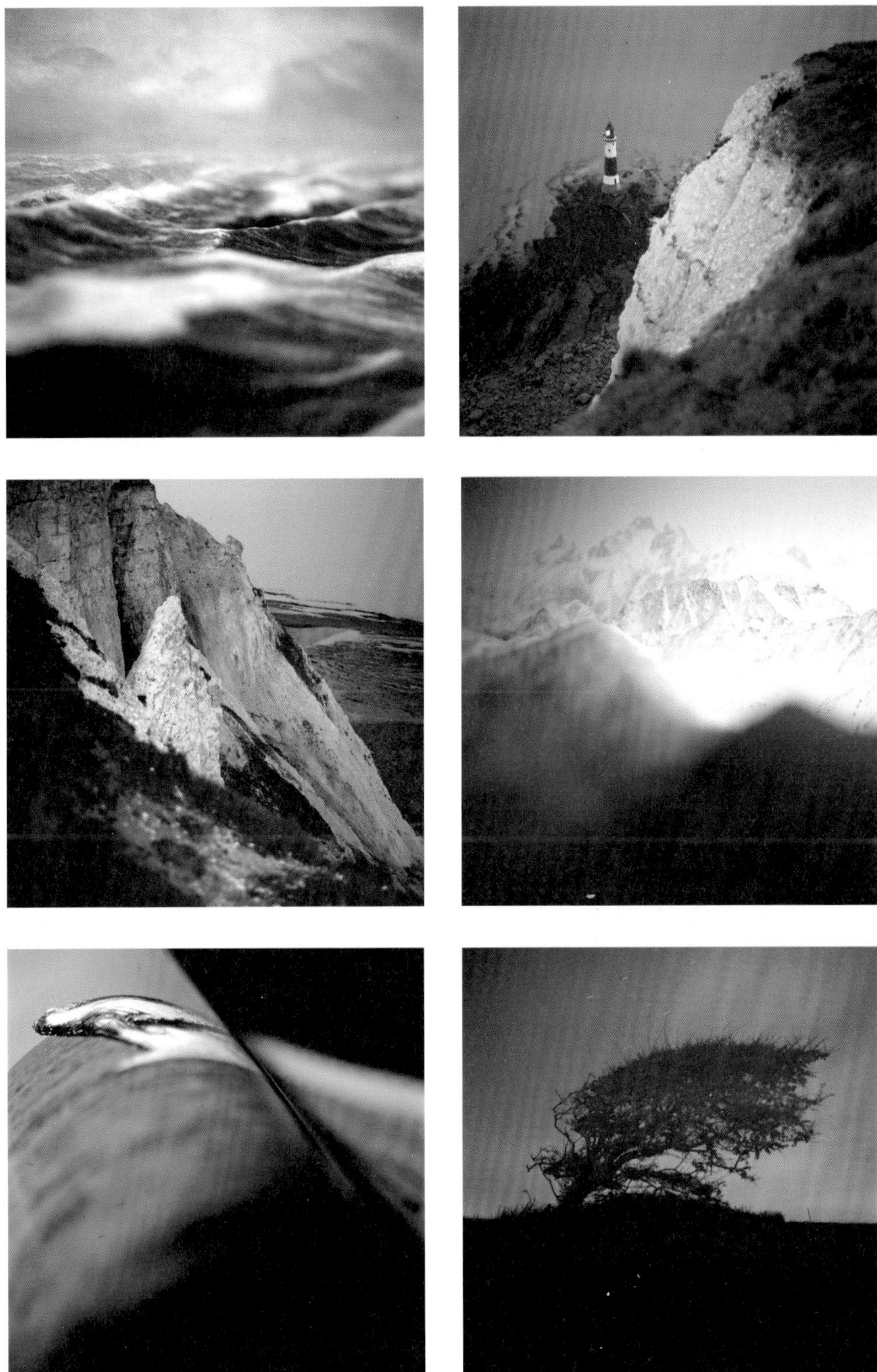

Southbank centre classical season 2007/2008 – catalogue – southbank centre – 2007

Apfel Zet

team:
Roman Bittner
Jarek Sierpinski
Julia Bittner
contact:
Brunnenstr. 7d
10119 Berlin, Germany
T + 49 30 68224853
F + 49 1805996262953
contact@apfelzet.de
www.apfelzet.de

Apfel Zet, which is Matthias Ernstberger and Roman Bittner, started designing together in 1996 and from 1997 they worked under the name of "Apfel Zet". They were students of the State Academy of Visual Arts Stuttgart. After graduating with a collaborative project in 2000, they re-designed the visual identity of the Academy. It was at this time that fine artist and web designer Jarek Sierpinski completed their team. In 2001, Matthias Ernstberger left the group and relocated to New York to work with Stefan Sagmeister while the remaining team members rented their first studio in Berlin. In 2008, Julia Bittner joined the two designers. Since then, Apfel Zet has worked primarily for cultural institutions, publishing houses and design labels. Among their customers are the "Center about art and media" in Karlsruhe, the Newspaper "Zeit", the "Filmwinter Stuttgart" and the "Deutsche Kinder- und Jugendtheaterzentrum", often one of their illustrations acting as the focus of the overall design. Parallel to their commercial commissions, they are constantly involved in personal projects such as the creation of the fictional web-cities of "Usonia and Zarovka", the independent comic "Sowy Park" and the large-format series "Ancient Cities for Tomorrow" for the Illustrative Berlin. Alongside their design ventures, they also deal with design, graphic design and architecture on a theoretical level, publishing articles on the topic across a diverse range of media. Their theoretical work has also led them to define their interpretation of a second modernity after the digital revolution and may place them among the pioneers of the german retro-movement. However, you would not be doing them any favour by classifying them in such a way as they would much rather be considered multi-stylists. After all, they are just as happy to develop modern, reduced design, where the only constant is a wealth of visual reference, this being the logical consequence of a flood of inspiration and impressions that since the printing press, and moreover since the advent of the internet, pours over today's designer.

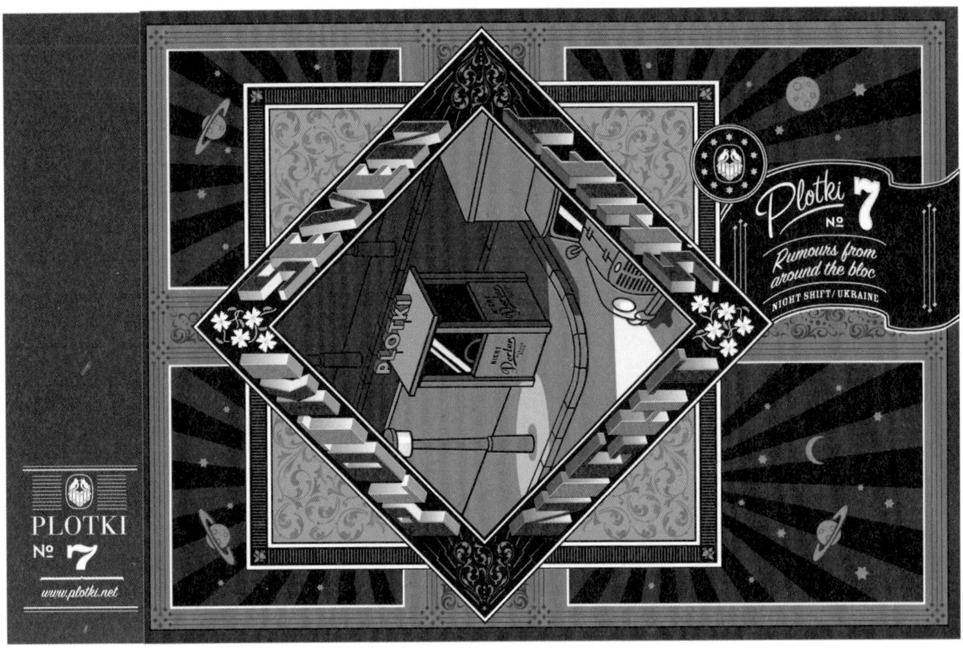

STAATLICHE
AKADEMIE DER
BILDENDEN KÜNSTE
STUTTGART

Plotki seven – magazin cover – plotki – 2006
National academy of fine arts Stuttgart – logo – ak Stuttgart – 2000
Happy new year – card – druckvogt – 2007

Interview with Apfel Zet

1. What led to the formation of your studio?

As students of the State Academy of Art and Design Stuttgart Roman Bittner and Matthias Ernstberger admired Studio Ott and Stein. They wanted to design posters like Ott and Stein, which lead to the formation of a small two-designers-studio in 1997. Soon they started working together as "Apfel Zet", primarily designing and screen printing posters for the Academy's events. After graduating with a collaborative project in 2000, they re-designed the visual identity of the Academy. It was at this point that fine artist and web-designer Jarek Sierpinski completed their team. In 2001 Matthias Ernstberger left the group and relocated to New York to work with Stefan Sagmeister while the remaining team members rented their first studio in Berlin.

2. How many staff people does your studio have and what are their main working fields?

We are four people: Roman, Jarek, Julia and one changing intern who usually stays for 3-6 months. Roman mainly works in the field of print design. He designs, typesets and illustrates mainly books, catalogues, brochures, folders, posters and develops corporate identities. Jarek's major working field is web design and programming but he also illustrates. Julia who graduated at the School of Art and Design Berlin Weissensee in the field of communication design joined the studio in 2007 and is engaged in designing, typesetting and illustration. The intern helps us with designing, typesetting, programming and is instructed in software skills, designing skills and design history.

3. How does a regular working day at your studio look like, how is the day structured?

Roman usually arrives at 9.30 a.m., Julia comes after taking the kids to the kindergarten, Jarek and the intern arrive at about 11 a.m. We often have breakfast together in the studio. Sometimes we take a break in the afternoon to go out for lunch, but often there's no time. Julia leaves at 2.30 to pick up the kids, Roman usually stays until 7.30. Sometimes we have to go on working at home. Jarek often stays late, sometimes 11 or 12 at night. One day a week Roman leaves at 2.30 to fetch the children and spends the rest of the day with them.

4. How much leisure time do you have during a year?

We try to take a vacation of about three weeks in the summer and two weeks in winter to see our families or go on holiday. Sometimes we take a day off to join design, comic or art events or see special exhibitions.

5. Which business areas do your clients mainly come from? Is the number of your clients increasing or rather declining?

Apfel Zet primarily works for cultural institutions, publishing houses and design labels. The number of clients is definitely increasing.

6. Do you have a specific corporate philosophy or maybe a mission statement like other companies, which is reflected in the way you steer the studio's course?

First of all – we're not the biggest fans of mission statements. For us it's important to make things that we're really enthusiastic about. We consider our style a multi-stylistic one – even though it's highly recognizable. We like to immerse ourselves in what we do and really enjoy discussing design and look for references in art, music, architecture or cinema, and also write about these things in a variety of publications.

7. What, from your point of view, makes the difference between a small studio and a big company?

Jean Luc Godard believed that, if you want control you need to make small films. Surely, this is one of the secrets but it all works very much like a mathematical equation. An idea has to position itself within the mechanism of the way the studio works. In a small studio the idea has more of a chance. You can see this with companies such as Google, Pixar and many others that started out small. Now you have employees leaving because they can find no room for the realization of their ideas.

Plotki – logo – plotki – 2004
Hear we go – logo – mega eins publishing – 2005
Pling – logo – sternform design – 2006

8. What kind of advantages and disadvantages does a small studio have compared to a big company?

As owners of our own small studio we can work independently and do a lot of non-commercial projects parallel to our commercial commissions, such as the illustrated series "Ancient Cities of Tomorrow", the online project "Zarovka" or the independent comic "Sowy Park". We are not in charge of employees. We can decide easily. We have a lot of fun because we've known each other for a long time and are good friends.

9. What is your idea about the future of small studios? Do you think that small studios do not have any other choice but to expand in order to survive in these times of globalization?

We're convinced that there will always be small studios like Ott and Stein, Sagmeister, Cyan, Buero Destruct or Cassarramona, which make the unique design we like best.

10. Please describe and elaborate on the goals or plans that you have for your studio for the next five years?

We are not planning to enlarge the studio and we are satisfied with our client list. However, we would like to earn more money and get more famous. We would love to teach at a design school.

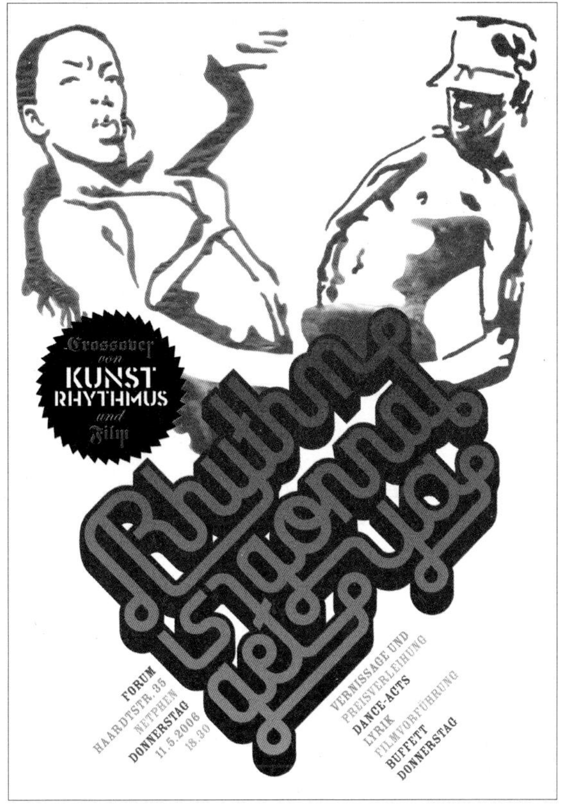

Rhythm is gonna get ya – poster – 2006

Sixtynine star love guitar – poster – 2000

Thunderbold – postcard – German technic museum Berlin – 2006

Sky harbour & train st. – illustration – illustrative 07 – 2007

AUDIAC

THANK YOU FOR NOT DISCUSSING THE OUTSIDE WORLD

... the outside world – cd cover – audiac – 2003

We are updating – website – privat job – 2005

Appetite Engineers

team:
Martin Venezky
contact:
165 Jessie Street
2nd Floor
94105 California, USA
T + 1 650 4155380059
martin@appetiteengineers.com
www.appetiteengineers.com

Martin Venezky has been the mastermind behind San Francisco-based Appetite Engineers, a small, intense and internationally recognized design firm, since 1997. Martin's work explores intricacy and complexity, and his process allows projects to flow in and out of different media – drawing, collage, photography, sculpture. Each step engages the hand and its link to the eye and body, with results that ask to be held, studied, and lived with. Appetite Engineers has had the good fortune to work with such esteemed clients as the Sundance Film Festival, San Francisco Museum of Modern Art, Reebok, Simon & Schuster, Princeton Architectural Press, and Chronicle Books among others. Martin was also art director of the late, great Speak, a magazine of popular culture, literature, music and art. Martin received an MFA in Design from Cranbrook Academy of Art in 1993 which followed an earlier BFA in Visual Studies from Dartmouth College. He currently teaches in the graduate and undergraduate design program at California College of the Arts (CCA) in San Francisco. Martin's work has been collected in magazines and books worldwide, and in 1997 he was listed among I.D. magazine's "ID40" list of influential designers. The San Francisco Museum of Modern Art has honoured Martin with an exhibition of his collected design work. "Martin Venezky: Selections from the Permanent Collection of Architecture and Design" ran from July 20 to October 14, 2001. It Is Beautiful... Then Gone, a monograph of Martin's work, has been published by Princeton Architectural Press.

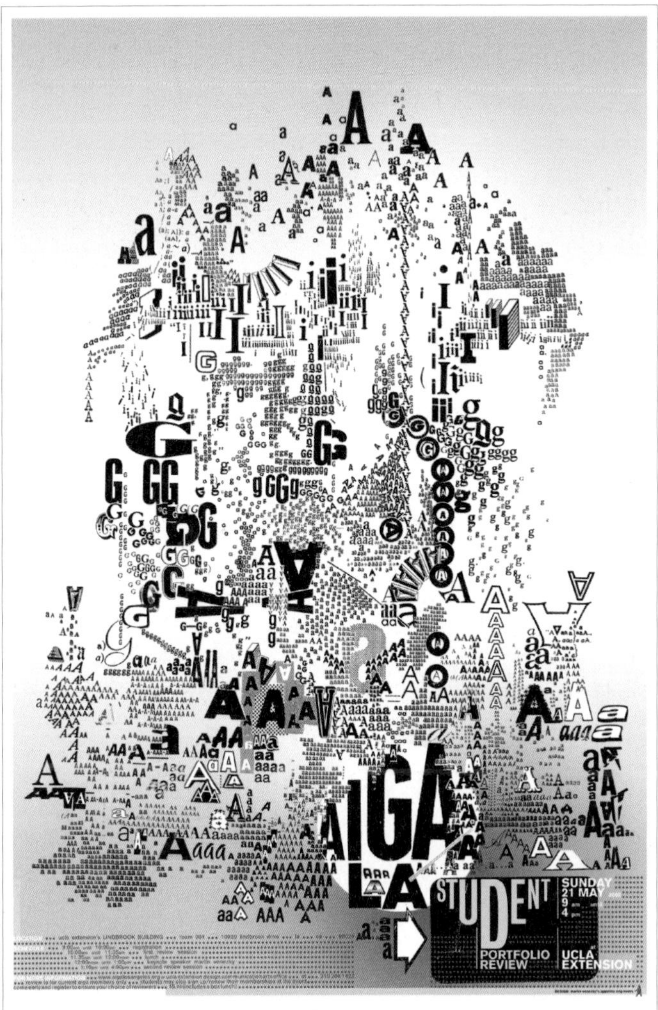

AIGA student portfolio review – poster – UCLA extension – 2006

Interview with Appetite Engineers

1. What led to the formation of your studio?

After working almost exclusively on Speak magazine for several years, I was beginning to take on more outside work. In 1997, I moved my operation into my apartment and named myself Appetite Engineers. The business was calm until I won a very large Reebok project. Appetite Engineers was hired to design the graphics for one of their primary trade show booths. I had to quickly move into a real office space, hire employees, buy computers, printers, scanners, telephones, desks and set up shop to begin the project immediately. I didn't even have stationery yet. I used the money we made on that big project to print letterhead and business cards and produce our first sales promotions.

2. How many staff people does your studio have and what are their main working fields?

At its peak in 2001, I had three employees plus a part-time intern. All of my employees were former students of mine, so we knew each other's work habits very well. Although each of my employees had particular specialties – one was exceptional in photography, another had a keen understanding of materials and architecture – they all helped with different phases of each project. Once the economy here began to falter in late 2001, my business slowed dramatically and I had to let each of my workers go. I am still in touch with them and consider them good friends. I moved my office back into my apartment, eventually leaving San Francisco for Providence, Rhode Island (where I taught full time at Rhode Island School of Design for a year and a half) and then Los Angeles. I am back in San Francisco now, sharing an office with two other designers and hoping to begin hiring again!

3. How dos a regular working day at your studio look like, how is the day structured?

Every day is different, and every day flies by too fast. Because I also teach full time at CCA (California College of the Arts), I am often racing back and forth between the campus and my office. Right now, working alone means that I am responsible for every part of every project – planning, designing, organizing, production. My working methods tend to be elaborate, involving slow processes, so I am always trying to make the most of every minute of the day. Part of every day is usually spent researching materials – finding a cheap source for small mirrors, looking up a new photographic method, visiting junk shops for old metal gears – that sort of thing. I am usually in the office by 8:00 am and stay until at least 8:00 pm, bringing some additional work or reading home with me.

4. How much leisure time do you have during the year?

Usually my vacation time is tied to a speaking engagement. Last year I was invited to lecture in Torino, so my partner and I added a few extra days and travelled on to Florence. That is unusual, though. Vacations are rare, and even day trips have to be planned in advance. I usually have to work around both the school schedule and my clients' deadlines.

5. Which business areas do your clients mainly come from? Is the number of your clients increasing or rather declining?

The biggest projects tend to be book projects. I'm lucky that they come from a wide range of subject matter, each of which is interesting to me. I really enjoy book design because I get to work with people who are deeply invested and passionate about their subject. I've done a number of poster projects recently, for museums and schools. I've also recently received a number of modest commissions for illustration projects, which I also enjoy a great deal. I think the number of clients is very slowly increasing, but as is the nature of small studios, one new client can drastically change the work flow.

6. Do you have a specific corporate philosophy or maybe a mission statement like other companies, which is reflected in the way you steer the studio's course?

I've just added our company philosophy to our web site (under the category "This Is Why We Do It"). Basically, it points out that design can do more than make things pretty and nice. It can reflect a world that is full of surprise, conflict, and drama. That's what makes design so vital to life, commerce, and art.

7. What, from your point of view, makes the difference between a small studio and a big company?

The scale of our operation does not allow us to perform as much sophisticated field research and testing. We often create through direct inspiration and experimentation. Small companies are often the testing ground for radical design which, when successful on a small scale, can find its way into larger companies.

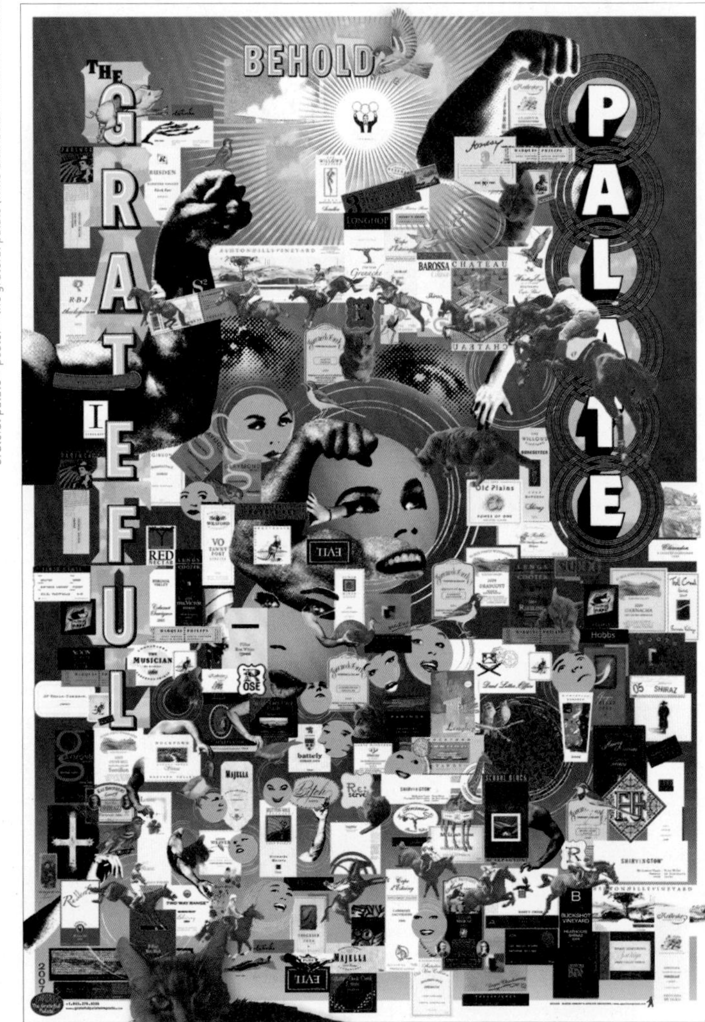

Grateful palate – poster – the grateful palate (wine distributor in southern California) – 2007

Cowboy Carl was offering to sharpen pocketknives, the Death Guilders shook out their clothes and came up with enough blades to cover the tailgate of his car. They aren't too surprised when strangers look at them suspiciously.

"The **Happiness-and-light** people view us as a **dark spot in the desert,"** says David King, a broad-shouldered, dreadlocked fellow who dreamed up the Thunderdome years ago. His story goes back to 1992, when he hitchhiked cross-country and ended up in San Francisco. "I was positive that if I stayed in New Jersey, I would either end up dead or in prison," he adds brightly. After he got to the West Coast, David started taking odd jobs at a club called the Pit, then started up a goth and industrial music night called Death Guild. The event's logo is a hanged man dangling from an oak tree. Nowadays, you can see that image adjacent to the Thunderdome, stretched across a banner on a scaffolding tower.

David ambled out to Burning Man in 1997 when, in his words, it was "uncoordinated artists' mayhem." Kurt Harland, a friend who sang in the tech-pop band Information Society, was there too, and Kurt decided to add to the bedlam by blowing up his car. Wrecking old cars at Burning Man is a hallowed tradition; to this day, a theme camp called Gigsville hosts an annual Car-B-Q. In any case, Kurt's car was a 1973 Plymouth Satellite Sebring, lovingly modified to look like the low-tech battle cars from the MAD MAX films. It was a hulking, matte black monster everyone called...... VECTOR.

The roof had pipes that **JUTTED OUT LIKE GUN BARRELS** along with a red laser sight **AND A DEER PELVIS ALL SPRAY-PAINTED BLACK.** The body was **A TANGLE OF TUBING** and expanded steel mesh, **WITH A PAIR OF PLASTER SKULLS** adorning the front bumper.

David convinced him not to destroy it. "You owe it to your fans," he insisted. So Kurt gave the car to him.

After getting the car, David explains, the next logical step was to build a THUNDERDOME to match it, in keeping with the MAD MAX theme. Two years later he made that happen with a group of around two dozen friends. They bought a geodesic dome in pieces. It took them four days to connect all the struts and hubs. It was so tall, they had to build an adjacent scaffolding to work on it, and a guy walking past on stilts stopped to help tighten the bolts. But when the dome was done, the battles began. Post apocalyptic gladiators defied gravity in the bungee harnesses. They hovered in the air and swooped down to deal crushing blows. The audience was mesmerized.

"It was basically a giant jungle gym with a TV in it, and if they screamed loud enough, blood would come spurting out," says David. He's exaggerating a little, but over the years contestants

164 DANGER DAYS DANGER DAYS 165

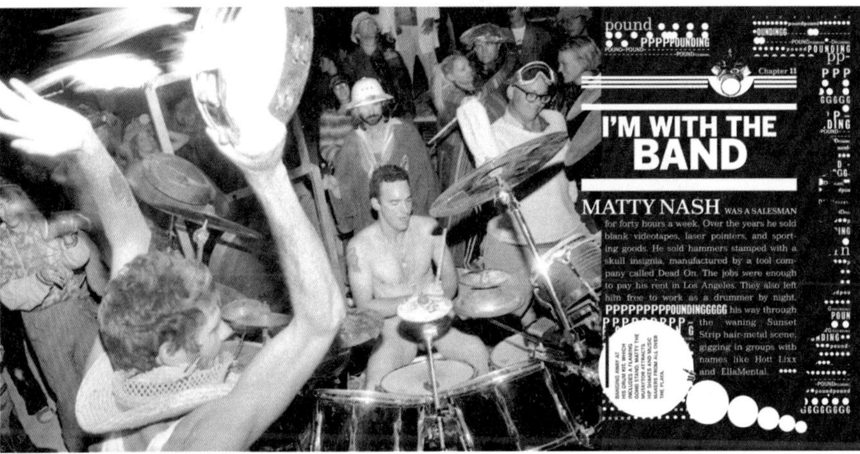

I'M WITH THE BAND

MATTY NASH WAS A SALESMAN for forty hours a week. Over the years he sold blank videotapes, laser pointers, and sporting goods. He sold hammers stamped with a skull insignia, manufactured by a tool company called Dead On. The jobs were enough to pay his rent in Los Angeles. They also left him free to work as a drummer by night. PPPPPPPPPOUNDINGGGGG his way through the waning Sunset Strip hair-metal scene, gigging in groups with names like Hott Lixx and EllaMental.

Burning book: a visual history of burning man – book – simon spotlight entertainment a division of simon & schuster – 2007

8. What kind of advantages and disadvantages does a small studio have compared to a big company?

While we don't often get to work with very large accounts that are seen by millions of viewers, we do get to work directly with creative individuals on a collaborative, meaningful basis. I've had the good fortune of making friends with artists, photographers, musicians, writers all of whom also work at a modest scale. The one-to-one direct contact, as well as shouldering the full responsibility of each project is both exciting and frightening. When a project is completed, there is an immense satisfaction to knowing that you brought something very special into the world. When I worked within larger companies, I never felt that kind of pride and responsibility.

9. What is your idea about the future of small studios? Do you think that small studios do not have any other choice but to expand in order to survive in these times of globalization?

No, I think that small studios can be productive and valuable in any economy. When necessary, small studios can collaborate on larger projects with ease. That's one of the newer trends in design education – to emphasize collaboration between disciplines, and among people within the same discipline but with different specialties. It is very hard, though, to do the sales and promotion side of a business at the same time as managing the actual design work. I hope that soon agencies will form to represent designers and small firms, like they do for illustrators and photographers. Then it would be much easier to connect with larger companies who are looking for specialty design services, or unusual points of view and processes.

10. Please describe and elaborate on the goals or plans that you have for your studio for the next five years.

I would ideally like Appetite Engineers to grow to be the same size that it was in its 2001 peak – maybe four or five employees who like each other and work well in an experimental/laboratory setting. Since I so enjoy working with materials, I'd like to be able to have separate areas within the firm for tools and building, photography, collage, and digital work. To have access to so many processes at my fingertips would be my dream studio – one that can fluidly move in and out of drawing, sculpture, photography and digital work on a single project. For me, that is the ultimate pleasure in design, and where I do my best work.

California College of the Arts PRESENTS
WORD.WORLD.2008
A LITERARY READING SERIES
MARCH 28
APRIL 4
APRIL 18
AND APRIL 25

THE GRADUATE PROGRAM IN
DESIGN
AT California College of the Arts PRESENTS
2008
THESIS EVENTS

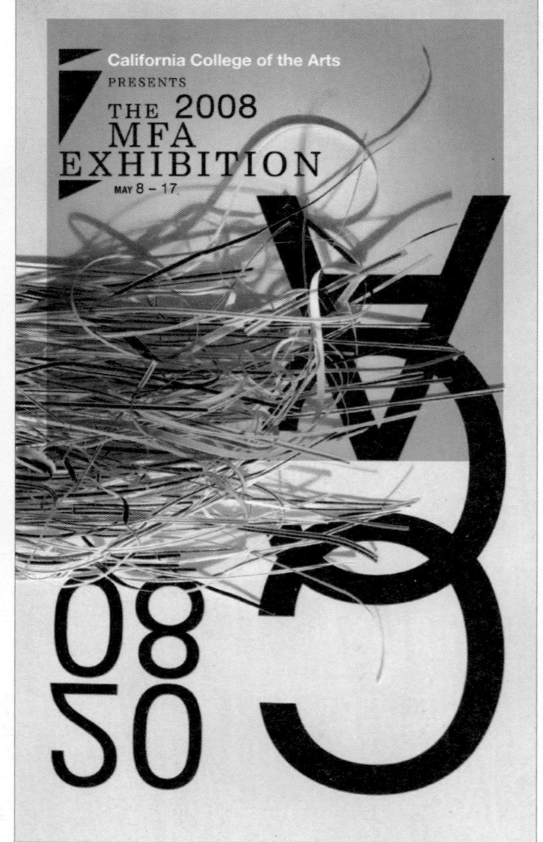

California College of the Arts
PRESENTS
THE 2008
MFA
EXHIBITION
MAY 8 – 17

GCCA gaduate thesis events – poster/flyer/postcard – CCA (California college of the arts), San Francisco, California – 2008

News for you from Martin Venezky's appetite engineers – newspaper – appetite engineers – 2008

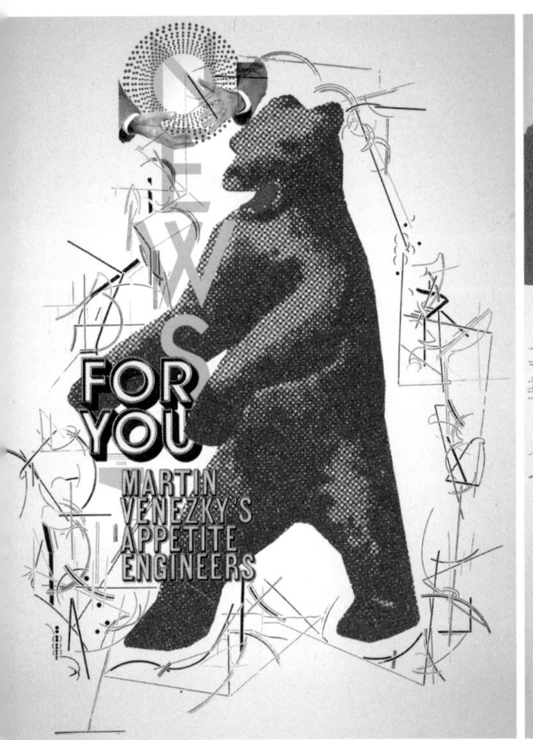

NEWS
FOR YOU
MARTIN VENEZKY'S APPETITE ENGINEERS

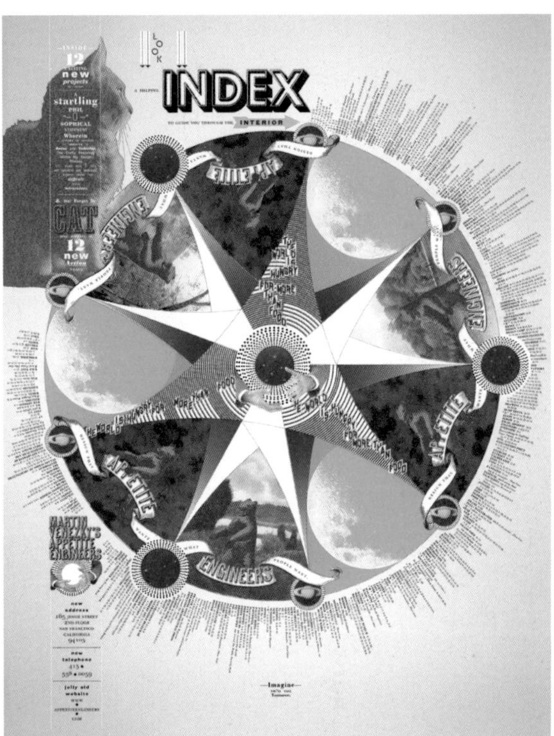

LOOK
INDEX
INTERIOR
CAT
ENGINEERS
APPETITE
MARTIN VENEZKY'S APPETITE ENGINEERS

APPETITE ENGINEERS
Oh no!
NEWS
LOOK
WILD WEST
SAN FRANCISCO
CALL
WRITE
VISIT
SEND
TRY
415 538 0059

BEHOLD
LOOK
CAT
BUILT
WOW
NOW
Mills College
AIGA

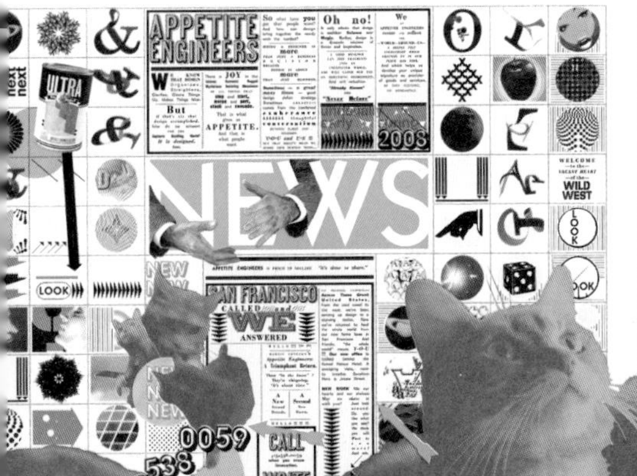

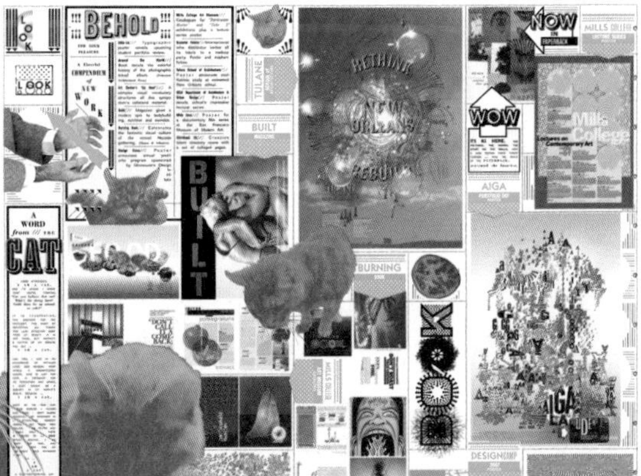

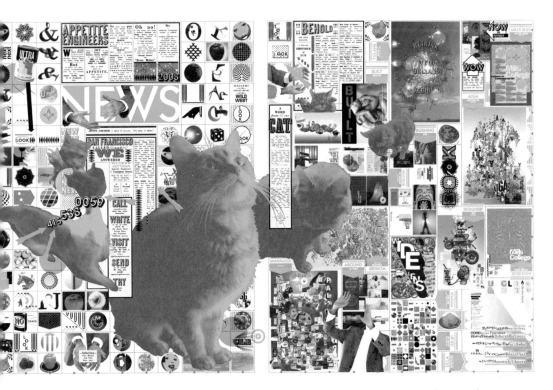

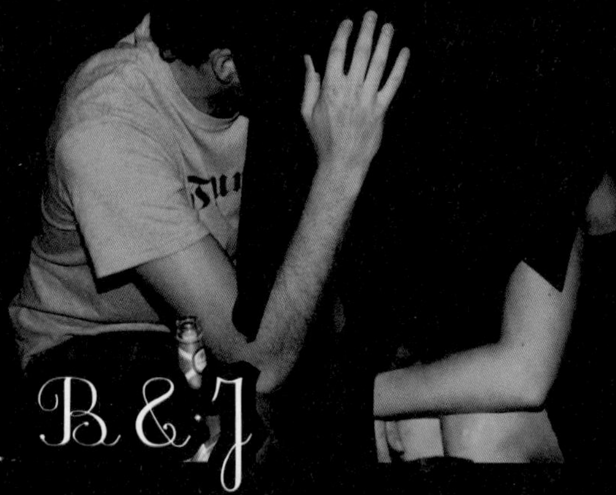

B & J

team:
Brigitte Speich
Jaques Magiera
contact:
Prinzessinnenstr. 16
10969 Berlin, Germany
T + 49 30 65705231
T + 49 30 65705232
F + 49 30 65705230
ja@materia.li
info@brigittespeich.com
www. materia.li
www.brigittespeich.com

B & J, "It's not about design – it's about love". Jacques et Brigitte is a Berlin-based graphic and illustration team, driven by the passion of design. Winner of Print magazine's European Design Annual 2007.

Nintedo´s wii-crib, Berlin – acrylic-hand paianted walls – nintendo and flip sellin – 2006

Interview with B & J

1. What led you to the formation of your studio?

Love. And the passion for what we're doing.

2. How many staff people does your studio have, and what are their working fields?

No fix staff. Depending on the work's size, interns or freelancers are helping us out.

3. How does a regular working day at your studio look like, what are your working schedules?

Small breakfast at the atelier. Checking emails, post. Project meeting. Work and try to remember to have lunch. Work harder, try to finish what needs to be done and go home when it's dark outside.

4. How much leisure time do you have during the year?

Around 6 weeks, but work's always in progress!

5. Which business areas do your clients mainly come from? Is the number of your clients increasing or declining?

Culture, fashion- and exhibition design, PR, music, etc. The number is increasing.

Create Berlin – invitationcard – create Berlin e.V., goethe institute Tokyo – 2006

Create Berlin - carpet – 220 m2 carpet – create Berlin e.V., goethe institute Tokyo – 2006

Smeilinener invitationscard – card – smeilinener (fashion label) – 2007

6. Do you have a specific corporate philosophy or maybe a mission statement like other companies, which is reflected in the way you steer your studio's course?
To understand your client; to be true to yourself; to surprise your client and yourself.

7. What, from your point of view, makes the difference between a small studio and a big company?
As a small studio you are doing everything from step one to the end.

8. What kind of advantages and disadvantages does a small studio have compared to a big company?
Advantages: It's definitively more personal and cheaper because of the lower fixed costs.

9. What is your idea about the future of small studios?
If you only see the money – expand! We think collaborations are the future. Networking with other studios' people to catch bigger job opportunities. being flexible, moving the studio if needed.

10. Please describe and elaborate on the goals or plans that you have for your studio for the next five years?
We would wish that it continues like it all started: Travelling to new places through projects and meeting interesting people, realizing our ideas and some crazy projects, collaborations with motivated and motivating persons, going to new scopes, to lecture, and keeping the dream alive!

Kaleidoskop partyseries – flyers – best works, Berlin – 2006

Hairbob – postcard – radio 3fach, Lucerne, Switzerland – 2006 / 07

Glitz and then some... – poster, a1 – schmuck2 and Suska Mackert – 2007

Jacques et Brigitte, what makes Berlin addictive? – poster – BCCB, vanguard gallery Shanghai, coordination Berlin – 2006

Coordination catalogue – chinese-bound book – coordination Berlin – 2007

Without title (trees) – poster – BCCB, vanguard gallery Shanghai, coordination Berlin – 2006

痴迷柏林

WHAT MAKES BERLIN ADDICTIVE?

展览日期：2006年9月14日－9月17日
开幕酒会：2006年9月14日18:00

SEPTEMBER 14. - 17. 2006
OPENING PARTY: 14.09. 2006, 6:00 PM

Address: No. 20 Cha Ling Bei Lu, Shanghai
Tel: 0086 21 525 22 551
www.vanguardgallery.com
www.outlooklook.com

Organizers:
Vanguard Gallery Shanghai;
Berlin China Cultural Bridges eV.;
Coordination Berlin

Co-organizer:
T. Win Creation
Sponsor:
Gold Huasheng Paper

展览地址：上海茶陵北路20号（近斜土路）
联系电话：0086 21 525 22 551

主办：
Vanguard Gallery Shanghai
柏林中国文化之桥协会
柏林 Coordination 事务所
协办：华瑶创意
赞助商：金华盛纸业

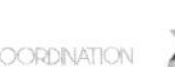

What makes Berlin addictive? – poster – BCCB, vanguard gallery Shanghai, coordination Berlin – 2006

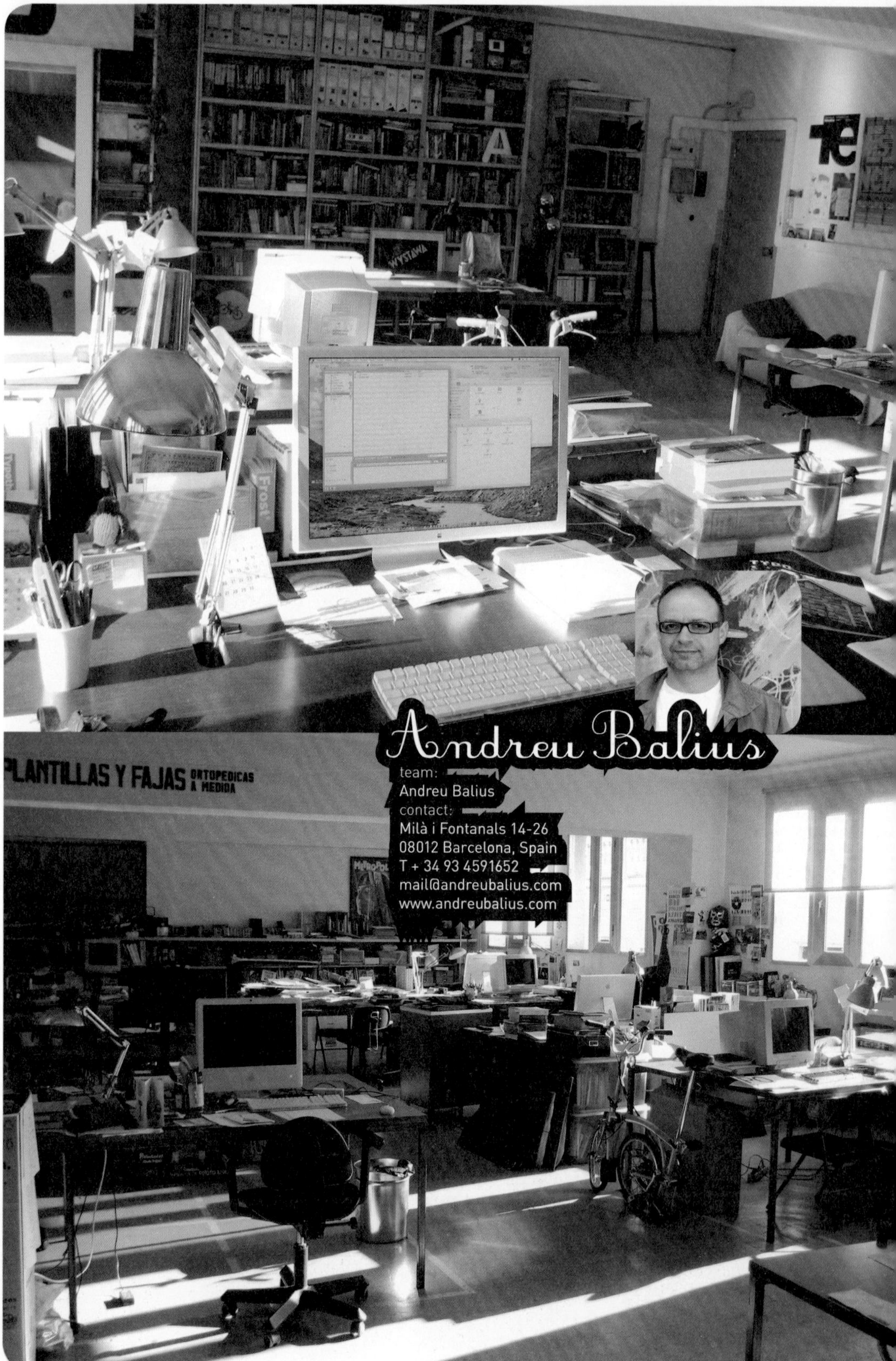

Andreu Balius

team:
Andreu Balius
contact:
Milà i Fontanals 14-26
08012 Barcelona, Spain
T + 34 93 4591652
mail@andreubalius.com
www.andreubalius.com

Andreu Balius Graphic Design studio based in Barcelona devoted to type design and font production from corporate typefaces to tailor-made fonts. They are especially qualified for those design projects where typography is the most important thing. They really love their work and they put their best at developing their projects.

Type at work – book – self published – 2004

Interview with Andreu Balius

1. What led to the formation of your studio?

According to my way to look at things and my early approach to graphic design and the early passion for typography, I felt in the mood to set up my own design studio. After getting some professional experience in graphic design and some work being selected to be part in an international design exhibition, I felt myself with the aim of running my own company. That was really hard in the beginning since my budget was very limited. A plain Macintosh LC and a Laser Writer were really expensive at that time (that was in the early 90's). But during the end of the 80's and the beginning of the 90's, my city – Barcelona – was living a very exciting moment. Graphic design was considered a quite brand new profession at that time. Some young designers were anxious to be part of those times and to use graphic design as a way to express ourselves, too. I set up my own studio but never missed the pleasant experience when working in collaboration with others. Collaborative work is something important when you decide to be small.

2. How many staff people does your studio have and what are their main working fields?

Actually, it's just me. I also have an assistant supporting me in final arts and little assignments, although sometimes I would like to get him more involved in certain projects. There was a time when I had the opportunity to grow, to become "bigger". There was a lot of work to do. My studio, named "Typerware" at that time, became quite "trendy". But things were not clear about the future. There came the time to make a decision. Me and my collaborative partner – who was one of my best pupils – decided to split since our point of view was quite different. I remained "small". And I feel comfortable with that situation.

3. How does a regular working day at your studio look like, how is the day structured?

Usually it's quiet. I mean, not too early, some pleasant music during the day, not long hours. I share my studio with three other designers. It's a nice way to share, not only the rent but also the net connections, printer machines, cleaning. It's not easy to enjoy from a luminous big room in Barcelona at a nice rental. Sharing makes it more affordable and funny, since you can keep good relationship with other designers and ask them for advice or some help, if needed.

4. How much leisure time do you have during a year?

I like to distribute my leisure time – let's say "holiday time" – in different dates along the year. In Spain, people use to enjoy holiday time in August. That makes a big stop. It's difficult to work in August since the large majority of your suppliers or clients are on holidays. But for me it's the best time to work. It's more quiet: no phone calls, no stress at all, you can really do good job! If I have the opportunity to be invited abroad (for a lecture, a workshop, a presentation), I try to organize my work in order to have some days off and visit the country or the city. Since I love my work I don't have the need to "stop" too much.

5. Which business areas do your clients mainly come from?

They mainly come from the cultural area. That is, Galleries, Museums, Festivals, Cultural departments. But in my type design work I use to work for other graphic studios and agencies, editorial companies and big corporations, too.

Is the number of your clients increasing or rather declining?

The number increases a bit. But according to my "small" condition, I prefer to choose the kind of work I like to do and not accept too much work I could not do.

6. Do you have a specific corporate philosophy or maybe a mission statement like other companies, which is reflected in the way you steer the studio's course?

I believe that my philosophy is more reflected in the work I do – and the way I do it – than how I steer my studio. Obviously, I try to do my work as best as possible. Trying to do my best is the main goal of my design work. And trying to behave in an ethical way within my profession.

7. What, from your point of view, makes the difference between a small studio and a big company?

Small studios normally take more care of every little thing they do. A small studio minds the client and tries to do its best for him. Good results help a small studio to become better known and get some kind of promotion (and get more commission work at the same time) and respect. Big companies are more interested in big business. Their marketing departments use to put pressure on designers. The result is not as important as the amount of money you could get from a specific project. Of course, that's not always that case: I know big studios that really mind their projects and do great design work. When you are small you value every little thing. You get control of the whole process, from the idea to the final result. And that's the real thing! Furthermore, a small studio can change its strategy faster than a big one.

8. What kind of advantages and disadvantages does a small studio have compared to a big company?

Well, the problem with small studios is that big companies don't trust your capability in assuming a big project. They think: you are small therefore you can do only small projects. But if you are specialized enough (and that's my case), then you can work in collaboration with somebody else, or even you can be part of a group working on a big project for a large company. I have designed typefaces for big companies (editorial, corporate, governmental). So, in my type of work (designing typefaces is a very specialized work) I believe I can get over some of those disadvantages (only some of them).

9. What is your idea about the future of small studios? Do you think that small studios do not have any other choice but to expand in order to survive in these times of globalization?

Small studio will survive as specialized studios. They should be good at certain things in a certain area in graphic design. They will always exist, although things are not easy for them in a neo-liberal economy. But they are useful anyway. I believe that collaborative work is the key to a pleasant survival – sharing professional experiences without loosing the freedom which a small studio (or a freelancer) usually has.

10. Please describe and elaborate on the goals or plans that you have for your studio for the next five years?

It's difficult for me to plan my future. I think about the future in a positive way. I'll try to get even more involved in type design commission work. Further producing my own type design projects, some personal work, and enjoying my work as much as I can.

Mecano- typeface - CCCB - 2007

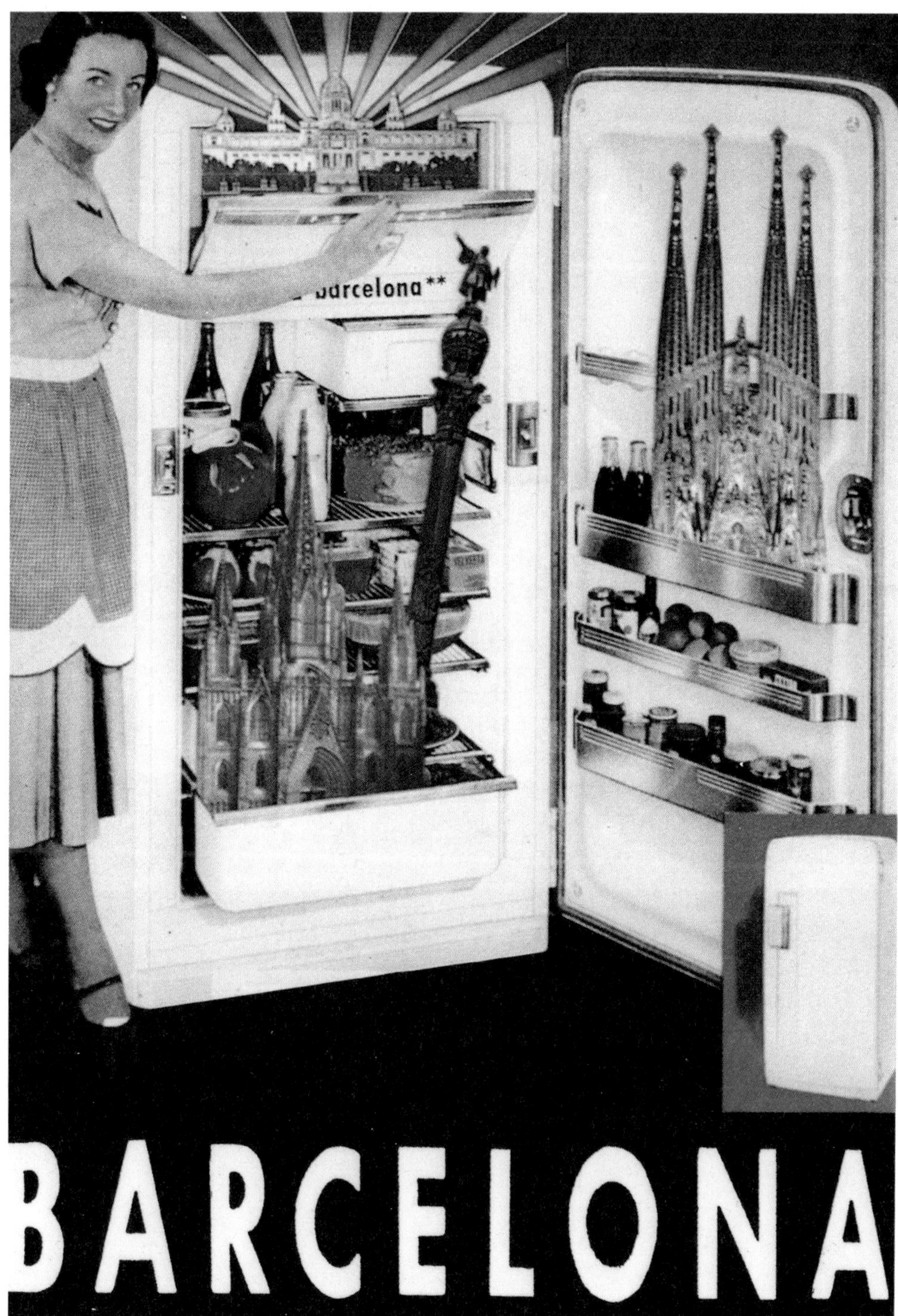

Barcelona – postcard – star – early 90´s

Diseño revista GRRR número 14 – magazine – GRRR magazine – CCCB – 2005

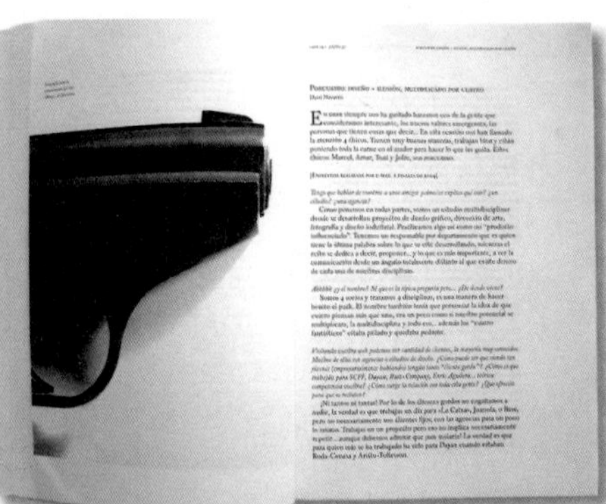

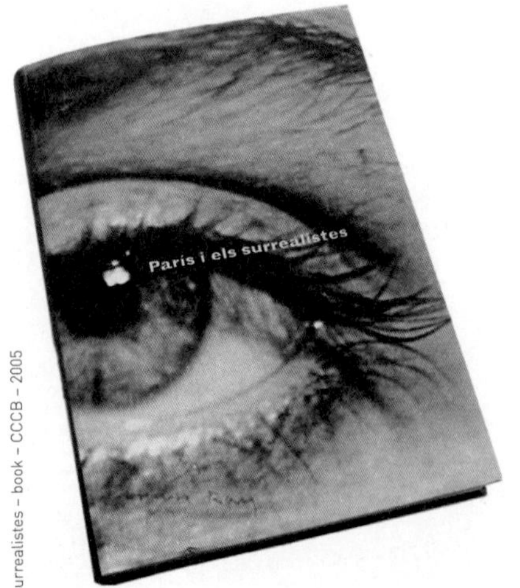

París i els surrealistes – book – CCCB – 2005

El salvathe europeu – book – CCCB – 2004

ELISABETH ANTIQUA

Roman – Italics & Swash capitals

GOETHE

Jack amazed a few girls by dropping the antique onyx vase

Heizölrückstoßabdämpfung

Two hardy boxing kangaroos jet from Sydney to Zanzibar on quicksilver pinions

AUDREY HEPBURN

Zwölf Boxkämpfer jagten Eva quer über den Sylter Deich

BERLIN

Six big juicy steaks sizzled in a pan as five workmen left the quarry

Der Ring des Nibelungen

TANNHÄUSER

Jove xef, porti whisky amb quinze glaçons d'hidrogen

El Perro de Roque no tiene Rabo

Bésame mucho

POLLO

HELADO DE MARACUYÁ

Aquest xicot està com una cabra

TYPOGRAPHY

Hace bastante calor en Madagascar

BERLIN

Mary Poppins fumaba canutos de marihuana

SUPERCALIFRAGILISTICOESPIALIDOSO

SÃO PAULO

PRADELL

Pradell Roman, *Italic* & **Bold.**

Latin text family inspired from 18th century spanish type specimens by Andreu Balius

ABC

DEFGHIJK

LMNOPQRSTUVWXYZ

abcdefghijklmnopqrstuvwxyz

ÀÁÂÃÄÅÆÈÉÊËÌÍÎÏÒÓÔÕÖØŒÙÚÛÜÇÑŸ

à á â ã ä å æ è é ê ë ì í î ï ò ó ô õ ö ø œ ù ú û ü ç ñ ÿ

1 2 3 4 5 6 7 8 9 0 0 € $ ¢ £ & ﬁ ﬂ ct ß @ © ® * † ‡ § ¶

Eudald Pradell (1721-1788) nació en Ripoll *(Barcelona)*, junto al Pirineo catalán. Aprendió de su padre el oficio de armero, adquiriendo conocimientos sobre el arte de grabar punzones. ¶ Pradell estableció su propio taller como maestro armero en Barcelona y abrió sus primeros punzones en el grado de letra «Peticano». *Dada la calidad del material realizado y la gran falta del mismo en España, Carlos III le pensionó para que diseñara nuevos tipos de letra para la Imprenta Real en Madrid, ciudad donde Pradell finalmente instaló su taller de fundición.* ¶

Eudald Pradell was born in Ripoll *(Catalunya, Spain)*, a little village under the Pyrenees, in 1721. He pertained to a family of gunsmiths and learned the practice of being an armourer with his father, adquiring the knowledge of making punches. ¶ Pradell established his own workshop in Barcelona. Despite he was illiterate, he was able to produce one of the most appreciated typefaces ever cut in Spain. *His fame as a punchcutter increased and King Carlos III gave him a pension in order to provide new type designs at the Imprenta Real in Madrid, where he finally moved and set up his foundry. He died in 1788.* ¶

HISPANIA

hamburguesa

ROMA

SOUP & NOODLES

Barcelona

Typography

Mont~Serrat

What would you like for dinner?

RAQUEL

Ultramarinos

Manuale Tipografico

cactus

Elisabeth/Lladro/Tipografía/Pradell – typeface – neuville digital – 2005

Lladró – typeface – pepe gimeno studio – 2006

Lladró – typeface – pepe gimeno studio – 2006

Banana Moon Studio Sapporo

team:
Hiroshi Maeda
contact:
312 Odori-Heim, Nishi-15, Kita-1
Chuo-ku, Sapporo 060-0001
Japan
T + 81 11 6418776
F + 81 11 6416443
maeda@bananamoon.jp
www.bananamoon.jp

Banana Moon Studio Sapporo was founded by Hiroshi Maeda. Born in Sapporo, Japan, he obtained a Masters degree at the graduate school of international media and communication, Hokkaido University. As an undergraduate student, he had begun to work as a designer, illustrator and writer for a publishing company. He founded Banana Moon Studio in 1990. He has been involved in many projects for local and global companies as designer, art director or strategic consultant. At present, the studio is located in Sapporo and Niseko, Japan. He creates posters for the Inter-cross Creative Center, and some of his works have been selected or awarded prizes in major international graphic design competitions such as the Biennale Warsaw, Biennale Brno, Biennale Lahti, Triennale Toyama, Biennale Korea, Chaumont Festival, New York ADC and others. He also won numerous prizes in domestic design awards. In 1996, Hiroshi Maeda became a member of the Tokyo-based Japan Graphic Designers Association (JAGDA) and has been an editorial member of Graphic Design in Japan (JAGDA Annual) since 2004. As one of the founding members he helped to establish the Sapporo Art Directors Club in 2001 and has been a committee member since then.

Interview with Banana Moon Studio Sapporo

1. What led to the formation of your studio?

I established Banana Moon Studio in 1990, at the age of 26. It was a fortunate moment because at that time Japan was still enjoying so-called "Bubble-Economy", there was much demand for design work even here in Sapporo, a city in northern Japan.

2. How many staff people does your studio have and what are their main working fields?

We have three staff people including myself: a director/designer, a writer and an accounting manager. Furthermore, we are working with independent creative people in various fields.

3. How does a regular working day at your studio look like, how is the day structured?

It starts with unlocking the door by the writer or me around 9:30 – this is the only guideline we have. The daily structure and quitting time is...it depends.

4. How much leisure time do you have during a year?

Every weekend and three week-long vacations during a year (in spring, summer and winter).

5. Which business areas do your clients mainly come from? Is the number of your clients increasing or rather declining?

increasing or rather declining?

Basically, clients come from my personal relationships, and the number is stable (increasing a little) for the past five years.

6. Do you have a specific corporate philosophy or maybe a mission statement like other companies, which is reflected in the way you steer the studio's course?

Helping small companies or local companies, getting deeply involved. Do offer unsolicited things. Become friends with clients, being more than just business partners. Do not rely on agencies. So, do not rely on agencies.

7. What, from your point of view, makes the difference between a small studio and a big company?

8. What kind of advantages and disadvantages does a small studio have compared to a big company?

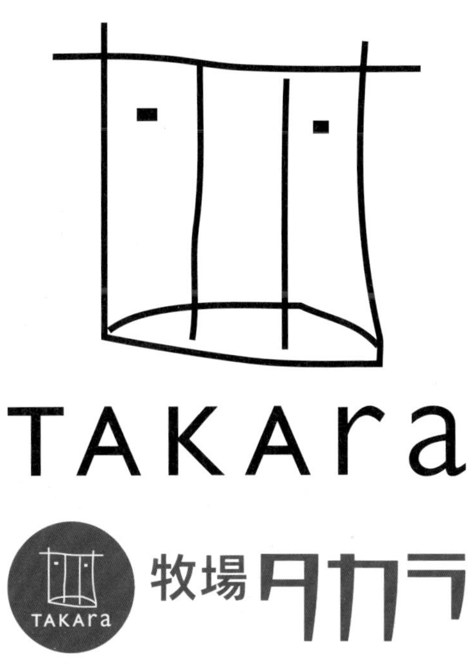

Farm takara – visual identity program – farm takara – 2001

In my case, I don't think of our studio's job as a business but the life now. I have no interest in big campaigns or projects which have stressful many layers of related-unrelated people and necessity of their approvals, sometimes don't see the objectives, although they would make big money. I started my career in a big company. It was nice and the business was very exciting. Then I studied marketing and communication scientifically in the context of large businesses which was also exciting. Now, in our small studio, all the projects are small but very exciting in terms of creativity. Small numbers of people involved and simple decision structures bring me days without stress.

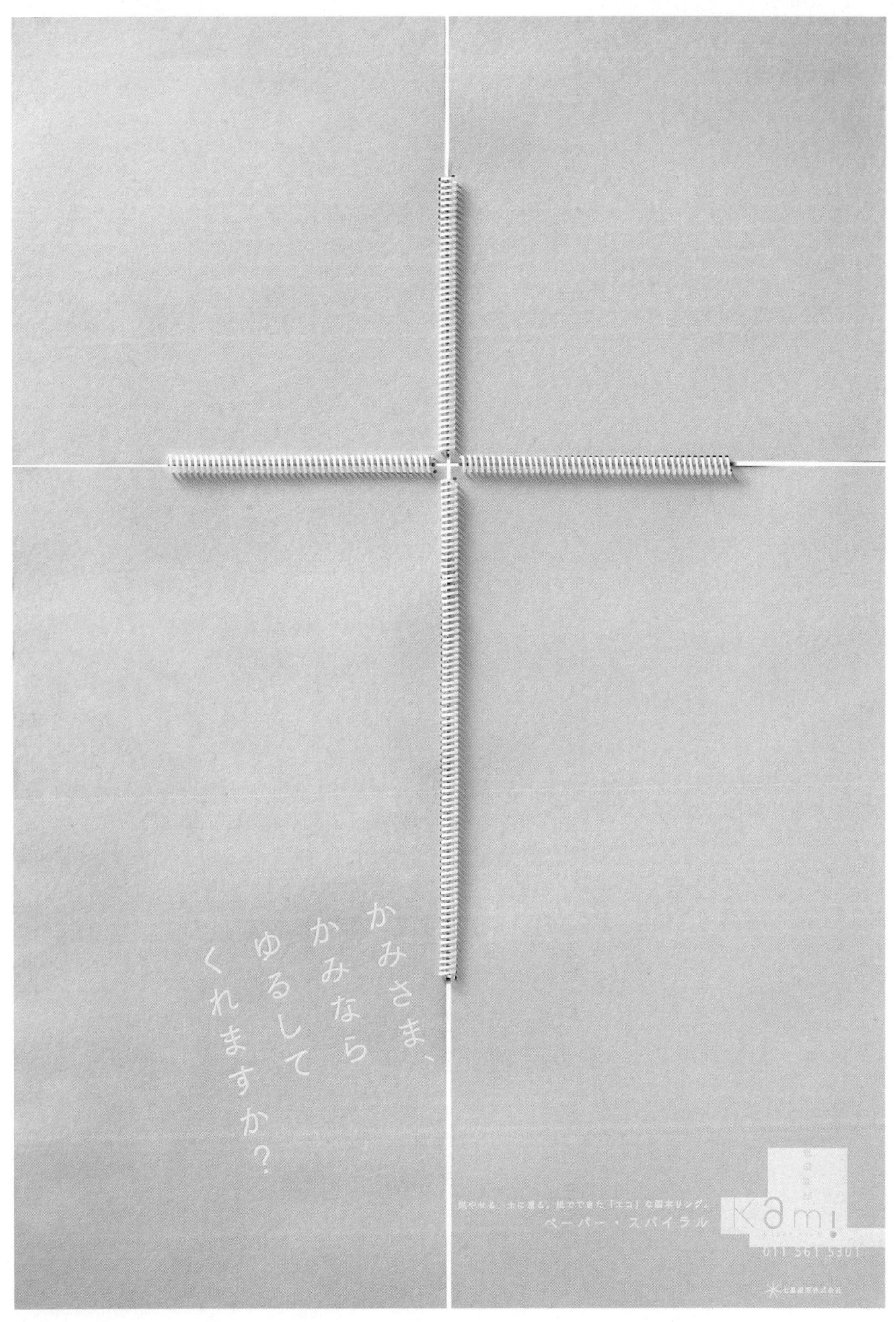

Eco-friendly binding rings – poster series – shichisei industry Sapporo – 2007

Kami – poster series – paper kami club – 2006

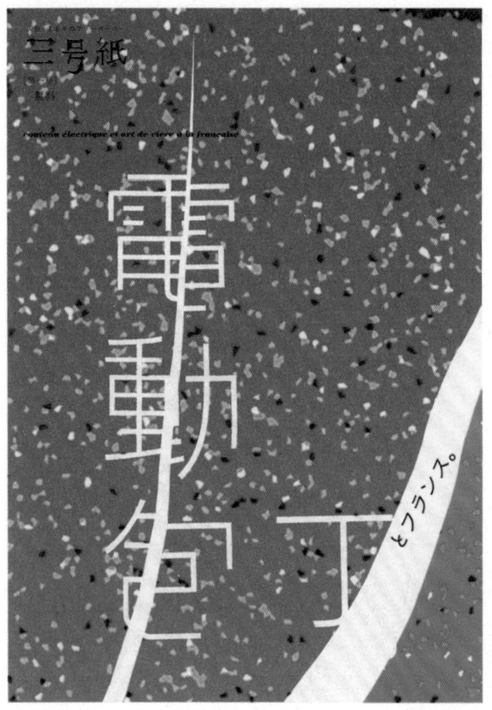

Sangoshi – free papers – banana moon studio – 2006-2008

9. What is your idea about the future of small studios?

The trend of globalization provides a convenient daily life, I enjoy to use my iPhone every day and sometimes I have lunch at McDonald's. At the same time, it opens our eyes to the distinctive and attractive aspects of localization. Many small companies have individualities in their products or services based on locality which global companies cannot acquire. I think it's the same situation in the field of creative business: small studios can be shining. Small business, but happy.

10. Please describe and elaborate on the goals or plans that you have for your studio for the next five years?

In the early years of our studio we had more staff. After one decade we steered to the opposite. We have no ambitions for a large unit or size expansion any more. Currently, we are aiming to be more of a stimulating place. For that, we are accepting international internship students to be the place uniting fresh and different ideas. By the way, Sapporo where we are based is just a local city, about 1,000 km away from Tokyo. It's not the centre place of Japanese things but getting to have the other position, especially in field of graphics, although not well known widely. Many international prize winners have come from Sapporo in the past. Only this year, for example, a gold prize at the Poster Biennial in Warsaw (8 designers were qualified), a 3rd prize at the Chaumont Festival, 4 designers won the Merit Award in New York ADC. In the domestic competition "Graphic Design in Japan (JAGDA Annual)" Sapporo has enjoyed the highest position in the percentage of selected designers within 3 years. The city provides an exciting and stimulating environment for me.

ICC – poster series – Inter-x-cross creative center – 2001

広告＋1ネタのフリーペーパー

三号紙

［第二号］

無料

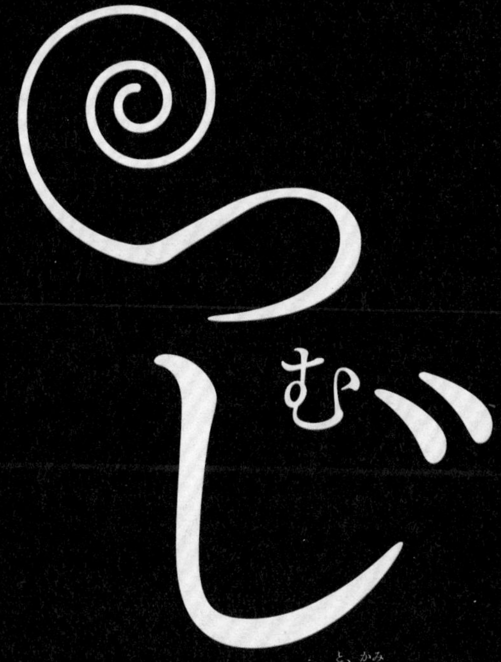

Sangoshi – free papers – banana moon studio – 2006-2008

BANK™
team:
Sebastian Bissinger
Laure Boer
contact:
Rungestr. 22-24
10179 Berlin, Germany
T + 49 30 24047570
F + 49 30 24047571
tellme@bankassociates.de
www.bankassociates.de
Photo by Adam Slowik

BANK™ was founded by Sebastian Bissinger and Willem Stratmann in 2004. Since 2007, BANK™ consists of Sebastian Bissinger and Laure Boer. We plan, develop and realize a wide range of design projects for cultural, institutional, and commercial clients. We are interested in unique approaches. And yes: what the client gets is different from what he expected. And it's more...

StudioNOW – self promotional (press kit)/sticker set/T-shirt – self promotional – 2006

Interview with BANK™

1. What led to the formation of your studio?

As thinking designers with experience in working for clients and agencies as freelancers, we liked the idea of being in contact with other points of view and other opinions while working on something. As a working group with an international network of designers/artists/musicians – call it creative people – you also have the big advantage to be able to connect talents from different fields for certain needs.

2. How many staff people does your studio have and what are their main working fields?

We are two – a French/German couple plus one intern and some associated designers. We work pretty free on different approaches, looking over it together, figuring out which way is the most interesting to go. We all work on different aspects of the job.

3. How does a regular working day at your studio look like, how is the day structured?

Our normal working day is: waking up at 10 o'clock, making love and feel full of energy for a good working day. Or to say it in other words: "Every day think when you wake up, today I am fortunate to have woken up, I am alive, I have a precious human life, I am not going to waste it, I am going to use all my energies to develop myself. To expand my heart out to others to achieve enlightenment for the benefit of all beings, I am going to have kind thoughts towards others, I am not going to get angry, or think badly about others, I am going to benefit others as much as I can." – H.H. The XIV Dalai Lama.

4. How much leisure time do you have during a year?

Three to four weeks leisure time per year. We stopped working every weekend some years ago. But if it is necessary, we don't sleep for a week or two...

5. Which business areas do your clients mainly come from? Is the number of your clients increasing or rather declining?

We do corporate and editorial design, we work a lot for the music, fashion and club scene as well as for cultural institutions, developing concepts and designing magazines, record sleeves, flyers, posters, self-promotions or T-shirts. We also create websites and campaigns. Each project demands an appropriate visual language the same as thinking about the content while developing ideas and copywriting.

Fumakilla – series of recordsleeves/front and three backsides with one-sided punchhole – Fumakilla – since 2004

6. Do you have a specific corporate philosophy or maybe a mission statement like other companies, which is reflected in the way you steer the studio's course?

Every assignment is somehow a new game for us, we try to invent new things in an unique way for each project. Therefore we do a lot of type design because we believe that the whole thing gets more interesting when you think about all the elements instead of using "presets". There is nothing more boring than designers who copy what is "trendy" or what is supposed to be "trendy" instead of having their own vision and their own vocabulary. Even if it turns out a bit crumpled or unconventional.

7. What, from your point of view, makes the difference between a small studio and a big company?

When working in a big studio you usually can't refuse to do a job. For us it is important to handle things how we want it and having a social and political responsibility instead of serving and not questioning the capitalistic stupidity surrounding us, like it is – sad but true – common in nearly all bigger ad-agencies (growing is very often related to more ad-work).

Fritzclub at postbahnhof – partyslides – 2007

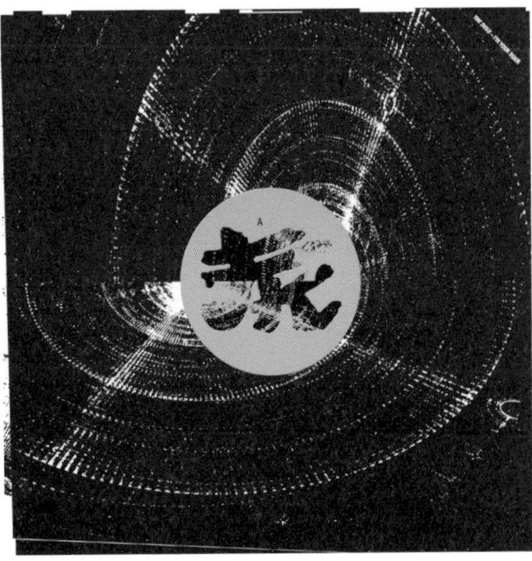

8. What kind of advantages and disadvantages does a small studio have compared to a big company?

These days nearly all innovation in graphic design comes from smaller studios or single persons (check the publications of the last few years). The output of bigger studios – concerning design, not concerning ideas or concepts – is rather boring. The situation in product or industrial design is different because in those fields the development and the whole process around the realization is – despite some exceptions – way more expensive.

9. What is your idea about the future of small studios?

It is essentially necessary for a society that younger talented people have chances to get bigger budgets and to work on a larger scale. Public competitions are often defined in a way which excludes many (not to say nearly all) interesting agencies. E.g. the practise to connect the financial income of an agency to the estimated ability to handle the responsibility of a big project must be changed.

10. Please describe and elaborate on the goals or plans that you have for your studio for the next five years?

We keep on pushing things forward. Maybe we grow a bit, let's say to up to 5 or 6 people

Good and Plenty – event and party series , flyers – self initiated project with Ian Warner/blotto – since 2002

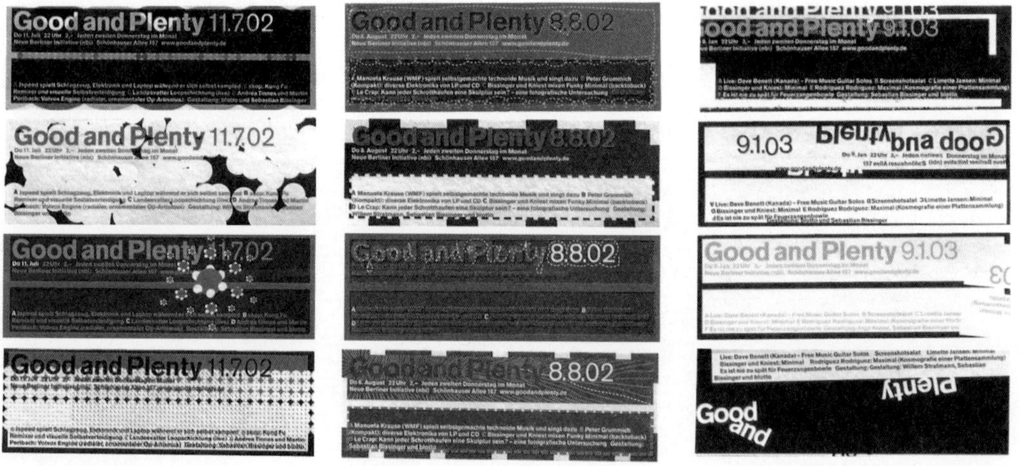

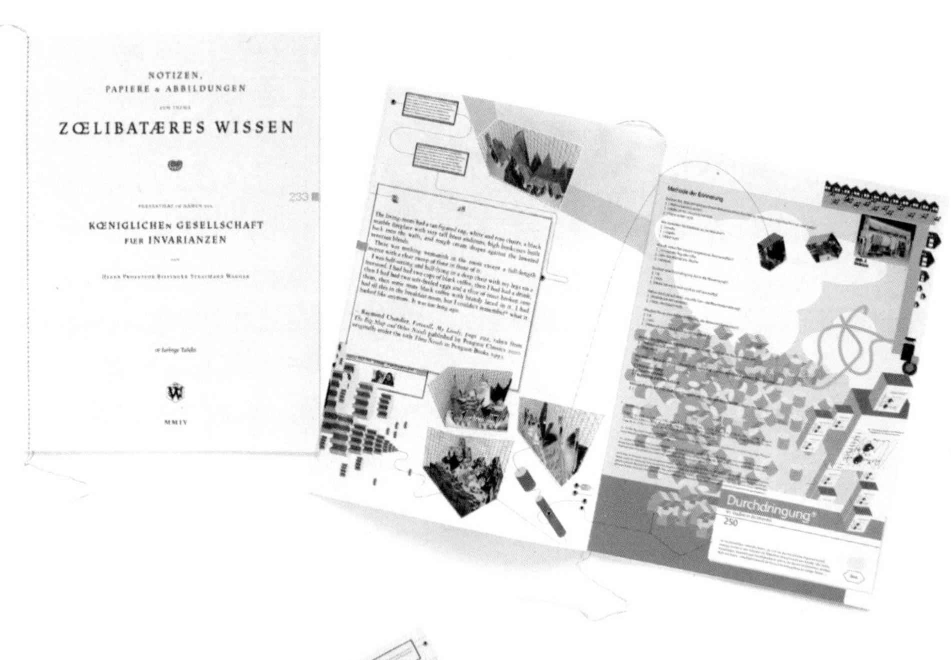

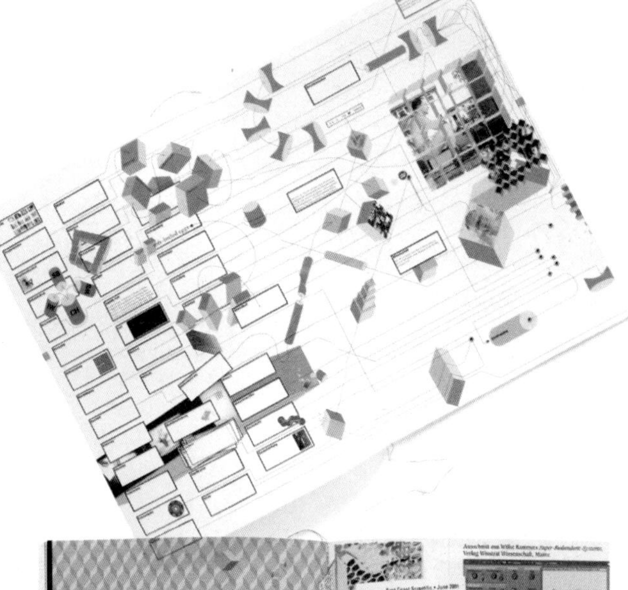

Zoelibataeres Wissen – 16 page contribution for the magazine DieKlasse, issue No. 2/with Ian Warner/blotto – published by museum of design Zürich – the contribution is also published seperately with a stiched binding – 2004

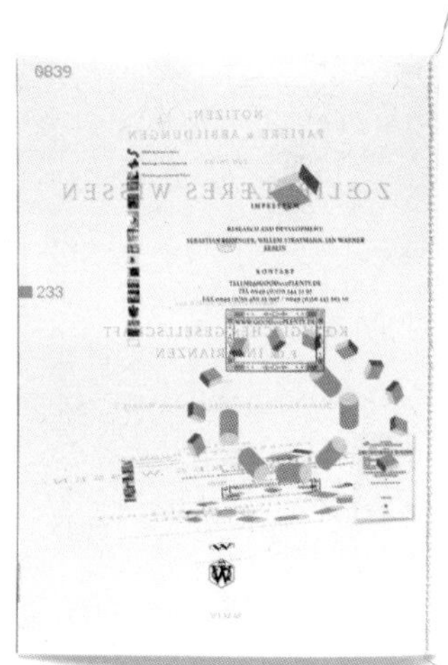

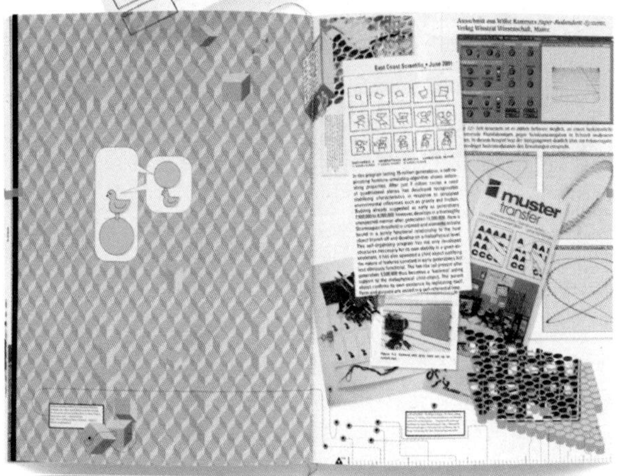

Alex Bec

team:
Alex Bec
contact:
1 Pavan Court
114-116 Sceptre Road
E2 0JS London
United Kingdom
T + 44 77 09105590
hello@alexbec.com
www.alexbec.com

Interview with Alex Bec

Alex Bec is an London-based independent graphic designer, art director and illustrator. He is also the co-founder of the design studio "HudsonBec" (www.hudsonbec.com) and the independent publishing house "If You Could" (www.ifyoucould.co.uk). Working on projects ranging from classic graphic design, exhibition curation, typography, book publishing and event management, Alex's real passion is hands-on, tangible design with distinct personality. Believing in the philosophy, "The Eye is Blind if the Mind is Absent" he always looks to add an extra, unexpected dimension to his work.

1. What led to the formation of your studio?

A desire to work independently on interesting projects. A small studio gives me the freedom to monitor everything that comes out of the studio.

2. How many staff people does your studio have and what are their main working fields?

One: Graphic Design/Illustration/Art Direction – although I regularly collaborate with graphic designer Will Hudson on design projects and "If You Could" (www.ifyoucould.co.uk).

3. How does a regular working day at your studio look like, how is the day structured?

Get in early, make a list of what needs to be done, do the work and finish when I need to!

4. How much leisure time do you have during a year?

As much as I can possibly fit in.

5. Which business areas do your clients mainly come from?

Magazines, editorial, small studios, record labels, galleries.

Is the number of your clients increasing or rather declining?

Increasing (I hope).

6. Do you have a specific corporate philosophy or maybe a mission statement like other companies, which is reflected in the way you steer the studio's course?

I believe very strongly in meeting the people that I work with in person. The personal touch which is so often forgotten in the email-filled world that we live in is completely priceless. Other than that I'm interested in doing work with integrity and honesty.

7. What, from your point of view, makes the difference between a small studio and a big company?

The amount of people working there!

8. What kind of advantages and disadvantages does a small studio have compared to a big company?

In a small studio you have total control on what work is being produced. You also have input in all aspects of the design process from idea generation, to art-working, to finishing projects. In a larger company the work gets passed around much more and your personality and style gets filtered out.

9. What is your idea about the future of small studios? Do you think that small studios do not have any other choice but to expand in order to survive in these times of globalization?

If the work being produced is good, the studio will always survive. Small studios will always exist as people will always want to react against large, more corporate companies. There will always be an opposition to everything. By taking on the right amount of people and the right amount of work a small studio can always survive if the work being produced is good.

10. Please describe and elaborate on the goals or plans that you have for your studio for the next five years?

I hope to expand a little bit – and start working with Will Hudson more closely. We have plans to set up a new small studio called "HudsonBec" (www.hudsonbec.com) but my personal work will always remain, regardless of other collaborations.

Football strips – hand cut paper – nike – 2008

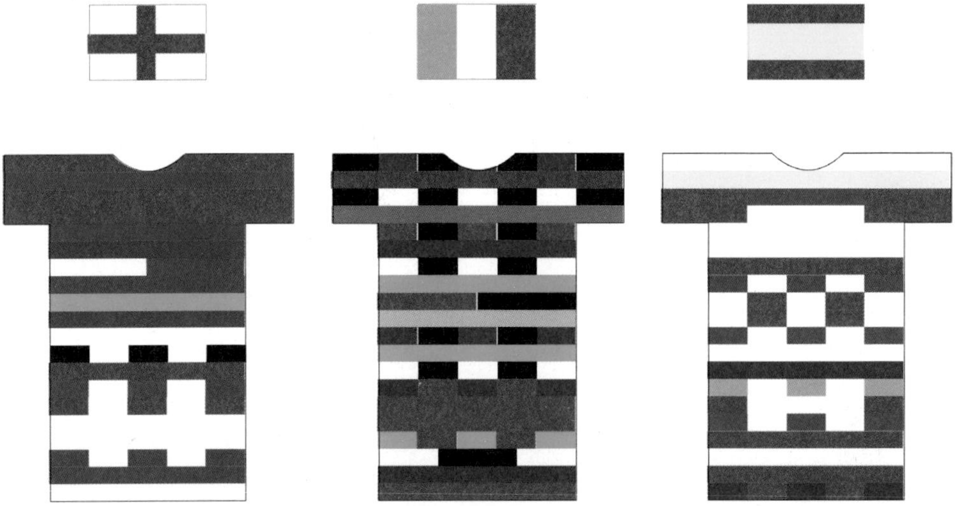

Seeing is believing – photograph – self initiated work – 2007

Too much – illustration – pocket sized – 2008

Sale graphics degree show poster – illustrator/fluro screen prints – personal work – 2007

TOO MUCH.
SEEING
IS
BELIEVING

University of Brighton graduate fashion show invitation – double foil blocked card – university of Brighton – 2007

Self – illustration/metallic screen print – art is proof press – 2008

You must judge a man by the work of his hands – hand cut paper – manystuff zine – 2008

Order is the shape upon which beauty depends – hand cut paper – polygon show – 2007

YOU
MUST
JUDGE
A MAN
BY THE
WORK
OF HIS
HANDS

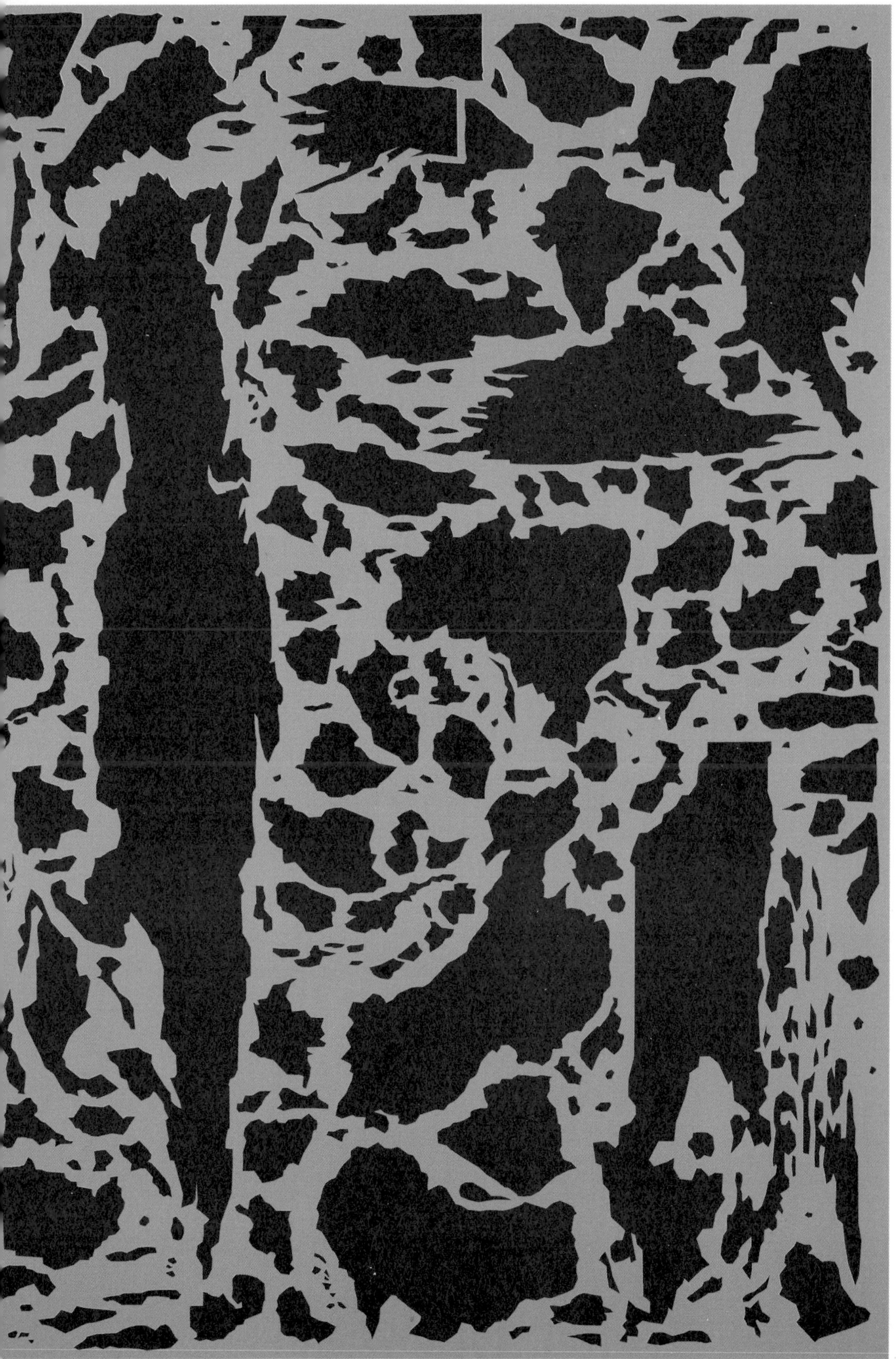

Better New World
team:
Kleon Medugorac
contact:
Mozartstr. 52
70180 Stuttgart, Germany
T + 49 711 2637443
kleon@gmx.net
www.better-new-world.com

Better New World – I always liked doing things. Doing anything feels better than doing nothing. People say I am very diligent, but I think I'm rather easily bored and so I got to keep myself busy. Plus I often have a pretty clear vision how things I create should look like in the end, and if the result shall be complex the work will be complex too. I probably live in my own world that is somehow flowing around in the ordinary world. Here it's more colourful and things happen in different ways. Music, emotions, animals and nature are more important over here. Style don't count too much. In my opinion a lot of people are either taking things too serious or not serious enough. I'm interested in almost everything. A good graphic designer should know as much as possible about life and all its situations and characters.

Crazy Horse – pictogram – class project college of art Stuttgart – 2003

Interview with Better New World

1. What led to the formation of your studio?

Interest in creative activity and the need for money. Somehow I was always used to work on my own, and not to execute the ideas of others. I did my first jobs at the age of 17, so I'm already ten years in business now.

2. How many staff people does your studio have and what are their main working fields?

Just me. For big projects I work together with good friends who are good graphic designers as well.

3. How does a regular working day at your studio look like, how is the day structured?

Most of the time, there are no regular working days, as each project deserves a different approach. But to structure it a bit I think I do more organizational stuff in the morning and more creation at nights.

4. How much leisure time do you have during a year?

Not very much. I can't tell it in hours, but somehow I always wait in the wings, even if I'm on holiday. But on the other hand I can plan my time the way I like it, which really makes you feel free somehow.

5. Which business areas do your clients mainly come from?

Until now my jobs vary from corporate designs and interface design for big international companies to flyers for the club next door or music videos. I hope it will stay this way. Personally I'm more interested in cultural jobs and illustration than in big business stuff, but I see this as a nice challenge. I like to work in various fields, because you always broaden your horizon with new experiences and learn something with every job.

Is the number of your clients increasing or rather declining?

Steadily increasing.

6. Do you have a specific corporate philosophy or maybe a mission statement like other companies, which is reflected in the way you steer the studio's course?

I do have an artistic philosophy which is certainly reflected by most of my works, the way I am working and the clients I am working with. It's the same philosophy that influences me in my way of making music or preparing a soup. I could talk for hours about my philosophy, there is so much from everyday life, that has to be considered in graphic works. It's a lot about feelings and semiotics. Pictures cause thoughts in people's brains... a lot is about those thoughts... things should be done with passion and heart. I believe that passion can be put into a lot of different tasks. Not just into those that I fancy personally. I like to communicate and reach people. I like to touch them somehow. I don't like graphic concepts just for the graphic designer's concepts sake. That's what a lot of graphic designers do at the moment. To me that is totally unprofessional. Graphic design is a very sensitive thing. There are a lot of components that influence ones perception of a book or website. A good graphic designer must know as much as possible about mankind, must have a big general knowledge, because he has to find pictures for thoughts and ideas that mankind comes up with. But this is also what makes it an interesting job!

7. What, from your point of view, makes the difference between a small studio and a big company?

8. What kind of advantages and disadvantages does a small studivo have compared to a big company?

In my opinion there are a lot of differences between small and big studios, those are probably reflected in the advantages and disadvantages listed below: Advantages of small studios:

- more freedom for the designer
- small studios are much faster and much more spontaneous.
- results from small studios are more individual and thus more unique
- very personal contact between client and designer
- more interesting work for the designer
- better prices for the client
- lower investments for the designer

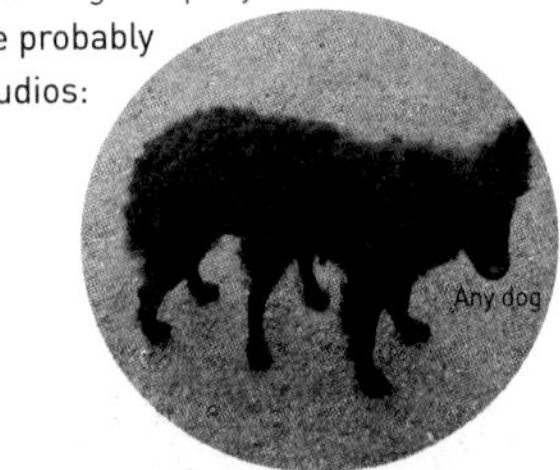

Any dog

Disadvantages of small studios:
- very big projects cannot be handled alone
- organization and book keeping has to be done by the designers
- less equipment
- working alone can be really boring after some time...

9. What is your idea about the future of small studios? Do you think that small studios do not have any other choice but to expand in order to survive in these times of globalization?

I don't think that small studios have to expand in general. The ones that think they should expand because of the globalization should do that. The small specialists will always have some work to do. And if all studios would expand there would be no more small studios. That's probably the chance for some new small studios. I think there might be kind of a renaissance of the small studios and individuals who do the jobs in their special way. In the globalized world, where everything gets exchangeable, individuality is a big value. One problem is that today there are often big teams who decide, and everything gets discussed down to a boring compromise, but that is a general problem and not just one for graphic designers. Companies shouldn't be so afraid of doing things.

10. Please describe and elaborate on the goals or plans that you have for your studio for the next five years?

Keep on rocking in a free world!

Heart to forget – magazine – degree – 2007

Max experimentell – poster – Max experimentell – 2008

Youth is great – poster – class for stage design/state academy of art and design – 2004

The most beautiful months – poster – study project – 2005

Snillingur – poster – Vincent Schmid, Linda Leifsdottir – 2007

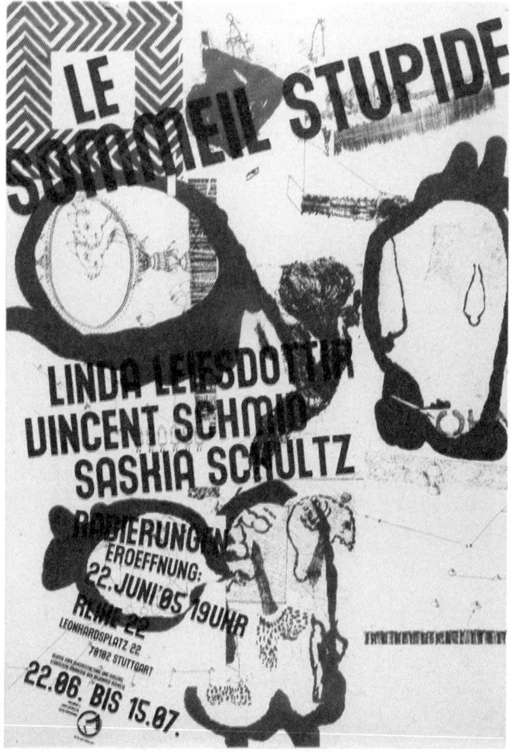

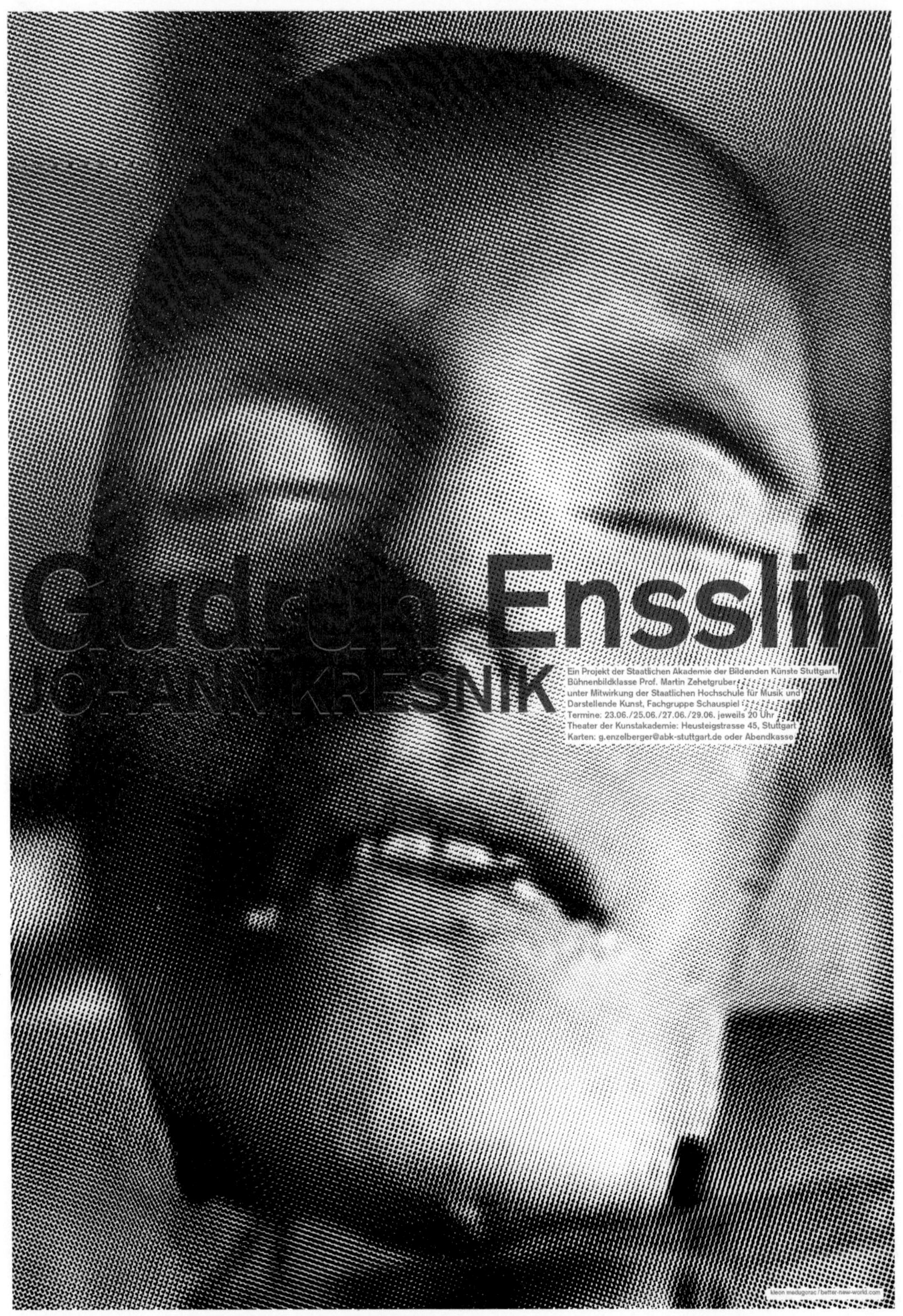

Gudrun Ensslin – poster – class for stage design/state academy of art and design – 2005

Anzeiga – poster – ellerhold druck ag – 2006

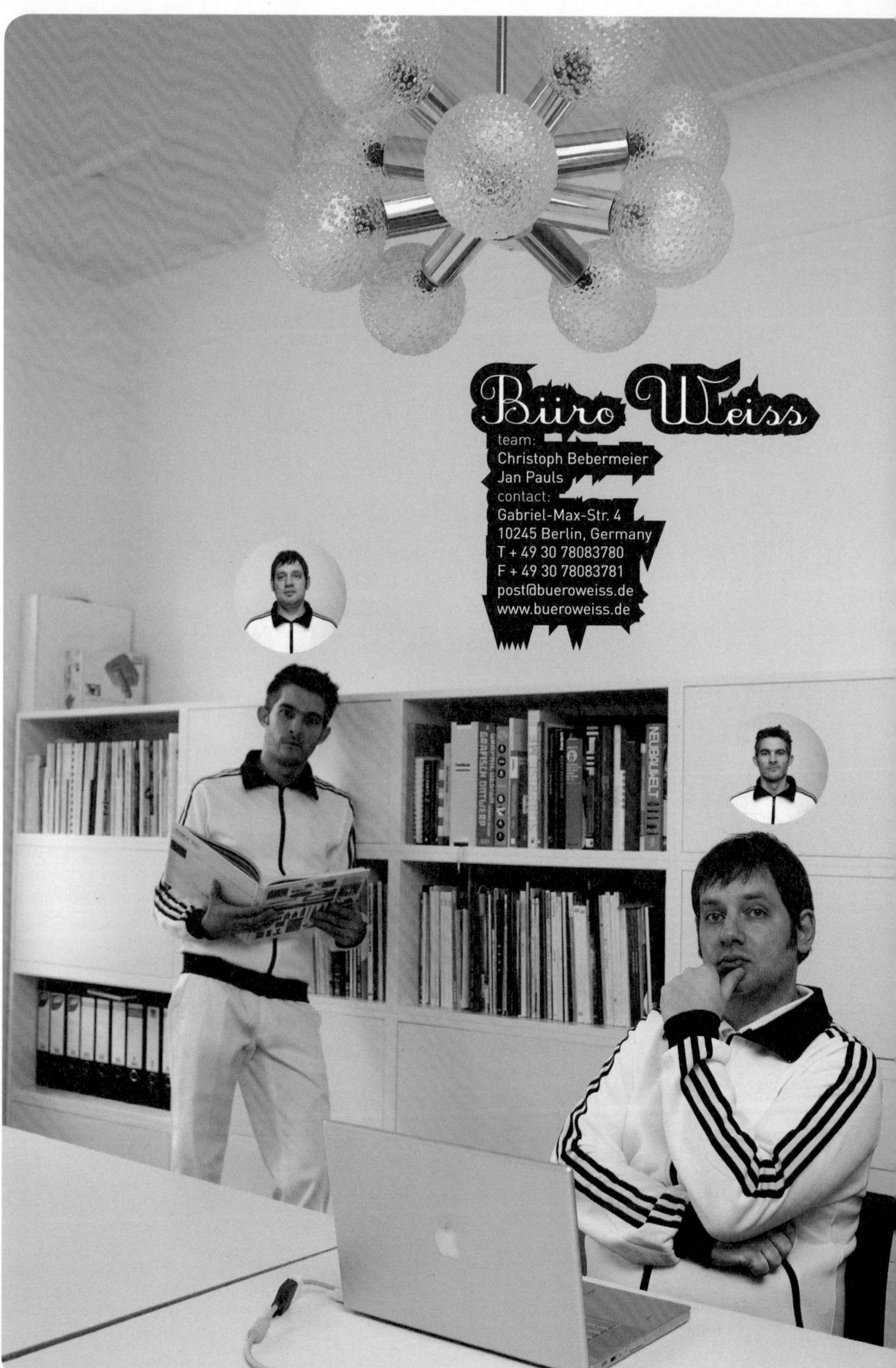
Büro Weiss
team:
Christoph Bebermeier
Jan Pauls
contact:
Gabriel-Max-Str. 4
10245 Berlin, Germany
T + 49 30 78083780
F + 49 30 78083781
post@bueroweiss.de
www.bueroweiss.de

Büro Weiss In 2004 the Berlin designers Christoph Bebermeier and Jan Pauls have joined in forming the design agency Büro Weiss. Büro Weiss offers its customers high-quality work in the fields of graphic design, multi-media and photography. The agency has a political-cultural focus in its work.

Hedwig Bollhagen/a life for ceramic – exhibition – haus der Brandenburgisch Preußischen geschichte – 2007

Interview with Büro Weiss

1. What led to the formation of your studio?

We didn't need any specific reason. We always knew that we wanted to build a small yet ambitious design studio. What was most important for us was to have control over the content and design of our work. Of course, this is most realistic in your own studio.

2. How many staff people does your studio have and what are their main working fields?

At the moment, there are two "bosses" and one intern. If the workload demands it, we also work with freelancers. Currently, we concentrate on developing corporate designs, posters and photography.

3. How does a regular working day at your studio look like, how is the day structured?

In case we`re not travelling for business, we have a 9 am to 6 pm office day. We put in extra hours if there still is work to do. Since our studio is very small, we don't need pre-defined structures. There's a kick off-meeting in the morning, and if there is a need, we get together for meetings spontaneously.

4. How much leisure time do you have during a year?

There's enough leisure time. Maybe that will change if we grow.

5. Which business areas do your clients mainly come from? Is the number of your clients increasing or rather declining?

We mostly work for clients from the cultural and political scene, but now we are also reaching out for clients in the classical field of corporate communications. At the moment, our client base is growing although the situation in the cultural scene continues to be difficult – in Berlin and elsewhere. This is why we want to expand our local and topical base.

The seeming everyday – photo – dummy magazine – 2004

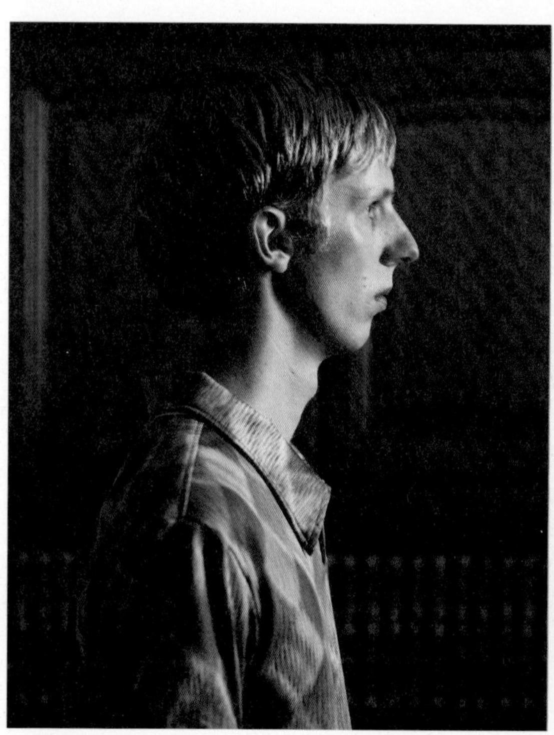

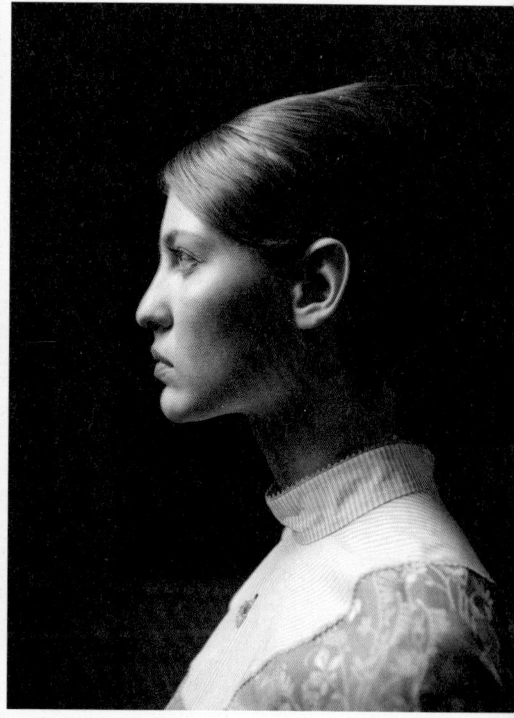

HUNDEKOT! HARALD SCHMIDT!! KLINGELTÖNE!!!

100 GRÜNDE, UM AUF DIE BARRIKADEN ZU GEHEN: 1. DAMIT HARALD SCHMIDT ENDLICH MAL WAS ANDERES MACHT 2. „PISA-STUDIE" AUF DEN INDEX! 3. CAMP CROPPER 4. GELDSTRAFE AUF DEN SPRUCH: „WER MIT 20 KEIN SOZIALIST IST, HAT KEIN HERZ. WER MIT 30 NOCH EINER IST, HAT KEINEN VERSTAND" 5. FÜR PRÄVENTIVES VERHANDELN STATT PRÄVENTIVER KRIEGSFÜHRUNG 6. DAMIT JAMBA ALS KÖRPERVERLETZUNG EINGESTUFT WIRD 7. FÜR DIE EINSCHLÄFERUNG ALLER KAMPFHUNDE 8. BERUFSVERBOT FÜR MAKLER! 9. KEIN VERLAG DARF MEHR ALS EIN FRAUENMAGAZIN MACHEN 10. WIDER DIE DIKTATUR DER TAGESAKTUALITÄT 11. ABSCHAFFUNG DER KOMMENTARE IN DEN „TAGESTHEMEN"! 12. WEIL DER MÜLL RAUS MUSS 13. SMART ROADSTER 14. DER HAUSMEISTER ALS SOLCHER 15. CHINA DARF WIEDER DIKTATUR GENANNT WERDEN 16. FÜR AUTOS, DIE NUR ZWEI LITER VERBRAUCHEN 17. KLAUS WOWEREIT ALS SOLCHER 18. WENIGER IKEA! 19. DAMIT DIE MACHT DES ÖLS NICHT NOCH GRÖSSER WIRD 20. BILD 21. DAMIT IMMER ÜBERALL 24 STUNDEN OFFEN IST 22. DAMIT GUIDO WESTERWELLE FAMILIENMINISTER WIRD 23. FÜR DIE BÜRGERPFLICHT, EINMAL PRO JAHR IN DIE FREMDE ZU REISEN 24. DAMIT DIE ARD NICHT NOCH MEHR WIE RTL WIRD 25. GETREIDEKAFFEE 26. BERLINER WEISSE 27. CHRISTIAN WULFF 28. WEIL ES IM OSTEN IMMER NOCH „CAPPUCHINO MIT SAHNE" GIBT 29. WEIL ES IM OSTEN AUCH SONST BESSER WERDEN MUSS 30. DAMIT DAS BUCH „SCHLUSS MIT LUSTIG" AUS DEM HANDEL GENOMMEN WIRD 31. ENDLICH FAIRE PROZESSE FÜR MICHAIL CHODORKOWSKI, ABDULLAH ÖCALAN, HELMUT KOHL! 32. FINGER WEG VON MICHAEL JACKSON! 33. DIE DEUTSCHE NACHKRIEGSLITERATUR 34. DIESEL-JEANS 35. LAMINAT 36. RAUHFASER 37. DAMIT SICH DIE FRAUEN IN BERLIN-MITTE NICHT MEHR SO HÄSSLICH MACHEN 38. FÜR KLARHEIT DARÜBER, WARUM EIN COMEBACK DER KAROTTENJEANS AUSGESCHLOSSEN IST 39. UNSER PAPST 40. DÖNER KEBAP 41. DAMIT RIO REISER AUFERSTEHT 42. DAMIT GERHARD MEYER-VORFELDER FÜR IMMER VERSCHWINDET 43. TIMO HILDEBRANDT STATT OLIVER KAHN! 44. FÜR DEN ABRISS DES POTSDAMER PLATZES 45. DAMIT HELMUT BERGER ZURÜCKKOMMT 46. WEIL WIM WENDERS IMMER NOCH GUT ANKOMMT 47. STOPPT HEINO FERCH, OSKAR ROEHLER, DIETER BOHLEN, DANIEL BRÜHL! 48. WEIL BULLY HERBIG DEUTSCHER HUMOR IST 49. WEIL SICH NIEMAND TRAUT, WONG KAR-WAI DOOF ZU FINDEN 50. WEIL JEDER NPD-WÄHLER EIN SOZIALES JAHR IN JERUSALEM MACHEN MUSS 51. HELMUT MARKWORTS TAGEBUCH 52. AUF DASS ULI WICKERT SICH NIE MEHR VERSPRICHT 53. FÜR EINIGKEIT DARÜBER, OB SABINE CHRISTIANSEN GUT ODER SCHLECHT GELIFTET IST 54. SPIRALEN AUF KRANKENSCHEIN! 55. WEIL ALLES IMMER SACH-

Dummy/revolution – magazine – dummy magazine – 2005

58
MUSKELN
WECK
SIE
AUF
POWER FÜR DEINE FÜSSE
NIKE FREE
nikefree.com
Offizieller Trainingsschuh des Deutschen Leichtathletik-Verbandes

DIE MEDIEN SIND SCHULD!

JOCHEN FÖRSTER UND OLIVER GEHRS

„MASSENMEDIEN ZERSTREUEN JEDES AUFKEIMEN ALTERNATIVER ENERGIEN, INDEM SIE ES UNTER DAS DIKTAT DER KURZWEILIGKEIT, DES UNTERHALTUNGSWERTS, DER TAGESAGENDA STELLEN", SAGT DER ENGLISCHE POLITIKWISSENSCHAFTLER DAVID HELD (S. 18) UND STELLT DAMIT DIE MASSGEBLICHE DIAGNOSE ZUR ZEIT. AUF DER EINEN SEITE JOURNALISTEN, DIE JEDE WOCHE EINE ANDERE SAU DURCHS DORF TREIBEN, AUF DER ANDEREN SEITE POLITIKER, DIE KEINE ZEIT HABEN, IRGENDWELCHE VISIONEN ZU ENTWICKELN, WEIL ENTWEDER DIE NÄCHSTE WAHL ANSTEHT ODER DIE NÄCHSTE SCHLAGZEILE, UND ZWISCHENDRIN WÄHLER, DIE ANGESICHTS DIESER BERICHTERSTATTUNG UND POLITIK, DIE KEINE BLEIBENDEN WERTE AUSSER DEM PUREN WACHSTUM ZU KENNEN SCHEINT, RATLOS BLEIBEN. DABEI HAT DIE SKANDALISIERUNG VON POLITIK AUSGERECHNET UNTER ROT-GRÜN ZUGENOMMEN. SCHULD DARAN TRÄGT AUCH GERHARD SCHRÖDER, DER ZAUBERLEHRLING, DER DIE GEISTER NICHT MEHR LOS WIRD, DIE ER EINST RIEF – ALS ER NOCH SPASS AN SEINEM JOB HATTE, ALS ER MIT ZIGARRE UND MASSANZUG POSIERTE, ALS ER SICH MIT BILD UND GLOTZE EINLIESS, DIE FERNSEHDUELLE BEINAHE SPIELEND GEWANN UND DEUTSCHLANDS ERSTER „MEDIENKANZLER" WURDE.

IN DEN VERGANGENEN JAHREN KONNTEN DIE ANLÄSSE GAR NICHT KLEIN GENUG SEIN, UM NICHT ZUR GROSSEN AFFÄRE HOCHGEJAZZT ZU WERDEN. MAN WIRD DEN EINDRUCK NICHT LOS, ALS OB DIE MEDIEN NUR NOCH FÜR SICH UND NICHT DIE MENSCHEN PRODUZIEREN. JEDER SCHAUT, WAS DER ANDERE MACHT, UND VERSUCHT ES DANN ZU TOPPEN. KEIN INNEHALTEN, KEINE MEINUNGSVIELFALT, VIEL PROFESSIONALISMUS, WENIG EHRLICHE AUFKLÄRUNG. DER AUSSTOSS AN INFORMATIONEN HAT DRAMATISCH ZUGENOMMEN, DER GEHALT DER INFORMATION SO GAR NICHT. WOHL NICHT UMSONST HAT DIE AUFLAGE ALLER ZEITUNGEN WELTWEIT ZUGELEGT, NUR IN DEUTSCHLAND WIRD SIE KLEINER: WIEVIEL JUNGE MENSCHEN DEN ZEITUNGEN UND DEM FERNSEHEN NOCH VERTRAUEN ENTGEGENBRINGEN – DIESE ERNÜCHTERNDE ZAHL SEI HIER AUSGESPART. DIE MEISTEN SUCHEN LÄNGST IM INTERNET NACH THEMEN UND INFORMATIONEN, DIE SIE WOANDERS NICHT BEKOMMEN.

FAKT IST, DASS ES LANGE NICHT MEHR SO VIELE GRÜNDE GAB, WÜTEND ZU SEIN, AUF DIE BARRIKADEN ZU GEHEN. DER UNTERSCHIED ZWISCHEN ARM UND REICH WÄCHST IMMER RASANTER – WENN ERSTMAL DIE CDU REGIERT, GEHT'S ERST RICHTIG LOS. ES GIBT WEDER EIN VERNÜNFTIGES EINWANDERUNGSGESETZ (NACHDEM ES DEN BUNDESRAT NICHT PASSIERTE, VERLOR DIE SPD DIE LUST AN DEM THEMA), DIE EUROPAPOLITIK IST VON INTERNEM STANDORTGESCHACHERE GEPRÄGT, DIE ENERGIEPOLITIK BEFINDET SICH AUF DEM WEG IN DIE VERGANGENHEIT. ANSTATT GESETZLICH GEZWUNGEN ZU WERDEN,

IN NEUE EXPORTFÄHIGE UMWELTSCHONENDE TECHNOLOGIEN ZU INVESTIEREN, DÜRFEN DIE ATOMKRAFTWERKSBETREIBER IHRE GELDDRUCKMASCHINEN BALD NOCH LÄNGER LAUFEN LASSEN. WENN VON POLITIK DIE REDE IST, GEHT ES UM WIRTSCHAFT, UM ARBEITSLOSENZAHLEN, UM BIP-QUOTE, RENDITEN UND EXPORTMARGEN. DIE ÖKONOMISIERUNG HAT DAZU GEFÜHRT, DASS ÜBER WANDEL AUF ANDEREN FELDERN NICHT MEHR GESPROCHEN WIRD. DAS LAND IST IN SIEBEN JAHREN ROT-GRÜN LIBERALER GEWORDEN, ABER DAS INTERESSIERT NIEMANDEN. IN DEN MEDIEN HERRSCHT DERWEIL ZUR ALTEN FRAGE FAST VOLLENDETE EINIGKEIT: SOZIALISMUS? ERLEDIGT. ARBEITERKLASSE FUTSCH. DEMOKRATIE LAUT LUHMANN AUF AUTOPILOT, HARTE ARBEIT EXPORTIERT, KONSUM DAS BESSERE OPIUM, DER MENSCH QUA LEKTION DER WELTREVOLUTION CHARAKTERLICH NICHT GEWACHSEN. REVOLUTION IST WAS FÜR SOFTWARE- ODER NANOTECHNOLOGEN, DER LINKEN FEHLT DAZU JEDE VISION, JEDES GESICHT. DIE MEDIEN TUN DERWEIL ALLES, UM GEWERKSCHAFTEN SCHLECHT ZU SCHREIBEN, UND DISKUTIEREN ALLES, WAS DIE ALTE FRAGE NACH SOZIALER GERECHTIGKEIT NICHT BETRIFFT. BILD UND ARD, SPIEGEL UND RTL SINGEN IM VEREIN DAS LIED VOM SIEGESZUG DER FREIEN MARKTWIRTSCHAFT IN DER WELT, PRODUZIEREN NACHRICHTEN VON STÜNDLICHER HALBWERTZEIT, DEBATTEN DAUERN UNWESENTLICH LÄNGER. JEDER WEISS, DASS DEMOKRATIE HEUTE MEHR DENN JE MEDIOKRATIE UND PLUTOKRATIE BEDEUTET. ABER WAS IST ELENDER ALS EINE ÖFFENTLICHKEIT, IN DER POLITISCHE IDEALE NICHT DISKUTIERT WERDEN? SOLLEN WIR SIE TOTSCHWEIGEN, WEIL ES BISHER NICHT GEKLAPPT HAT? DIE RECHTE IST DER UNBOTMÄSSIGE GEWINNER DER GLOBALISIERUNG. DIE LINKE MUSS SICH ZU IHREN IDEALEN BEKENNEN. MUSS RAUS AUS IHRER JAHRZEHNTE WÄHRENDEN DEFENSIVE, AUS LETHARGIE UND ÜBERDRUSS AN DEN HOHLKÖPFEN, DIE REVOLUTION HEUTE STALINISTISCH REPRÄSENTIEREN. SIE MUSS SMART SEIN, UND SIE MUSS SICH ENDLICH GLOBALISIEREN.

DAS SIEBTE DUMMY WILL ANREGEN, SICH MIT DER GESTALTBARKEIT DER WELT WIEDER MEHR ZU BESCHÄFTIGEN. REVOLUTIONEN DES AUTODESIGNS KOMMEN EBENSO VOR WIE EIN PLÄDOYER ZUGUNSTEN DES VERMUTLICH EINZIGEN VOLKSTRIBUNS AN DER MACHT, VENEZUELAS PRÄSIDENT HUGO CHAVEZ. UND WEIL REVOLUTIONEN PLATZ BRAUCHEN, HABEN WIR DIESMAL – AUSNAHMSWEISE – EIN EXTRA GROSSES FORMAT GEWÄHLT. GESTALTET WURDE DIESE AUSGABE VOM BERLINER „BÜRO WEISS". DAS NÄCHSTE DUMMY ERSCHEINT AM 19. SEPTEMBER.

6. Do you have a specific corporate philosophy or maybe a mission statement like other companies, which is reflected in the way you steer the studio's course?

Of course! Our mission statement isn't really short, but it describes our understanding of design pretty well: Design is more than a facade. Design catches the eye. Design is beautiful, exciting and intelligent. It tells stories and gives you food for thought. Design is different. It is not entirely customer – oriented. It may, for instance, be hard to read. If design permanently caters to the consumer's taste, it creates weak, undefined brands with no clear direction.

7. What, from your point of view, makes the difference between a small studio and a big company?

Naturally, we are fans of (good) small design studios. We think that small studios are more flexible, more creative and more striking than big agencies. Small design studios are more able to keep up quality standards because the people at the top still are in the loop of things and know what's going on.

8. What kind of advantages and disadvantages does a small studio have compared to a big company?

First of all, small design studios have significantly lower costs than big agencies. Using this advantage, we take greater liberties at choosing exciting clients and creating exciting designs. In doing so, small agencies are able to develop more accurate profiles than big agencies that offer full-service. Full-service, in turn, suggests safety that big accounts look for. Of course, big agencies also have the capacity to handle large-scale projects.

9. What is your idea about the future of small studios? Do you think that small studios do not have any other choice but to expand in order to survive in these times of globalization?

In the future, small agencies will have to focus more on their strengths than before. Instead of competing with the "top dogs" and offering services that these big shots are better equipped to fulfil, small agencies should concentrate on what they are best at. They should focus on establishing clear profiles because this may distinguish them in a very positive way from similar big agencies.

10. Please describe and elaborate on the goals or plans that you have for your studio for the next five years?

Of course, we want to grow although not too much! We think that – as a small studio – we are able to put our strengths best to work, i.e. to create good, intelligent and striking designs and still have fun!

Internet presence büro weiss – internet site – büro weiss – 2007

Against the oblivion – poster – büro weiss – 2004

bueronardin
team:
Christof Nardin
contact:
Mariahilferstr. 9/7
1060 Wien, Austria
T + 43 699 19432298
cn@christofnardin.com
www.bueronardin.com

Photo by Kramar – 2007

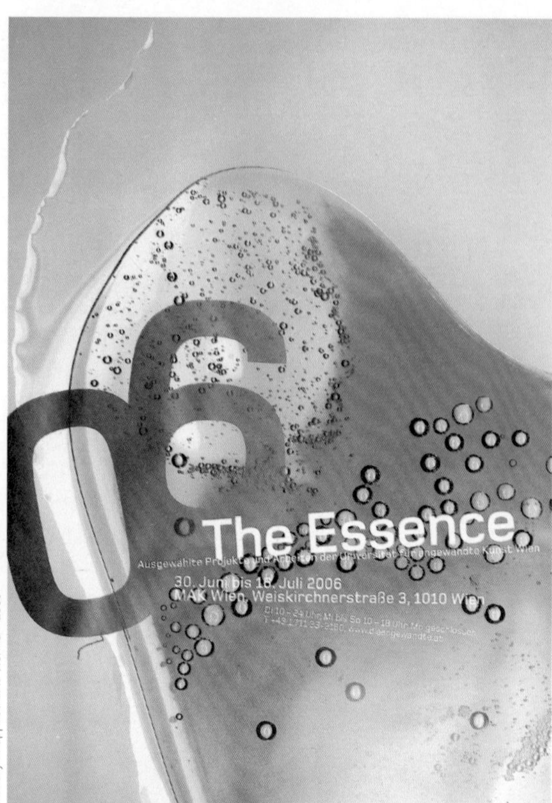

The Essence 06 – poster – university of applied arts Vienna – 2006

Christof Nardin born in Bregenz (AT), grown up in the 1980ies surrounded by mountains. Information Design studies in Ravensburg (DE), in between Berlin (DE); graduation 2007 (Graphic Design) at the University for Applied Arts Vienna (AT). As a designer he is developing visual worlds for all kinds of media. His extensive portfolio comprises posters, magazines, books, typographies, corporate designs, websites as well as exhibition – and interior design. In the last years he achieved a lot of appreciation for his assignment. Nardin lives and works in Vienna. Amongst others he received awards from the Type Directors Cl b New York, ED-Awards, Red Dot Award, Communication Design (Best of the Best), ADC New York, ADC Germany, the one hundred best posters D/A/CH, Design Austria (Joseph Binder Award), the output Foundation, and multiple nominations for the Design Award in Germany.

Alsterhaus Hamburg – Showcase – SDBI – 2007

Photo by Martin Veit

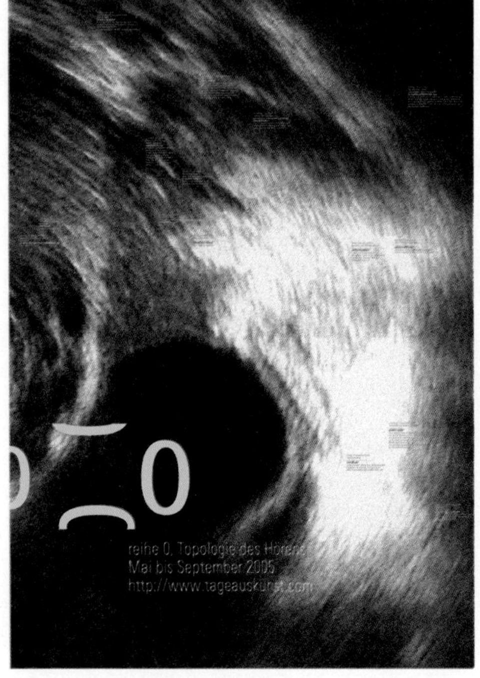

Photographer – Kramar – 2007

Reihe 0 – poster – kunstverein – 2003/2005/2007

Interview with bueronardin

1. What led to the formation of your studio?

The formation is just me. After my graduation in January 2007 there was not too much time to think about that. I got an offer of my friend Robert Ruef to share an office with him. Some requests of clients and my own book project compelled me to start soon.

2. How many staff people does your studio have and what are their main working fields?

I am the studio, but the work is not just mine. I'm working in an open network – asking friends and getting asked to share jobs on different requests in the field of communication and design.

3. How does a regular working day at your studio look like, how is the day structured?

Checking mails – all other things are different each day. That's amazing, expensive and precarious.

4. How much leisure time do you have during a year?

What is leisure? And what is time?

5. Which business areas do your clients mainly come from? Is the number of your clients increasing or rather declining?

Most of my clients are working in or with design, arts or in another cultural environment.

I don't know about the number of my clients, but the work is increasing.

6. Do you have a specific corporate philosophy or maybe a mission statement like other companies, which is reflected in the way you steer the studio's course?

Being a designer means having visions and wishes – I want to communicate, force knowledge, show links in a more and more complex world and think about context. No "corporate philosophy", running my own design studio is a very personal thing. I want to have a good time on this planet, not just a business-wise.

7. What, from your point of view, makes the difference between a small studio and a big company?

The size.

8. What kind of advantages and disadvantages does a small studio have compared to a big company?

Very small companies have difficulties with their budget and effort, because one single person has to do all the work.

9. What is your idea about the future of small studios? Do you think that small studios do not have any other choice but to expand in order to survive in these times of globalization?

I don't know.

10. Please describe and elaborate on the goals or plans that you have for your studio for the next five years?

I want to make the world a nicer place, do more interesting jobs, and have fun going my way. Five years? What will happen next Monday?

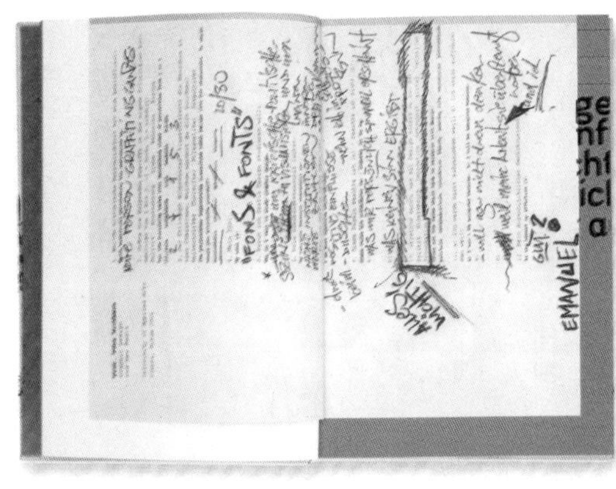

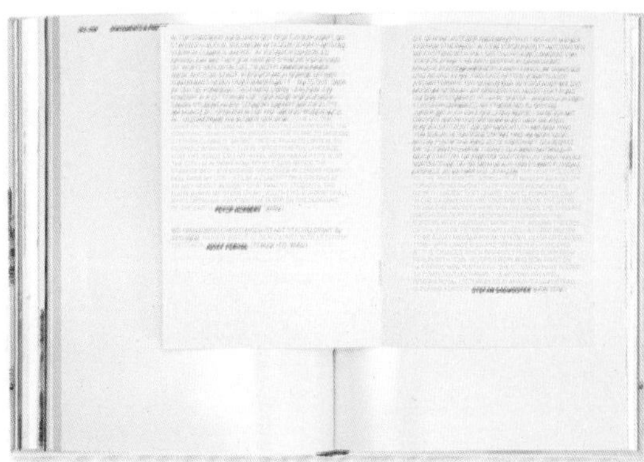

Beyond graphic design – book – university of applied arts Vienna – 2007

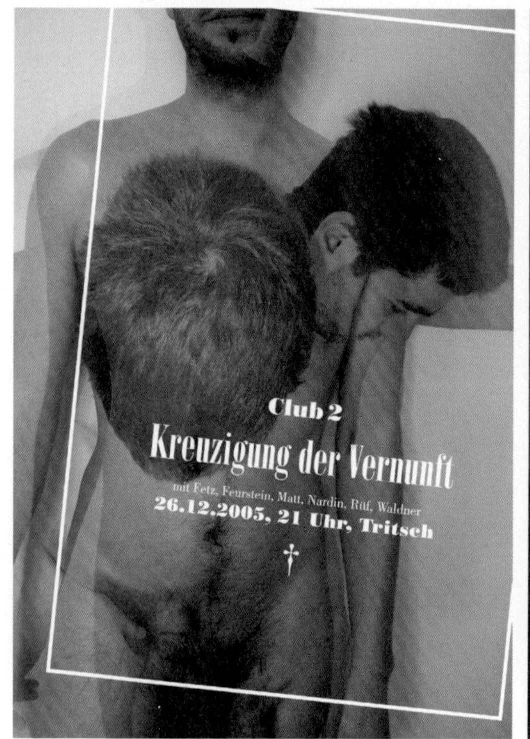

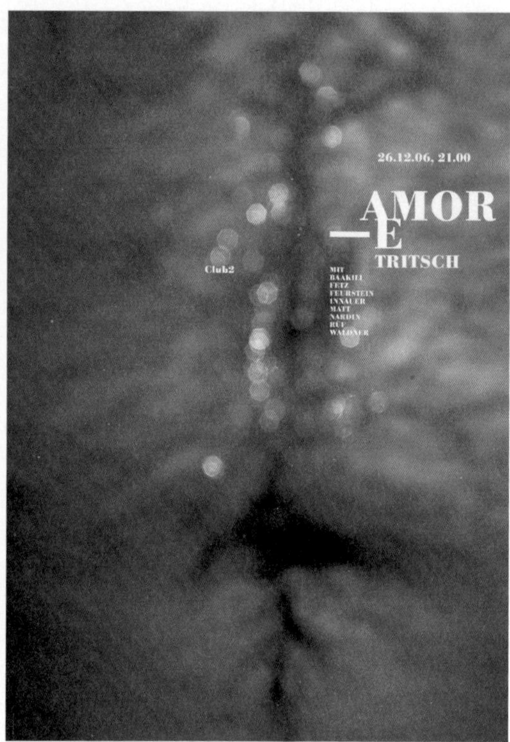

Landjäger No.3 – magazine – verein landjäger – 2007

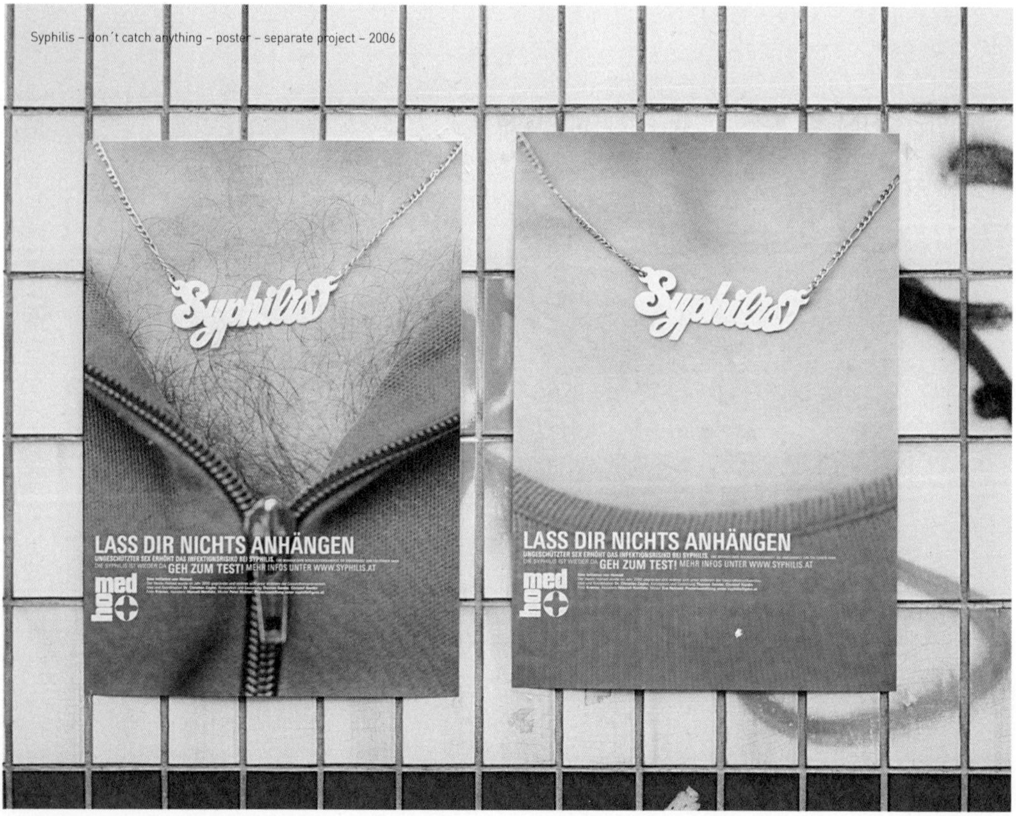

Syphilis – don´t catch anything – poster – separate project – 2006

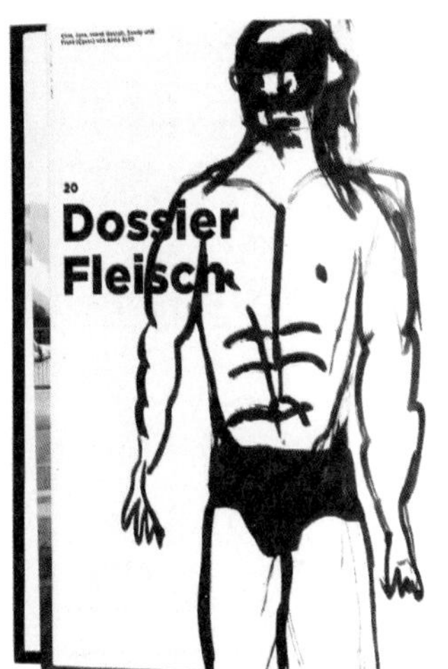

Club2 - book - no client - 2005/2006/2007

C2F: Cybu Richli & Fabienne Burri

team:
Cybu Richli
Fabienne Burri
contact:
Kasimir Pfyfferstr. 18a
6003 Luzern, Switzerland
T + 41 41 240 44 24
to@c2f.to
www.c2f.to

Fabienne Burri (www.c2f.to) and Cybu Richli is a graphic design studio in Switzerland focusing on design for art, architecture, science, education, cultural clients, etc. The members are working on projects such as books, catalogues, magazines, exhibitions, posters, info graphics, identities, case studies, critical thinking and research projects. They were awarded the Swiss Federal Design Grant, The Most Beautiful Swiss Books, 100 Best Posters, the Lucky Strike Junior Designer Award, Prints New Visual Artist, New York.

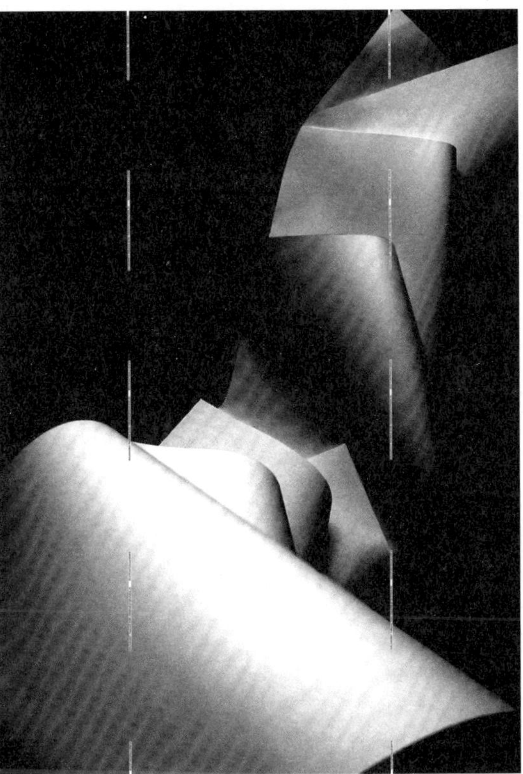

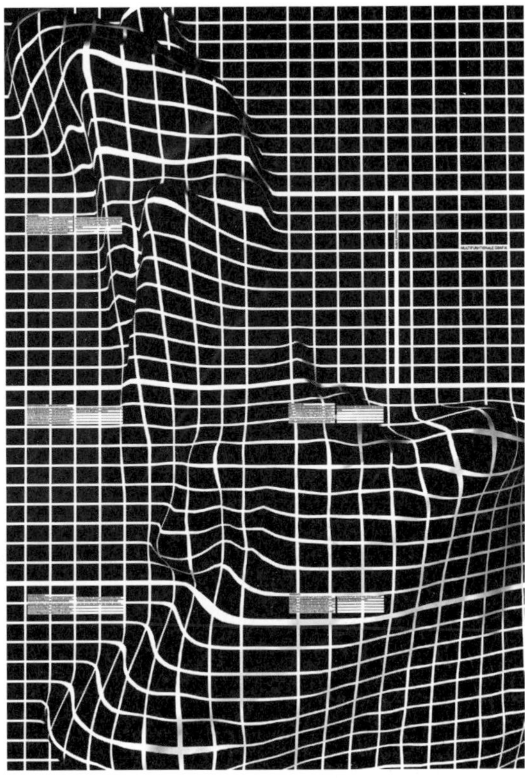

Multifunctional – poster – separate project – 2005

Interview with Fabienne Burri

1. What led to the formation of your studio?

We already collaborated for projects during our studies. After that, we took different ways at first. Cybu followed an invitation to Chicago to work in a research project on information graphics for half a year. After his return to Switzerland he chose to open his own studio. Fabienne worked for different studios. Two years later we met again while working on a shared project. Since then both of us work at the same studio, recently more often on collective projects.

2. How many staff people does your studio have and what are their main working fields?

We work alone or in pairs. Depending on the contracting work, we decide about the division of tasks each time.

3. How does a regular working day at your studio look like, how is the day structured?

Working, sleeping, working again.

4. How much leisure time do you have during a year?

100 percent. However, we work a lot during our leisure time.

5. Which business areas do your clients mainly come from? Is the number of your clients increasing or rather declining?

Many of our clients come from the domains of culture, education, science and journalism. We do not exclude other fields though as long as we are interested in the assignment and the client. We like to start working on new tasks, which makes our job even more fascinating. The number of our clients is increasing.

6. Do you have a specific corporate philosophy or maybe a mission statement like other companies, which is reflected in the way you steer the studio's course?

We did not really think about that yet. Our highest priority is always the creative quality of the design. And we love to work for clients who have high demands on the design.

7. What, from your point of view, makes the difference between a small studio and a big company?

A big agency provides safety and is able to offer its clients a wide range of services. A small studio on the other hand, has more character and as a general rule more individuality. New or even totally crazy ideas can be realized faster and more easily.

8. What kind of advantages and disadvantages does a small studio have compared to a big company?

Generally speaking, we see only advantages in a small studio. We really appreciate to be able to oversee the whole designing process until the final production. One disadvantage of small studios might be the lack of capacity with regard to large projects. We have a good network with excellent designers, photographers, illustrators, printing agencies, etc., collaborating with us on bigger projects. This offers the important advantage that we get into contact with very different people, different styles of working and new ideas all the time. Thus, we enhance our own work constantly.

9. What is your idea about the future of small studios? Do you think that small studios do not have any other choice but to expand in order to survive in these times of globalization?

For many people designing is a great passion, a passion which motivates you and keeps you running. Large agencies have identified the quality of small studios long ago and outsource designing work by co-operating with smaller studios. Big agencies more and more become design managers, juggling financial numbers instead of typography and pictures. For that reason, small studios which maintain high quality will always be able to survive – through contracting works of their own clients or through collaborations in networks.

10. Please describe and elaborate on the goals or plans that you have for your studio for the next five years?

We hope to get great assignments and to keep on enjoying our work. Furthermore, we work on our own projects and reserve a certain amount of time for that. A lot of new ideas develop in such projects, which are again used in contracting assignments.

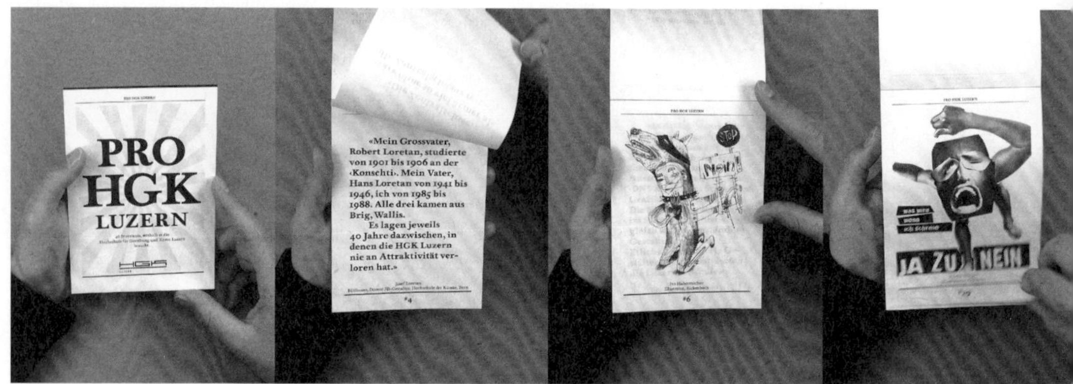

Pro hgk Luzern– calender – Lucerne university of art/design – 2007

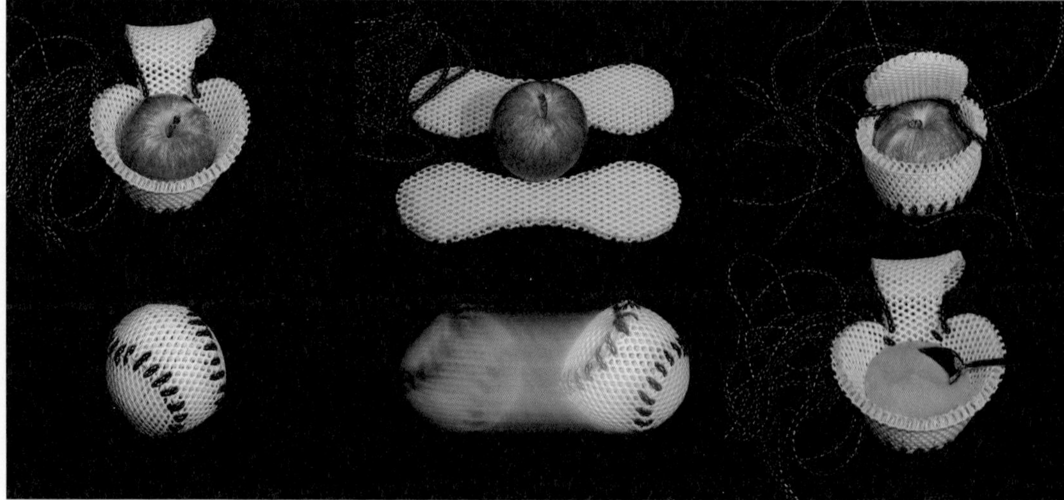

Designer: Cybu Richli

Emil Manser – poster – b verlag Luzern – 2006

Infotag – poster – Lucerne university of art and design – 2005

Werkbeiträge 2007 – art-design-culture competition organized by the city and the canton of Lucerne – 2007

Signal – poster – self briefing project – 2005

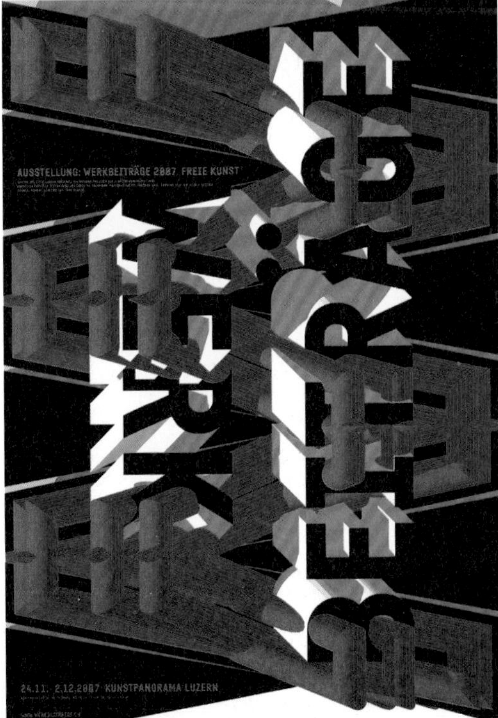

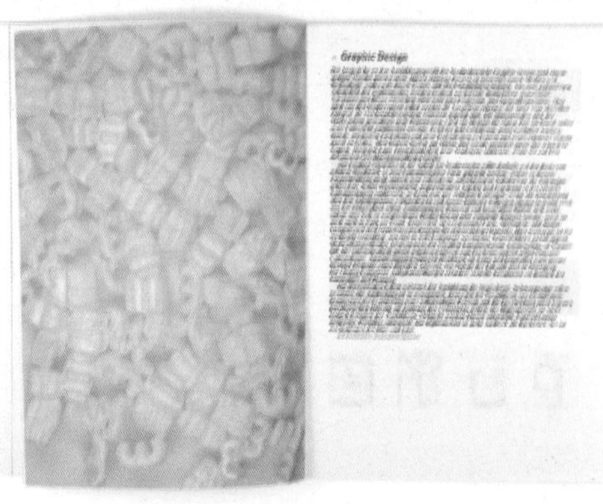

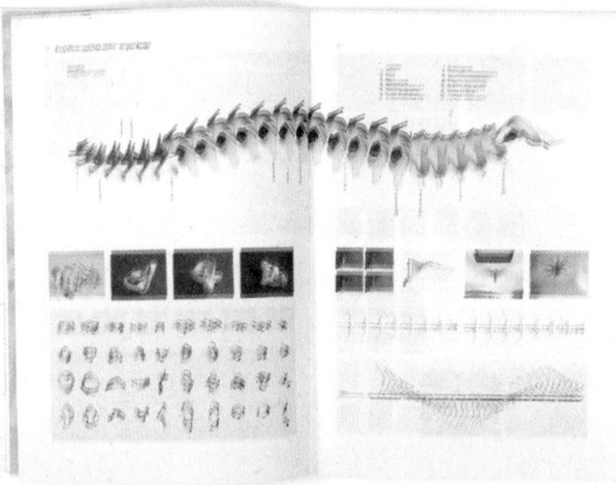

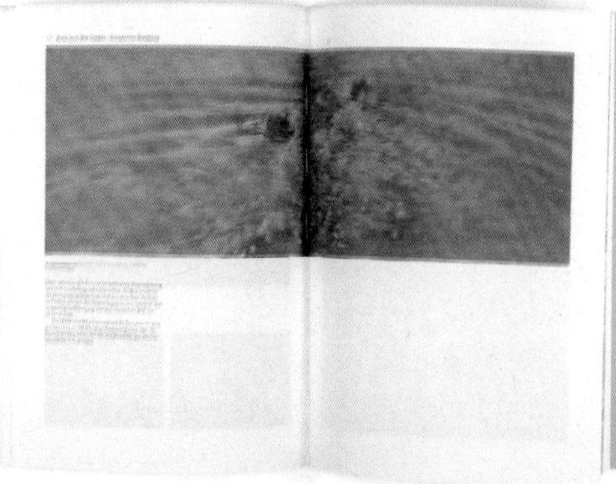

Diplomiert – book – degree – 2004

New York magazine high priority – magazine – New York magazine – 2007

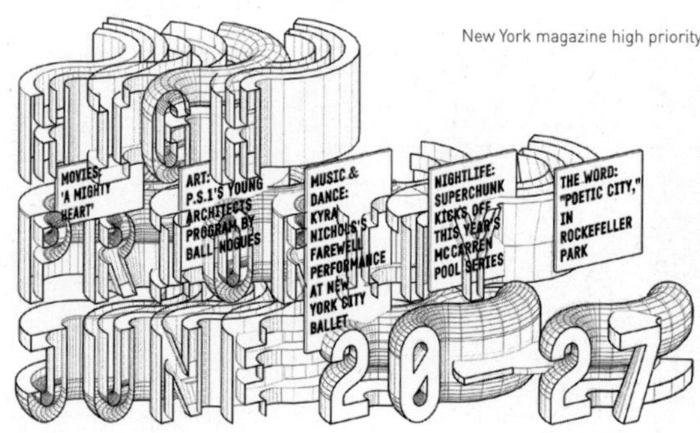

Osram – poster – self briefing project – 2005

Bouwe van der Molen graphic design

team:
Bouwe van der Molen
contact:
Kramatweg 90-2
1095 KD, Amsterdam
The Netherlands
M + 31 6 49309255
info@bouwevandermolen.com
www.bouwevandermolen.com

Studio- & portraitphoto by Anneke Hymmen

Bouwe van der Molen Graphic Design

Bouwe started his studio because being independent gives him the freedom to do the work he loves. His focus lies on editorial and concept-driven design and illustration. He is interested in cross-cultural (visual) communication. In the globalizing world, there is a growing need for knowledge in this area. By working on both a local and a global level, he hopes to gain a broader understanding of the relevant factors. At the Institute for Art and Design Arnhem (ArtEZ) and the Gerrit Rietveld Academy in Amsterdam he learned to remap the boundaries of design so as to coincide with his other interests. His internship at the graphic design agency NLXL in The Hague inspired him to strive for innovation and originality in the visualization of ideas. While working at LAVA graphic designers in Amsterdam, he developed methods for applying his ideas and graphics to editorial design in dynamic collaborative efforts. He received a stipend from the Netherlands Foundation for the Arts, Design and Architecture, which enabled him to start-up his business. As an independent creative he continues his explorations with an unquenchable thirst for knowledge.

Freaky fauna – screen-printed card – free work/self-promotional card – 2008

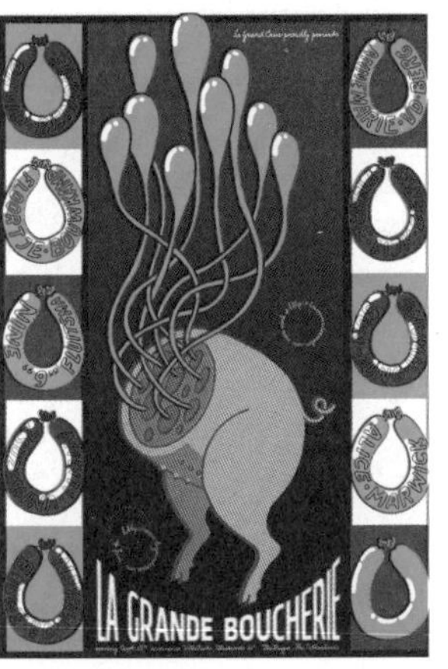

La grande boucherie – screen-printed poster – villanuts gallery – 2008

Interview with Bouwe van der Molen

1. What led to the formation of your studio?

After graduating from art academy in 2005, I decided to get a job for a few years. That way I could gain experience and learn the ins and outs of a design company before starting my own. I was very lucky to find a job at Lava graphic designers in Amsterdam. After two and a half years I left with a lot of knowledge and a network of helpful colleagues. It was great to work there, but being my own boss has always been my goal. I received a stipend from the Netherlands Foundation for the Arts, Design and Architecture which enabled me to start-up. I specialize in print-based editorial design and illustration, but have also designed and art-directed several video productions and websites. Collaborating with other designers, illustrators, writers, programmers, editors and photographers enables me to be as versatile as my imagination.

2. How many staff people does your studio have and what are their main working fields?

I have not yet felt the need to employ anyone. In the future, a partnership with one or two other professionals could be an option.

3. What does a regular working day at your studio look like, how is the day structured?

I currently work at home. Appointments often require me to travel. I spend a lot of time with my laptop on the train. I enjoy working at the same place with whomever I collaborate at that moment.

4. How much leisure time do you have during a year?

Being independent means always having time to do the thing I enjoy most: design. That is leisure to me.

5. Which business areas do your clients mainly come from?

I have a healthy mix of corporate and cultural clients. Occasionally, I do freelance work for larger design companies to gain an extra income. Apart from my assignments I also enjoy working on personal projects. I co-edit and publish O.K. Publications (a magazine), organize events with the art/illustration collective Le Grand Crew, and often do screen-printing projects. Although I don't profit from them directly, self-initiated projects are important. People that saw my free work have brought me several jobs.

Is the number of your clients increasing or rather declining?

The number of clients is steadily increasing.

6. Do you have a specific corporate philosophy or maybe a mission statement like other companies, which is reflected in the way you steer the studio's course?

I enjoy being my own boss. A corporate philosophy is probably more relevant for a company that consists of more than one person. This being said, it would be great to form a partnership with one or two other professionals. Their expertise would compliment my own and enable us to accomplish bigger things than we could do by ourselves. I would like to meet like-minded people from the fields of programming, writing and photography. Apart from broadening my own horizon, such an arrangement could be very attractive to clients. Many assignments cross a whole range of media. Being able to offer the whole package offers obvious advantages.

7. What, from your point of view, makes the difference between a small studio and a big company?

Tha five elements – flyer for online platform for hip hop culture – tha5elements.com – 2008

O.K. collections – magazine/design, magazine design, art direction and publishing in collaboration with O.K. Parking and Jeremy Jansen – free work – 2008

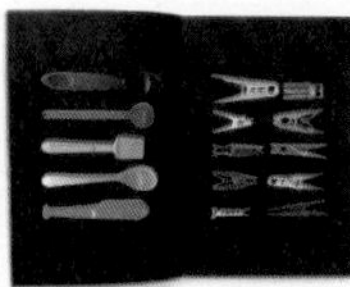

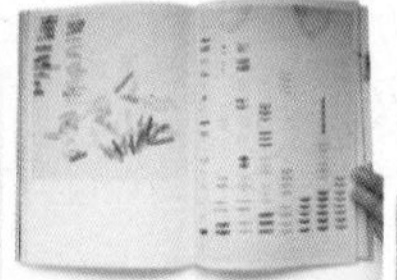

The book of perception – book/ texts on perception collected in collaboration with philosopher Patric Healy – graduation project – 2005

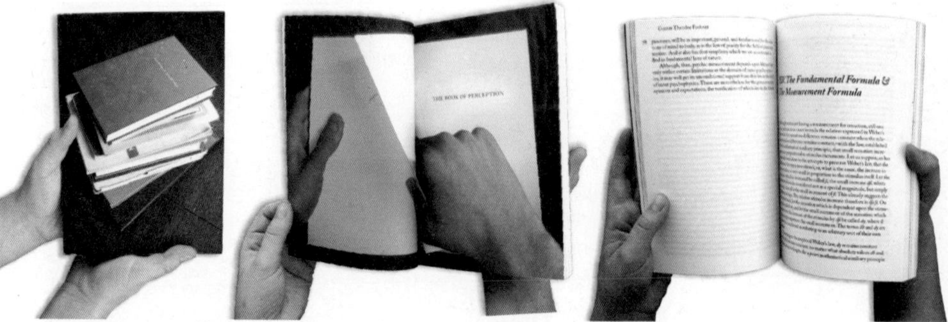

Corresponding vessels – screen-printed card – free work – 2008

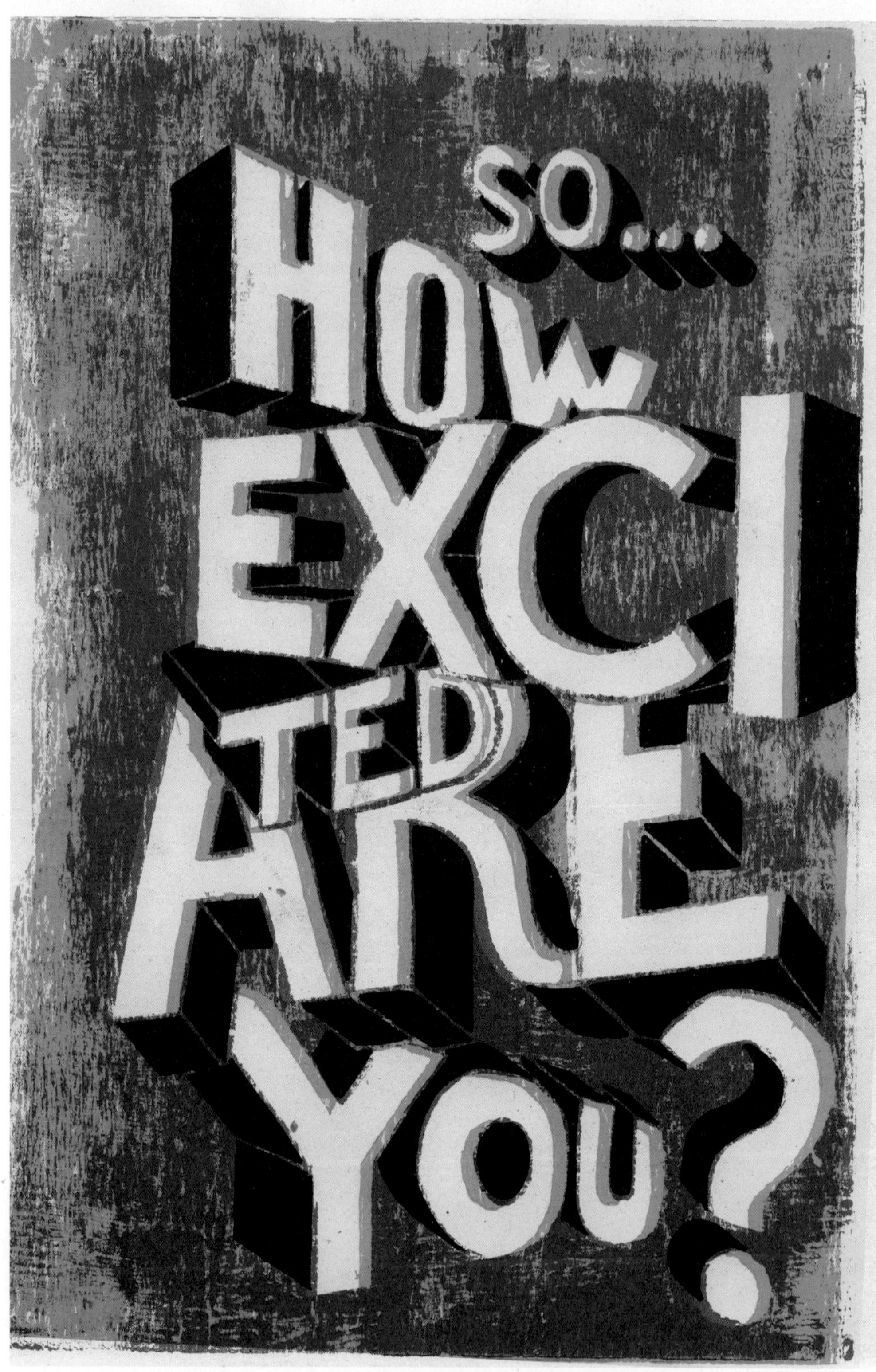

So... how excited are you? – woodblock printed poster – free work – 2008

Revolution – illustration – DUF2, bookazine for teenagers – 2008

Unplug – poster/advertising for a one-room hotel in my garden – free work – 2005

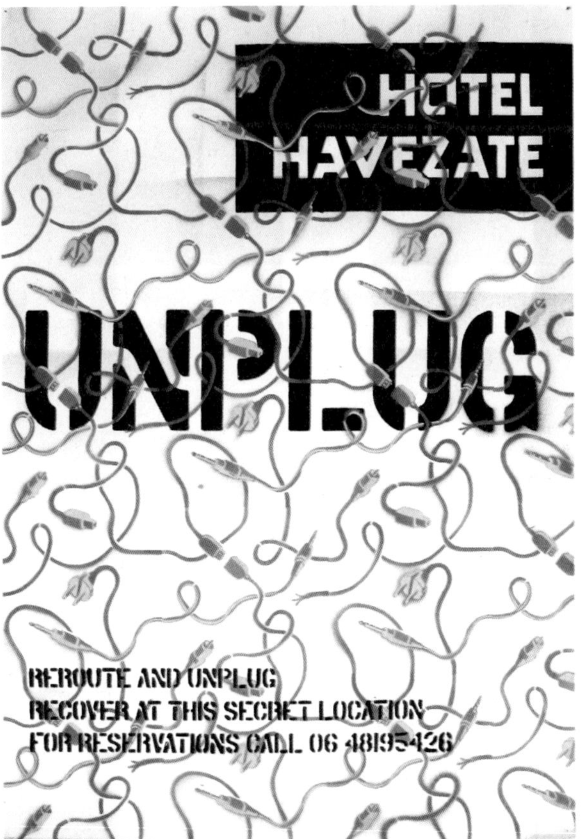

8. What kind of advantages and disadvantages does a small studio have compared to a big company?

I am much more flexible than any studio that is also an employer. Their fixed costs are much higher than mine. There is also a difference in assignments. Even though I know a small company could take the workload, more often than not, big projects usually end up with larger design firms. Clients simply do not see us as an option. At my previous employer, and when I do freelance work for other large design companies, I single-handedly, or perhaps with the help of one other designer, tackle assignments from large corporate clients. These clients often think that a whole design team is working on their commission, but this is usually not the case. I think it is this (false) sense of security that drives the clients to the big companies. A weakness of large design firms is that presentations to the client are usually not made by the designers, but by art directors or project managers. Concessions in concept and design are more likely to be made this way. No one can explain and defend a proposal as strongly as the person who has made it. Personal contact with a client can greatly improve communication, and so the quality of the design. This is the reason why the most sincere and groundbreaking design is still coming out of small design studios.

9. What is your idea about the future of small studios? Do you think that small studios do not have any other choice but to expand in order to survive in these times of globalization?

Small studios need to collaborate. By pooling their talents and being aware of each other's specialties, they can do almost any design job. Clients look for reputation and security. Anyone who is good at their job can provide that needed trust. There will always be plenty of companies and institutions looking for that one small creative studio. Small studios and large studios will continue to exist side by side.

10. Please describe and elaborate on the goals or plans that you have for your studio for the next five years?

I hope the current economic situation will not have too much influence on my business. Many (potential) clients still see good design as a luxury rather than a means to increase efficiency and returns on investment. Luckily, most good clients are aware of this and realize that investing in communication might be what gets them through this crisis. My interests lie in cross-cultural (visual) communication. In the globalizing world there will be an increased need for knowledge in this area. By working on both a local and a global level, I hope to gain a broader understanding of the relevant factors. Every project is a challenge to innovate. As long as I'm learning, I must be getting better at something.

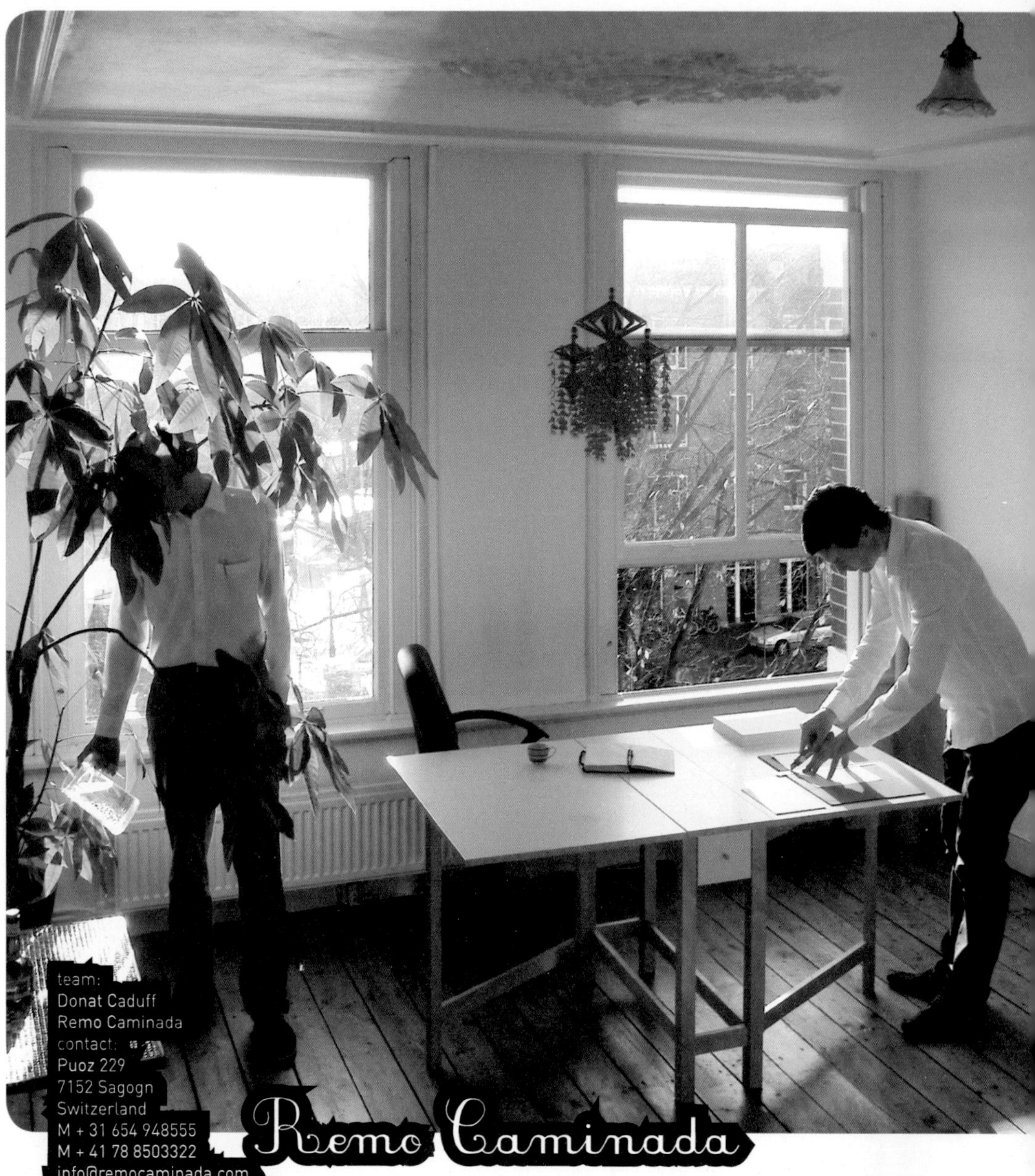

team:
Donat Caduff
Remo Caminada
contact:
Puoz 229
7152 Sagogn
Switzerland
M + 31 654 948555
M + 41 78 8503322
info@remocaminada.com
www.remocaminada.com

Remo Caminada

Remo Caminada — We are a small studio, but our interests are broad. It is not really important whether a job which is offered to us comes from a client with a commercial or a cultural background. Far more important is that we are able to transfer the potential of an assignment in accordance with our creative agenda into a meaningful work. This implies that we do not from the very beginning think of a logo, a book or a website, but leave open the specific choice of media in the first place. Actually, we want to reflect an atmosphere, provide an interesting idea to take along. That's the core of our work. By the way we analyze and guide the stream of our impressions and wishes arise the adequate products getting to the core of the client's needs.

Interview with Remo Caminada

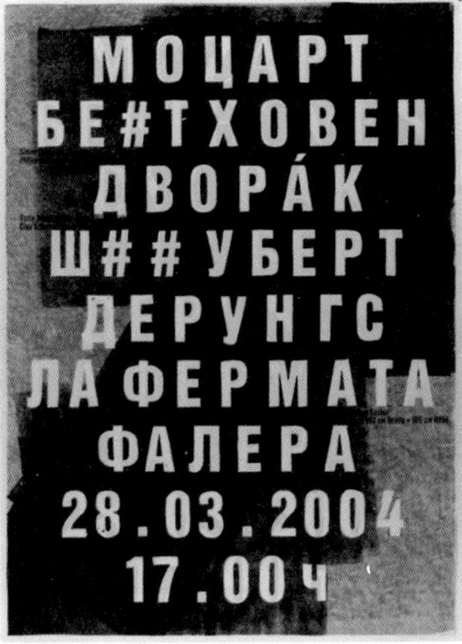

Cyrillic meets latin – poster – la fermeta, cultura Falera – 2004

1. What led to the formation of your studio?

During the time of my studies I have worked as an independent graphic designer. It was the only way to support myself financially while being a student. So I had the chance to gradually build up my own stock of customers. After graduating I had to decide if I wanted to keep up this network or rather try to find a job in an agency. My decision was to stay independent. Would I have I opted for the agency job at that time, the last two years would probably have been easier. However, I was curious to see what was needed to establish your own business from the start and solely on your own initiative – with all the success and all the setbacks involved.

2. How many staff people does your studio have and what are their main working fields?

We are 1-3 people. Each one of us has to cover all different work areas.

3. How does a regular working day at your studio look like, how is the day structured?

We start between 8.00 - 8.30 a.m., and we have a one-hour lunch break around 1.00. In the afternoon, I go singing for an hour. We work until 6.00 or 7.00 p.m., rarely longer until midnight, depending on the work load.

4. How much leisure time do you have during a year?

I do not draw a rigid line between work and leisure time. Your free time is at your own command. But I behave the same when I am working – for that reason I became an entrepreneur.

5. Which business areas do your clients mainly come from? Is the number of your clients increasing or rather declining?

Our clients come from very different areas. No matter if it is a hotel, somebody engaged in the cultural sector, or a supermarket approaching us – everybody is welcome. The number of clients, however, is currently rather decreasing. Is that a bad sign?

6. Do you have a specific corporate philosophy or maybe a mission statement like other companies, which is reflected in the way you steer the studio's course?

I enjoy working with curious people who want to accomplish something. That's probably the most important thing. To my mind, the best collaboration is reached when the client perceives me as a designer, not just as a service provider – and when I return do not treat him as a client in the basic commercial sense, but as a partner with a very interesting idea. In such a given case, a lot of things are possible, more than what is indicated at first glance. What seemed unrealistic in the first moment becomes solvable. I do not begin a work process with an idea of a specific end product, but with the imagination of a new world. The products come up as a logical and authentic consequence of that. Further, I do not think much about creating works so that many people like them. The most important point is when a work distinguishes itself by its uniqueness.

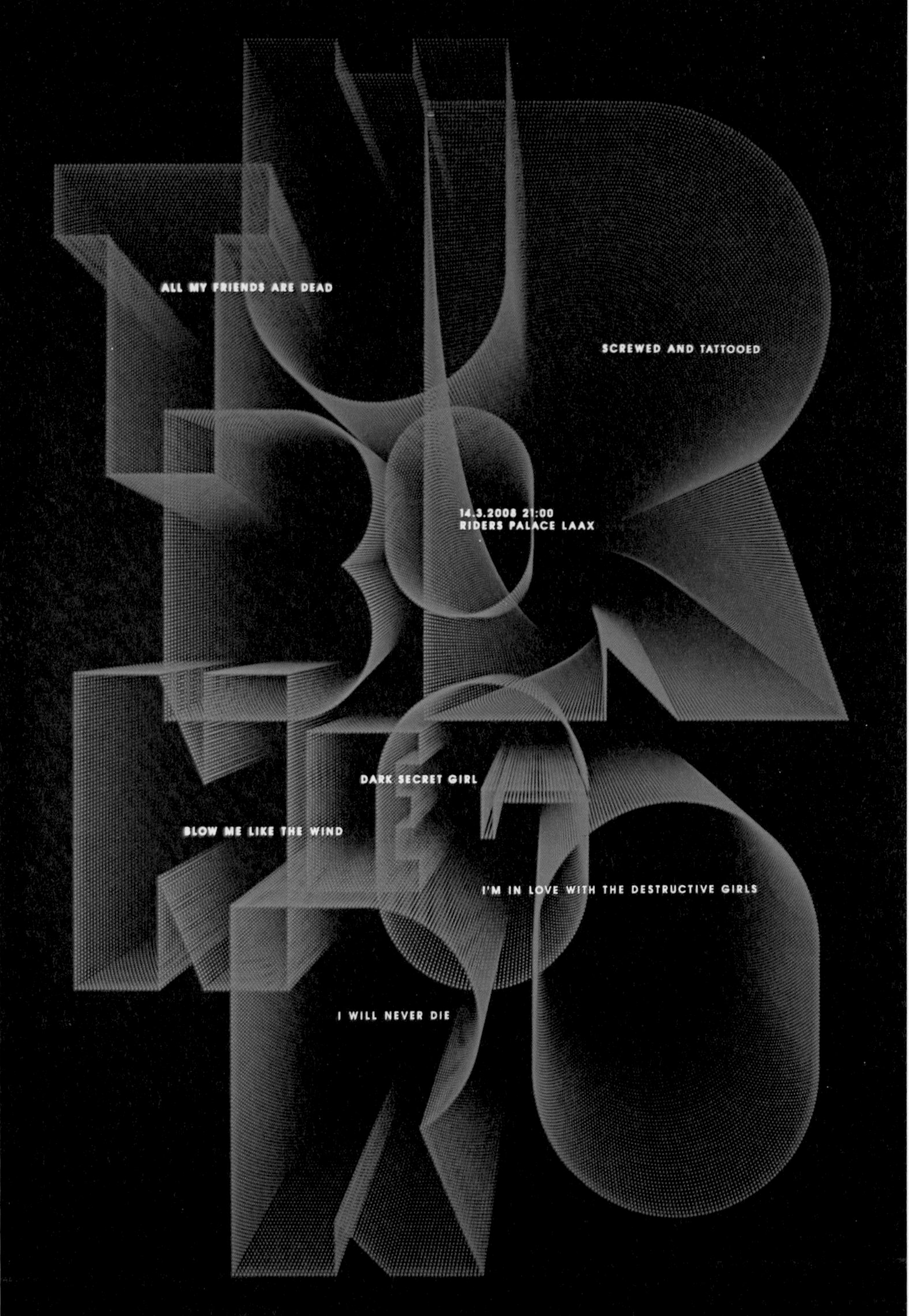

Turbonegro – poster – riders palace, weisse arena group – 2008

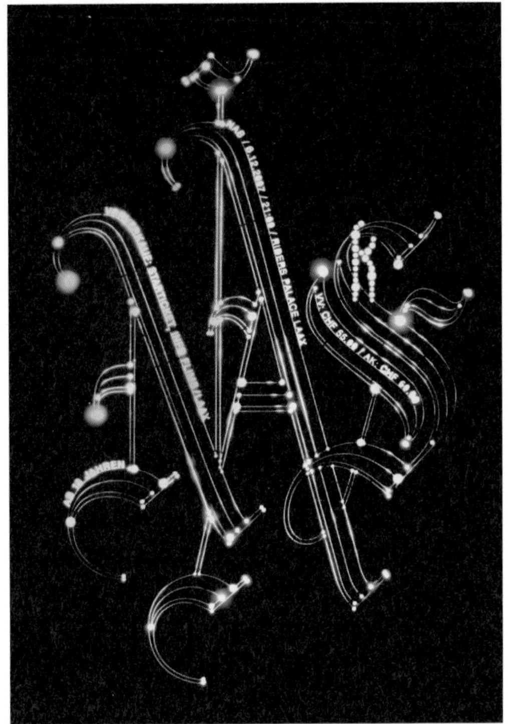

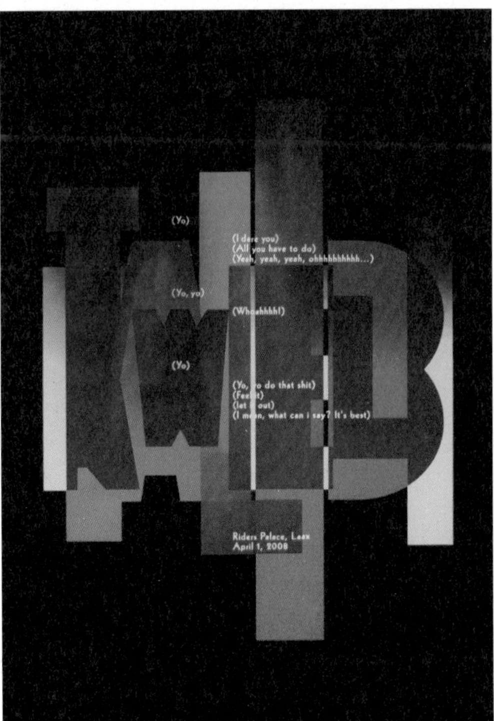

7. What, from your point of view, makes the difference between a small studio and a big company?

An employee in a small company is quickly involved in every stage of a work process. Thus everybody develops a close relationship to the whole project. Everybody is aware of the ups and downs of all ongoing projects. A job in a small company can therefore be more stressful and intense compared to a bigger enterprise.

8. What kind of advantages and disadvantages does a small studio have compared to a big company?

A small studio must invest a lot of energy to win a client's confidence. That is definitely a disadvantage at first sight. On the other hand, skepticism on behalf of a client also provokes reassessment and self-reflection. You discuss, struggling for solutions. And exactly this uncomfortable situation can prove to be a plus for the designing quality of a product. In the ideal case it is very thorough, and obtains an individual expression. A bigger company functions under different circumstances. Confidence is provided much more easily. The workflows are more professional and tight, also more standardized. But all of this comes with the danger that a product suffers with regard to its peculiarity.

9. What is your idea about the future of small studios? Do you think that small studios do not have any other choice but to expand in order to survive in these times of globalization?

I don't think that a small studio needs to expand to survive. There are, in my view, two ways for a small studio to go: either you systematically follow projects that you are interested in and strive for a designing perfection in order to realize personal, independent works. Or, you produce a lot and fast, and put less emphasis on the sophistication of your design. The perfectionist offers better quality. The economically thinking person has more financial freedom for a certain time span. He may also quickly realize, however, that he is not really satisfied by his work. Personally, I am only interested in the first scenario. Why? Nowadays, it is trendy that everybody wants to be a designer and tries to exert him/herself as an accentuated individual human being. Many people are convinced that they can stand their ground in creative discussions. I think this is a dangerous development with regard to projects which are not too complex for a long time. The graphic designer is often turned into the deliveryman for inputs and a technical henchman. The handwriting of a project, the concept, the style belongs to client. The trained perception of the graphic designer and his experiences assembled in daily life are on the verge of being ignored. I believe that the main task for small studios today is to stop that development. This is only possible if we as graphic designers make sure that we exclusively deliver high-quality work, instead of looking for a benefiting financial balance. Unfortunately, one may also be out of favor as a designer then.

10. Please describe and elaborate on the goals or plans that you have for your studio for the next five years?

That's our only project which shall never get beyond the phase of sketching.

NAS – poster – riders palace, weisse arena group – 2007

Talib Kweli – poster – riders palace, weisse arena group – 2008

ALPS AND ARTS

Alps and Arts – logo – alps and arts – 2008

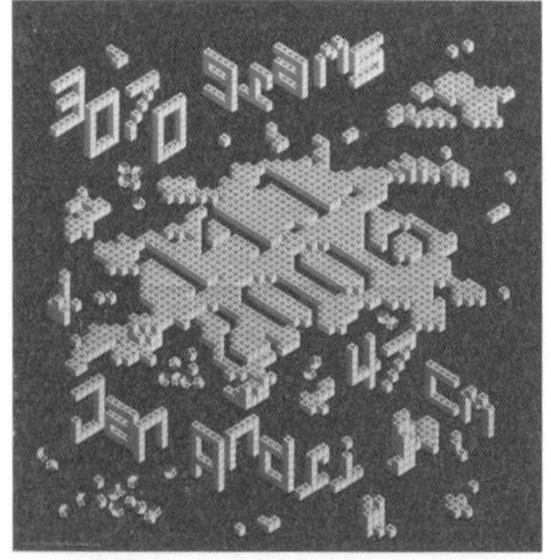

Happa birthday Jan Andri – birthday flyer – family tuor – 2006

Study abroad – poster – self-initiated – 2005

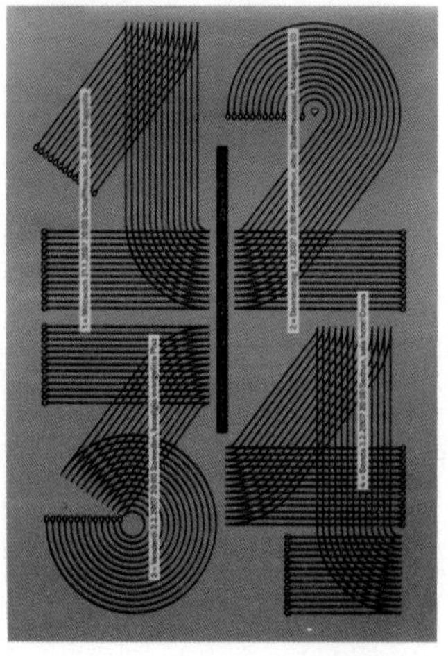

4 concerts, ensemble amanita – poster – ensemble amanita – 2007

Wedding of Sereina & Ervin – flyer – family Huonder – 2006

To death with a smile – poster – self-initiated – 2007

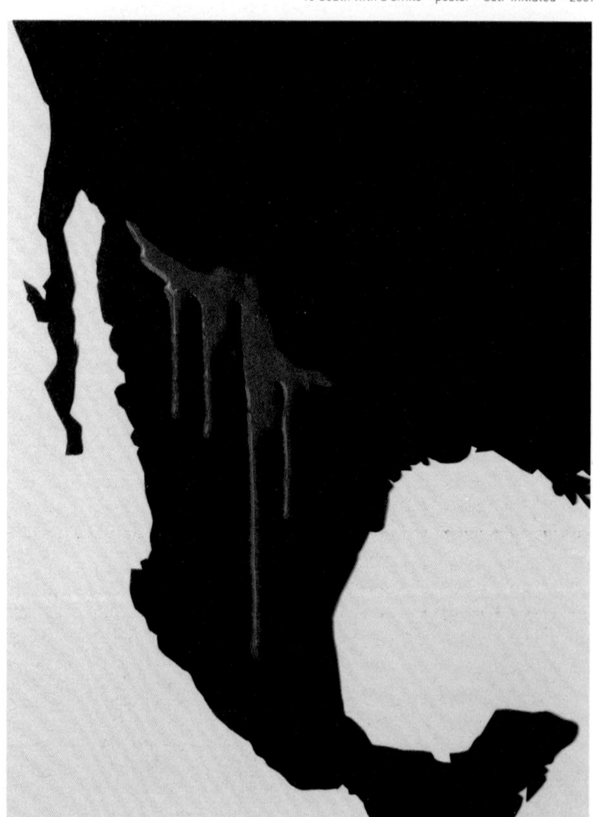

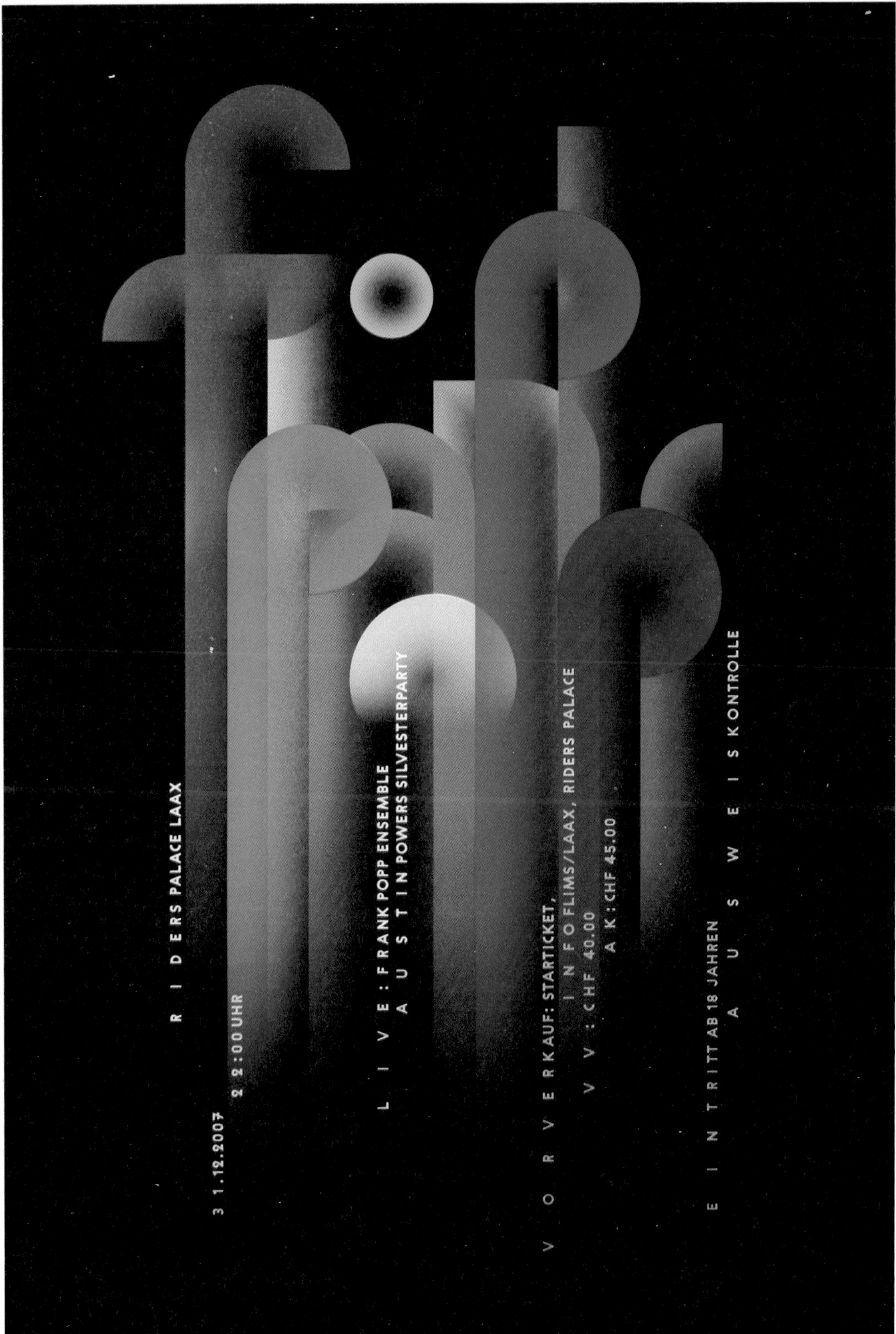

4 concerts, ensemble amanita – poster – 2007

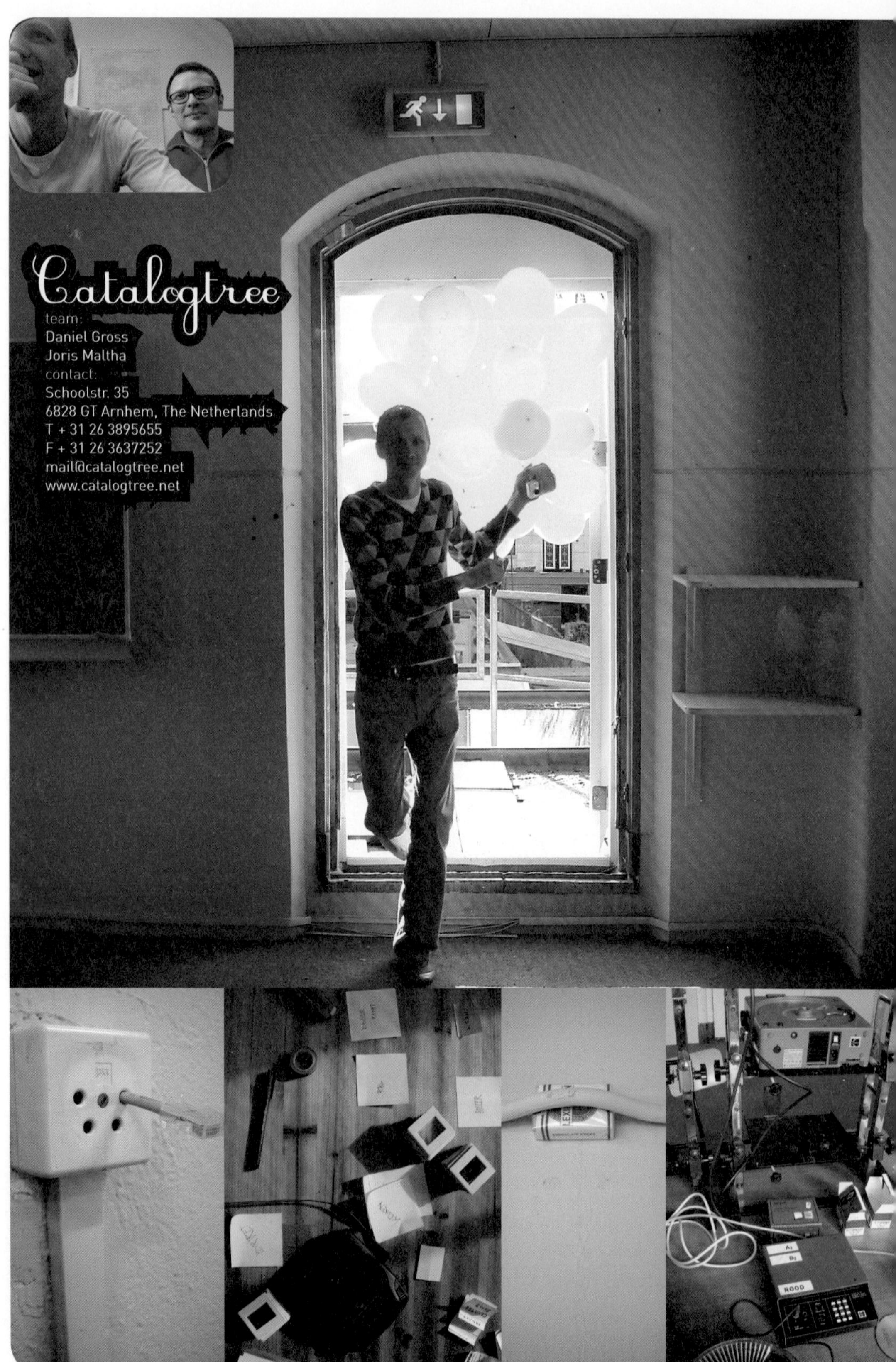

Catalogtree

team:
Daniel Gross
Joris Maltha
contact:
Schoolstr. 35
6828 GT Arnhem, The Netherlands
T + 31 26 3895655
F + 31 26 3637252
mail@catalogtree.net
www.catalogtree.net

Catalogtree is a multi-disciplinary graphic design studio founded in 2001 by Daniel Gross and Joris Maltha. The studio works continuously on commissioned and self-initiated design projects, being convinced that form equals behaviour. Medium independent design, programming, typography and the visualization of quantitative data are part of our daily routine. Recent endeavours include: Helium ballooning, i-pod-controlled slide projecting and visualizing the parking habits of New York Diplomats.

BUREAU
BUREAU
BUREAU LOFVERS
BUREAU LOFVERS

Bureau lofvers – logo – bureau lofvers – 2006

Interview with Catalogtree

1. What led to the formation of your studio?

When we started out with the first assignments in 2001, we did not really have the feeling as if we were launching a studio. We worked together on most of the projects, and also made a joint appearance when meeting customers. In the course of time we got used to that habit, but it never became a formality. Catalogtree, originally intended to be the name for a website on which we and a couple of friends wanted to show some of our works, finally became "our" name. While in the aftermath the regularity was increasing, the teamwork remained informal and based on friendship.

2. How many staff people does your studio have and what are their main working fields?

It's just the two of us – without having a clear or consequent division of tasks. Recently, however, project-oriented co-operation with others became more numerous and common to us.

3. How does a regular working day at your studio look like, how is the day structured?

Writing emails, sketching on the blackboard, eating soup, listening to Faur© and Liam Gillick at the maximum volume, working, playing Unreal – in a variable order.

4. How much leisure time do you have during a year?

Three weeks during the winter, three weeks during the summer.

5. Which business areas do your clients mainly come from?

Magazines in the U.S., architects in Holland, and artists in Germany. Is the number of your clients increasing or rather declining? The number is increasing.

6. Do you have a specific corporate philosophy or maybe a mission statement like other companies, which is reflected in the way you steer the studio's course?

Form equals behaviour.

7. What, from your point of view, makes the difference between a small studio and a big company?

More liberties due to lower fixed costs.

8. What kind of advantages and disadvantages does a small studio have compared to a big company?

See above.

9. What is your idea about the future of small studios? Do you think that small studios do not have any other choice but to expand in order to survive in these times of globalization?

On the contrary. Due to the globalization small studios can stay small and join forces with other small studios to handle big projects.

10. Please describe and elaborate on the goals or plans that you have for your studio for the next five years?

Becoming world-famous, fashioning film titles, collaborate with architects, teaching, new working cooperation bonds.

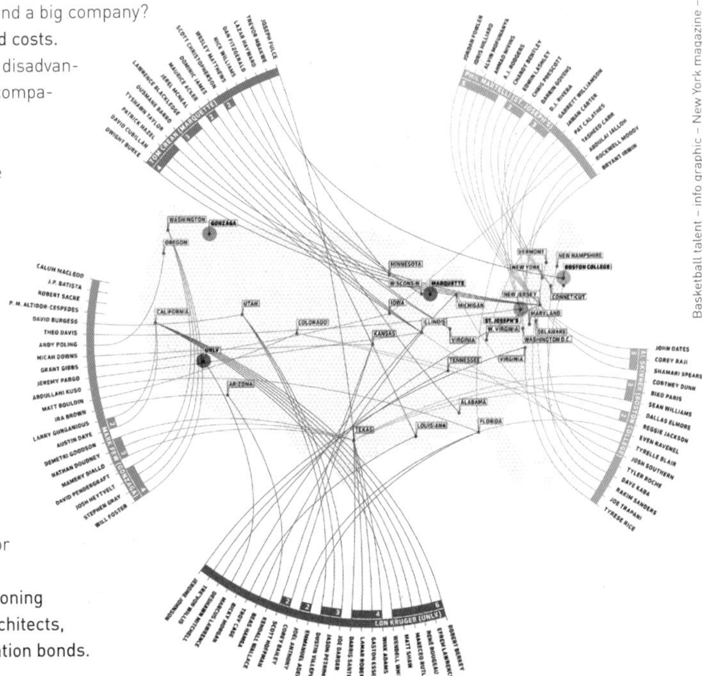

Basketball talent – info graphic – New York magazine – 2007

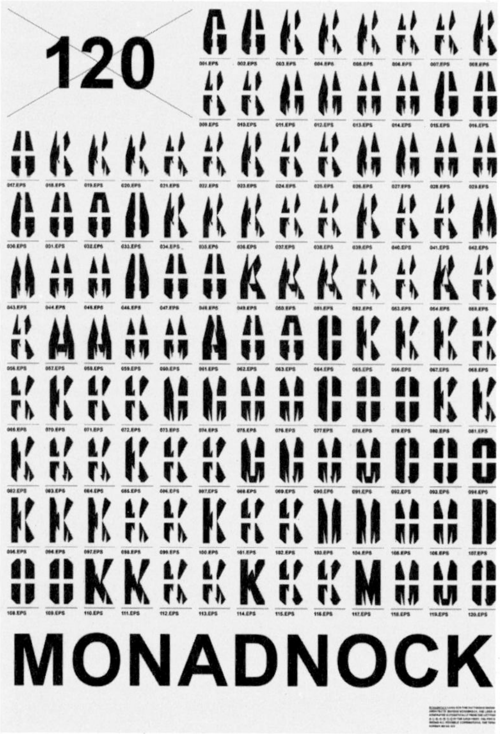

120

MONADNOCK

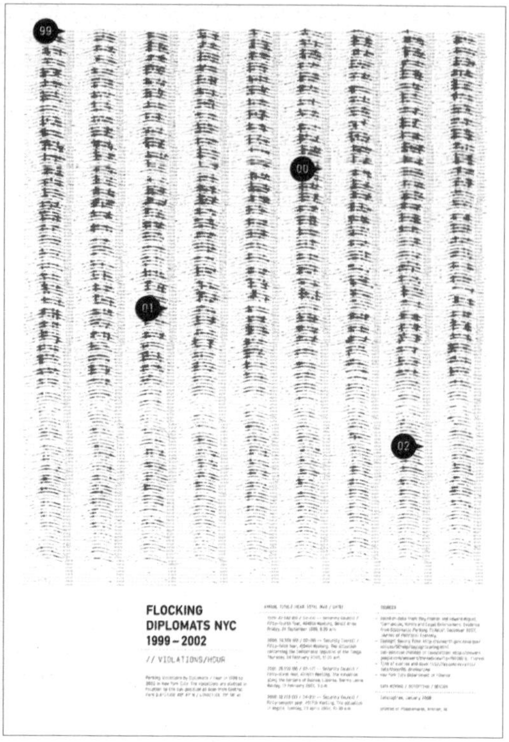

FLOCKING DIPLOMATS NYC 1999 – 2002

// VIOLATIONS/HOUR

Monadnock – logo – monadnock architects – 2007

Flocking diplomats – poster – self initiated project – 2007

Nepotism – info graphic – the Knoxville voice – 2007

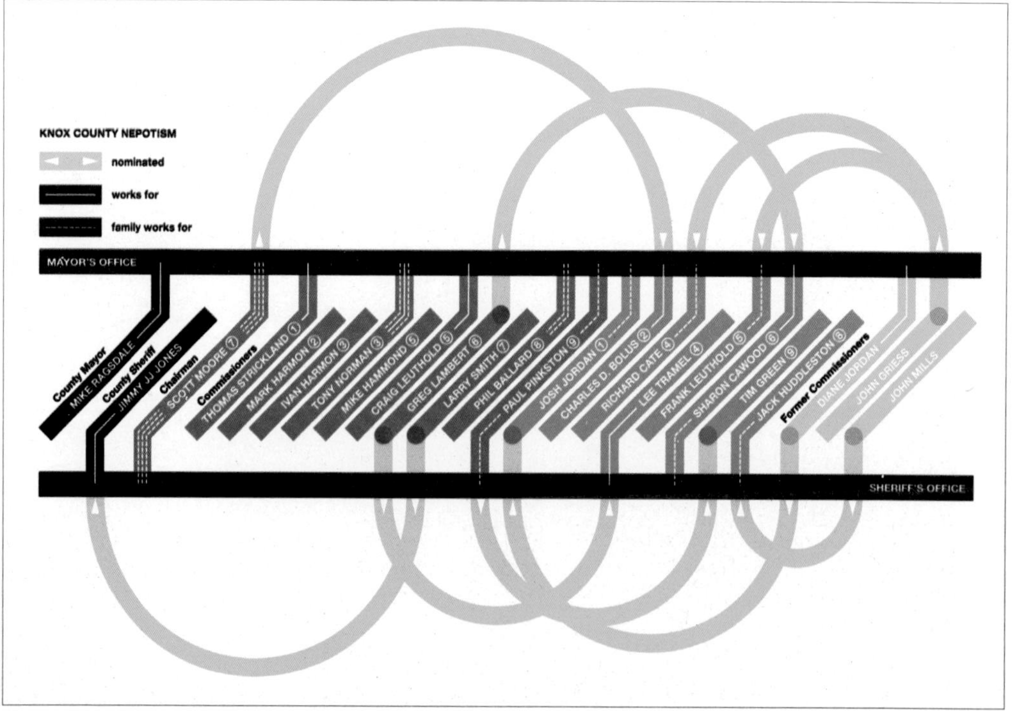

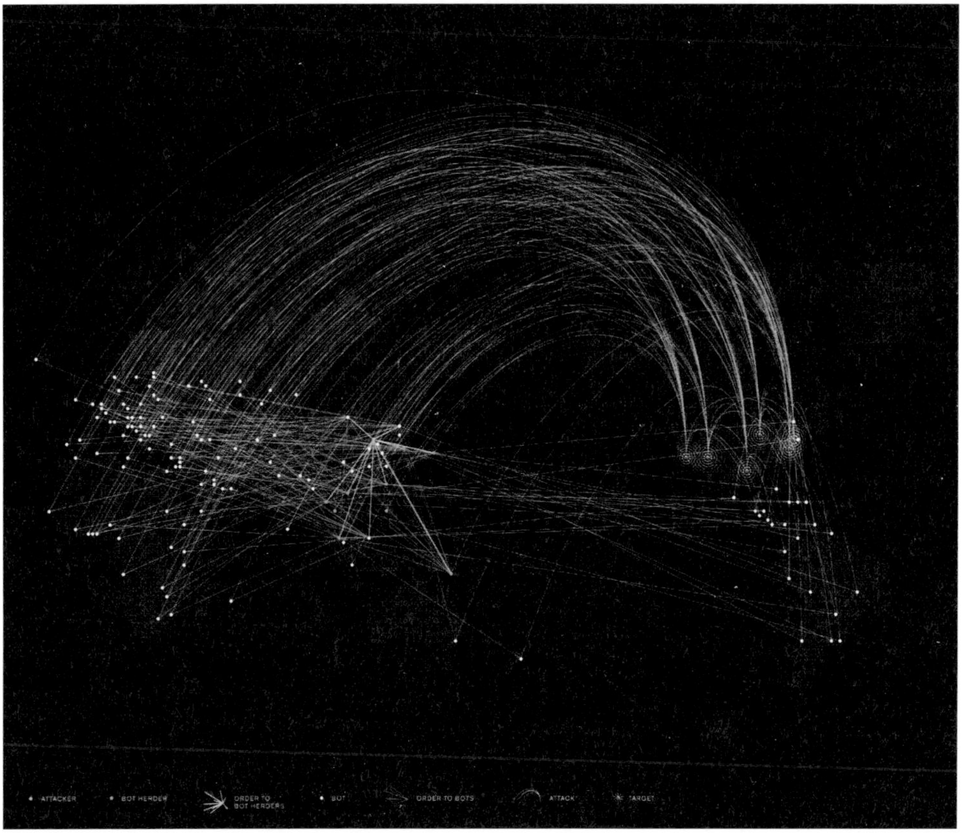

ATTACKER BOT HERDER ORDER TO BOT HERDERS BOT ORDER TO BOTS ATTACK TARGET

Cyberwar – info graphic – wired magazine – 2007

Infoporn – info graphic – wired magazine – 2007

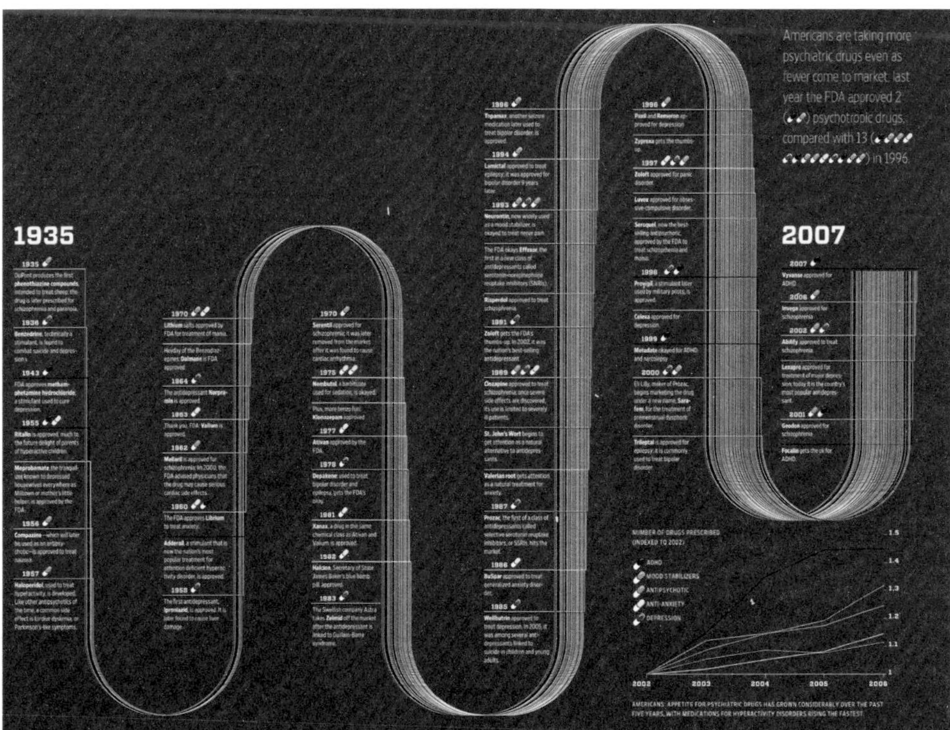

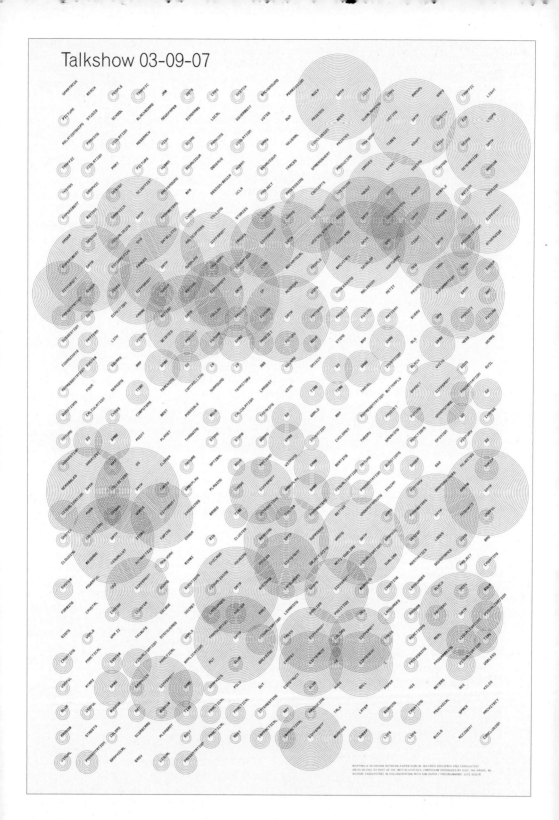

Talkshow – mapping – info aesthetics symposium – 2007

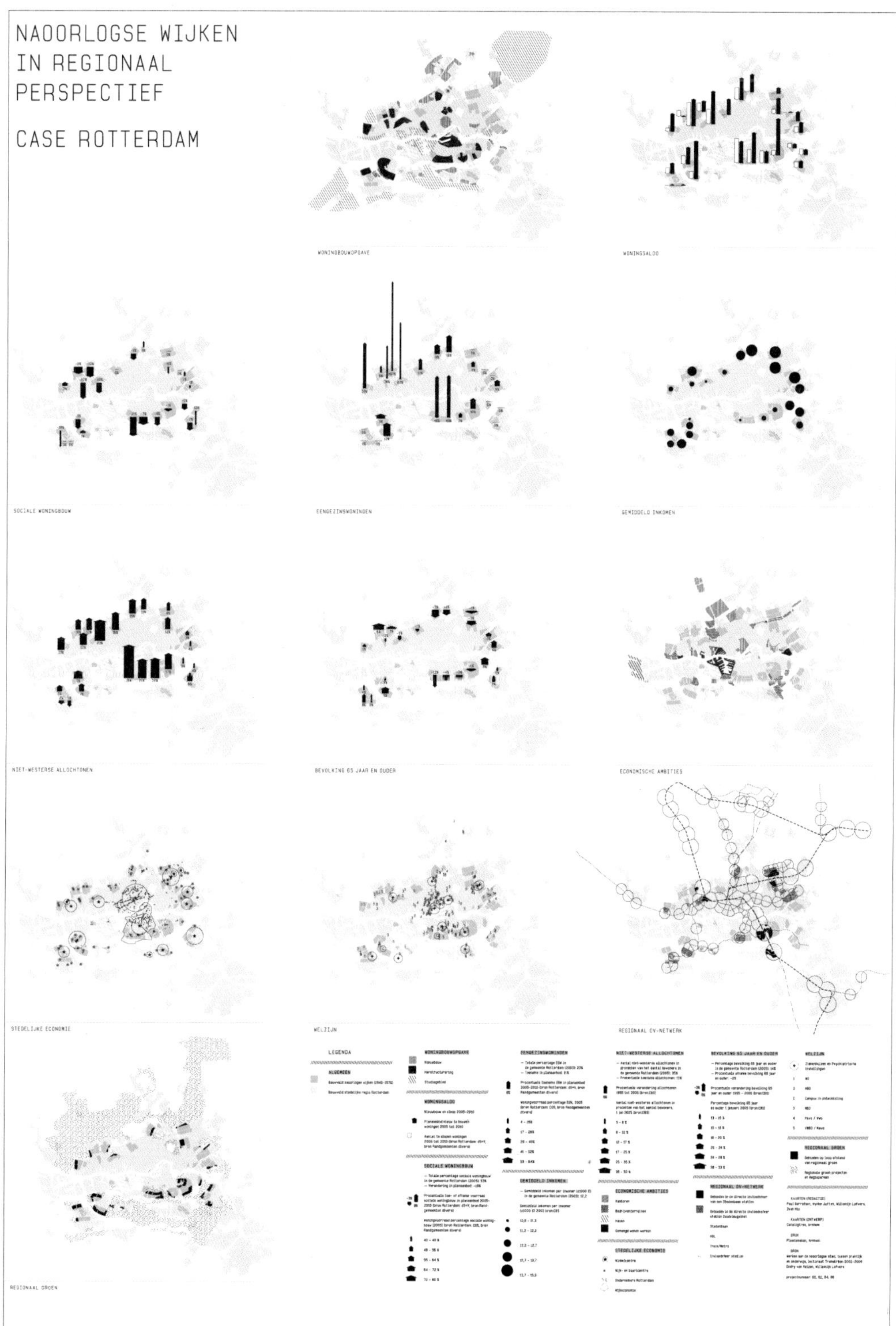

Transurban – poster – endry van velzen/willemijn lofvers – 2006

team:
Savas Cekic
Sendogan Yazici
contact:
Havyar Sk. No: 27/4
Cihangir 34433
Beyoglu Istanbul
Turkey
T + 21 224 96918
F + 21 224 55009
info@savascekric.com
www.savascekric.com

Savas Cekic

Savas Cekic was established in 1987 by Savas Cekic and has been producing graphic design for twenty years. It is better to consider this studio as a small design school rather than a small working place. This studio has an impact on many new age designers in Turkey since the day it was founded. Without discriminating against designers or the designs they produce, our goal has always been to find the most appropriate design for the respective needs. The main productions are: posters, corporate identities, brochures, catalogues, annual reports, calendars, diaries, packaging, books, book covers, magazines and magazine covers. During the last 5 years, we specialized on book design in our studio.

Interview with Savas Cekic

1. What led to the formation of your studio?

After graduating from the academy, I found myself with two paths ahead of me. The first was to get myself into an advertisement agency and to carry on as a commercial designer. The second was to set up my own studio in order to produce works that suited my philosophy, to pursue my own design enthusiasm, and to say what I wanted to say through design. I chose the second.

Savas Cekic's poster exhibition – poster – 2004

2. How many staff people does your studio have and what are their main working fields?

Our staff changes according to the project we're working on. Actually, most of the time it's only my assistant and me. Depending on the project, we get a few more people involved. We're also publishing a design magazine with my students called "No Design". When the magazine staff adds up, we become quite a number of people.

3. How does a regular working day at your studio look like, how is the day structured?

Our studio is mainly a discussion platform resembling a small design school, which is frequented by writers, activists, actors, painters, poets, and students.

4. How much leisure time do you have during a year?

Three weeks, distributed to various times over the year.

5. Which business areas do your clients mainly come from? Is the number of your clients increasing or rather declining?

Generally, the demand we encounter from our clientele splits into 40% cultural, 40% social, and 20% commercial content. As for the quantity of customers, it's highly correspondent with the economical state of the country at any given time. In case of economical decline, we deal with a lot of social works while in economically more favourable times, we have a decent amount of commercial work on our hands. Cultural works are not really dependent on the economy. Since the general economic state is constantly in decline nowadays, our clientele also constantly diminishes.

Savas Cekic's communication design exhibition – poster – 2003

6. Do you have a specific corporate philosophy or maybe a mission statement like other companies, which is reflected in the way you steer the studio's course?

Of course. Personally, I oppose the system. It's quite obvious that the biggest problem in the world is excessive consumption, and one of the foremost driving factors of this consumption are designers. The importance of designers realizing this fact while practicing their trade is paramount. Taking social roles for social responsibilities and using our creativity for humanity instead of the system are inevitable obligations. We try to evaluate our work according to this responsibility. Therefore, we turn down commissions that we don't agree with. Unfortunately, this reflects on our economy. Even though this becomes difficult to endure from time to time, it doesn't really bother us that much since it was never our goal to live in opulent luxury. The contentment resulting from producing the designs we like makes up for economic shortcomings.

7. What, from your point of view, makes the difference between a small studio and a big company?

The production mentality of a big company relies on money. For that, ends justify the means, so to speak. To produce designs with integrity we have to make compromises. Small design offices on the other hand, have a spirit keeping them alive. They seek to infuse that spirit into everything they create. In short, on one hand you have money, whereas on the other, you have philosophy.

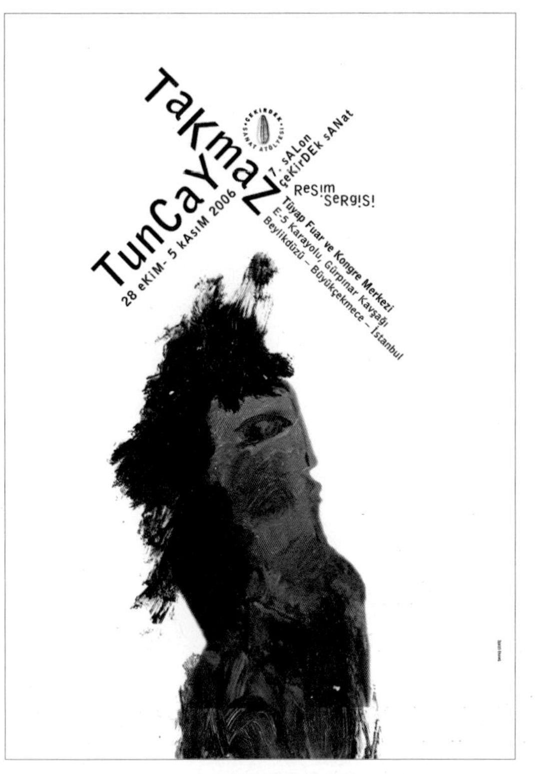

Tuncay Takmaz – exhibition poster – 2004/2006

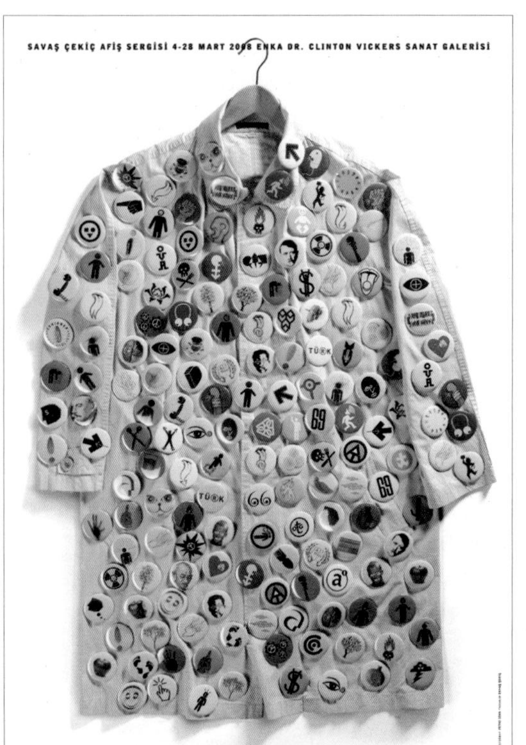

Savas Cekic's poster exhibition – poster – 2008

A play that is formed from the stories of Sait Faik – poster – 2007

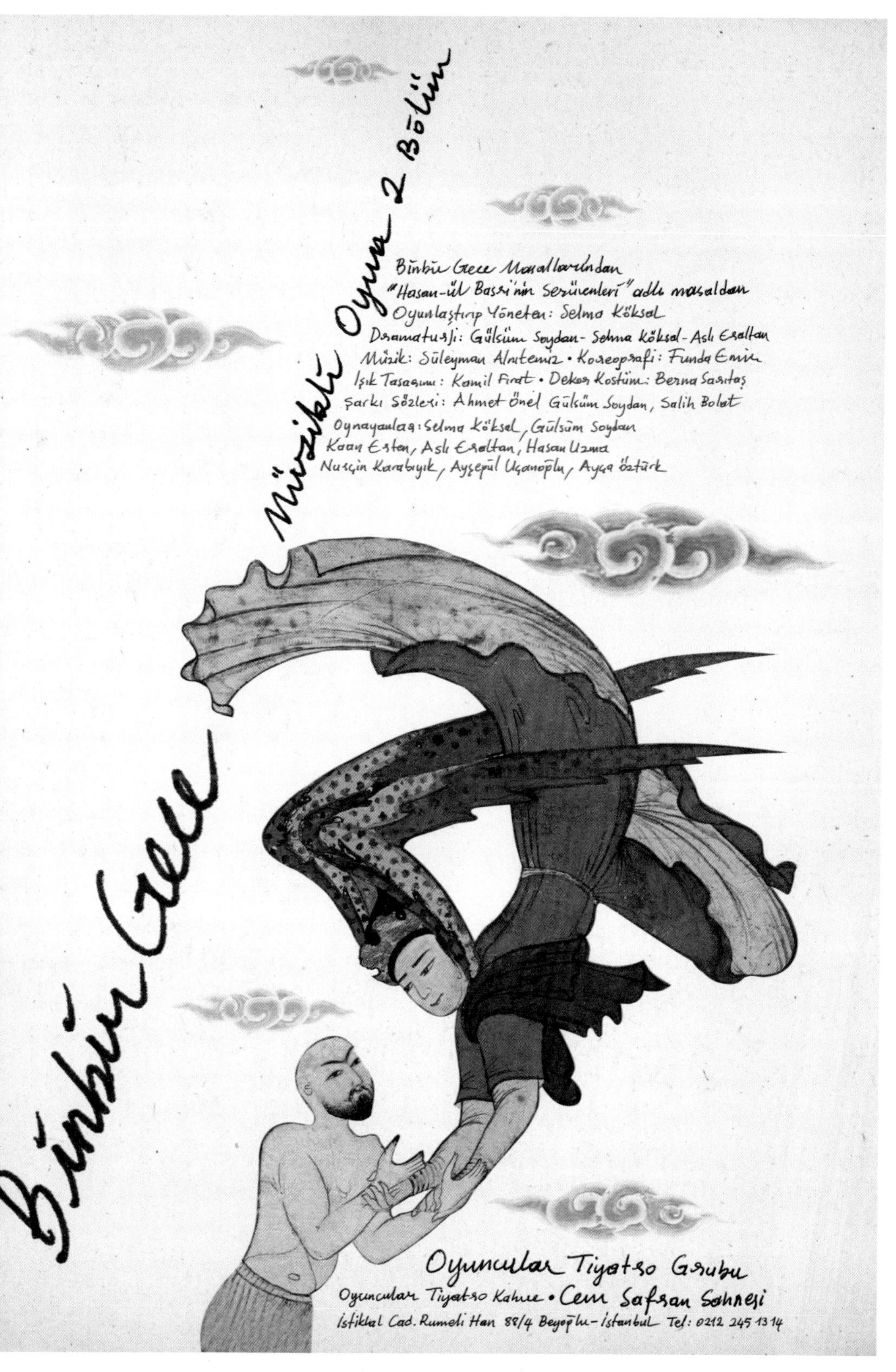

Binbir Gece
Müzikli Oyun 2 Bölüm
Binbir Gece Masallarından
"Hasan-ül Basri'nin Serüvenleri" adlı masaldan
Oyunlaştırıp Yöneten: Selma Köksal
Dramaturji: Gülsüm Soydan - Selma Köksal - Aslı Eraltan
Müzik: Süleyman Altıntemiz • Koreografi: Funda Emir
Işık Tasarımı: Kamil Fırat • Dekor Kostüm: Berna Sarıtaş
Şarkı Sözleri: Ahmet Önel Gülsüm Soydan, Salih Bolat
Oynayanlar: Selma Köksal, Gülsüm Soydan
Kaan Esten, Aslı Eraltan, Hasan Uzma
Nurçin Karabıyık, Ayşegül Uçanoğlu, Ayça Öztürk
Oyuncular Tiyatro Grubu
Oyuncular Tiyatro Kahve • Cem Safran Sahnesi
İstiklal Cad. Rumeli Han 88/4 Beyoğlu - İstanbul Tel: 0212 245 13 14

Arabian nights – poster – 2004

8. What kind of advantages and disadvantages does a small studio have compared to a big company?

If it's a greedy corporation that you're looking for, it doesn't make a difference if it's big or small. You can benefit from the perks of both. That being said, both sides also have drawbacks. It's all about the perspective you take to observe the issue. A big company brings big responsibility. To support your employees' responsibility, you may have to compromise your own beliefs and ideals. Your client's demands may turn your world upside down, or you may become incredibly rich if you go for the big projects which are being commissioned. As long as you don't mind the "ethical" inconsistencies, you might as well live "a perfect life". Small studios, on the other hand, are relatively easy to operate, given their better conditions of economical survival. It's possible for designers to form fraternities among their ranks and to construct their own way of life in their designs. In my opinion, to be able to reject a commission is the utmost luxury for a designer. Who doesn't want to enjoy such a luxury? I think this is a concept that can only be possible in small studios.

9. What is your idea about the future of small studios? Do you think that small studios do not have any other choice but to expand in order to survive in these times of globalization?

I don't agree and personally I don't consider expanding. I always have a dream for design and a better world. I'm sure there are and there will always be people or companies that understand us, and who will come to us for design. I put my trust in them.

10. Please describe and elaborate on the goals or plans that you have for your studio for the next five years?

In this country, it's a bit of a pipe dream to make plans for the next five years. However, first and foremost, we're aiming to maintain the demands we put to our own work. To be able to carry on designing in order to inform, enlighten and encourage the public about social problems. To publish "No Design", the magazine project to inform our colleagues.

Poetry books cover – book cover – cekirdek publisher – 2007

The book of chosen social designs – book design – 2007

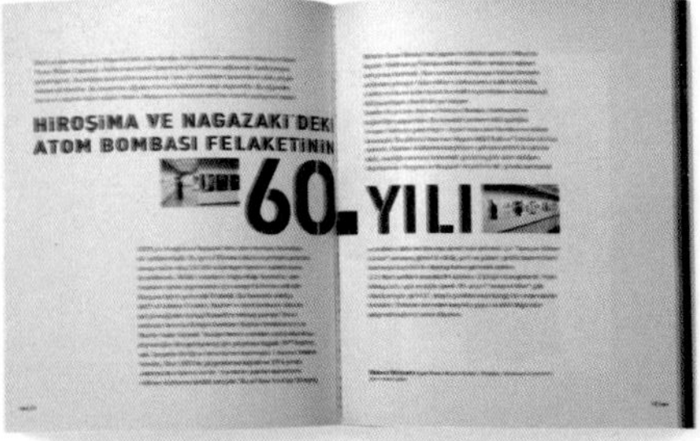

A play that is formed from the stories of Kafka – poster – 2000

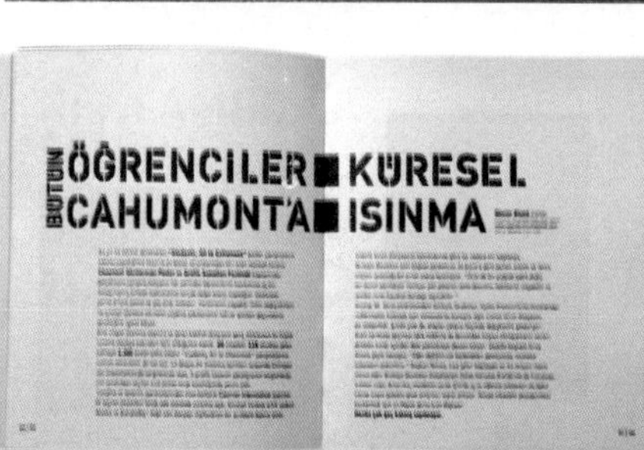

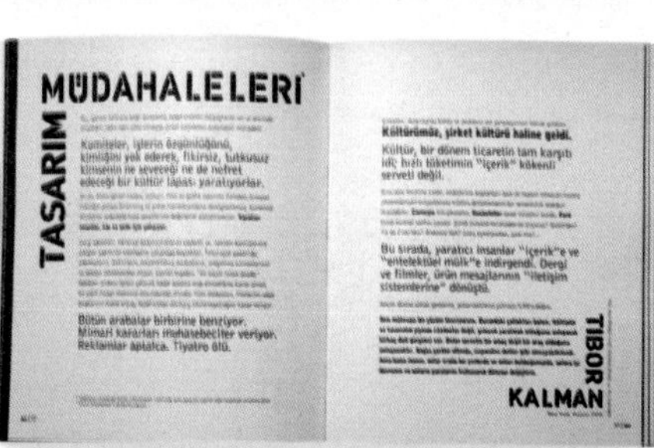

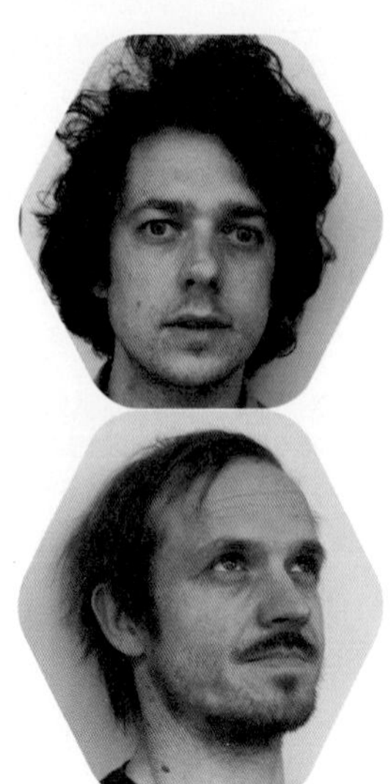

Change is good

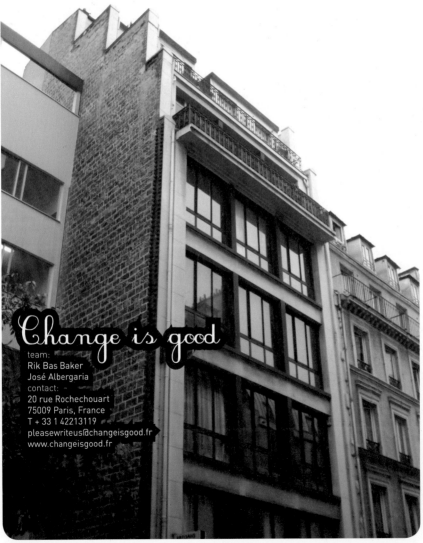

team:
Rik Bas Baker
José Albergaria
contact:
20 rue Rochechouart
75009 Paris, France
T + 33 1 42213119
pleasewriteus@changeisgood.fr
www.changeisgood.fr

Change is good – One makes it change, the other makes it good. Two graphic designers, one from the Netherlands, the other from the islands of the Azores. The chances of meeting in a city like Paris were very small, but notwithstanding, circumstances made these two graphic designers meet in Paris in 1999 and establish a small studio. These two designers share a wide range of interests from music, cooking, surfing to hockey, subjects that reveal a lot and remain graphic references for them. Change is good has an intuitive way of designing and dealing with projects, the result of each project is the consequence of a permanent laboratory of techniques and ideas. Rules or no rules, this is not a dilemma, the experiment brings out the most impulsive and closely related to the commission. The idea of a big studio is only an idea in their minds, that's why they keep their studio small.

Interview with Change is good

1. What led to the formation of your studio?

We were studio mates, working separately, until one of us was offered a big job.

2. How many staff people does your studio have and what are their main working fields?

The two of us plus one stagiaire, and many other people that assist us on various tasks, all of them are graphic designers.

3. How does a regular working day at your studio look like, how is the day structured?

It depends on each different project. But in general, as long as we are a small studio, we all take part in every stage of the process from the concept to working out the technical details.

4. How much leisure time do you have during a year?

About 4 weeks all in all.

5. Which business areas do your clients mainly come from?

What in France is called the institutional area, like museums, art centres, a Belgian beer producer, independent publishers.

Is the number of your clients increasing or rather declining?

It is difficult to say as we have several permanent clients, but also some booking us only once.

6. Do you have a specific corporate philosophy or maybe a mission statement like other companies, which is reflected in the way you steer the studio's course?

Trying to be very open-minded, trying to create a team work structure with the client, trying not to have a pre-defined style or way of working. Trying to break hierarchies.

7. What, from your point of view, makes the difference between a small studio and a big company?

Everybody works with everybody, everyone knows everyone.

8. What kind of advantages and disadvantages does a small studio have compared to a big company?

Small companies are maybe less dependent on a money flow on a monthly basis, but a lack of money hits harder. There are no holidays without sacrificing some work.

9. What is your idea about the future of small studios?

We hope they'll always be the "engines" of a graphic avant-garde (like the French would say).

Do you think that small studios do not have any other choice but to expand in order to survive in these times of globalization?

No, you just need a network of other designers who are able to give a hand, and clients that understand that you're only two doing the job.

10. Please describe and elaborate on the goals or plans that you have for your studio for the next five years?

Evolve from working together with freelancers towards a small company structure.

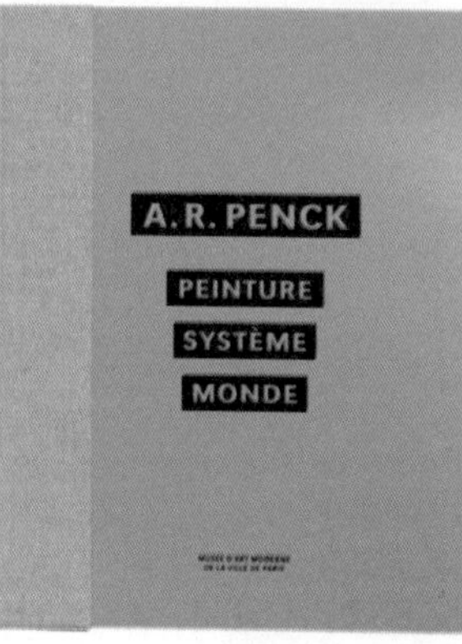

A.R.Penck – catalog – musée d'art moderne de la ville de Paris, Paris musées – 2006

Festival international de l'affiche – poster – ADCEP – 2004

Fête de la musique – poster – ADCEP – 2006

Image to come – catalog – magnum/steidle, cinémathèque Française – 2007

Stefan Claudius

team:
Stefan Claudius
contact:
Savignystr. 59
45147 Essen, Germany
T + 49 201 7268210
stefan@claudius-design.de
www.claudius-design.de

Stefan Claudius is running his one-man show since 2000. After his studies, he rather slipped into independency. His main focus is always type. On the one hand, he is making fonts of his own and distributing them through his foundry Cape Arcona. On the other hand, he creates logos and corporate designs. When he is not in his little office, he is at the Folkwang University in Essen or the University of Applied Sciences in Dortmund, where he is teaching type and typography.

Knickelkopp – corporate design/website/ci – Yvonne Frieß – 2007

Interview with Stefan Claudius

1. What led to the formation of your studio?

During my dissertation I worked in a medium-sized company and was for the first time confronted with the phenomenon of mobbing. This led to the decision not to have a boss again and to try it on my own.

2. How many staff people does your studio have and what are their main working fields?

The studio is just me. And I do everything. In fact, the thought to have people working for me really occurs from time to time, but if I have too much to do I don't want to spend my time introducing others into my work. I have the concept of being "small but fine" and hope it will work out for me.

3. How does a regular working day at your studio look like, how is the day structured?

I walk to the studio, which takes a quarter of an hour. During that time I think about what to do during that day. When I arrive I read and answer the mail. Then I start working. From time to time I eat something but I don't really have a regular lunch break, because too much food makes me tired. In the evening when the official work is done, I start working on fonts. Since I am now teaching at the university, two days of the week look different. On Mondays I go to the university of Essen and teach type, while on Wednesdays I drive to Dortmund to hold a course on conception and design.

4. How much leisure time do you have during a year?

I take my time, that is my kind of luxury. Others drive a Mercedes, I go on holidays. But my kind of holidays are not luxury. Once a year I take a two-week trip with a group of mentally retarded people. And once I go on holidays for two or three weeks on my own. And then, there can be weekends when I am taking a day off or so.

5. Which business areas do your clients mainly come from?

From all kinds of businesses. A part is from the social sector, but I also work for some agencies, and these jobs can be about everything. Some clients have a cultural background and these jobs are pretty nice, because they offer more freedom, usually.

Is the number of your clients increasing or rather declining?

All in all, it is increasing but it comes in waves. There are always times when there is way too much work and then there are times when it is pretty relaxed. But the teaching jobs and a monthly magazine that I produce bring some regularity into my business.

6. Do you have a specific corporate philosophy or maybe a mission statement like other companies, which is reflected in the way you steer the studio's course?

I have the vision that I will be mainly making and teaching type in the future, and I am trying to take measures to make this happen. Concerning my clients I have the philosophy that I want to make them happy. I take their opinion very seriously and I am very likely to question mine if we do not agree on something. But I think I should change that. I have to become stronger and more austere with my clients. But I try to do that in a way they can understand. I try to find reasons for the things I do, and I think they are more likely to follow me if I give them good reasons.

7. What, from your point of view, makes the difference between a small studio and a big company?

Both can do good and crappy work. A big company can offer more durability and can handle larger jobs.

8. What kind of advantages and disadvantages does a small studio have compared to a big company?

I think the work is more diversified. If I would work in a large company, I would probably do the same stuff every day. I would be bored and get fat. Right now, I have to struggle for my existence, which keeps me alive. And I can hope to steer in a direction I like. And I can hope for miracles, like great customers with lots of money. In terms of working the main difference is that big companies have big clients. Big clients often offer well-paid, boring jobs, but sometimes also well-paid exciting jobs. It makes me sad to think that I will never get these jobs.

9. What is your idea about the future of small studios? Do you think that small studios do not have any other choice but to expand in order to survive in these times of globalization?

As I said I have a different concept. If you grow with your studio, you will end up one day organizing work and getting jobs instead of designing. I don't want that. I try to make my work as profitable as possible while keeping my size. I would like to have a partner, but not an employee. I think both large and small studios are needed. And for that reasons both will survive in the times of globalization.

10. Please describe and elaborate on the goals or plans that you have for your studio for the next five years?

I will try to focus on type design even more than in the past. On the one hand, I will work on new text fonts and try to publish them through the best font labels, on the other I will try to get clients for custom–fonts. In the meantime I would like to continue teaching, because I learn a lot from that – things that I have in my mind but which need to be structured. The process of structuring has taught me a lot. If eventually, this will lead me to become a professor, I would not object.

Duisburg film week – poster – adult education center of Duisburg – 2007/2004

I could lend me a bicycle – cd – ludwig records – 2006

3. bis 9. nov 2003
DEMAG
STAHLBAU
DEMAG
DUISBURGER FILMWOCHE 27
das festival des deutschsprachigen dokumentarfilms
echt falsch
filmforum der VHS am dellplatz | T (+49) 203.283.4187/-4171 | F (+49) 203.283.4130 | www.duisburger-filmwoche.de | filmwoche.vhs@duisburg.de
DUISBURG
NRW.
arte
3sat
Sparkasse Duisburg
dfi

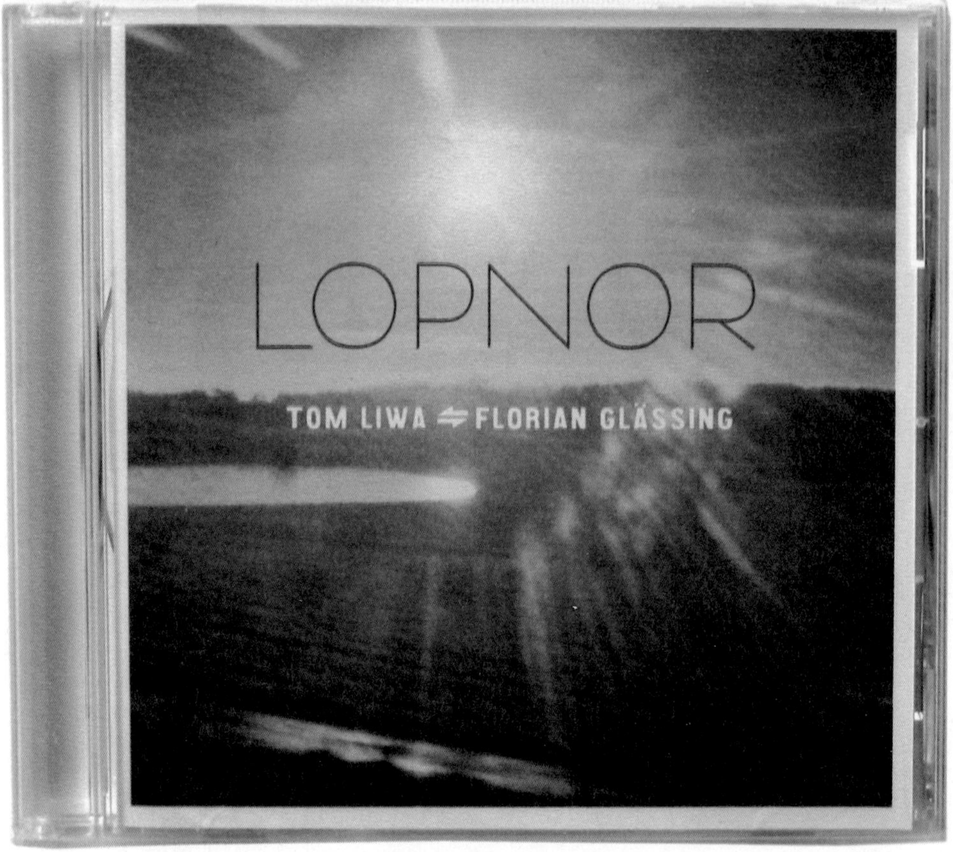

Lopnor – cd – normal records – 2002
The sound of animals fighting – logo – ths design – 2006
Firescape – logo – ths design – 2007
Marienorgel Witten – logo – catholic church St. Marien Witten – 2007

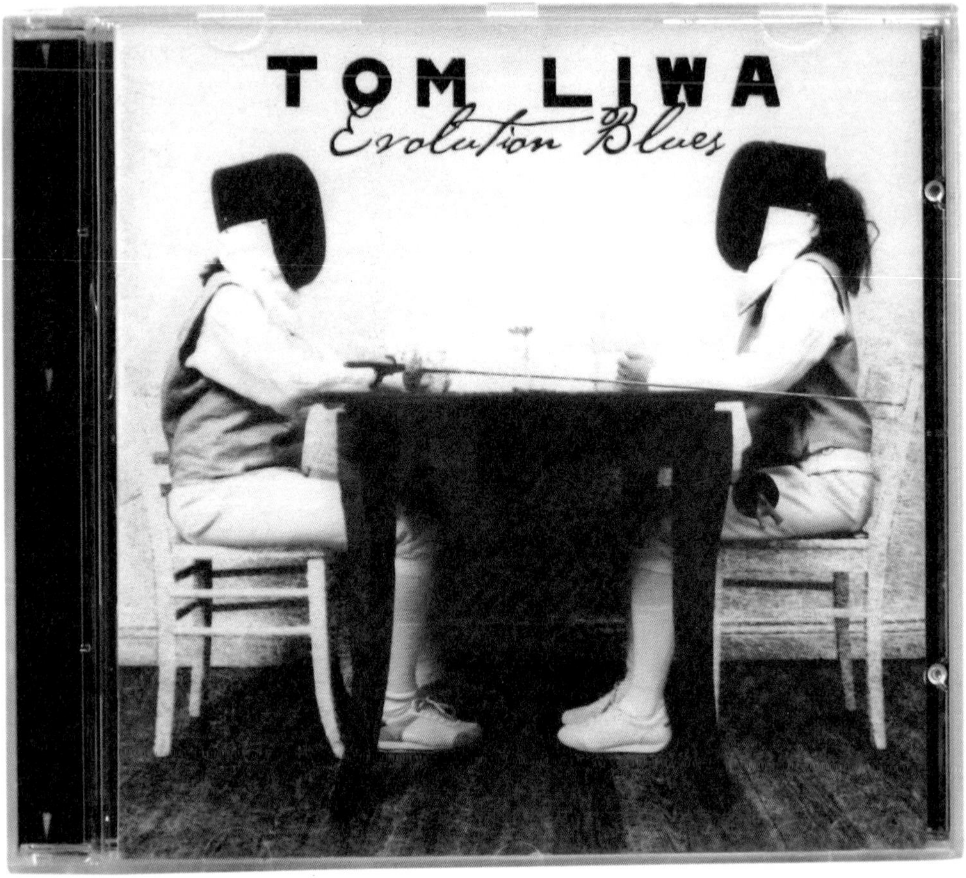

Tom Liwa - evolution blues - cd - normal records - 2001
Seeleninsel - logo - seeleninsel - 2007
The city drive - logo - ths design - 2007
Argiope - logo - ETH Zürich - 2007

collerette coco fill lsd

team:
Constant Mathieu
Laurent Baudoux
Fabrizio Terranova
contact:
98 rue du Coq
1180 Brussels
Belgium
F + 32 2 3721710
M + 32 485433146
constant@collerettecocofilllsd.com
www.collerettecocofilllsd.com

collerette coco fill lsd consists of Dr. Collerette who is a graphic designer, animator, producer and medical doctor, although he never practiced medicine. Collerette, son of a Trinidadian mother and a Zimbabwean father was born in Brussels, Belgium. He employs numerous pseudonyms, such as "Pipecock Jaxxon", etc. According to interviews with Collerette, he was also "recovering from his wounds" and swearing revenge "to the industry that so badly deformed him". In 1973, Collerette built a studio in his back yard. In 1998, he attended a spontaneous meeting to create a record sleeve for the first Fan Club Orchestra LP. With the help of the professor Jihad Spiridon he later developed a system for random language generation, which led to the discovery of these four words: Collerette Coco Fill Lsd. Collerette's design often incorporates common themes, such as humanity's relationship to nature and technology. This often led to radical choices that are, unfortunately, often disliked by "clients". But, as Collerette puts it: "the client might be the king, but we are the emperors of our universe".

Interview with collerette coco fill lsd

1. What led to the formation of your studio?
Buying a couple of pioneer CDJ turntables and being the best dressed guys in town. Dreaming of building a whole city with containers, buying a van, collecting the whole discography of Drexciya galaxy.

2. How many staff people does your studio have and what are their main working fields?
We are three brains with two hands. We manage computer magnetic fields, contradictory propositions, spontaneous collages, client conflicts and dream considerations.

3. How does a regular working day at your studio look like, how is the day structured?
To begin with, we don't have a studio (workplace), the first decision to make is: do we work at your place or at mine? Every day is structured differently; shifted phases, in the long run, be happy. Make time to go downtown. One more coffee?

4. How much leisure time do you have during a year?
Latitude Degrée : 38°53'59"N, Longitude Degrée : 1°25'59"E

5. Which business areas do your clients mainly come from? Is the number of your clients increasing or rather declining?
Most of them are from the cultural sector, the non profit scene or just crazy people, and yes, the number is increasing. Gus Van Sant has contacted us for his new film poster.

6. Do you have a specific corporate philosophy or maybe a mission statement like other companies, which is reflected in the way you steer the studio's course?
Yes, we practice hypnosis! Self support! Enthusiasm! Tantric love!

7. What, from your point of view, makes the difference between a small studio and a big company?
The small studios still have the hope to work for friends, small structures with small budgets, to educate they clients... Big companies are stuck in the barbaric capitalist logic.

8. What kind of advantages and disadvantages does a small studio have compared to a big company?
Big or small, we're always looking for ways to uplift our vital energy, our strength.

9. What is your idea about the future of small studios? Do you think that small studios do not have any other choice but to expand in order to survive in these times of globalization?
It would be good to create connections between small studios everywhere, at every time. To be dispersed as much as possible.

10. Please describe and elaborate on the goals or plans that you have for your studio for the next five years?
Our goal for this year is to accept everything. If we feel bad, lazy or zombified we will change our goal for the future. Also, we want to buy an American letter board and are going to live in Alabama and create some magic quilt in the little town of Gee's Bend.

Electrosold collectif – cd sleeves – electosold collectif – 2003

RADIOPHONIC

LES RENCONTRES DE L'ATELIER DE CREATION SONORE RADIOPHONIQUE
DU 1ER AU 8 NOVEMBRE 2003 - BRUXELLES

88.8FM

Radiophonic – paper collage – atelier de création sonore radiophonique – 2003

sun ok papi k.o. – record sleeve – sun ok papi.o. – 2004

Bli:b – poster/logo – bibliothéque de forest – 2008

ENTRE-
OUVERT
BLI:B
STAAT
OPEN

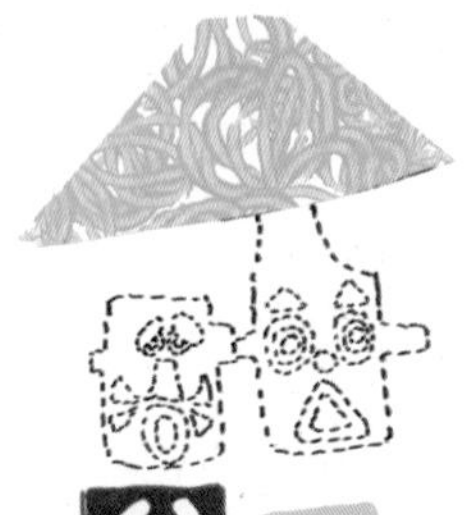

Quarantaine shop – flyers, price tags – quarantaine – 2006

Silence radio – logo – paper collage – atelier de création sonore radiophonique – 2008

Cinema NOVA – magazine – cinéma NOVA – 2003

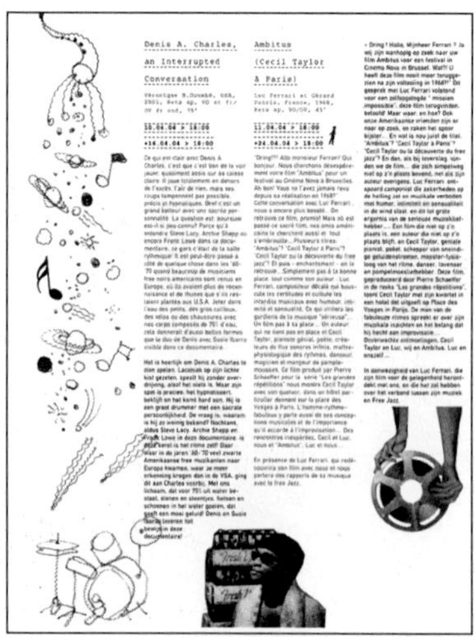
Denis A. Charles, an Interrupted Conversation

Ambitus (Cecil Taylor à Paris)

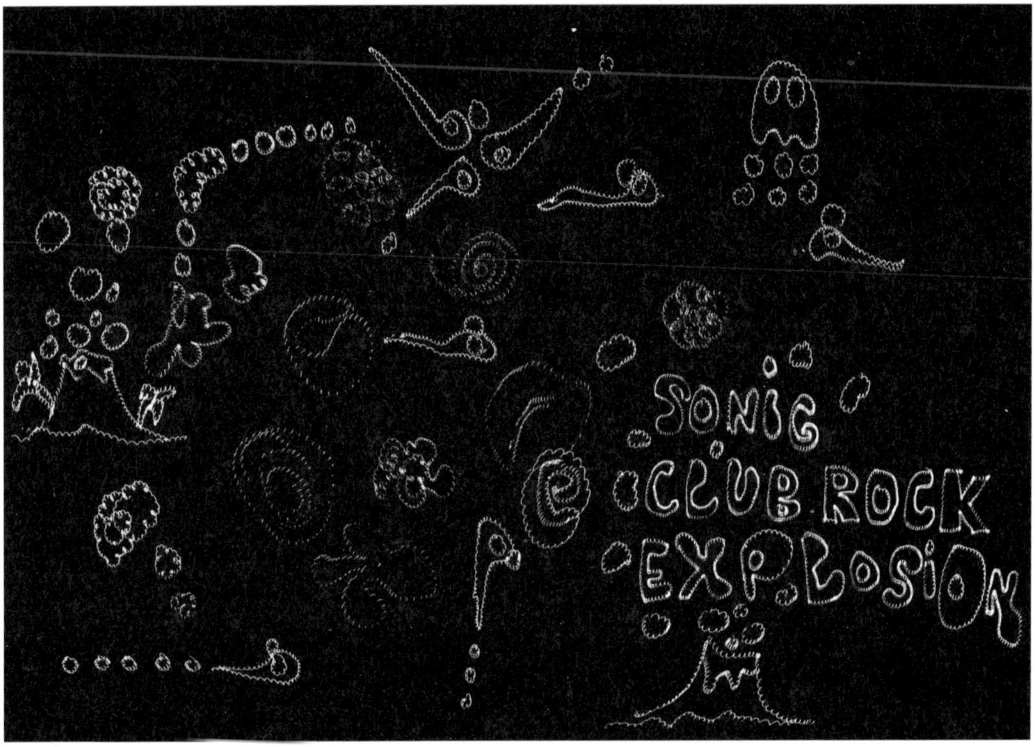

Sonig - club rock explosion - flyer - sonic record/Cologne - 2003

Radiophonique - paper collage - atelier de création sonore radiophonique - 2007

Coup

team:
Peter van Denhoogen
Erica Terpstra

contact:
Zeeburgerpad 51bg
1019 Ab Amsterdam, The Netherlands
T + 31 20 4272584
hello@coup.nl
www.coup.nl/hello.html

Coup is a conceptual design couple. It consists of Peter van den Hoogen and Erica Terpstra. They focus on developing visual concepts. Their design approach is medium-driven: the message is often emphasized by inventive use of the intrinsic qualities of the given medium. Although they grew up with Dutch design and were inspired by strong typographic movements like Modernism, Futurism, Bauhaus, French Deco, American Sophistication and Punk/New Wave, the visual ideas of Coup are not limited to a certain style. It's an ever changing eclectic constellation of communicative elements, especially invented to serve the concept. Erica has an extensive technical background in the graphic industry. Peter worked as an illustrator and interaction designer. He studied graphic design at the HKU in Utrecht, where he later worked as a teacher himself. He also taught at the Willem de Kooning Academie in Rotterdam and the Academie van Bouwkunst in Amsterdam. He gave seminars, lectures and workshops. Peter and Erica worked for the Stedelijk Museum Amsterdam, Rijksmuseum Amsterdam, Kunsthalle Fredericianum, Felix Meritis, International Film Festival Rotterdam, ArchiNed, Submarine, VPRO, TPG Post, KPN Telecom, SKOR and others.

Interview with Coup

1. What led to the formation of your studio?

We were already working on projects together long before the studio was founded.

2. How many staff people does your studio have and what are their main working fields?

Two staff members. Peter is working on concepts, graphic design projects, typography and interaction projects. Erica is working on graphic design projects and technical support.

3. How does a regular working day at your studio look like, how is the day structured?

We start between 9 and half past 9 in the morning. Erica works until 17.30, Peter works until six or seven. In between, we are working on projects, visiting printers, and teaching students.

4. How much leisure time do you have during a year?

Not enough.

5. Which business areas do your clients mainly come from?

Clients are mostly cultural. The number of clients is increasing.

6. Do you have a specific corporate philosophy or maybe a mission statement like other companies, which is reflected in the way you steer the studio's course?

We want to work on projects in which we get a lot of freedom from clients to be able to make the best product for them.

7/8. What, from your point of view, makes the difference between a small studio and a big company?
What kind of advantages and disadvantages does a small studio have compared to a big company?

Small studios: Clients don't have to deal with project managers: they get into direct contact with the experts and pay less money. Also, a small studio is more involved and more flexible in general.

9. What is your idea about the future of small studios? Do you think that small studios do not have any other choice but to expand in order to survive in these times of globalization?

We don't hope so. Maybe it will turn out to be the other way around.

10. Please describe and elaborate on the goals or plans that you have for your studio for the next five years?

We would like to have periodic assignments, like magazines, and do more self initiated work.

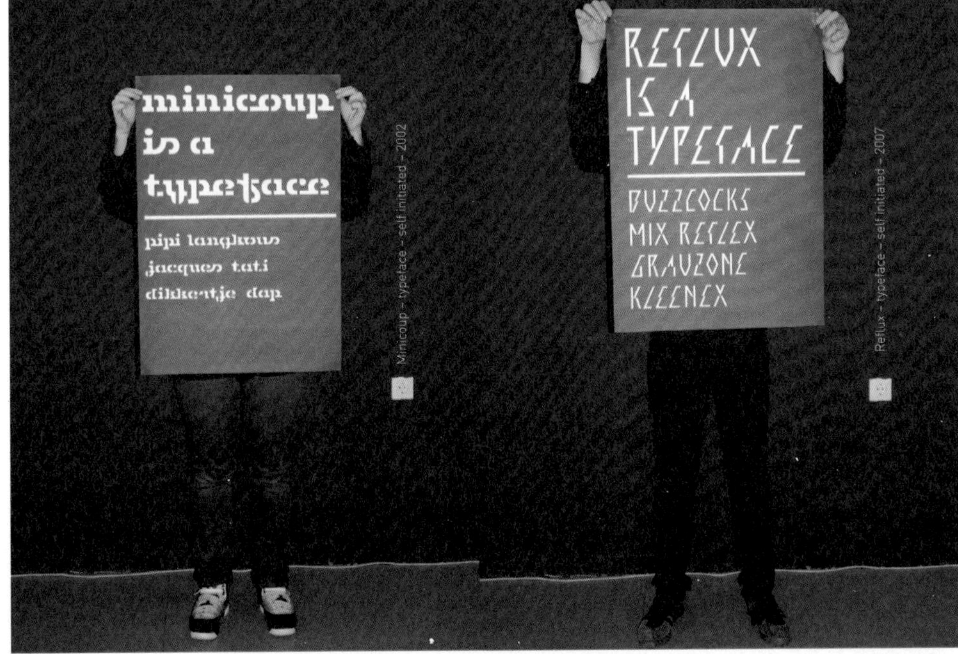

Minicoup – typeface – self initiated – 2002

Reflux – typeface – self initiated – 2007

Fris 3 – magazine – city of Utrecht, cultural affairs – 2007

Beyond was er vroeg bij in de Utrechtse nieuwbouwwijk Leidsche Rijn, met een ambitieus en internationaal georiënteerd kunstprogramma. Iets te vroeg en te ambitieus volgens sommige inwoners van Leidsche Rijn. Zij vroegen zich af waarom er zoveel aandacht en geld naar de beeldende kunst ging, terwijl andere voorzieningen op zich lieten wachten. Toch heeft Beyond menig aanzet gegeven tot een ontginning van cultureel braakliggend terrein. Een tussenstand.

VELD ONDERZOEK IN LEIDSCHE RIJN

DOOR LOTTE HAAGSMA

BEELD VERHALEN

DE DIGITALISERING VAN KUNST IN DE OPENBARE RUIMTE

INGRID COMMANDEUR

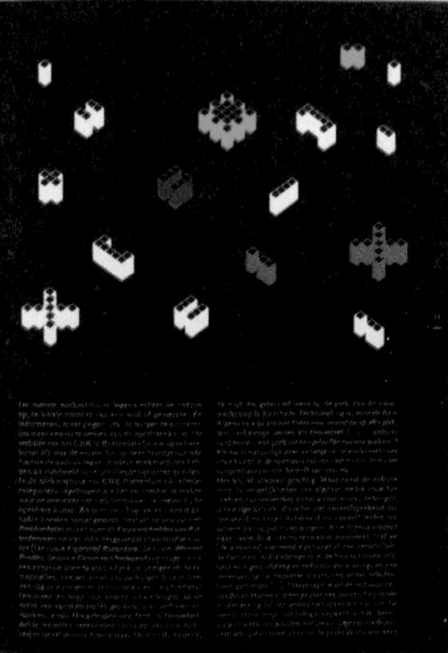

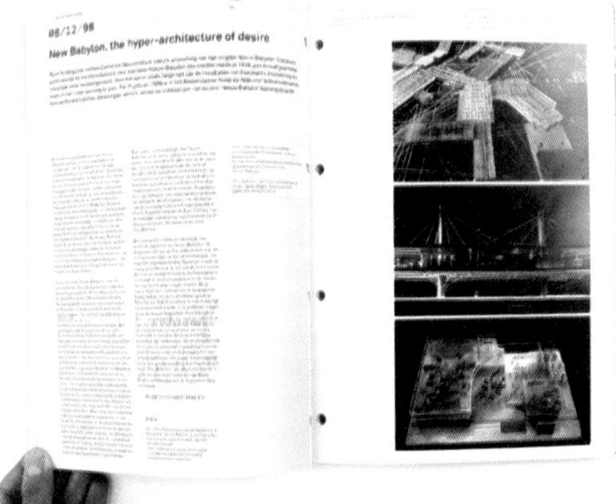

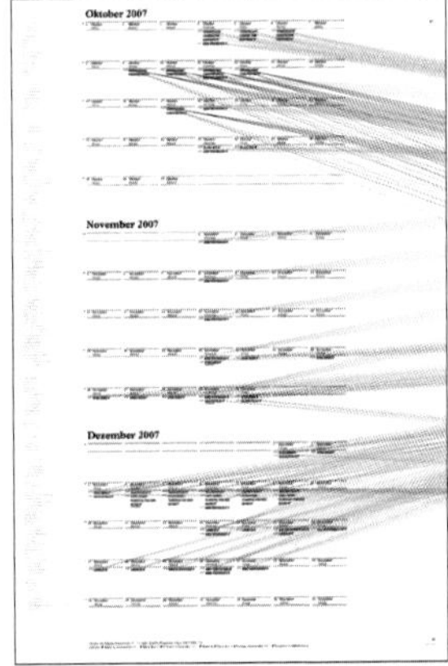

Archined archief – book – city of Utrecht, cultural affairs – 2007

PLAY AROUND WITH SOUND

REC SOUND'S PLAY GROUND

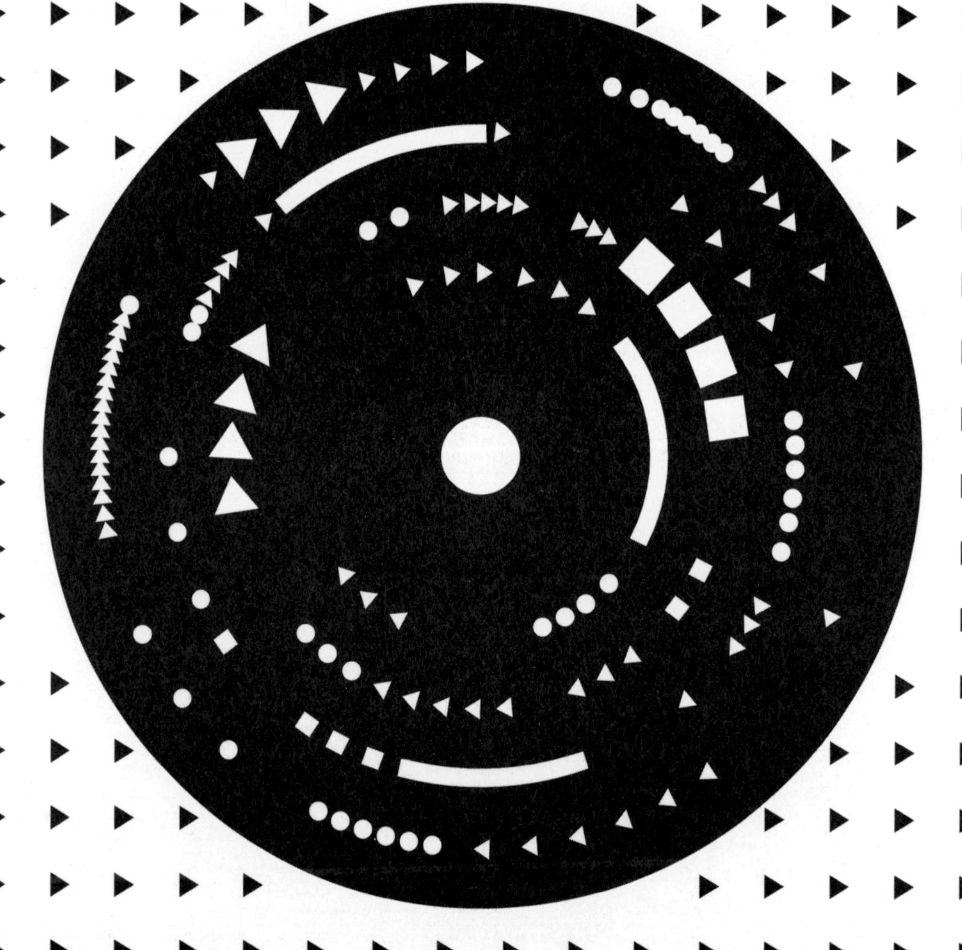

REC | MUSIC | SOUNDDESIGN

HAZENSTRAAT 4 1016 SP AMSTERDAM T +31 20 6272726 F +31 20 6272826 E INFO@RECSOUND.NL WWW.RECSOUND.NL

SonicActsXI
THE ANTHOLOGY OF COMPUTER ART
23-26 February 2006
Paradiso & De Balie, Amsterdam
www.sonicacts.com
Design by Coup, Amsterdam. http://www.coup.nl

The Anthology
of Computer Art
Sonic Acts XI

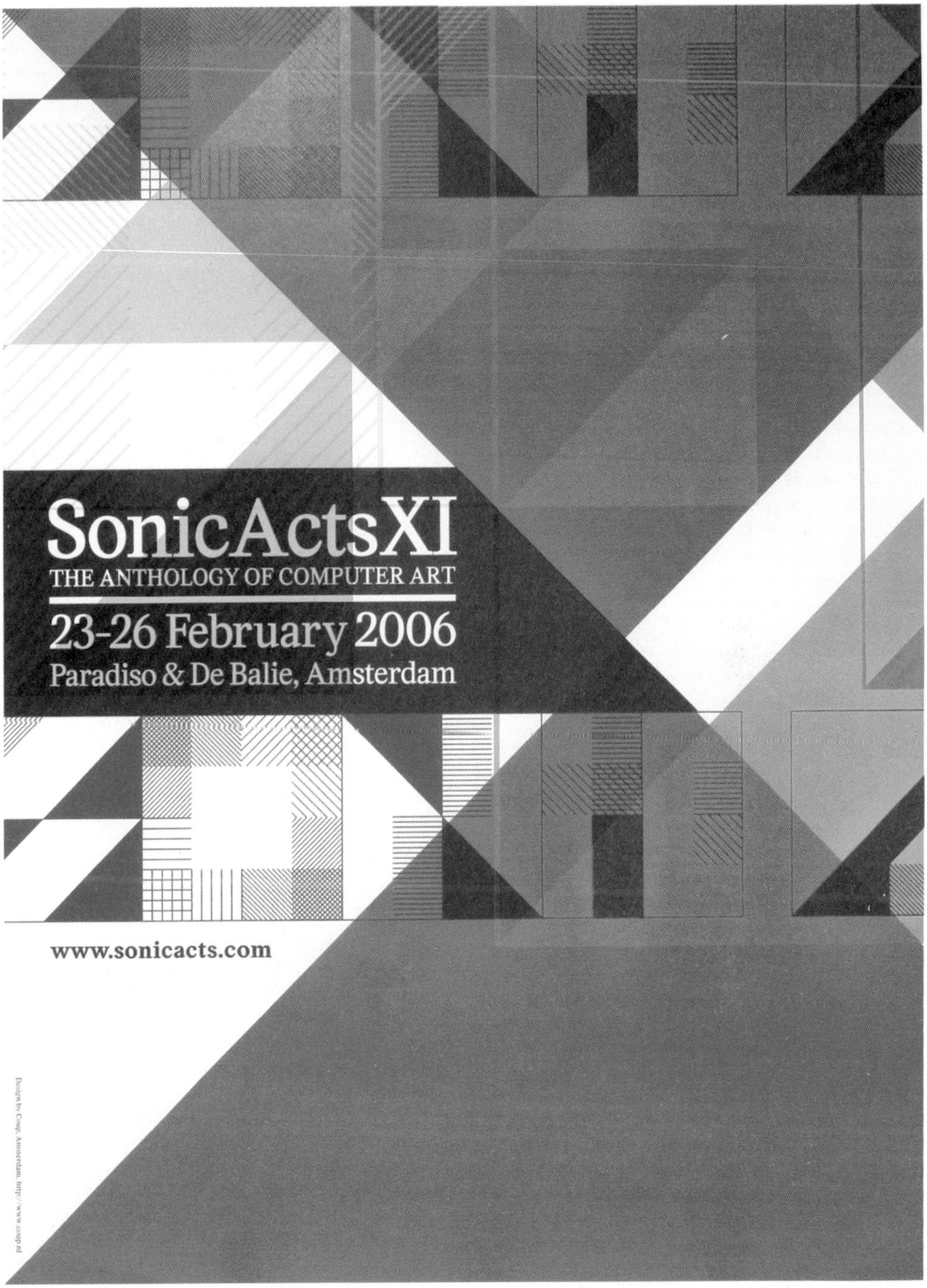

Play around with sound – poster – rec sso und design, Amste·dam – 2008

New dawn fades – logo – CS.M.A.K, Gent, Belgium – 2006

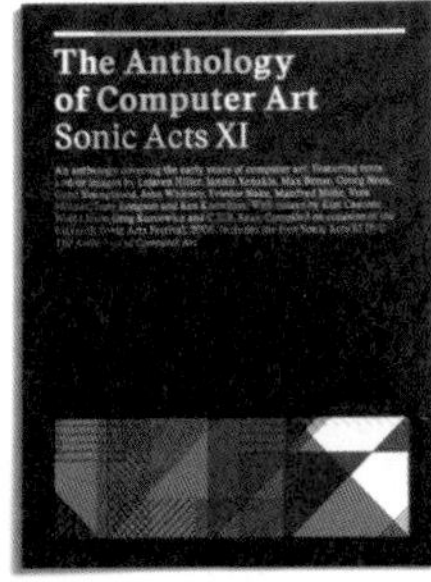

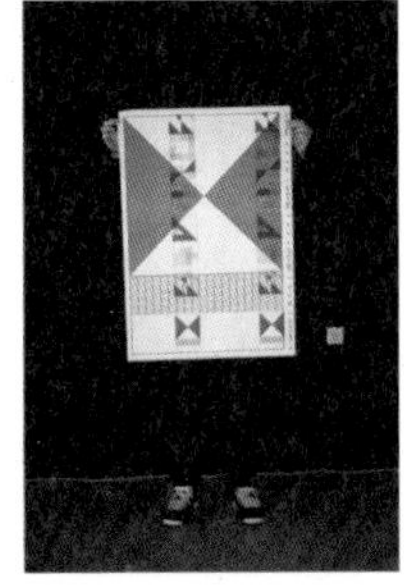

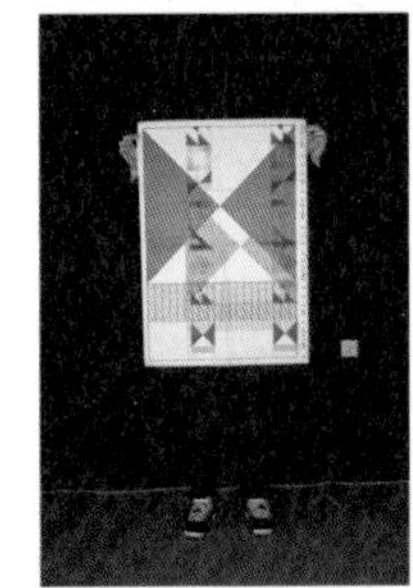

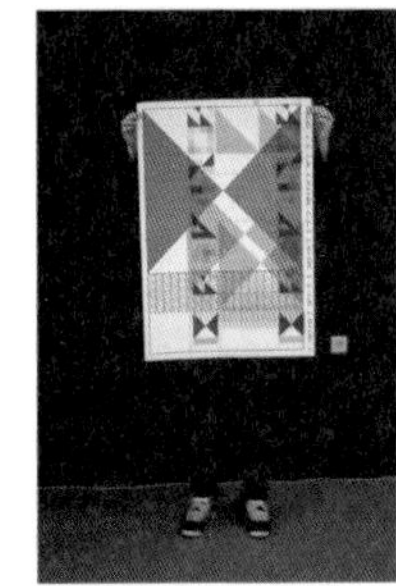

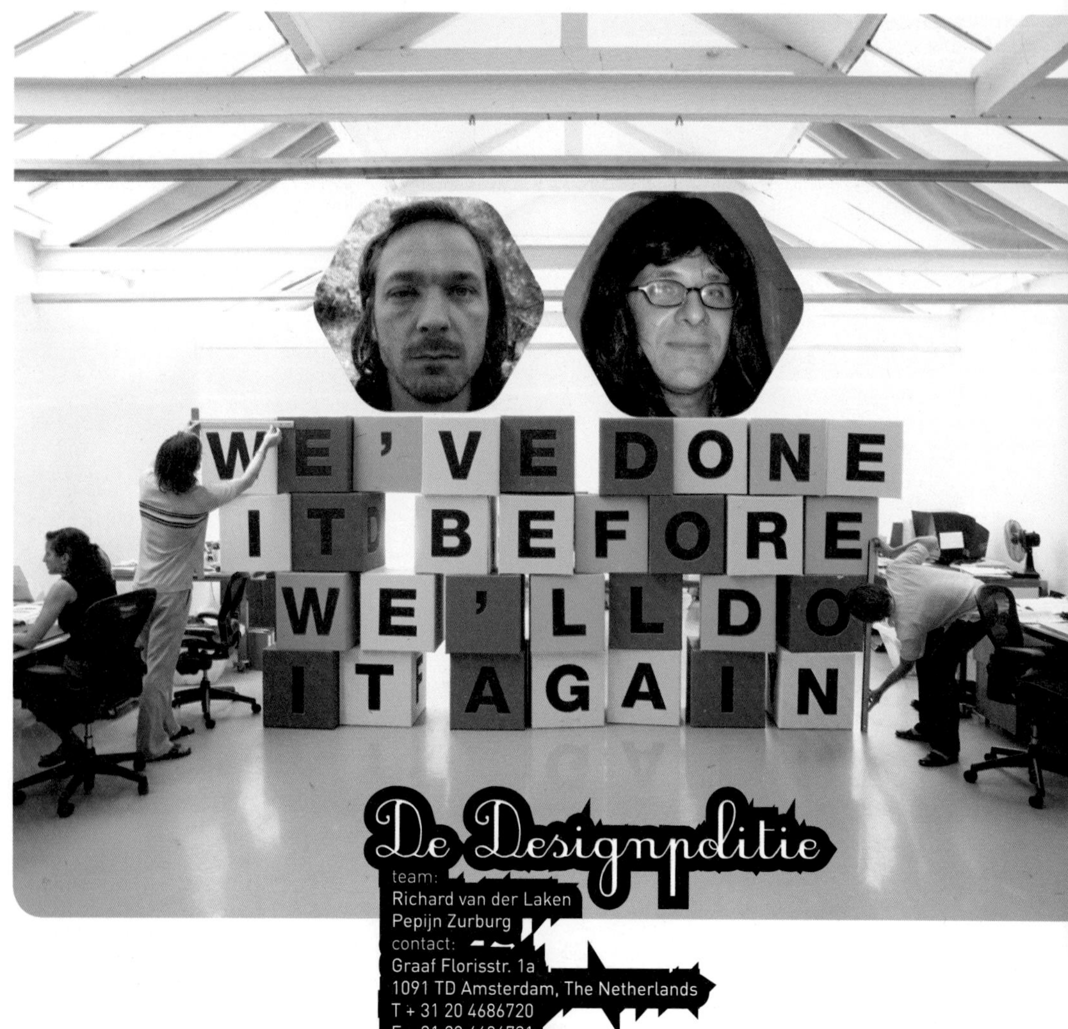
WE'VE DONE
IT BEFORE
WE'LL DO
IT AGAIN
De Designpolitie

team:
Richard van der Laken
Pepijn Zurburg
contact:
Graaf Florisstr. 1a
1091 TD Amsterdam, The Netherlands
T + 31 20 4686720
F + 31 20 4686721
info@designpolitie.nl
www.designpolitie.nl

De Designpolitie is a graphic design agency, based in Amsterdam, in the Netherlands. De Designpolitie belongs to the "Dutch design" family. Its members were brought up in the Dutch design culture and rich tradition of Dutch art, design and tolerance. In keeping with these traditions, De Designpolitie follows simple but ruthless methods. Their working process often ends in a stripped image which is a critical but always communicative solution. De Designpolitie works for various small and big clients in the non-profit and commercial sectors. De Designpolitie also initiates exhibitions, festivals, books, lectures and workshops. De Designpolitie consists of a small group of ambitious and talented creative people, and was founded by Richard van der Laken and Pepijn Zurburg.

Interview with De Designpolitie

1. What led to the formation of your studio?

Richard van der Laken and Pepijn Zurburg are the founders of De Designpolitie. They know each other from the art academy in Utrecht, in the Netherlands.

2. How many staff people does your studio have and what are their main working fields?

De Designpolitie's staff is not very consistent, but they do have a DTP-er Wout (Netherlands), a designer named Sebastian (Germany) and the office manager Patti (South Africa). Next to that, young designers and interns from the Netherlands and from abroad are flying in and out.

3. How does a regular working day at your studio look like, how is the day structured?

Is this a serious question?

4. How much leisure time do you have during a year?

Is this a serious question???

5. Which business areas do your clients mainly come from?

After 12 years in the "design business", we work and worked for a lot of different clients in the commercial and non-commercial sector, the government, artists, writers, publishers, insurance companies, etc. We like the mix.

6. Do you have a specific corporate philosophy or maybe a mission statement like other companies, which is reflected in the way you steer the studio's course?

Think small, act big. Most of the time, the treasure of a concept or a project can be found in the small place. Blow that up, focus on it, make it big.

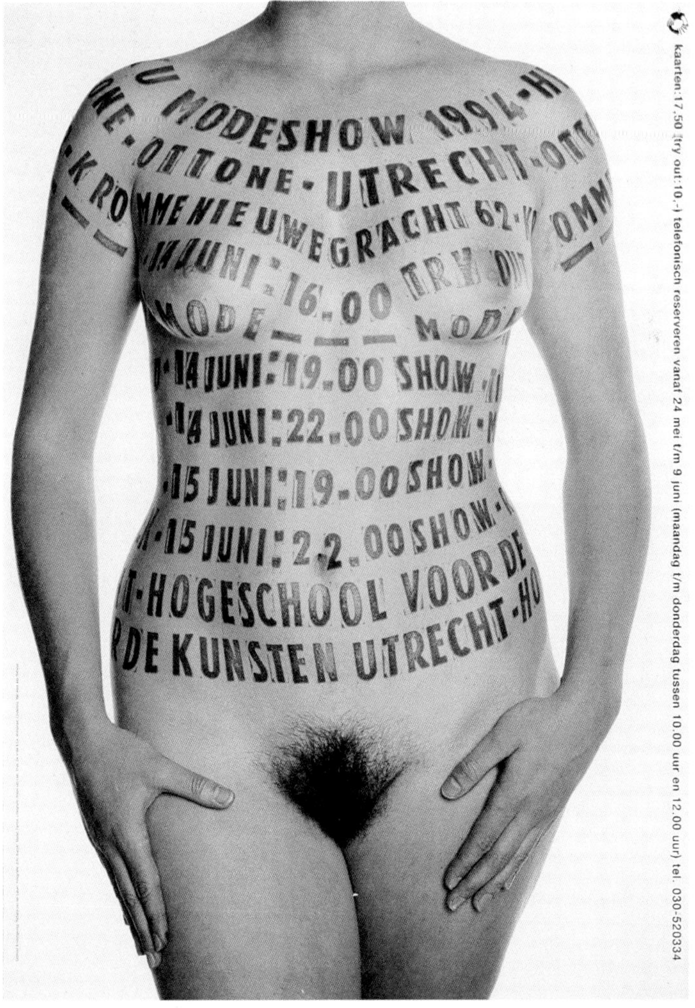

7. What, from your point of view, makes the difference between a small studio and a big company?

Personal signature. And that is in our opinion a very precious thing. Without personalit there is no good design.

8. What kind of advantages and disadvantages does a small studio have compared to a big company?

It is difficult to handle the work load when pressure is increasing. You have to do a lot by yourself. Next to that, there is a certain limit to the size of projects you are being offered, and the accounting management you can do. Sometimes we disappoint clients because we do not pamper them enough. But we do our best!

9. What is your idea about the future of small studios?

Smallstudios and globalization have nothing in common. A specific voice, opinion or style will always be appreciated. But you do have to re-invent yourself once in a while. Otherwise you will drown in your own vocabulary.

10. Please describe and elaborate on the goals or plans that you have for your studio for the next five years?

Keeping up the good work.

HKU final exam catalog – catalog – separate project – 2004

Art = zoo – posters – artis zoo – 2001

ART

ARTIS

AMSTERDAM

ART=

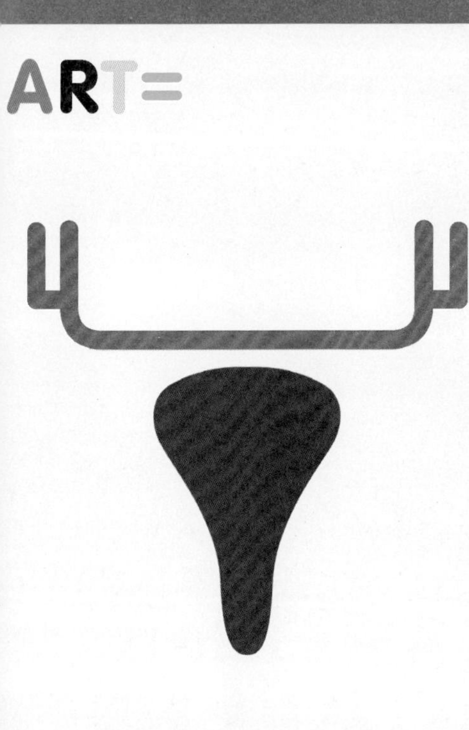

ART=

Springdance – poster – springdance – 1999

Amsterdam Calling – flyer/cd cover – Dutch POP institute – 2003

Art and Technology

COMPUTERS CAN DO THAT?

HKU final exam – catalogue – separate project – 2003/2005

'Never miss a good chance to shut up'
Will Rogers

team:
Ilona Ilottu
Petri Salmela
Eeva Sivula
contact:
Tallberginkatu 1 C 145
00180 Helsinki, Finland
T + 358 9 6932343
M + 358 50 3545910
dog@dogdesign.fi
www.dogdesign.fi

dog design is a Finnish design trio offering a wide range of graphic design, illustrations and art direction services from concept to completion. The members, Ilona Ilottu, Petri Salmela und Eeva Sivula, have worked in close co-operation since 1994. dog design seeks to provide its clients with innovative, open-minded and in-depth solutions, always with a playful attitude. Its functionalist expression manifests contemporary, pure, subtle Finnish design. The company's clientele varies from large, established companies to experimental underground projects. dog design boasts several awards from the Association of Professional Graphic Designers in Finland and the Finnish Book Arts Committee's annual competitions. The agency has also represented Finnish graphic design in several exhibitions and publications in Finland and abroad. Striving to move smoothly in the border areas between art and design, dog design finds inspiration from both everyday life and holiday.

Hardcore – visual identity – new Finnish design exhibition – 2008

Interview with dog design

1. What led to the formation of your studio?

We started to study graphic design same year in the University Of Art and Design Helsinki. The collaboration between the three of us started already then. We share taste, vision and style. We are also good friends.

2. How many staff people does your studio have and what are their main working fields?

Our studio consists of three designers, one assistant, and occasional trainees. Designers not only design but also lead the projects, communicate with the clients, take care of the public relations and write offers and bills. The assistant has various jobs, depending on the ongoing projects. He takes care of the pre-press work and deals with printers, sometimes he makes coffee, sometimes he drills holes or paints the wall. We try to keep our trainees busy as best we can, too.

3. How does a regular working day at your studio look like, how is the day structured?

The days in our office vary a lot. Sometimes we have meetings all day long, sometimes the days are spent in peace and silence concentrated on work. Normally, we start by checking the incoming mail and try to answer them in needed order. Quite often it seems that there is hardly any time left for the most important thing, the design work. After "office hours" though, when the phones stop ringing, one can find some time for that.

4. How much leisure time do you have during a year?

We have four weeks of holidays in the summer and one week in the winter. And we try to keep the weekends free of work, too.

5. Which business areas do your clients mainly come from? Is the number of your clients increasing or rather declining?

Quite many of our clients are from the fields of culture, design or publishing. But we do have customers from all kinds of business fields, too. It makes the work interesting. The number of our briefs is increasing, but the number of clients is quite stable.

6. Do you have a specific corporate philosophy or maybe a mission statement like other companies, which is reflected in the way you steer the studio's course?

Communication is our key word. We communicate with our clients and inside the studio. We try to provide our clients with innovative, open-minded and in-depth solutions, always with a playful attitude. Our design's functionalist expression manifests pure subtle Finnish design. We hope that our designs will endure over time.

7. What, from your point of view, makes the difference between a small studio and a big company?

In small studios designers have a bigger responsibility for the whole project. Also, there is the financial side of the work.

8. What kind of advantages and disadvantages does a small studio have compared to a big company?

Small studios are flexible and easy to communicate with. There are not too many middle hands in the project – the client is able to communicate his needs straight to the designer. Small studios can also work very effectively. Sometimes the small size of a studio frightens the customer. Client might think that small studios cannot handle big projects well enough, even though there is quite often a way to built a bigger network for bigger projects.

9. What is your idea about the future of small studios? Do you think that small studios do not have any other choice but to expand in order to survive in these times of globalization?

We trust in small studios! Small can be effective and more personal. We also think that the flexibility of a small organization has a good value in the midst of the ever growing bureaucracy.

10. Please describe and elaborate on the goals or plans that you have for your studio for the next five years?

In the future we hope good design will be more and more considered to be an important value in life. And we hope that designers will be commissioned in fields where they haven't earlier. In our studio, we have not "locked" an official 5-year plan, we like to keep the door open, there might be surprises knocking...

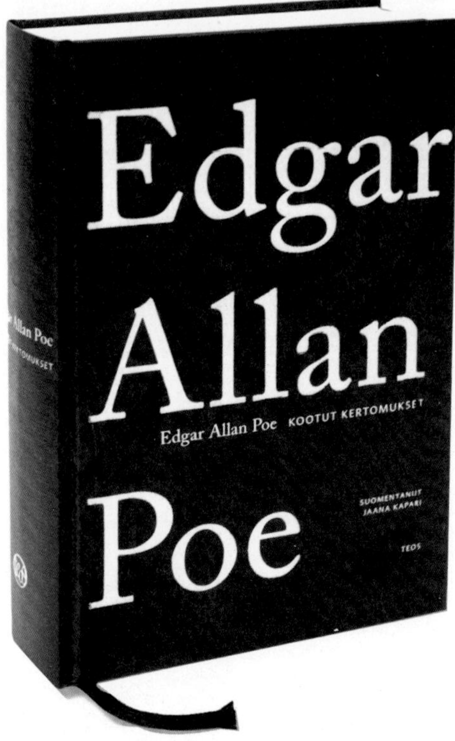

Leena Krohn – book cover – teos publishing – 2006/2008

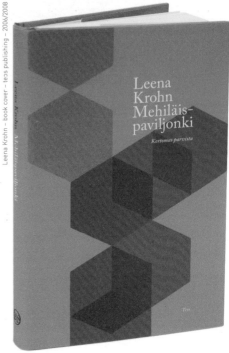

Edgar Allan Poe – book cover – kustannusosakeyhtiö teosteos the publishing house Teos – 2006/2008

Riikka Pelo – book cover – kustannusosakeyhtiö teos/the publishing house teos – 2006/2008

Finnish design yearbook – book cover – design forum Finland – 2008/2009

Birds package – package – Iittala – 2006

New Finnish design exhibition – visual identity – new Finnish design exhibition – 2008

Kartio package – package – Iittala – 2006

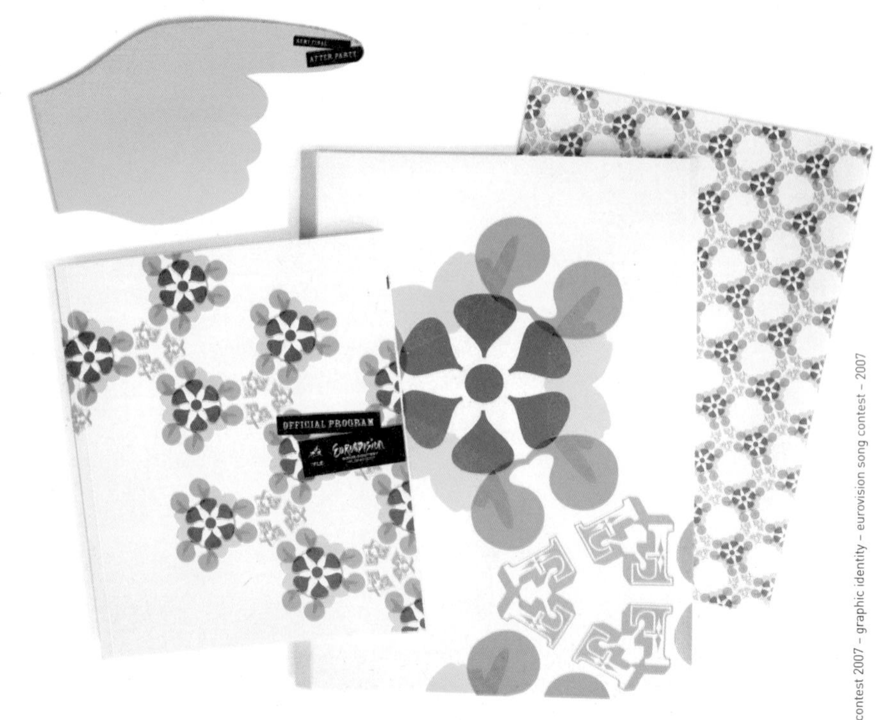

Eurovision song contest 2007 – graphic identity – eurovision song contest – 2007

Simple recepies – magnets – Iittala refrigerator – 2003

Aika espresso mug – product design – pattern & color design – 2006

Drop
team:
João Faria
João Guedes
contact:
Rua de Pedro Hispano
1271, 1º
4250-368 Porto, Portugal
T + 351 228300678
jfaria@drop.pt
www.drop.pt

Drop Design Design e Realização de Objectos Perfeitos is a graphic design studio from Porto, Portugal. Formed in 1996 by João Faria (born 1971), the studio mainly works in cultural production areas such as music and theatre. João Guedes (born 1982) joined Drop in 2004.

Interview with Drop

1. What led to the formation of your studio?

In the middle of the 1990s, public investment created a relatively interesting cultural environment in Porto. The appearance of small production companies working in areas such as music and theatre turned out to be the opportunity for young designers to get regular work from these areas. Forming a studio seemed the best way to get our design practice structured to deal with these opportunities.

2. How many staff people does your studio have and what are their main working fields?

We are two – João & João. Both graphic designers. Different music tastes. Separated rooms. But both working on the same projects. The older João gets the paperwork and the meeting tasks, too.

3. How does a regular working day at your studio look like, how is the day structured?

Monday - Friday's regular working day usually lasts from 7 am to 7 pm. Mornings are more peaceful and productive. The afternoons are more chaotic and more connected to the "real" world.

4. How much leisure time do you have during a year?

We stop working for 2 weeks in summer. During the rest of the year we try hard not work until late at night, neither on weekends nor on holidays. But one side effect of the job is the mixing of leisure with work, and work with leisure. We never really know if it is one or the other, or both at the same time, or none of them.

5. Which business areas do your clients mainly come from? Is the number of your clients increasing or rather declining?

The cultural "business". Public institutions and (mainly small) production companies. As we never got a big client list, the number is more or less the same as twelve years ago, when we started. This doesn't mean that we always had the same clients during this time.

6. Do you have a specific corporate philosophy or maybe a mission statement like other companies, which is reflected in the way you steer the studio's course?

Probably is the first principle for us is to refuse work offers that we feel we are not able to do, whatever the reason for this might be. It's the only basis we know to get honest communication done.

7. What, from your point of view, makes the difference between a small studio and a big company?

To work with and for people or to work with and for numbers means a big difference for us.

Mind da gap/Matéria Prima – cd/poster – Edições Valentim de Carvalho – 2008

8. What kind of advantages and disadvantages does a small studio have compared to a big company?

Small studios can easily do better work for small clients. To keep big, these companies just have to forget how to get things done without money as the main goal. If the client's needs and expectations are the opposite, things turn the other way and the disadvantage turns out to be an advantage.

9. What is your idea about the future of small studios?

We can't think of any reason why small studios could stop existing. At least not as long as small and medium business still exist.

Do you think that small studios do not have any other choice but to expand in order to survive in these times of globalization?

Why should that happen? Are local relationships really disappearing? We don't think so.

10. Please describe and elaborate on the goals or plans that you have for your studio for the next five years?

We would like to have a lot of sports-related projects. We are not very interested in new media projects.

Fassbinder – poster – teatro nacional – 2008

Caruma – poster – teatro nacional São João – 2007

RHX4/rui horta x quatro – poster – teatro nacional São João – 2006

Curtas Vila do Conde/international short film festival 2007's theme: highway to hell – poster – Curtas Vila do Conde – 2007

Curtas Vila do Conde
7-15 JUL 2007

Curtas Vila do Conde/international short film festival 2007's theme: highway to hell – poster – Curtas Vila do Conde – 2007

Plasticina - poster - teatro nacional São João - 2006

Desmontagem 4.1 - poster - teatro nacional São João - 2007

O Coronel Pássaro - poster - teatro nacional São João - 2007

Beiras - poster - teatro nacional São João - 2007

Vladimir Dubko

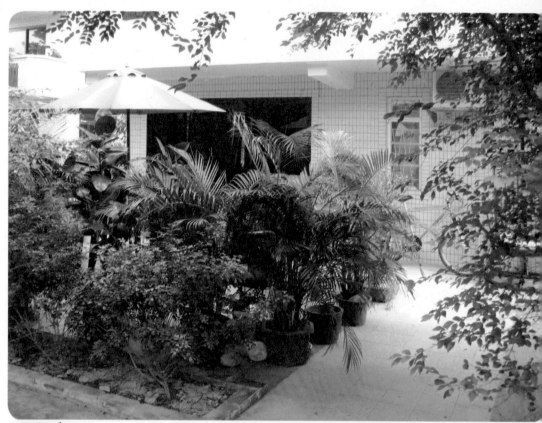

team:
Vladimir Dubko
contact:
Room 502, 100/1, Chang Shu Rd.
200031 Shanghai (Jing An), China
M + 86 15800468357 (Shanghai)
M + 85 267429870 (Hong Kong)
mailbox@vladimirdubko.com
www.vladimirdubko.com

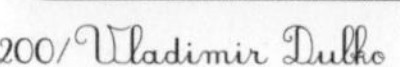

Vladimir Dulko hails from Vitebsk, Belarus, where he got a degree in communication design. After working as an art-director in advertising in Moscow, he was awarded a grant at the Benetton's Research Centre Fabrica and spent two years in the interactive department working for Benetton and Killer Loop, and on self-initiated illustrative projects. After Fabrica, Vladimir moved back to Moscow to work as art director for a Russian fashion holding on three lines of designer clothes. Today, Vladimir lives in Hong Kong where he does illustrative, designing and interactive jobs for a number of the world's best-known fashion companies. His works were exhibited in Moscow, Stockholm, San Francisco, and in the Pompidou in Paris among others.

Beef – illustration – German art director club/beef magazine – 2007

Wish list – illustration – lane crawford, Hong Kong magazine – 2007

Black and white – illustration and typography – fashion collection – 2005

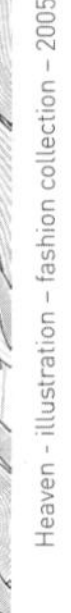

Heaven - illustration – fashion collection – 2005

English picnic – illustration and typography – fashion collection – 2005

Interview with Vladimir Dubko

1. What led to the formation of your studio?

Obviously the main reason was finding comfort in doing my own work and organizing my personal time. I tried quite a few studios and agencies, which was a really useful experience but it was hard to do anything different from what clients expected from the agency they hired. And then it just happened that I quit my job in Moscow and moved to Hong Kong, so it was a natural way and the right time to start a studio of my own.

2. How many staff people does your studio have and what are their main working fields?

The studio is really young and exists in form of a collaboration between me and my friends. We do it through e-mails and chats in which I'm the one permanent member here. Most people are ex-Fabrica of Benetton. So quite simply, if the project requires it, I'm getting some friends hooked on it. Generally, I need help with interactive projects, and then I work with my friend Linus Nilsson – who is a great mind in programming ideas and making everything happen. For now, there isn't enough specific or routine technical work, like multi-paged catalogs, etc., to hire some permanent junior designers. And after all, doing illustrations is a one-man craft.

3. How does a regular working day at your studio look like, how is the day structured?

I'm not an early bird, so I prefer to use my mornings for something different than work. The day is usually reserved for client meetings and some research or pressing jobs. The most productive time is the evening. Recently my working hours have shifted towards the night, because of the time difference – I live in Hong Kong and most of my co-workers and some clients are back in Europe and Russia.

4. How much leisure time do you have during a year?

As a newcomer among those who sail alone, so far I cannot draw a line where my work ends and where my leisure time begins. It's like being haunted by a single thought – you keep thinking about work almost constantly, even if you actually do nothing for the whole day. But all in all I do have more free time than I used to have working in someone else's office, because I am not obliged to just sit around and wait if I don't feel like it, and then to stay up late for no good reason.

5. Which business areas do your clients mainly come from? Is the number of your clients increasing or rather declining?

We do a lot of jobs for fashion companies. Some art-direction for photo-shootings, some catalogs. And a lot of graphics for garment and illustration projects – that's the main part. The most exciting jobs are interactive installations like the one we are doing for Lane Crawford here in Hong Kong. Magazines are a big part of my job as an illustrator. They are mostly international dealing with fashion,

OVS – cover illustration – OVS live more! magazine – 2007

culture, design etc. The number of our clients is rather increasing, thanks to a bit of exposure my work got this year. Having more clients of my own was actually another reason to go ahead with my own studio.

6. Do you have a specific corporate philosophy or maybe a mission statement like other companies, which is reflected in the way you steer the studio's course?

No, not at all. I just care about doing great work in an appropriate time.

7. What, from your point of view, makes the difference between a small studio and a big company?

The management – the more people you hire the more people you need to regulate everything. Hence, much more politics involved in a work process.

8. What kind of advantages and disadvantages does a small studio have compared to a big company?

A small studio is more flexible in taking on new routes or clients, trying out something different. It is usually driven by the passion of its owner. A big company is more like an organized business machine where people come and go, and where it's important to produce a lot of work of a certain quality or level. But big companies can realize big projects for big clients. For a small studio it's rather difficult to provide full service. Its lot is to have smaller-scale projects, even though for big clients, but it's easier for them to do some outstanding, creative jobs, and to have pleasure to be hired for their own approach.

9. What is your idea about the future of small studios? Do you think that small studios do not have any other choice but to expand in order to survive in these times of globalization?

I have no doubt small studios will continue existing. I can't predict how successful they are going to be, but there'll always be people craving for independence. Not that many creative people can cope with corporate policies and spend days at meetings, quietly being rendered meaningless and slowly getting burned out. For designers and illustrators a small studio is often their own turf, where they can be focused on the work they like, and where balancing on the edge between commercial and artistic projects is easier, just because they can decide for themselves. After all, the designing process is intimate for many of us.

10. Please describe and elaborate on the goals or plans that you have for your studio for the next five years?

For sure, one of the most desirable goals is to keep the studio stable with regard to business. Stable clients, safe projects and good income are important to keep spirits high, preferably in a great office space with hardwood floors and high ceilings. Then just to do amazing work, to be passionate about it and to try going new ways.

OVS – cover illustration – OVS live more! magazine – 2007

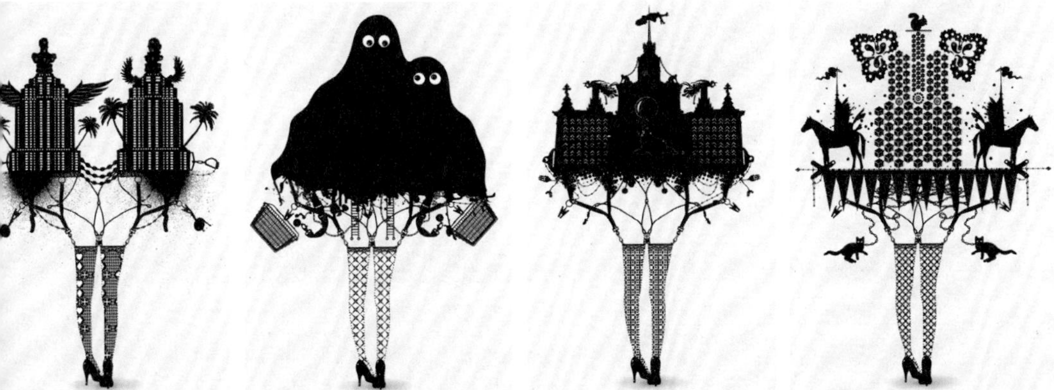

Bend aid head – artwork – personal project – 2007

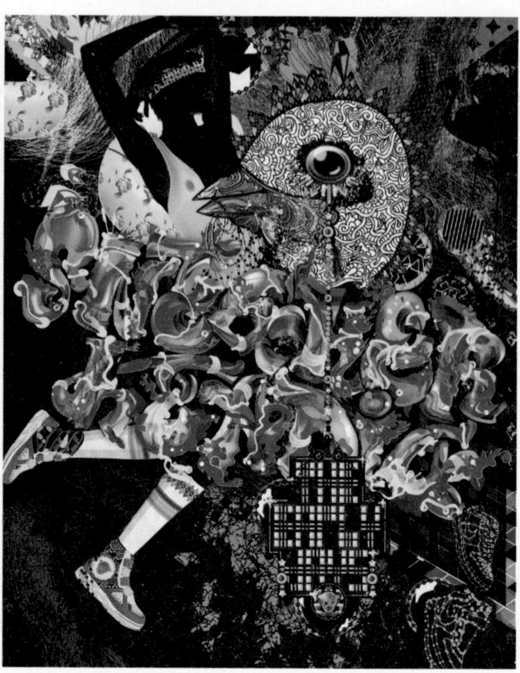

Sneakerheadia – artwork – personal project – 2007

Good night, city hawks! – artwork – personal project – 2007

Xmas – illustration – belorussian beer syabr – 2007

Boris Dworschak

team:
Boris Dworschak
contact:
Theaterstr. 9a
75175 Pforzheim, Germany
T + 49 7231 1398778
F + 49 7231 1398776
info@borisdworschak.de
www.borisdworschak.de

Buero Boris Dworschak founded in 2004 by Boris Dworschak (*1974), is an internationally operating graphic design studio focusing on corporate design, book & magazine design, exhibition graphics, type design and digital media, working with clients who mostly have cultural or artistic backgrounds. The studio also provides services in consulting and overall project management

Olio santo – logo – olio santo, Karlsruhe – 2007

Universe - logo – IdN, Hong Kong – 2008

Adieu tristesse – illustration – design t-shirt store graphic, Tokyo – 2008

At home records – logo – at home records, Paris – 2006

Forever is nothing! – poster – personal project – 2004

Splash – poster – personal project – 2005

Interview with Boris Dworschak

1. What led to the formation of your studio?

After finishing university in 2004 it was clear for me to start my own studio, I couldn't imagine to work as a permanent employee from 9 to 5 for someone else.

2. How many staff people does your studio have and what are their main working fields?

Most of the time I'm on my own, but for special work like coding, etc., I'm temporary working with others.

3. How does a regular working day at your studio look like, how is the day structured?

Checking mails and drinking coffee, taking a look at my calendar to decide what has to be done today. Start working on projects. Taking a break for lunch, working, scheduling, making calls, having meetings, leaving the office.

4. How much leisure time do you have during a year?

I have 2-3 weeks leisure time during a year.

5. Which business areas do your clients mainly come from? Is the number of your clients increasing or rather declining?

My clients mostly have cultural and artistic backgrounds. The number of clients is increasing with every year.

6. Do you have a specific corporate philosophy or maybe a mission statement like other companies, which is reflected in the way you steer the studio's course?

There is no specific philosophy or mission, just a definition of what I'm doing: "Buero Boris Dworschak" is a graphic design studio focusing on corporate design, book & magazine design, exhibition graphics, type design and digital media. I would characterize my style or my direction in graphic design as clear, conceptual, multidisciplinary and type-oriented. The starting point of my design is always content; everything else is a result of the content. Maybe that's my course.

7. What, from your point of view, makes the difference between a small studio and a big company?

A small studio can respond very, very fast. A big company acts very, very slow.

8. What kind of advantages and disadvantages does a small studio have compared to a big company?

The advantage of a small studio is that there is a very personal relationship between the client and the studio. Decisions can be made quickly. A big company can offer and handle a wider range of works, small studios are more specialized.

9. What is your idea about the future of small studios? Do you think that small studios do not have any other choice but to expand in order to survive in these times of globalization?

Small studios should focus on finding appropriate clients, they need to find the right kind of client with the right kind of work for them to have a bright future. I think the advantage of small studios is that they are small. I think small studios have to stay small to use that advantage.

10. Please describe and elaborate on the goals or plans that you have for your studio for the next five years?

Keep all things simple and straightforward. Acquire more interesting clients and do more very good work.

www.borisdworschak.de
"ONLY THE DILETTANTE
IS THE EXEMPLAR
OF REALISM"
-ALLEN GINSBERG

For Allen – poster – personal project – 2005

– IkiruSerif Thin

ABCDEFGHIJKLMNOPQRSTUVWXYZ

abcdefghijklmnopqrstuvwxyz

1234567890 ½¼¾ ¹²³ €$¢£¥ #-+×÷=≠

<>*±≤≥°%‰¦√≈¬∆/∞µ∂ΩΠπ◊∫!?¡¿&§

ß/@Øøþþ‡†•©®™ªº^¶|‹«{[(/|\)]}»› .:,;

ÆŒÁÀÂÄÃÅÇÉÈÊËÍÌÎÏÑÓÒÔÖÕÚÙÛÜŸÝŽŠŁĐ

æœáàâäãåçéèêëíìîïñóòôöõúùûüÿýžšłđ ƒfifl ı

Ikiruserif – typeface – gestalten fonts, Berlin – 2007

Diamonds and bars – card – ZKM | museum für neue kunst Karlsruhe – 2008

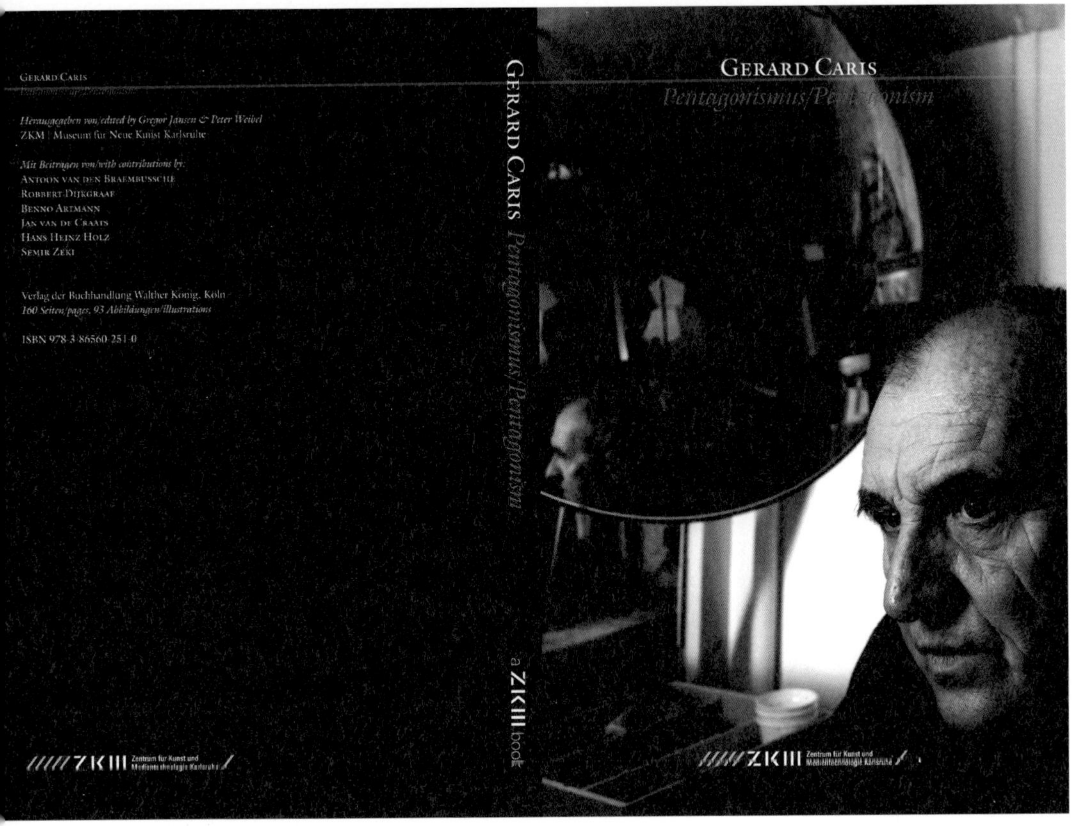

GERARD CARIS

Herausgegeben von/edited by Gregor Jansen & Peter Weibel
ZKM | Museum für Neue Kunst Karlsruhe

Mit Beiträgen von/with contributions by:
ANTOON VAN DEN BRAEMBUSSCHE
ROBBERT DIJKGRAAF
BENNO ARTMANN
JAN VAN DE CRAATS
HANS HEINZ HOLZ
SEMIR ZEKI

Verlag der Buchhandlung Walther König, Köln
160 Seiten/pages, 93 Abbildungen/illustrations

ISBN 978-3-86560-251-0

ZKM Zentrum für Kunst und Medientechnologie Karlsruhe

GERARD CARIS *Pentagonismus/Pentagonism* a ZKM book

GERARD CARIS
Pentagonismus/Pentagonism

ZKM Zentrum für Kunst und Medientechnologie Karlsruhe

Gerard Caris – book cover – Gerard Carished pentagonism – 2007

Michael Kunze – card – ZKM | museum für neue kunst Karlsruhe – 2007

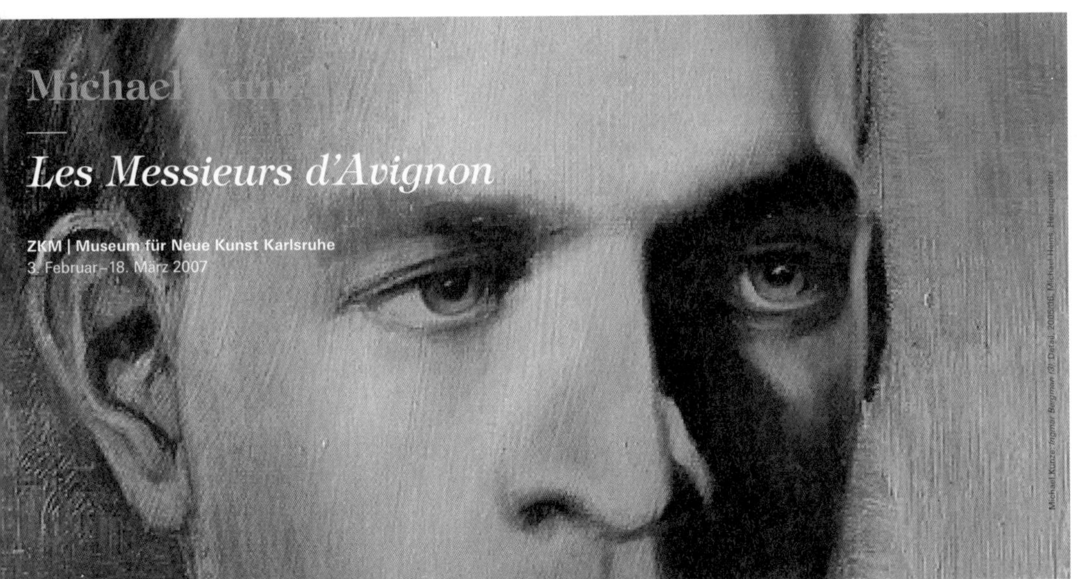

eBoy was founded in 1997 by Steffen Sauerteig, Svend Smital and Kai Vermehr with the acquisition of the eBoy.com domain. The basic idea driving eBoy was the embracement of the new possibilities brought up by the emerging digital world. The decision to work directly on and for the screen led to the use of pixels. A modular working system started to evolve and resulted in complex, object-rich artwork. eBoy is fortunate of having the chance to work with some of the finest clients and partners. Among them are Adidas, Coca Cola, Pepsi, Paul Smith, DKNY, Kidrobot, MTV, The New York Times, Wired Magazine, and many others.

PPM – illustration – punk magazine – 2003

eBoy
team:
Steffen Sauerteig
Svend Smital
Kai Vermehr
contact:
Gerichtstr. 12-13
Aufgang 2
13347 Berlin, Germany
T + 49 30 44008715
eboy@eboy.com
www.eboy.com

Eboyprickies – sticker – prickies – 2006

Interview with eBoy

1. What led to the formation of your studio?

We started in 1998 with eboy.com. The concept was to show only our free projects.

2. How many staff people does your studio have and what are their main working fields?

We are three people, and we are doing graphics and illustrations for magazines, advertising agencies, fashion companies, and we do toys.

3. How does a regular working day at your studio look like, how is the day structured?

We are working in three different places but are connected via video and text chat. Sometimes we meet in our main office to see visitors and clients. Our days usually start at 10 am with emails, then we talk via video, and then everybody works until night (with some breaks of course).

4. How much leisure time do you have during a year?

About four weeks.

5. Which business areas do your clients mainly come from? Is the number of your clients increasing or rather declining?

Hard to say, it's changing all the time. If we get more job requests than we can handle, we rather turn them down. We don't hire people because we prefer to stay small and independent.

6. Do you have a specific corporate philosophy or maybe a mission statement like other companies, which is reflected in the way you steer the studio's course?

Not really...maybe having fun and keep being curious.

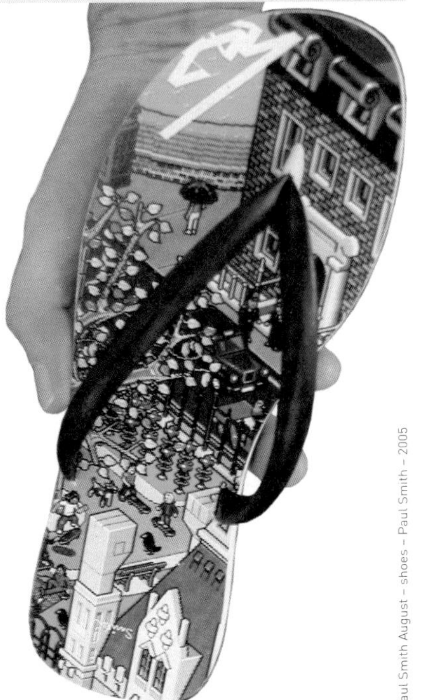

Paul Smith August – shoes – Paul Smith – 2005

7. What, from your point of view, makes the difference between a small studio and a big company?

We are much more flexible and free to do what we like than a big company. Also, decisions can be made really fast!

8. What kind of advantages and disadvantages does a small studio have compared to a big company?

A big advantage for us is to have 100% control over everything we do. A disadvantage might be that there are less money resources to be invested in new products. Oh, and an office in a skyscraper would be fun.

9. What is your idea about the future of small studios? Do you think that small studios do not have any other choice but to expand in order to survive in these times of globalization?

Thanks to the internet it has become much easier to reach clients and to get jobs even for small companies. Many of our clients probably have no idea how big or small we are. It doesn't matter anymore. What matters are your work and the respect for the people you are working with.

10. Please describe and elaborate on the goals or plans that you have for your studio for the next five years?

We don't have fixed planes, just some ideas which we are following. Basically expanding our range of products. And two of us are planning to move to Vancouver, Canada.

Berlin poster – poster – personal project – 2002

Fullmap – promotion – t-mobile, UK – 2005

Jumping guys – drawing – eBoy – 2007

Paul Smith – portrait – Paul Smith, UK – 2005

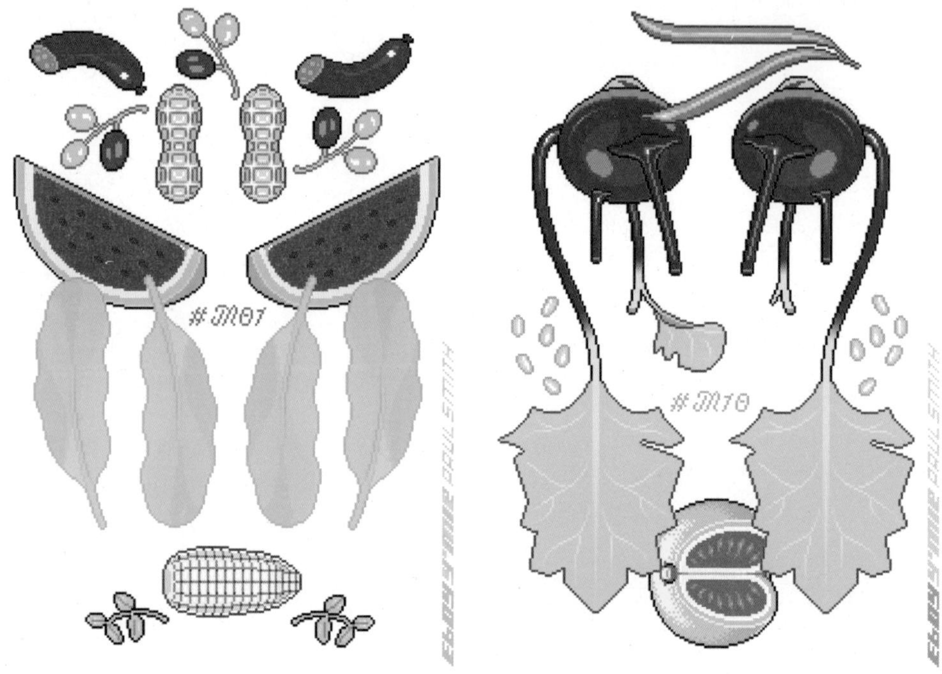

PSM_y´mie – poster – Paul Smith – 2005

Peecol – packaging – kidrobot – 2007

Peecol – poster/toys – kidrobot – 2007 / 2008

Eric and Marie

team:
Éric Gaspar
Marie Bertholle
contact:
45 Avenue Montaigne
75008 Paris, France
T + 33 1 47235127
info@ericandmarie.com
www.ericandmarie.com

Éric and Marie is Éric Gaspar and Marie Bertholle, who teamed up in 2002, but have known each other and worked together since the early days of their graphic design education. After a first qualification in France, both obtained the Bachelor of Arts degree at the Central Saint Martins College of Art in London, and then extended their graphic design training for two more years, obtaining their MAs from the Royal College of Art. Through each new project, Éric and Marie seek to develop a different, singular approach to graphic design. Parallel to their commissioned work, they research a personal grammar of ideas and forms, a sort of keep-fit gymnastics, which often proves useful at certain moments. Convinced that the idea should dictate the form, Éric and Marie stay clear of immediately seductive images and attach great importance to choosing the materials as well as the printing and production methods for their projects. Experimentation has its place in every stage of their work, from conception to production. They have carried out commissions for the French Foreign Ministry ADPF, Central Saint Martins College of Art and Design, the Royal College of Art, the Dutch Ministry of Social Affairs and Employment, le Musée de la Mode in Paris, Ronan and Erwan Bouroullec, and the Akadêmia, Culturesfrance.

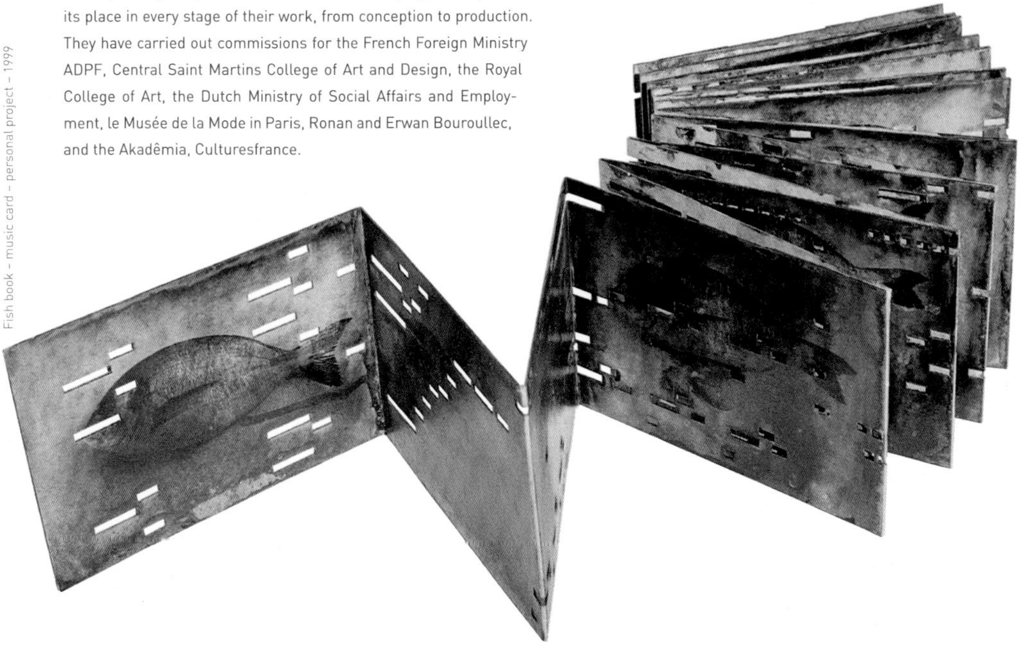

Fish book – music card – personal project – 1999

Interview with Éric and Marie

1. What led to the formation of your studio?

We studied Graphic Design together. During our time in London at Central Saint Martins and then at the Royal College of Art, both of us started working on the same projects. When we left college and came back to France, we naturally continued working together. Also, we are a couple. This can also justify the formation of our studio.

2. How many staff people does your studio have and what are their main working fields?

Our studio is only the two of us, and we work indifferently on everything.

3. How does a regular working day at your studio look like, how is the day structured?

That's the beauty of small studios: there is no regular day as such. It depends on the amount of work we have to do. We could say that we are disciplined, but we don't really follow regular working hours.

4. How much leisure time do you have during a year?

We cannot say how much leisure time we have during a year. We usually go on holidays when there is a break between large projects. And as we answered in the last question, it is very easy to take day breaks at anytime without needing somebody's permission.

5. Which business areas do your clients mainly come from? Is the number of your clients increasing or rather declining?

We mainly work for people involved in culture. For the last couple of years we have been working for the same clients.

6. Do you have a specific corporate philosophy or maybe a mission statement like other companies, which is reflected in the way you steer the studio's course?

We have a personal point of view on graphic design and also some ideals, but not a philosophy as such. In general, we like when the work contains a bit of thinking and when it is well-considered (and we don't mean by that clean and pretty). We are not attracted by decorative-surface design. When we have a brief, we like to rethink it, even to rewrite it to be able to find the most accurate and sensible answer. Of course, this is not always possible for every work we get.

7. What, from your point of view, makes the difference between a small studio and a big company?

As long as we are smaller, we usually move faster. Small studios gain in flexibility. There are less expenses and less responsibility. We can afford to do more personal work. We feel more like two designers/artists rather than one single entity.

8. What kind of advantages and disadvantages does a small studio have compared to a big company?

The disadvantage being a small studio is that it is very difficult to get big clients. They feel more confident with large companies. The advantage is that you can organize your daily life the way you want. This is a luxury.

9. What is your idea about the future of small studios? Do you think that small studios do not have any other choice but to expand in order to survive in these times of globalization?

A studio usually gets bigger when it is offered a lot of work. We don't really see the link to the globalization. To our minds, at this (fairly low) economic level it doesn't make any sense to talk about globalization.

10. Please describe and elaborate on the goals or plans that you have for your studio for the next five years?

We don't want to get bigger at any price, despite the fact that we would be glad to work for a larger range of clients. But most of all, we would like to produce more interesting and juicy pieces of work.

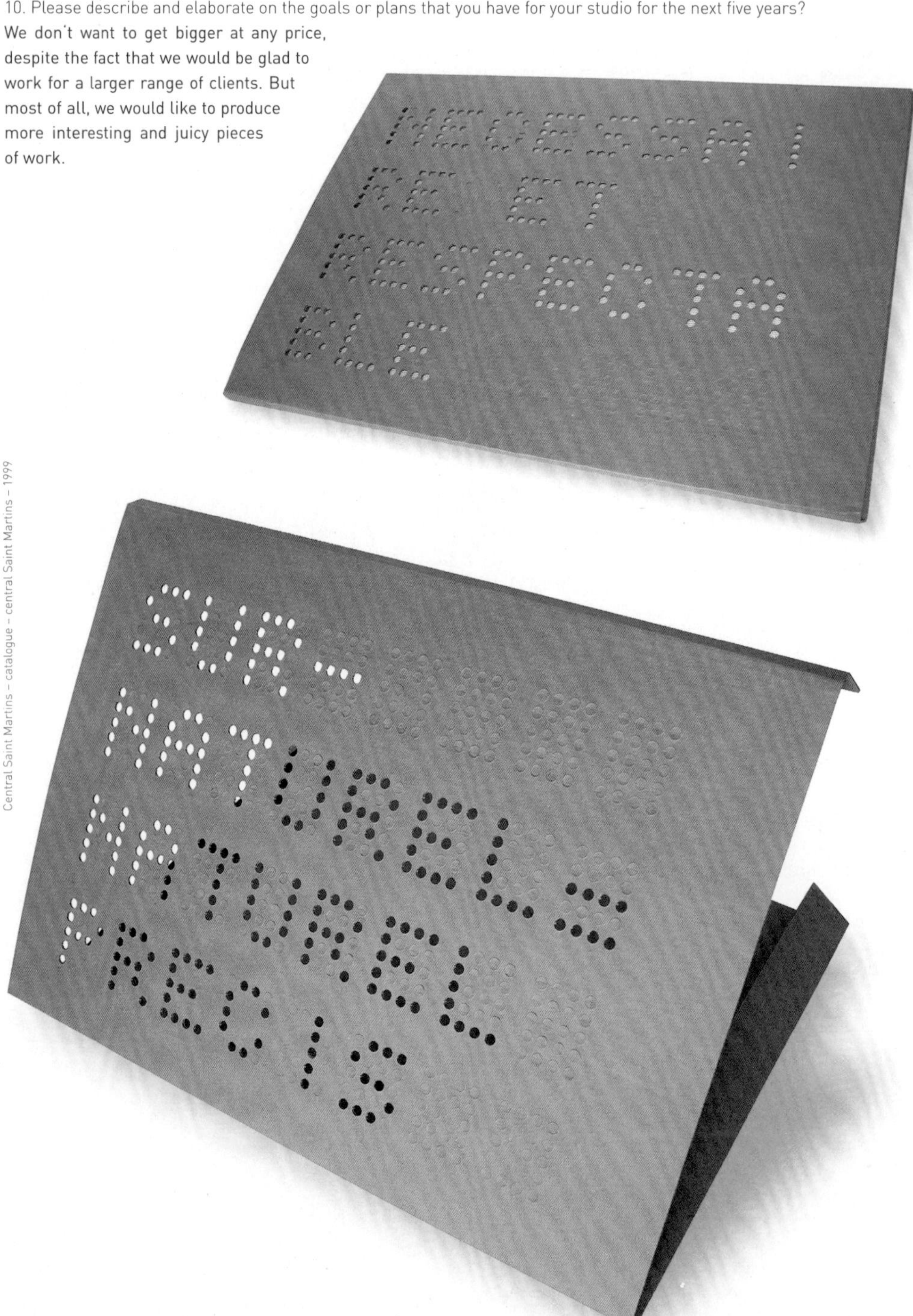

Central Saint Martins – catalogue – central Saint Martins – 1999

A story of graphic design in France – book cover – les arts décoratifs et carré éditions

RCA architecture – book – royal college of arts – 2001

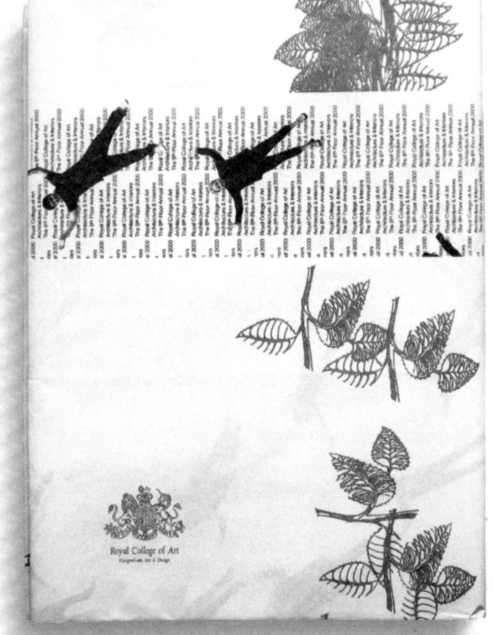

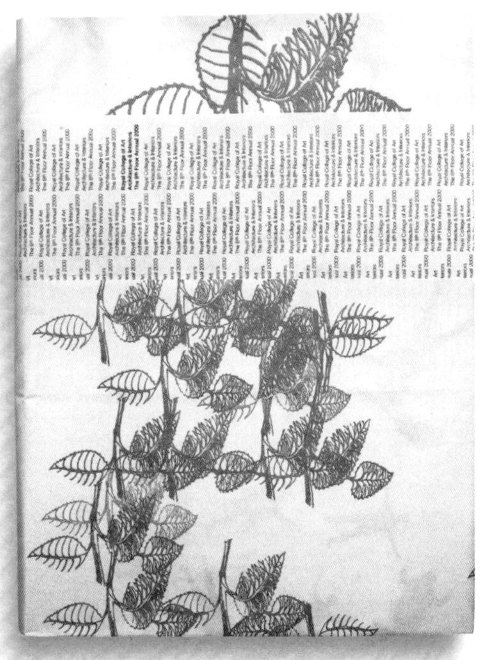

Manual binding – portfolio book – personal project – 2000

George Sand – book – culturesfrance – 2004

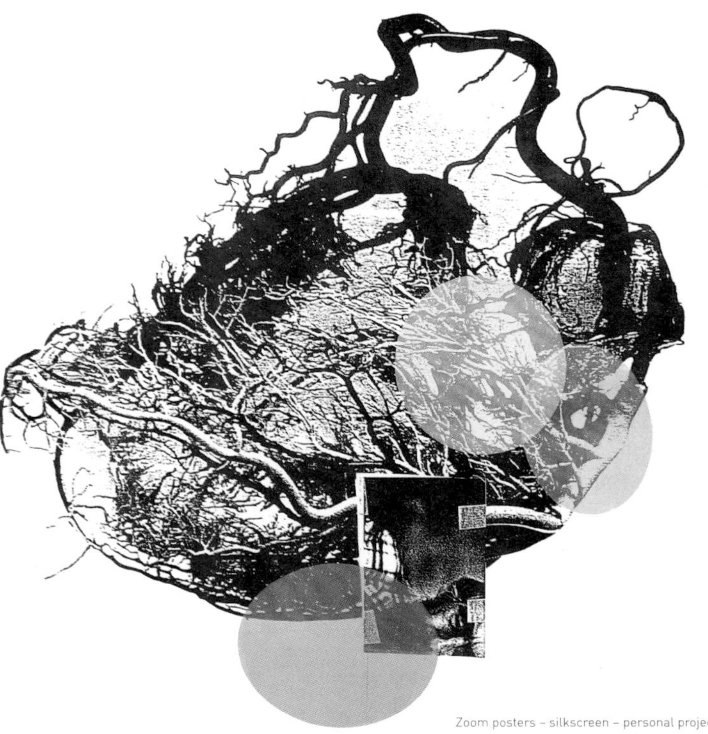

Zoom posters – silkscreen – personal project – 1999

Oded Ezer is an Israeli typographer, type designer and lecturer. Graduated at the V.C.D Dep. of the Bezalel Academy of Art and Design, Jerusalem, Ezer founded his own independent studio in Givatayim, Israel (2000), specializing in the typographic aspects of branding and publication designs. A member of the DCI (Designers Community of Israel), Ezer teaches at several academies in Israel, e.g. the Shenkar College of Design, Ramat Gan, one of the most distinguished design academies in Israel. While constantly working as a commercial designer, Ezer also runs experimental typo art projects to explore the non-conventional solutions in Hebrew typography.

Interview with Oded Ezer

1. What led to the formation of your studio?

What led to my decision to become an independent designer and open my studio was my desire to create an intimate work space where I could work on both commercial and experimental projects.

2. How many staff people does your studio have and what are their main working fields?

Right now, I am the only one in the studio. From time to time I hire freelancers (mostly photographers, web specialists, and illustrators), but most of the work is done by myself.

3. How does a regular working day at your studio look like, how is the day structured?

A regular working day can be composed of teaching at the design academy in the early morning (08:30), driving back to my studio on my scooter (around 12:30), stopping for a quick Falafel on the way (lunch time), answering some urgent e-mails (13:30), making some logo sketches for a client (14:00-16:30), thinking about ideas for a possible future experimental project (16:30-17:30), chatting with some friends on skype (17:30-18:00), surfing through the internet (18:00-18:30), having a cup of black coffee and cheese toasts with a friend at a café near my studio (18:00-18:30), going back to one more round of commercial sketches (18:30-20:00), burning a backup CD of the work, arranging the studio (20:00-20:30), and driving back home (20:30-21:00).

4. How much leisure time do you have during a year?

I usually work (and play) for about 10 hours every day, 5 days a week. The rest of the time is mostly dedicated to my family.

5. Which business areas do your clients mainly come from? Is the number of your clients increasing or rather declining?

My clients come from different business areas, such as high-tech, architecture, culture, electronic, printed media, and entertainment. I also get commissions from big design companies who need my typographic skills for certain projects. The number of my client has increased slowly but steadily in the last 7 years.

6. Do you have a specific corporate philosophy or maybe a mission statement like other companies, which is reflected in the way you steer the studio's course?

Be honest, select your projects carefully, work only for clients you like, and put your maximum efforts into fewer projects.

7. What, from your point of view, makes the difference between a small studio and a big company?

A small studio is much more flexible and able to adjust to changing market conditions. For me, it gives the designer the opportunity to have more artistic and financial freedom.

8. What kind of advantages and disadvantages does a small studio have compared to a big company?

The advantages of a small studio are a more intimate work space, smaller but often more creative projects, and less technical and administrative problems. The disadvantage of a small studio is that you make less money.

9. What is your idea about the future of small studios? Do you think that small studios do not have any other choice but to expand in order to survive in these times of globalization?

Well... I don't know about other small studios, but I hope that I won't have to expand too much in order to survive. Maybe it is a naive point of view, but I think that the solution will not be found in quantity (increasing the number of the people working in the studio) but in quality (improving my own skills).

10. Please describe and elaborate on the goals or plans that you have for your studio for the next five years?

In the next five years I hope to improve the studio's conceptual and technical skills, and to initiate more and more creative collaborations worldwide, constantly blurring the borders between the commercial and the experimental activities of the studio. And of course, to have fun.

Biotypography – experimental typography – personal project – 2005/2006

The rooms – typography – personal project – 2004/2005

Helvetica

Helvetica – poster – personal project – 2008

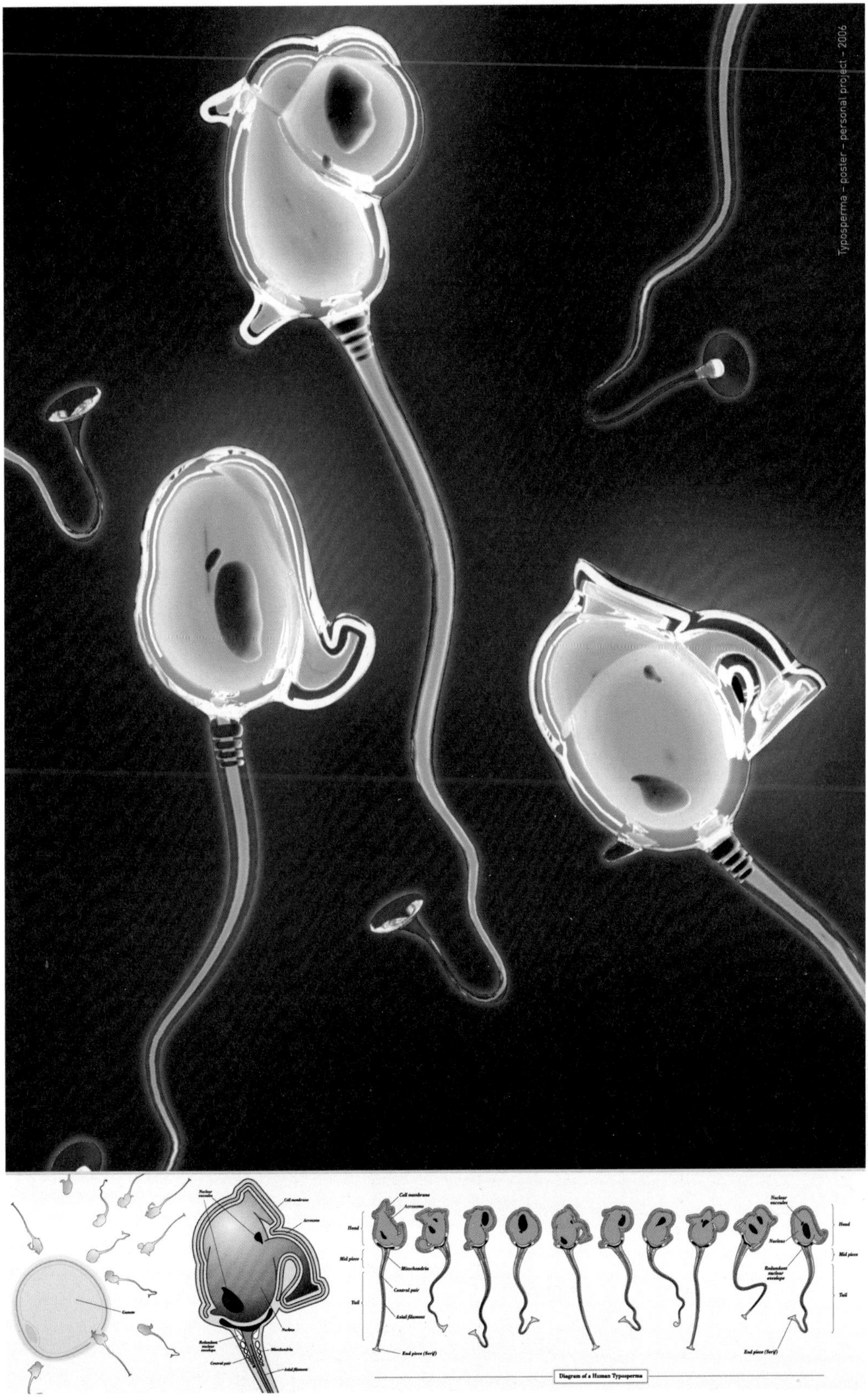

Typosperma – poster – personal project – 2006

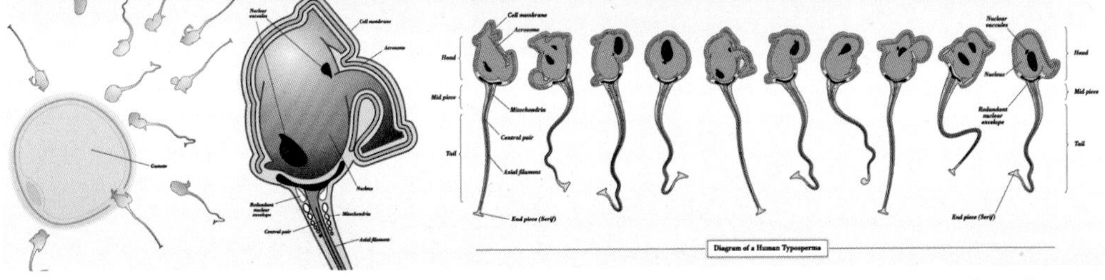

Diagram of a Human Typosperma

Temporary type - experimental typography - self produced - 2006

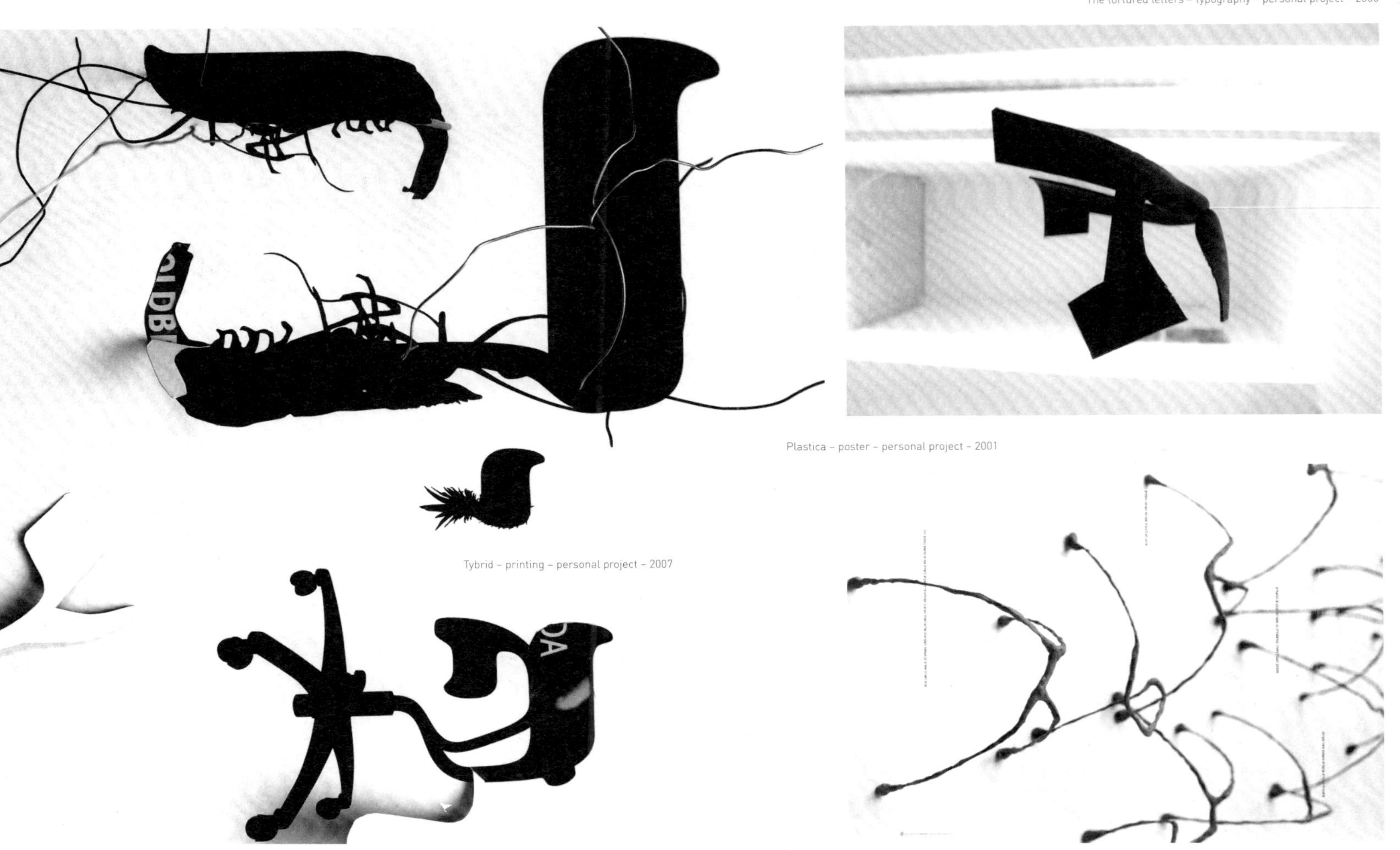

The tortured letters – typography – personal project – 2006

Plastica – poster – personal project – 2001

Tybrid – printing – personal project – 2007

Floor 5

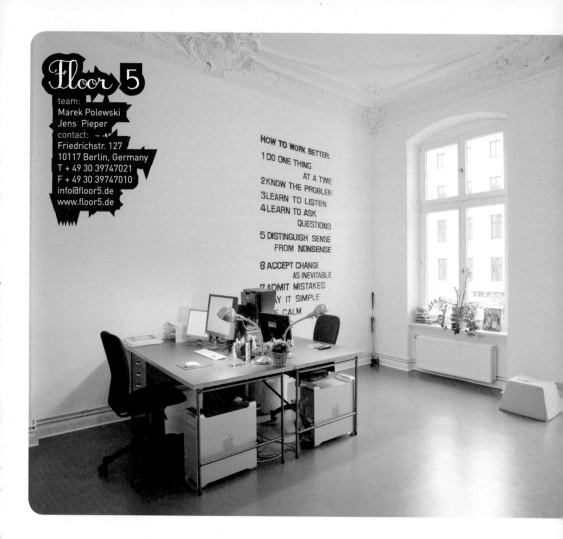

team:
Marek Polewski
Jens Pieper
contact:
Friedrichstr. 127
10117 Berlin, Germany
T + 49 30 39747021
F + 49 30 39747010
info@floor5.de
www.floor5.de

Floor 5, which is Marek Polewski and Jens Pieper, met in Berlin ten years ago. Marek was studying Fine Art in London while Jens was already in Berlin studying Visual Communication. On Marek's birthday, Jens presented a website to him to display his work – and they soon realized that together they could develop projects with a shared sense of humour and a ton of enthusiasm. In 2002, they founded the Floor5 agency, so they could start billing people. They used Marek's studio as an office, located on the fifth floor of a factory building in Berlin where a huge "5" was painted on the elevator. Further projects quickly ensued, meaning they could now work for themselves independently. Since then, with eyes wide open and with heads bursting with creativity, Floor 5 has been developing countless innovative design concepts for clients mainly from the fields of fashion, art, and music. The first step is always to establish a personal association with a project, out of which a more specific idea is developed. The content dictates the form, and anything unforeseen transforms into something new. Every task is imbued with heartfelt emotion and always contains an element of surprise; humour is, then, an essential tool. In 2004, Floor 5 moved its office to Berlin-Mitte, where the studio forms an integral part of a creative network and the artistic energy which the city of Berlin exudes today.

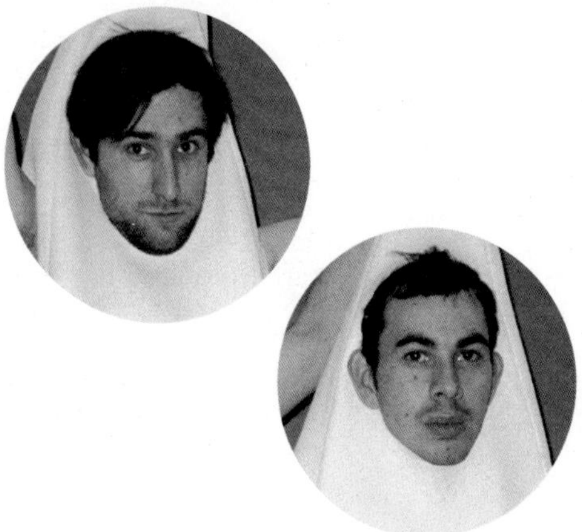

Interview with Floor 5

Tausend – logo/ci – bar tausend – 2007

1. What led to the formation of your studio?

I met Jens Pieper about 10 years ago when Jens was studying Visual Communications in Berlin and I was in London studying Fine Arts. As a birthday present Jens gave me a small portfolio-website for my paintings, and soon we discovered a similar sense of humour and our excitement to realize projects together. We founded Floor 5 in 2002, so that we could write the first invoices. At that point I had my studio on the 5th floor of a factory building with a big "5" painted on the elevator door. This quickly became our office. The first assignments came in pretty fast, which enabled us to work on an independent level.

2. How many staff people does your studio have and what are their main working fields?

The two main members of Floor 5 are Jens Pieper and Marek Polewski. Both of us are in charge of the conceptualization and the realization of projects. We also employ illustrators, graphic designers and photographers on a freelancer basis and have regular 3-6 month interns.

3. How does a regular working day at your studio look like, how is the day structured?

Jens usually opens the studio around 10:45. I come in at about 11:30, as I find it very hard to get up in the morning. After checking our emails and having a small meeting to discuss ideas and plans, we start working very hard on the current projects. This goes on until about 14:00 when we usually have lunch at a Vietnamese place called "Manngo" or an Italian restaurant in a former pharmacy. After the lunch-break, we continue working until about 19:00. Apart from sitting at the computer, we drive to printers, meet with clients and interview the tons of applicants who would die to become interns at Floor 5. And because we believe in giving something back to the community, we teach graphic design at the "Academy for Fashion and Design" twice a week.

4. How much leisure time do you have during a year?

Depending on the money we earned and the spare time we have, we enjoy travelling around the world for about four weeks a year. As much as we'd love to spend our vacations together, someone needs to watch the office. Good thing that one of us is Christian and the other is Jewish. So it works out pretty well.

5. Which business areas do your clients mainly come from? Is the number of your clients increasing or rather declining?

We mostly work for clients from the fashion and music industry, but lately more artistic and cultural projects have been realized. The number of our clients is increasing rapidly.

6. Do you have a specific corporate philosophy or maybe a mission statement like other companies, which is reflected in the way you steer the studio's course?

Our philosophy is very simple: In every job that must be done, there is an element of fun. Thank you Mary Poppins.

7. What, from your point of view, makes the difference between a small studio and a big company?

A big company has lots of employees, a small company doesn't. Less people mean less trouble and most of all fewer egos to satisfy. Big clients tend to go to big companies and give them big boring jobs with limited amount of creative freedom. Also, in a big company with many creative people, everyone has an opinion. Of course, we sometimes think to ourselves that a few more employees taking care of the extra work would be great, but this way you can actually feel like you created and produced the whole thing. This way we'll never have to fire anyone either. That makes us feel good.

8. What kind of advantages and disadvantages does a small studio have compared to a big company?

Since neither of us has ever worked in a big company we can only guess. We only have to get along with one person and that seems very easy compared to a hierarchy of a big company with many employees. We have the freedom to choose our projects and realize ideas less compromised.

9. What is your idea about the future of small studios?

We think that expanding only leads to bigger projects with limited amount of creativity and less self-involvement. Instead of directly working on your ideas you direct projects, and that way the essential details might get lost. Sagmeister Inc. is the living proof for a small studio with interesting clients and an impressive body of work.

10. Please describe and elaborate on the goals or plans that you have for your studio for the next five years?

Same projects – better payment!

Impulse – corporate design/poster campain – theater festival Impulse – photo by Daniel Josefsohn – 2007

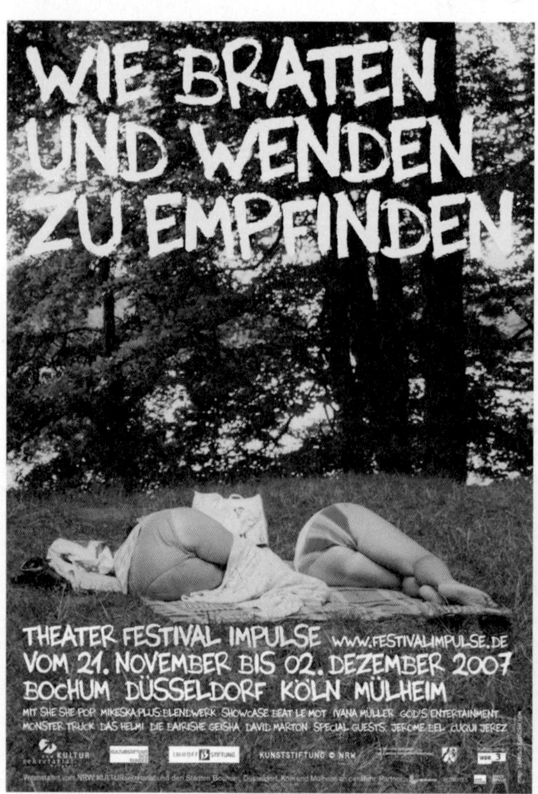

Exploited – record covers – music label exploited – 2008

ALLE MEINE FREUNDE SIND HUNDE

WENN KINDER ZWÖLF SIND, KANNST DU DICH VIELLEICHT MIT IHNEN UNTERHALTEN. MIT HUNDEN KANNST DU DICH NIE UNTERHALTEN UND WENN SIE ZWÖLF SIND, STERBEN SIE.

Fotos: Jan Friese, Text: Marc Fischer, Casting: Pauline Hoch/THEFOXPROJECT

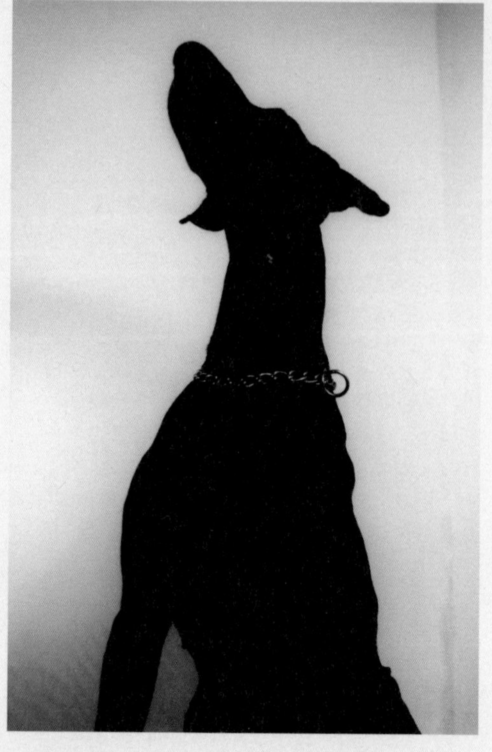

BAHNHOF ZOO

EINE BERLINER LIEBESGESCHICHTE

Fotos: Howard Sheronas, Text: Heiko Zwirner

Liebling – magazine – liebling verlag GmbH – 2005

Friday 13th – invitation card – Ingrid Junker/Katahrina Kemmler/Niki Pauls – 2008

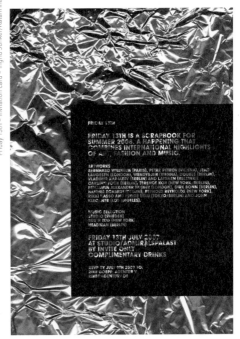

Christina Föllmer

team:
Christina Föllmer
contact:
Bernardstraße 47-49
63067 Offenbach, Germany
T + 49 69 17511792
M + 49 179 5267515
hallo@christinafoellmer.de
www.christinafoellmer.de

Christina Föllmer studied interdisciplinary at the Academy of Art and Design, Offenbach. She developed wide skills in the field of graphic design as well as in fine art (video and photography). Because of this orientation, she developed her own style, which moves somewhere between design and artistic expression. In the course of her studies she was awarded a one-year stipend by Fabrica, the International Research Centre of Art and Design of Benetton, Italy, and has worked there on diverse projects in a highly creative and international environment.

Greeting card – type – personal project – 2003/2007

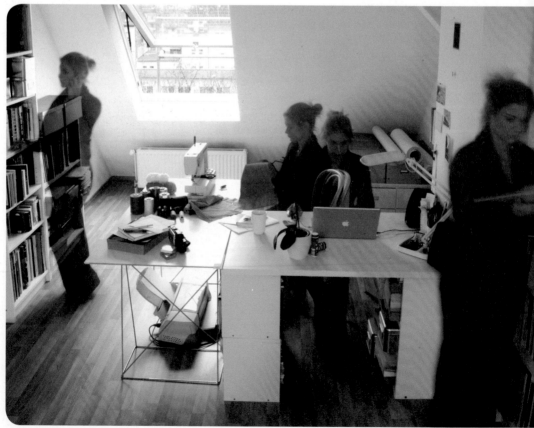

Interview with Christina Föllmer

1. What led to the formation of your studio?

I went into business as a freelancer in order to achieve my individual style and to realize experimental as well as artistic goals. In doing so, it is particularly important to me to have room for personal projects.

2. How many staff people does your studio have and what are their main working fields?

My regular workforce is constituted by my excellent network, which I have built up during my working year in Fabrica, the International Research Centre of Communication of Benetton (Italy), and at the German academy HfG Offenbach.

3. How does a regular working day at your studio look like, how is the day structured?

I prefer concentrating on one single project per day to be able to advance this as much as possible.

4. How much leisure time do you have during a year?

Two to five weeks.

5. Which business areas do your clients mainly come from? Is the number of clients increasing or rather declining?

I have customers from totally different domains – from the theatre sector, from the industry, from the design and art scene, from the medical sector, etc., because I advocate working on very different topics which are intriguing me. The number of my clients is increasing significantly.

6. Do you have a specific corporate philosophy or maybe a mission statement like other companies, which is reflected in the way you steer the studio's course?

What constitutes my work is the combination of art and design in a conceptual manner, linked to the enjoyment of experimenting, coherent in detail with regard to content and composition.

7. What, from your point of view, makes the difference between a small studio and a big company?

I prefer a certain creative freedom and a self-determined style of working, organizing and realizing all work steps, having room for experiments and artistic projects, the liberty to pick my working partners as well as the option to choose projects on the basis of content.

Festival junger talente/in cooperation with Catrin Sonnabend - poster/catalog/orientation system - festival junger talente - 2006

FESTHALTEN *

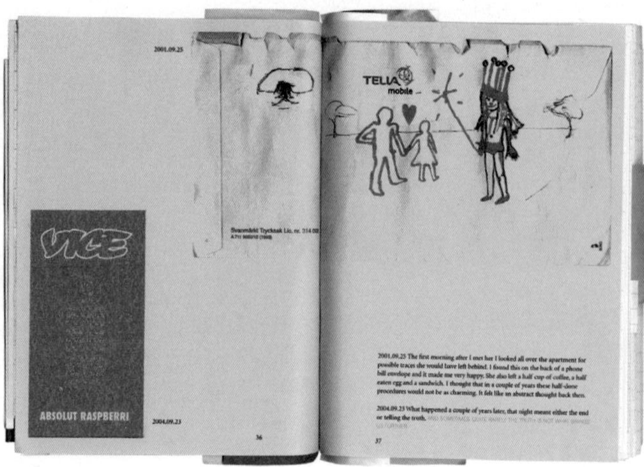

2001.09.25

2004.09.23

36

2001.09.25 The first morning after I met her I looked all over the apartment for possible traces she would have left behind. I found this on the back of a phone bill envelope and it made me very happy. She also left a half cup of coffee, a half eaten egg and a sandwich. I thought that in a couple of years these half-done procedures would not be as charming. It felt like an abstract thought back then.

2004.09.23 What happened a couple of years later, that night meant either the end or telling the truth.

37

ZUM GLÜCK BESANN ICH MICH DANN DOCH
EINES TAGES UND BEHIELT DIE LETZTE ROSE, DIE ICH
FÜR SIE GEKAUFT HATTE, FÜR MICH.

Kei

Am Rückspiegel meines Autos hängt eine kleine getrocknete Rose. Ich kann nicht mehr exakt sagen, wann ich sie dahin gehängt habe, doch weiß ich noch, woran sie mich erinnert. Ihr Name war Daniela, ein Mädchen aus meiner Straße, und für mich war es Liebe auf den ersten Blick! Ich lernte sie während des Firmunterrichts kennen und, auch wenn wir nichts gemein hatten und auch nie über einen gehemmten Smalltalk hinaus kamen, verfiel ich ihrem Lächeln und dem Glanz ihrer Augen. Verwirrt von so vielen Gefühlen doch unerfahren im Umgang mit Frauen beschloss ich eines Abends, ihr meine Gefühle zu offenbaren.
Wäre ich nicht so feige gewesen, hätte ich sie direkt angesprochen, doch so mussten eine Rose und ein kleiner Liebesbrief vor ihrer Tür die Boten mimen.
Zitternd und mit Herzklopfen erwartete ich eine Antwort, ein Zeichen, irgendwas, das mir Klarheit verschaffen könnte … doch verblendet durch verklärten Blick übersah ich ihre Antwort, die deutlicher hätte nicht sein können – sie sagte nichts!
Und so quälte ich mich fast zwei Jahre in der vagen Hoffnung, doch noch eines Tages eine Antwort zu erhalten, zu weiteren unbeantworteten Rosengängen. Zum Glück besann ich mich dann doch eines Tages und behielt die letzte Rose, die ich für sie gekauft hatte, für mich. Ich kann nicht genau sagen, warum ich diese Rose nach fast zehn Jahren noch besitze, aber vielleicht sollte sie mich daran erinnern, dass man seine Liebe nicht leichtfertig vor fremden Türen hinterlegt …

15

Suzanne

I'm really sentimental – I keep everything. This is my treasure because it reminds me of my mum and dad. For Christmas last year my brother and I booked my parents flights to Venice and a hotel for Valentines weekend. I didn't realize at the time, but it was also carnival time. They hadn't been out of Belfast together, well Ireland, since the 1970s – and never abroad together. When they arrived in Venice – they landed in Treviso – I missed them and was really worried. I had lived in Treviso at that time already. I managed to get them on my dad's phone and he was all cheerful: „Yeah, we're in Venice. Just going to the hotel now." I was so relieved! They married years before I was born – funny thing to remember!
Anyway, I missed them again and again, I called the hotel, they weren't in, and I eventually got a phone call where they were.
We met the next night in the middle of mad carnival fireworks at St. Marcus Square. My mum was wearing this mask and my dad had a big hat with feathers and they both had their faces painted and they were full of fun … it was great as well because I hadn't seen them in so long and I knew that things had been difficult for them recently – my dad was diagnosed with Parkinson's Disease. They had such a great time and we ended up getting soaked on the Vaporetto under the stars at night time back to their hotel. That night they'd met Holger for the first time as well but it was just so special to see them again.
When they went home I wore the mask for the next carnival and IT'S HUNG ON MY WALL EVER SINCE. IT MAKES ME SMILE.

Conventionalism* – book – personal project – 2005

Maike Häusling exhibition – catalog – Maike Häusling – 2007

9. What is your idea about the future of small studios? Do you think that small studios do not have any other choice but to expand in order to survive in these times of globalization?

The future of both small and big studios will eventually depend on their quality. In the first place, however, it will be a much greater challenge to small studios to position themselves on the market. Probably, a distinct office concept becomes more and more important. Still I am sure that small studios will not get dispensable, since every trend – and so the trend of globalization – generates counter-movements in the long run.

10. Please describe and elaborate on the goals of plans that you have for your studio for the next five years?

My ambition is a varied, high-quality mixture of cultural, artistic, social and "exotic" projects. My ideal working conception consists of 50 percent contracting work and 50 percent realizing my own, free projects. At long sight, I want to establish a flexible, transnational office.

Silk – type – personal project – 2003

Hier vorne – exhibition/catalogue/poster – Frankfurter buchmesse – 2006

voila
ENSEMBLE
ab jetzt
SCIENCE-FICTION-KOMÖDIE VON ALAN AYCKBOURNE
PREMIERE AM 24. MAI 2007, 20 UHR
GALLUS THEATER, KLEYERSTRASSE 15
VORSTELLUNGEN 25. UND 26. MAI UM 20 UHR
REGIE ALEXANDER BUSSMANN
DARSTELLER REGINA BROWN, ALEXANDER BUSSMANN, JENNY HEMPEL,
MIKE KESS, JULIA LERCH, KATJA SIMON
MIT FREUNDLICHER UNTERSTÜTZUNG DES AMTS FÜR WISSENSCHAFT UND KUNST DER STADT FRANKFURT.
Frankfurter Sparkasse 1822
PIZZERIA EL-SAN

Ab jetzt – poster – play ab jetzt by Alan Ayckbourn – 2007

Fontef

team:
Lahav Iontef
Yanek Halevy
contact:
31 Rothschild Blvd.
Room 35
66883 Tel Aviv
Israel
T + 972 3 5605801
F + 972 3 5602501
info@fontef.com
www.fontef.com

Fontef is specialized in brand identity, systematic typographic design as well as Hebrew and Latin typeface design. Among the studio's clients are the Strauss Group, Bank Hapoalim, Yedioth Aharonoth, Arcaffe, Calcalist and many more. Yanek Iontef worked as a graphic designer in London and as a Senior Designer at Metamark International, Tel Aviv. Since 1995, he has taught typography and type design at the Bezalel Academy. He currently works in Tel Aviv as a freelance designer specializing in type design, corporate identity, and editorial design. An award-winning type designer (2000, TDC Type Design Competition. 2001 bukva:raz! Type Design Competition), he also has his own type foundry, producing a range of Hebrew and Latin fonts. Lahav Halevy used to be a newspaper graphic editor in the early 90s and moved to New York in 1995 as a correspondent of an Israeli newspaper. After returning to Tel Aviv in 2000, he worked as a freelance designer under the name BigEyes Design. Focusing on poster design, he works for cultural and political organizations (also some radical left-wing and human rights organizations) on both commercial and social-political issues, and editorial design. He participates in exhibitions and shows all around the world (Warsaw Biennial; Lahti Biennial; Ningbo Biennial, etc.).

הנפטנוסקהמחירשל$2
חבית→עלה€35 זהו טקסט
דמי המדגים את תפקוד האותיות והסימנים
השונים של פונט זה. 257₪ סימן קריאה! כוכבית
פונט אשתי, למטבח
8.5% מניות

Shual font – headlines font – financial newspaper – 2008

Fontef – logo design – type foundry fontef – 2005

Interview with Lahav Yontef

1. What led to the formation of your studio?

Each one of us was working at different places during the previous years, feeling the need to work on his own to be independent and free from struggling with both the client AND a boss. So we joined and rented a space to share facilities and knowledge.

2. How many staff people does your studio have and what are their main working fields?

We are two independent designers sharing the same office space and sometimes collaborating on big projects. Yanek Iontef is a typographer in his heart and bones. He specializes in Hebrew type design, and trying very hard to keep all his "commercial" work as close as possible to his type-related projects, such as type design for newspapers, corporations, and logotype design. Lahav Halevy mainly works for social-cultural customers. He is specialized on poster design on political and cultural issues.

3. How does a regular working day at your studio look like, how is the day structured?

After having morning coffee in the café four floors below, we turn on our computers and "sink" into the chairs. On lucky days there are no disturbances from the outside world. That means – no meetings inside or outside the studio, no visits to the printing house. Then we can just sit and do the work, which is something we are both trained to do – and do gladly. Lunch is an important event of the day, as we tend to stroll up and down the streets of southern Tel-Aviv, "hunting" for old neglected signs and street graphics. The second half of the day looks very much like the first, only with the need to fight the tiredness showing up after lunch. On many days we spend long hours at the office, definitely exceeding the average of working hours.

4. How much leisure time do you have during a year?

Usually, it sums up to two-three weeks per year.

5. Which business areas do your clients mainly come from? Is the number of your clients increasing or rather declining?

Yanek mostly deals with type design and corporate identities. Lahav mainly deals with the Israeli film industry and small-scale "street" businesses, like restaurants, etc. Fortunately, the number of our clients did not decline through the years, and it hopefully never will. Since we both have made the decision not to hire staff on a regular basis, we have limited the number of clients we can deal with. What we were trying to do over the years, though, was to "improve" the quality of our clients which means to spend the greater part of our working time on work we like to do, rather than doing every job just to make a living.

6. Do you have a specific corporate philosophy or maybe a mission statement like other companies, which is reflected in the way you steer the studio's course?

Keeping a philosophy is very hard when it comes to clashes with everyday life. We do have our "red lines" with regard the type of work we don't want to do or the kind of customers we will not agree to serve.

7. What, from your point of view, makes the difference between a small studio and a big company?

Apart from the mere idea that one cannot get rich when working alone, we both strongly believe that keeping the studio small, or "thin" as we call it, provides us with a freedom that does not exist in larger business entities.

8. What kind of advantages and disadvantages does a small studio have compared to a big company?

The main advantage is this sense of freedom, maybe even a slightly nihilistic way of life you can create by working on your own. The main disadvantage is the inability to grow financially.

The last 40 years – exhibition poster – exhibition the last 40 years – 2007

Coffeebar – restaurant design – very famous upscale restaurant in Tel-Aviv – 2007

Domestic violence – series of posters of human issues – fight – 2007

AIDS – series of posters of human issues – fight – 2007

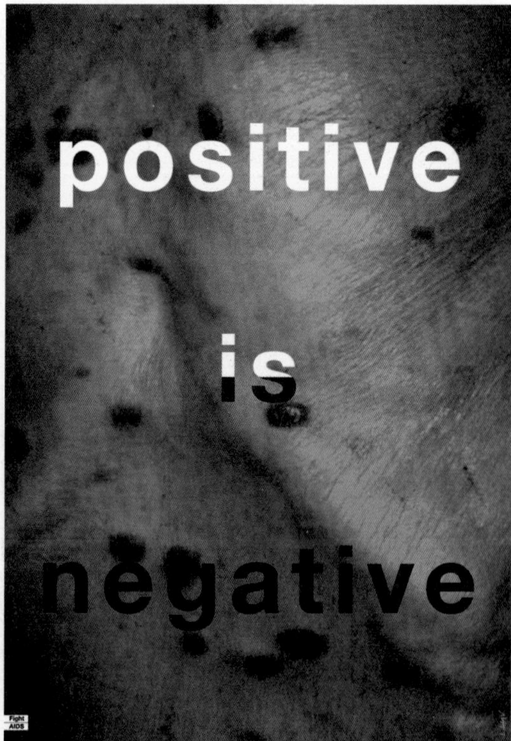

The last 40 years – exhibition poster – exhibition the last 40 years – 2007

9. What is your idea about the future of small studios? Do you think that small studios do not have any other choice but to expand in order to survive in these times of globalization?

Luckily for us, we don't buy into the globalization concept entirely. We are not worried about the future of any small studio around the world. Like people want to drink an espresso in a café nearby, this café or (restaurant, book publisher, local newspaper, etc.) will always need a designer nearby. It is true that there was a shift during the last 20 years in the way big corporations work, and their ability to import graphic design as a part of branding from afar. But we deal with people who walk the same streets which we walk, breath the same air, and deal with the same issues. That makes us – and our work – part of the actual world we all live in.

10. Please describe and elaborate on the goals or plans that you have for your studio for the next five years?

I think that we both wish to be able to focus more on the issues (both graphic and human) that we have a personal interest in. And that means being able to make a living out of it without compromising on our vision and work. Yanek wishes to have the terms to start working on a new serif typeface in Hebrew, something that was not done in the Hebrew language for many years, and which is seriously needed. Lahav hopes to deepen his work in the field of poster design, especially on social and political issues, as well as increasing his involvement in the artistic world

Impressia – corporate logo – hitech company – 2007

FFcartonage font – font – FF cartonage – 2003

Meitar font – font – Yad Vashem holocaust museum, for a video installation of the artist Uri Zeig – 2007

28.04.04:גרסה [5] תאריך | מלל לדוגמה | האות | שם הפרנט

26/24 פרנקט

דאת הדפסת נסיון לבדיקת גופן חדש
של אותיות. דה רעך יצחק הטייס
מתעופף כנשר גדול בין שמיים וארץ.
1000%. סימן קריאה! כוכבית להערת
שוליים* נקודתיים: נקודה ופסיק;
מי מפחד מדקדוק? גבעת־החבצלת עם
מקף עליון. הישוב מאכלס 28,590
תושבים, בתוכם 6,943 ילדים. יום
א', יום ד', יום ה'. תשר"ק, אה"ל,
צל"מ, אג"ד. "מדף". "איזהו חכם –

צ

מיתר מדבר

פריסת סימנים סטנדרטית

אבגדהוזחטיכלמנסעפצקרשתךםןףץ
(*:/.,;?!)1234567890#
{[|"$%₪'>=<-+]}

15/12 פרנקט

פיסקה דו מהווה דוגמה לטקסט שסודר
במרווח אחיד בין השורות. המונח אחיד
מתייחס לקומפוזיציה טיפוגרפית ללא
רווח נוסף בין השורות. במונחים
חדותיים, סדר זה מעניק מידה אחידה של
צבע אפור הנעים מבחינה אסתטית, אך
מאמץ את עיני הקורא בקריאה מתמשכת.
אף על פי כן, הבחירה ב-אחיד המוכתבת
על ידי איכות החדותית הרצויה. פיסקה
דו מהווה דוגמה לטקסט שסודר במרווח
אחיד בין השורות. המונח אחיד מתייחס

12.5/10 פרנקט

פיסקה דו מהווה דוגמה לטקסט שסודר
במרווח אחיד בין השורות. המונח אחיד
מתייחס לקומפודיציה טיפוגרפית ללא
רווח נוסף בין השורות. במונחים
חדותיים, סדר זה מעניק מידה אחידה של
צבע אפור הנעים מבחינה אסתטית, אך
מאמץ את עיני הקורא בקריאה מתמשכת.
אף על פי כן, הבחירה ב-אחיד המוכתבת
על ידי איכות החדותית הרצויה. פיסקה
דו מהווה דוגמה לטקסט שסודר במרווח
אחיד בין השורות. המונח אחיד מתייחס
לקומפודיציה טיפוגרפית ללא רווח נוסף
בין השורות. במונחים חדותיים, סדר זה
מעניק מידה אחידה של צבע אפור הנעים

עברית מול לועזית

Consectetuer adipiscing	פיסקה דו מהווה דוגמה לטק
lorem elit, sed diam	סט שסודר במרווח אחיד בין
nonummy nibh euismod tinc	השורות. המונח אחיד מתייחס
idunt ut laoreet. Enim ad	לקומפודיציה טיפוגרפית ללא
minim veniam. Sed diam non	רווח נוסף בין השורות.
ummy nibh euismod tincid	במונחים חדותיים, סדר זה
unt ut laoreet dolore	מעניק מידה אחידה של צבע
magna aliquam erat volu	אפור הנעים מבחינה אסתטית,
tpat luis autem veleum	אך מאמץ את עיני הקורא
dolor magna aliquam volutp	בקריאה מתמשכת. אף על פי
at lorem ipsum dolor. Euis	כן, הבחירה ב-אחיד המוכתבת
mod tincidunt ut laoreet	על ידי איכות החדותית
dolore magna aliquam erat	הרצויה. פיסקה דו מהווה
volutpat luis veleum dolor	דוגמה לטקסט שסודר במרווח

Jelly fish – poster – for a movie by Etgar Keret, Cannes film festival – 2007

A film by

Etgar Keret & Shira Geffen

JELLYFISH

Etgar Keret & Shira Geffen

A film by

Lama Films etc.

Lama Films etc.

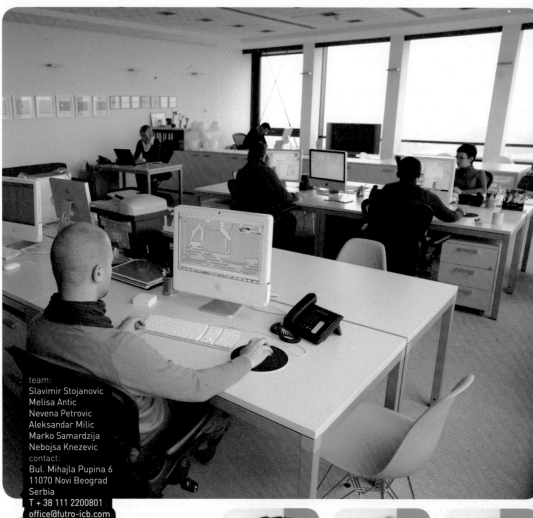

team:
Slavimir Stojanovic
Melisa Antic
Nevena Petrovic
Aleksandar Milic
Marko Samardzija
Nebojsa Knezevic

contact:
Bul. Mihajla Pupina 6
11070 Novi Beograd
Serbia
T + 38 111 2200801
office@futro-icb.com
www.futro-icb.com

Futro ICB

Futro was founded in 2003 in Ljubljana, Slovenia by the award-winning graphic designer Slavimir Stojanovic. It was conceived as a small creative service unit working for clients in the region and abroad. Futro is divided into three different areas of interest: Futro Art, Futro Work, and Futro Design. Futro Art is published through a monthly publication, the Futro Fanzine. Futro Work represents our daily commercial business in the area of designing and branding, while Futro Design constitutes our latest venture into the design of usable, everyday products like chairs, lights, tables, clocks, paper products and pottery. In 2007, Futro moved to Belgrade, the capitol of Serbia, offering a bigger market hungry for contemporary design. Our work ethic is best described by our daily mantra: To complicate simply.

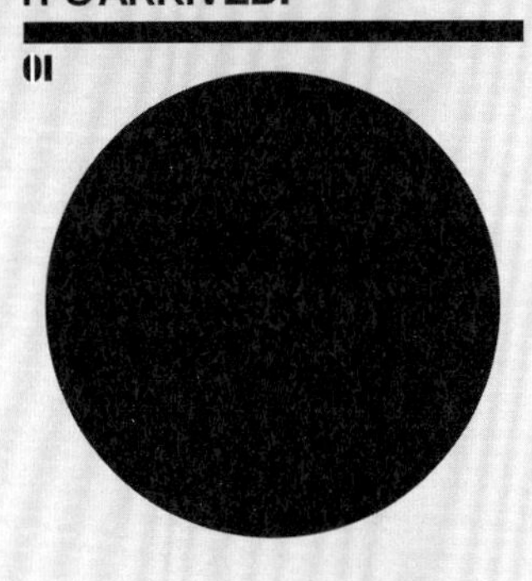

FOR THOSE WAITING
FOR THE FUTURE,
WE HAVE GOOD NEWS:
IT'S ARRIVED.
01

Interview with Futro ICB

1. What led to the formation of your studio?

I was working in advertising industry for more than 10 years, winning more than 200 awards, and beginning to feel frustrated by the creative limitations involved. Graphic design was my zone of interest since I attended Design High School, and I always dreamed of having my own studio. During the 1990s living in former Yugoslavia was hell. The only place a creative person could work and live on his or her own creativity was in advertising agencies. Soon the whole region blew up in a bloody war, which ended after a couple of years, but somehow Serbia remained in that mode for years to come. Just a few years ago, normality and democracy became everyday habits, and thus, also the profession of design got back into the picture. I formed Futro – Creative Service Unit in Ljubljana, Slovenia in 2003, and one year ago I opened Futro ICB – Design & Branding Agency in Belgrade, Serbia.

2. How many staff people does your studio have and what are their main working fields?

We are 6 people: one director, one creative director, one project manager, and three designers.

3. How does a regular working day at your studio look like, how is the day structured?

Every day around 9.00 we go through the daily briefing. All meetings with clients are finished by lunchtime around 13.00. After that we become creative. We stay at work as long as we need to, usually until 17.00, but sometimes we sleep at work.

FOR THOSE SEARCHING
FOR LOVE,
WE HAVE GOOD NEWS:
IT'S WITHIN YOU.
02

Good news – poster triptich – U.G F.I.A – 2007

4. How much leisure time do you have during a year?

As much as we can afford. In most cases, it is about 4 - 6 weeks.

5. Which business areas do your clients mainly come from? Is the number of your clients increasing or rather declining?

We have clients from construction, retail, fashion and the food industry. Also, we do a lot of editorial design as well as projects for cultural institutions. Since the Serbian design industry is very young, we can say that the number of clients is growing – daily.

6. Do you have a specific corporate philosophy or maybe a mission statement like other companies, which is reflected in the way you steer the studio's course?

Our design philosophy is to complicate simply. Our business philosophy is to be honest and to grow with your clients. Behind both philosophies there is truth. We don't use design as a seducing tool, but rather as a device to clear communication.

7. What, from your point of view, makes the difference between a small studio and a big company?

I think that the number of people is irrelevant as long as we all stick to the same philosophy. That is the hardest thing to achieve because people are different, so what usually happens is that you lose some of your core substance when you grow.

8. What kind of advantages and disadvantages does a small studio have compared to a big company?

Small studios have the opportunity to be more creative, more experimental, but most of the time not on socially important projects. It is a matter of choice. You can stay small and have more freedom, or you can work on big and important projects, but loose your identity in a big team. Freedom is most expensive thing, and there are people who are only good as team players.

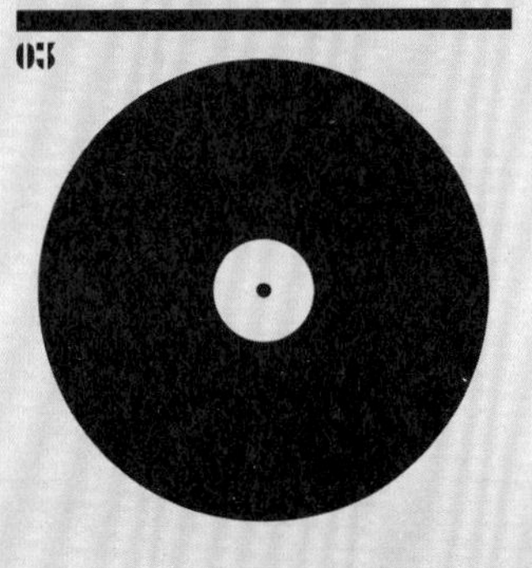

FOR THOSE LOOKING
FOR WEALTH,
WE HAVE GOOD NEWS:
IT'S AROUND YOU.
03

9. What is your idea about the future of small studios?

The future is in our heads. It is individuality. That is why a client is going to choose you. And if a big design company can achieve that same individuality, it is o.k. to grow. It is easier to work alone or in a small team, but as we can see in design annuals every year, brilliant work can be done by big teams, too. In these times of globalization, small design companies can survive as small teams within bigger companies if they only have the strength to keep their substance alive.

10. Please describe and elaborate on the goals or plans that you have for your studio for the next five years?

My plan is to make Futro a design brand. We will develop our own product line, while keeping the hands on the daily client services. We are working on a line of furniture, lights, carpets, and clothing, using 2D graphic design elements and making them 3D.

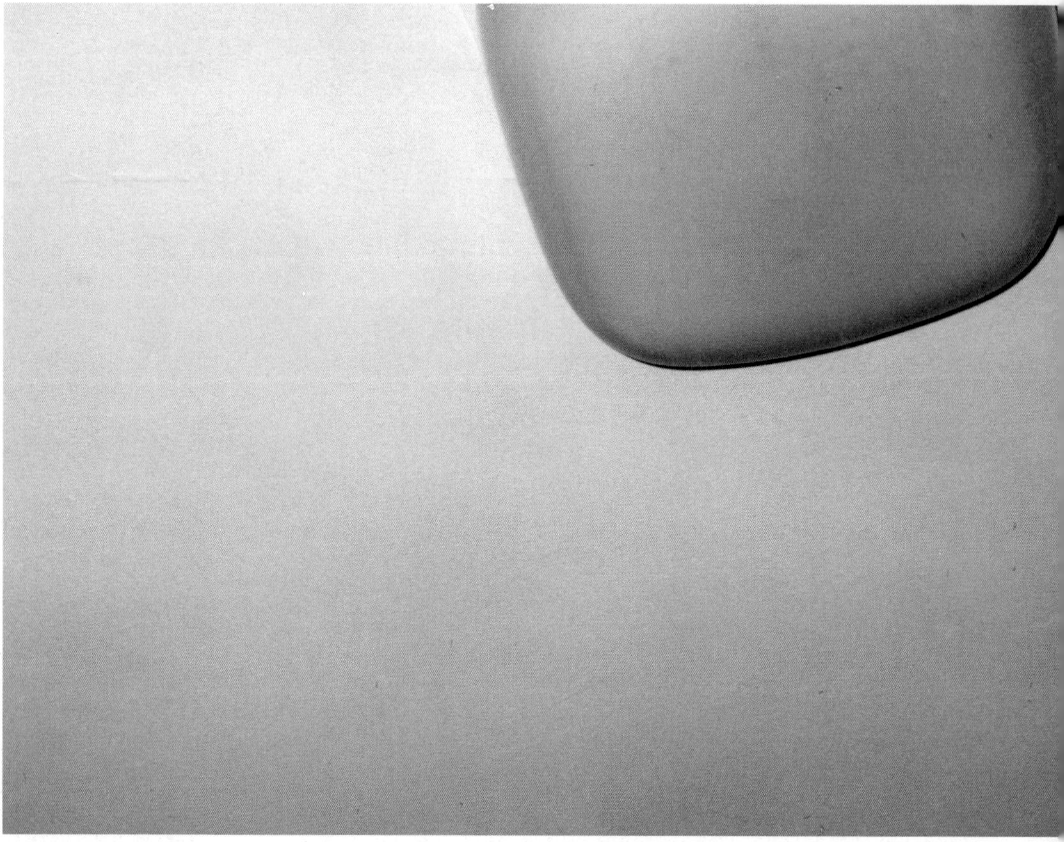

Private public – digital print on canvas – superspace gallery – 2007

Faar magazine – magazine – Belgrade's fashion art monthly magazine – 2007/2008

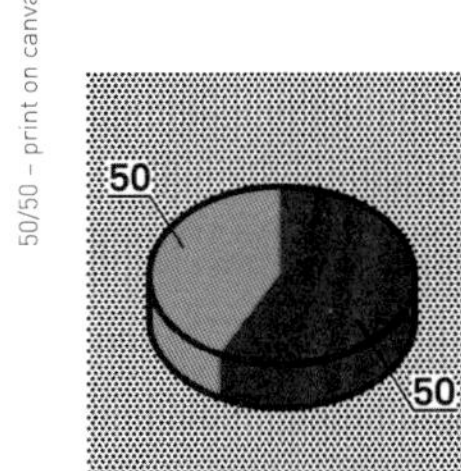

50/50 – print on canvas – worx office design – 2008

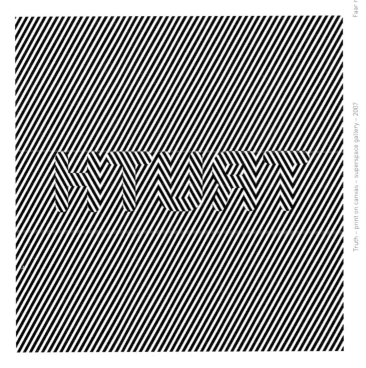
Truth – print on canvas – superspace gallery – 2007

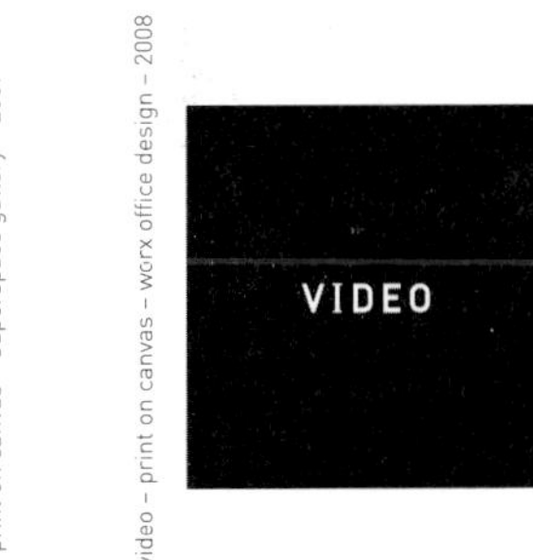

Audio/video – print on canvas – worx office design – 2008

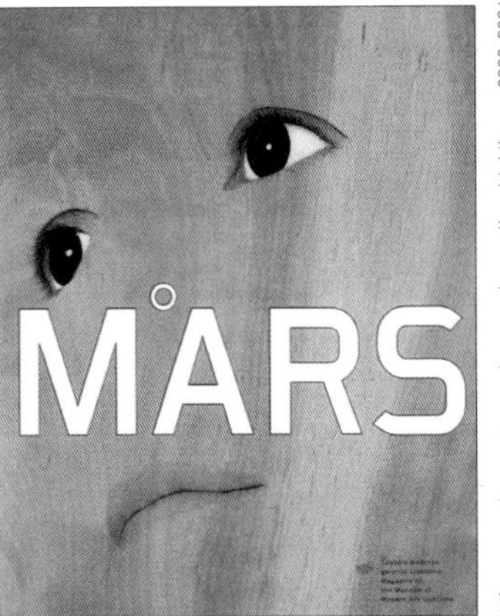

M'ars magazine – art magazine – modern gallery Ljubljana – 2002-2004

Futro stories – book – futro books – 2006

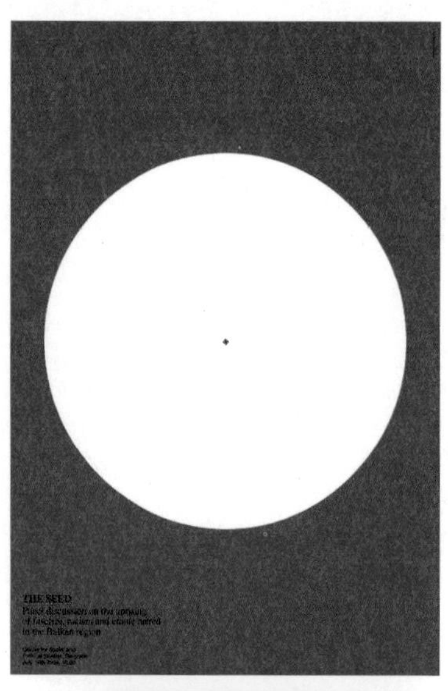

The Seed – poster – center for social and political studies – 2008

Fame magazine – magazine – press publishing group – 2008

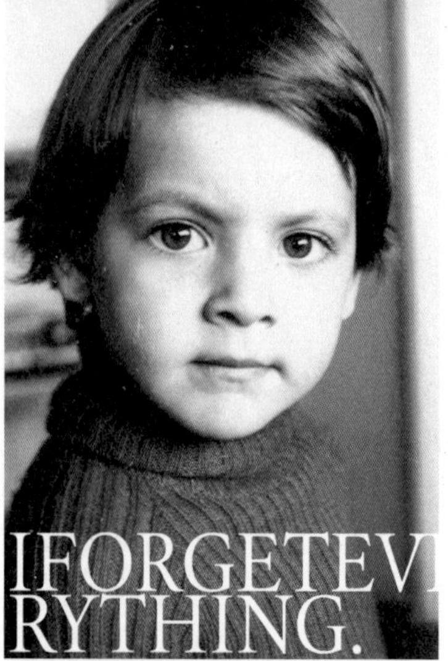

I forget everything – print on plexiglass – superspace gallery – 2007

Worx – identity – worx office design – 2008

New talent show – tv show identity – MTV Adria – 2006

Fedra's love – poster – JPD – 2008

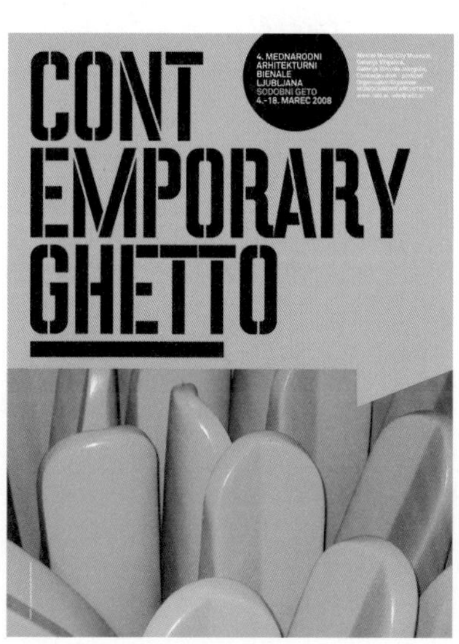

Contemporary ghetto – poster – monochrome architects – 2008

MTV:
NEW TALENT
SHOW

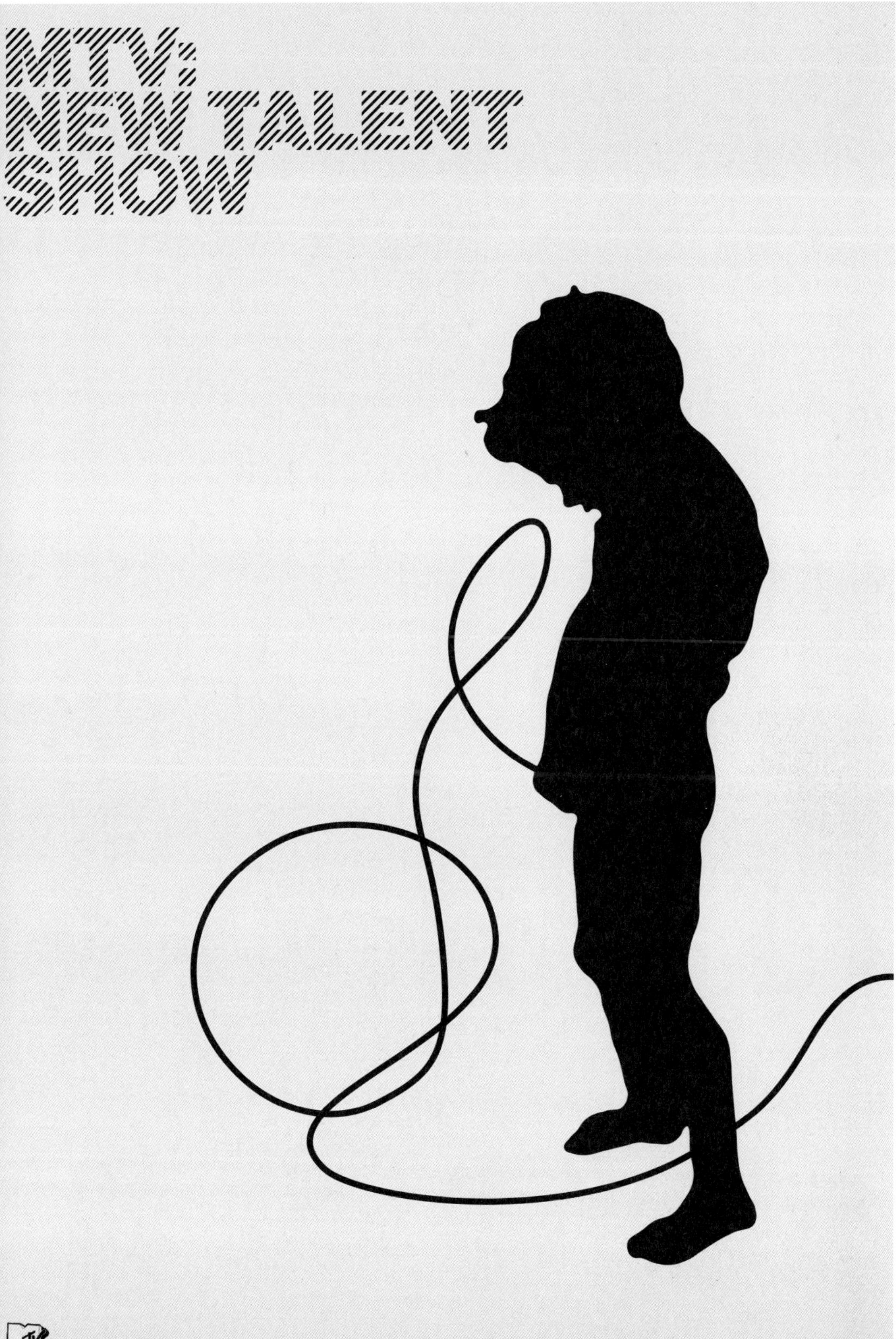

WWW.MTVADRIA.COM

General Working Group

team:
Geoff Kaplan
contact:
178 Amber Drive
94131 San Francisco, USA
T + 1 415 5581745
geoff@generalworkinggroup.com
www.generalworkinggroup.com

General Working Group is Geoff Kaplan and has realized projects for a wide range of academic and cultural institutions. He received his MFA from Cranbrook and teaches in the Graduate Program of Design at CCA, and the TransMedia program in Brussels. Geoff is currently writing, editing and designing his forthcoming book "Power of the People: The Graphic Design of Radical Press and the Rise of the Counter-Culture, 1964-1974", which will be published by the University of Chicago Press in the fall of 2009.

Incest - type - personal project - 2004

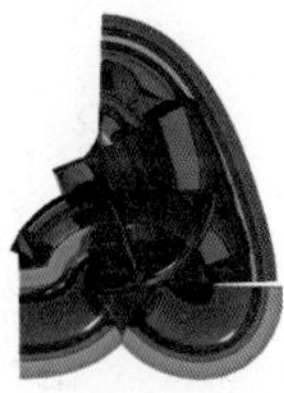

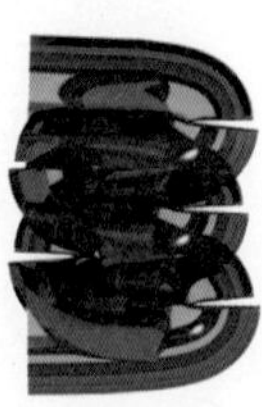

Interview with General Working Group

1. What led to the formation of your studio?

Control.

2. How many staff people does your studio have and what are their main working fields?

Myself, a part-time studio assistant plus an intern.

3. How does a regular working day at your studio look like, how is the day structured?

There is no structure.

4. How much leisure time do you have during a year?

It's all leisure. Work and leisure are one in the same.

5. Which business areas do your clients mainly come from?

Art. Or I just like to imagine that most of my clients are coming from the world of art.

Is the number of your clients increasing or rather declining?

See #10.

6. Do you have a specific corporate philosophy or maybe a mission statement like other companies, which is reflected in the way you steer the studio's course?

Mantra for 2008: Less fear.

7. What, from your point of view, makes the difference between a small studio and a big company?

It takes all types. My particular flavour of solo practice is a deliberate decision.

8. What kind of advantages and disadvantages does a small studio have compared to a big company?

I know maybe a dozen independent or single-person studios. We like to gang up in various constellations around particular projects; team up, and then disperse again. This is a major advantage which a network of small studios has over big lumbering companies.

9. What is your idea about the future of small studios?

More of the same: collaborative efforts.

Do you think that small studios do not have any other choice but to expand in order to survive in these times of globalization?

No, just the opposite.

10. Please describe and elaborate on the goals or plans that you have for your studio for the next five years?

More self initiated projects – and onto a self-sustained studio existence.

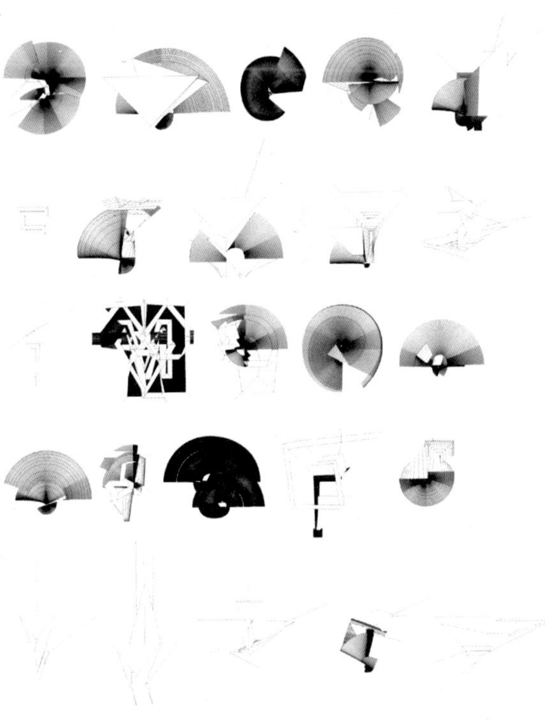

Letter(s) to ed (fella) – type – personal project – 2005

Icest – type – personal project – 2004

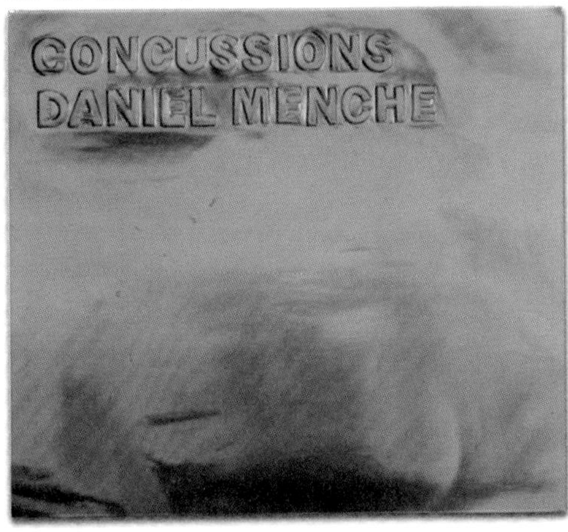

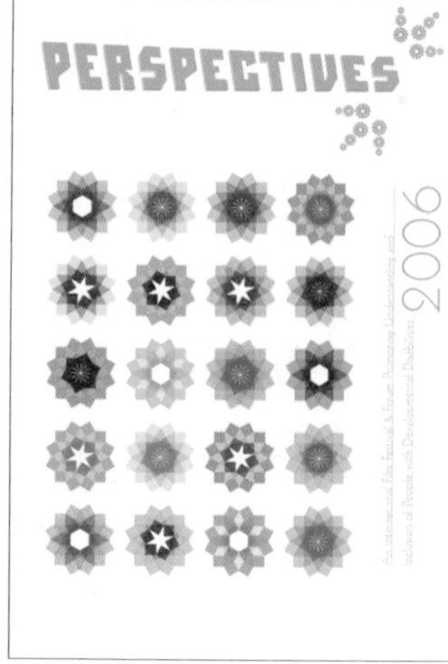

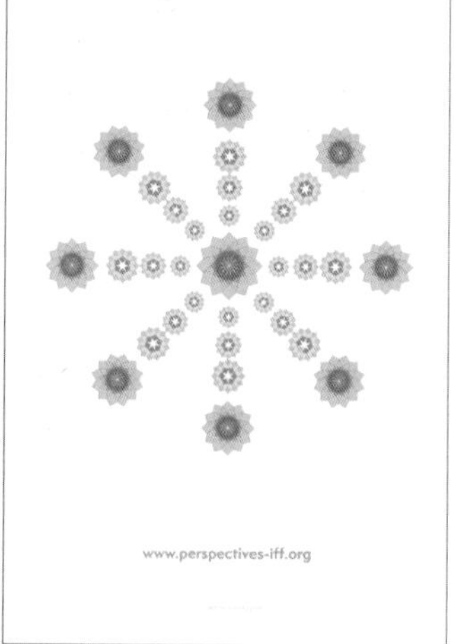

Perspectives – poster – Frank d. Lanterman – 2006

Dewey – website – Dewey Ambrosino – 2002

da sites
song poems lounge

da objects
fertile flesh croissant

Design currency – poster – aia – 2001

DESIGN CURRENCY

AIA California Council
1303 J Street, Suite 200
Sacramento, CA 95814-2935

THE 15TH AIACC

MONTEREY DESIGN CONFERENCE

April 6 – 8, 2001 Asilomar Conference Center
Pacific Grove, California

www.aiacc.org

Visit the AIACC web site for more information or email mdc2001@softcom.net

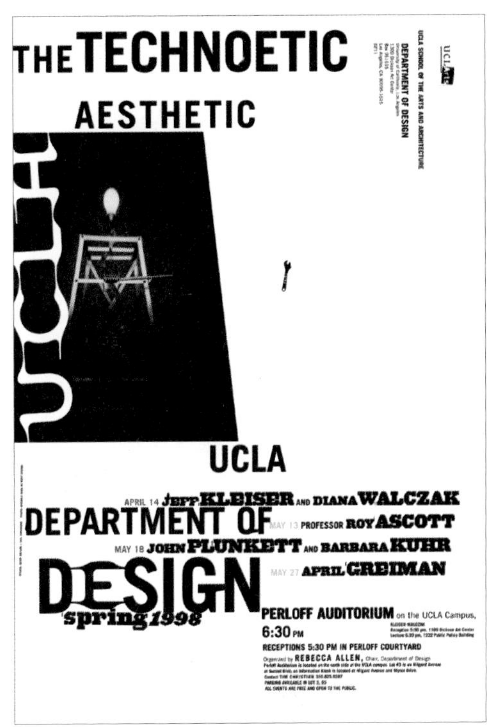

Tuesday, January 15
Co-Founder of the Nielsen Norman Group, Educator, & Writer.
The Design of Everyday Things.

Monday, January 28
Designer, Experimentalist, & Educator.
Exit-Level Designer.

Thursday, February 14
Curator, Writer, Educator, Graphic Designer, & Partner, Design/Writing/Research.
Skin: Surface, Substance and Design.

Monday, February 25
Co-Founder & General Manager of Westwood Studios, Game Designer.
Game Design Process, Examples From Westwood Studios.

Monday, March 11
Artist, Designer, & Curator.
The Museum of Jurassic Technology.

All lectures are at 6 p.m. in the EDA on the campus of UCLA.
Lectures are Free and Open to the Public.

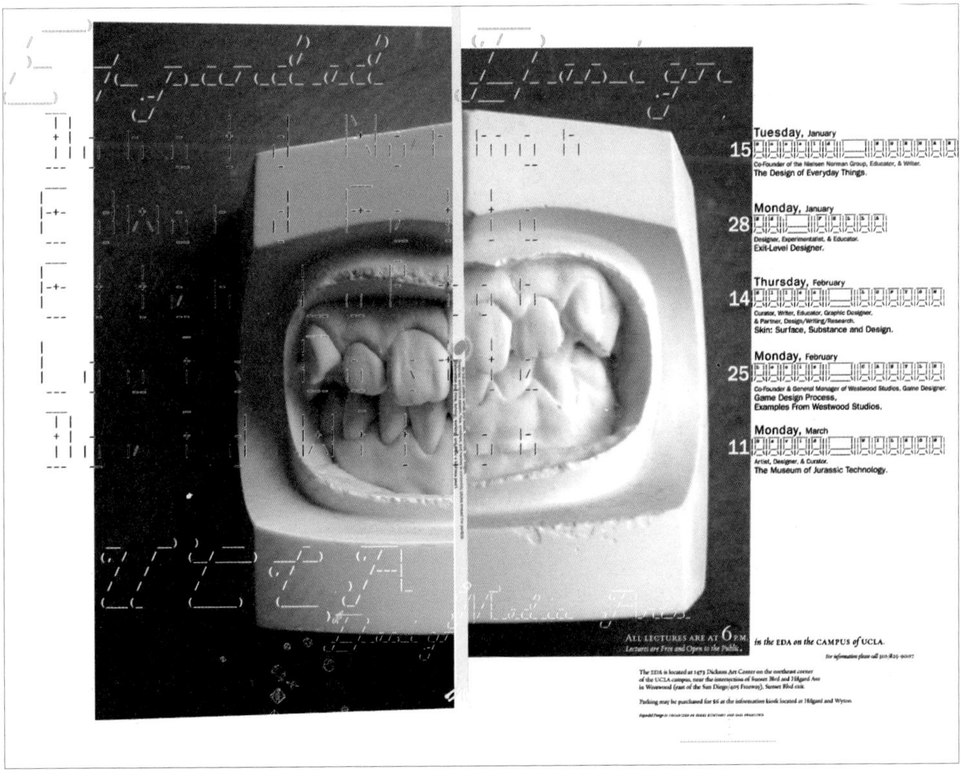

The technoetic aesthetic – poster – ucla – 2008/with Gail Swanlund

Gluekit is Christopher and Kathleen. They create illustrations, graphics and lettering, and also make products and work on interesting projects which sometimes are difficult to define. They think glue is good. They have worked for many nice people, including Wired, New York, GQ, Esquire, Rolling Stone, Spin, The New York Times, Readymade, Good, Nylon, Urban Outfitters, Entertainment Weekly, and Business Week.

Interview with Gluekit

1. What led to the formation of your studio?

Gluekit emerged from Christopher Sleboda's design practice in graduate school, building a bridge between the freelance work he had been doing since college and the methodology and ideas he had developed during the MFA Design program at Yale. When Gluekit opened its doors in 2002, Sleboda was able to merge grounded conceptual explorations with a pragmatic-driven approach for clients.

2. How many staff people does your studio have and what are their main working fields?

At present, Gluekit consists of two people: Christopher Sleboda and Kathleen Burns. Sleboda is the owner and Gluekit's principal designer. He handles art direction, graphic design, photography, and illustration. Burns' main areas are photo research, inventory management, writing, editing, and graphic production assistance. Brainstorming, bookkeeping and project management are cooperative tasks shared by both. Gluekit has evolved into a close partnership that focuses on our complementary strengths in order to maximize efficiency and to help keeping projects inspired, exciting, and fresh. The staffing model is flexible, however, and we are equipped to expand our staff as needed for client projects. Gluekit also welcomes opportunities for collaboration.

3. How does a regular working day at your studio look like, how is the day structured?

Work at our studio starts in the early morning, usually with cups of tea. A typical workday involves work in short shifts, a varied selection of music (we like indie pop, hardcore punk, and anything we can sing along with), and breaks for meals and snacks. We like making sure to include some free time into our schedule, and usually end up cutting up magazines, sketching, exercising with the studio's Wii, taking a quick bike ride, or walking along the path behind our studio space. It's really important to both of us to make things, and even on off-days we find ourselves sketching out ideas and brainstorming while travelling. Of course, in addition to the projects that we're hired to do, we have a number of self-directed projects that occupy our time. There's not a huge separation between work and play, since we both find a lot of enjoyment in the projects that we take on, and find that our creative playtime often spills back into our workflow in unexpected but serendipitous ways.

4. How much leisure time do you have during the year?

Gluekit keeps to a strict schedule of leisure. We take weeklong holidays during the summer and winter (even though, however, we often bring along a laptop or sketch pads to move projects along). In general, we tend to have flexible plans to respond to client needs, but we make a focused and conscious effort to keep ourselves stimulated. It's important to avoid burnout and to recharge. Gluekit believes that a rich cultural life can strengthen our work, imbuing it with a kind of immediacy and humour which is valuable. We receive inspiration from music and movies, from museum and gallery visits, from reading novels and magazines, and from taking part in University events in our neighbourhood. We're lucky to live close to a thriving academic community, affording us lots of opportunities to attend lectures and talks of all kinds. Since much of our work also responds to pop culture, we try to make time to indulge ourselves in that, too. But in the end, it's difficult to quantify leisure time – our work is fun, and our fun oftentimes is work. That's one of the joys working in a small studio environment.

T-shirt designs – t-shirts – personal project – 2006

5. What business areas do your clients mainly come from? Is the number of your clients increasing or rather declining?

Gluekit clients tend to be centred on the publishing industry, and we do regular illustration work for a number of major U.S.-based magazines such as GQ, Wired, The New York Times, and Esquire. Our past clients have also included book publishing houses, music labels, and museums or other cultural heritage organizations. We have seen a marked increase in the number of our clients over the past two years which we hope will continue.

6. Do you have a specific corporate philosophy or maybe a mission statement like other companies, which is reflected in the way you steer the studio's course?

Our mission is to create work that is good, responsible, and intelligent. The studio's name, "Gluekit," references the cut and paste mechanics of historical graphic design processes, and the contemporary nature of ad hoc imagery – how the juxtaposition and re-composition of elements can transform, challenge and subvert expectations and messages, revealing the unanticipated. Today, Gluekit strives to inject both a sense of rupture and dislocation, as well as a sense of connectivity and cohesion, into the projects that come our way. Much of our work is a purposeful collision of fragments that refines and deliberately exposes latent connections. We are committed to bringing a sense of play to fragmentation, and to exploring the complexities of image-making and image-reproduction.

7. What, from your point of view, makes the difference between a small studio and big company?

It seems that a small company can really do whatever it wants; big companies may have to take on projects in order to sustain operations and make ends meet. It's possible that the passion and energy which a small studio brings into projects might be diffused within a larger organization andcertainly, that the vision of an individual might ultimately be compromised Perhaps there's also a sense that a big company might be impersonal, or less focused on smaller jobs from lesser-known clients. But of course, these are generalizations and there are very possibly small studios and big companies for whom the reverse is true. Neither of us has ever worked for a big design company so we can only speculate on the differences. Gluekit is a small studio, not because that size is a specific goal, but because that's what we are at the moment. What's important to us is that we do work that we are happy with and that the client is happy with. For us, at the moment, that seems most attainable in a small studio environment, where we can focus and tailor our work to the clients we currently have.

8. What kind of advantages and disadvantages does a small studio have compared to a big company?

When a small studio works for a client, there's definitely a sense of personalized service. A small studio also has agility, and flexibility – Gluekit, for instance, doesn't have a huge overhead, so we are able to take on projects we feel strongly about which don't necessarily pay well. Projects are handled carefully and personally. There's a Gluekit feeling to everything being produced by our studio – a kind of consistency and tone that infuses our work, even when we're building out the client's vision. There's no aesthetic desaturation that might happen with "project trickle-down" in a big company, where projects and clients are passed to different teams or where there may be a number of people working on the same project. For us, a small studio also provides us with room for experimentation. We're not filling a specific design niche within a large company, so we are free to explore new avenues and introduce new techniques whenever we feel inclined. On the other hand, we do have to think creatively when approaching specific projects because we don't necessarily have the reservoir of resources that a bigger studio might have. And of course, we are always looking for ways to profile our studio and build relationships with new clients – but it's difficult to balance that effort when we are absorbed in projects we've been hired to do.

9. What is your idea about the future of small studios? Do you think that small studios do not have any other choice but to expand in order to survive in these times of globalization?

Small studios will likely exist as long as there are projects and clients looking for fresh perspectives, individualized service, and distinctive aesthetics that aren't necessarily present within a stereotypical monolithic design company. Just considering the Long Tail phenomenon, which predicates the success of services and products catered to minority tastes and the growth of catered markets, it certainly seems like there are and will be more opportunities than ever for small studios to establish themselves and flourish. There's also a certain cultural caché associated with small studios – a kind of boutique design culture that makes working one-on-one with a designer who owns their own studio appealing to clients.

10. Please describe and elaborate on the goals or plans that you have for your studio for the next five years?

In 2007, Gluekit launched our passion project: Part of It (www.partofit.org). Part of It is a charity-based t-shirt initiative that works with artists to design products about causes they want to support and draw attention to. A portion of the profits from each sale goes to the charity or non-profit identified by the artist. Over the next half decade, we hope to grow and nurture Part of It by inviting more artists to participate, broadening our range of designs and products, promoting more causes and charities, and scaling up the entire enterprise. Over the next five years, we would also like to: mount a show of our work, design more books, illustrate like crazy, do a cover for a major magazine, design a magazine ourselves, launch our imprint, Good Boys and Girls, be happy, be healthy, travel often, learn constantly, and take on many new challenges new challenges!

Detroit rock city – magazine – clear magazine – 2005

That's great,
it starts with an
earthquake,
birds and snakes,
an aeroplane
and Lenny Bruce
is not afraid.

Hurry down,
Doomsday.
The bugs are
taking over.

Doomsday – photography – faesthetic magazine – 2007

Marvelous – poster – Yale school of art – 2003

Fragments bag – bag – personal project – 2004

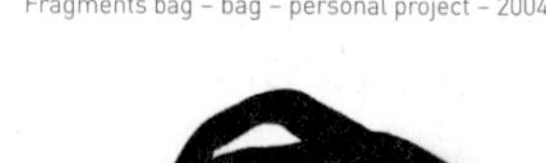

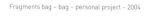

Road to ruins – magazine – wired magazine – 2007

Grain Studio

team:
Imaya Wong
Hsueh-Yin Lin
contact:
33-1 Bangsar Heights
59100 Kuala. Lumpur, Malaysia
T + 60 3 22872208
imaya.wong@gmail.com

Grain Studio is a creative seed which has been lovingly nurtured by its founder Imaya Wong – the inspirational soul of the studio – since 2006. Grain Studio consists of a dedicated and skilful team of two full-time designers, each of them embracing a unique style of creativity. They possess a balanced measure of the concept of "Yin & Yang" – one with a keen eye on designing details and a deep feeling for Chinese literature, art and music; while the other holds an in-depth perspective on contemporary visual dynamics, publication, poster design, and art-based projects. Grain Studio's philosophy is inspired by William Blake's "Auguries of Innocence" and its line "To see the World in a Grain of Sand", which allows them to see the "big picture" in a gritty grain – be it a seed or a speck of dust. The grain is small but totally significant. Taken from the design introspect: no matter how small or simple an idea might be, it can become a great solution. This has developed into their positioning as a "boutique design studio". It allows them to organically collaborate with associate teams of specialists given the case that a project requires distinct fields of creative expertise. The resources encompass photographers, typographers, illustrators, artists, writers and publishers. Grain Studio's aim is to deliver cutting-edge and thoughtful design. At the beginning of Imaya Wong's career as a young designer, her works had been exhibited in critically acclaimed local, regional, and international graphic design events in Singapore, Hong Kong, China, Taiwan, Switzerland, France, Czech Republic, Poland, Ukraine, and the USA. Many of her works have also been featured and published in Communication Arts, New Graphic Volume, The Rise of Asian Design, All Men are Brothers and Poster Collection 13: Typo China.

Art 1000 – postcards – valentine willie fine art – 2006

Interview with Grain Studio

1. What led to the formation of your studio?

After working for more than seven years at three local design companies, it was an eventual or normal step to try and set up my own design studio. The seed of Grain Studio was planted in 2006, a creative design and art studio. We specialize in print-based designs, including visual identity, publication, art projects and information design.

2. How many staff people does your studio have and what are their main working fields?

There are two permanent designers including myself, but when the studio is overflowed with too many projects, one or two freelance designers will be engaged to help out. The studio also tends to collaborate with another small studio to work on bigger corporate identity projects. Each designer's role is quite different – Yin has a fair working experience, and she started with me from the beginning. She acquires a keen eye on design details and greater interests in Chinese literature, art and music. As for myself, I have a vast experience in visual identity, publication, poster design and art-based projects. I have participated in many international graphic design competitions and exhibitions and have as well won numerous awards for my poster designs. Currently, I am also teaching part time at a local university.

3. How does a regular working day at your studio look like, how is the day structured?

The working hours are quite flexible. The first half of the day is mostly spent on checking emails and answering calls, whereas the second half is spent on designing and sometimes meeting with clients. During less busy days, we tend to have a longer lunch break, and whenever we feel like it, we hang out at cafés, bookshops, galleries, or watch a movie. We try to make our daily routine a little less mundane.

4. How much leisure time do you have during a year?

It depends. I try to get away three or four times to an island whenever I can. Short trips in-between projects are easily organized as we only need one designer in the studio. The studio will also be closed at the end of the year for a long holiday.

5. Which business areas do your clients mainly come from? Is the number of your clients increasing or rather declining?

We started out mainly with hotels and resorts, food and beverage, and publication projects. Over the last year, we have established a good relationship with some publication and art gallery clients – designing books and art catalogues is our main scope of work. We do not get new clients very often, however. It is more important that our existing clients are comfortable working with us and provide us with more projects. Having said this, it can also lead to a bad situation if we would stop getting regular projects from them. That's why I constantly have to look out for potential new clients. Occasionally, we also get jobs from clients' recommendation.

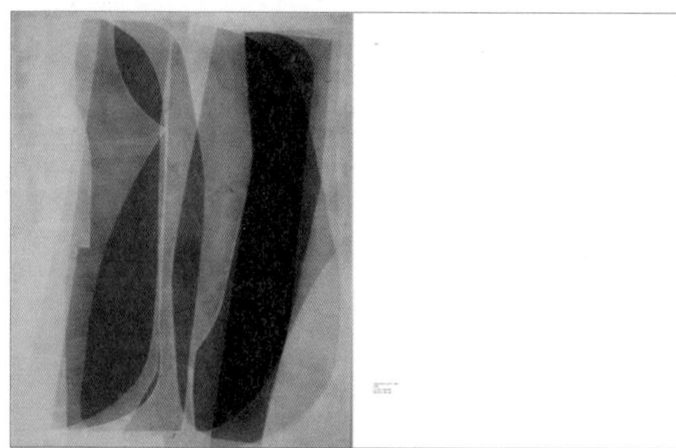

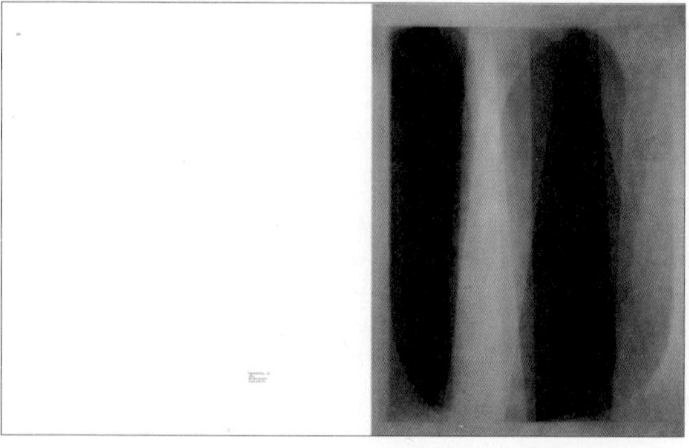

Romulo Olazo: the truth is still in the beautiful – artist catalogue – valentine willie fine art – 2007

6. Do you have a specific corporate philosophy or maybe a mission statement like other companies, which is reflected in the way you steer the studio's course?

Grain Studio was set up to bring together a gifted garden of talents – designers, artists, photographers, writers, who bring along added creative strength and dynamism, and work closely on high-quality design projects. To me, a grain – of rice, seed and dust – is so small and yet significant. This is my understanding from Eastern teachings. In the sense of design this means that no matter how small or simple an idea might be, it can become a great solution.

7. What, from your point of view, makes the difference between a small studio and a big company?

Small studios or "boutique" design studios are more selective on their clients and projects, and thus, tend to view themselves as niche businesses, more cutting-edge and less commercialized. The term "boutique" also suggests more individualized, one-to-one service and better design quality.

8. What kind of advantages and disadvantages does a small studio have compared to a big company?

Advantages: First, the costs of running a small studio are much lower. Second, there is less hierarchy in the organizational structure of a small studio. Third, flexible working hours and holiday breaks.

Disadvantages: None. I always preferred working in smaller design companies before setting up my own small studio.

9. What is your idea about the future of small studios? Do you think that small studios do not have any other choice but to expand in order to survive in these times of globalization?

I think that more and more small studios are forming as a form of rejection of corporations taking over the world. No doubt, many designers have no other choices but to attach themselves to big companies, but for those who can afford to make a choice, those who do not mind taking risks, those who are capable of running their own businesses, and those who dislike big companies or agencies, a small studio is the way to go. Clients will start to realize that small studios are more affordable and can deliver better services and design quality. Globalization will only create a greater need for small, individualized studios.

Uzen – book (unpublished) – uzen – 2006

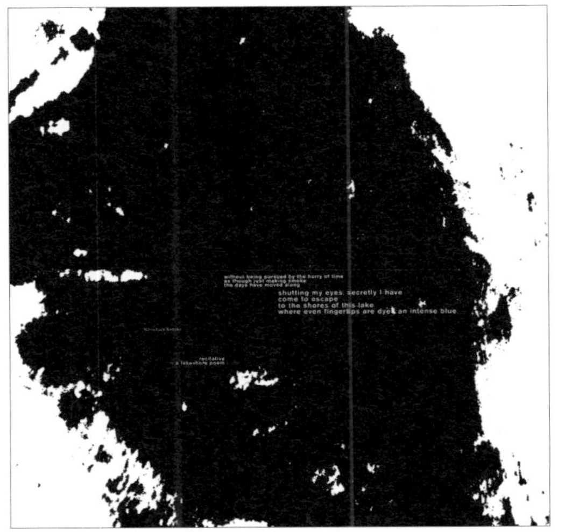

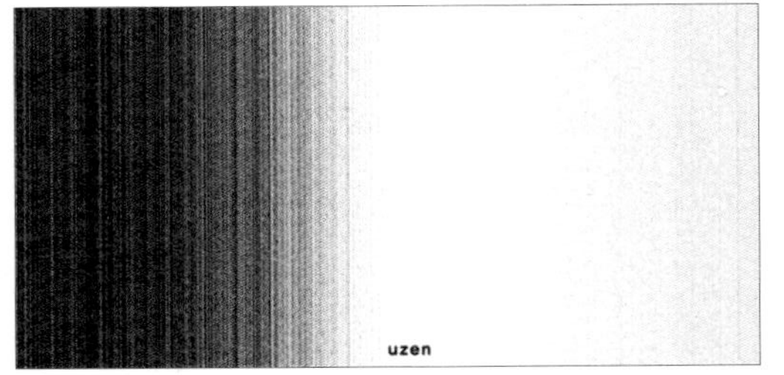

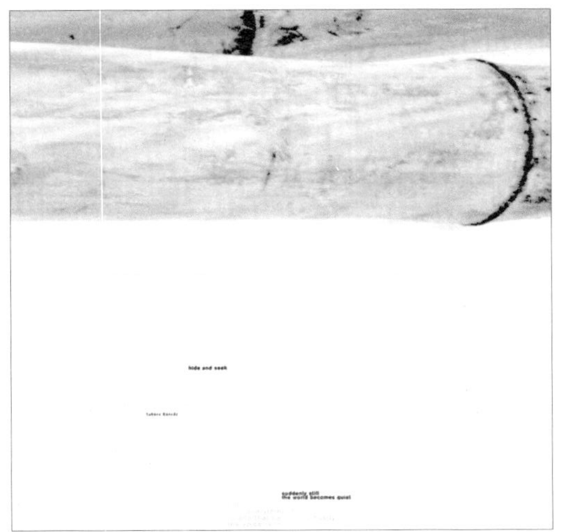

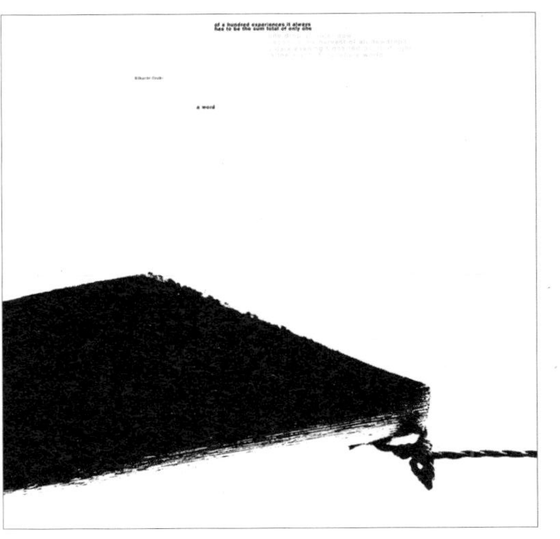

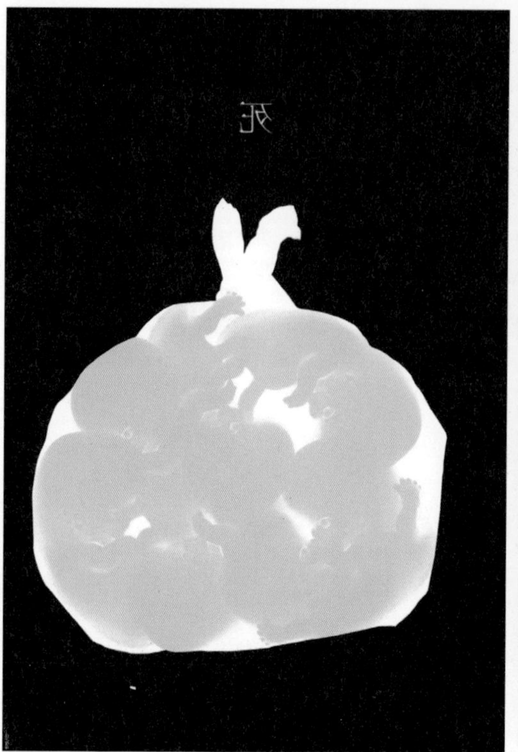

To live – poster – self promotion – 2006

Peekaboo!: jendela art group – postcard – Valentine Willie fine art – 2007

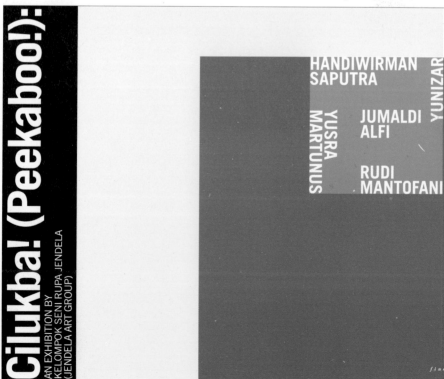

Cilukba! (Peekaboo!):

AN EXHIBITION BY
KELOMPOK SENI RUPA JENDELA
(JENDELA ART GROUP)

HANDIWIRMAN
SAPUTRA

YUNIZAR

YUSRA
MARTUNUS

JUMALDI
ALFI

RUDI
MANTOFANI

VALENTINE
WILLIE
fine ART

genes's

Genesis – identity – genesis colour separation – 2006

10. Please describe and elaborate on the goals or plans that you have for your studio for the next five years?

I have a lot of plans for my studio and myself for the next five years. What is clear to me is that I will continue to keep my studio small, and to work on book projects. I have always enjoyed designing books. If all goes well, Grain Studio will get more involved in collaborating with an art-based team to work on art projects. It has always been my goal to merge art and design, to cross boundaries and to contribute to the local art and design communities. I am also looking forward to publishing our own collectable items.

Gilding the lily: everyday portraits of Malaysian women (photographer: Sc Shekar) – book – ministry of women, family and community development, Malaysia – 2007

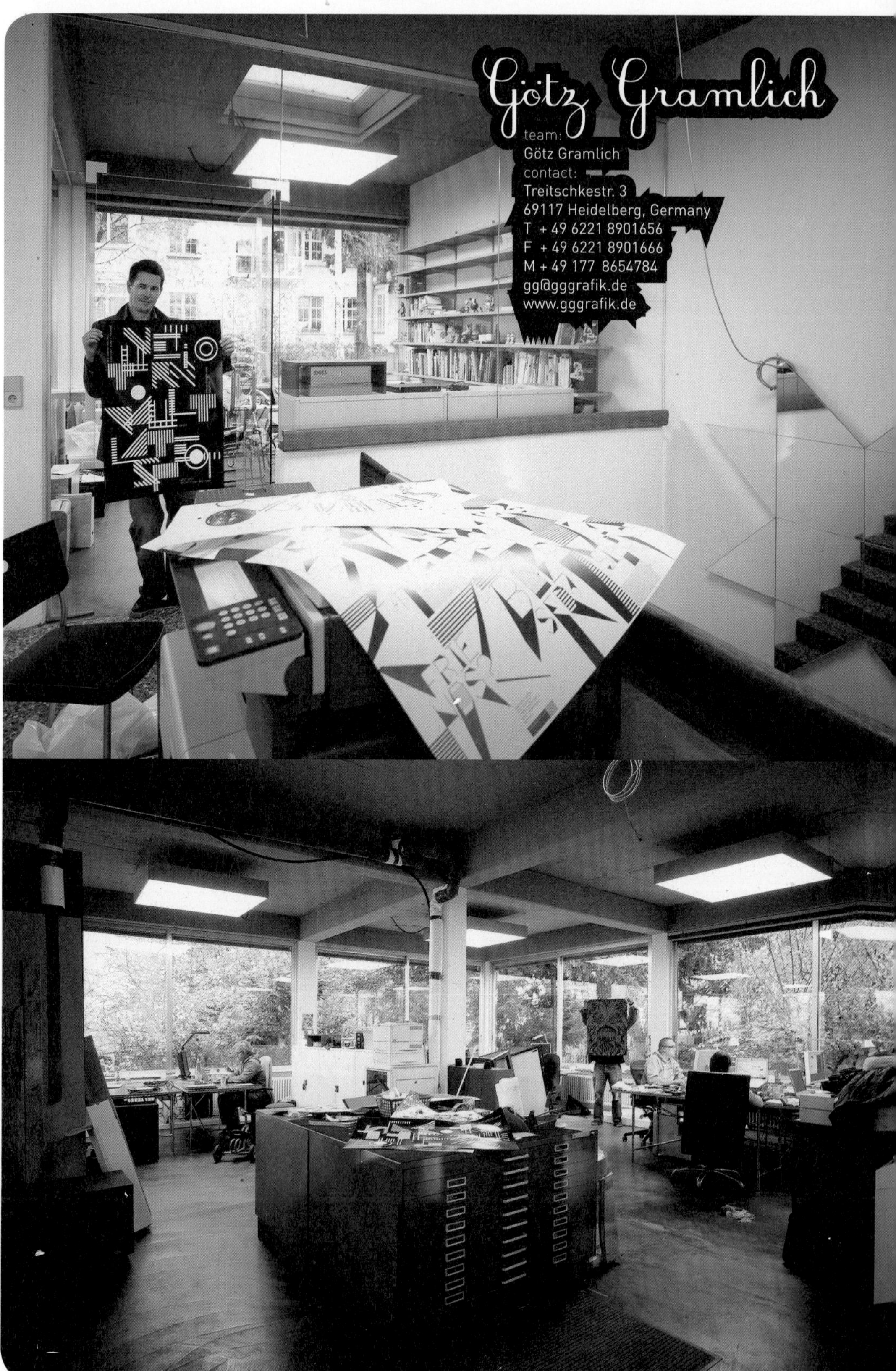
Götz Gramlich
team:
Götz Gramlich
contact:
Treitschkestr. 3
69117 Heidelberg, Germany
T + 49 6221 8901656
F + 49 6221 8901666
M + 49 177 8654784
gg@gggrafik.de
www.gggrafik.de

Götz Gramlich formed ggg design in 2005. Niklaus Troxler was his diploma mentor, and he has a degree in Communication Design from the Darmstadt University of Applied Sciences in his pocket. Besides working for some major clients and agencies in Germany, Gramlich has earned international critical acclaim for his poster designs – both for commercial and non-profit purposes – and magazine covers. Bold, fearless and universal in their graphic vocabulary, Gramlich's designs speak an easy-to-understand, eye-catching language that can be termed iconographic in its simplicity and its impact of message.

Interview with Götz Gramlich

1. What led to the formation of your studio?

ggrafik is one of several smaller studios in our shared office space, known as "TDrei". We are all independent, yet work together on various projects. Originally, a good friend and long-term colleague of mine rented the space. I had just returned from a long stay in Switzerland, where I completed my diploma thesis at the studio Troxler in Willisau. He asked me whether I wanted to get on board. It was a perfect start and a decision I don't regret.

2. How many staff people does your studio have and what are their main working fields?

gggrafik is actually a one-man show. But we have quite a few of them at TDrei. I work a lot with Ronald from infotectures and with Romero Steinhauser from romerror design – which diversifies the range of services I can cover. From the concept and draft to the final product we do all sorts of projects for all forms of media.

3. How does a regular working day at your studio look like, how is the day structured?

The day normally starts at 9 a.m. with a cup of coffee. The mornings are usually reserved for all the bureaucracy: opening post, reading and answering e-mails, packing packets, paying bills, writing invoices, doing taxes, etc. At around 1 p.m. we go for lunch or cook something; then I take my dog for a walk. Sometimes we play ping pong or Wii in the meeting room. After that, it's time to concentrate on work; often until long after 8 p.m. and on weekends.

4. How much leisure time do you have during a year?

Long holidays are something of a rarity, but short trips are taken frequently. In general, there is little leisure time, but we make up for that with the fun we are having at work. Sometimes it feels like a school outing or like a playing group.

5. Which business areas do your clients mainly come from?

Clients come from all over the place: from renowned international corporations to small, local culture venues.

Is the number of your clients increasing or rather declining?

Increasing.

6. Do you have a specific corporate philosophy or maybe a mission statement like other companies, which is reflected in the way you steer the studio's course?

The general credo is: If it feels good, it is good.

Trolls – poster – fun fiction Heidelberg – 2006

Going all the way – poster – loft Ludwigshafen – 2007

Body moving – poster – halle02 Heidelberg – 2007

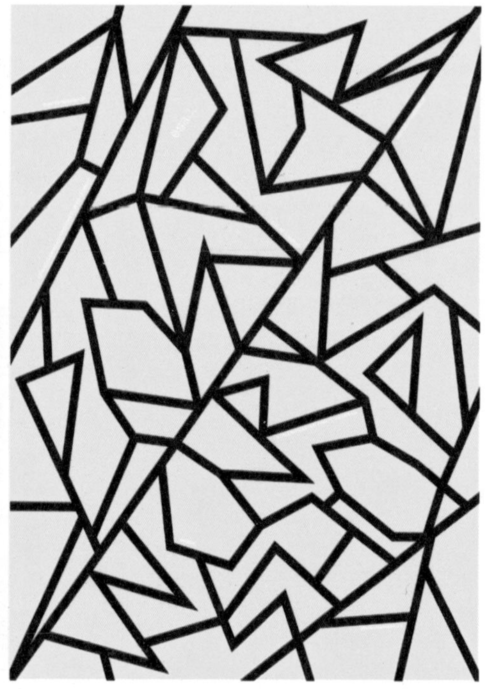

Posterworkshop – poster – esad amiens – 2008

7. What, from your point of view, makes the difference between a small studio and a big company?

The greatest advantage of a small studio lies in the short (communication) distances. Ideas aren't as diluted because they don't have to pass through so many instances. That's the sort of thing I normally experience working as a freelancer for larger agencies. And obviously, the great difference is the independence you enjoy as a freelancer.

8. What kind of advantages and disadvantages does a small studio have compared to a big company?

See above.

9. What is your idea about the future of small studios?

As long as there are individual graphic designers and independent-thinking artists, small studios will pop up like mushrooms.

Do you think that small studios do not have any other choice but to expand in order to survive in these times of globalization?

No. After all, it's the quality of the work that is decisive, not the number of people who participated. And if we do need extra hands for specific projects, we can always collaborate with other small (specialized) agencies or studios on a temporary basis.

10. Please describe and elaborate on the goals or plans that you have for your studio for the next five years?

To keep on enjoying my work as much as I do now, and to continue learning new things.

Suite city oasis – poster – suite Mannheim – 2006

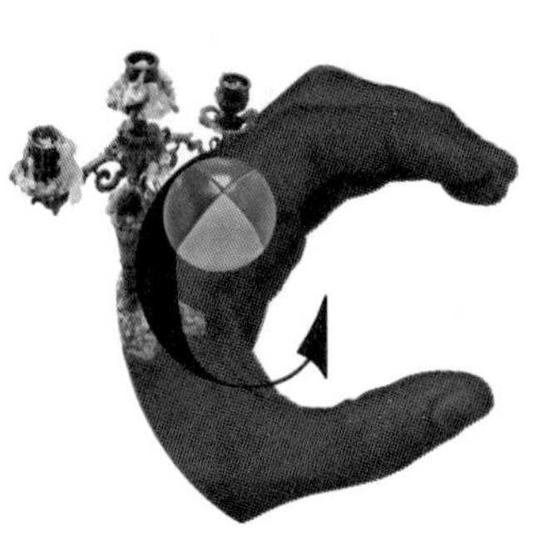

KABARETT & KLEINKUNSTFESTIVAL

KARLSTORBAHNHOF HEIDELBERG

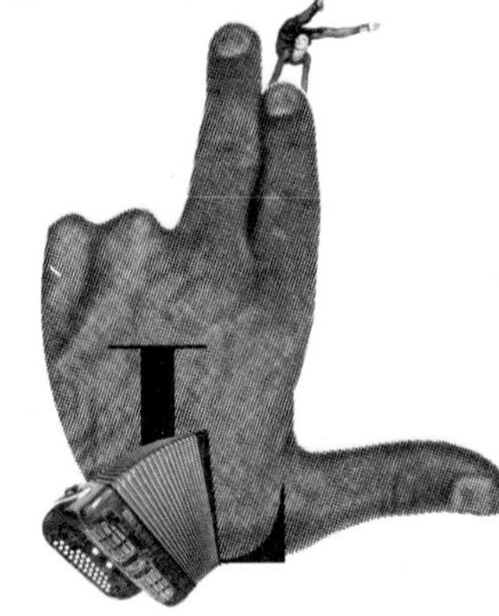
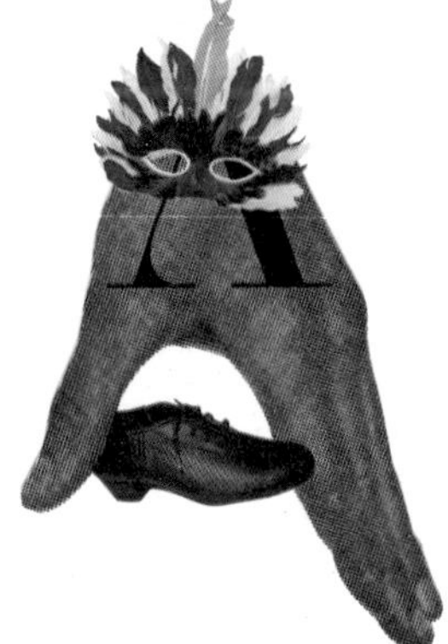

DONNERSTAG 17.01 – SAMSTAG 02.02

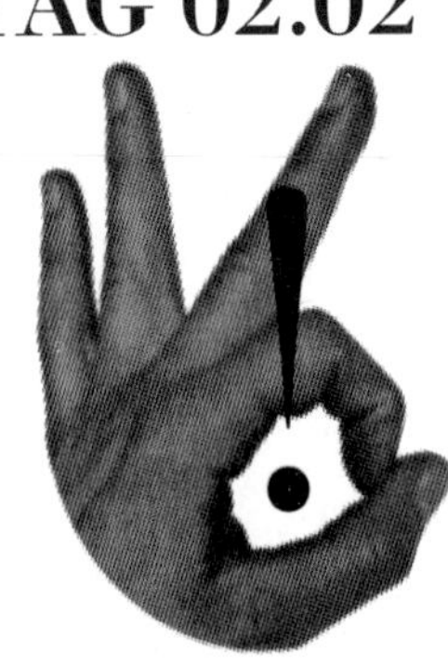

Carambolage – poster – karlstorbahnhof Heidelberg – 2007

JET TURINO AND HIS
FABULOUS DANCE MASHINE
FR.31.08
SA.01.09
PROJEKTIONEN VON
GGGROM!
VAULT
LATE SPOT
JAZZFESTIVAL WILLISAU
Latespotposter – poster – jazzfestival Willisau – 2007

SEEBASE

GOING ALL THE WAY

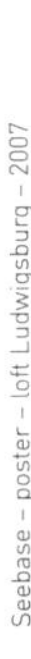

Seebase – poster – loft Ludwigsburg – 2007

Hi
team:
Megi Zumstein
Claudio Barandun
contact:
Neustadtstrasse 28
6003 Luzern, Switzerland
T + 41 41 3604366
megi.zumstein@hi-mail.ch
claudio.barandun@hi-mail.ch
www.hi-web.ch

Hi was founded in January 2007 by Megi Zumstein and Claudio Barandun. Megi, born in 1973, studied Visual Communication at the University of Art + Design in Zurich (HGKZ). Her diploma thesis "Visualization of Language" (2001) has been awarded several prizes. A grant of the Federal Office of Culture brought her to London and to work with Graphic Thought Facility (www.graphicthoughtfacility.com) in 2002/03. After her return to Zurich she worked with Bringolf Irion Voegeli (www.bivgrafik.ch) until November 2006. Since 2004, she teaches at the University of Art + Design in Lucerne (HGKL) covering the field of graphic gesign. She participated in exhibitions in Zurich (CH), Sarnen (CH), Paris (FR), Tehran (IR), and Ingolstadt (GER). Claudio Barandun, born in 1979, studied graphic design at the University of Art + Design in Lucerne, and started his first company "Monster & Bauchweh" (www.monsterundbauchweh.ch) together with Michel Steiner after his graduation in 2003. Their clients included the Universities of Applied Sciences of central Switzerland and different small private companies. Some of Claudio's posters have been awarded among the "100-best-posters in Germany, Austria and Switzerland", the "ADC Prize Switzerland", and the "Poster-Biennial in Tehran". He is also the co-editor of the comic magazine "Strapazin". Both of them are mainly working on book and poster design as well as signage systems for clients such as Lucerne University of Applied Sciences and Arts, Museum of Art Lucerne, Modemuseum Antwerpen, Zurich University of the Arts, and Gaswerk Winterthur.

Excerpts of diploma works – book – hochschule für soziale arbeit – 2007

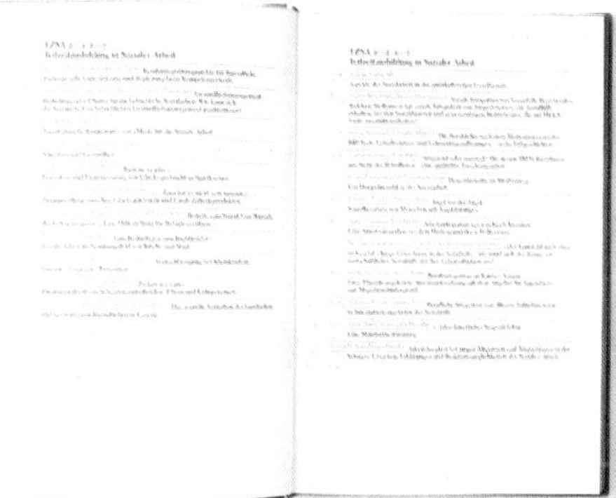

Interview with Hi

1. What led to the formation of your studio?

Our love and passion for graphic design.

2. How many staff people does your studio have and what are their main working fields?

We are a pair and share most of our projects. We either work collectively on the same project or we criticize each other up to the point at which both of us are satisfied with the results.

3. How does a regular working day at your studio look like, how is the day structured?

We usually begin at 9 a.m., reading post and e-mails, and start working on our projects. In between we play table top soccer with the people sharing the studio rooms with us. If required, days are extended into the nights and work weeks into the weekends.

4. How much leisure time do you have during a year?

Since this was our first year, we cannot give an average number. During the first six months our working hours were quite regular, while in the second half of the year we almost never left the studio. We just stopped counting the hours at some point.

5. Which business areas do your clients mainly come from?

Educational institutions, hosts and organizers from the cultural sector, small independent companies, arch tects, public buildings, etc.

Is the number of your clients increasing or rather decl ning?

Our studio is only one year old, so the number of clients simply has to be on the rise.

6. Do you have a specific corporate philosophy or maybe a mission statement like other companies, which is reflected in the way you steer the studio's course?

Calling it a real "corporate philosophy" would probably be exaggerated. We have, however, defined a certain guideline for ourselves saying that on every assignment we take, we will search for individual, modern answers to the questions raised, naturally reflected from our own personal viewpoint. Our goal is to improve with each project, and, if that is possible at all, not to repeat ourselves. The amount of joy, curiosity and accuracy developed by us during a designing process shall be openly visible in the solutions we come up with – and the most important thing is that we hopefully will never stop loving our job.

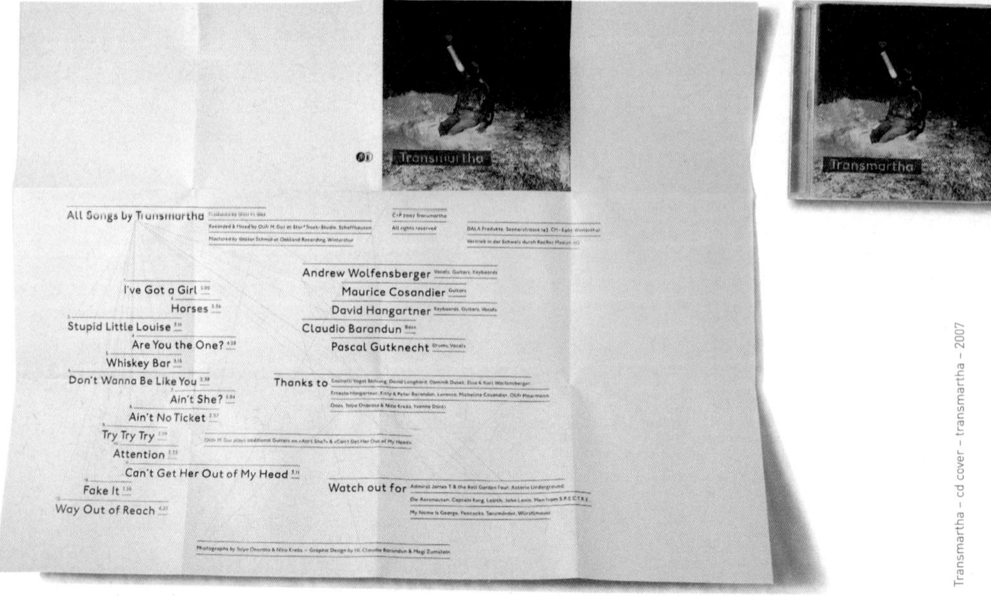

Transmartha – cd cover – transmartha – 2007

7. What, from your point of view, makes the difference between a small studio and a big company?

The structures are different: In big-sized agencies, the employees are more specialized, working rather team-orientated, structured in a more thoroughly way, one could say. But since both of us have never worked in large companies, we can only speculate about that point.

8. What kind of advantages and disadvantages does a small studio have compared to a big company?

As already mentioned, we assume that small-sized bureaus might be more flexible or able to react faster, because there is less handling time required in the face of new projects. On the other hand, this implies that in comparison our work time capacity reaches its limits rather quickly. For that reason, we focus on other areas than the big agencies, build project teams outside of our studio, and ultimately work on smaller projects.

Top – exhibition catalogue – exhibition top of central Switzerland, museum of art Lucerne – 2007

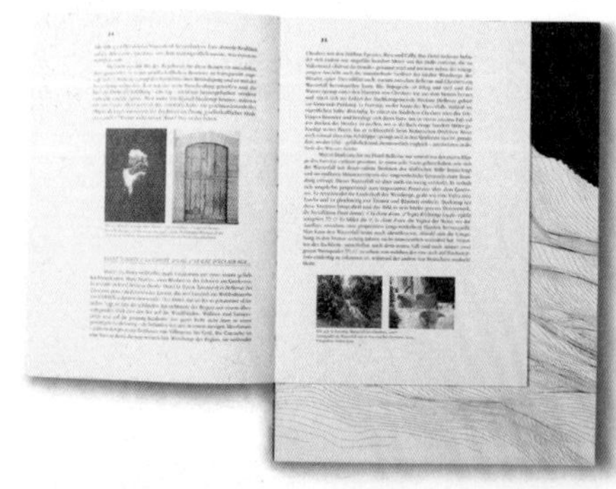

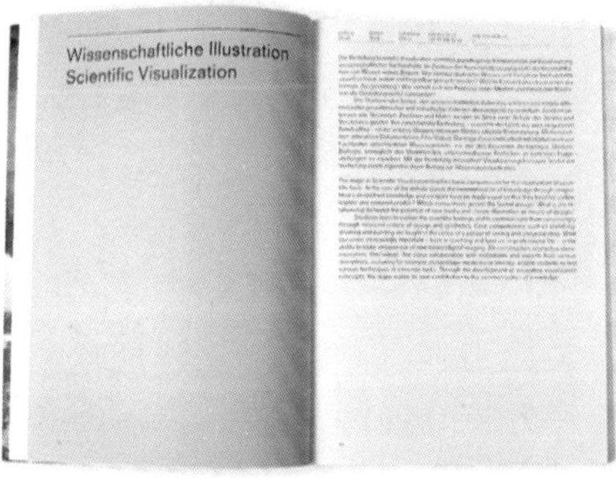

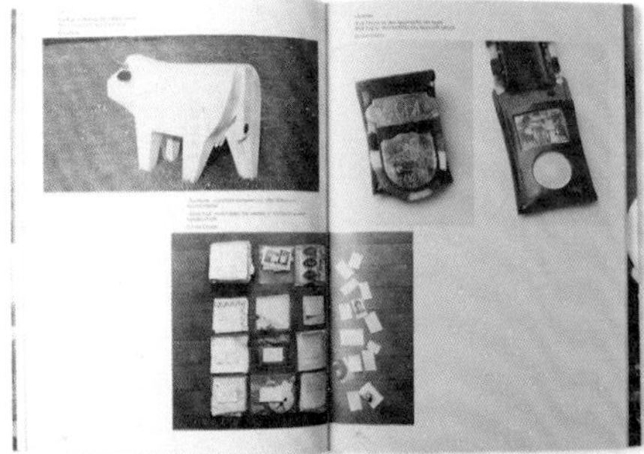

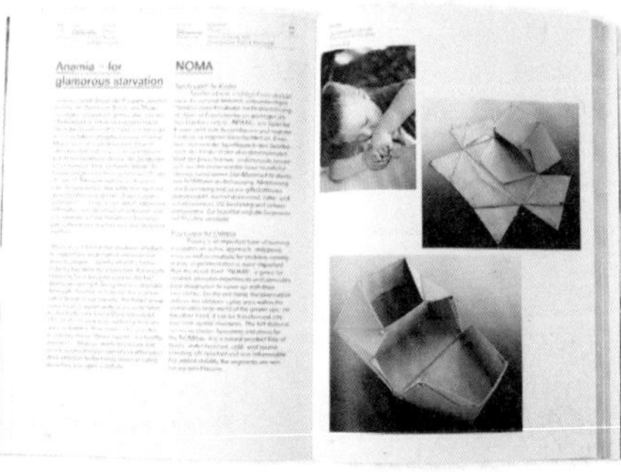

Design_Z 2007 – yearbook – Zurich university of the arts – 2007

Invitation for series of lectures first thursday – invitation – Lucerne university of applied sciences and arts – 2005/2006

Camp1 – cd cover – camp1 – 2005

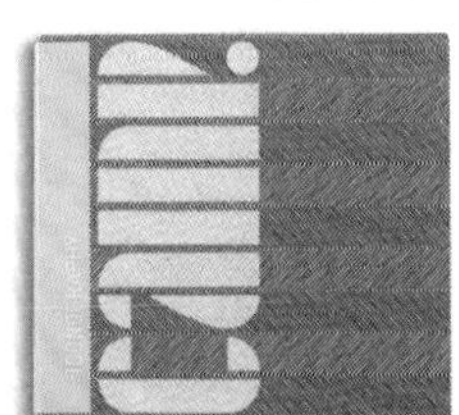

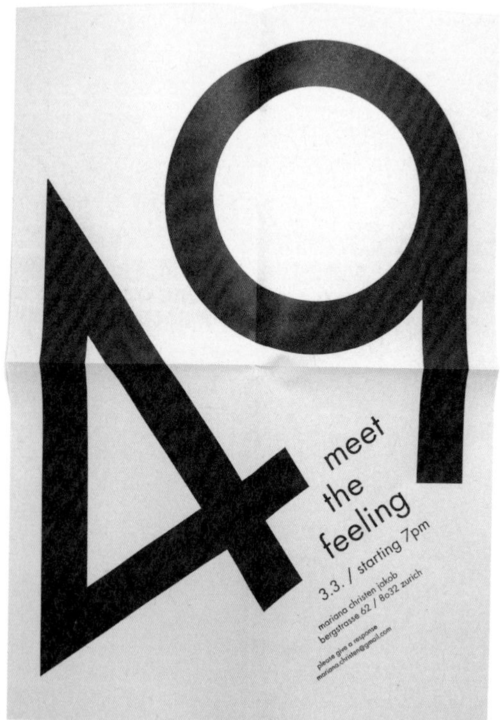

9. What is your idea about the future of small studios? Do you think that small studios do not have any other choice but to expand in order to survive in these times of globalization?

Being small and agile is a realistic survival strategy. Customized, individualized solutions do not depend on the size of a business enterprise. When a customer is looking for something different than standardized products, the investments in time and effort for small and big agencies are almost the same. The market is both global and local, and there is a lot of work to be done.

10. Please describe and elaborate on the goals or plans that you have for your studio for the next five years?

We are already working on expanding our repertoire in the areas of book & poster design, and signage. In the long run, we want to have the liberty to realize more self-initiated projects. Our idea is to operate actively within our local environment, but also to become internationally involved.

Invitation for a 49th birthday – invitation – Mariana Christen Jakob – 2006

HOCH
SCHUL
STUDIUM
UNDER
GRADUATE
COURSES

Prospectus 06 – prospect – Lucerne university of applied sciences and arts – 2006/2007

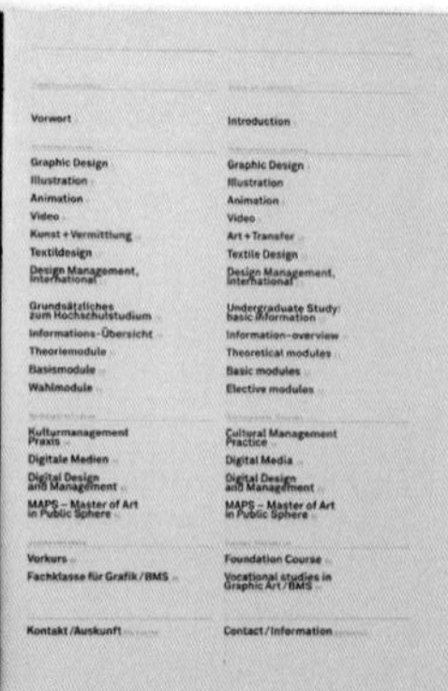

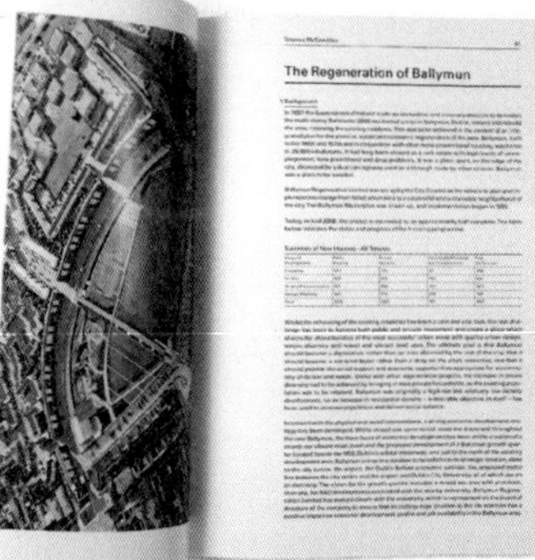

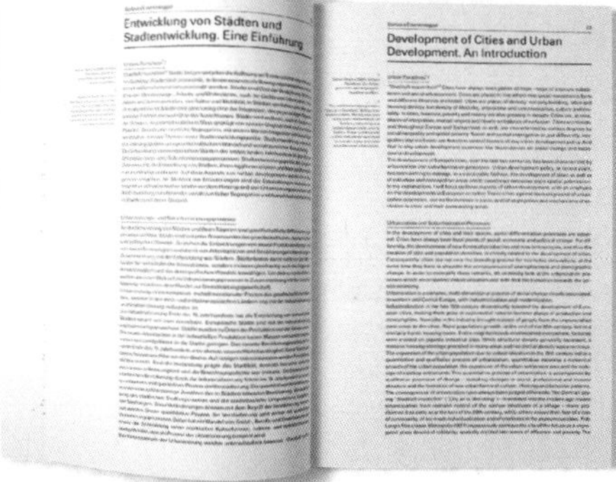

Reader of workshops – prospect – Lucerne university of applied sciences and arts – 2006/2007

Flyer for Lucerne university of applied sciences and arts – flyer – Lucerne university of applied sciences and arts – 2005

Homework

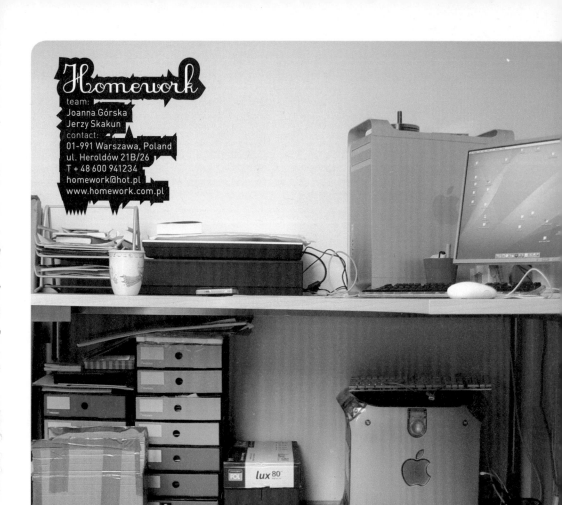

team:
Joanna Górska
Jerzy Skakun
contact:
01-991 Warszawa, Poland
ul. Heroldów 21B/26
T + 48 600 941234
homework@hot.pl
www.homework.com.pl

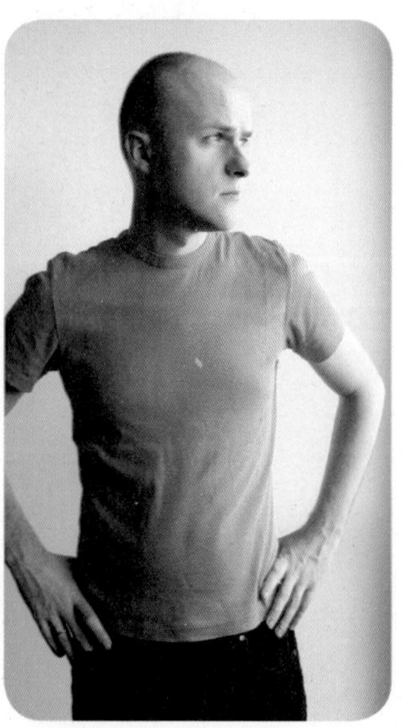

Homework – Joanna Górska and Jerzy Skakun both graduated from the painting faculty of Fine Arts Academy in Gdansk. Since 2003 they have been working in their own graphic studio named Homework. They design posters, work on printing graphics, and graphic works for cultural events. Their works were exhibited (among other places) in Paris, Berlin, Oslo, Mexico, Sofia, and Hong Kong, and have won prizes in several competitions. Their most important achievements are: the sliver medal at the Poster Biennial in Mexico, Grand Prix for the Akobi calendar in VIDICAL competition, 1st prize at the AMS competition "Be wise, read the press", and the Józef Mroszczak Honorary Award at the XXI Poster Biennial in Warsaw. Joanna Górska and Jerzy Skakun are working with cultural institutions such as: the Polish Theater in Bydgoszcz, Vivarto, the advertising agency Mañana, and the Pulaski Museum in Warsaw.

Interview with Homework

1. What led to the formation of your studio?

We set up our studio in 2003. Previously, Joanna had been working in another studio, and I used to work in a small advertising agency. Although I considered the people in that agency to be good friends of mine, I didn't like working there, because I could not do what I really wanted to do. There was plenty of work, but it was done according to manuals. There was no room left for experiments. Apart from this regular work, we had some additional projects, and soon I realized that we did not have enough time to work on them, especially because we could only work on them in the afternoons. So Joanna left the agency she was working at and set up our own studio named Homework, and I joined her soon after that.

2. How many staff people does your studio have and what are their main working fields?

There are just the two of us. Privately, we are a couple. We both work on the same projects or swap jobs sometimes with one exception – Jerzy takes most of the pictures and does the bulk of illustrative work. Joanna works on text and layouts. Sometimes we cooperate with other people when it comes to web work, redaction, or DTP work.

3. How does a regular working day at your studio look like, how is the day structured?

As long as the studio is also our home, our private life is mixed up with graphic design. We usually start working at 9am and finish around 4 or 5 pm. In case of a project with a tight deadline, we also work in the evenings, but we are trying to avoid that. We have one break (for about 15 minutes) around 1 or 2 pm.

47th Krakow film festival – poster – Krakow film foundation – 2007

Charlie Chaplin/the great dictator – movie poster – vivarto – 2008

Charlie Chaplin/the kid – movie poster – vivarto – 2008

Motortown – poster – Polski theatre in Bydgoszcz – 2007 About the animals – poster – Polski theatre in Bydgoszcz – 2007

Movies of the world – movie festival poster – mañ – 2007

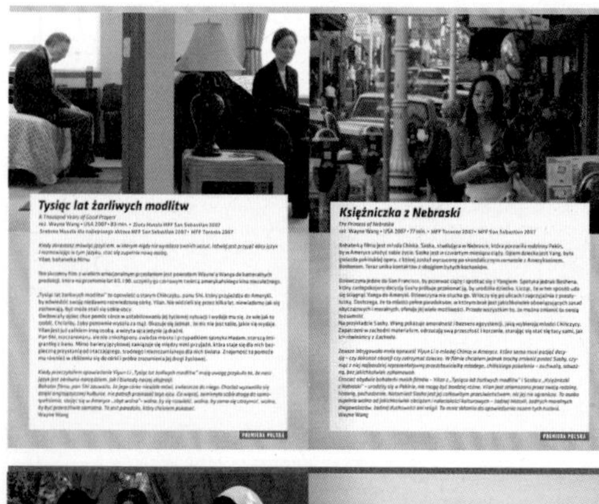

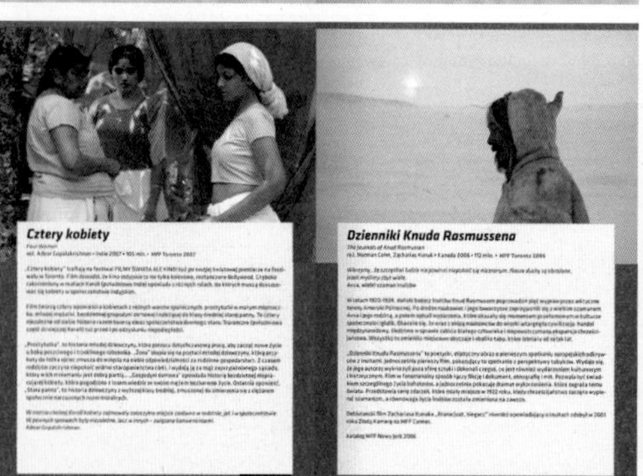

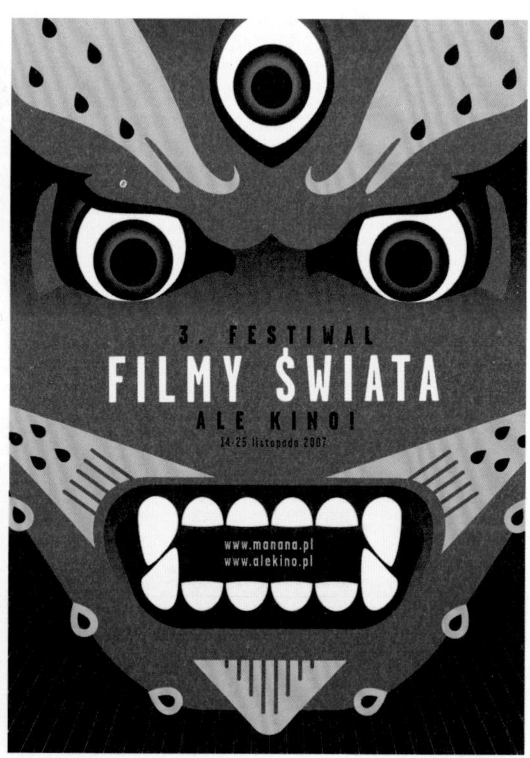

4. How much leisure time do you have during a year?

About 3 to 4 weeks.

5. Which business areas do your clients mainly come from?

Most of our clients are film distributors, theatres, museums, and we work for the Polish post.

Is the number of your clients increasing or rather declining?

It looks as if it is increasing gradually.

6. Do you have a specific corporate philosophy or maybe a mission statement like other companies, which is reflected in the way you steer the studio's course?

We prefer clients who give us a lot of freedom, like i.e. the cultural institutions. It is much more fun to work for them than for business clients who have plenty of money but offer projects often dealing with boring, less creative subjects.

7. What, from your point of view, makes the difference between a small studio and a big company?

A big company usually has strict rules and a tight schedule. They have a certain amount of money to spend on a project, and have a specific deadline. They have enormous costs, so they cannot take less-paid jobs with crazy deadlines. Usually, people who work in such a company specialize on a specific field. When you work in a small studio, on the other hand, you can organize your work the way you like it. You have a lot more freedom. If there are no jobs for you to do for a couple of days, you can take your time and rest. It is not an issue. On the other hand, you have to deal with a lot of things on your own.

The danton case – poster – Polski theatre in Bydgoszcz – 2008

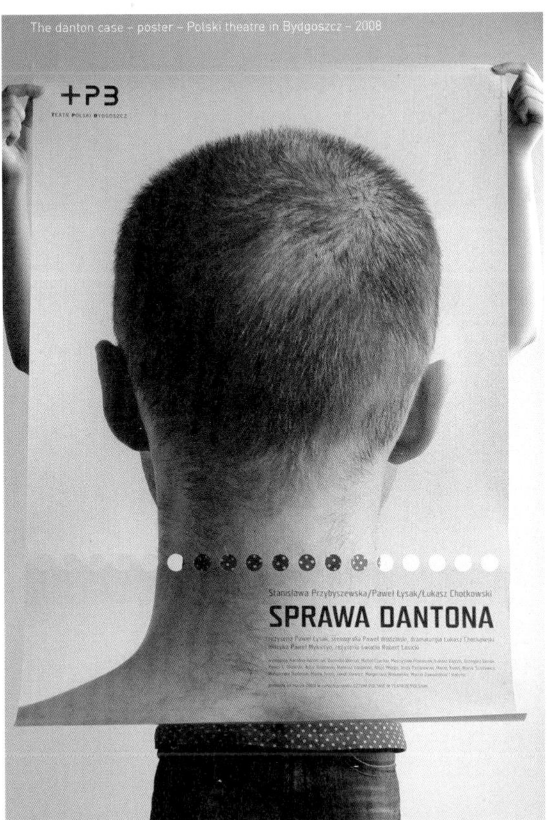

The return of oldys – poster – Polski theatre in Bydgoszcz – 2007

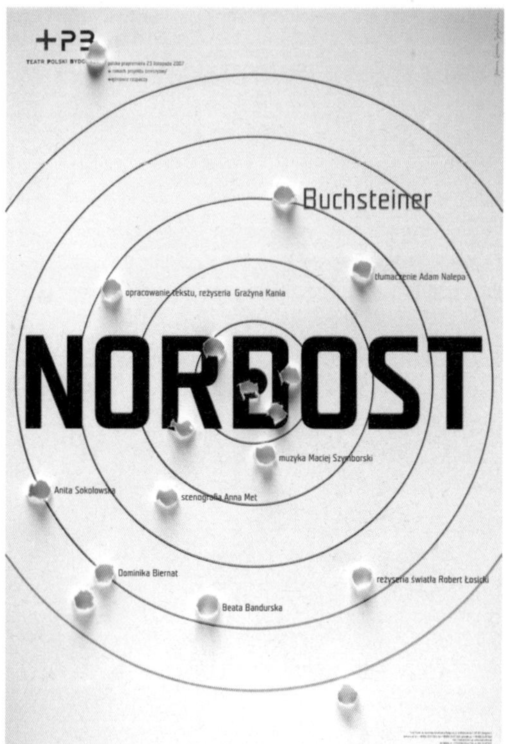

Northeast – poster – Polski theatre in Bydgoszcz – 2007

40th anniversary of Pułaski museum in Warka – poster – Pułaski museum – 2007

Shut up and shoot me – movie poster – Vivarto – 2006

8. What kind of advantages and disadvantages does a small studio have compared to a big company?

Advantages: You can take jobs that are not paid very well, or just have smaller budgets; you can organize your time; you can have a better, more personal contact with a client, which means that both sides can communicate their ideas more easily, as there is no agent, no third person in between; you can follow more radical, courageous solutions; you can decide what to do by yourself, for there is no boss above telling you to do something in a certain way.

Disadvantages: irregular salaries; difficulties to plan and take vacations; lots of things to manage on your own.

9. What is your idea about the future of small studios? Do you think that small studios do not have any other choice but to expand in order to survive in these times of globalization?

I think there's plenty of space for small studios. I have found that even big clients sometimes prefer to work with small studios as they can guarantee better communication and higher quality.

10. Please describe and elaborate on the goals or plans that you have for your studio for the next five years?

We don't have any specific plans. We are thinking about moving the job out of our home apartment, or to exchange it for a bigger place like a house to have more space for the studio. We would like to get some nice interesting projects to work on, just like it has been happening in the past – or maybe even something better.

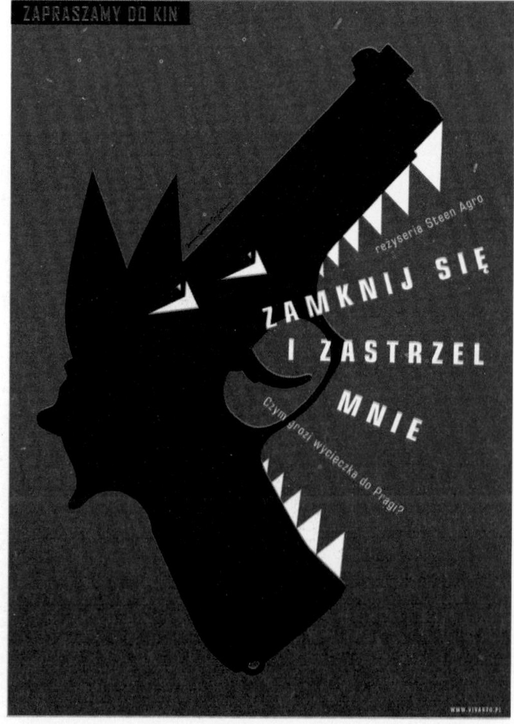

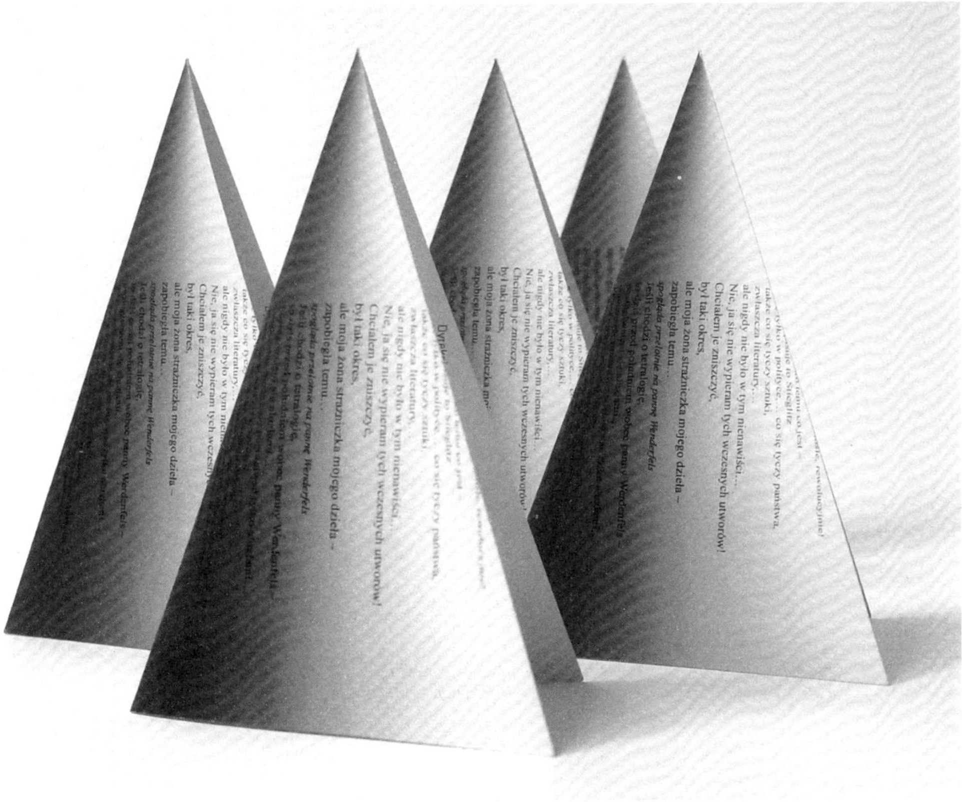

Over the mountain silence prevails – invitation, program, bilboard – dramatyczny theatre – 2006

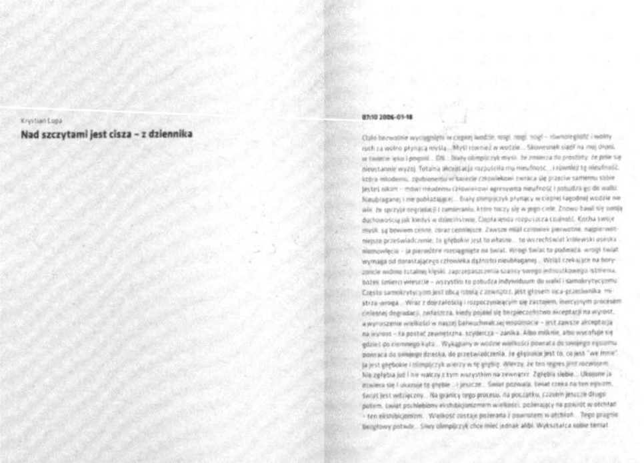

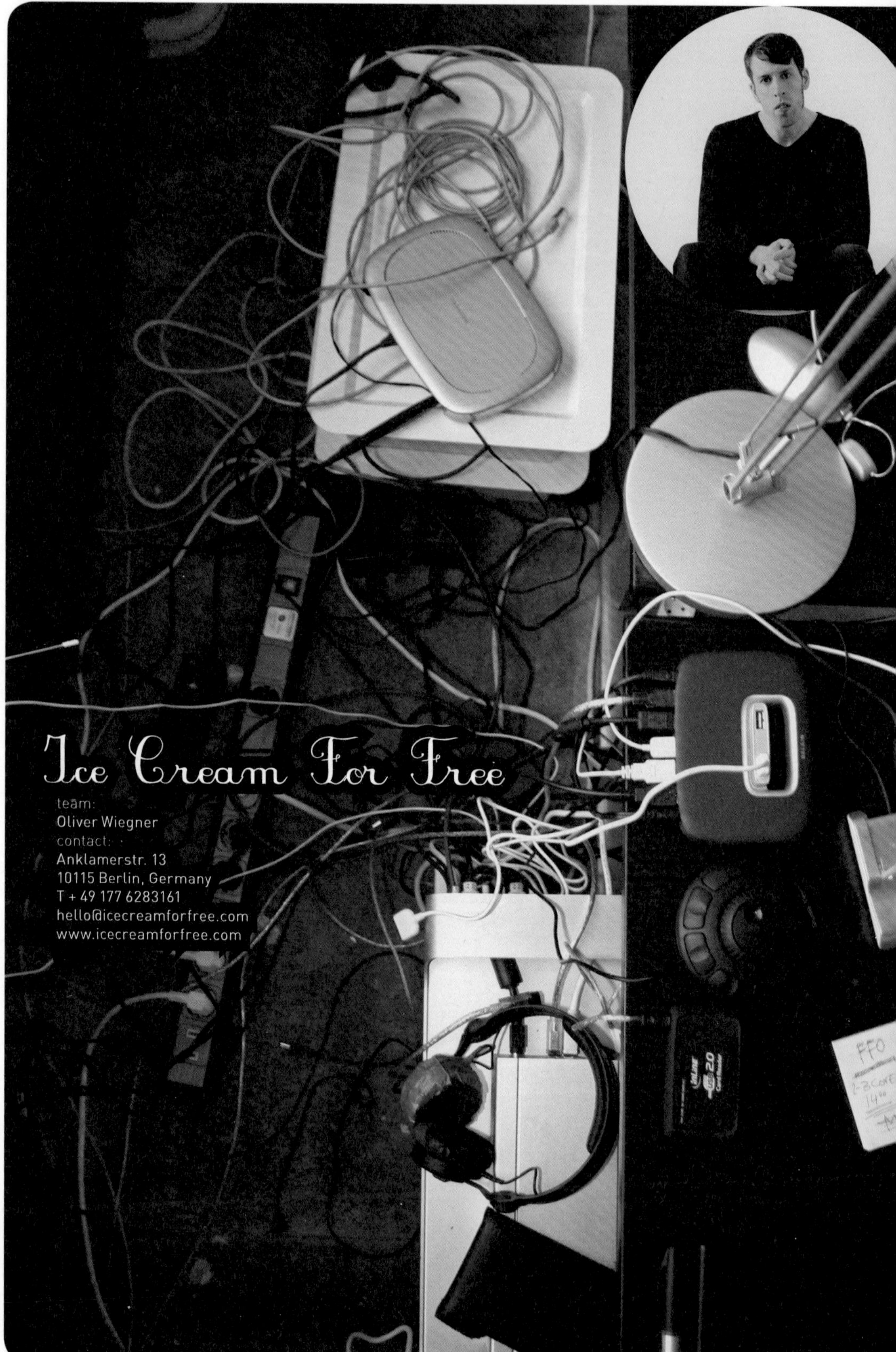

Ice Cream For Free

team:
Oliver Wiegner
contact:
Anklamerstr. 13
10115 Berlin, Germany
T + 49 177 6283161
hello@icecreamforfree.com
www.icecreamforfree.com

Ice Cream For Free – His talent for graphic design already became obvious at the early age of six – or maybe it didn't. Taking part in a drawing competition for "Haribo Gummibaerchen" – a sweet like jelly babies – in Germany, he totally missed out. Instead, his sister won the main price, a golden necklace with a Gummibear pendant. Unabashed by this childhood experience, he moved to New York City to gather experience and inspiration. This gave him the final impulse and the energy to conquer Berlin. Germany's contemporary source of life offered the perfect surroundings for all forms of subculture and talented artists. At the end of 2005, he became the founding member of the design studio Ice Cream for Free. Ice Cream for Free is a Berlin-based design studio founded b Oliver Wiegner in 2005. Having developed from a collective, ICFFTM has access to a multidisciplinary team of designers mainly focusing on print. Their style is influenced by current impressions from the streets of Berlin, the fine art scene of the city, and from all over the world. Bubbling with ideas, ICFF-TM is ready to go.

Flash008/Koletzki & Meindl/tiger – 12" record sleeve – flash recordings – 2008

Interview with Ice Cream For Free

1. What led to the formation of your studio?

In 2004, I moved to Berlin together with some friends, and we started working jointly on some project. This way we sort of developed into a collective, but at the same time each one of us followed his own way. And I started the studio ICE CREAM FOR FREE.

2. How many staff people does your studio have and what are their main working fields?

At the moment it is just me, and my main fields are illustration and print design.

3. How does a regular working day at your studio look like, how is the day structured?

Having a very structured working day is not always easy, as clients often come up with a job at the very last minute, and then I have to meet the deadline, even if that involves working until late at night. I mostly start my day early and come home in the evenings. Once in a while I work at parties as a VJ, then the next day begins later, of course. Apart from that the first thing I do when I get up in the morning is checking my emails from home. Later I go to my office and start working on current projects. Unfortunately, the administrative office work takes a great deal of the time.

4. How much leisure time do you have during a year?

That's a good question. Counting Sundays, I have 52 free days this year. Basically, I work most of the time, and it is not easy to make a clear cut between working and private life. For me, real leisure time means being away on vacation when nobody can get hold of me.

5. Which business areas do your clients mainly come from? Is the number of your clients increasing or rather declining?

I prefer to work with clients from the music industry, because it's easier to work together with people having an artistic background, such as musicians, DJs, music loving event managers or other design studios. Most of these people are open-minded and have a feeling for what it means to connect arts, design and music. That is pretty helpful. But of course, it's not always like this. The number of my clients has been increasing in the last couple of months, for I get a lot of new jobs on recommendation.

Flash003/Koletzki & Meindl/kolibri – 12" record sleeve – flash recordings – 2007

Flash007/lützenkirch/micro boy ep – 12" record sleeve – flash recordings – 2007

Milk – poster – neverest – 2007

Dog/horse – t-shirt – and a/Tokyo – 2007

6. Do you have a specific corporate philosophy or maybe a mission statement like other companies, which is reflected in the way you steer the studio's course?

Not a real philosophy, more a feeling or an attitude. Every time I do a project I want to take a step forward. Every time I am trying to get more provocative using oddness or beauty in a strange way. I like to create a lack of understanding. It's more interesting for me if people do not understand my work immediately.

7. What, from your point of view, makes the difference between a small studio and a big company?

Most studios start off as small companies, and while they are growing, they lose their independence and naivety. Many small studios try to stay small in order to avoid this development. The bigger a studio is and the more people it employs, the bigger becomes the responsibility. The focus shifts over to financial aspects, and exciting projects which don't bring a lot of money, get neglected or disappear completely from the studio's radar.

8. What kind of advantages and disadvantages does a small studio have compared to a big company?

A small studio can concentrate on a few projects and act flexible. Therefore, it keeps the possibility of intensive exchange alive. Most of these studios, though, don't have a lot of money in the background and have to fight hard to survive. But I think it's better to fight than to sell your independence.

Light - poster - die krieger des lichts - 2006

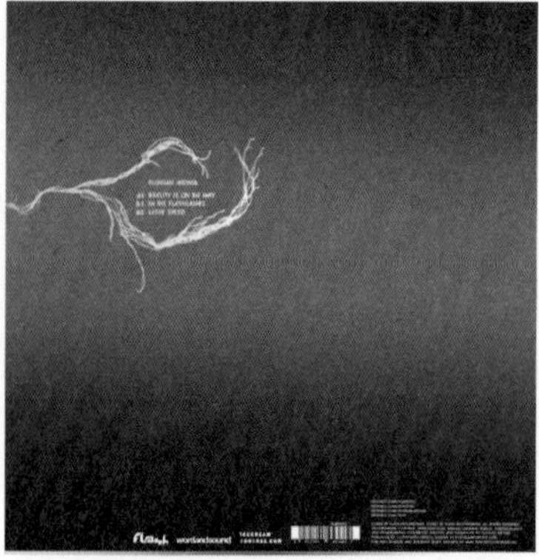

Flash004/Florian Meindl/my way – 12" record sleeve – flash recordings – 2007

Flash002/Florian Meindl/reality is on the way – 12" record sleeve – lash recordings – 2007

9. What is your idea about the future of small studios? Do you think that small studios do not have any other choice but to expand in order to survive in these times of globalization?

I am convinced that there are a lot of clients who have to deal with small budgets and who are willing to work with fresh and cheeky studios. So there will be always a demand for small studios. And I think there are quite a few examples of studios staying small on purpose, which have come up with great art over the years. But I cannot judge how difficult their struggle really is.

10. Please describe and elaborate on the goals or plans that you have for your studio for the next five years?

I have moved to a new office some month ago, and right now I concentrate a lot of my energy on doing some self-promotion. After that I hope to get a lot of new jobs, more than I can handle by myself, so that I have to hire some freelancers. In five years, you will find ICFF in Berlin, London, Tokyo, New York, Barcelona, and of course in Shanghai. Besides the design studio, I would like to push my VJ career a little bit. That is a nice way to party and work at the same time.

Flash009/lützenkirchen/moonlight ep – 12" record sleeve – flash recordings – 2008

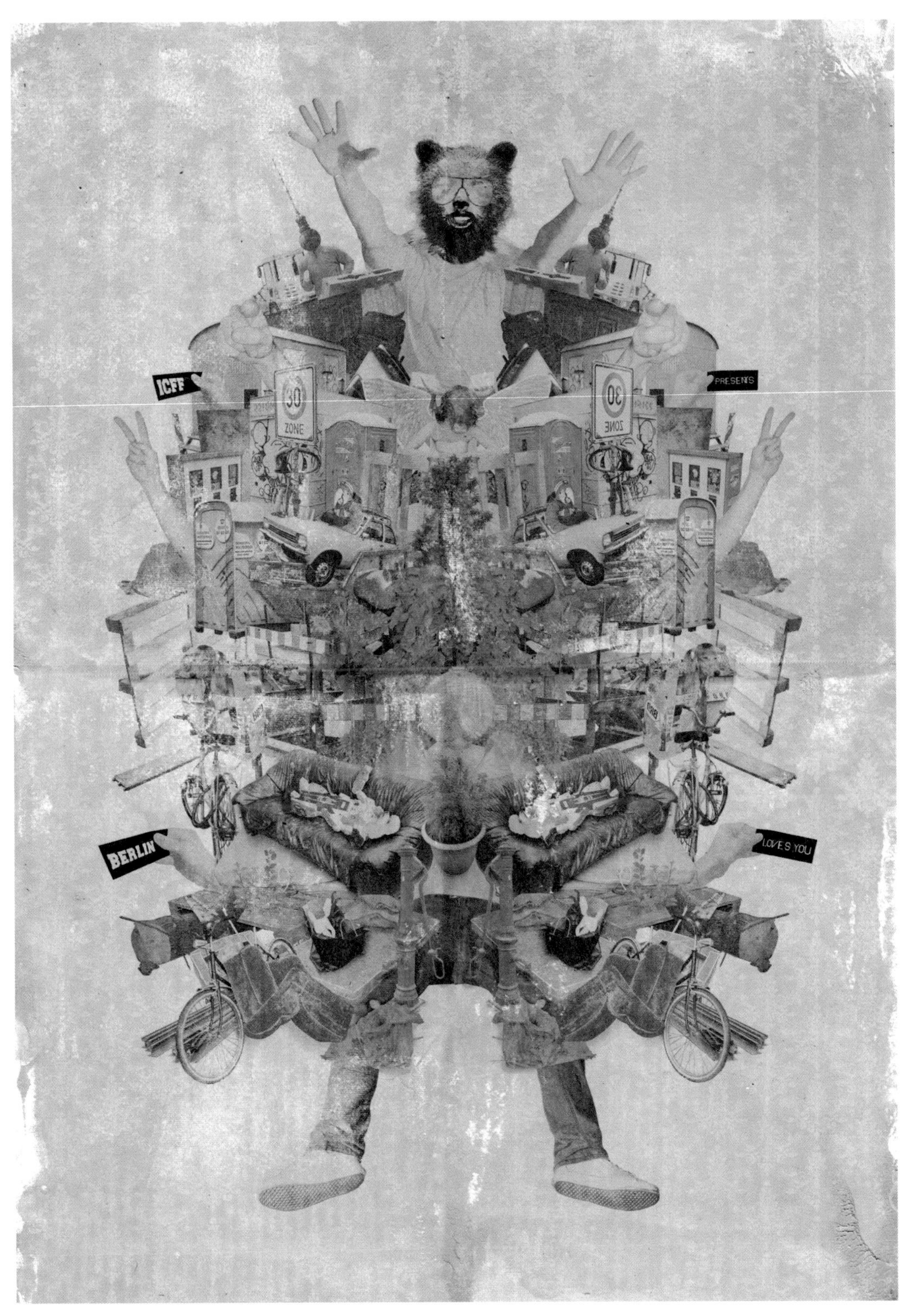

What makes Berlin addictive? – poster, printed on uncoated paper – China cultural bridge – 2006

Hiroshi Iguchi

team:
Hiroshi Iguchi
contact:
1-38-11, Chateau Yoyogi Uehara #103,
Uehara, Shibuya-Ku,
151-0064 Tokyo, Japan
T/F + 81 3 34816481
info@thebwoy.com

Hiroshi Iguchi was born in 1973. In 1999, he joined the graphic team ILL-DOZER in Tokyo before gradually starting to produce solo works such as the project THE BWOY. His art work is being used in various media around music, fashion and books.

Exhibitions:

2001 - "MOVEMENT" at SENDAI MEDIATHEQUE (Sendai Japan)
2003 - "VERSUS EXHIBITION 02" at PARCO MUSEUM (Tokyo Japan)
2003 - "GIGEI" at BRAZEN GALLERY (Singapore)
2006 - "TRAX GROUP SHOW" at GALLERY TRAX (Yamanashi Japan)
2007 - "2027" at Trancepop Gallery (Kyoto Japan)

Spikewave/reserge – cd – crue-l records – 2007

Interview with Hiroshi Iguchi

1. What led to the formation of your studio?

When I started designing party flyers for my friends, people who saw my works offered jobs to me and encouraged me to do my own exhibitions.

2. How many staff people does your studio have and what are their main working fields?

I am the only studio member at the moment. I handle art directions, graphic designs, and illustrations.

3. How does a regular working day at your studio look like, how is the day structured?

After waking up in the morning, I make a schedule for the day, check my e-mails, and read the news. When I am invited to a party, I work extra hard for it.

4. How much leisure time do you have during a year?

I try giving myself some leisure time every night, even if it is for a short time. People often told me that I have to play and have fun, but it took me 5 years since I started my studio to understand what that means.

5. Which business areas do your clients mainly come from? Is the number of your clients increasing or rather declining?

My clients mainly come from the music and fashion industry. Fortunately, the number of clients I am working for is increasing. I am very proud of the great quality of the CD designs I did in recent years. I put much faith in quality instead of quantity.

6. Do you have a specific corporate philosophy or maybe a mission statement like other companies, which is reflected in the way you steer the studio's course?

Some years ago, a taxi driver told me: "You must take a more difficult and more challenging path when you are stranded."

V.A./Kahimi Karie presents crue-l crystallization – cd – crue-l records – 2006

Sound x vision logo – logo – gas as interface – 2004

2027 logo – logo – blues interactions, inc. – 2006

Bonobos/thank you for the music – cd – dreamusic – 2005

Nike Osaka 8.27 – poster – W+K Tokyo lab – 2005

7. What, from your point of view, makes the difference between a small studio and a big company?

I have never really compared small and big studios. Perhaps one difference is the budget which the studio holds. I meet people owning small studios at parties, we discuss, and sometimes we work together.

8. What kind of advantages and disadvantages does a small studio have compared to a big company?

The job flow is smoothly manageable. I enjoy an exceptional situation at work. I can stay flexible at any time. In London a designer once told me: "It is interesting that you are able to work as a graphic designer without affiliating with an agency". Tokyo is such a unique place. I can work without an agency, and it has been quite normal for me to cling to the style I have established.

Cool wise men/salty dinner – cd – galactic – 2006

Bonobos/grove me – cd – dreamusic – 2005

Rub-A-Dub market/digikal rockers – cd – BMG Japan – 2007

9. What is your idea about the future of small studios? Do you think that small studios do not have any other choice but to expand in order to survive in these times of globalization?

I do not think that a studio's size is a problem. When I see someone's creation and feel that the designer is enjoying the work, it is such a pleasing experience. Having fun at work is not an easy choice for me. I have a deep respect for creative people capable of expressing joy, which has less to do with content or a size of a studio.

10. Please describe and elaborate on the goals or plans that you have for your studio for the next five years?

I am working on a music CD which is going to be released by a label called SKIN TRAXX in London. I am also working on some design works at the same time.

Pencil & missile – illustration – private work – 2005

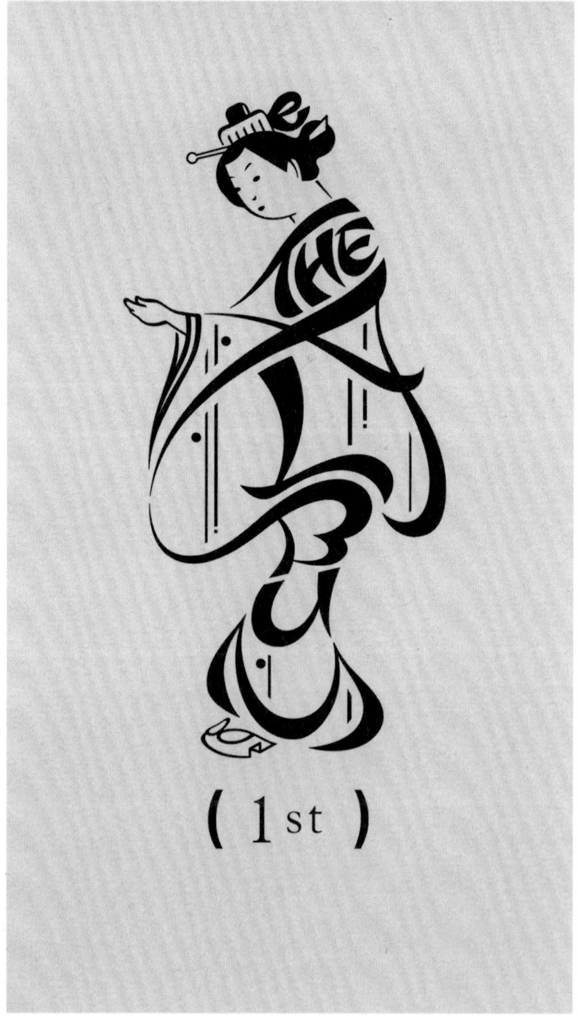

V.A./the album(1st) – book, cd – beamst – 2005

The zoot16/right out! – cd – zoot sunrise sounds – 2004

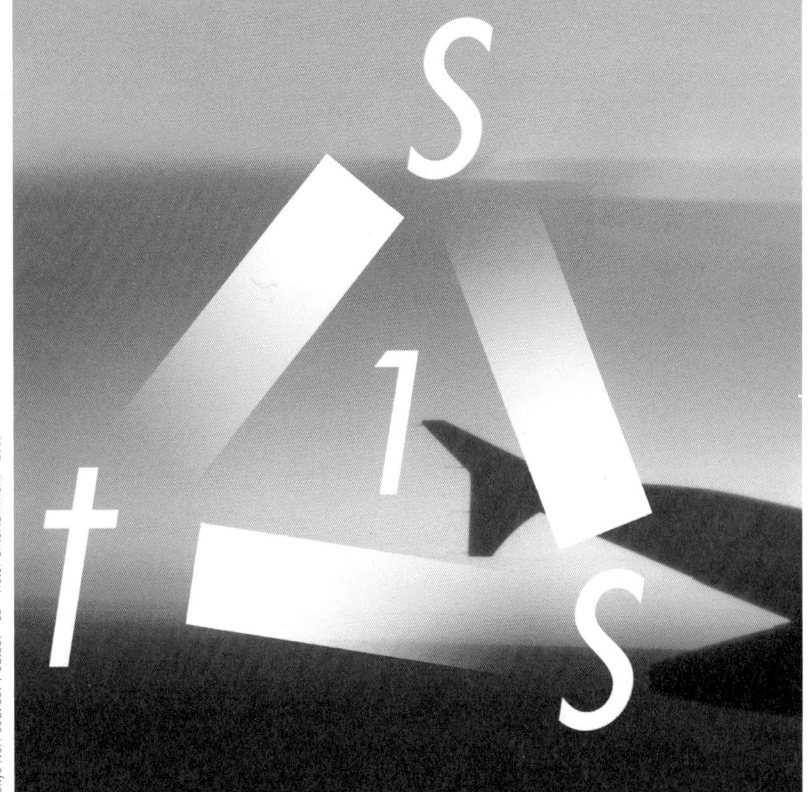

Tokyo No.1 soul set / outset – cd – Victor entertainment – 2005

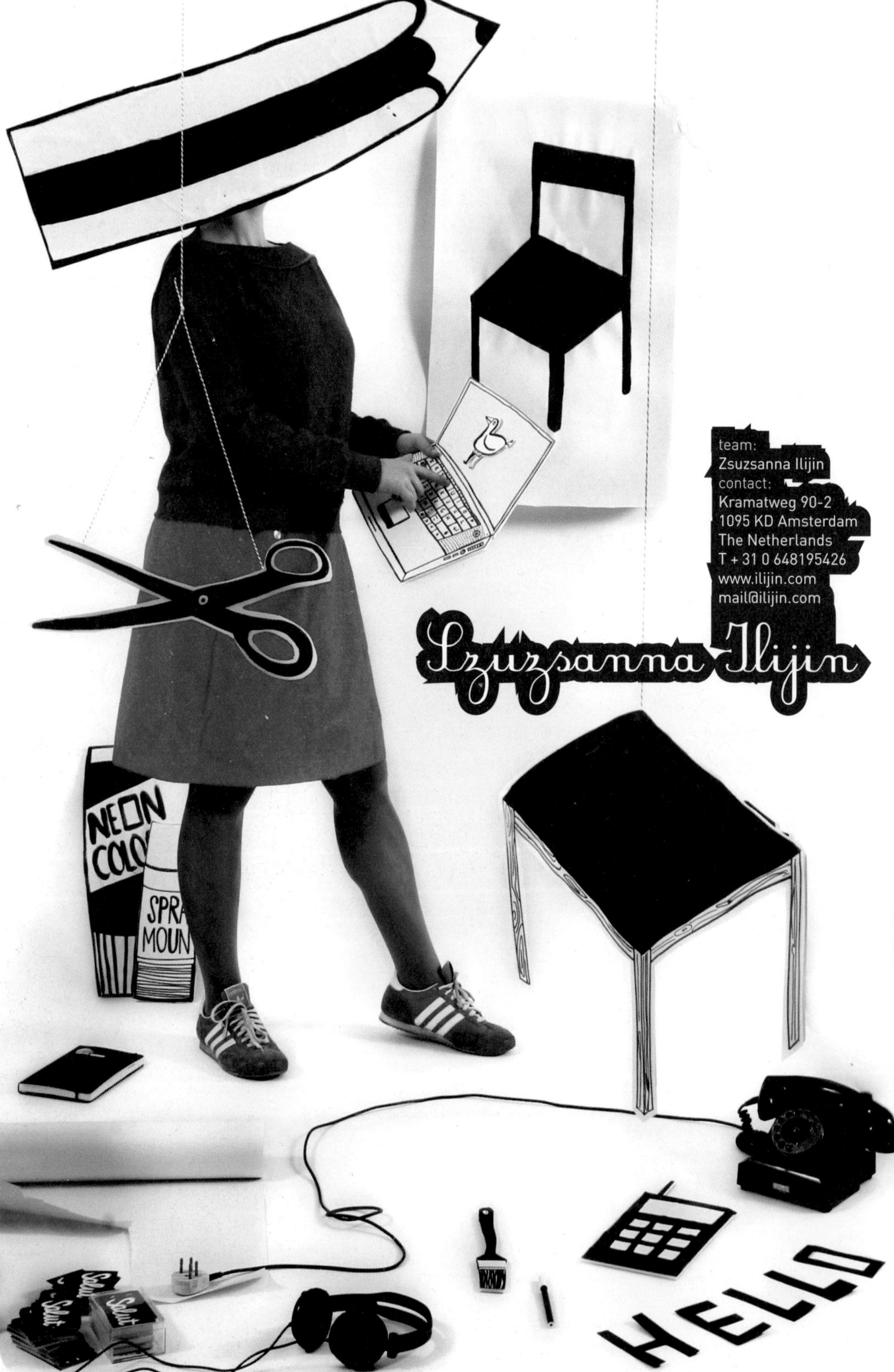
team:
Zsuzsanna Ilijin
contact:
Kramatweg 90-2
1095 KD Amsterdam
The Netherlands
T + 31 0 648195426
www.ilijin.com
mail@ilijin.com
Szuzsanna Ilijin
NEON
COLO
SPRA
MOUN
HELLO

Zsuzsanna Ilijin is originally from Germany and has Hungarian roots. She founded her studio in Amsterdam one year after graduating from the Academy of Art and Design in Stuttgart, Germany. Her focus lies on print-based projects like posters, visual identities, books and book covers. Her studio also does illustrations and drawings for editorials, advertising and event-styles. From time to time she exhibits her silkscreen-prints, which she produces in a small workshop in the heart of Amsterdam.

Interview with Zsuzsanna Ilijin

1. What led to the formation of your studio?

I studied at the state Academy of Art and Design in Stuttgart, where I had many inspiring teachers such as Prof. Niklaus Troxler, Jan Bazing and Prof. Gerwin Schmidt. They all work in a small studio. I was also affected by the small studio called NLXL (Bob van Dijk, Joost Roozekrans, Oscar Smeulders) where I did my internship. All these influences inspired me to start my own studio. I also worked at a big company, but that just convinced me more of my plan to do my own thing. So here I am.

2. How many staff people does your studio have and what are their main working fields?

My studio does graphic design and illustration, mostly for print. I usually get booked for my design. I collaborate with other designers and people from other fields like photography, writing, film etc.

3. How does a regular working day at your studio look like, how is the day structured?

I have a coffee and then start to work. It is not like a nine-to-five job. I try to structure and plan my week. But especially the jobs I do for magazines come unexpected and have narrow deadlines. I have a to-do-list every day.

4. How much leisure time do you have during a year?

The nice thing about being a designer as well as your own boss is that work feels like leisure time, so I kind of always have leisure time. When I travel, I see a lot of things giving me inspiration for my work. It fills my sketchbook with many ideas for upcoming projects.

5. Which business areas do your clients mainly come from? Is the number of your clients increasing or rather declining?

Currently I work for clients with a cultural and editorial background. It is increasing constantly.

6. Do you have a specific corporate philosophy or maybe a mission statement like other companies, which is reflected in the way you steer the studio's course?

I don't have a "corporate philosophy". I like to tell stories, create little worlds, look at the big picture and pay attention to tiny details. I research, experiment, surprise, irritate, innovate... My studio is known for a unique visual and a convincing concept.

7. What, from your point of view, makes the difference between a small studio and a big company?

8. What kind of advantages and disadvantages does a small studio have compared to a big company?

I worked for both: a big company and for small studios. A big studio needs to make a huge amount of money to pay for all the expenses. They need big clients with big project so there is enough work for all the employees. Most jobs are not so creative, because there are a lot of things to execute. Of course it depends on the client, and how the company deals with assignments, but the size makes them less flexible. One the other hand, they can offer more safety. They can put more designers on a project or just the brainstorming. This can be good or bad. In my experience, I felt like too many heads are involved in a project. I believe in the German saying: "Zu viele Köche verderben den Brei" – "Too many cooks spoil the broth". I rather have direct contact with the client and present my work directly. That works out better for my small studio.

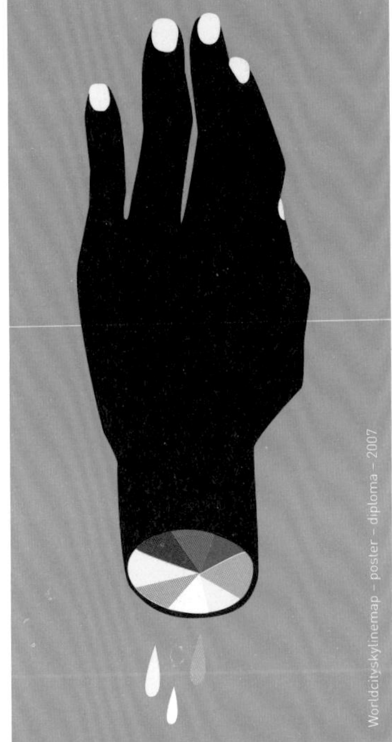

Worldcityskylinemap – poster – diploma – 2007

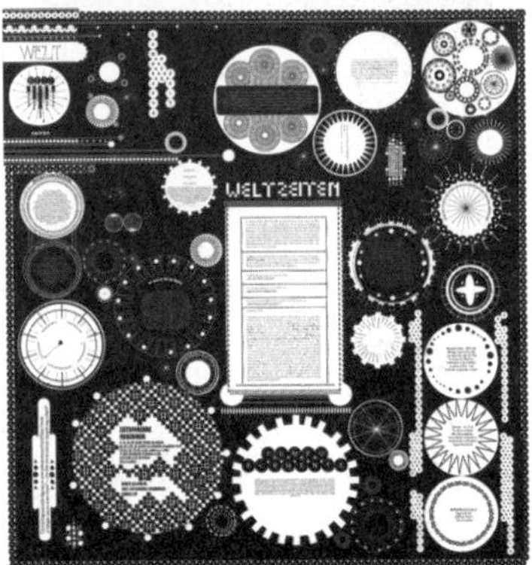

Timemap – poster – diploma – 2007

Worldcityskylinemap – poster – diploma – 2007

The rocker and the record – poster/flyer – legrandcrew – 2008

Medical care expert conference – poster – academy for social welfare – 2005

La grande boucherie – poster – legrandcrew – 2008

The perfect plan – poster – music school St. Georgen – 2007

DESIGN: ZSUZSANNA IL

Hänsel
und
Gretel

Humperdinck

MIT
DEN
MFG-KINDERN

TAG DER OFFENEN TÜR

SAMSTAG
7. JULI 07

10.00 UHR
11.30 UHR

The perfect plan – illustration – sz-magazin – 2008

9. What is your idea about the future of small studios? Do you think that small studios do not have any other choice but to expand in order to survive in these times of globalization?

There will always be a need for good design. Most designers I admire are busy working in a small studio. I think it will be even easier to survive, I am very optimistic about that. People are tired of seeing the same stuff all over the world made by the same big brands or companies. Through globalization, we are loosing much of our cultural diversity. There is a big need for fresh, outstanding ideas. And it seems like it is easier to create those in a small studio. Small Studios: Yes we can!

10. Please describe and elaborate on the goals or plans that you have for your studio for the next five years?

Keep on working in the same size studio and enlarge the list of clients and groundbreaking projects.

Diploma show – illustration – sadbk – 2006

Musicmap – poster – diploma – 2007

Hellomap – poster – diploma – 2007

Jan en Randoald

team:
Randoald Sabbe
Jan W. Hespeel
contact:
Randoald Sabbe
S. de Mirabellostr. 28
9000 Gent, Belgium
T + 32 4 79296733

Jan W. Hespeel
Wezestr. 30a
8850 Ardooie, Belgium
T + 32 4 86756857
www.janenrandoald.be
info@janenrandoald.be

Jan en Randoald studied free graphics and/or graphic design at the High School for Visual Arts Sint-Lucas Ghent, Belgium, where they teach graphic design today. They started collaborating in 2004 and had the fortune to work for open-minded clients such as: the concert hall De Bijloke, several museums (Museums of Antwerp, STAM, Museum Dr. Ghuislain), Veronique Branquinho, Witte Zaal, Hans De Pelsmacker, les ballets C de la B, Sofie Lachaert, Young Artists, and so on. Both Jan and Randoald consider the client's input with regard to the content to be extremely important. The two designers also like to recuperate trivial photos, using older, proven typefaces, the pure CMYK coloring, and the tactility of paper. Their partnership is a very positive and enriching journey. So far...

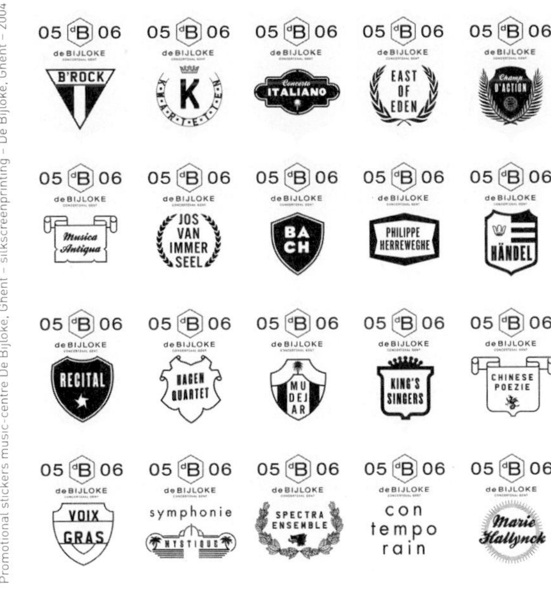

Promotional stickers music-centre De Bijloke, Ghent – silkscreenprinting – De Bijloke, Ghent – 2004

Cover magazine Nr. 6 De Bijloke Ghent – cover – cover magazine Nr. 6 De Bijloke Ghent – 2005

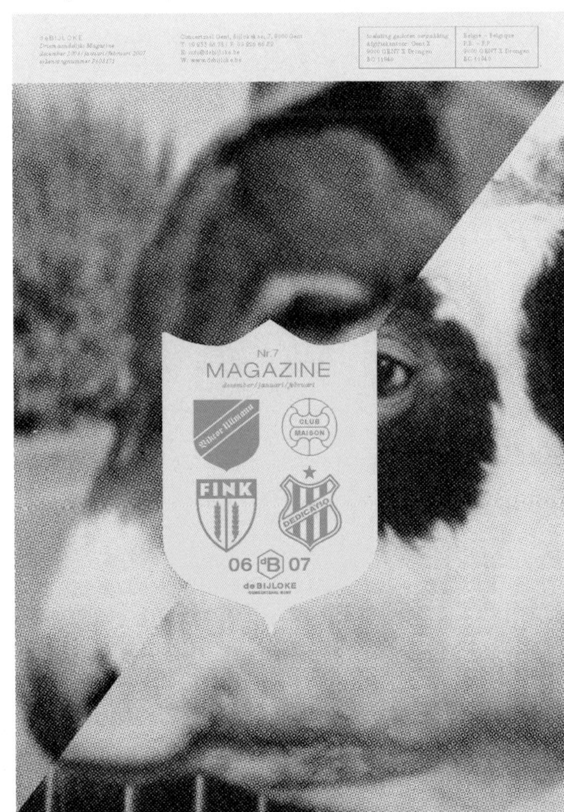

Interview with Jan en Randoald

1. What led to the formation of your studio?

We studied (and now teach) graphic design and free graphics at the Sint-Lucas school for visual arts in Ghent. During our education we were very polite to each other, but we never had a conversation. In 1999, we became colleagues at Sint-Lucas, so conversations were unavoidable. To our surprise, we shared lots of interests and got along quite well. A collaboration – starting in 2004 – was obvious.

2. How many staff people does your studio have and what are their main working fields?

Just the two of us with some logistical help from our wife and girlfriend.

3. How does a regular working day at your studio look like, how is the day structured?

There isn't a well-defined structure. Meetings, project work and deadlines determine our daily structure.

4. How much leisure time do you have during a year?

For the last couple of years, the leisure time was stipulated by deadlines and the frequency of projects (which is not always easy to combine with family and social life).

5. Which business areas do your clients mainly come from?

Mainly from the cultural sector and some companies. Generally, the amount of work is increasing, which is not necessarily the same with regard to the client list. Sometimes we have a client with a large project running for several years, and sometimes clients with small one-off projects or a mixture of both. Thanks to our teaching assignments, we have the luxury of being able to turn down projects we don't want to do.

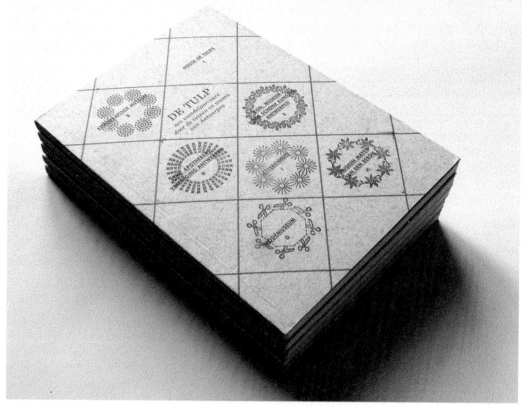

TULP brochure (TULLIP brochure) – brochure – museums of Antwerp – 2006

Campaign image exhibition ZIEK (ILL), museum Dr. Guislain, Ghent – poster – museum Dr. Guislain – 2007

STAM-invitation (museum of the city Ghent) – invitation, offset – STAM-team – 2004

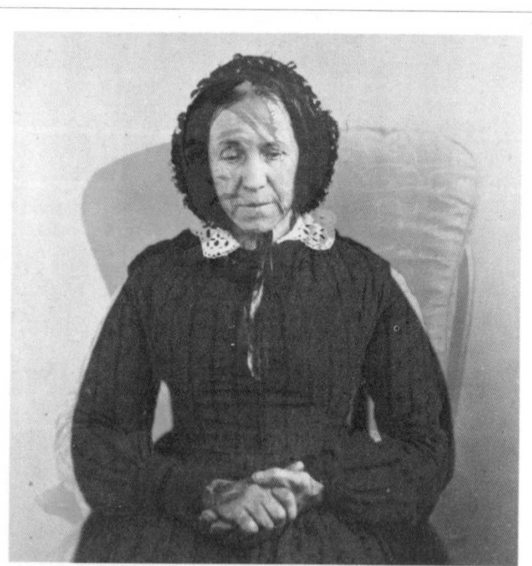

6. Do you have a specific corporate philosophy or maybe a mission statement like other companies, which is reflected in the way you steer the studio's course?

Our philosophy: Having fun with every new assignment!

7. What, from your point of view, makes the difference between a small studio and a big company?

8. What kind of advantages and disadvantages does a small studio have compared to a big company?

A big advantage for small studios is their flexibility. A big disadvantage is not always taken seriously.

9. What is your idea about the future of small studios? Do you think that small studios do not have any other choice but to expand in order to survive in these times of globalization?

There will always be an interest in small studios, and there will always be small studios. Please do not expand! Expansion leads to uniformity and mediocrity.

10. Please describe and elaborate on the goals or plans that you have for your studio for the next five years?

To receive a lot of interesting projects from open-minded clients.

Antwerpen lonkt – cover catalog – museum of Antwerp – 2005

Spread seasonnal-brochure De Bijloke, Ghent – brochure, offset on signaset-paper – De Bijloke Ghent – 2005

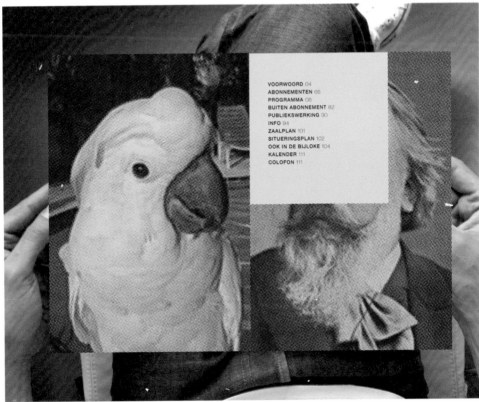

Dummies, theater-production De Werf, Bruges – poster – De Werf – 2007   Cover catalogue young artists – poster – De Werf – 2007

Youngster festival De Werf, Bruges – cover – Witte Zaal, Ghent – 2007

Season-poster art-centre De Werf, Bruges – poster – De Werf – 2007

John Morgan Studio

team:
John Morgan
Michael Evidon
Catarina Pereira
Daniel Chehade

contact:
Room B.128
MacMillan House
Platform 1
Paddington Station
London W2 1FT
United Kingdom
F + 44 20 74026622
info@morganstudio.co.uk
www.morganstudio.co.uk

John Morgan Studio From the Typography department at Reading University, John Morgan assisted Derek Birdsall at Omnific, London. In 2000 he established John Morgan studio where he works with a small team on Platform 1 Paddington Station. Alongside studio work, he has tutored at Central St Martins and the University of Reading and co-founded Workplace Co-operative 115 with Robin Kinross, a new building for designers and makers. Morgan's projects include prayer books for the Church of England, granite poetry for the BBC, exhibition design for the Design Museum, art direction for Phillips de Pury, and in progress a new graphic identity for David Chipperfield Architects. He has written for various journals including Typography Papers and Dot Dot Dot.

Blumfeld, an elderly bachelor by Franz Kafka – book design – four corners books – 2008

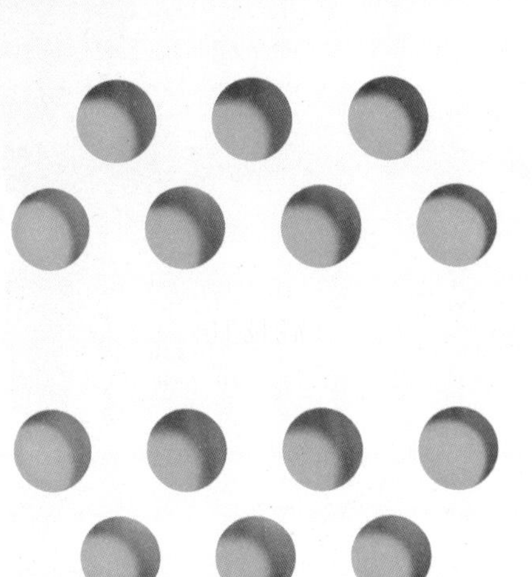

Design – auction catalogue – Phillips de Pury & company – 2008

Interview with John Morgan Studio

1. What led to the formation of your studio?

After my time with Derek Birdsall at Omnific there was nobody else I wanted to work with. I also wanted to be in control of my work and time. When the amount of work was growing I took on assistants.

2. How many staff people does your studio have and what are their main working fields?

Michael and I have always been at the core – other positions have changed over the years. Currently, there are four people at the studio, all graphic designers.

3. How does a regular working day at your studio look like, how is the day structured?

There is no regular working day. In a studio of our scale there is little need to formalize working method and relationships. I try to avoid the telephone as much as possible. We try to have lunch together outside the studio.

4. How much leisure time do you have during the year?

I don't like to distinguish too much between work and play. I've never met a good designer with a hobby. My family has grown parallel to the studio – three children are a guarantee for life balance.

5. Which business areas do your clients mainly come from?

From the cultural and the publishing sector.

Is the number of your clients increasing or rather declining?

Increasing.

6. Do you have a specific corporate philosophy or maybe a mission statement like other companies, which is reflected in the way you steer the studio's course?

No mission statement. Rather a desire to work with intelligent, responsive human beings.

7. What, from your point of view, makes the difference between a small studio and a big company?

Apart from scale – it's presentation. Pentagram, for example, effectively combines many small practices under a shared name and in shared facilities. That's appealing and can serve as a role model for other small studios to follow.

PHILLIPS KYŌBAI 3 APRIL 2008 LONDON
競売

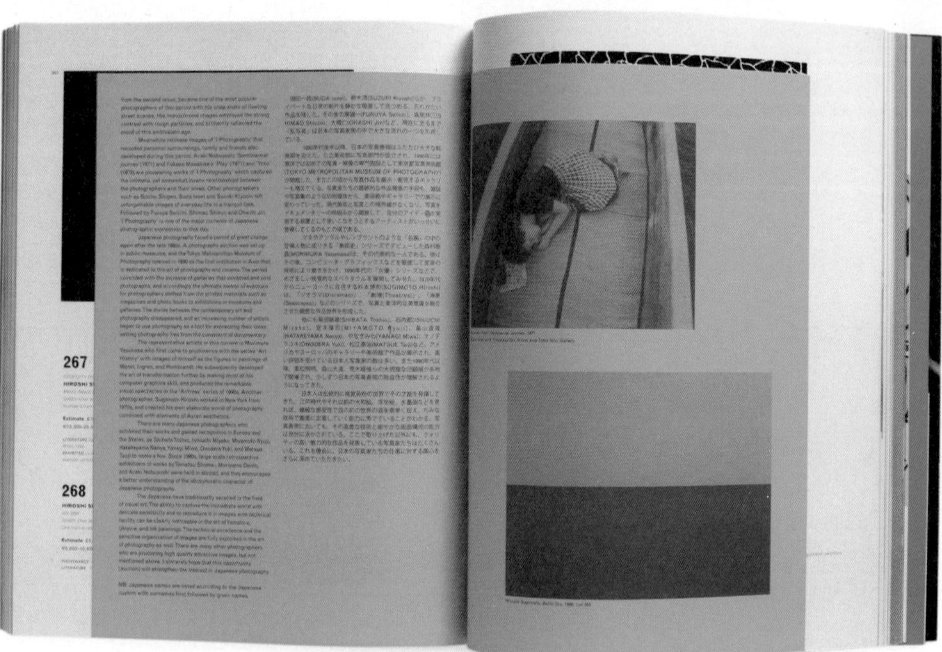

Kyobai – auction catalogue – Phillips de Pury & company – 2008

The Invisible University and its historical values:

I. U. means learning as an ecosystem (what on earth might this mean?).
I. U. means being carbon positive.
I. U. all data is everywhere, all the time.
I. U. means architecture is no substitute for face-to-face contact.
I. U. means a new relationship between man and nature.
I. U. needs no new buildings.
I. U. means tune up kits (small robots, cyber-pets and neuro-gardening – see catalogue available from caretaker).
I. U. means knowing what time it is, is more important than knowing where you are.
I. U. uses less fuel per hour than any other university.

I. U.

Ljubljana – visual identity – Ljubljana tourist board – 2008

Plečnik

Prešeren

Žižek

Vices of white city – 10000 sticker, hoarding project – bbc – 2005

HELMUT
NEWTON

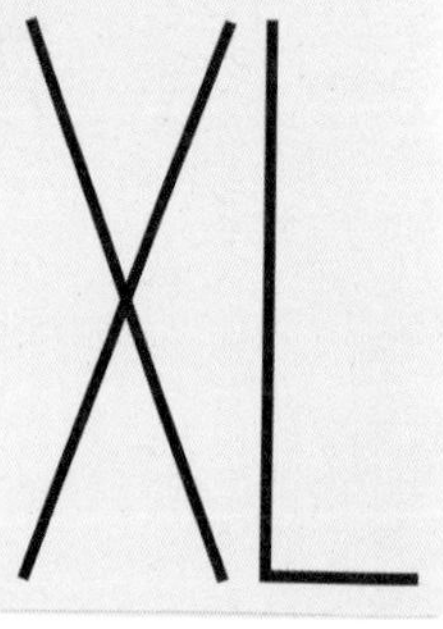

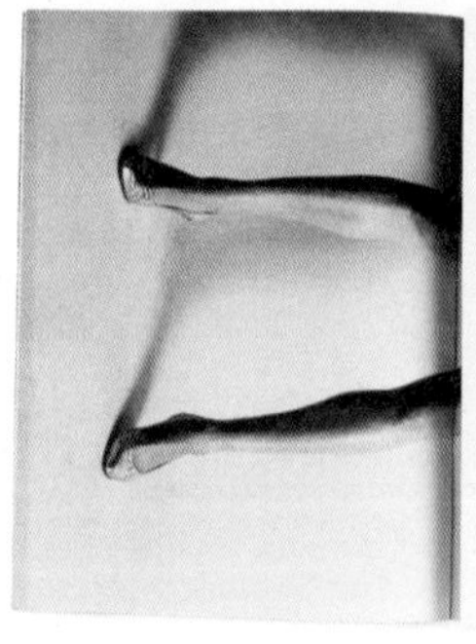

Helmut Newton XL – exhibition catalogue – Hamiltons gallery, Jefferies Cowan – 2007

Contemporary art – auction catalogue – Phillips de Pury & company – 2008

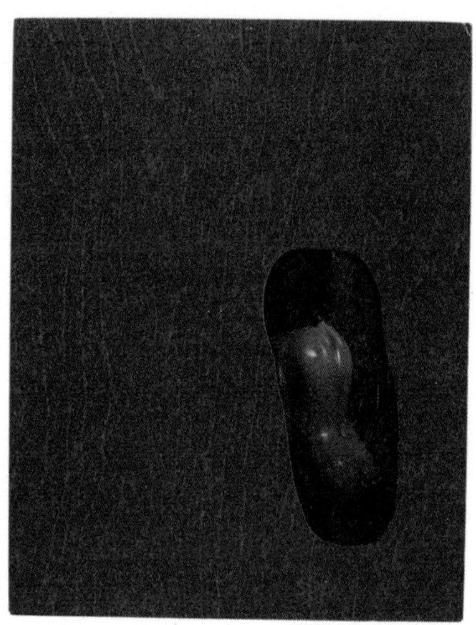

Associates

in

NEW
YORK

Associates in New York – exhibition catalogue – Phillips de Pury & company – 2008

ASSOCIATES
IN
New York

PHILLIPS
de PURY & COMPANY

A young man of extra-ordinary personal beauty

When his servant entered, he looked at him steadfastly and wondered if he had thought of peering behind the screen. The man was quite impassive and waited for his orders. Dorian lit a cigarette and walked over to the glass and glanced into it.

All art is quite useless.

For years, Dorian Gray could not free himself from the influence of this book. Or perhaps it would be more accurate to say that he never sought to free himself from it. He procured from Paris no less than nine large-paper copies of the first edition, and had them bound in different colours, so that they might suit his various moods and the changing fancies of a nature over which he seemed, at times, to have almost entirely lost control. The hero, the wonderful young Parisian in whom the romantic and the scientific temperaments were so strangely blended, became to him a kind of prefiguring type of himself. And, indeed, the whole book seemed to him to contain the story of his own life, written before he had lived it.

The picture of Dorian Gray by Oscar Wilde, art by Gareth Jones – book – four corners books – 2007

8. What kind of advantages and disadvantages does a small studio have compared to a big company?

Small is beautiful. Less politics, easier communication, and most important, every client knows that I will be actively involved in their job. It won't be handed to a junior or intern. On the other hand, jobs of a certain scale demand a larger team. The risk in working with large scale companies is that you could easily get swallowed up by them.

9. What is your idea about the future of small studios? Do you think that small studios do not have any other choice but to expand in order to survive in these times of globalization?

I have learnt a lot from our architectural clients. It is normal for architectural firms to expand and hire people according to the demands. This is a good model to follow. The other possible route for small studios is to collaborate and to share facilities. The challenge is to find like-minded people.

10. Please describe and elaborate on the goals or plans that you have for your studio for the next five years.

Over the last five years my studio has grown from one person to four people. If growth continues at this rate, there would be eight people working at the studio in five years. This is unlikely, however, and undesirable at the same time. Instead, we have become more selective in the work we do and learnt to say "no".

Jung und Wenig

team:
Christopher Jung
Tobias Wenig
contact:
Naumburgerstr. 44
Haus E
04229 Leipzig, Germany
info@jungundwenig.com
www.jungundwenig.com

Jung und Wenig – We work in the wilderness of Leipzig. It's the old horse stable of a former soap factory. We are fortunate to have so much space to hang up our posters, spread out all our layouts, read some books, or to play bowling. Berlin is just around the corner – the city where we started our new office – yuchee. We want our design to match the project; and eventually, it should look good and make the client, viewers and ourselves happy. We cannot deny, though, that the environment surrounding the HGB influenced the look of our designs. People like Cyan, Guenter Karl Bose, Markus Dressen, and, of course, the famous Leipzig typographic experts Jan Tschichold and Walter Tiemann left their mark. It is important not to forget the roots of everything. So many people make fancy and sometimes even good-looking stuff, but for how long will it last? Form more and more becomes a matter of public interest. Unfortunately, content and the objective view deciding about good or bad are not debated to the same degree.

Interview with Jung und Wenig

1. What led to the formation of your studio?

We (Christopher Jung and Tobias Wenig) met in Leipzig in 1999 at the admission test of the Academy Of Visual Arts Leipzig. In 2000, we started studying at the HGB. Among our professors were Cyan, Daniela Haufe and Detlef Fiedler (System Design and Foundation Studies) or Guenter Karl Bose (typography), just to mention some of the outstanding teachers of our academy. Since then, we have worked together on almost all of our projects. In 2004, we founded Jung und Wenig (jung=young, und=and, wenig=little). Our work includes books, magazines, CD covers, film, and multimedia works for clients from the cultural sector.

2. How many staff people does your studio have and what are their main working fields?

Just the two of us – our main field is graphic design.

3. How does a regular working day at your studio look like, how is the day structured?

It's always different. On most days we start at 9. And then we work.

4. How much leisure time do you have during a year?

?

5. Which business areas do your clients mainly come from? Is the number of your clients increasing or rather declining?

a) See answer 1.

b) Rather increasing.

6. Do you have a specific corporate philosophy or maybe a mission statement like other companies, which is reflected in the way you steer the studio's course?

We don't have a certain corporate philosophy or a mission statement, we just want our design to match the project; and eventually, it should look good making the client, other viewers and ourselves happy. It is important not to forget the roots of everything. So many people make fancy and sometimes even good looking stuff, but for how long will it last? Form more and more becomes a matter of public interest.

7. What, from your point of view, makes the difference between a small studio and a big company?

The size?!

8. What kind of advantages and disadvantages does a small studio have compared to a big company?

It would take way too much time to answer this question, and we don't even care about the answer.

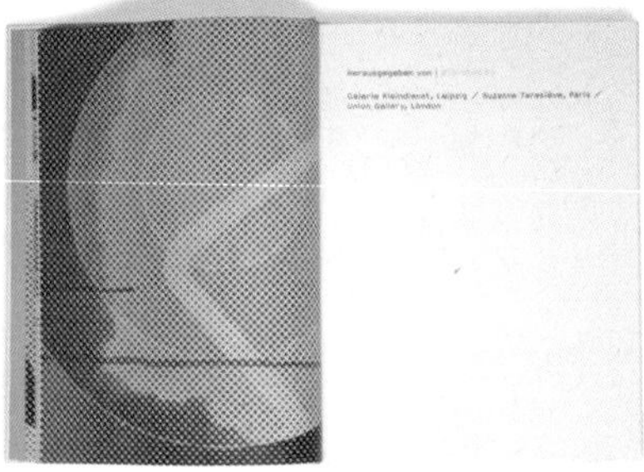

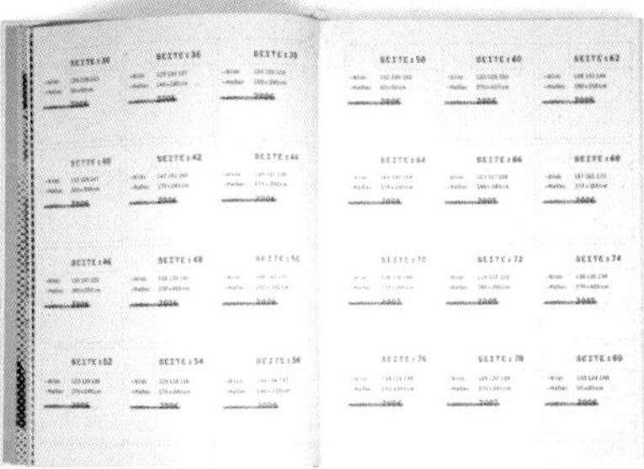

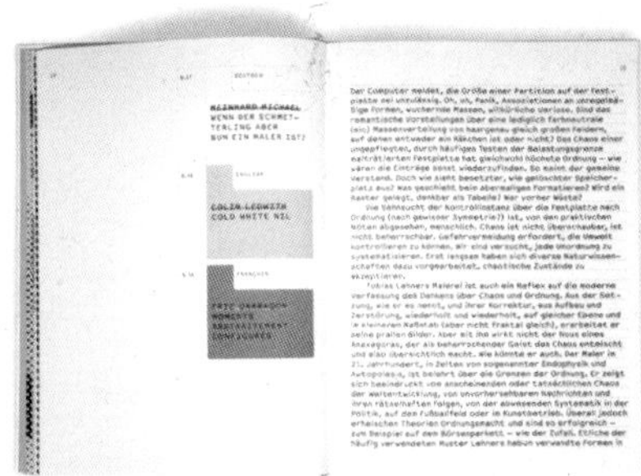

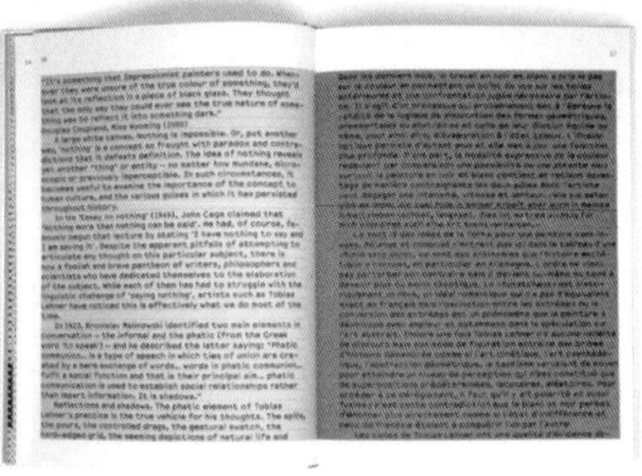

Tobias Lehner – exhibition catalogue – galerie kleindienst – 2007

Zbyněk Baladrán
Michael Beutler
Luca Buvoli
Simon Dybbroe Møller
Cyprien Gaillard
Dionisio González
Konsortium
Ciprian Mureșan
Deimantas Narkevicius
Veit Stratmann

FUSION//CONFUSION
12.01. – 30.03.2008

Di bis So 10 bis 18 Uhr, Fr bis 21 Uhr

Museum Folkwang

Kahrstraße 16
45128 Essen

www.museum-folkwang.de

Exhibition poster fusion//confusion – poster (collaboration: Markus Dressen/Pascal Storz) – Museum Folkwang – 2008

Exhibition catalogue fusion//confusion – catalogue [collaboration: Markus Dressen/Pascal Storz – museum Folkwang – 2008

9. What is your idea about the future of small studios? Do you think that small studios do not have any other choice but to expand in order to survive in these times of globalization?

Running a small studio is not a problem at all. Unfortunately, content and the objective view deciding about the quality of a piece of work are not debated to the same degree.

10. Please describe and elaborate on the goals or plans that you have for your studio for the next five years?

We hope to earn enough money to make a decent living, doing the things we love to do, so that we will never have to turn to one of the big advertising agencies and sell our souls.

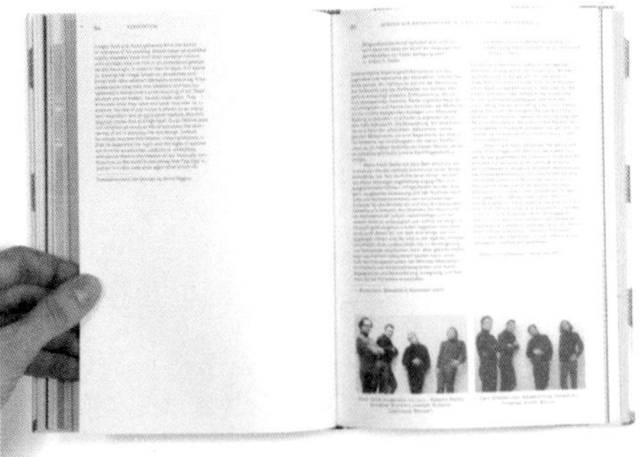

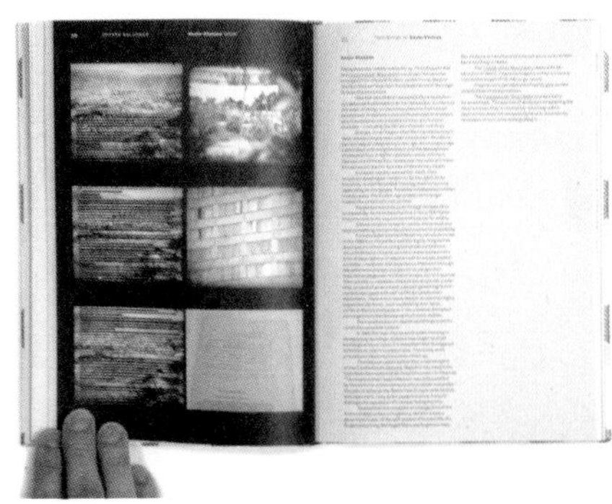

The strange case Dr. Jekyll and Mr. Hyde – poster – self publisher – 2007

Bunny lake is gone – exhibition card – gallery ritter zamet – 2006

Without titel – illustration – self publisher – 2007

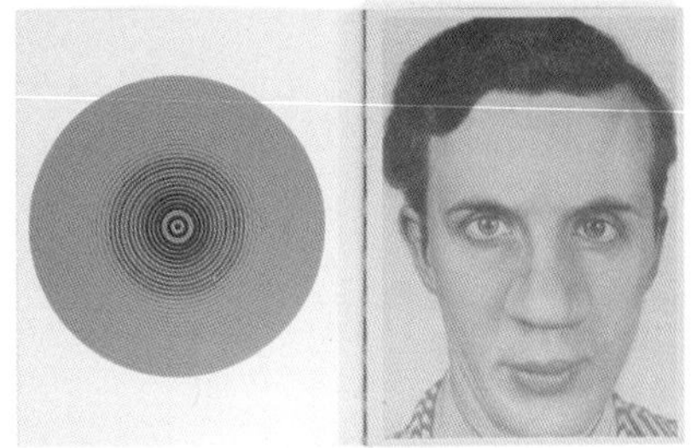

Schlummers, Oberhand gewann und ihn aus dem Leben drängte. Hydes Haß gegen Jekyll war ganz anderer Art. Seine Angst vor dem Galgen veranlaßte ihn immer wieder, vorübergehenden Selbstmord zu begehen und in die untergeordnete Stellung eines Teiles zurückzukehren, statt eine selbständige Persönlichkeit darzustellen. Doch fluchte er der Notwendigkeit, er fluchte der Verzagtheit, die Jekyll jetzt befallen hatte, und er war beleidigt über die Abneigung, mit der er betrachtet wurde. Daher auch die unwürdigen Possen, die er mir spielte, indem er in meiner Handschrift Gotteslästerungen an die Seiten meiner Bücher schrieb, Briefe meines Vaters verbrannte und sein Porträt vernichtete, und wenn er nicht Angst vor dem Tode gehabt hätte, so hätte er sich schon längst zugrunde gerichtet, um mich mitzureißen. Aber seine Liebe zum Leben ist wunderbar; ich gehe sogar weiter: obgleich mich eine Schwäche befällt und ich zu Eis erstarre beim bloßen Gedanken an ihn, bringe ich es fertig, ihn von Herzen zu bemitleiden, wenn ich mir die Verworfenheit und Leidenschaft seines Hanges zum Leben vergegenwärtige und wenn ich daran denke, wie er sich vor meiner Macht fürchtet, ihn durch Selbstmord auszulöschen. Es ist sinnlos,

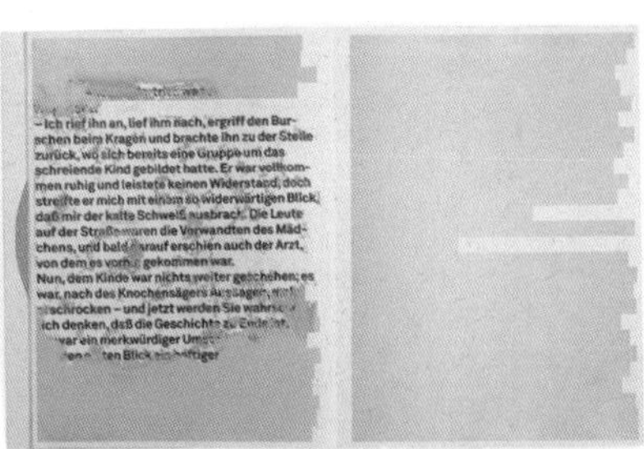

– Ich rief ihn an, lief ihm nach, ergriff den Burschen beim Kragen und brachte ihn zu der Stelle zurück, wo sich bereits eine Gruppe um das schreiende Kind gebildet hatte. Er war vollkommen ruhig und leistete keinen Widerstand, doch streifte er mich mit einem so widerwärtigen Blick, daß mir der kalte Schweiß ausbrach. Die Leute auf der Straße waren die Verwandten des Mädchens, und bald darauf erschien auch der Arzt, von dem es vorher gekommen war.
Nun, dem Kinde war nichts weiter geschehen; es war, nach des Knochensägers Aussagen,
schrocken – und jetzt werden Sie wahr
ich denken, daß die Geschichte zu Ende ist.
war ein merkwürdiger Um
ten Blick

The strange case Dr. Jekyll and Mr. Hyde – book – self publisher – 2007

karlssonwilker

team:
Hjalti Karlsson
Jan Wilker

contact:
karlssonwilker inc
536 6th avenue
New York City 10011
USA
T + 1 212 9298064
F + 1 212 9298063
tellmewhy@karlssonwilker.com
www.karlssonwilker.com

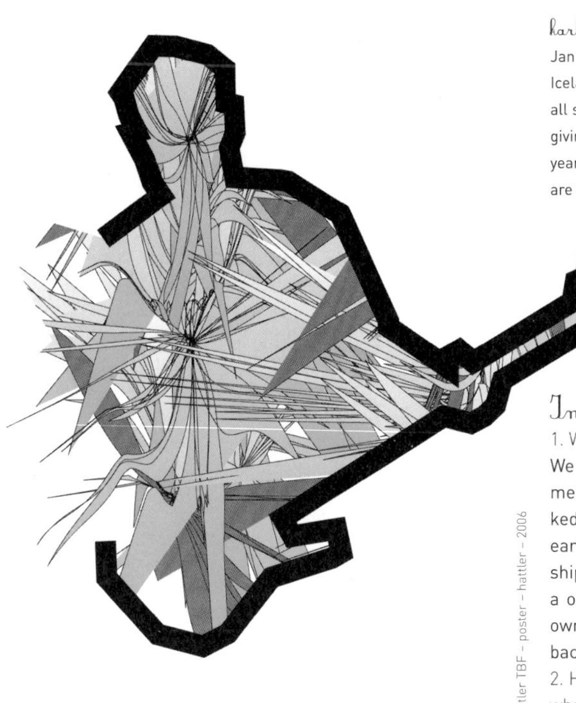

karlssonwilker is the design studio of Hjalti Karlsson and Jan Wilker, located in the heart of Manhattan. Originally from Iceland and Germany respectively, the two of them work on all sorts of projects with a wide range of clients. Both enjoy giving talks and workshops. Combined, they have over 90 years of experience ahead of them. From time to time there are parties on their backyard rooftop.

Hattler TBF – poster – hattler – 2006

Interview with karlssonwilker

1. What led to the formation of your studio?

We met while working with the great Stefan Sagmeister at Sagmeister Inc.. Hjalti had already worked with him from 1996 to 2000, and Jan arrived in early 2000 and did his three-month design internship. Around this time, Stefan had decided to go on a one-year sabbatical later that year. Starting our own design firm was the only thing we could think of back then, even though we hardly knew each other.

2. How many staff people does your studio have and what are their main working fields?

It's Hjalti Karlsson, Jan Wilker and one intern who changes every three months. And right now we have the amazing Frank DeRose working with us, since Hjalti became a father recently and is not working full time these days. We all do the same, and that is designing and trying to have a good time.

3. How does a regular working day at your studio look like, how is the day structured?

We all come in around 10 a.m., talk a little, have some breakfast if needed, then slowly sit down and start the day, at our desks. We walk around the office a lot during the day, because we cannot sit for too long. We sit in the back room, or sit at our in-house bar, change the music, watch the things the others are doing, talk, and/or anything else. Then, around 2 or 3pm, someone becomes so hungry that he or she goes out and gets lunch for everyone else. We work until 8 p.m., but on many days much longer. Quite often we also come in during weekends, at least for a short day.

4. How much leisure time do you have during a year?

We lecture and give workshops a lot, so we travel to all kinds of places. This is the only way we get out of New York, and it's a great way to see new places, since there are always people waiting for you at the airport: instant access to the "natives".

5. Which business areas do your clients mainly come from? Is the number of your clients increasing or rather declining?

These days, most of our clients come from the cultural sector. We didn't push for this, it just happened that way. Regarding the number of clients, it feels like it has been pretty much the same for the past few years. No big changes in here.

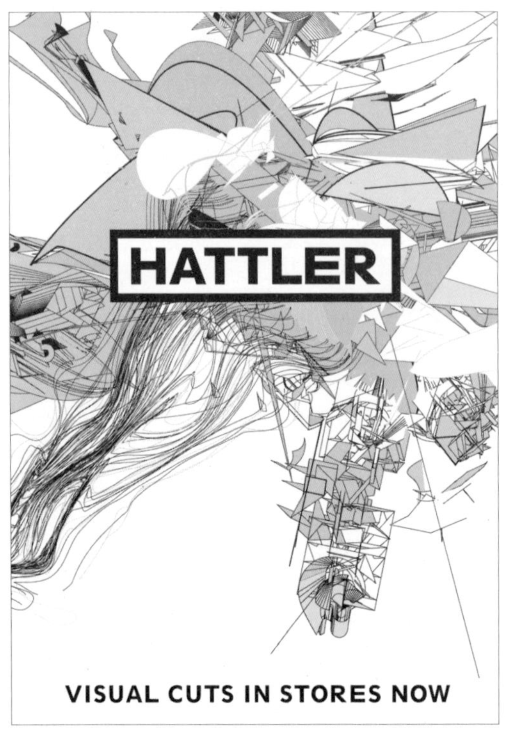

Hattler VC – poster – hattler – 2007

Hattler HK – poster – hattler – 2005

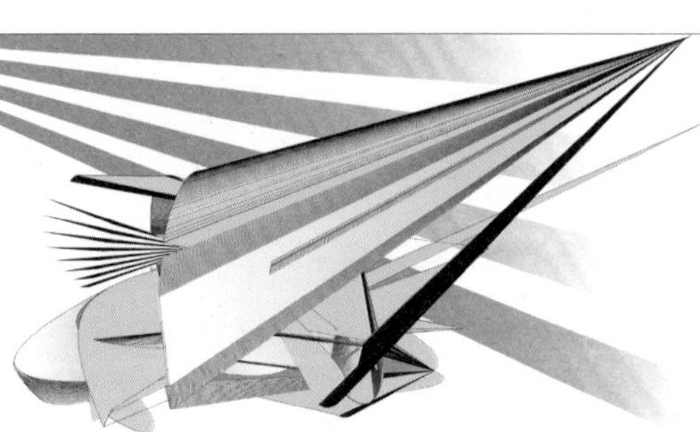

Hattler BC – poster, cd cover – hattler – 2004

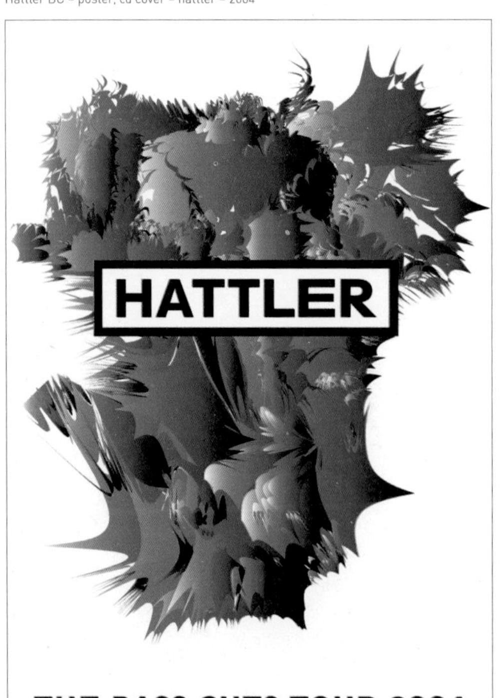

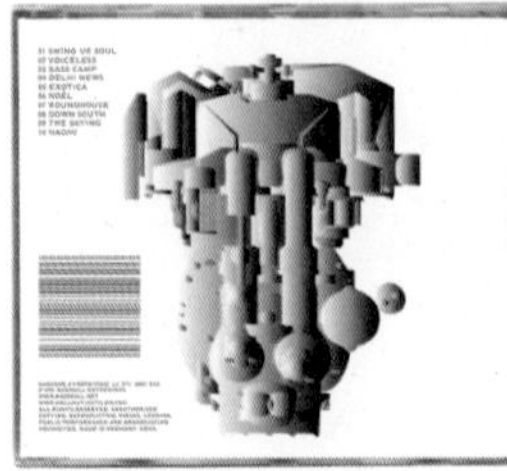

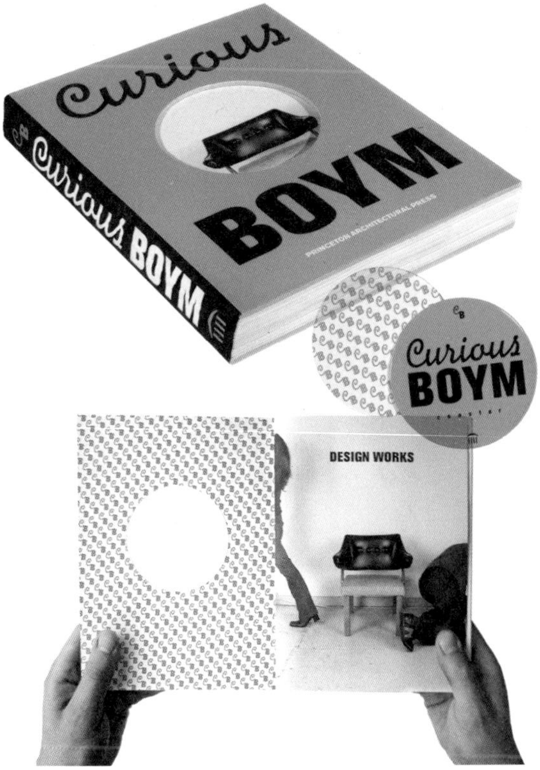

Boym – book – Princeton architectural press – 2003

6. Do you have a specific corporate philosophy or maybe a mission statement like other companies, which is reflected in the way you steer the studio's course?

We answer this question in two parts:

a) We don't have a written, well-phrased paragraph about how "multi-disciplinary, award-winning, successful and special" we are; all designers' mission statements usually suck, and they all sound exactly the same. We couldn't write something we were happy with, so we just live without one.

b) Every year in January, the two of us go out for drinks to talk about the year ahead, and make some kind of a one-and-a-half-year plan. That's as far as we go.

7. What, from your point of view, makes the difference between a small studio and a big company?

As a small company, one can be more risky and personally involved or vulnerable, but obviously not necessarily. There is more variety in small companies. Big companies lack strong personality or strong points of view, because that doesn't mix well with big money, hence they're all the same.

8. What kind of advantages and disadvantages does a small studio have compared to a big company?

See above 7.

Creative time – book – creative time, inc. – 2007

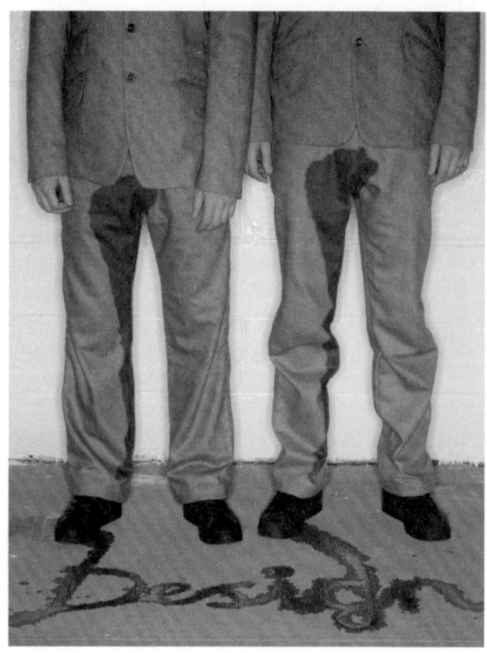

Creativity magazine – magazine (photography: Elisabeth Smolarz) – creativity magazine – 2004

Guggenheim hugo boss prize – book – the guggenheim foundation – 2006

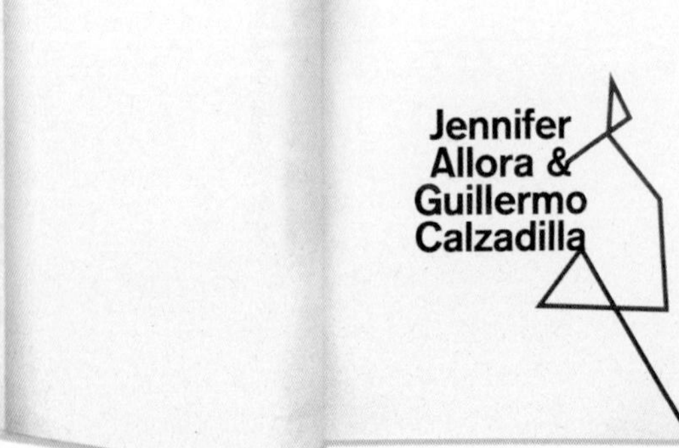

9. What is your idea about the future of small studios? Do you think that small studios do not have any other choice but to expand in order to survive in these times of globalization?
There will always be small studios. The more small studios out there the better. Globalization will have no negative effect on the number of small studios. To the contrary, over the past few years we convinced ourselves that an increase in small studios was detectable, and it will continue.

10. Please describe and elaborate on the goals or plans that you have for your studio for the next five years?
See above 6. We will continue to try to make each day a good day here in the office. And we'll do our best to do good work.

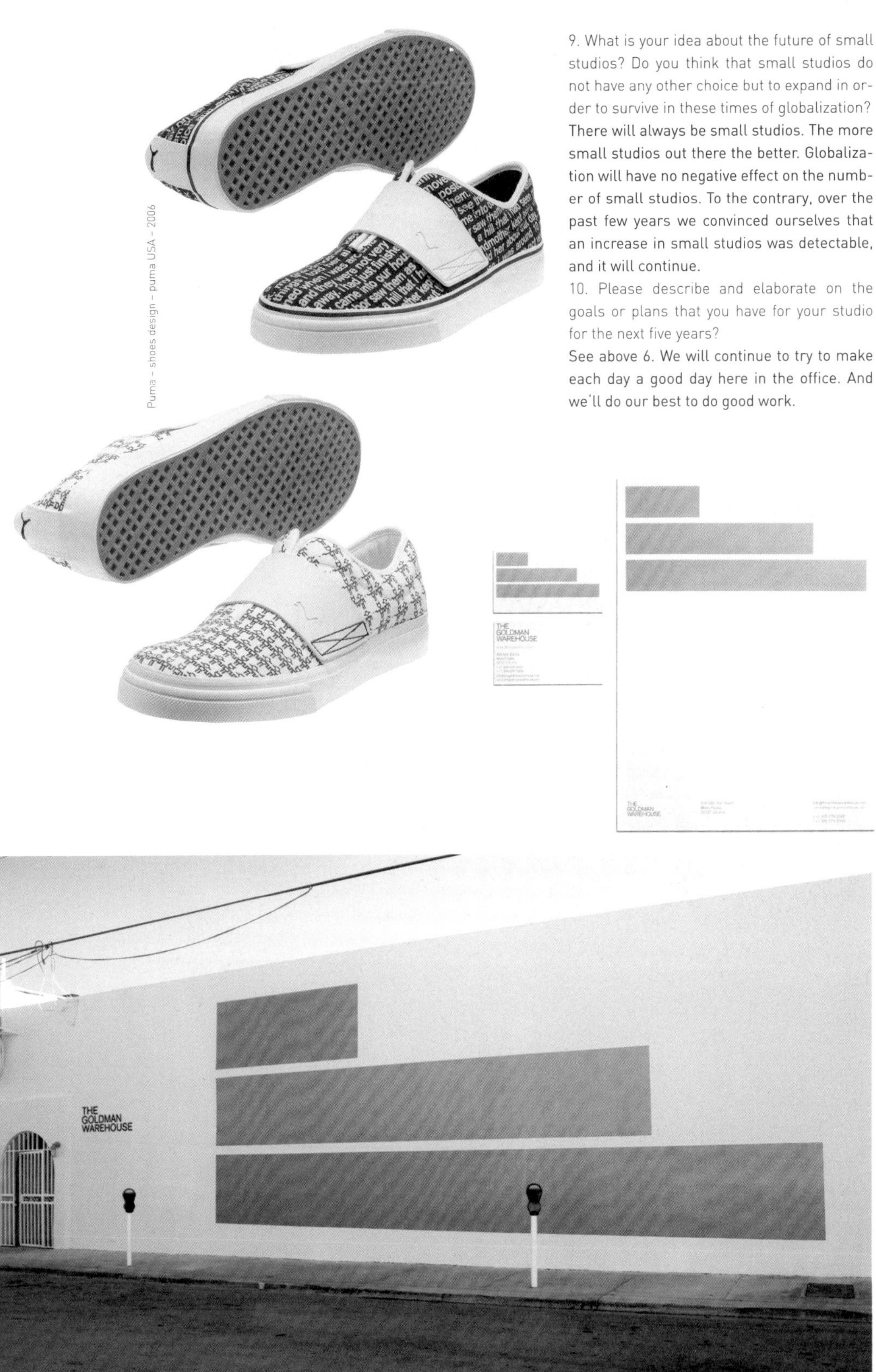

Puma – shoes design – puma USA – 2006

Goldman warehouse – corporate identity – goldman properties – 2006

Oliver Kartak
team:
Oliver Kartak
contact:
Gersthoferstr. 126/10
1180 Wien, Austria
T + 43 195 77127
M + 43 699 10410690
office@oliverkartak.com
www.oliverkartak.com

Oliver Kartak – I always wanted to be self-employed, it was already my plan during design school. After 4 ½ years of gathering experience at a design studio co-owned by Neville Brody, where I focused mainly on on-screen graphics and channel identities, I started my own small studio. I had done quite a number of channel designs as creative director and felt ready for something new. In the following years I continued working in my area of expertise, while being able to experiment and expand my abilities. I took on photography on a completely self-educated path, directed commercials, sharpened my editing senses, flew all over the world as director/camera man for a cultural TV series, wrote a couple of screenplays, and directed and edited my first short feature film. None of this would have been possible had I stayed in a steady job. It is the joy of being able to choose what you want to do, whenever you want to do it, and whom you want to have as partners. Since 2007, I am professor for graphic design at the University Of Applied Arts in Vienna. It is a joy as well and my goal is to support young designers to develop an open mind about cutting their own paths. I invite fellow minds to travel with me (www.klaasekartak.com). Merrits of distinction and nominations at: Promax/BDA, ARC Awards NY, Trend Austrian Annual Report Awards, ArtDirectorsClub NY, Creative Club Austria, Art Directors Club Germany.

Friendly travelers – cd cover – material records – 2007

Interview with Oliver Kartak

1. What led to the formation of your studio?

I knew very early on, that I wanted to work self-employed, mainly because I found all the larger company structures I encountered as a freelancer to be poisoned by intrigues and mini-wars. As a result of this, the quality of work was usually compromised. After four and a half years employment at DMC Design for media and communication Vienna, where we started out as a four-member "band", basically building it from scratch, I left the studio at a time when it was growing rapidly and became self-employed.

2. How many staff people does your studio have and what are their main working fields?

There is only one fully employed person in my studio, and that's me. I work with a changing number of field specialists and freelance workers. I find this strategy very suitable for my needs as it leaves me great freedom in choosing my assignments.

3. How does a regular working day at your studio look like, how is the day structured?

We get up quite early due to our two-year old daughter. Then the family has breakfast together and I leave to see my class for graphic design at the University Of Applied Arts in Vienna or I go into my working room to tackle the issues of the day. Lunch and dinner time is family time, and I usually take some hours off everyday for my daughter. Music is a steady companion throughout the day.

4. How much leisure time do you have during a year?

It depends on ongoing projects, of course. I can basically say, that I have and take more leisure time than I had when I was employed, although I frequently work on weekends.

Glow – cd cover – material records – 2008

Joris Roelofs – cd cover – material records – 2008

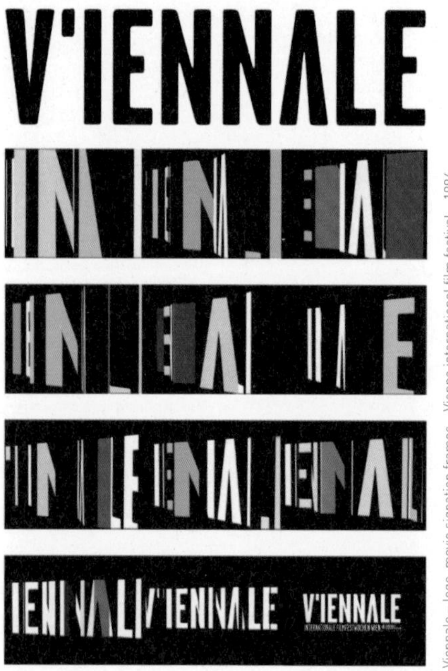

Viennale – logo, movie signation frames – Vienna international film festival – 1994

VIVA logo – channel identity – VIVA – 1994-1999

5. Which business areas do your clients mainly come from? Is the number of your clients increasing or rather declining?
I am working in different fields, be it music industry, broadcast industry or cultural affairs. I do print, motion graphics, or corporate stuff on various scales, as well as photography and directing. I am happy to say, that my work load is steady, and I try to choose wisely what assignments I am taking on.

6. Do you have a specific corporate philosophy or maybe a mission statement like other companies, which is reflected in the way you steer the studio's course?
I see graphic design as way of thinking and an attitude towards life, rather than a specific field of work.

7. What, from your point of view, makes the difference between a small studio and a big company?
Creative concepts can be more daring, and should be.

8. What kind of advantages and disadvantages does a small studio have compared to a big company?
Creative concepts can be more daring, and should be.

X13 – opener frames – experimental clip magazin for red bull tv – 2008

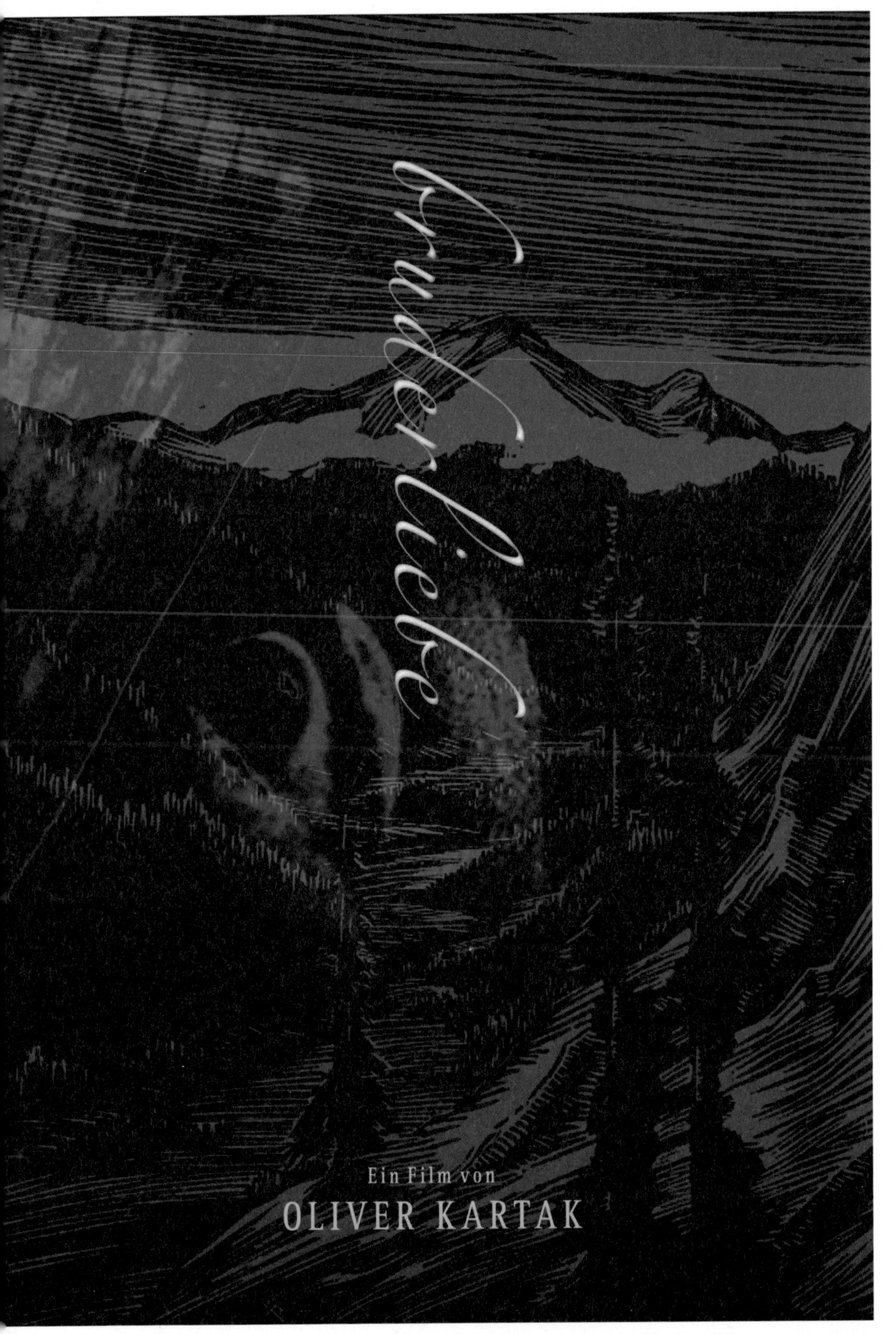

A brothers love – film poster – 45 min feature film for television script. director, editor: Oliver Kartak – 2006

Sincerely yours – record cover – klein records – 2005

9. What is your idea about the future of small studios? Do you think that small studios do not have any other choice but to expand in order to survive in these times of globalization?

There will always be creative structures on a small scale, and their present and future do not lie in expansion, but in their creative force.

10. Please describe and elaborate on the goals or plans that you have for your studio for the next five years?

I had a very demanding and wonderful time writing, directing, and editing my 45 min feature film. I would love to take this experience further into a full length feature film.

Princess Him – record cover, inner spread – klein records – 2005

MUM - leader of monkey – record cover, inner sleeves – klein records – 2004

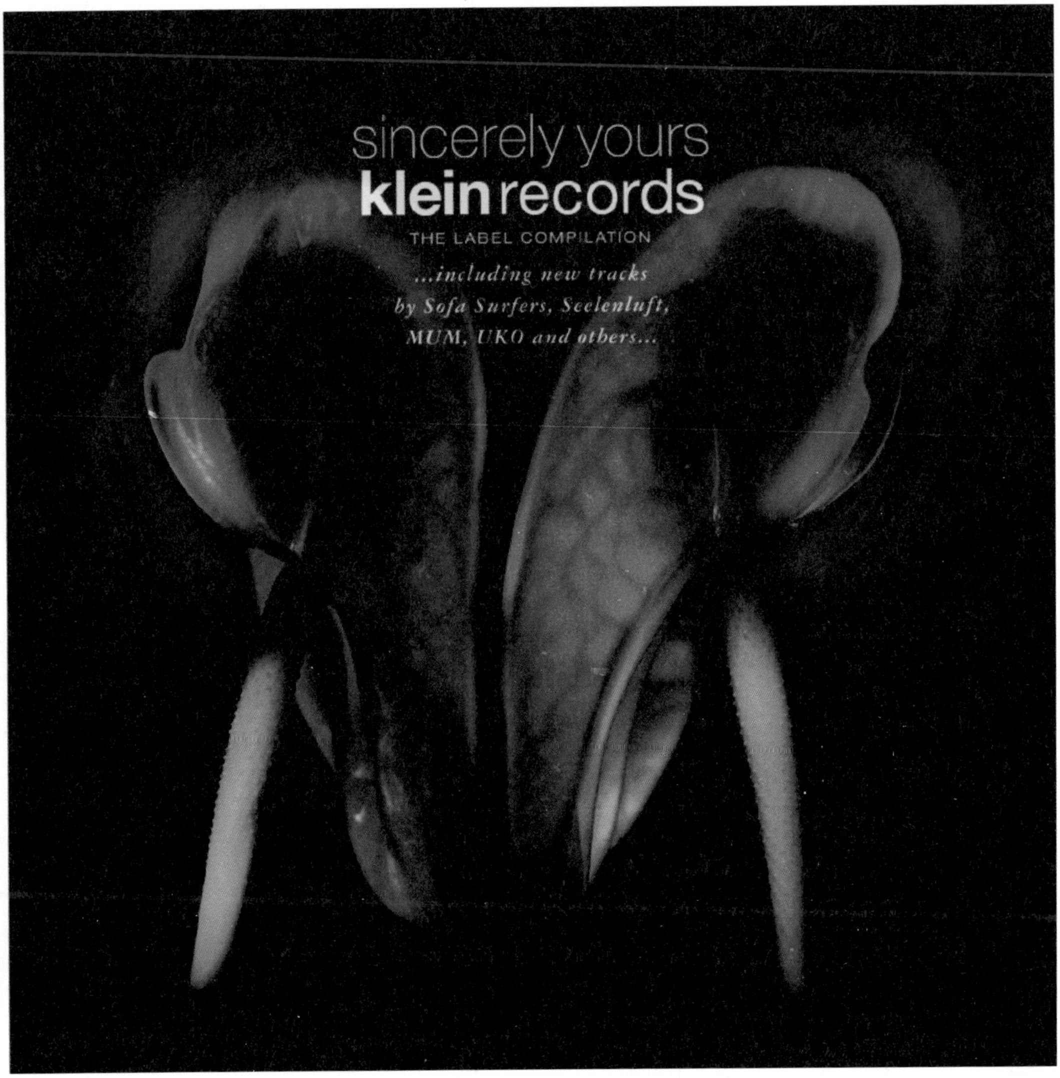

sincerely yours
klein records
THE LABEL COMPILATION
...including new tracks by Sofa Surfers, Seelenluft, MUM, UKO and others...

Sincerely yours – record cover – klein records – 2005

Kawakong designworks

team:
Ong Chung Ping
Ng Ai Beng (Ming)

contact:
sunwaymas commercial centre
92-A-3B, Jalan PJU1/3B
47301 Petaling Jaya
Selangor, Malaysia
T /F + 603 78809971
info@kawakong.com
www.kawakong.com

Commercial laundry consultant – identity design, company profile – BCL marketing – 2004

Kawakong designworks started in September 1999. His name is Chung and his partner and wife is Ming. The name kawakong means "talk to me" in Hokkien, a Chinese dialect, commonly used among their family, friends and people in their hometown. The name is about who they are and what they do, and they considered it to reflect them perfectly, and it still does. As a working motto, "talk to us" simply means that the more effort they make to listen to their clients, the better their clients will understand their work. Both of them have completed their studies at the Malaysian Institute of Art. Like many others, they started in the advertising industry, doing paste-up work and providing assistance to art directors, without knowing exactly what they really wanted. About a year later, they realized that their hearts belong to graphic design, and this led them to study graphic design in Curtin University, Western Australia. In 1996, they returned to Kuala Lumpur, and for the first time they got paid as designers. But the real reward still comes from job satisfaction. Their passion in graphic design grew each and everyday which led them to form kawakong designworks, a graphic and identity design studio. The studio is a chance for them to discover their own destiny as designers, and more even important, to free them from the traffic of business. They like doing identity design, especially starting from print work like business cards, company profiles, posters, calendars, or even web design. They have also started the B-sides project, an illustration series inspired by movies, music, scenes from the streets, silly jokes, unexplained dreams, and people who dress for themselves – or maybe ourselves – which somehow find ways to appear in our minds. For them, design is categorized into two sections, firstly, "design for clients" and secondly, "design for ourselves"; and their mission is to make the gap closer each everyday.

Interview with Kawakong designworks

1. What led to the formation of your studio?

Freedom is something we want more than anything else. Being in charge of our time as much as possible. To choose what we want to do, and most important, working in our own space. These are the most luxury things that we can have, and that has led us to form our studio.

2. How many staff people does your studio have and what are their main working fields?

Just the two of us and designers.

3. How does a regular working day at your studio look like, how is the day structured?

We never really "structured" our day. It depends on the job load and on how productive we are.

4. How much leisure time do you have during a year?

Not much, but it is good enough.

5. Which business areas do your clients mainly come from? Is the number of your clients increasing or rather declining?

There are no specific business areas which we are targeting. Most of our interesting clients come from the new generation of business entrepreneurs, who are ready to listen to what we can really offer. Since we started in 1999, the number of our clients has never really increased or decreased but the type of clients has changed quite a bit, and they began to get more involved in the design process which has made the designs more meaningful.

6. Do you have a specific corporate philosophy or maybe a mission statement like other companies, which is reflected in the way you steer the studio's course?

Always to make sure that the client knows who we are and how we work before hiring us.

Beauty & skin care centre – calendar – serenity skin therapy – 2007
Diva - classical music concert – poster, program booklet – artists platform – 2006

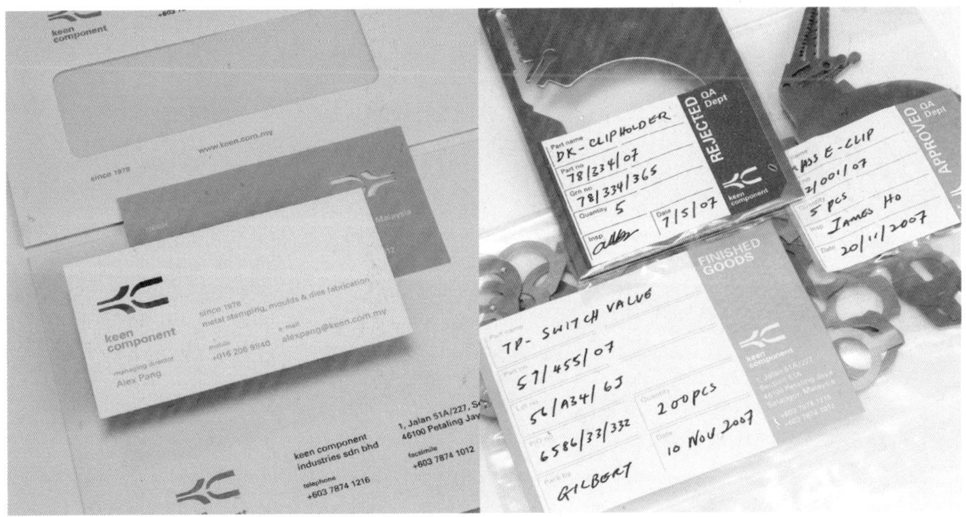

Metal stamping factory – identity design – keen component – 2008

Longing - classical music concert – poster – Peter Ong – 2006

7. What from your point of view, makes the difference between a small studio and a big company?

A small studio is like a 100 meter run and a bigger company is like a 4 x 100 meter hurdle run.

8. What kind of advantages and disadvantages does a small studio have compare to a big company?

As a small company, we don't always get enough support from suppliers but throughout the years we have worked with some reliable smaller suppliers. Sometimes clients expect us to charge less.

9. What is your idea about the future of small studios? Do you think small studios do not have any other choice but to expand in order to survive in these times of globalization?

For us, the future is very unpredictable but the choice is always in our hand. As a small studio we see that it is a great way to make design works, and balance our time with our everyday life. In my country, some small restaurants from our grandfather's generation survived and are successful without much expansion simply because they still serve great food. This has really inspired and encouraged us to continue doing what we know best.

10. Please describe and elaborate on the goals or plans that you have for your studio for the next five years?

We wish to meet more clients who appreciate our work and to produce designs that make us happy. In 5 years, we will be 13 years young, and we do feel the need to do something in order to continue enjoying what we are doing now. Probably, it is time for us to "expand", yet to stay small.

Kids wear – poster – gaagookids – 2004
Kids menu – menu design – mandarin oriental hotel – 2004

Calender 2005 - paper merchandise, calendar - fine paper takeo - 2005&2004
Melody of evening/classical music concert - poster, program booklet - artists platform - 2004

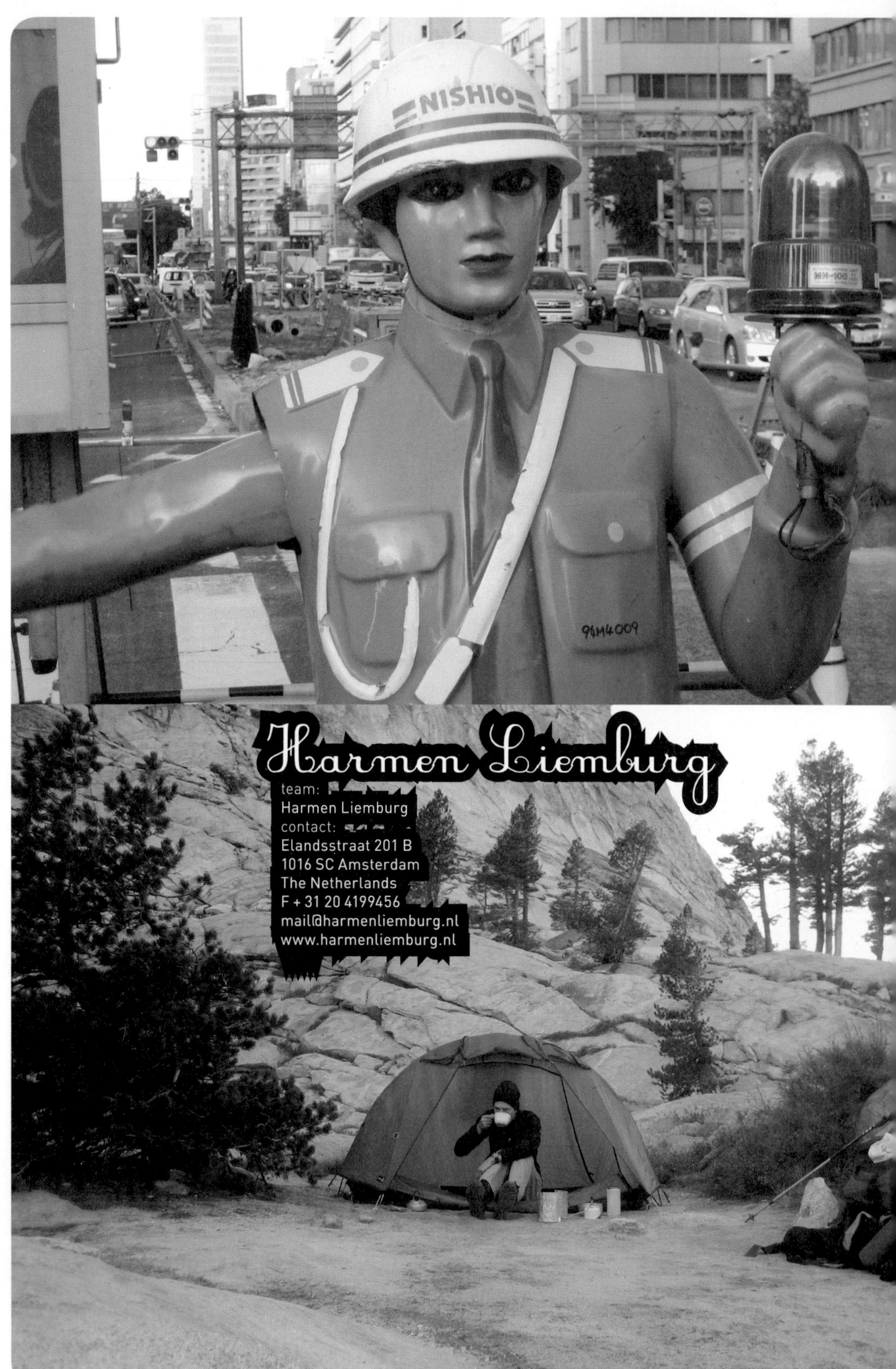

Harmen Liemburg

team:
Harmen Liemburg

contact:
Elandsstraat 201 B
1016 SC Amsterdam
The Netherlands
F + 31 20 4199456
mail@harmenliemburg.nl
www.harmenliemburg.nl

Harmen Liemburg – After graduating as a social geographer/cartographer from Utrecht University in 1992, Harmen Liemburg set out to become a graphic designer. Freshly graduated from the Gerrit Rietveld Academie in 1998, he started a collaboration with Richard Niessen as the "Golden Masters". Since 2002, Liemburg is working solo again. His projects frequently involve collaborations with other (graphic) artists and result in elaborate and layered images that are often silkscreen-printed by himself. His designs and illustrations are utilized in print and architecture, and have been exhibited in numerous group exhibitions and publications.

Interview with Harmen Liemburg

1. What led to the formation of your studio?

First of all, my graduation as a graphic designer at the Gerrit Rietveld Academie in 1998, after that a collaboration with Richard Niessen. I had my role models in the field of graphic design, too, in the form of friends who started small studios together. Stubborn individuals as Max Kisman (NL) or J. Otto Seibold (USA), for example, who where doing their very specific "thing" at that time, encouraged me to pursue a similar career.

2. How many staff people does your studio have and what are their main working fields?

I currently work alone, which means I create all concepts and the artwork, and do screen printing work as well. No interns or other staff. I like to see myself as a designer, researcher, printmaker, and journalist.

3. How does a regular working day at your studio look like, how is the day structured?

I'm fairly disciplined but also extremely flexible. I spend a lot of time communicating with many different people about past and current projects, future plans and other stuff. Sometimes it's hard to focus and actually create new things. I really need a rock-hard deadline or a practical necessity. I enjoy doing my own screen printing because it gives me a break from the computer, plus the opportunity to work with graphic materials in a very physical way.

4. How much leisure time do you have during a year?

I cannot tell exactly. I never count my hours, and most of the time work and leisure time completely run over into each other. Most ideas come when I'm lying in bed, anyway, or when I'm hiking. Maybe I should spend more time sleeping! These days, however, I'm trying to make a clearer mark by spending more time outside. I started kayaking, and when it's time for that, I drop everything else.

5. Which business areas do your clients mainly come from?

Most of my clients are from the cultural field. Some are institutional, but in that case there's usually a cultural advisor involved. An important part my work is self-initiated, though. Somehow I always seem to have sufficient (non-)commercial projects going to keep things running.

6. Do you have a specific corporate philosophy or maybe a mission statement like other companies, which is reflected in the way you steer the studio's course?

Like any other artist, my work is strongly connected to my life and personality. I can only say what I'm aspiring in terms of artistic goals, not so much what I could do for my client in terms of solutions or stuff like that. But if you like to make your life more beautiful, rewarding and interesting, try me!

Riesling – illustration – Hollands diep magazine – 2007

The recordshow – poster – the recordshow – 2006

Crispy cloud kombini – poster – sieboldhouse, Leiden/self commissioned – 2007

Offshore (a tip of the liemberg...) – poster – northeastern university, department of visual arts – 2006

At random – poster – at random/self commissioned – 2006

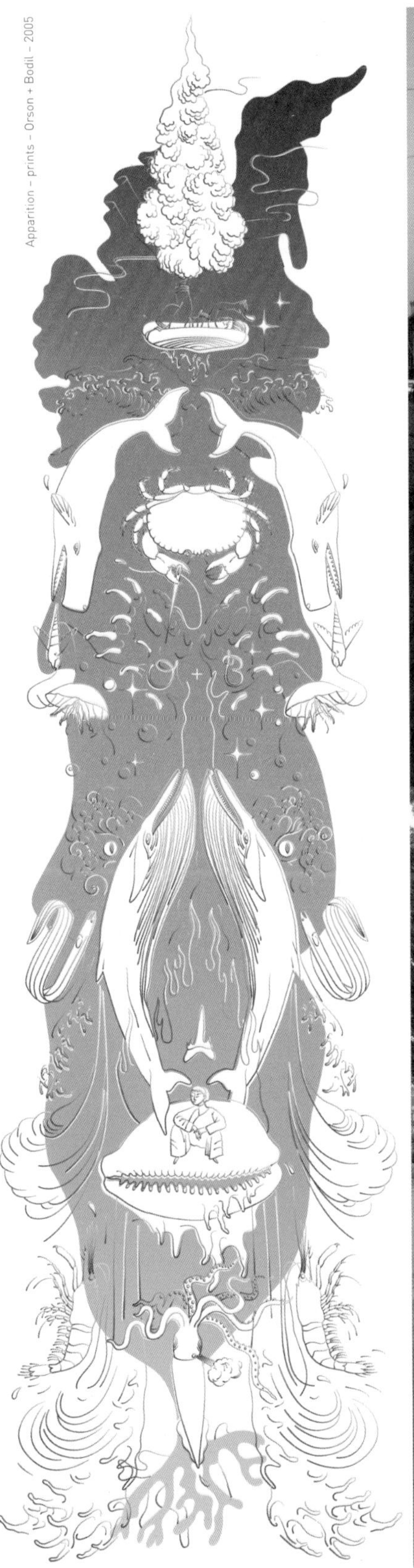

Apparition – prints – Orson + Bodil – 2005

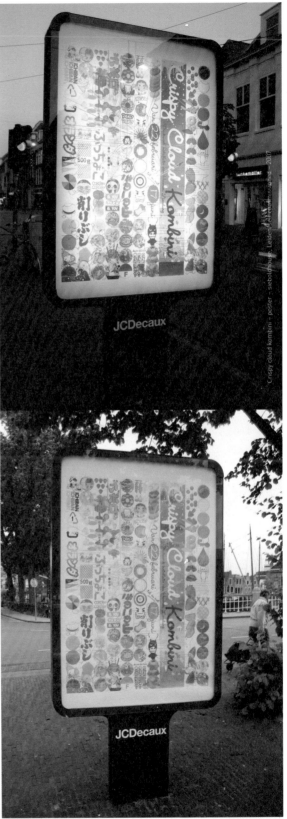

Crispy cloud kombini – poster – sieboldhouse, Leiden/self commissioned – 2007

7. What, from your point of view, makes the difference between a small studio and a big company?

Well, it's all about scale and organization, isn't it? I have to be multifunctional and multitasking, working with two hands and only 24 hours, so there's a limit to what I can achieve single-handedly.

8. What kind of advantages and disadvantages does a small studio have compared to a big company?

Think only of what I could do using more and better resources, meaning assistants. Sometimes it's a real challenge to do everything by myself, but in general I very much enjoy the creative and practical freedom. Nobody tells me what to do, and I don't have to make sure others are not running out of work either.

9. What is your idea about the future of small studios? Do you think that small studios do not have any other choice but to expand in order to survive in these times of globalization?

I really don't know. For me, there's simply no other choice than doing what I'm doing, except for doing it better and preferably faster.

10. Please describe and elaborate on the goals or plans that you have for your studio for the next five years?

One of the main challenges is to keep innovating one's own creative output instead of getting stuck in routines and well-paved paths. I'm striving for an even more intuitive way of working and having a larger output, combining my two passions – outdoor life and graphics – in a powerful way.

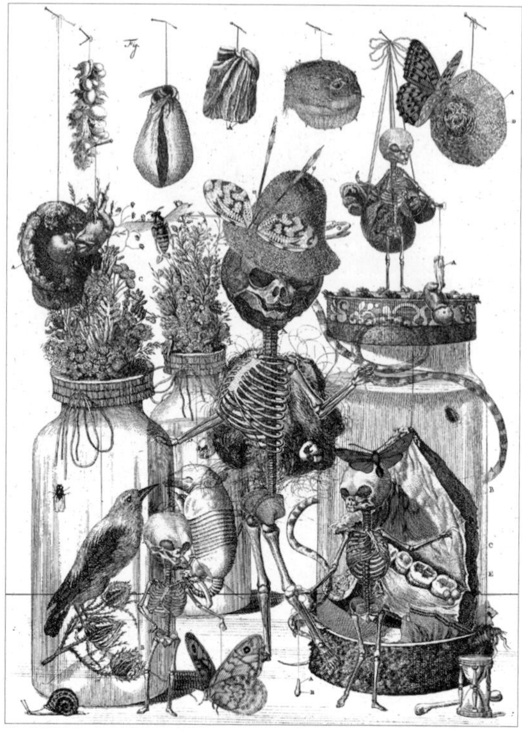

Hollands diep – illustration – Hollands diep (a new cultural magazine with an old name) – 2007

Speed – poster – seeing red – 2006

So long Santiago – commemorative poster – mcad – 2006

Fall 2005 visiting artist lecture series – poster – northeastern university Boston – 2005

Lighthouse Media

team:
Dimitris Karaiskos
contact:
115 Zoodohou Pigis Str,
Athens 11473, Greece
T + 30 6948084263
dkaraisk@gmail.com

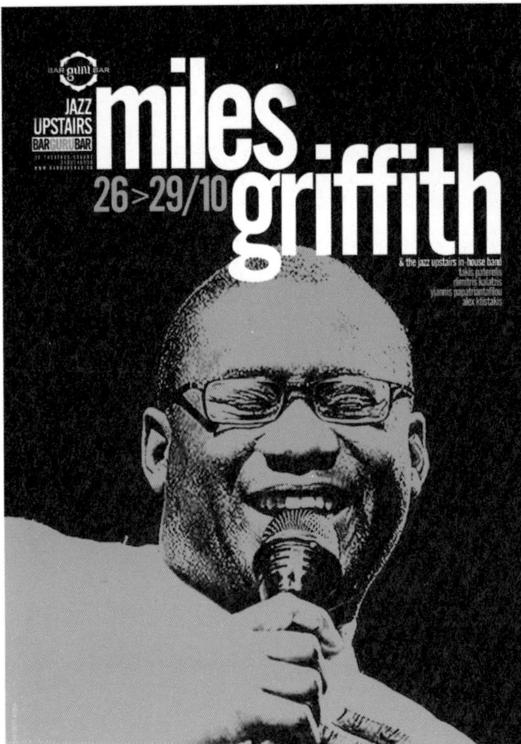

Jazz live by Miles Griffith – poster – guru bar – 2004

Jazz upstairs live venue – poster – guru bar – 2003

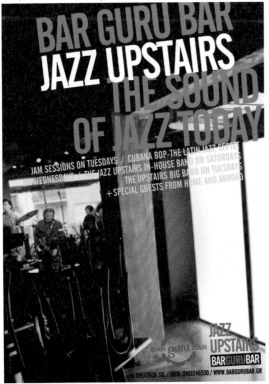

Lighthouse Media – I was born in Athens in 1973. I studied and worked in Athens and London before opening my own graphic design studio, Lighthouse Media, in Athens in 2000. I have worked for various international clients across different formats, from websites to multimedia, mobile phone interfaces to illustration and print. I take most pleasure in designing posters, especially for music events, for which I have designed a large number of them. In 2007, I won the first prize for a poster design at the "EVGE" design awards in Greece. I collect rare publications and old books. My collection of strange objects washed up by the sea was photographed and turned into a book called "Flotsam & Jetsam" in 2007 (published by Gema Editions, Athens). I currently work on two more forthcoming books, "Everyday Typography" and "Secret Athens", to be published by Editions Jonglez. I was chosen to represent my country at a poster exhibition for the "European Cultural Season" of the French Ministry of Culture which will be hosted at the airports of Paris from July to December 2008. Since January 2008, I collaborate with AGI designer Dimitris Arvanitis. I love jazz, surfing, boxing, running, trekking and my dog, Oro.

Interview with Lighthouse Media

1. What led to the formation of your studio?

After studying and working for a bit at London design firms, I grew sick of the lack of sunshine there and decided to get back to my hometown Athens and start a small studio.

2. How many stuff people does your studio have and what are their main working fields?

Two – me and a graphic designer, plus my dog. We do work, though, with a group of carefully picked freelance designers, photographers, animators, authors and programmers according to every project's needs.

3. How does a regular day at your studio look like, how is the day structured?

A regular day at my studio consists of me listening to lots of music while working, walking the dog and spending large amounts of time designing and browsing through design-related publications. There's no specific pattern of working or timetable. Days can start at 7 a.m. or 10 a.m. and can end up at 6 p.m. or 10 p.m., or even the next morning.

4. How much leisure time do you have during a year?

Normally 2-3 weeks during the summer and hopefully another 2 weeks in winter.

5. Which business areas do your clients mainly come from? Is the number of your clients increasing or rather decreasing?

Most of my clients come from the field of culture/arts/music although they also tend to come from everywhere.

6. Do you have a specific corporate philosophy or maybe a mission statement like other companies, which is reflected in the way you steer the studio's course?

Be honest, true and happy when designing. Listen to a lot of inspiring music. Learn about the great ones of the past and honor them through your work. Stay alert and well-informed about anything related to contemporary culture. Read a lot of theory and watch lots of good movies. Try not to forget the social role of design. Collect everything design-related. Collect as much info on anything as possible – there's no useless info. Everything has its role, everything is somehow related to everything. Never loose your sense of humor, that's lethal. A touch of randomness and surrealism never hurts anyone. Don't take yourself too seriously. Try to be unpredictable in a cleverly familiar way. Love what you're doing. Take care of your body – working out and eating well helps your design to get better. It's later than you think.

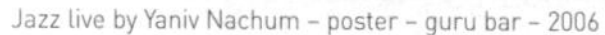
Jazz live by Yaniv Nachum – poster – guru bar – 2006

Jazz live by Joel Soto – poster – guru bar – 2005

7. What, from your point of view, makes the difference between a small studio and a big company?
Small studios are closer on the human scale and they tend to produce very unique material. Big companies are more efficient but tend to be humorless.
8. What kind of advantages and disadvantages does a small studio have compared to a big company?
A small studio can be relaxed, design-driven, sui generis, and a great value for a client's money, but there's a limit to the number of assignments it can handle. A big company can be more expensive, less original and less "human" than a small studio, but it certainly beats it with regard to the load of work it can handle.
9. What is your idea about the future of small studios? Do you think that small studios do not have any other choice but to expand in order to survive in these times of globalization?
Not necessarily. By exploiting all tools the internet has to offer, a small studio could be quite flexible and productive on a global scale.
10. Please describe and elaborate on the goals or plans that you have for your studio for the next five years.
I've recently been involved in book authoring and I enjoyed it. So I would like to go on experimenting on this field for the following two or three years. Researching unusual themes or design books and producing them sounds like a good idea. I've also been into poster design a lot, so working on these two fields at the same time would be an ideal goal. It would also be great if lots of traveling could be part of the plan.

Leaflet for jazz events – 3-fold flyer – jazz upstairs live venue – 2005

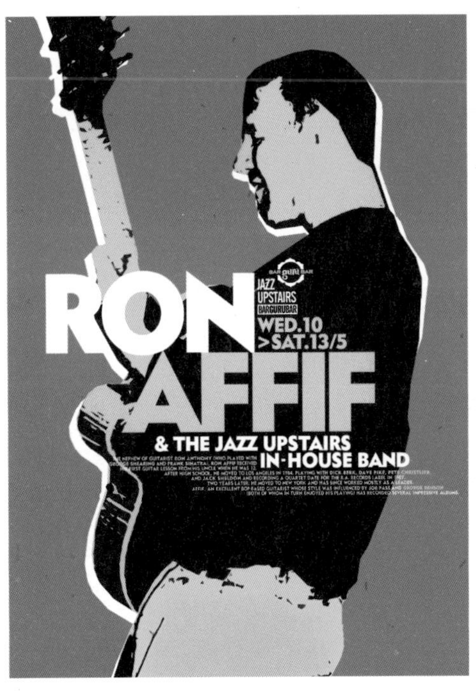

Jazz live by Ron Affif – poster – guru bar – 2006

Flotsam & jetsam – 180-page book showing objects washed up by the sea on various beaches around the world – gema publications – 2007

BAR guru BAR
SUNDAY 13.03.05
LE BAL MASQUÉ
DJ WILLI THE BEE, DJ JACKIE "NOMAMAZ" TREEHORN AND DJ AKU-AKU ON THE DECKS!

Costume party poster – poster – guru bar – 2004

Jazz band buzz sextet – poster – Guru Bar – 2003

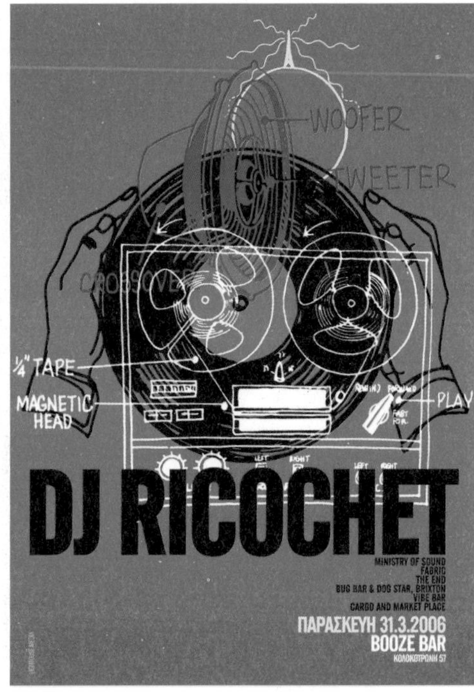

DJ sessions – poster – dj ricochet – 2005

Costume party poser – poster – guru bar – 2004

Lo Siento

team:
Borja Martinez Perez
Carolina Rodriguez
contact:
Comunicación gráfica
Palo Alto
Pellaires 30-38
08019 Barcelona, Spain
T + 34 933036492
www.losiento.net
borja@losiento.net

Lo Siento is the creative agency based in Barcelona run by Borja Martinez, who graduated from the London College of Communication with a BA in graphic design in 2003. The agency was born in 2005. Our philosophy it is about humor and the idea to have fun in any project. We think that graphic design needs to be accurate in terms of quality. Graphic excellence is one of our main standards in order to achieve good results. Part of the work produced by the agency is self-initiated, experimentation becomes a fundamental process to reinforce the media. We have designed print products and environmental graphics for the following purposes: music covers, publishing, marketing, packaging, signage, websites, corporate communications, corporate identity, and branding. Lo Siento has worked on a wide range of projects from the packaging design for Italian pasta & ice cream company Sandro Desii, the identity of the photographer's gallery La Camara Lucida, the design of the latest recipe book by Ferran Adria (2005), a booklet for the Spanish formula-one pilot Pedro de la Rosa, design covers for the electronic band The Pinker Tones, welcome packaging for the perfume company Antonio Puig, to corporate identities for the film company Alguienvolo or the shoe retail store company Vermont. We are still working in personal projects like experimental graffiti made of glue or sand, 3D typefaces made of mirror or food, and reactive photography with strong messages about injustice and climate change problems. Lo Siento means "to be passionate" but also "to be sorry".

Interview with Lo Siento

1. What led to the formation of your studio?

To have absolute freedom and control over the projects I do for different kinds of clients. Also, the idea to get more time for self-initiated projects.

2. How many staff people does your studio have and what are their main working fields?

We are two people in total: A middleweight designer and myself in person of an art director-designer.

3. How does a regular working day at your studio look like, how is the day structured?

In the morning: General planning of projects we are working on. I used to carry on with these projects, updating all the information and doing the presentations for the clients. Further, we deal with printers and production stuff. In the afternoon: The middleweight designer works in the afternoons on the projects I started in the morning.

4. How much leisure time do you have during a year?

Not too much. Lo Siento works on many weekends to update projects. We are small but we have a certain "worker activity".

5. Which business areas do your clients mainly come from?

Mostly from the fields of music, food, fashion, art.

Is the number of your clients increasing or rather declining?

The number is increasing.

6. Do you have a specific corporate philosophy or maybe a mission statement like other companies, which is reflected in the way you steer the studio's course?

To have fun. Keep it simple, but with a strong message. My personal goal is to see my clients laughing after a project presentation. Work like a craftsman and keep the work warm, sensitive, dynamic, clear.

7. What, from your point of view, makes the difference between a small studio and a big company?

Budgets? Better budget, better projects? Maybe. I think bigger budgets give you the possibility of producing more sophisticated results, more specialized collaborations with good illustrators, photographers and printers. You have the access to realizing big projects because of the budget. Big clients are looking for big companies to get big results – not small ones. They just want to get in contact with small studios when the budget is limited. Small studios have less pressure at his point. They have to explore different ways to transform a small budget into a project of high quality. One important thing for me is that in a big company there is normally no time for personal stuff, no time to practice or experimental processes in order to develop new ideas. Everything is going very fast. Everything is for tomorrow. Rush! Rush!

Bazaar Bajo Terra/bazaar under de land – packaging – bazaar – 2006

Tekko 04 – moody queuing packs – tekko 04 – 2005

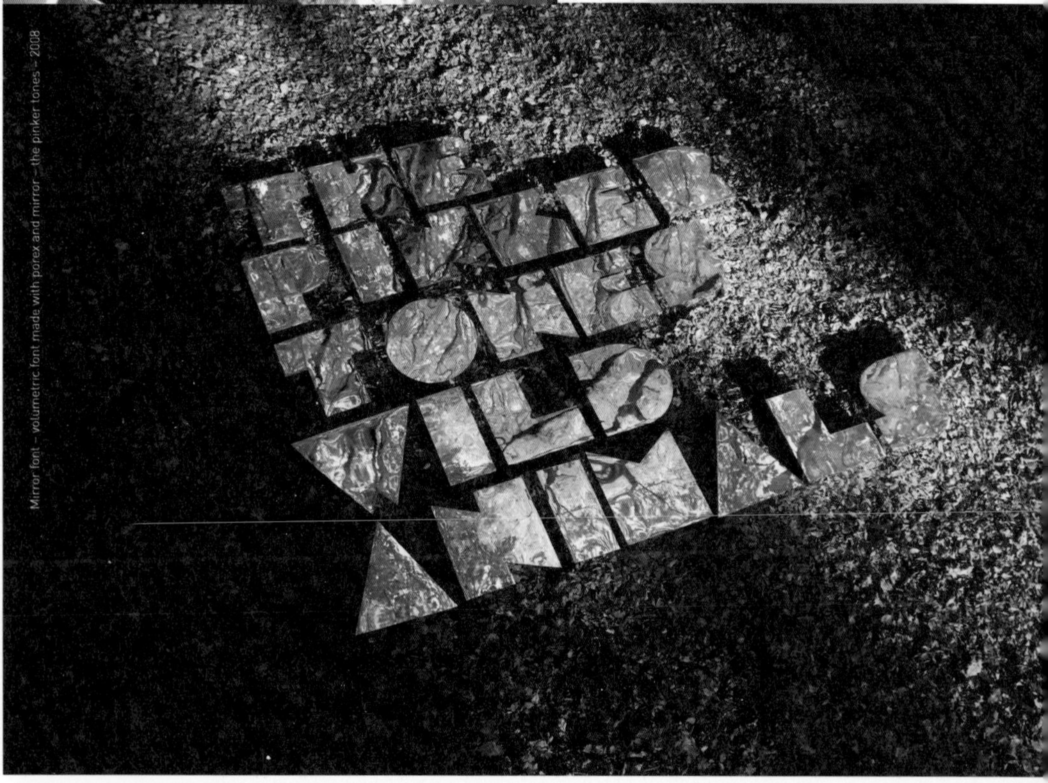

Mirror font – volumetric font made with porex and mirror – the pinker tones – 2008

Lamarca – identity – lamarca – 2004

Sandro Desii – identity packaging and general image – Sandro Desii – 2007/2008

Vermont – general identity – vermont, Barcelona shoe shop company – 2008

VERMONT
Siempre calzados

The million colour revolution – pack design – the pinker tones – 2005/06

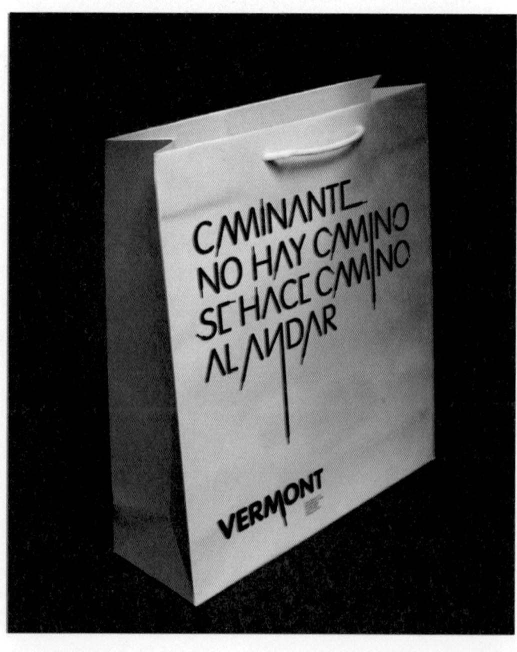

THE
UNFINISHED
SYMPATHY
THIS LIVING
KILLS

Rock for food – album cover – the unfinished – 2005

We push you pull – album cover – the unfinished – 2007

8. What kind of advantages and disadvantages does a small studio have compared to a big company?
Big studios get big clients, big projects, institutional projects; it's about big structures, big spaces, big everything!!!
9. What is your idea about the future of small studios? Do you think that small studios do not have any other choice but to expand in order to survive in these times of globalization?
I think we will grow. We will survive by making connections with good collaborators like photographers, illustrators, printers, web designers, and with other small studios. Due to the new technologies this happens frequently nowadays.
10. Please describe and elaborate on the goals or plans that you have for your studio for the next five years?
I would like to keep on doing the same work, but to have the chance of reinforcing the results in terms of quality, ideas, collaborations, and client satisfaction. And the main thing is: to have fun.

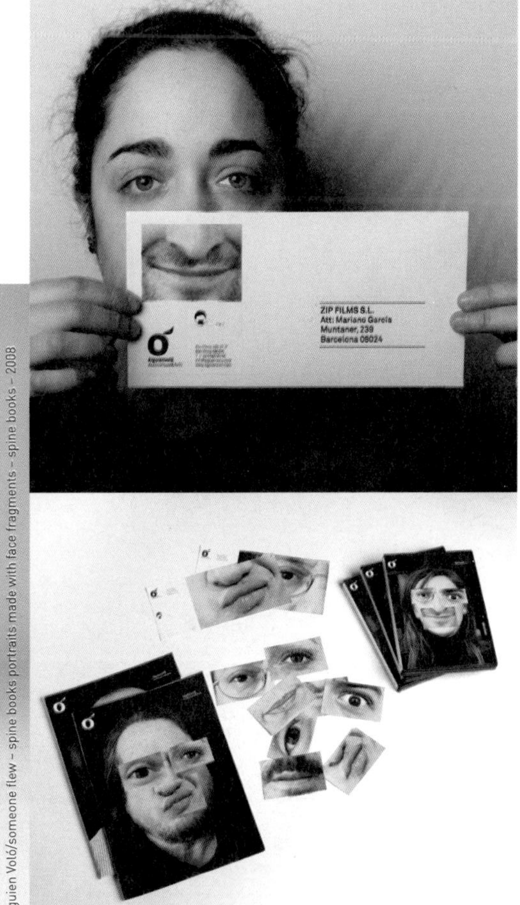

Alguien Voló/someone flew – spine books portraits made with face fragments – spine books – 2008

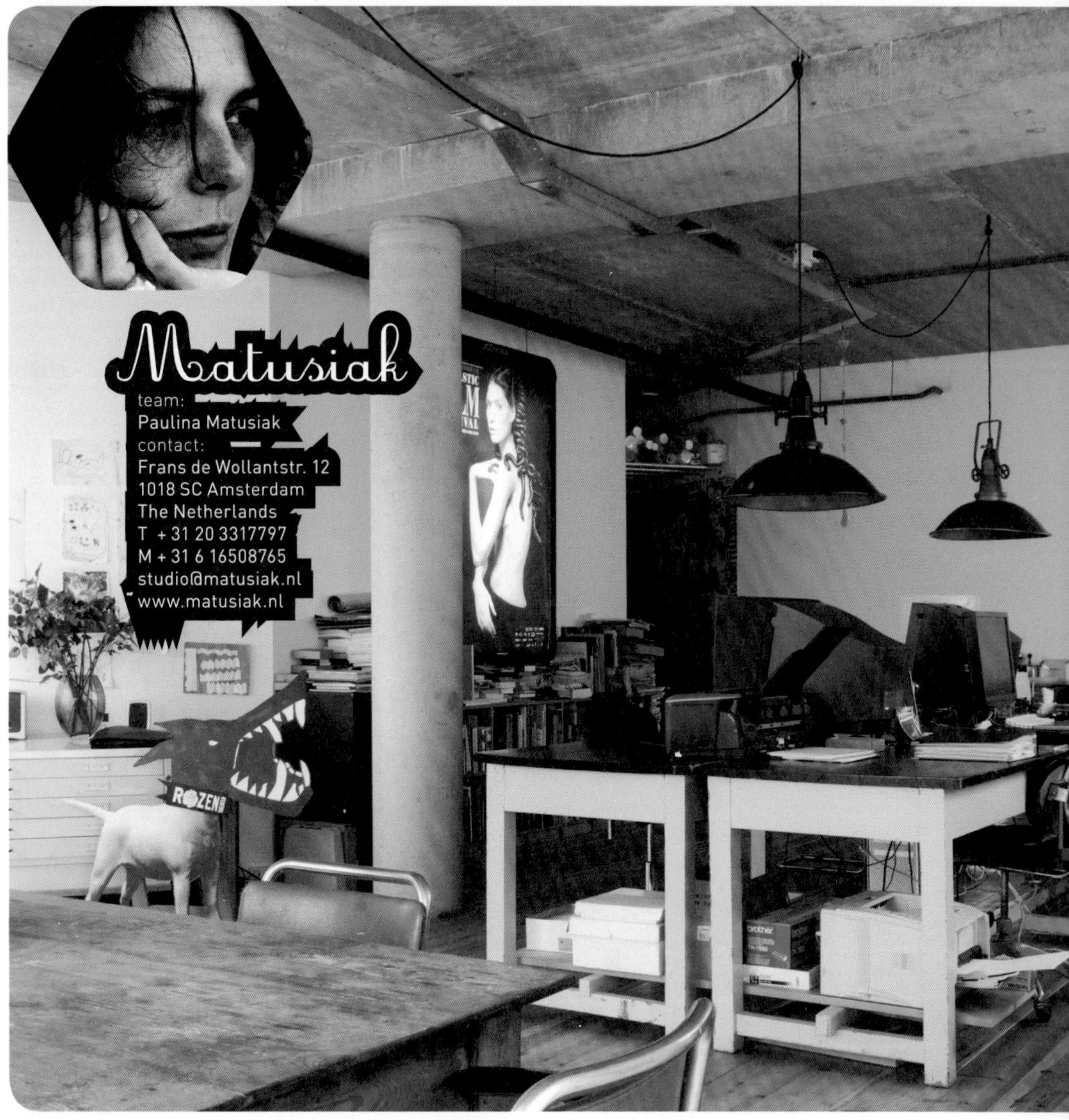

Matusiak is Paulina Matusiak's creative playground in Amsterdam. Since its inception in 2002, Paulina's signature works thrive in their own niche. Almost exclusively finding her partners in the cultural sector in the Netherlands, her visuals typically elicit strong responses. The subtle disparities evident in the work hint at an affinity with the works of Tim Burton; a certain quaintness is present in the undertone, lending a particular nuance to the visuals of her clients' performances. The studio is multidisciplinary, offering art direction, graphic and interactive design, photography and illustration. Having strong ties with the performing arts, the accent lies primarily on printed publicity. Next to designing commercial and cultural identities, Studio Matusiak predominantly develops large scale theatre posters, programs, promotional flyers and book- and CD covers. Clients include national theatre- and dance companies, performance artists active in music and stand-up comedy and various national film festivals. A much sought after designer, Paulina Matusiak is the recipient of several awards. Nominations received include those for Best Verzorgde Boeken (Best Book Design) awarded by Het Stedelijk Museum Amsterdam and the annually awarded Theater Affiche Prijs Amsterdam (Theatre Poster Prize), for which she was nominated four years consecutively. A two-time nominee in 2005 and 2006, she recently participated as sole European representative in judging the 18th Festival d'Affiches de Chaumont in France. Paulina Matusiak (1971) hails from Zgierz, Poland. After completing the secondary School of Arts in Lodz, she relocated to The Netherlands where she is accepted into the Royal Academy of Visual Arts in The Hague, graduating in Graphic and Typographic Design. Upon invitation she then worked at Matzwart, the former in-house studio of the academy. Several graphic studios followed, during which time she works as Head Designer. A four-year stint as senior designer at the prestigious, Amsterdam based studio of Anthon Beeke prepared her for a new chapter in her career. In 2002, she struck out on her own to pursue her creative independence and established Studio Matusiak in Amsterdam.

Rozentheater – poster – rozentheater – 2006

Life rituals – poster – productiehuis frascati – 2004

Interview with Paulina Matusiak

1. What led to the formation of your studio?

Like most independents I started my career in a larger studio. I had been fortunate enough to be invited to join the team at the prestigious Anthon Beeke Studio who has been distinguished as one of the Five Designers of the Century. I spent four years there. It gave me the necessary practical experience and the confirmation that my work was commercially viable. Striking out on my own was a natural consequence, not in the least because it also afforded me the freedom to regulate my own hours! Not long after Studio Matusiak was a fact.

2. How many staff people does your studio have and what are their main working fields?

Studio Matusiak is a small venture. In the past I have had one assistant. I currently have several trainees who mainly concern themselves with the research for the projects at hand. As is usually the case with smaller studios, tasks are not clearly limited by set boundaries. It's very much a wide hands-on a proach: photographing, sketching, going out there and collecting impressions.

3. How does a regular working day at your studio look like, how is the day structured?

A regular day in my studio can be typified by one word: hectic! Generally there are always 1001 things going on simultaneously. The keyword here is multi-tasking. It leaves less room for a rigid structure for anyone to adhere to, neither do we have set times for specific activities. Those are the benefits reserved for large companies, I'm afraid. We generally start at 9:30 and work until 18:30. It's a happy rat race, but I am currently looking at how I can increase the efficiency by implementing some form of guideline.

4. How much leisure time do you have during a year?

Leisure time? I strive for five weeks a year; four weeks of summer holidays and one week during the Christmas season. Nevertheless it remains an aspiration. As any small business owner I tend to take my work with me on holidays. As such I can say that I reserve the time but do tend to shortchange myself when it comes to leisure! I do reserve Mondays and Tuesdays for my creative playtime. Those are the days that I am alone in the studio and re-energize. Sometimes by doing assigned work simply at a slower pace, other times by freely exploring new ideas.

5. Which business areas do your clients mainly come from? Is the number of your clients increasing or rather declining?

The majority of my clients are active in the arts themselves. These are predominantly national theatre companies. They are the most obvious partners because of my background as an artist and my predilection for performance. We strike a natural chord in each other in that respect. Translating the essence of a theatre piece into a single image is not only gratifying, it allows graphic art to reach beyond typography to explore a larger world using multiple disciplines. My client list is growing. I do find that long-term relationships fluctuate. Theatre companies in the Netherlands are generally dependant upon government subsidies that are evaluated every four years. The upside is a contract for four years; a possible drawback is that potentially long-term relationships are dependent upon outside factors rather than the merit of my studio. Nevertheless, the Dutch cultural community is constantly evolving and growing and I expect to benefit from the positive conjuncture.

6. Do you have a specific corporate philosophy or maybe a mission statement like other companies, which is reflected in the way you steer the studio's course?

Creative integrity is my mainstay. In a sense this could be interpreted as a corporate philosophy because it does account for the direction in which the studio is focused. More than anything it's a natural compliance to my own personal nature rather than a prefabricated strategy. So essentially you could say it's a mission statement by default. By staying true to my own voice my work has developed a recognizable signature without it being defined by a particular concept. People intuitively recognize the maker without being able to put their finger on it. It's important to me, if not a condition, that the artist remains consistently present in the work, as a kind of trademark if you will, but closer to home it just means that this allows me to function optimally by av iding a situation in which I feel I'm selling out. Commercially this translates into the strategy of steering Studio Matusiak towards evolving into a marketable, artistic identity. At the end of the day I am my own product. I don't subscribe to the idea of the graphic designer as ghostwriter. Expression has a source and therefore a clear identity; paramount is the ability to remain versatile. It's a niche attitude, but I find the market is increasingly appreciative of this kind of integrity.

7. What, from your point of view, makes the difference between a small studio and a big company?

I feel that one big difference between small studios and large companies lies in the approach to clients. In small studios communication lines are shorter. There are many clients who abhor having to get past the reception to get to the secretary in order to eventually get a possible appointment with the art director. Having worked for a large company in the past I found there was a clear demarcation between decisions and output. The top generally decides on the style. This causes a lessening of personal involvement because you aren't working on your own baby, as it were. Another possible pitfall is the repetition of concepts through which the work may end up becoming predictable. Nevertheless there are advantages that big companies have.

8. What kind of advantages and disadvantages does a small studio have compared to a big company?

The advantages of a small studio are myriad: the freedom to create your own style, direct contact with your clients, being able to pull your own cart. It's definitely a plus to be able to decide about your own target group. Larger companies have the benefit of an organizational backbone and administrative support. Canvassing is generally done for you. It allows for efficiency that smaller studios, through lack of hands and by association, lack of time, still struggle with. Larger projects tend to go to the bigger companies. But whether this is a clear disadvantage to smaller studios I'm not so sure of. I've found that the larger the project, the more restrictions are imposed. If you like the challenge, that's fine. If you prefer more freedom, a smaller studio would be a natural alternative.

Crave – poster – teatro – 2006

Heads – poster – anoukvandijkdc – 2006

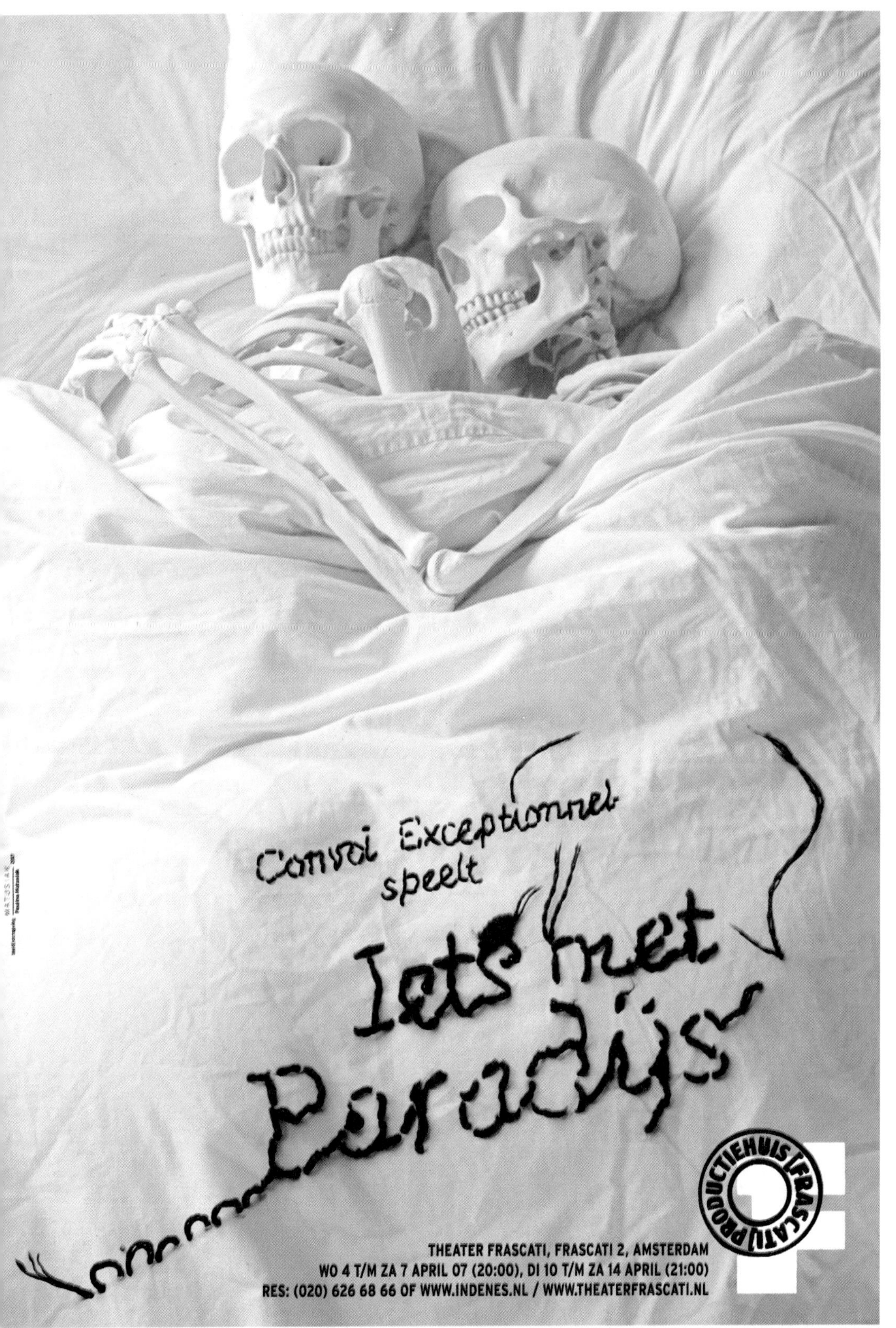

Lets met paradijs – poster – productiehuis frascati – 2006

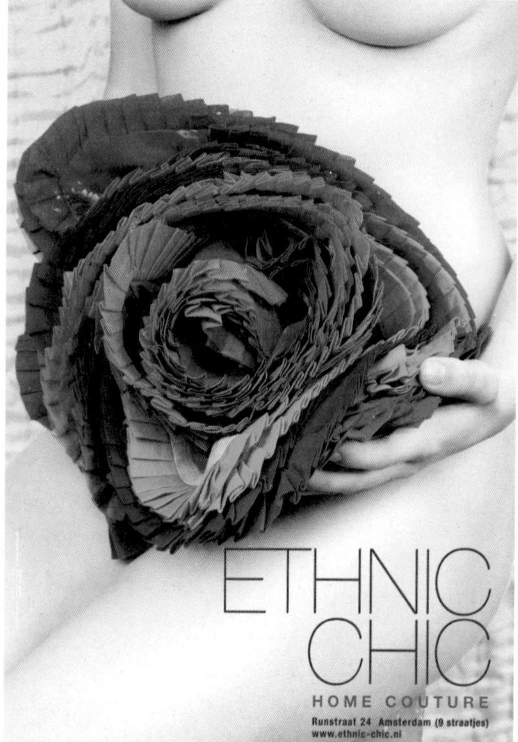

Ethnic chic – poster – ethnic chic – 2007

Sunna no onna – poster – anoukvandijkdc – 2005

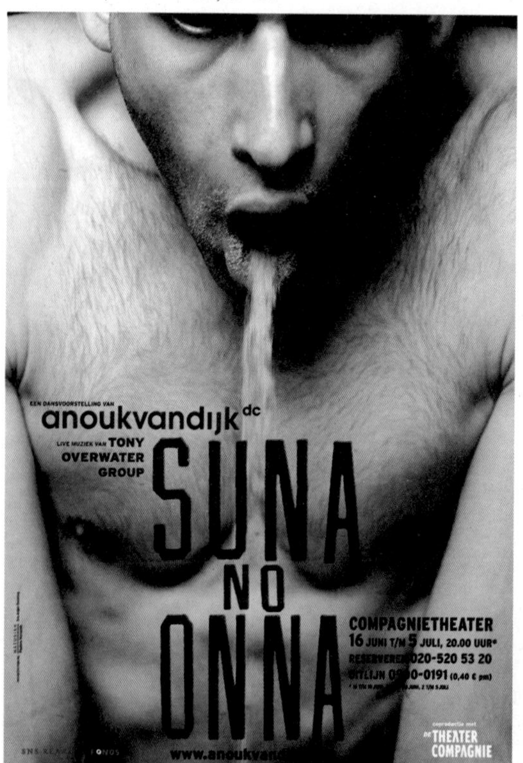

9. What is your idea about the future of small studios? Do you think that small studios do not have any other choice but to expand in order to survive in these times of globalization?

The future of small studios is safeguarded by the advantages it offers. There will always be clients who prefer the direct contact of a small studio. Important is that you are clear about your long-term objectives and target group. Do you wish to go for the large commercial accounts? Are you happy catering to smaller businesses or projects? The course you set out should be based on the answers to these fundamental questions. Many small studios in Amsterdam work as a kind of unofficial collective in which, for reasons of efficiency, assignments are sometimes passed on. It's a practical solution for the time limit many of us are up against. Collectives are a good alternative to large companies. They allow you to retain your own studio identity while giving you access to other professional services you may not be able to offer yourself. Perhaps a more official collective would be a good alternative to large companies. It would be interesting to see if there could be enough streamlining to allow for an umbrella organization without foregoing on the idiosyncrasies of the studios involved.

10. Please describe and elaborate on the goals or plans that you have for your studio for the next five years?

I've been operating Studio Matusiak for approximately six years now and have come to the point where I have to make choices. Do I expand? Or should I lessen my work load? Which scenario affords me the greatest creative satisfaction? What is about my personal life? Where is it? Mainly based on these questions I've decided that the most natural course would be to take the path of least resistance. By this I mean doing that which is closest to me. I love my work and the most natural expansion would be to create a situation in which I can work freely and still enjoy time off to pursue other passions like painting. For this reason I'm currently working with a marketing bureau. It's important to realize that a designer is also his/her own product. Like any product a solid marketing strategy is imperative to its success. My aim is to steer Studio Matusiak into a becoming a clearly defined creative identity, much in the line of an autonomous artist; to make my niche my strength. The personality Matusiak is then just as relevant as the Matusiak work. I'm wont to use the word branding, but essentially that would be the most logical step to take. We're turning the tables as it were: You know the work. You know what I stand for. Buy Matusiak and wear it with a proud smile on your face. With a little luck I can soon start painting again!

Rozentheater – poster – rozentheater – 2004

merkwürdig

team:
Nadine Häfner
Jennifer Staudacher
Kai Staudacher
contact:
merkwürdig GmbH
Hanauer Landstr. 161-173
60314 Frankfurt am Main
Germany
T + 49 69 94943315
F + 48 69 94943309
www.merkwuerdig.com
info@merkwuerdig.com

merkwürdig – Nadine Häfner, Jennifer Staudacher and Kai Staudacher gained experience working in a wide variety of graphic design firms and agencies after completing their studies at the Fachhochschule Wiesbaden (university of applied sciences). In April 2002, they joined to form a studio. The German word "merkwürdig" means "unusual", "memorable" or perhaps "weird", terms which the founding trio believes correctly describe their professional endeavors. Right from the outset, merkwuerdig specialized in the development of corporate designs and the creation and illustration of brochures and catalogues. Their clients come from the areas of traveling, fashion, art and culture. All of them benefit from merkwuerdig's particularly close communication and their love of details. Parallel to their day-to-day business they invest a great deal of time and passion in non-profit and experimental projects.

EWTC – corporate design – EWTC, travel agency from Cologne – 2005

Interview with merkwürdig

1. What led to the formation of your studio?

The desire for the freedom to develop our own projects and to allow ourselves the maximum creative margin.

2. How many staff people does your studio have and what are their main working fields?

There are three partners/designers, plus one intern and freelancers: Nadine: design, project management, finances, Jenny: design, project management, production, Kai: design, project management, new business and public relations. One trainee: design Freelancers: photography, web programming, design

3. How does a regular working day at your studio look like, how is the day structured?

We treat every day as new and each project as different. The week's timetable is planned on each Monday. From Monday to Friday we brainstorm, design, talk, cook together, and present our ideas and projects.

4. How much leisure time do you have during a year?

Approximately three weeks per year.

5. Which business areas do your clients mainly come from? Is the number of your clients increasing or rather declining?

We have a broad client base ranging from traveling over city marketing to music, art and culture. We find that established clients are happy to stay with us, and the number of new clients is increasing steadily.

Bicykon – corporate design – bicykon, extreme sports event – 2006

Herzsprung – brochure – Typotron AG – 2005

12 minutes – brochure – AKRIS/typtron AG – 2005

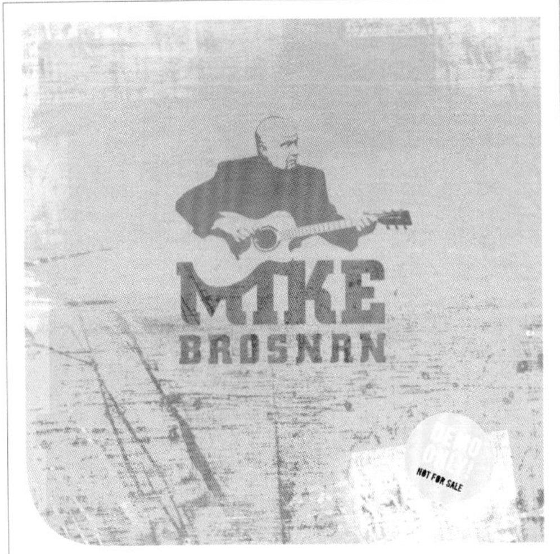

01 End of the Game* 3.38 **02** Good Liquor, Bad Company** 3:08 **03** Handyman** 3:20 **04** Ain't Gonna Be Your Antidote* 2:45 **05** Streets of Glass** 3:23 **06** Tuatapere* 4:18 **07** Slide Action* 4:34 **08** Duagh Memories** 5:03 **09** Home To You* 3:44 **10** All Fall Down* 3:34 **11** Wasted Time* 4:07 **12** Love so Good* 2:32 **13** Such A Shame*** 3:29 **14** Long Gone*** 2:44 **15** Home To You*** 2:21 **16** Night Train**** 5:15

*taken from the album "Wasted Time" **taken from the album "Streets of Glass" ***solo ****duo/live

All songs written by Mike Brosnan | www.mikebrosnan.com

Contact: Flying Kiwi Music | Henriette Guth | Heidelberger Landstraße 93 | 64297 Darmstadt/Germany
Phone: + 49 (0) 61 51.1 01 70 04 | Fax: + 49 (0) 61 51.1 01 70 05 | Mail: henriette@flyingkiwimusic.com

FKMDEMO401 **© 2004** Flying Kiwi Music. All rights reserved. **Design** www.merkwuerdig.com

GEMA DDD LC 12554

Mike Brosnan-demo cd – cd cover – kiwi music – 2005

LUDWIGSHAFEN diskutiert baut kauft handelt inszeniert wohnt spielt blüht beschließt gräbt denkt plant informiert steht erweitert musiziert lernt befragt pflanzt besitzt produziert handelt **HEUTE FÜR MORGEN**

Today for tomorrow – corporate design – city Ludwigshafen – 2006

Soccer cards – illustration – merkwürdig – 2006

Luise Amstrup, collection 2003 – brochure – Luise Amstrup – 2003

Stage ahead – corporate design – stage ahead-school for popular music – 2007

6. Do you have a specific corporate philosophy or maybe a mission statement like other companies, which is reflected in the way you steer the studio's course?

Our "merkwuerdige" philosophy: All ideas and concepts go through three heads and six hands. We believe that a great idea is nothing without an excellent presentation. Our design always has to excite the client, the client's client, and ourselves.

7. What, from your point of view, makes the difference between a small studio and a big company?

In our way of working the creative process is streamlined to a great extent. In large agencies a meeting is needed for every little change, whereas here we are able to solve problems as they occur. Thus, everything remains manageable. We believe this is the only way to fulfill our commitment to design, and the main reason why many of the larger companies have been down-sizing in the last few years.

8. What kind of advantages and disadvantages does a small studio have compared to a big company?

Big advantage: Our reaction to short notice job requests is quicker, and we are in constant communication, important information do not get lost. Small disadvantage: Our overall project capacity is limited and reached quickly.

9. What is your idea about the future of small studios? Do you think that small studios do not have any other choice but to expand in order to survive in these times of globalization?

As long as there are medium-sized companies as well as new companies opening regularly, there will be a need for small design studios. Even the large companies whose project load is still manageable tend to go back to smaller studios in order to save precious time. And even within the current trend towards globalization, these niches will not disappear. To have a well-attuned team with competent partners is the most important thing.

10. Please describe and elaborate on the goals or plans that you have for your studio for the next five years?

Extending the team with fresh talent within the next two years. To take on one non-profit project each year. To have our own company helicopter. To have even more fun at work.

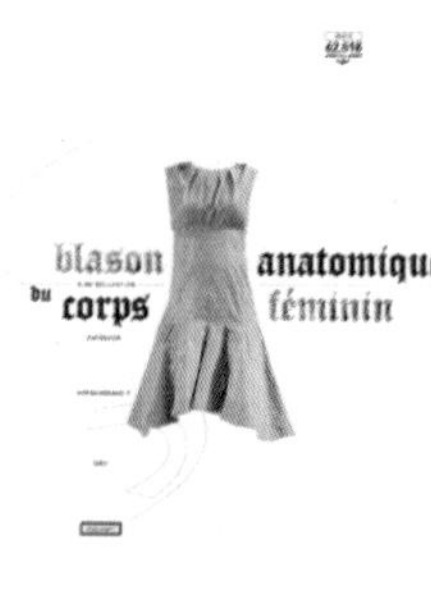

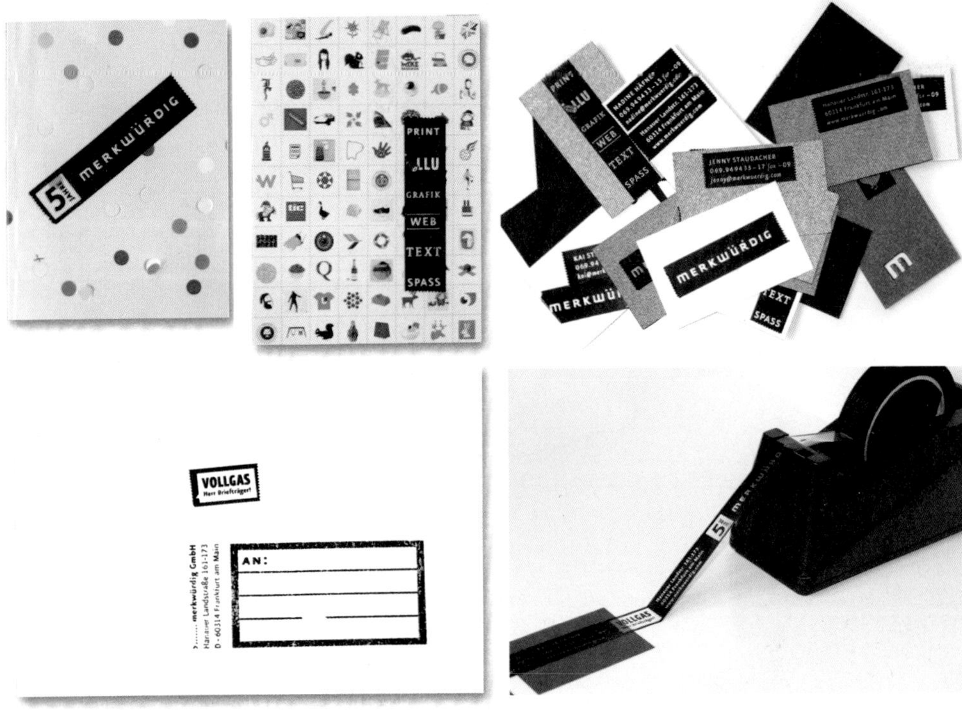

Tape to remember us by – tape – merkwürdig – 2007

Metamorphoses – poster – city Ludwigshafen, city marketing – 2005

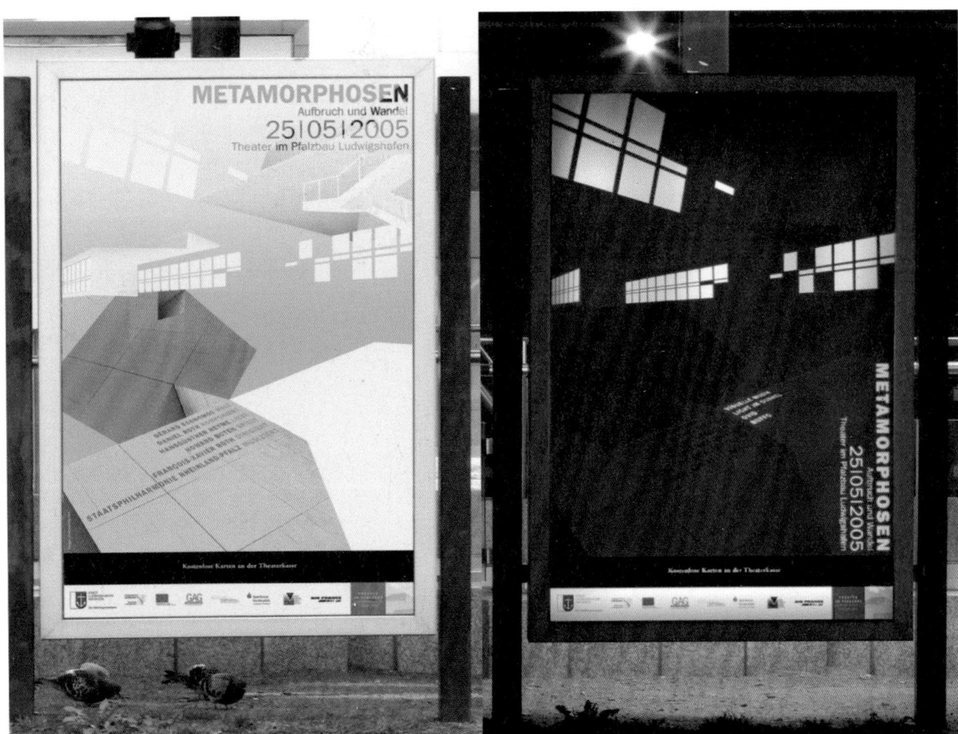

Milkxhake

team:
Javin Mo
Wilson Tang
contact:
3/F, B, Lam Shan Bldg,
113-119 Belcher's St.,
Kennedy Town,
Hong Kong, China
www.milkxhake.org
mix@aa.org

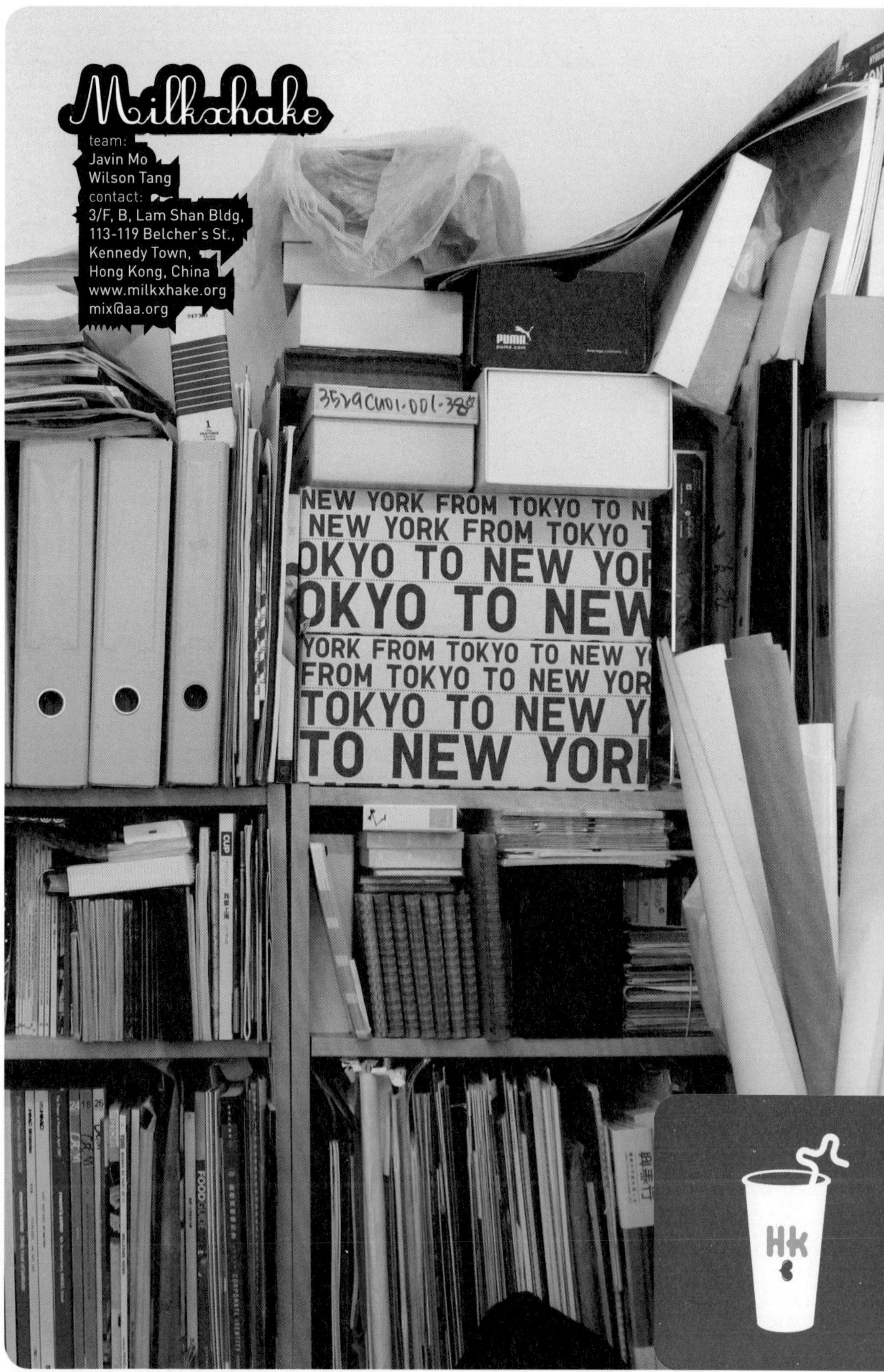

Milkxhake is a young Hong Kong-based design unit co-founded by graphic designer Javin Mo and interactive designer Wilson Tang in 2002. The studio mainly focuses on graphic and interactive mixtures. In 2004, Javin was invited to join FABRICA, the Benetton Research and Communication Center in Italy. He was also art director of the FABRICA quarterly magazine FAB launched between 2004 and 2005. In 2005, he revived Milkxhake together with Wilson as one of the most energetic design collectives in Hong Kong. Their works have been selected for numerous design competitions, including the Tokyo Type Directors Club Awards (04/06) and the Hong Kong Designers Association Awards (05/07) with gold, silver and bronze prizes. In 2006, Javin was awarded the Young Gun 5 from the New York ADC. In 2007, the two designers received merit from the 86th New York ADC and British D&AD Awards. Their works have been widely published in international design magazines and journals. In 2008, Javin edited his first book under the title "New Graphic Design in China", published by 3030 Press in Shanghai which features 30 young graphic designers from China.

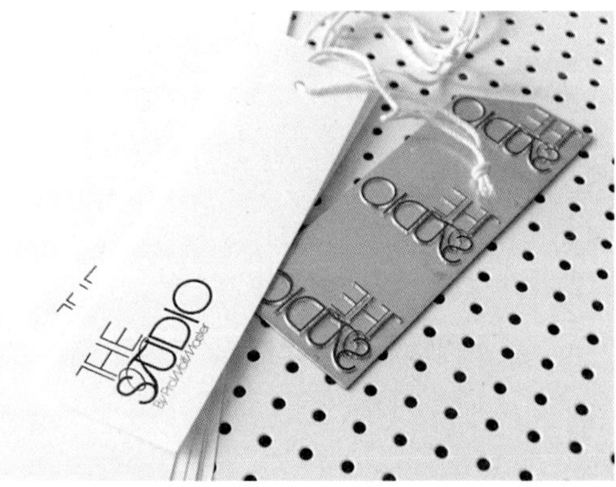

The studio by pro Wolf Master – corporate identity – the studio by pro Wolf Master – 2005

Interview with Milkxhake

1. What led to the formation of your studio?

Milkxhake was co-founded by graphic designer Javin Mo and interactive designer Wilson Tang. It was our final-year project and the brief was to set up a design company with a creative strategy. We came up with "milkshake" but we changed to "milkxhake" in 2002 to include the meaning of the "mix". We think it's a good name as long as we believe design should mix up ideas apart from the physical appearances. At that time both of us had full-time jobs and spared extra-time to create our first creative online portfolio. In 2004, Javin was invited to join FABRICA, the Benetton Research and Communication Center in Italy for a one-year grant scholarship. After his return in 2005, we found that it was time to do our own stuff and revived milkxhake to become one of the most energetic design collectives in Hong Kong.

2. How many staff people does your studio have and what are their main working fields?

We have only 2 people at this stage, Wilson is a talented interactive designer and I focus mainly on art direction and graphic design.

3. How does a regular working day at your studio look like, how is the day structured?

We start working after breakfast at 10 a.m., checking e-mails and working until 2 p.m. when we have tea-lunch. Then we work again till late everyday, it depends on our projects.

4. How much leisure time do you have during a year?

We need to have more leisure time here in Hong Kong. To be honest, our city is not as perfect as other creative cities and we have to rush for everything everyday. Sometimes you definitely get lost. The best arrangement is to have two trips per year no matter where you go. Starting in summer of 2007, I have had the great chance to go to different cities in China for design exhibitions, which inspired me a lot, and actually it was a very good chance to have a break!

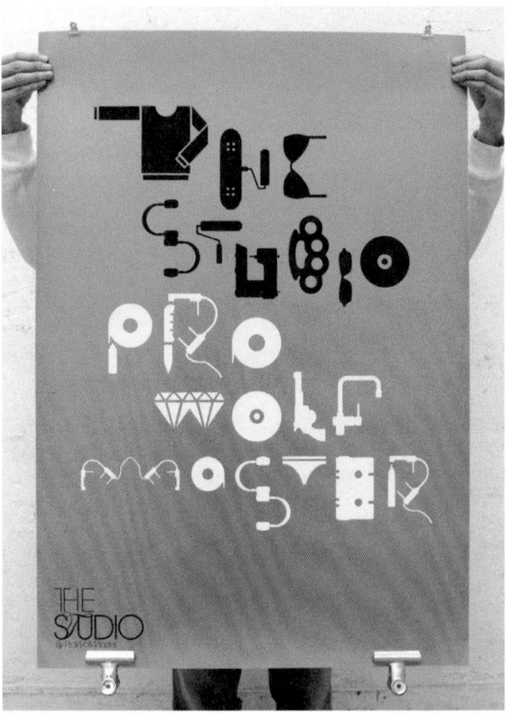

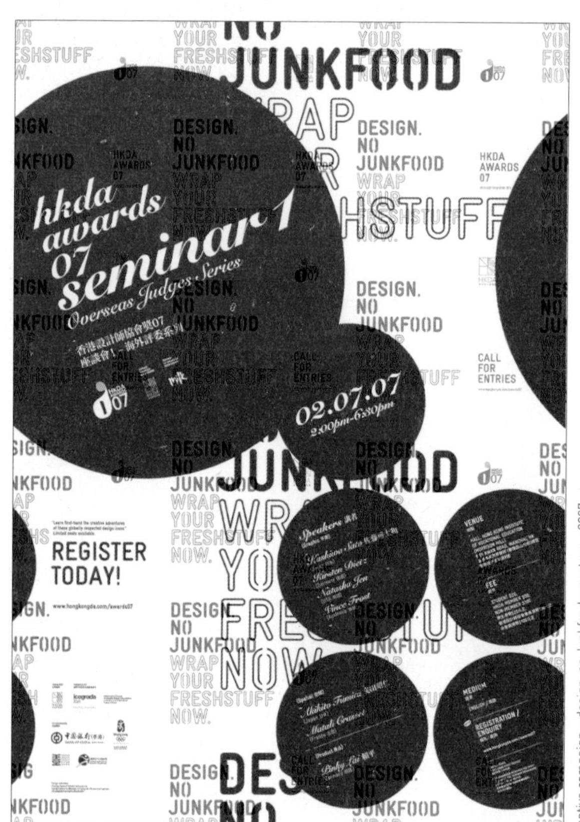

5. Which business areas do your clients mainly come from?

Right now, we do not have a really diverse range of clients. Most of them come from the local art- and cultural sector in Hong Kong, where we did whole campaigns for them. Further, we have some commercial and some oversea clients for whom we are working on identity issues and websites.

Is the number of your clients increasing or rather declining?

It was decent, especially in 2007, and still is. We did quite a few creative campaigns for clients from the local art- and design sectors and aroused some positive attention. This also attracted other clients, which was good for us anyway.

6. Do you have a specific corporate philosophy or maybe a mission statement like other companies, which is reflected in the way you steer the studio's course?

We try our best to make design to be more fun and meaningful in our city! We believe that a good design should speak for itself, and our motto "Mix it a better world" reflects the ultimate dream we hope to come true through design one day.

JHKDA awards 07 creative campaign – design. no Junkfood – posters – 2007

JMW summer arts & dance program 2006 – event logotype, promotional posters – JMW, school of ballet in Hong Kong – 2006

Make-up bag – book – artist collaboration project – 2007

7. What, from your point of view, makes the difference between a small studio and a big company?

A small studio can easily generate something creative without much complexity, while a big company would have a lot of pressure in terms of policy and strategy. Sometimes small studio may be more effective in that sense.

8. What kind of advantages and disadvantages does a small studio have compared to a big company?

Simplicity, less pressure, more fun.

9. What is your idea about the future of small studios?

Right now, there are so many small studios in Europe and Asia producing really good works. I am sure there will be more and more within the next few years, and especially the bulk of fresh graduates will certainly enjoy this creative scene.

Do you think that small studios do not have any other choice but to expand in order to survive in these times of globalization?

Not really. Clients are really clever nowadays, they will definitely compare the pro and cons of both kinds of studios with regard to their marketing needs and the project scale. So I definitely think that small studios can survive and still play a role for the industry.

10. Please describe and elaborate on the goals or plans that you have for your studio for the next five years?

It's hard to predict at the moment, but the production of interesting, high-quality work is still our primary concern. Doing some self-publications in the near future sounds like a good idea, too.

October contemporary 2007 – poster – art4soul, Malaysia – 2007

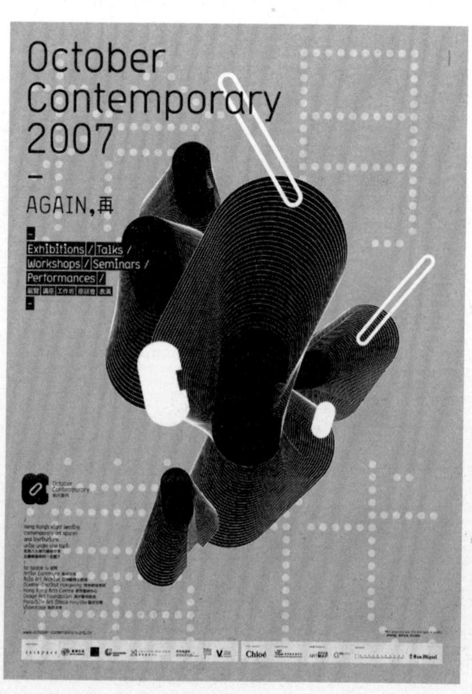

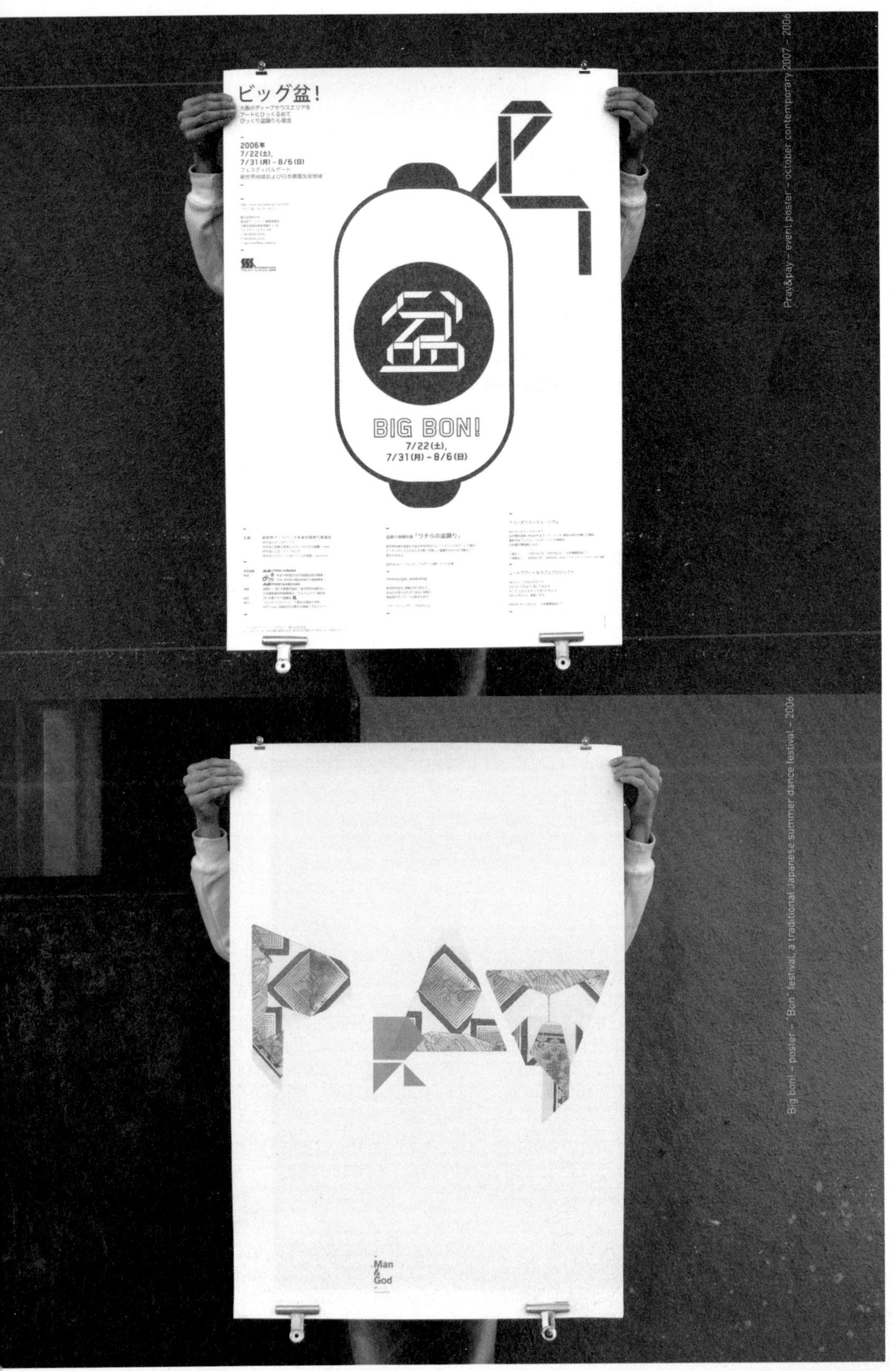

Pray&pay – event poster – october contemporary 2007 – 2006

Big bon! – poster – "Bon" festival, a traditional Japanese summer dance festival – 2006

mischen
team:
Barbara Bättig
Harri Kuhn
Vera Rammelmeyer
contact:
Erkelenzdamm 11-13
10999 Berlin, Germany
T + 49 30 44042082
F + 49 30 44042083
studio@mischen-berlin.de
www.mischen-berlin.de

mischen was founded in October 2005 by Barbara Baettig, Harri Kuhn and Vera Rammelmeyer. All three have gathered their experience in diverse offices in Germany and abroad. Barbara has studied graphic design in Lucerne and has since then worked with Die Gestalten Verlag, Leonardi. Wollein, and for the past four years at Fons Hickmann M23 in Berlin. Harri has studied communication design in Mannheim and Berlin. He had been art director at Luna in Barcelona for two years after having worked with Josep Bagà and *S,C,P,F. In Berlin he joined Leonardi. Wollein for one year. Vera has studied communication design in Mannheim and has designed for the publishing house Kehrer Verlag in Heidelberg after having worked at MRGL in New York. Before joining mischen, she had worked as a designer for the DB Station & Service AG in Berlin.

Over limits – catalogue, slipcase, invitation – mart-stam gesellschaft Berlin – 2007

Interview with mischen

1. What led to the formation of your studio?

Knowing we could make it by ourselves and the feeling that something was missing.

2. How many staff people does your studio have and what are their main working fields?

mischen are Barbara Baettig, Harri Kuhn and Vera Rammelmeyer. We are inventors and accountants, philosophers and craftsmen, managers and spiritual guides.

3. How does a regular working day at your studio look like, how is the day structured?

On – standby – on – off.

4. How much leisure time do you have during a year?

As much as we need. Free time is just as important as work for us. A waste bin should be emptied now and then, and a fire will go out if you don't tend to it.

5. Which business areas do your clients mainly come from? Is the number of your clients increasing or rather declining?

mischen is open to everything. Our clients are active in all different fields, although there is an increasing number coming from the cultural sphere. mischen's pool of clients continues to grow steadily.

6. Do you have a specific corporate philosophy or maybe a mission statement like other companies, which is reflected in the way you steer the studio's course?

mischen's mission is to achieve a balance of opposites. Our concepts and designs are individual and public, creative and focused, emotional and intelligent, unusual and familiar, continuous and spontaneous, profound and beautiful.

7. What, from your point of view, makes the difference between a small studio and a big company?

8. What kind of advantages and disadvantages does a small studio have compared to a big company?

A small office provides more space for the personal development of everyone involved. Our relationship to the client is also more direct and intense. Flat hierarchies and quick and uncompromising decision-making processes enable small offices to create unique and strong profiles for themselves. One disadvantage is that size is often equated with quality – so that the potential of smaller agencies is often left undiscovered.

Perceptions – catalogue, invitation – allianz – 2007

Power plant earth – poster series – free project – 2007

LUZERNER GRAFIK IST HIMMEL UND HÖLLE.
KREATIVITÄT UND FUNKTION, KÜR UND PFLICHT, WAHNSINN UND GESELLSCHAFT, DENKEN UND ZEIGEN, GESTALTEN UND WALTEN, SPONTANEITÄT UND PRÄZISION, SATZ UND FLATTERSATZ, CHAOS UND ORDNUNG, WEG UND ZIEL.
LUZERNER GRAFIK BIETET KREATIVEN RAUM.

Lucerne graphic – poster – Lucerne university of applied sciences and arts – 2007

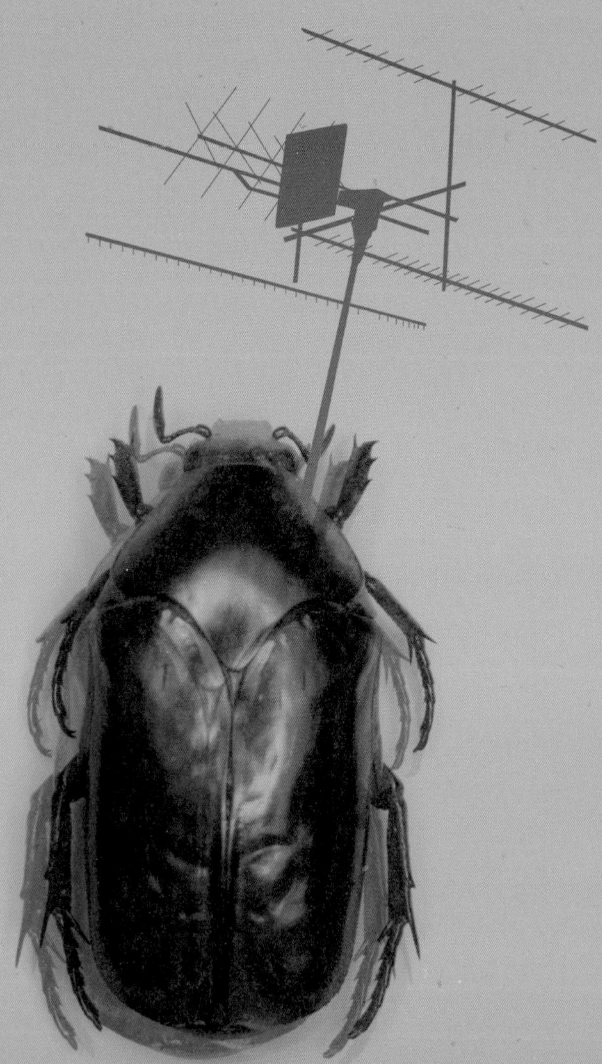

Radiovisions – website – tesla Berlin – 2007

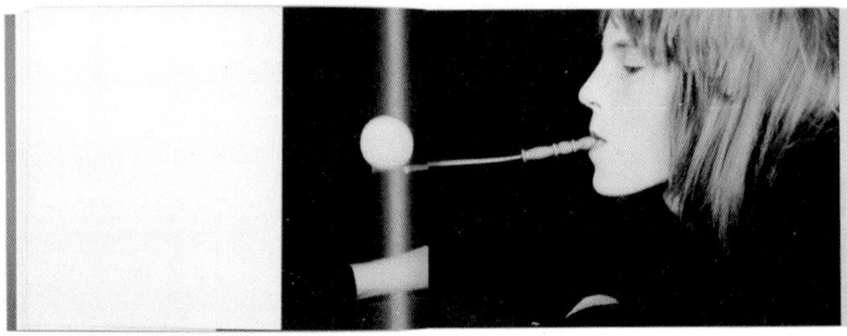

La vagabonde – catalogue – goldrausch, Judith Karcheter – 2006

Klemm´s – corporate design – klemm´s – 2007

KLEMM'S

9. What is your idea about the future of small studios? Do you think that small studios do not have any other choice but to expand in order to survive in these times of globalization?

Expansion is necessary, but not necessarily in terms of the size of the office or the number of employees. Rather, expansion in terms of "inner growth" is what we're striving for.

10. Please describe and elaborate on the goals or plans that you have for your studio for the next five years?

Get big but stay small.

Mixer
team:
Erich Brechbühl
Marco Sieber
Maurus Domeisen
Remko van Hoof
contact:
Löwenplatz 5
6004 Luzern,
Switzerland
T + 41 41 4103535
F + 41 41 4601504
erich@mixer.ch
www.mixer.ch

Mixer – Once started as a young filmmakers group, Mixer has become a professional communication network, located in Lucerne. The group was founded in 2003 and consists of four core members, all coming from the communication domain: Remko van Hoof (concept), Erich Brechbuehl (graphic design), Marco Sieber (photography), and Maurus Domeisen (display). What makes Mixer special is the possibility to hire the entire team, creating working units or working on an individual basis. Amongst other awards, Mixer was honored with a publication about their work in 2007, published by the French editor Pyramyd.

Interview with Mixer

1. What led to the formation of your studio?

One of the best things and greatest coincidences in life - to find friends that have the same ideas and visions and then just go for it.

2. How many staff people does your studio have and what are their main working fields?

Mixer consists of four individuals, each one of us with a specific field of expertise: concept, display, graphic design and photography. Each of Mixer's members is the owner and the person fully responsible of his business field. If required, we hire freelancers or work with external partners to fulfill the task.

3. How does a regular working day at your studio look like, how is the day structured?

We meet at 9 in the morning and start the day with a good breakfast. Ongoing and upcoming projects are discussed or reviewed. From then on everything is handled on a very individual basis. In case everything goes well, a regular working day finishes around 6.30 p.m., if not maybe around 8.30 p.m..

4. How much leisure time do you have during a year?

It really depends on the amount of ongoing projects. We try to have as much leisure time as possible.

5. Which business areas do your clients mainly come from?

From small and medium-sized businesses. The spectrum is quite wide and goes from commercial brands over cultural institutions to the music and sports market. It is the rich mix of clients and projects that makes it challenging and exiting.

Is the number of your clients increasing or rather declining?

We are fortunate to say that the number of our clients is increasing continuously.

6. Do you have a specific corporate philosophy or maybe a mission statement like other companies, which is reflected in the way you steer the studio's course?

We all share the philosophy to always create surprisingly new solutions and to focus on the individual needs of each client. What we don't want is to create a corporate agency style to stick to on every job we do. Branding belongs to the client and costumer and not to us.

7. What, from your point of view, makes the difference between a small studio and a big company?

Small studios are more focused and less distracted by in-house social-political factors. Because of their own background small studios have a much better understanding of how to get the maximum out of the project with limited resources.

100 best posters 06 Germany Austria Switzerland – book and poster
– poster competition 100 best posters 06 – Germany Austria Switzerland – 2007

8. What kind of advantages and disadvantages does a small studio have compared to a big company?

Small studios dare to come up and try new things. Big studios pretend to dare. The downside is that companies with larger budgets choose work with big studios to protect their internal and external status.

9. What is your idea about the future of small studios?

The sky is the limit. Mixer believes that as long as there is human mankind, there will be individualism and the wish to change things constantly in all dimensions and life circumstances. Therefore small studios have a great future potential.

Do you think that small studios do not have any other choice but to expand in order to survive in these times of globalization?

We think that there is more and more space for small agencies. As the big studios have to focus on the big projects and brands there is a rather large potential for small studios focusing on small and middle-sized companies.

10. Please describe and elaborate on the goals or plans that you have for your studio for the next five years?

Our goal is to work more for clients that dare to go new ways in the field of communication. We want to focus on jobs where we think we can make a real difference.

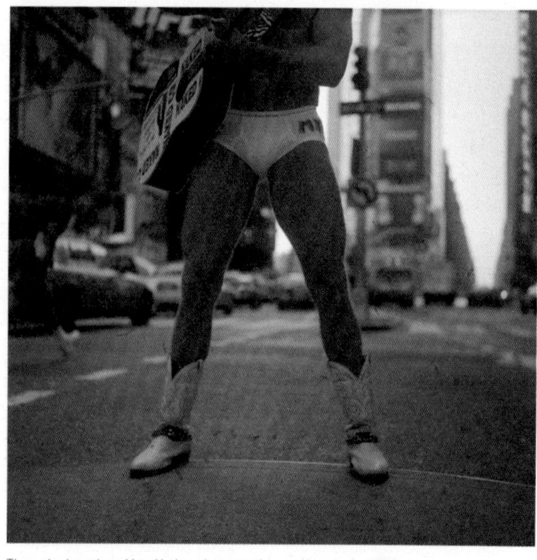

The naked cowboy, New York – photography – self project – 2007

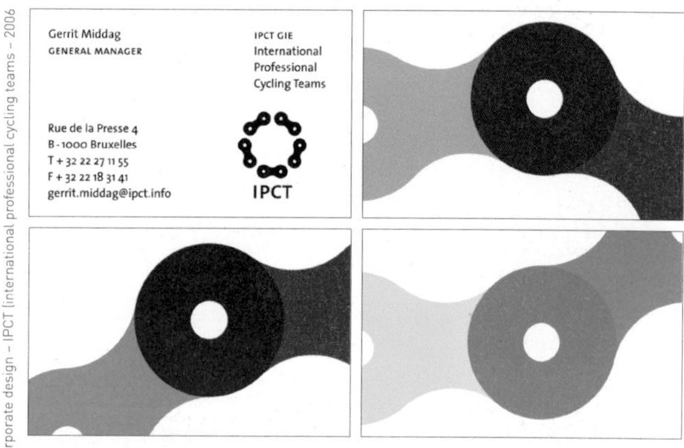

Gerrit Middag
GENERAL MANAGER
IPCT GIE
International
Professional
Cycling Teams
Rue de la Presse 4
B-1000 Bruxelles
T +32 22 27 11 55
F +32 22 18 31 41
gerrit.middag@ipct.info
IPCT

IPCT – corporate design – IPCT [international professional cycling teams] – 2006

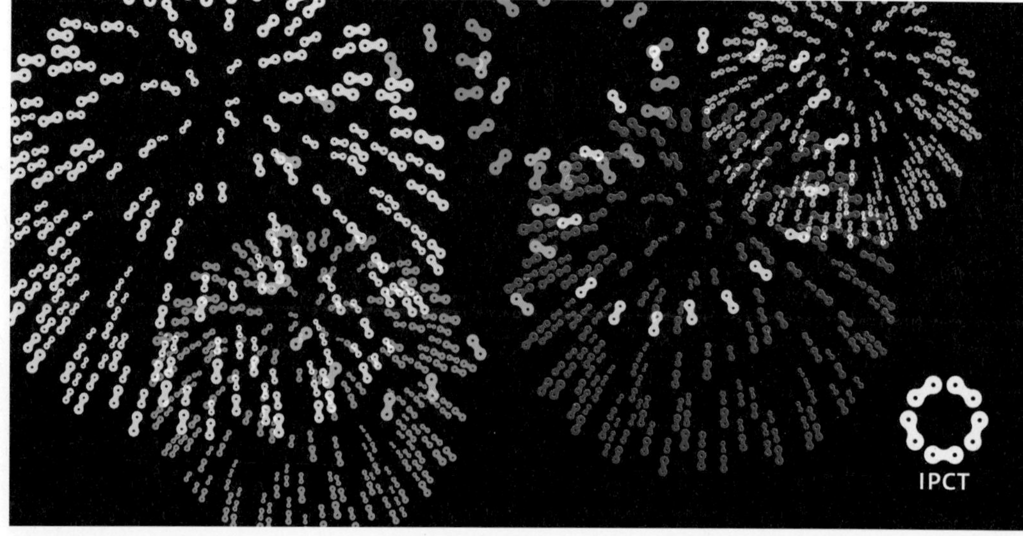

The arabien night – theatre poster – theater aeternam, Lucerne – 2006

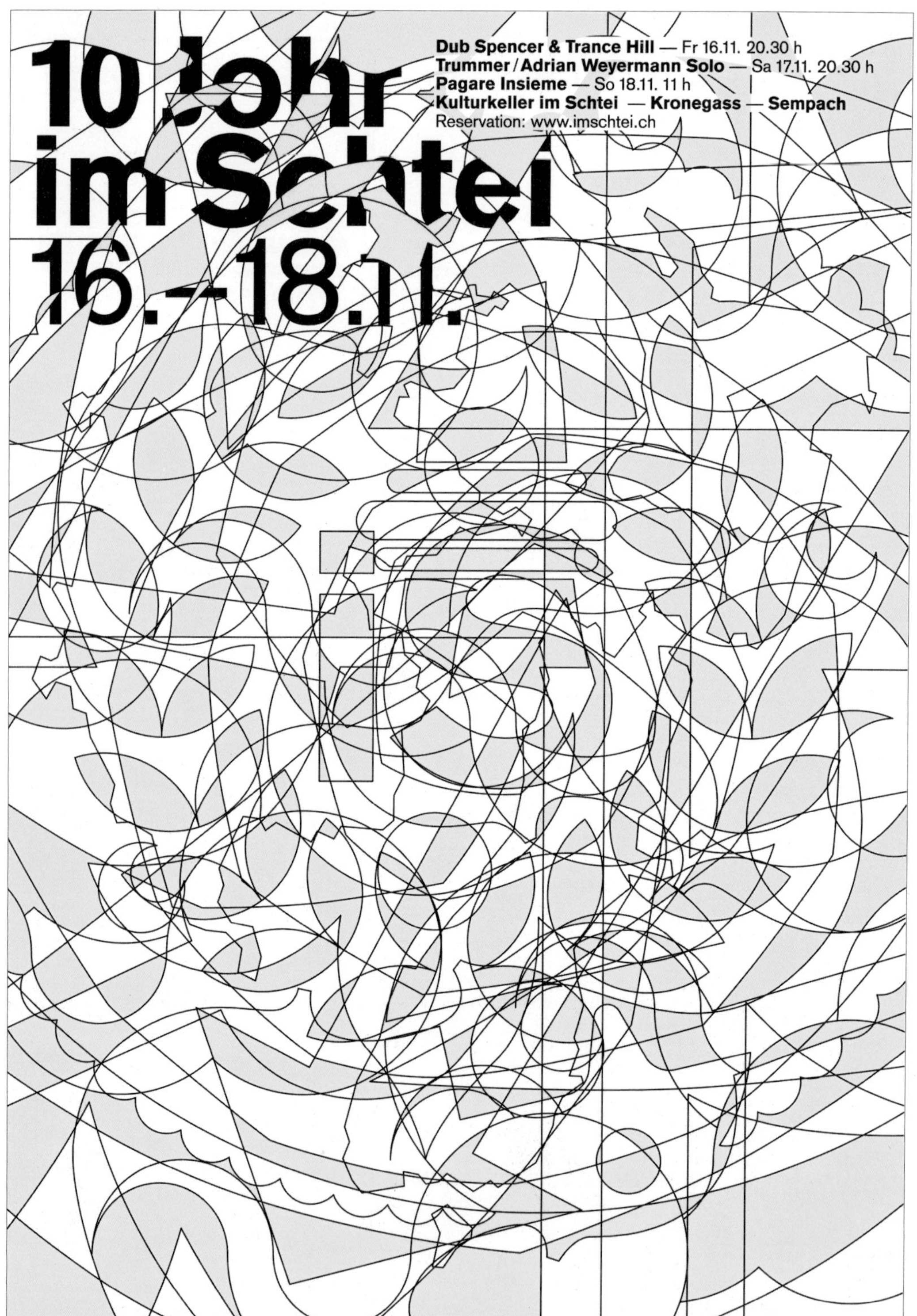

10 years im schtei – anniversary poster – cultural place im schtei, Sempach – 2007

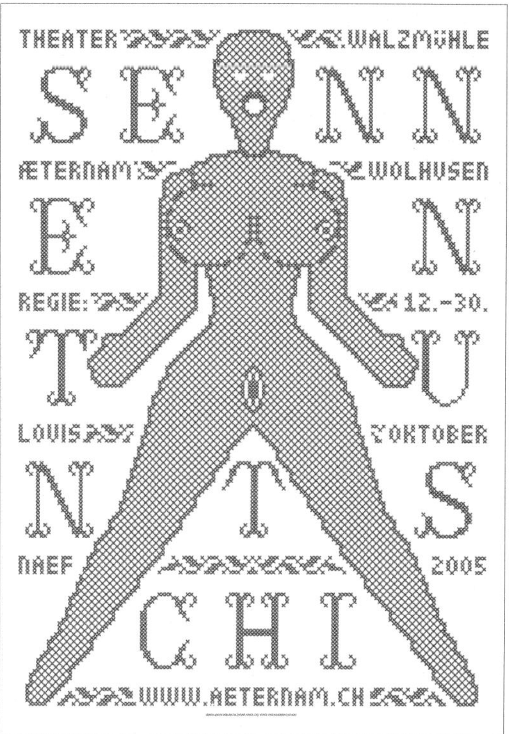

Sennentuntschi – theatre poster – theater aeternam, Lucerne – 2005

100 times im schtei – event poster – cultural place im schtei, Sempach – 2005

Room of little Constantine – interior design – Constantine – 2007

Monsters

team:
Pavel Frič
Lukáš Müller/lumír
Michaela Labudová/mlsa
Bery/dog
contact:
Michaela Labudová
U Blaženky 14
150 00 Prague 5
Czech Republic
T + 420 605 973498
pavelfricz@yahoo.co.uk
www.monsters.cz

Monsters members all studied at the Faculty of Art and Design of J. E. Purkyně University in Ústí nad Labem, Graphic Design Department. Since 2005, they are freely connected to each other and work on common projects. At the same time, they are going abroad to study, for example in Warszawa, Duesseldorf, Budapest, Praha or Brno. After finishing their studies, Pavel and LukásĐ started to teach graphic design and typography at the UJEP (University). Their studio is profiled in CID, poster design, publication design and illustration.

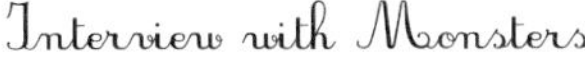

Interview with Monsters

1. What led to the formation of your studio?

We all like pancakes, what we got to know when we studied together.

2. How many staff people does your studio have and what are their main working fields?

We are three graphic designers and one dog. The graphic designers are doing everything around the projects.

3. How does a regular working day at your studio look like, how is the day structured?

The same as the working-night does look like.

4. How much leisure time do you have during a year?

27,3 % leisure time, we guess.

5. Which business areas do your clients mainly come from?

By now, the focus is on clients from the cultural sector.

Is the number of your clients increasing or rather declining?

Our clients mainly come from the cultural and educational area. We are happy that the number of them is still increasing.

6. Do you have a specific corporate philosophy or maybe a mission statement like other companies, which is reflected in the way you steer the studio's course?

We want to do nice things without loosing our minds.

7. What, from your point of view, makes the difference between a small studio and a big company?

We believe that we are able to do more progressive works in a small studio than it is possible in a big one.

8. What kind of advantages and disadvantages does a small studio have compared to a big company?

We are coming in and leaving the studio whenever we like, what is both advantage and disadvantage at the same time.

9. What is your idea about the future of small studios? Do you think that small studios do not have any other choice but to expand in order to survive in these times of globalization?

We hope it will not be absolutely necessary.

10. Please describe and elaborate on the goals or plans that you have for your studio for the next five years?

That is pretty long time, but we think we will start with finding some nice new working place full of light. We want to work and enjoy our lives.

Dělej, co musíš! (do what you gotta do!) – book A6 – monsters – 2008

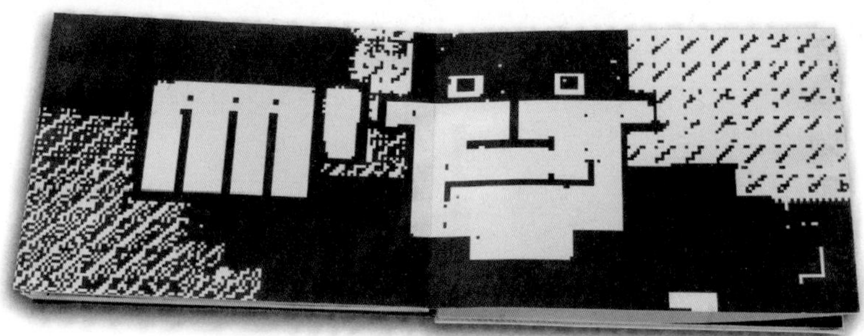

Dělej, co musíš! (do what you gotta do!) – book A6 – monsters – 2008

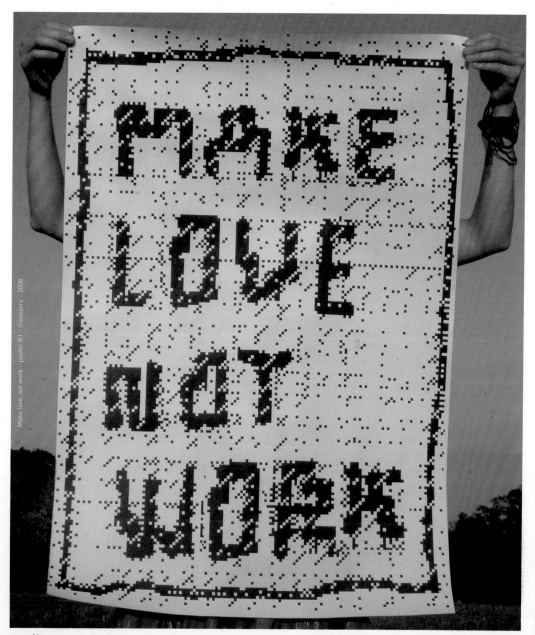

Make love, not work – poster B1 – monsters – 2008

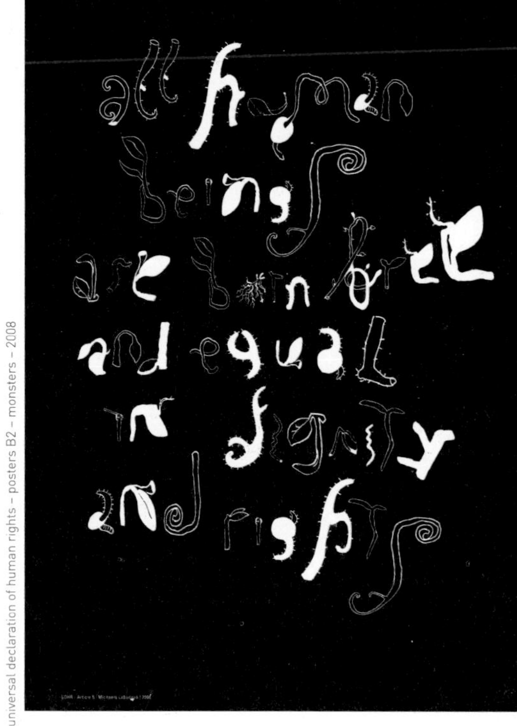

NO ONE SHALL BE
SUBJECTED TO
TORTURE OR TO
CRUEL, INHUMAN
OR DEGRADING
TREATMENT OR
PUNISHMENT.

all human
beings
are born free
and equal
in dignity
and rights

UDHR – universal declaration of human rights – posters B2 – monsters – 2008

NADECHNI SE
A ROZHLÍDNI
OKOLO SEBE
TVOJE ULICE,
TVOJE MĚSTO,
TVŮJ PROSTOR,

grafický design na ulici
workshopy
výstavy
přednášky
www.pro.tebe.cz
pro@tebe.cz

Supermarket – poster B1 – protebe live o.s. Karlovy Vary (n.g.o) – 2006

Univerzita J. E. Purkyně
v Ústí nad Labem

Univerzita J. E. Purkyně
v Ústí nad Labem
Pedagogická fakulta

Univerzita J. E. Purkyně
v Ústí nad Labem
Fakulta sociálně ekonomická

Univerzita J. E. Purkyně
v Ústí nad Labem
Přírodovědecká fakulta

Univerzita J. E. Purkyně
v Ústí nad Labem
Ústav zdravotnických studií

Univerzita J. E. Purkyně
v Ústí nad Labem
Fakulta životního prostředí

otevřený vizuální prostor

UJEP –logos, ci – J.E. purkyně university in Ústí nad Labem – 2007

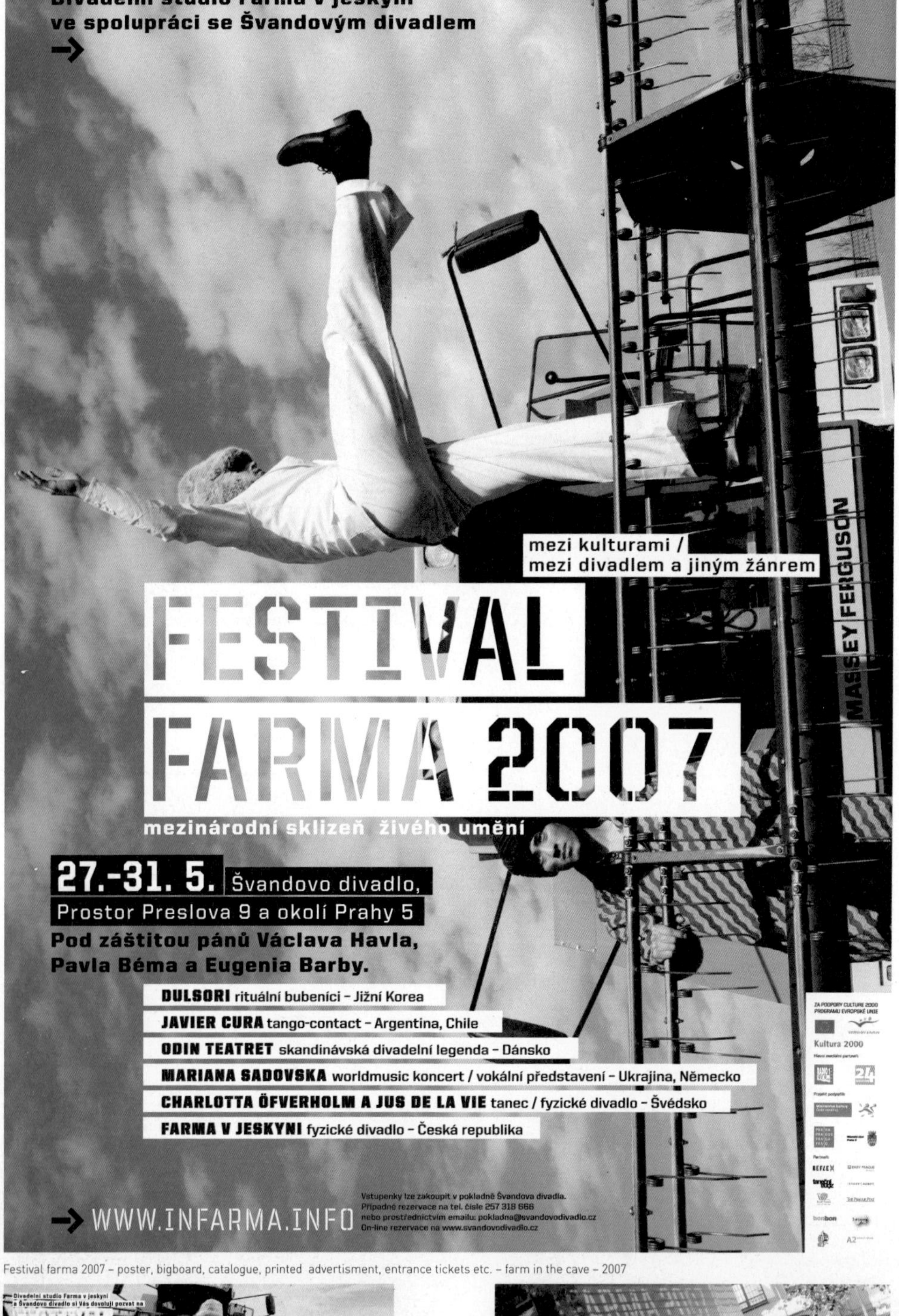

Divadelní studio Farma v jeskyni
ve spolupráci se Švandovým divadlem
→

mezi kulturami /
mezi divadlem a jiným žánrem

FESTIVAL
FARMA 2007

mezinárodní sklizeň živého umění

MASSEY FERGUSON

27.–31. 5. Švandovo divadlo,
Prostor Preslova 9 a okolí Prahy 5

Pod záštitou pánů Václava Havla, Pavla Béma a Eugenia Barby.

DULSORI rituální bubeníci – Jižní Korea
JAVIER CURA tango-contact – Argentina, Chile
ODIN TEATRET skandinávská divadelní legenda – Dánsko
MARIANA SADOVSKA worldmusic koncert / vokální představení – Ukrajina, Německo
CHARLOTTA ÖFVERHOLM A JUS DE LA VIE tanec / fyzické divadlo – Švédsko
FARMA V JESKYNI fyzické divadlo – Česká republika

Kultura 2000

→ WWW.INFARMA.INFO

Vstupenky lze zakoupit v pokladně Švandova divadla.
Případné rezervace na tel. čísle 257 318 666
nebo prostřednictvím emailu: pokladna@svandovodivadlo.cz
On-line rezervace na www.svandovodivadlo.cz

Festival farma 2007 – poster, bigboard, catalogue, printed advertisment, entrance tickets etc. – farm in the cave – 2007

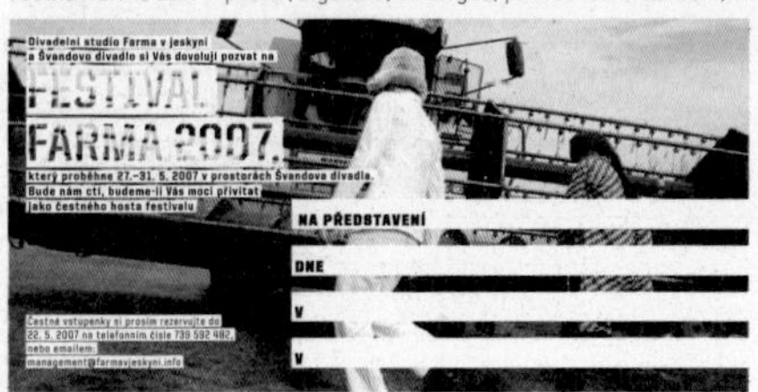

Don't panic! – street art installation, wallpaper – monsters – 2008

Lesley Moore
team:
Alex Clay
Karin van den Brandt
contact:
Graphic Designers
Tweede Atjehstraat 60hs
1094 LK Amsterdam
The Netherlands
T + 31 20 6635110
mail@lesley-moore.nl
www.lesley-moore.nl

Lesley Moore is an Amsterdam-based graphic design agency, founded in May 2004 by Karin van den Brandt (born 1975 in Blerick, The Netherlands) and Alex Clay (born 1974 in Lørenskog, Norway). Van den Brandt and Clay both studied at the Arnhem Academy of the Arts (The Netherlands). Current clients include: BIS publishers, Centraal Museum Utrecht, Wilfried Lentz, Mark Magazine, MTV, De Volkskrant, Gorilla (in collaboration with Herman van Bostelen and De Designpolitie), and Warmoesmarkt.

Lesley Moore – logos created by visitors to www.lesley-moore.nl – Lesley Moore – 2004

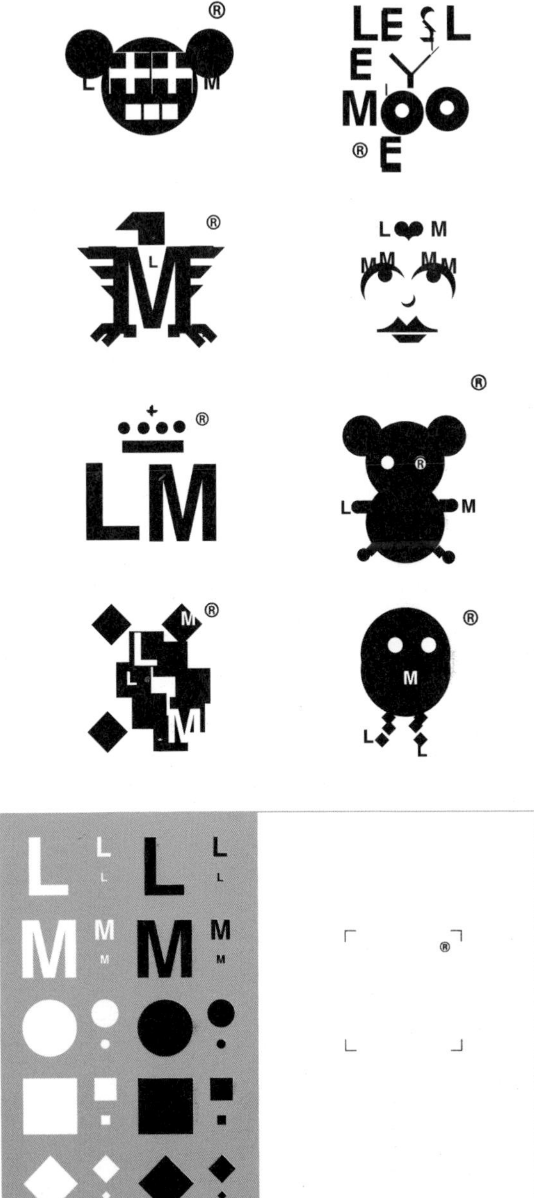

Interview with Lesley Moore

1. What led to the formation of your studio?

We had been working as designers for an agency for 4 years. The time was ripe to give it a try on our own.

2. How many staff people does your studio have and what are their main working fields?

Lesley Moore currently has no staff, but occasionally we take on interns. An intern takes part in the design process under our supervision, so his/her skills have to be rather developed. We do, however, work with freelancers in different fields like photography, film and music.

3. How does a regular working day at your studio look like, how is the day structured?

One of the advantages of being a small studio is that one is very flexible. In other words, we don't need to structure everything we do. When we feel the need to discuss something with each other, we just do it. Truth being told: on Monday mornings we take a look at the coming week to see which deadlines are coming up and so on.

4. How much leisure time do you have during a year?

The last couple of years were very busy in terms of working, so leisure paid the price. At the moment, it looks like we are managing to balance it a bit more. But it's always difficult to say "no" if a nice assignment comes along, even if you already have plenty of work. This can be one of the disadvantages for a small agency.

5. Which business areas do your clients mainly come from? Is the number of your clients increasing or rather declining?

Mainly from the commercial area, but with a strong cultural influence. In the beginning it was very hard to get any clients at all – our network was largely connected to the agency we were previously working for. As a gentleman's agreement you stay clear of these connections. But it basically meant we had to meet a lot of new people and try to convince them that we were the one for the job. We chose to put our energy into artistically interesting jobs as opposed to the financially lucrative ones. After a while this started to pay off, because we attracted clients who appreciated our approach.

6. Do you have a specific corporate philosophy or maybe a mission statement like other companies, which is reflected in the way you steer the studio's course?

Our name, Lesley Moore, refers to "less is more". It doesn't mean that we are minimalists in a formal kind of way – on the contrary. But we try to approach every assignment by defining the essence of the task which has been given to us. In our choices we try to stay as close to this essence as possible. When we succeed in doing this, the result is always strong.

the ideal stencil letter for lazy dogs

7. What, from your point of view, makes the difference between a small studio and a big company?

Freedom. As a small studio we have all the freedom we could wish for in the design process. Our personal contact with our clients is an important factor in that regard. In most big agencies, the designer is not actually the person talking with the client. In a way the design process is a lot like a conversation – with a lot of people involved it doesn't work that well.

8. What kind of advantages and disadvantages does a small studio have compared to a big company?

As mentioned earlier, flexibility is a big plus for us. We also feel that the more an agency grows the less original the design gets. For us the process of making things is very important. If we would grow into a big studio, we would have to supervise much more. It's quite difficult doing that without losing something (a personal touch) in the design along the way.

9. What is your idea about the future of small studios?

Small studios are the future! Seriously, with globalization the need for "personal design" is only increasing. As mentioned earlier, it's difficult to accomplish that being a large agency. But 90% of all companies go for the safe side, so there is room enough for both of us. The challenge for small studios is to build up networks with professionals in different fields, so that they also can handle complex assignments. This way they can hand-pick the best man or woman for the job.

10. Please describe and elaborate on the goals or plans that you have for your studio for the next five years?

Becoming the biggest small studio in the world.

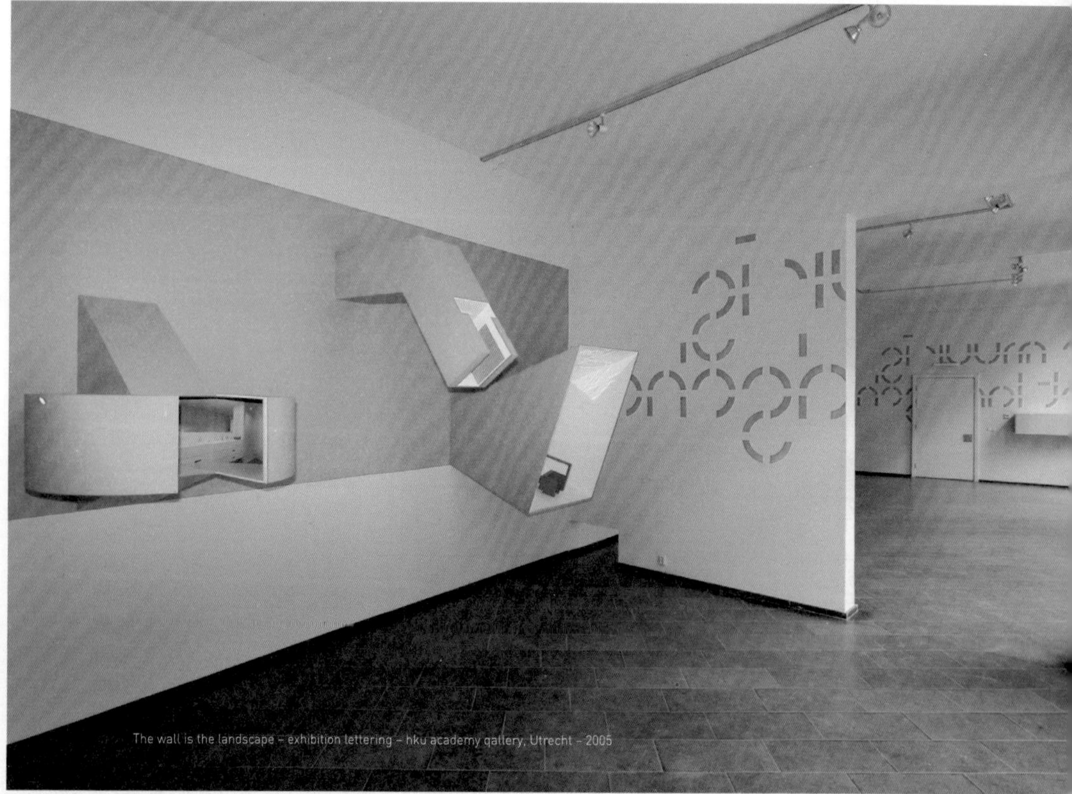

The wall is the landscape – exhibition lettering – hku academy gallery, Utrecht – 2005

Genesis – poster [photography by Lard Buurman] – central museum utrecht – 2007

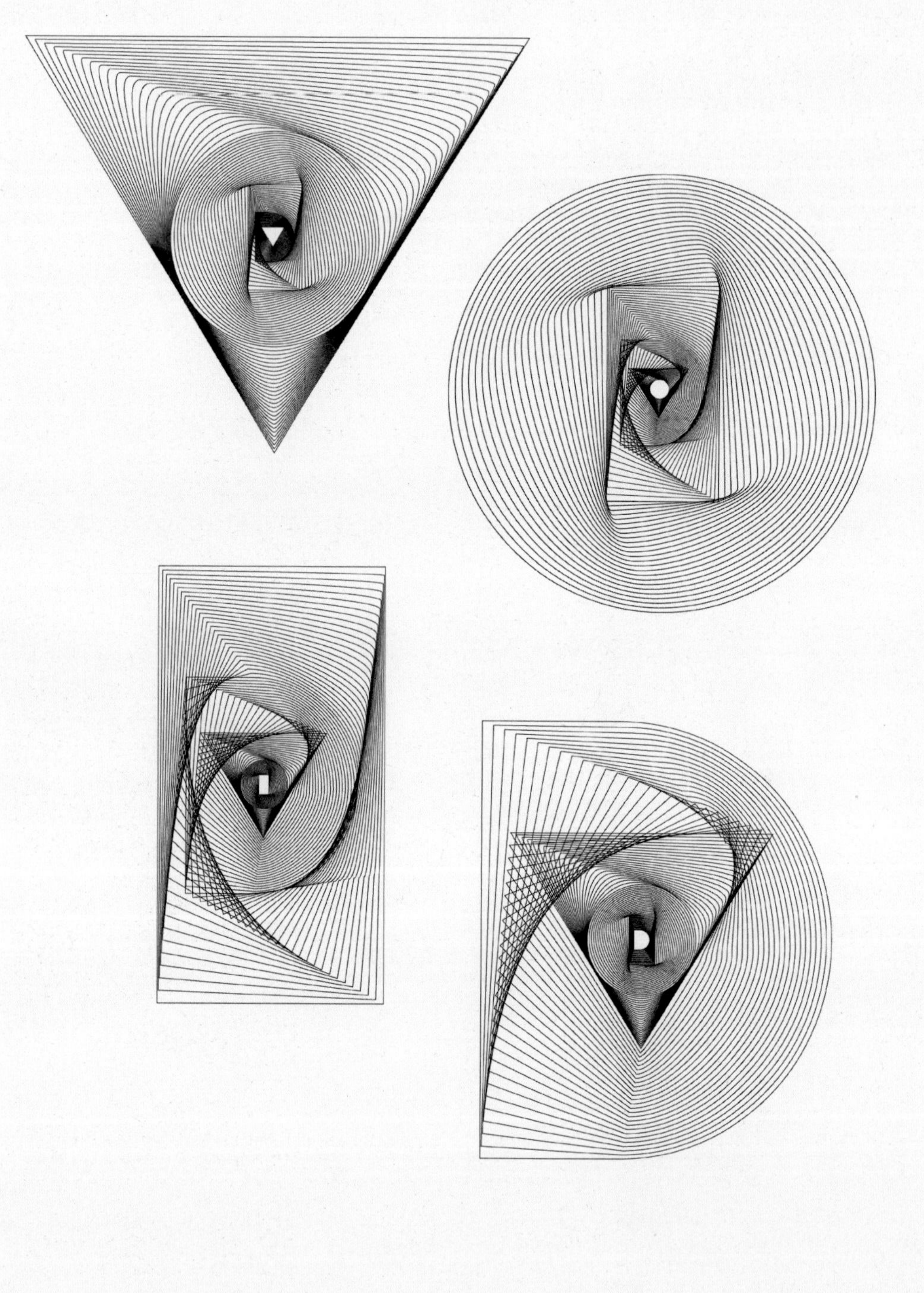

VOID – poster – poster in an autonomous series of publications on the theme VOID – 2008

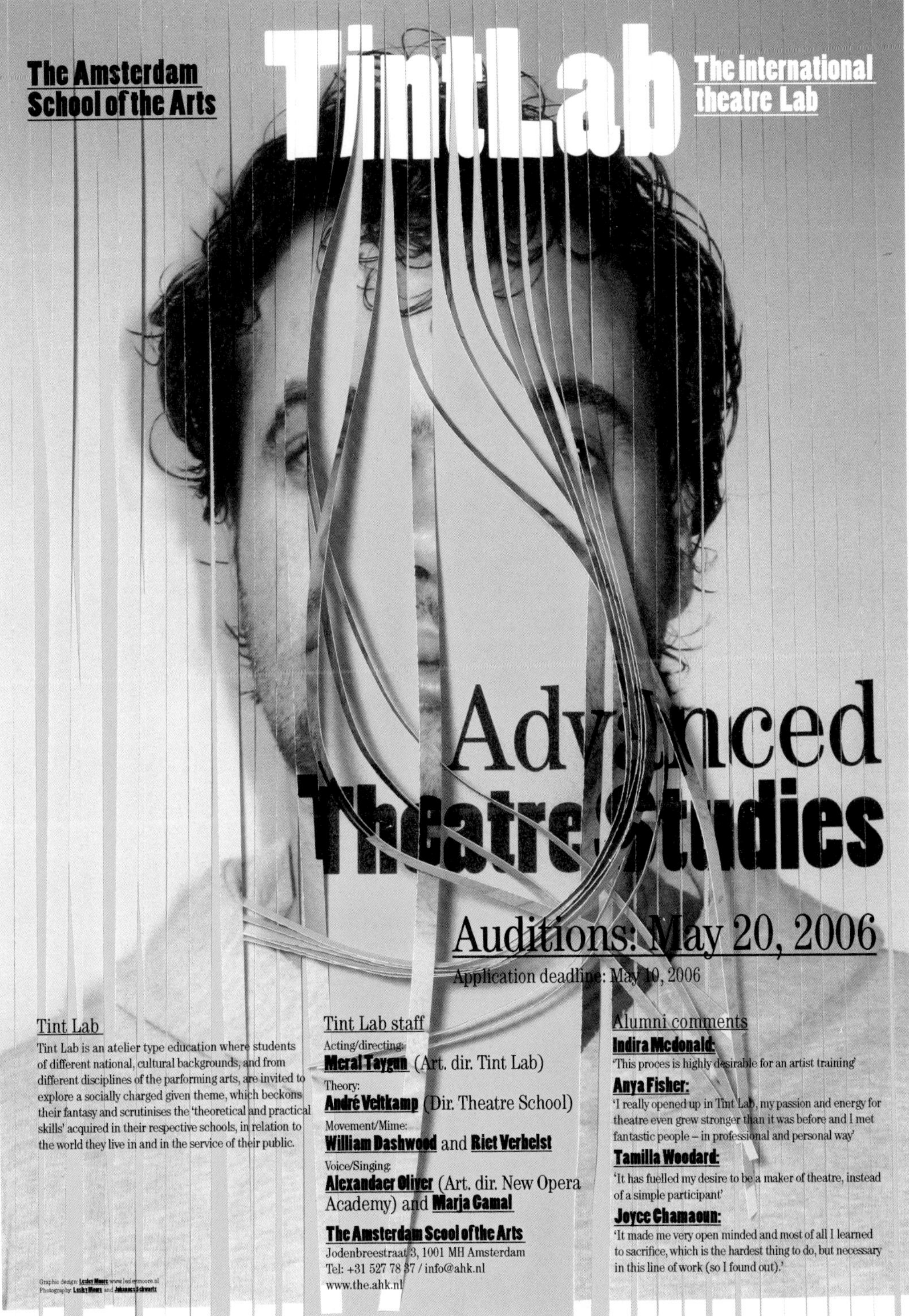

The Amsterdam School of the Arts
TintLab
The international theatre Lab
Advanced Theatre Studies
Auditions: May 20, 2006
Application deadline: May 10, 2006
Tint Lab
Tint Lab is an atelier type education where students of different national, cultural backgrounds, and from different disciplines of the parforming arts, are invited to explore a socially charged given theme, which beckons their fantasy and scrutinises the 'theoretical and practical skills' acquired in their respective schools, in relation to the world they live in and in the service of their public.
Tint Lab staff
Acting/directing:
Meral Taygun (Art. dir. Tint Lab)
Theory:
André Veltkamp (Dir. Theatre School)
Movement/Mime:
William Dashwood and Riet Verhelst
Voice/Singing:
Alexandaer Oliver (Art. dir. New Opera Academy) and Marja Camal
The Amsterdam Scool of the Arts
Jodenbreestraat 3, 1001 MH Amsterdam
Tel: +31 527 78 37 / info@ahk.nl
www.the.ahk.nl
Alumni comments
Indira Mcdonald:
'This proces is highly desirable for an artist training'
Anya Fisher:
'I really opened up in Tint Lab, my passion and energy for theatre even grew stronger than it was before and I met fantastic people – in professional and personal way'
Tamilla Woodard:
'It has fuelled my desire to be a maker of theatre, instead of a simple participant'
Joyce Chamaoun:
'It made me very open minded and most of all I learned to sacrifice, which is the hardest thing to do, but necessary in this line of work (so I found out).'

TintLab – poster (photography by Johannes Schwartz) – the Amsterdam school of the arts – 2006

Julia Müller

team:
Julia Müller
Arjan Groot
contact:
Donker Curtiusstr. 25c
1051 JM Amsterdam
The Netherlands
M + 31 630047753
M + 49 163278874
jule@gmx.de
www.hellojulia.com

Julia Müller after studying fine arts in Germany (Hochschule für Gestaltung Offenbach), I started working as a sound artist. I had some solo exhibitions and especially one of my works received a great deal of attention ("Plaques", illegal sound installation, Museum of Modern Art, Frankfurt, 2002). This was fantastic, but I still felt I needed more and exchanged Frankfurt for Amsterdam to study graphic design (Gerrit Rietveld Academie, Amsterdam). I realized that my conceptual thinking was also of great use here. Two weeks after I got my diploma, I got on my bike to see one of my favourite designers in Amsterdam (Arjan Groot). We became friends and started to work together and still do. Since then I've also worked together with my best friend, Julia Neuroth, in Cologne, earning an award (Type Directors Club New York) for the design of a literary magazine and just being happy with my boyfriend and my cat.

1. What led to the formation of your studio?

After graduation in 2004, I cycled around Amsterdam, meeting my favorite designers and having a talk with them. This resulted in a friendship with Arjan Groot and a work place with him sitting right next to me.

2. How many staff people does your studio have and what are their main working fields?

1, me myself and I. Apart from that I often work in collaborations with Arjan Groot and Julia Neuroth.

3. How does a regular working day at your studio look like, how is the day structured?

Every day is different, depending on the work load.

4. How much leisure time do you have during a year?

3-4 weeks each year.

5. Which business areas do your clients mainly come from?

My clients mainly come from the architectural field. I have been doing an architectural exhibition for the Architecture triennal in Lissabon with Arjan Groot, several architecture books last year and the magazine A10, magazine for new european architecture, which I am doing every two months. Apart from that I have clients from the fashion industry, art and cultural sector.

Is the number of your clients increasing or rather declining?

Increasing as it gets busier each year.

6. Do you have a specific corporate philosophy or maybe a mission statement like other companies, which is reflected in the way you steer the studio's course?

All these mission statements bore me. In the end they all sound the same. I guess if I have to give a philosophy on how I work, then thats starting out with a concept whenever possible to develop a specific graphic look.

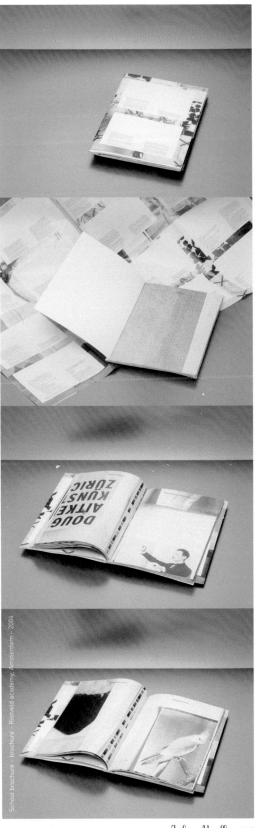

School brochure – brochure – Rietveld academy, Amsterdam – 2004

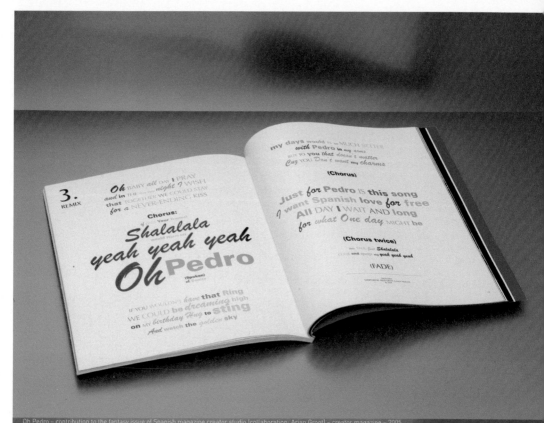

Oh Pedro – contribution to the fantasy issue of Spanish magazine creator studio (collaboration: Arjan Groot) – creator magazine – 2005

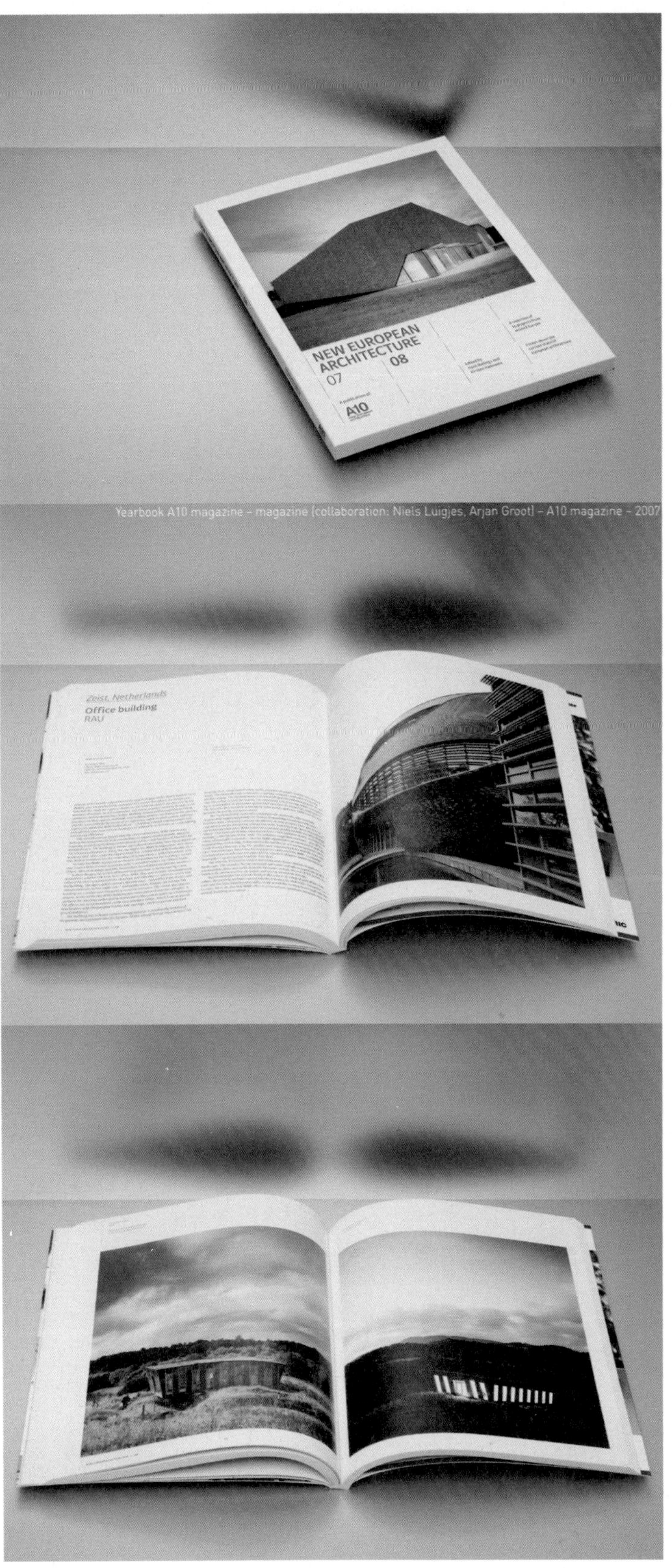

Yearbook A10 magazine – magazine (collaboration: Niels Luijges, Arjan Groot) – A10 magazine – 2007

7. What, from your point of view, makes the difference between a small studio and a big company?

When you are working on your own and in collaborations, you have to fulfill all the functions, from book keeper, secretary, art director, public relation etc. that a big company consists of, yourself. That can be nice but also tiring sometimes.

8. What is your idea about the future of small studios?

In Amsterdam you can find a lot of very small studios, it seems like a trend that will go on. Graduates immediately start their own studio, successfully or not. I think it is very valuable to know the big company's structures for your own small studio use.

9. Do you think that small studios do not have any other choice but to expand in order to survive in these times of globalization?

No. Both studio forms can coexist fine.

10. Please describe and elaborate on the goals or plans that you have for your studio for the next five years?

Eventually I want to merge with on specific collaborator in germany to build a bigger studio and expand.

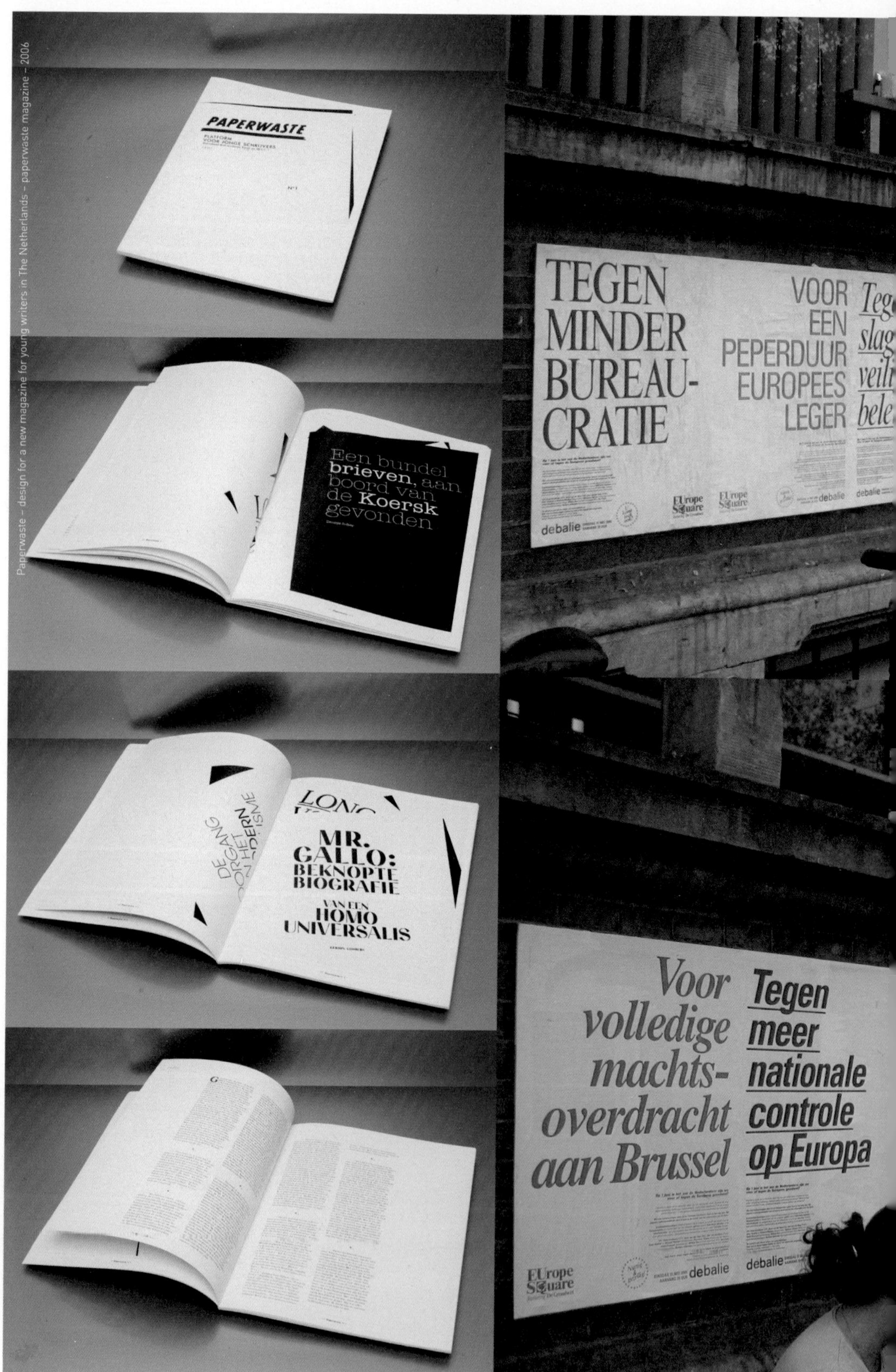

Paperwaste – design for a new magazine for young writers in The Netherlands – paperwaste magazine – 2006

De Balie – publicity campaign (collaboration: Arjan Groot) – De Balie – 2005

Niessen & de Vries

team:
Richard Niessen
Esther de Vries
contact:
Florijn 34
1102 BA Amsterdam
The Netherlands
T + 31 20 6633323
richard@tm-online.nl
www.niessendevries.nl

Niessen & de Vries is Esther de Vries and Richard Niessen who have been working together since 2005. Besides being designers Esther runs a small publishing house (Uitgeverij Boek) and Richard makes music (The Howtoplays). Together they share the interest in dense collaborations with clients. They do not just believe in representation, but always tend to produce "new" works, making use of the printing process (like Uroboros, the snake biting into its own tail). Instead of one clear concept they seek durability through richness in layers, they like to emphasize the materiality of the printwork and avoid references: each work generates its own universe. Richard Niessen graduated from the Gerrit Rietveld Academy in Amsterdam in 1996. He has mostly worked alone except for the time between 1999 and 2002 when he worked with designer Harmen Liemburg under the name "Golden Masters". Niessen is also a musician, and designed the packaging, typography and artwork for each of the albums by his band The Howtoplays. Inspired by the likes of Ettore Sottsass (founder of the Memphis group) and the Scottish-Italian sculptor Eduardo Paolozzi – artists who similarly seek out the tension between structure and going overboard – Niessen developed his own systematic approach to design. He chose the name Typographic Masonry (TM) in 2002 after hearing the term used to describe the work of one of his major influences, the Dutch designer and architect Hendrik Th. Wijdeveld. Since graduating from the Gerrit Rietveld Academy in Amsterdam in 1998, Esther de Vries has been self-employed. She soon moved into publishing, specializing in the design of artist books and educational books on art for childeren. She has an intense approach to each of her projects, which leads her to cooperate with her clients, taking a stance on the content and often adding personal stories connected to the subject being addressed. Since she began freelancing, she has carried out commissions for the Stedelijk Museum, the Dutch post office, the Gemeente Museum in The Haque, De Balie, and several artists.

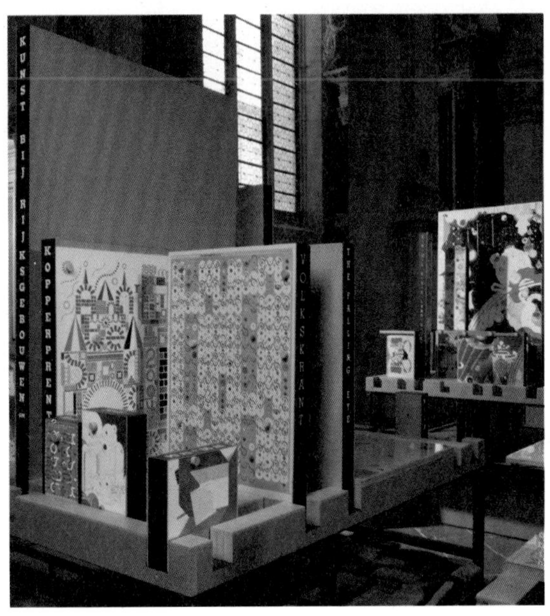

TM City - poster - TM city - 2007

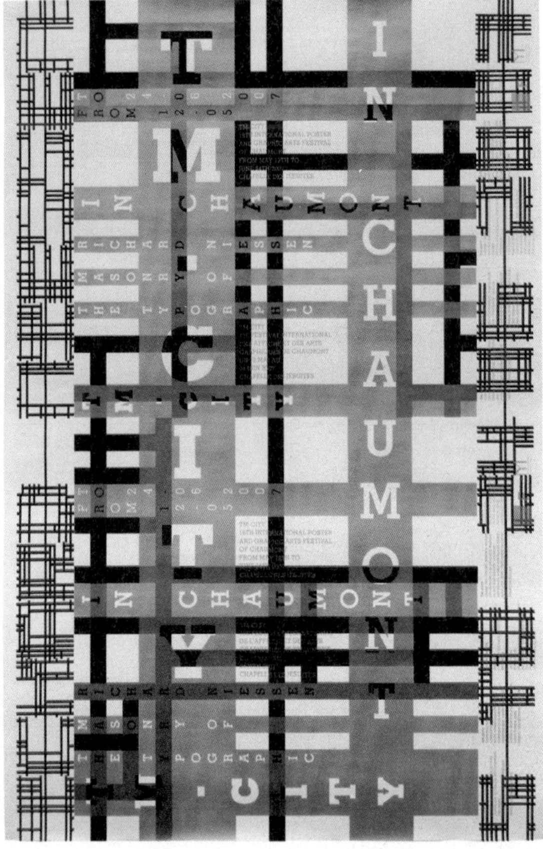

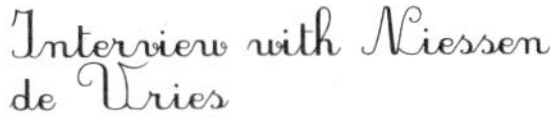

Interview with Niessen de Vries

1. What led to the formation of your studio?

The coorporation between me and Esther de Vries. We started working together on one project in 2005, and from then on we did more work together. At the end of 2007 we decided to start to work under one name: Niessen & de Vries.

2. How many staff people does your studio have and what are their main working fields?

We work with the two of us. We work mainly for cultural clients: artists and cultural institutes, museums, foundations, books, stationaries, typefaces, CD-covers, flyers, festoons, wedding cakes, birth announcement cards, silkscreened posters, DVDs, animations, etc.

3. How does a regular working day at your studio look like, how is the day structured?

It's chaotic from 8 until 6.

4. How much leisure time do you have during a year?
Not much, but then again we do not need that much since we do nice work.

5. Which business areas do your clients mainly come from? Is the number of your clients increasing or rather declining?
As I said, we mainly work for cultural clients. And the number is increasing.

6. Do you have a specific corporate philosophy or maybe a mission statement like other companies, which is reflected in the way you steer the studio's course?
We both emphasise originality and a vast quantity of subject matter, we allow the work to evolve from itself, often creating every component from scratch. The density of our work stands out.

7. What, from your point of view, makes the difference between a small studio and a big company?
Personal involvement.

8. What kind of advantages and disadvantages does a small studio have compared to a big company?
I don't know, I guess our day is more varied. We have to make coffee ourselves, talk to the clients and answer all emails.

SCB The thing that wears my ring – cd, font design – scram c baby –2007

Big art for small humans part 2 – package design – dvd grote kunst voor kleine mensen – 2007

De droomintendant – brochure – fonds BKVB – 2007

Stedelijk New Years card – card – stedelijk museum Amsterdam – 2008

TM-city – textildesign – TM city – 2007

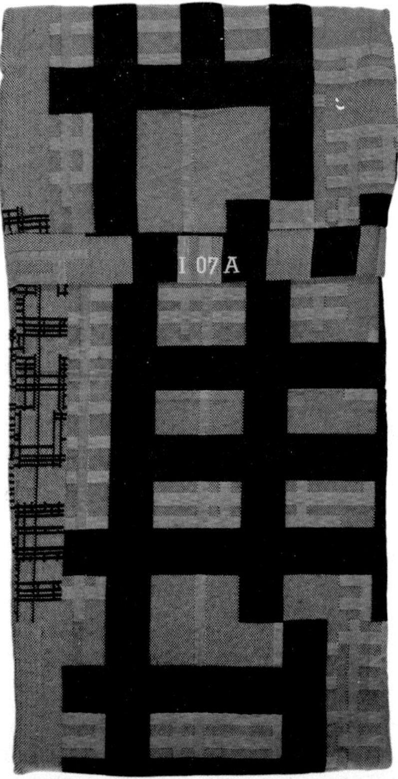

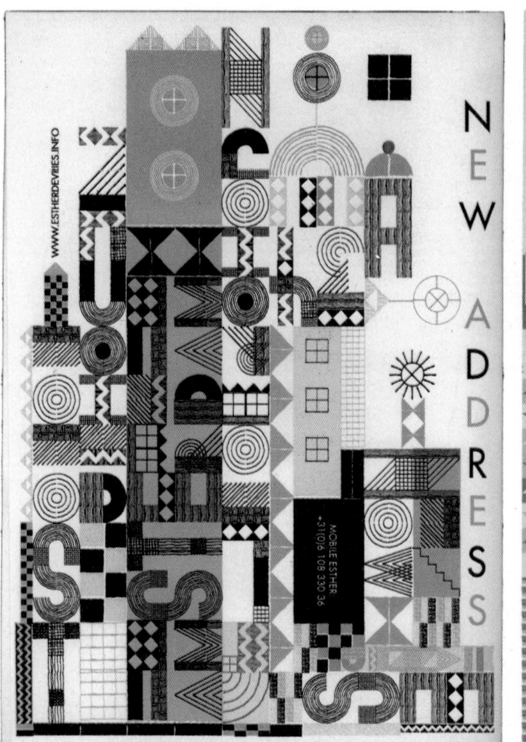

New adress – poster – self published – 2007

Fiep – birth announcement card – fiep – 2008

Cooper – birth announcement card – cooper – 2007

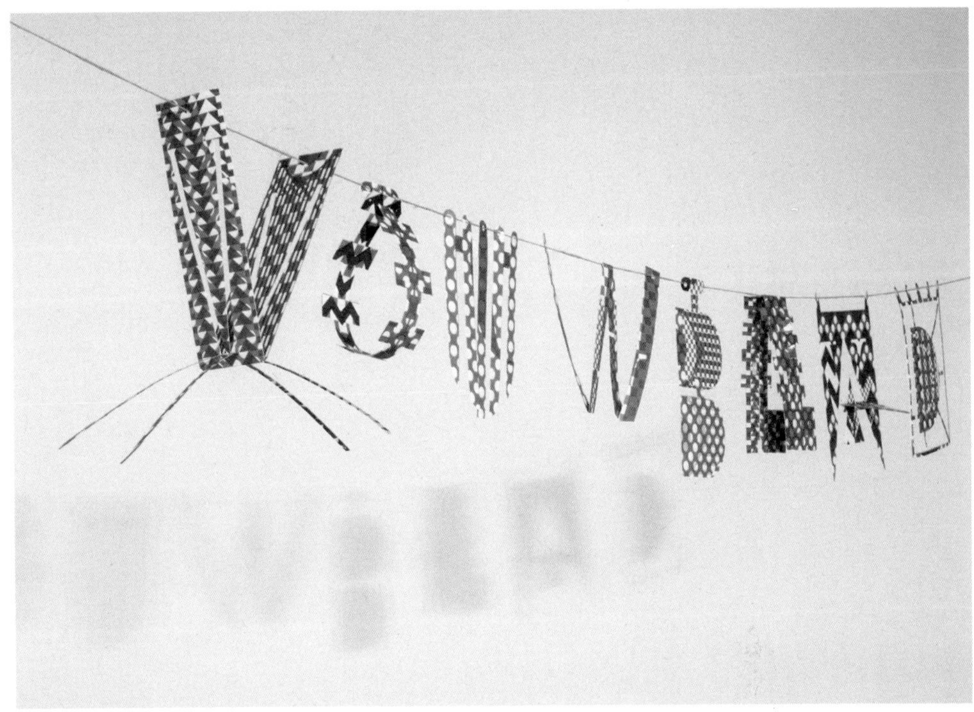

9. What is your idea about the future of small studios? Do you think that small studios do not have any other choice but to expand in order to survive in these times of globalization?

No way! Why?

10. Please describe and elaborate on the goals or plans that you have for your studio for the next five years?

We would like to have better paid, more serious assignments.

Vouwblad – series of publication – lenoirSchuring printers in Amstelveen – 2007

nlxl
team:
Bob van Dijk
Oscar Smeulders
Joost Roozekrans
contact:
Paviljoensgracht 70
2512 BR The Hague
The Netherlands
T + 31 70 3601770
F + 31 70 3469557
info@nlxl.com
www.nlxl.com

nlxl is a design studio for visual communication and interaction design. The strength of the studio lies on the development side of design projects. NLXL explores and experiments with the possibilities of combining visual and interactive elements within single design solutions. Content, form and technique are carefully considered in each and every solution. The three partners of NLXL, Bob van Dijk, Oscar Smeulders and Joost Roozekrans worked together for several years before founding NLXL. The studio is able to produce advanced and original cross media design solutions. Continually challenging boundaries with innovative and original design concepts is paramount to NLXL's philosophy. In short: NLXL designs logos, corporate and visual identities, web sites and webidentities, event styles, forms, posters, animations, books, content management systems, digital presentations and other digital applications.

Poster for the volksbuurtmuseum, The Hague – poster – volksbuurtmuseum – 2003

Interview with nlxl

1. What led to the formation of your studio?

The partners of NLXL worked together for several years at Studio Dumbar before starting NLXL. This studio became famous for the dentity of the Dutch railways, KPN, and the Dutch police force. Besides that, Studio Dumbar was also well known for their work in the cultural field. Besides being colleagues, Bob, Oscar & Joost also became friends over the years. They have a mixture of different interests. Being different as persons in the studio is something that they see as a strength and what they encourage amongst their staff, too. It also means that everyone can learn from each other. Never look into the same direction.

2. How many staff people does your studio have and what are their main working fields?

There are 3 partners and 8 people in total working at NLXL. The work is a mix of traditional media, such as print and digital media, like websites, digital presentations, and even VJ-ing. In the end it is all about visual communication and not just graphic design. Designing ceilings, or traveling around the world with artists for a light-project or making theatre-plays are not things that you traditionally find in this profession. We are curious and always have young people in our studio from all over the globe, both as employees and as interns. We are quite often asked to travel abroad to lecture or do workshops.

3. How does a regular working day at your studio look like, how is the day structured?

Although everyone works in one big space there is always (loud) music playing. The studio is more structured than people would think at the first glance. Our former business manager always saw us with a glass of wine in our hands before starting to work with us – there were always a lot of visitors. Then, when he started working for us, he was amazed at how hard and serious we can work. If the back office is well organized, with proper ICT tools, there is more time to de creative work, to play and develop.

4. How much leisure time do you have during a year?

As much as everybody can, a couple of weeks. Being your own boss gives freedom on one hand while on the other, you always take the work or the profession with you.

International affiche gallery – poster – schoon of schijn institute – 2008

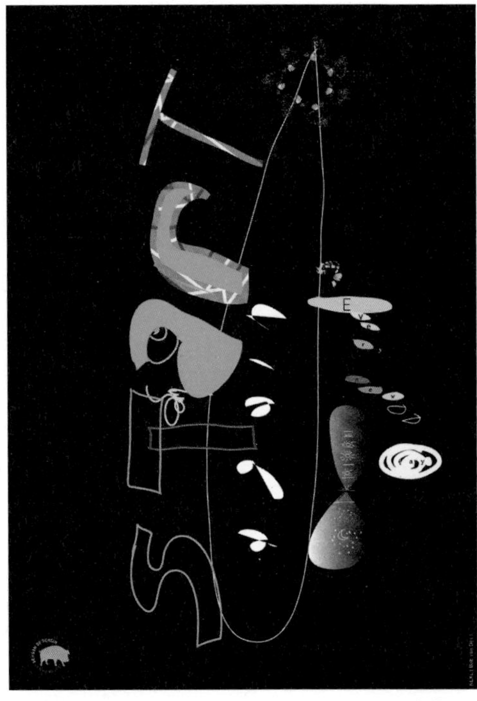

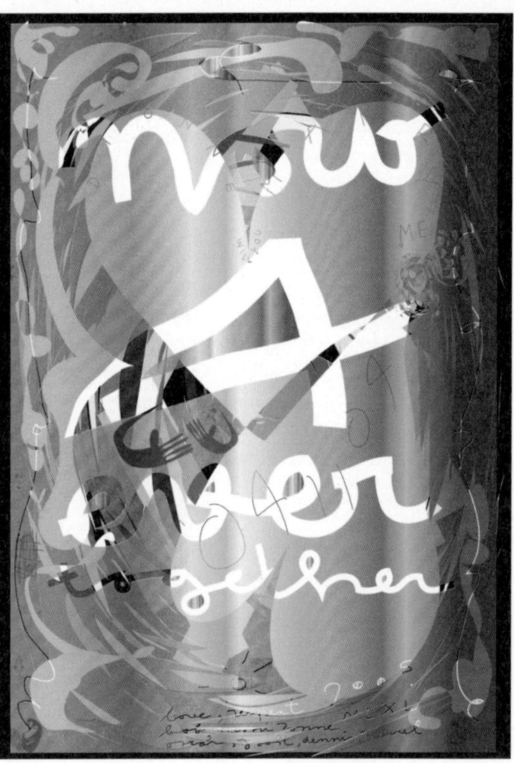

Love poster – poster – Marc Shillum, London – 2004

Poster for the international AGI - congress unknown land in Amsterdam – poster – AGI/alliance graphique internationale – 2007

Event style vrijheidsfestival Den Haag – poster – bureau discriminatiezaken Den Haag – 2006

1000 graphics for airports Milan and Rome - poster - goodby, silverstein and partners, San Francisco - 2003

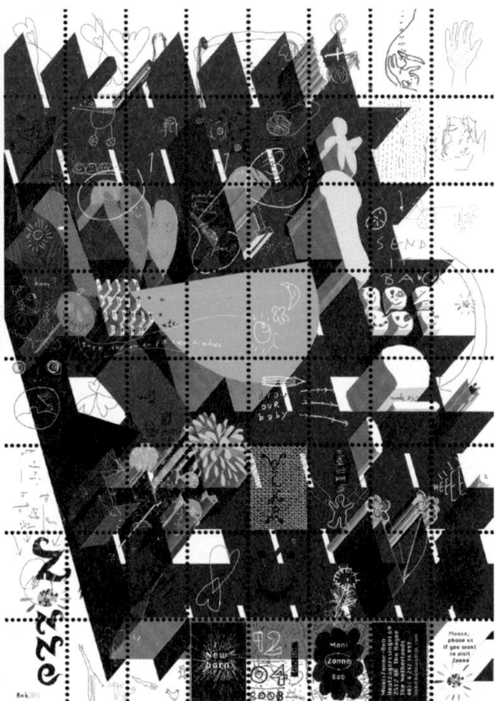

Birth stamps – stamps – Zonne van Dijk – 2003

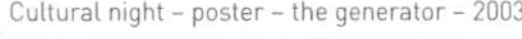

Cultural night – poster – the generator – 2003

5. Which business areas do your clients mainly come from? Is the number of your clients increasing or rather declining?

The clients come from all sorts of fields. Big and small, national and international. We like to work with different sorts of people and do projects that are complex or start from scratch. We call ourselves a development-studio, which means that we do not do a lot of production work. Of course, we do the production work for the projects we realize, but we hardly implement magazines or brochures monthlies. The good thing is that we put our energy on creativity and development. The downside is that once the initial development is done we might not work for this client again until they need something completely new. This means that we always have to look for this type of new business. It's a choice we have made because this is the type of work making us happy end this is what we are good at.

6. Do you have a special corporate philosophy or maybe a mission statement like other companies, which is reected in the way you steer the studio's course?

Yes, we do! It's the 3 F-words: Fun, Fame & Fortune. Fun is: do we like the topic, the challenge, the people. Fame is: does it potentially generate airplay. Is it something we could be proud of. Fortune is: does it generate money. Although it is not just the money, but also if we can learn from it. These words should apply to finding project, clients, people we work with and work for. At least 2 of the 3 words should apply to any selection of project or people. If not, we turn down the project. Ideally all 3 should apply, than we are the most happy and we have had that quite often.

7. What, from your point of view, makes the difference between a small studio and a big company?

The way we go about something in a small studio gives us more freedom and variety with regard to the kind of work we do. A small studio is more flexible in the type of work that they want to accept or let go. You don't always have to say "yes" just because of financial reasons and because of all the salaries having to be paid every month. Also working with freelance specialists is often better than just to pick the designer that happens to be available at that given moment. On the other hand, bigger organizations often want to work with a bigger studio. So, sometimes you don't get a project, because organizations want a bigger studio to level with and to do their creative communication work. However we do see that with the current development of new techniques it becomes easier to be organized in an efficient way with little effort, and to communicate fast from whereever you are. In the end, it's about being eager, being curious, nor being afraid to make mistakes or coming up with good ideas.

8. What kind of advantages and disadvantages does a small studio have compared to a big company?

I think we have aswered this already in the previous question.

9. What is your idea about the future of small studios? Do you think that small studios do not have any other choice but to expand in order to survive in these times of globalization?

Not only in design there is the tendency that people will work more and more in collaborations, instead of (traditional) organizations. Think of Linux open source technology, Wikipedia and the like. It's likely that in the near future people in the creative and services industries will operate more and more in small groups or even solo and collaborate depending on the size and complexity of any given project.

10. Please describe and elaborate on the goals or plans that you have for your studio for the next years?

We will do different projects for various (new) clients with the same design development mentality.

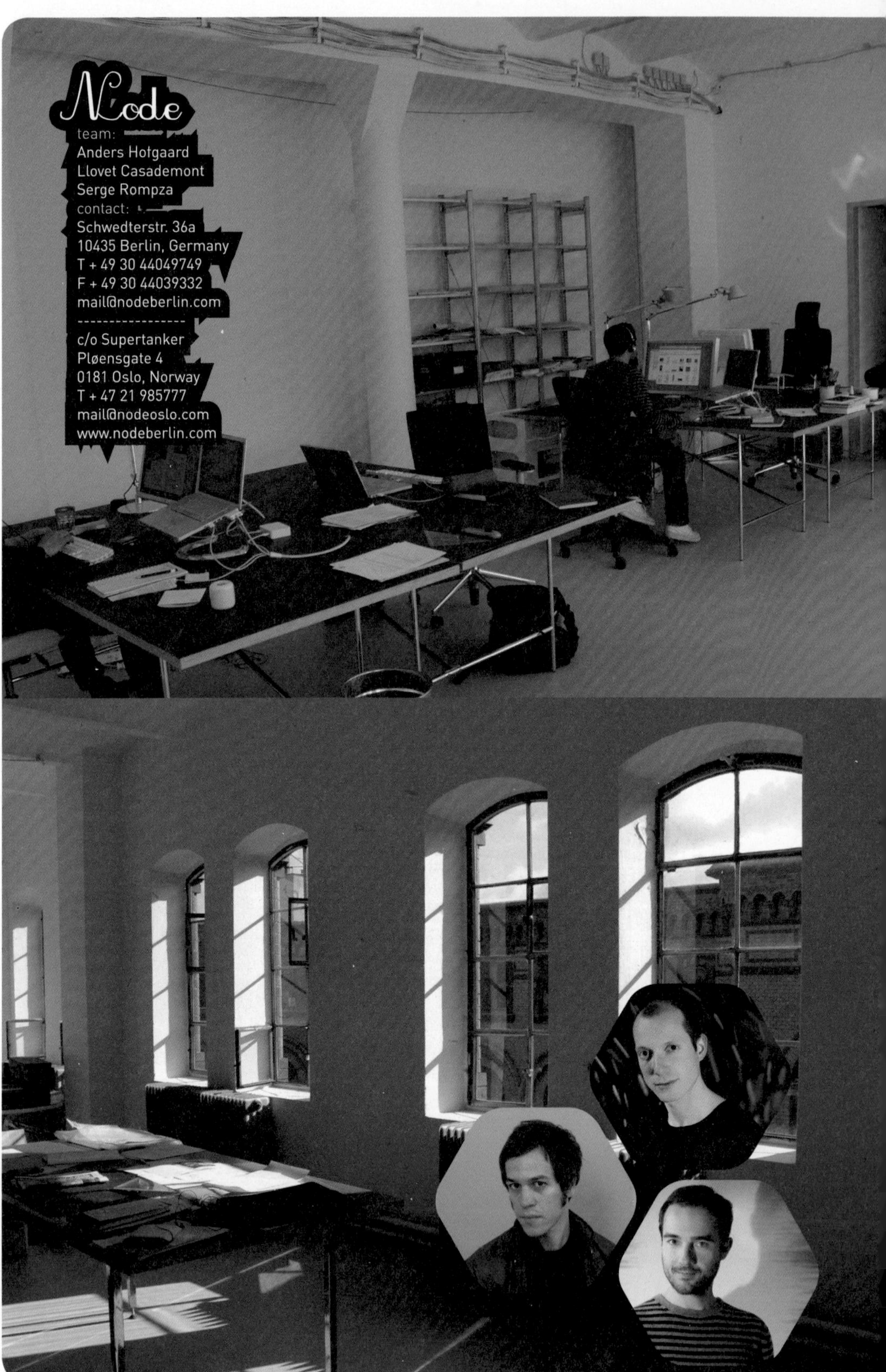
Node
team:
Anders Hofgaard
Llovet Casademont
Serge Rompza
contact:
Schwedterstr. 36a
10435 Berlin, Germany
T + 49 30 44049749
F + 49 30 44039332
mail@nodeberlin.com
----
c/o Supertanker
Pløensgate 4
0181 Oslo, Norway
T + 47 21 985777
mail@nodeoslo.com
www.nodeberlin.com

Node is a Berlin- and Oslo-based graphic design studio, founded in 2003 by Anders Hofgaard (NO) and Serge Rompza (DE). Vladimir Llovet Casademont (DE/ES) joined the collaboration in 2006. All three studied at the Gerrit Rietveld Academy, Amsterdam. The studio works for international clients and on self-initiated projects across various media: books, magazines, posters, typefaces, identities, exhibition design, signage and websites. NODE collaborates with freelance designers, illustrators, photographers and programmers.

Interview with Node

1. What led to the formation of your studio?

NODE was founded as Serge Rompza and Anders Hofgaard got to know each other at the Rietveld Academy in Amsterdam. We had this idea of going to Berlin because we thought it would be interesting to live and work in a city which is still very much in development, with certain structures that haven't been fixed yet. We appreciate the freedom this gives us. In Berlin, we got to know Vladimir Llovet Casademont who joined NODE. At an earlier point he had also been at the Rietveld Academy. We have a common background, and therefore also a similar view on design.

2. How many staff people does your studio have and what are their main working fields?

At the moment we are three designers and one intern. We all take part in the entire process of running the studio. This means one cannot solely focus on design, but we do believe that this makes our workplace more interesting, as it is entirely shaped by us. However, we also appreciate working with external designers, like Felix Weigand who has been collaborating with us on several projects.

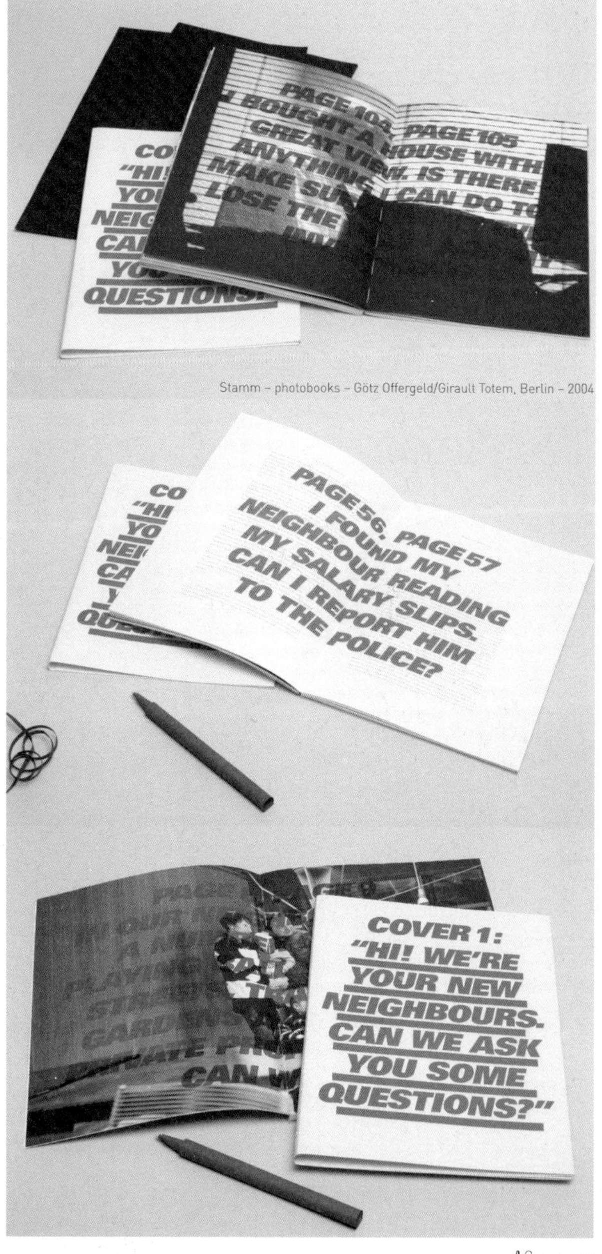

Stamm – photobooks – Götz Offergeld/Girault Totem, Berlin – 2004

3. How does a regular working day at your studio look like, how is the day structured?

We do spend quite some time at the office – usually 10–12 hours per day, sometimes more. The first part of the day may include more administrative work, whereas the second part may be more focused on developing ideas and designing. The day is determined by the projects, and the structure may be shifting. As we all take part in the entire process, our roles shift from project to project.

4. How much leisure time do you have during a year?

We try to keep Sundays free of work (but often fail). We do combine traveling and working, which often makes work and leisure overlap. In addition we try to get 2-3 weeks of "real" holidays.

5. Which business areas do your clients mainly come from? Is the number of your clients increasing or rather declining?

We do quite some work for the cultural sector and different non-commercial organizations. In addition, we do some very commercial work, for instance for StatoilHydro, a Fortune-fifty company. Our number of clients is increasing and we do have quite a lot to do at the moment.

6. Do you have a specific corporate philosophy or maybe a mission statement like other companies, which is reflected in the way you steer the studio's course?

No, if there is something that guides us, it is to create the studio where we would like to work ourselves.

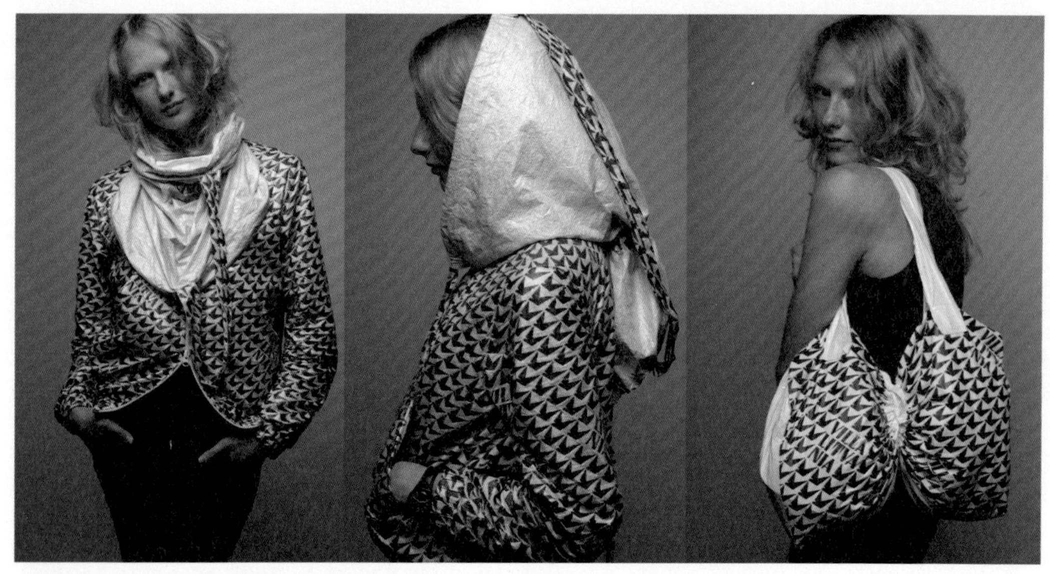

Villa Lituania, Venice Biennale – book, textil design – contemporary art centre, Cilnius – 2007

Villa Lituania, Venice Biennale – packaging – contemporary art centre, Cilnius – 2007

Heitere weitere polterei, tere recarens – artist momograph – galeria Toni Tàpies, Barcelona – 2005

Gerrit – artist catalogue – Gerrit Rietveld academy – 1997

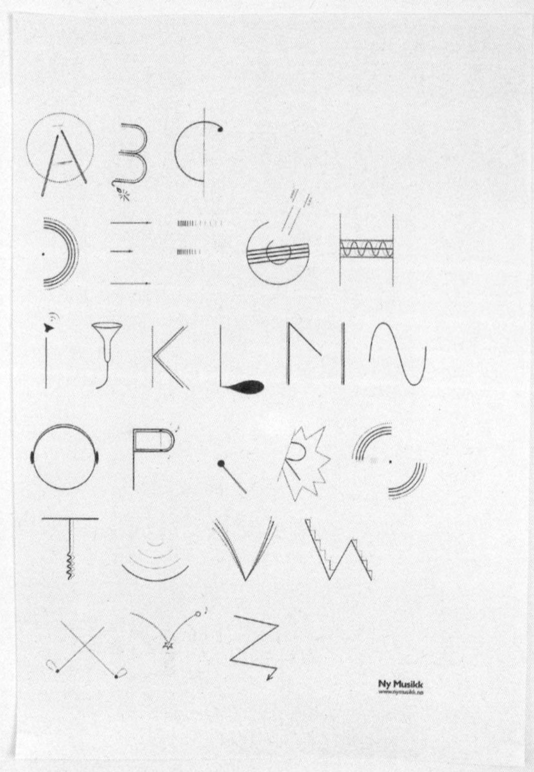

Audio alphabet – poster – ny musikk – 2007

032c – magazine – 032c workshop/Jörg Koch – 2002

7. What, from your point of view, makes the difference between a small studio and a big company?

The way we see it, there is a major difference. Everything we do is filtered through a few people with similar value sets. Once a company passes a given size, there are certain (power) structures arising, making it more of an organization and less individual.

8. What kind of advantages and disadvantages does a small studio have compared to a big company?

By being small we have much more freedom to prioritize the projects we want to realize – and decide what we don't want to do. The advantage of being big may be the ability to handle bigger projects.

9. What is your idea about the future of small studios? Do you think that small studios do not have any other choice but to expand in order to survive in these times of globalization?

It depends on what one pursues. Globalization also offers some very interesting possibilities for small companies. Working transnationally was previously a privilege for big "multinationals". The way we work now, with clients in several countries, is only possible because of certain developments within the last ten years.

10. Please describe and elaborate on the goals or plans that you have for your studio for the next five years?

It is very difficult to tell how the studio will develop, as it is intertwined with our own development. Some more stability is maybe desirable but we are still looking for the right balance between interesting and financially rewarding projects. We wish to remain able to do the kind of work we are interested in.

Happy Days 2007 – visual identity – ny musikk – 2007

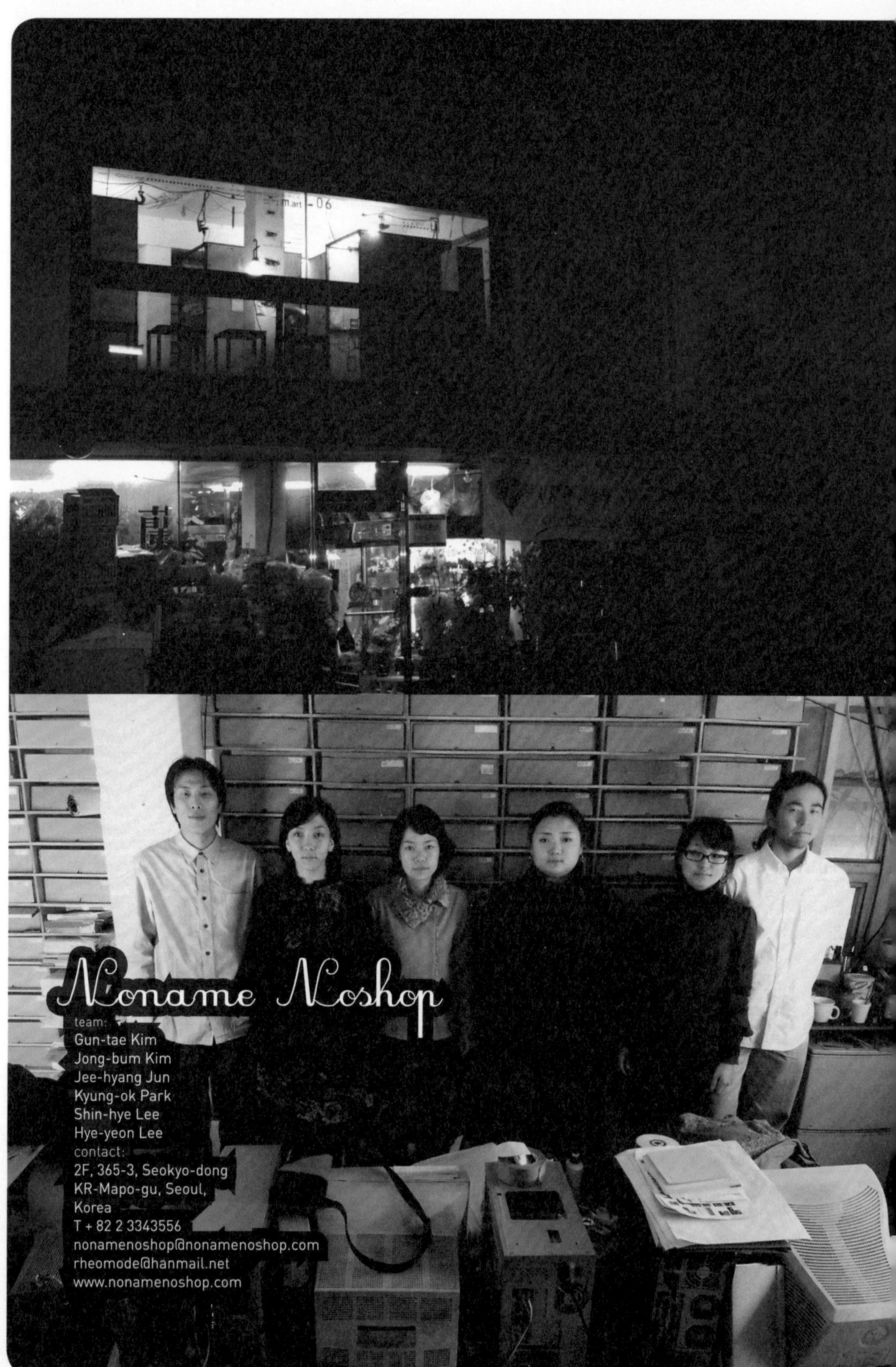

Noname Noshop

team:
Gun-tae Kim
Jong-bum Kim
Jee-hyang Jun
Kyung-ok Park
Shin-hye Lee
Hye-yeon Lee

contact:
2F, 365-3, Seokyo-dong
KR-Mapo-gu, Seoul,
Korea
T + 82 2 3343556
nonamenoshop@nonamenoshop.com
rheomode@hanmail.net
www.nonamenoshop.com

Noname Noshop is a Seoul-based independent design studio consisting of 6 members (Kim Geun-tae, Kim Jong-beom, Lee Shinhye, Lee Hye-yeon, Chun Ji-hyang and Park Kyung-oak). The studio was established in 2003 to give names to things that have "no name" and to make products with things and ideas considered by "no shop". Noname Noshop has been working across a wide range of disciplines including graphics, exhibition planning, space design, and product design.

Noname: Too many names given and scarce names to be found.

Noshop: Too many products given and scarce products to be found.

Nonamenoshop: Naming for the unnamed (lost, deprived or uncalled) and producing something that never was (couldn't be) produced.

Interview with Noname Noshop

1. What led to the formation of your studio?

First of all, we were urged to build a place where we could just ponder a lot of things after graduation from college. We also questioned ourselves about whether or not we should live our lives, doing what we really wanted in reality.

2. How many staff people does your studio have and what are their main working fields?

We have six artists in total. We all work together and the main roles change depending on the projects we get to work on.

3. How does a regular working day at your studio look like, how is the day structured?

We pretty much just stay there and work at the studio. We usually start a day after brunch.

4. How much leisure time do you have during a year?

As much as he/she wants, whenever it's possible.

5. Which business areas do your clients mainly come from? Is the number of your clients increasing or rather declining?

We've been having more clients associated with public projects lately.

6. Do you have a specific corporate philosophy or maybe a mission statement like othercompanies, which is reflected in the way you steer the studio's course?

Noname: Too many names given and scarce names to be found. Noshop: Too many products given and scarce products to be found. Nonamenoshop: Naming for the unnamed (lost, deprived or uncalled) producing something never was (couldn't be) produced. This is our own definition of "noname noshop". We still lack a full understanding of the complicated reality and the personal ability to grasp or criticize that reality with a clear sense of direction. We just want to find our identity gradually.

7. What, from your point of view, makes the difference between a small studio and a big company?

Thinking of a big company just a fancy symbol comes to our minds, whereas humanity exists in a small studio.

8. What kind of advantages and disadvantages does a small studio have comparedto a big company?

Every one of us is fully responsible for the whole process from the beginning to the end. That's the advantage but also a disadvantage.

9. What is your idea about the future of small studios? Do you think that small studios do not have any other choice but to expand in order to survive in these times of globalization?

We're not really sure about the future. But we hope that eventually small studios will expand and balance out in order to make the industry more comfortable with small studios and trust them, because it is our fundamental belief that sensibility is more important. We think that we can change the world with the strong belief in human values.

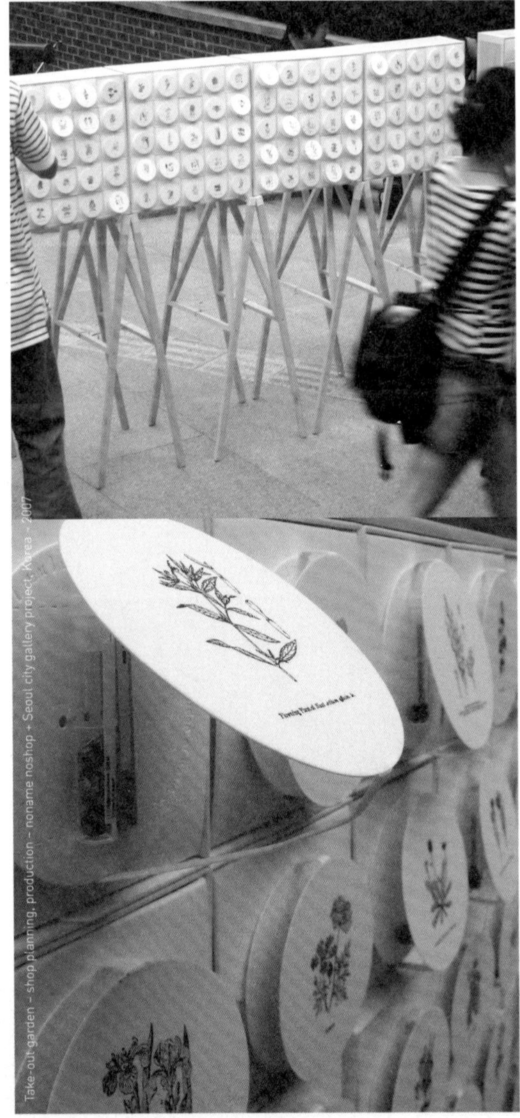

Take-out garden – shop planning, production – noname noshop + Seoul city gallery project, Korea – 2007

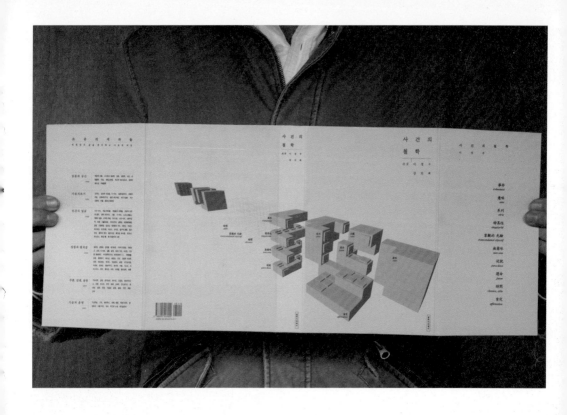

Philosophy of event – book – academy of philosophy – 2003

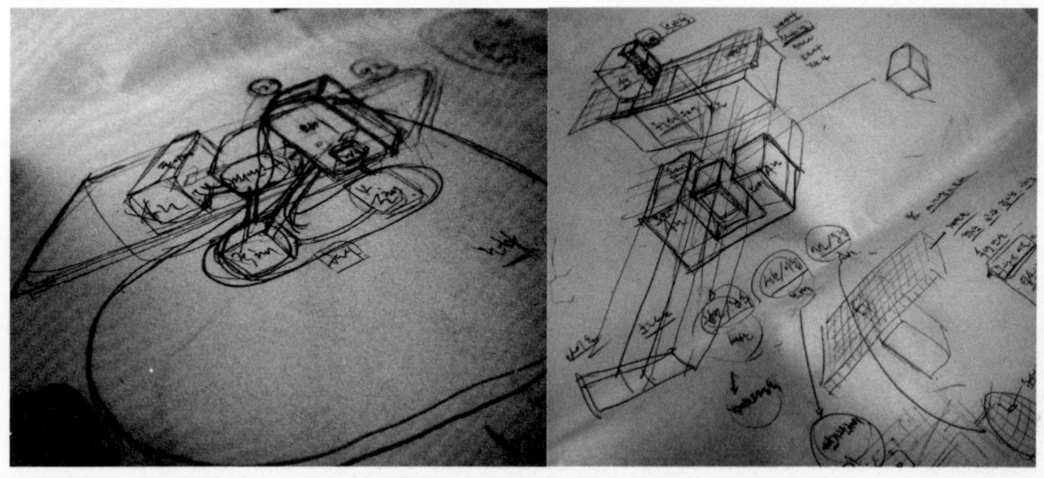

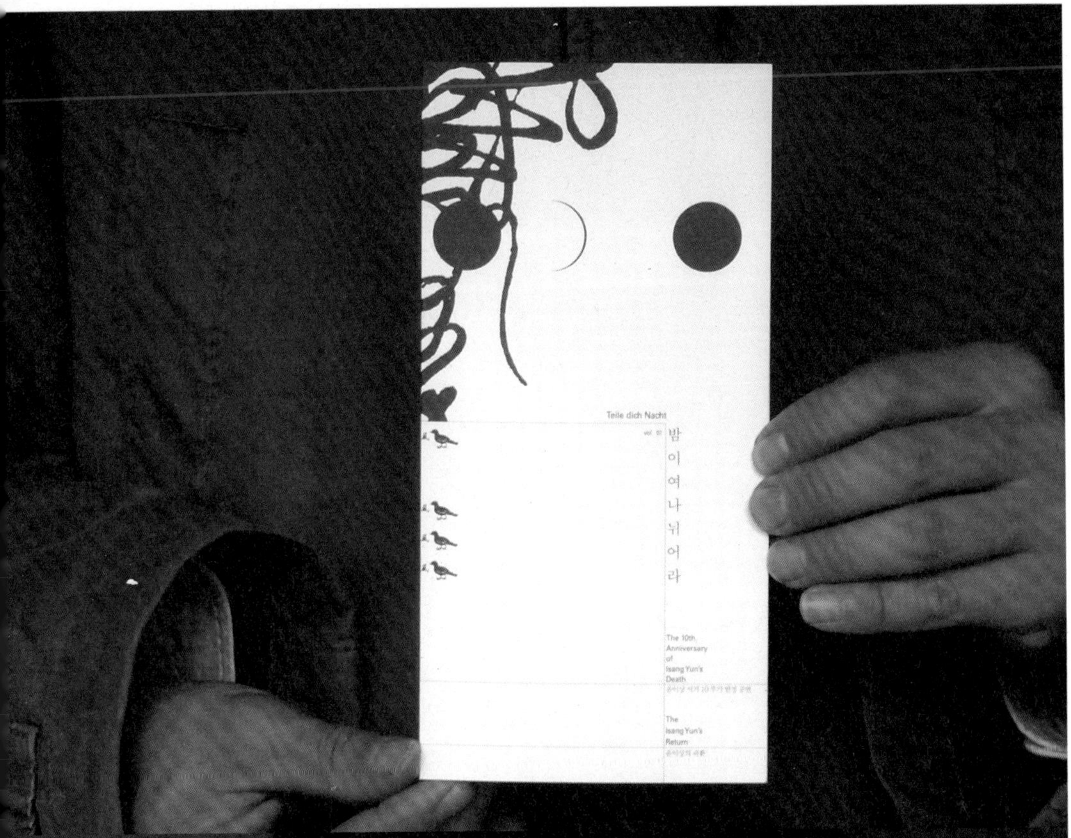

The 10th. anniversary of Isang Yun´s death – poster, flyer – Isang Yun Peace foundation – 2005

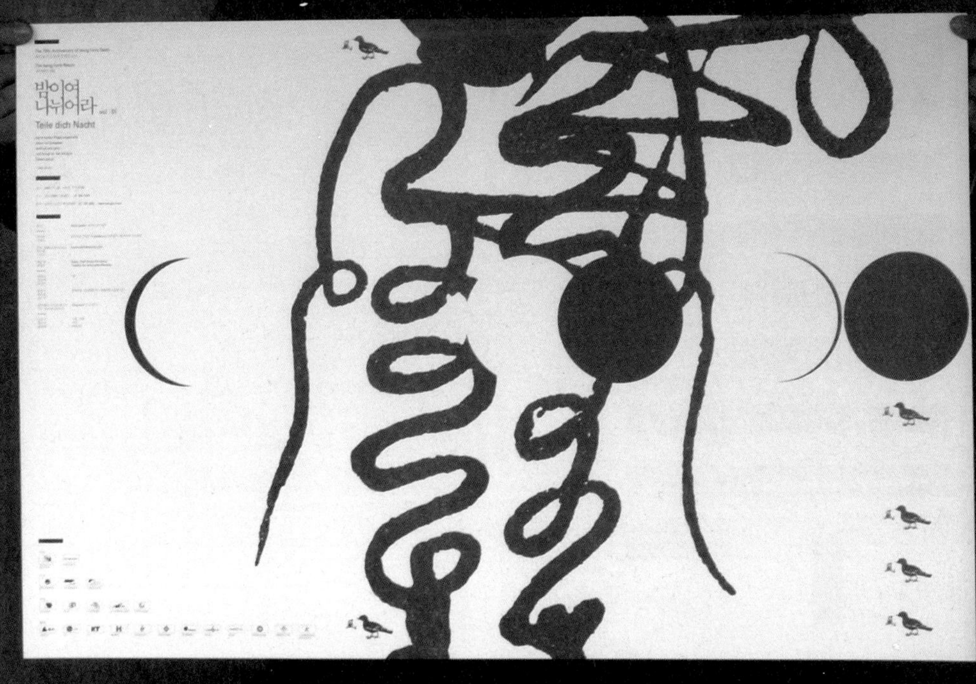

help-y christmas_help-y new year – production – noname noshop + earth project, Korea – 2006

00 market – shop planning, production – noname noshop + Munhwaro Norizzang, Korea – 2006

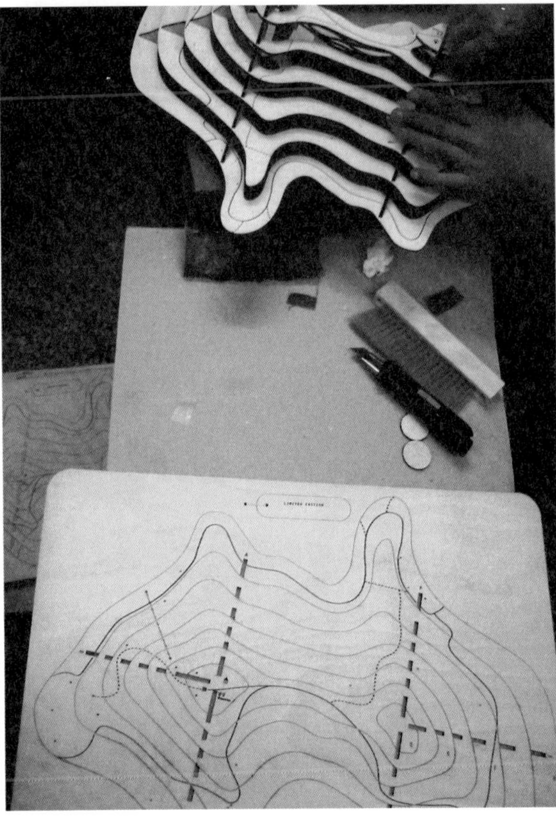

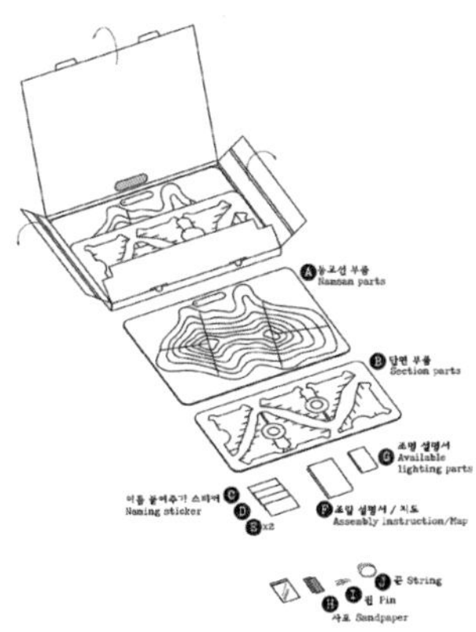

10. Please describe and elaborate on the goals or plans that you have for your studiofor the next five years?

We are planning to turn some ideas we've been having into actual works. The main idea is to open small-sized markets where products are made to influence the act of consuming in positive ways. It would be called the 00 market (the numerical term 00 is pronounced the same way as the word "public" in Korean). In that market there will be the "Help-y Christmas Shop" and "Switch House Shop" which encourage donation, the "Take-out Garden Shop" which is about afforesting a city, the "Silver Garden Shop" to help the elders healing physically and mentally. And also the "Hamadryades Shop" and "Little Earth Shop" which are based on ecological ideas.

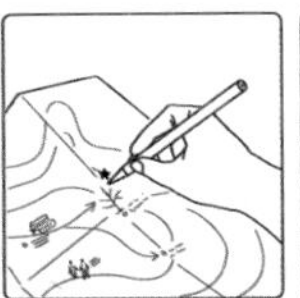

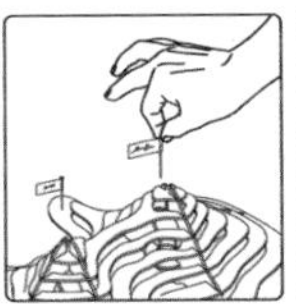

namsan – product design – CJ group, Korea – 2005

Parallax Design Pty Ltd

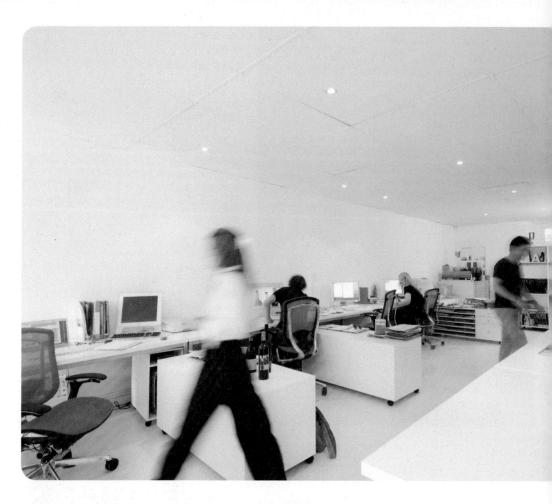

team:
Matthew Remphrey
Kellie Campbell
Sam Barrat
Lucy Fox
contact:
447 Pulteney Street
Adelaide SA 5000
Australia
T + 61 8 82328066
F + 61 8 82328055
matt@parallaxdesign.com.au
hello@parallaxdesign.com.au
www.parallaxdesign.com.au

Parallax Design Pty Ltd is a small design studio located in Adelaide, Australia, established in 2001. Specializing in identity and packaging design, the studio works for some of the biggest companies in the world, to some of the smallest. Creative Director Matthew Remphrey is currently Chair of the Advisory Committee to the South Australian School of Art and Design, University of South Australia. He is a past president of the South Australian chapter of the Australian Graphic Design Association (AGDA) and a past vice president of AGDA's national council. He lives in Adelaide with his wife Abra, 4 year old daughter Grace and 1 year old son Harrison.

Henry's drive reserve magnum – packaging – Henry's drive vignerons – 2003

Interview with Parallax Design Pty Ltd

1.What led to the formation of your studio?

I had been working as the Creative Manager for a large design studio for 7 years and was beginning to get itchy feet. I used a trip to the USA to have a look at studios in San Francisco and New York, mainly to see what work they were doing and how I might fit in. On the flight back to Australia (lots of thinking time – 18 hour flight), I realized that what I really wanted to do was work for myself. Once back in Australia, I resigned from my job and set up Parallax. We opened for business on 1 July 2001.

2. How many staff people does your studio have and what are their main working fields?

Including me, 4 staff. Matthew Remphrey – Managing and Creative Director. Kellie Campbell – Senior Designer. Sam Barratt – Designer. Lucy Fox – Administration Manager.

Cover Drive – packaging – Jim Barry wines – 2002

The epilepsy centre – identity program – the epilepsy centre – 2004

ABCDEF
GHIJKL
MNOPQR
STUVWX
YZ1234
567890

Adelaide festival of arts 2006 – identitiy program – Adelaide festival corporation – 2006

3. How does a regular working day at your studio look like, how is the day structured?

The days are really structured around what projects the studio is handling. There is no "standard" day, workflow dictates how our days look. One thing that we try to do is get out of the office by 6 p.m.. Obviously work load sometimes means that is impossible, but there is so much more to life than work. Having a rich life outside of the studio makes for a better informed designer. We aim for a healthy work-life balance.

4. How much leisure time do you have during a year?

We all try to take 4 weeks holiday during the year. We always close for 2 weeks at Christmas so the other 2 weeks are fitted around work flow.

5. Which business areas do your clients mainly come from? Is the number of your clients increasing or rather declining?

At the moment, most of our work is coming from the wine industry (South Australia produces about 65% of Australia's total wine production). The number of new clients in this area is increasing, as are the amount of new projects from existing clients.

canopy

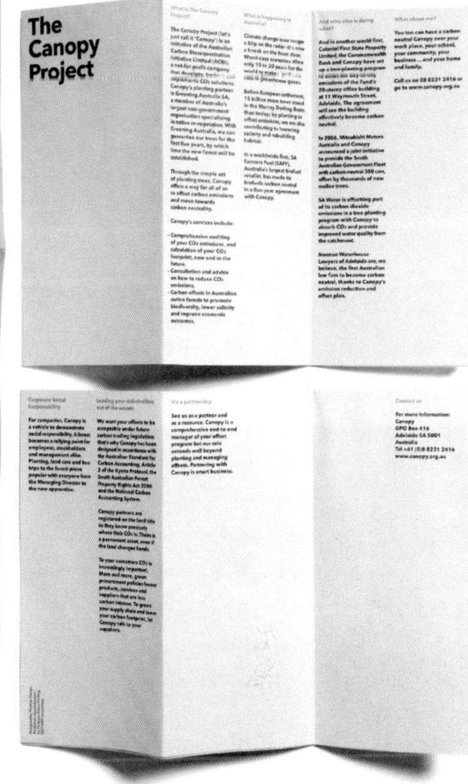

Canopy – identitiy program – canopy – 2007

Planting a seed is an infinitesimally small act. Growing a tree may seem futile. And a forest may be insignificant. But with a Canopy of forests, we can begin to change the world.

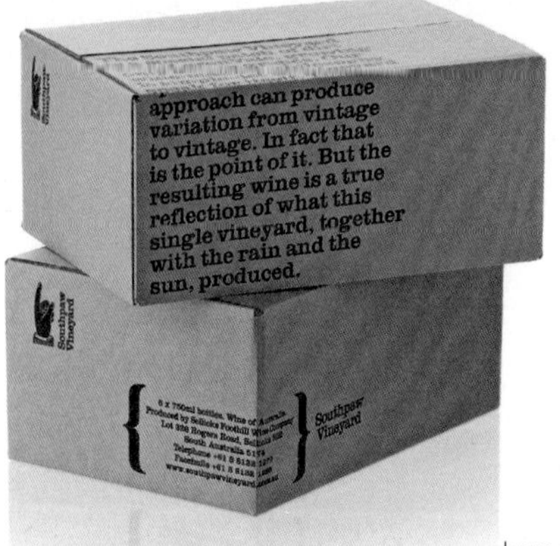

Southpaw vineyards – packaging and identity program – southpaw vineyards – 2006

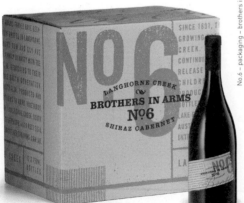

6. Do you have a specific corporate philosophy or maybe a mission statement like other companies, which is reflected in the way you steer the studio's course?

Not really a corporate philosophy, but we believe what we sell is imagination. Much of what we do as designers has become commodified, but imagination is rare and valuable. I also believe that clients are employing us to develop a unique language for them, rather than using their projects to develop our own language, or studio style. We spend a lot of project time getting to know our clients and understand their communication problems, before embarking on any development.

7. What, from your point of view, makes the difference between a small studio and a big company?

Size only.

8. What kind of advantages and disadvantages does a small studio have compared to a big company?

Advantages: No middle managers or account service people. Designers work directly with the client. Small size = low overheads = do not have to take on work just to cover overheads = can be choosey with projects taken on. Disadvantages: Sometimes it's hard to convince large clients you can handle their work

9. What is your idea about the future of small studios?

The design industry globally is incredibly fragmented, with the vast majority of firms under 5 people. There are many reasons for this, but probably the low cost of entry in setting up a studio the driving one. There will continue to be some consolidation, but there will always be small studios filling the gaps between the large ones. Also, many clients cannot afford or do not wish to work with large agencies, and there are some fantastic clients among this group.

Do you think that small studios do not have any other choice but to expand in order to survive in these times of globalization?

No. Small studios need to work the gaps in the market.

10. Please describe and elaborate on the goals or plans that you have for your studio for the next five years?

Buy and renovate studio space. Grow organically as work dictates, but limit size to 6 or 7 staff members. Open business partnership up to staff. Keep doing work that we and our clients are proud of.

No.6 – packaging – brothers in arms – 2003

Limbo haircutters – business card – limbo haircutters – 2002

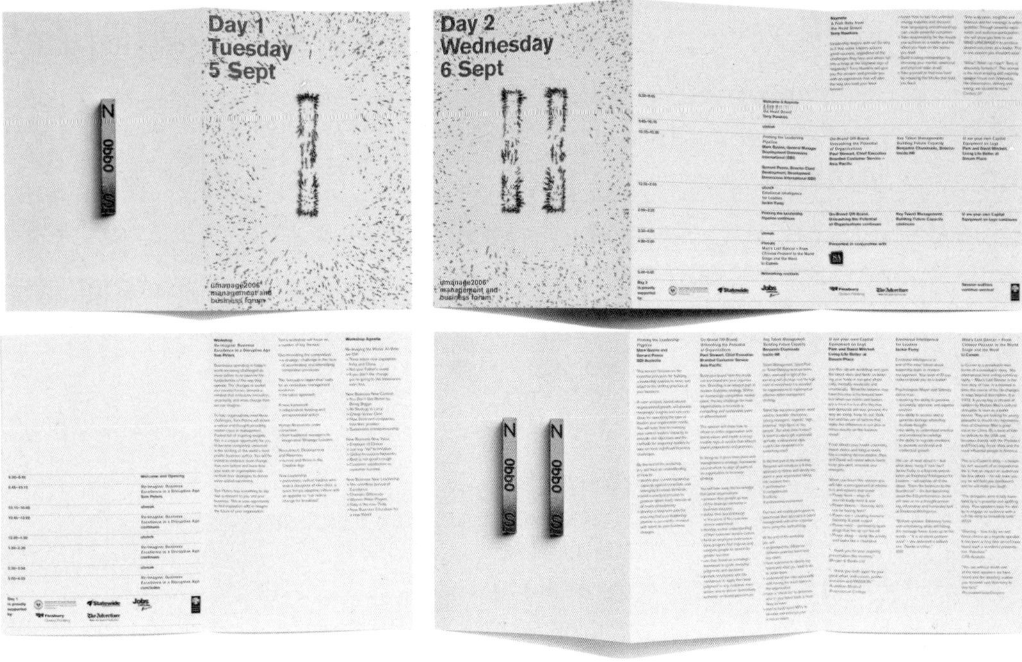

Umanage – event identity and collateral – Australian institute of management – 2006

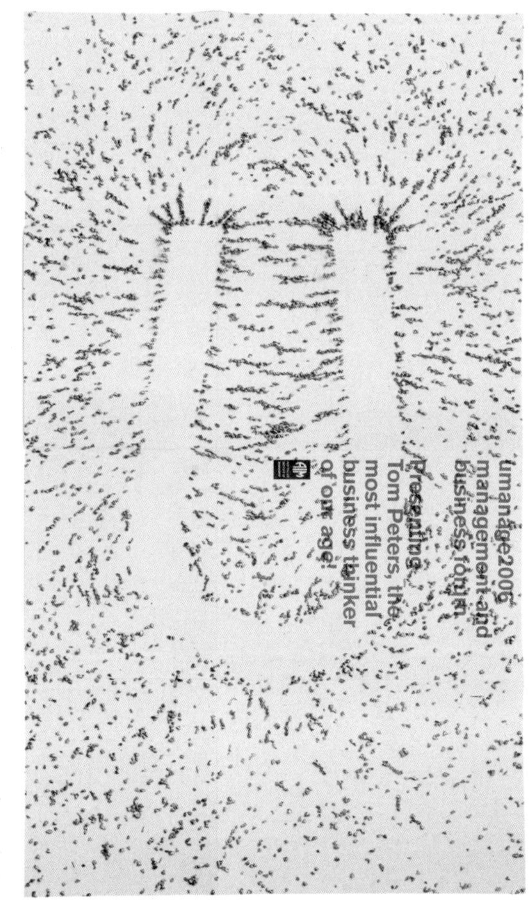

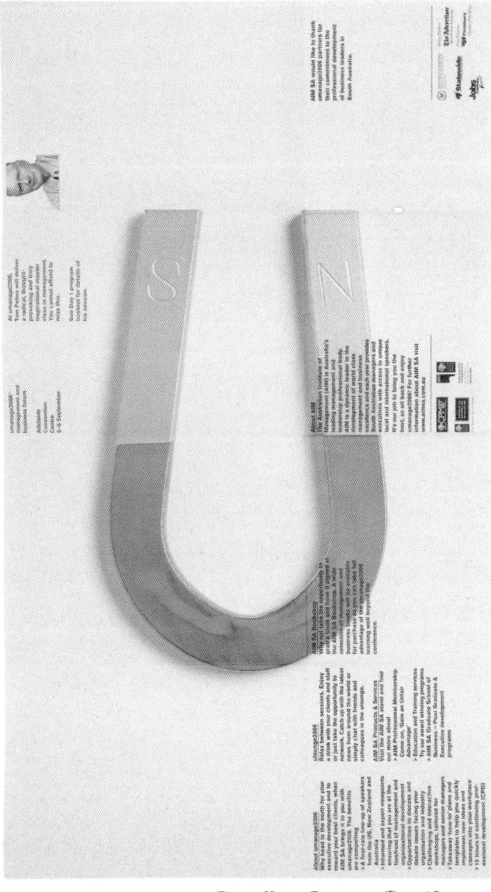

Rose Pistola

team:
Karin Höfling
Holger Felten
Frank von Grafenstein
Beate Pietrek
Helene Kargruber

contact:
Neureutherstraße 19
80799 München
Germany
T +49 89 28701314
F +49 89 28701305
Lippmannstraße 53
22769 Hamburg
Germany
T +49 40 23517646
F +49 40 23517649
kh@rosepistola.de
www.rosepistola.de

Rose Pistola was founded by Holger Felten and Karin Hoefling in 2002. With its two locations in the cities of Hamburg and Munich the agency proves to be a role model for the potential success of close business cooperation across the ideologically charged boundaries between Northern and Southern Germany. In the view of the staff at Rose Pistola, an act of designing stands for the deliberate transfer of content. They create statements in word and vision challenging the observer: attracting interest, establishing communication, starting thinking processes. Their final working results are preceded by a considerably conceptual consideration of the subject, attempting to filter the "good", the adequate idea out of the multitude of possible solutions. The majority of the bureau's clients come from the sectors of culture, fashion and publishing: Rose Pistola is specialized on the conception and design of print products such as books, brochures, magazines, posters focused on corporate and editorial design, as well as the realization of ideas within the available space of the corresponding medium. Samples of the agency's works are shown in a weekly changing exhibition in the showcase of the Munich bureau – a rather small stage which occasionally can even sustain the employee's spontaneous display window shows. The fees charged by Rose Pistola are measured in appropriate relation to the quality of the agency's work, which has already been recognized several times in the past: Karin Hoefling led the way, receiving the gold medal of the Art Director's Club Germany (Art Directors Club Deutschland) for her diploma thesis in 1997. In 2006, Holger Felten was appointed to a professorship for Visual Communication at the Academy of Fine Arts (Akademie der Bildenden Kuenste) in Nuremberg. Competitions calls linked to high participation fees appear to be more than questionable at best, especially for small bureaus. Across the board interests at Rose Pistola center on the life-encompassing triad soccer – art – cooking. This is amended by a clear position: against the dictatorship of self-exploitation, against postural deformities, against segregation – for more integrity, relevance, and most of all humor.

oui | set – catalog – oui | set – 2006

Cultural need – poster – Bayerischer rundfunk – 2005

Interview with Rose Pistola

1. What led to the formation of your studio?

During our student days at the Academy of Fine Arts in Stuttgart (Akademie der Bildenden Kuenste, Stuttgart) we already worked together on numerous joint projects, and while doing so, we were quite often talking about opening a bureau of our own. Then, just a few years after graduating – in the year 2002 – we simply did it.

2. How many staff people does your studio have and what are their main working fields?

We usually work in teams of three or four people, reinforced by an intern at best. One positive effect resulting from our bureau's limited size is the possibility of continuous supervision of a certain job from the first sketch to the realization and the final production by at least one person. Thus, the quality management remains in the same hands all the time. There is no separation of different working processes in our studio, everybody has to do everything.

3. How does a regular working day at your studio look like, how is the day structured?

The daily work includes: starting the computer, reading a lot of mails, sketching, preparing presentations, thinking, supervising the production, cooking; planning, designing, making many telephone calls, reflecting, turning off the lights and locking up the doors.

4. How much leisure time do you have during a year?

Between 14 and 25 days.

5. Which business areas do your clients mainly come from?

Our clients mainly come from the cultural sector and the fashion industry.

Is the number of your clients increasing or rather declining?

It is increasing.

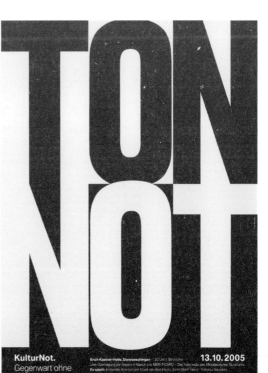

6. Do you have a specific corporate philosophy or maybe a mission statement like other companies, which is reflected in the way you steer the studio's course?

What camouflages itself as "philosophy" is frequently clouding simple work which shouldn't be overestimated in comparison to other parts of life. A very important aspect of our actions concerns the examination of a subject with regard to its contents: a form impressing primarily by its looks will be scrutinized by us very critically. We spent a lot of time debating the ideas and solutions we come up with. During its course, this analysis stays very open, for in rigid hierarchies (even when they are called "flat") it is impossible to unfold. In the end, a final decision or selection is to be made which shouldn't reflect the least common opinion but which is nonetheless the logical consequence of the previous discussion.

7. What, from your point of view, makes the difference between a small studio and a big company?

A small studio is always faster and more flexible, providing better chances for radical ideas. Furthermore, a personal and friendly work atmosphere is very important to us. Growth at an excessive speed is more likely to turn out to be a burden instead of having a liberating effect – be it that a large team has lost parts of its harmony, or be it that financial constraints prohibit the rejection of contract jobs.

8. What kind of advantages and disadvantages does a small studio have compared to a big company?

Advantages: You are living your own demands and you are self-determined in terms of your style of working (within the by all means limited scope of a "service provider").

Club21 – poster – jugendfreizeitstätte blumenau in München – 2007

SWR2 – magazine – SWR2 – 2007

JANUAR – MÄRZ NR.1/2007

DAS MAGAZIN DES SWR2 RADIOCLUBS

SWR2 MAGAZIN

WAS BLEIBT? WAS IST NEU? – SWR2-PROGRAMMCHEFIN MICAELA LÄMMLE IM GESPRÄCH /// SÖHNE MANNHEIMS UND SWR SINFONIEORCHESTER – GIPFELTREFFEN AUF AUGENHÖHE /// RADIOERZÄHLER GÜNTER EICH ZUM 100. /// HINTER DEN KULISSEN – SWR2 AM MORGEN

Hören Sie mal rein!

SWR2: Das neue Programm – alles bleibt anders.

LUST AUF KULTUR SWR2

THEMA

SWR2: DAS PROGRAMM 2007

LEBENDIG, OFFEN, VIELFÄLTIG

VON HÄNDEWEG BIS HINDEMITH

THEMA

»WIR SPIELEN NICHT EINFACH NUR MUSIK, WIR VERMITTELN MUSIK«

Die Musikchefin des Kultursenders über Qualität und Profil des Musikangebots in SWR2

Disadvantages: You are living your own demands and exploit yourself. No, on the contrary, survival depends on determining the adequate parameters for oneself. When a small studio delivers works of high quality, this will be noticed by others, too, and the studio will get more clients. At the same time, you have to ensure that an increased volume of contract work faced with the self-defined limits of capacity does not induce a decline of quality or the rampant exploitation of your own effort. In such a case, the better choice is to decline further jobs. Working in small-sized bureaus, which naturally require more personal responsibility by all people involved, is more fulfilling if the team is working smoothly and harmonious. Globalization does not have an impact in this context, unless your aim is the formation of a global agency with countless branches worldwide. The act of self-definition is exclusively a question of attitude.

10. Please describe and elaborate on the goals or plans that you have for your studio for the next five years?

Our goals are to enjoy our work, to be free from stress, worries or other burdens when going to the office, and to keep alive the feeling of being free to decide for ourselves what we want to do at a certain point of time.

Rose Pistola – visual identity – rose pistola – 2007

Sperl hairdresser – corporate design and room design – sperl – 2007

WerteWandel

Thema Musik *Live* Spezial: Fragen an die Zukunft – Wohin wir uns bewegen
Eine Reihe des Bayerischen Rundfunks und der BMW Group

14.10.

Donnerstag, 14. Oktober 2004, 20:05 - 21:30 Uhr, Bayern 4 Klassik,
Direktsendung aus der Erich Kästner-Halle, Donaueschingen

Musik von Wolfgang Rihm, Giacinto Scelsi, Manos Tsangaris, Jörg Widmann

Jörg Widmann, Klarinette
Münchener Kammerorchester
Leitung: Christoph Poppen

Es diskutieren:

Ulrich Dibelius, Schriftsteller
Max Nyffeler, Publizist
Wolfgang Rihm, Komponist
Manos Tsangaris, Komponist

Moderation:

Christine Lemke-Matwey
Peter Arp

In Zusammenarbeit mit: mdr FIGARO – das Kulturradio des MITTELDEUTSCHEN RUNDFUNKS | SWR 2 | Kulturamt Donaueschingen

Wertewandel – poster – Bayerischer rundfunk – 2007

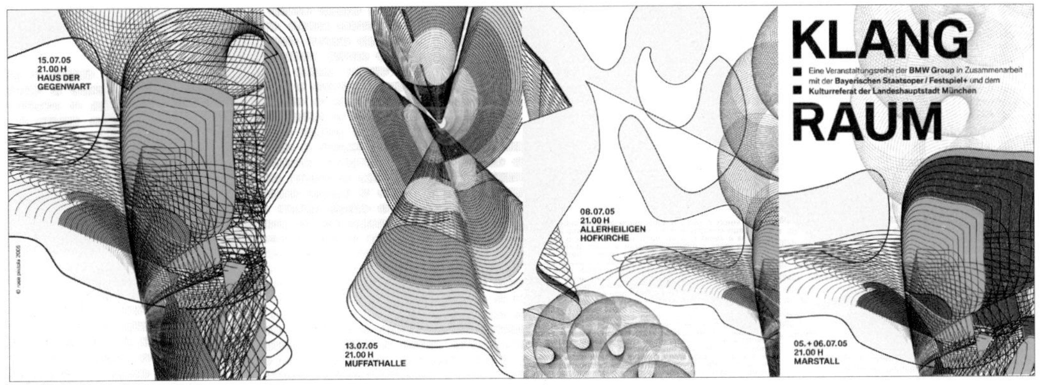

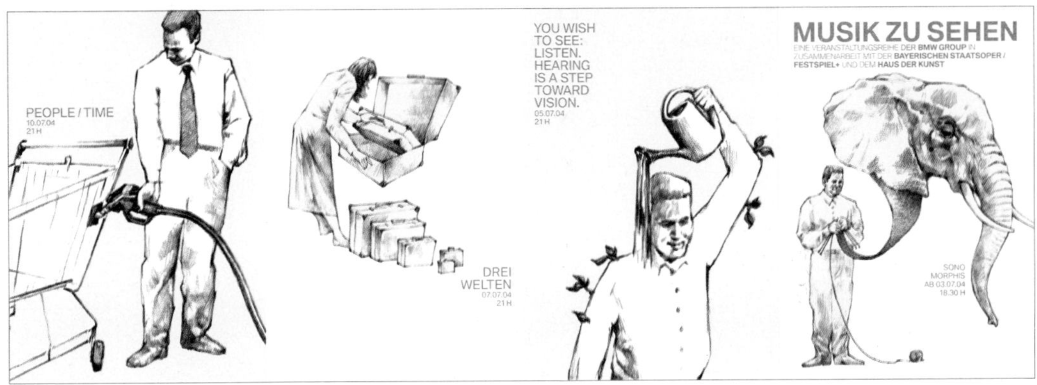

Sound:room – posters – BMW group – 2007

Music to see – leporello – BMW group – 2007

Areas of conflict – posters – Bayerischer rundfunk – 2007

Music to see – posters – illustration: Bernd Schifferdecker – BMW group – 2007

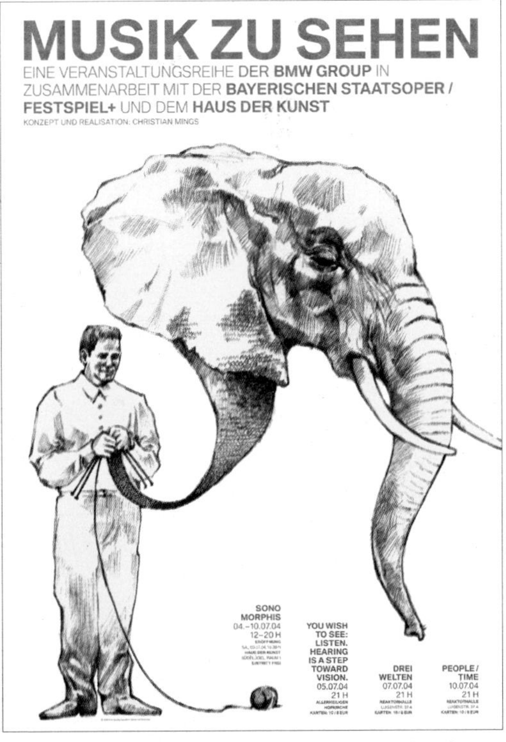

pixelgarten
team:
Adrian Nießler
Catrin Altenbrandt
contact:
c/o basis frankfurt
Elbestrasse 10 HH
60329 Frankfurt
Germany
T + 49 69 80087940/34
M + 49 160 7257997
info@pixelgarten.de
www.pixelgarten.de

pixelgarten is no classical design studio. Pixelgarten is a multidisciplinary studio run by Adrian Niessler and Catrin Altenbrandt. Both met while studying at University of Applied Arts Offenbach. Catrin and Adrian have a fine art background which definetly influences their work and the way they do it. Their projects are sometimes on the border between fine art and design. Crossing this border in either direction is the key to generating new ideas and finding new ways of visual communication. Pixelgarten is not only specialized in art direction and illustration, they also do installations, animation, fashion and are always open for new challenges. Catrin and Adrian mainly work together on their projects: "We love to combine analogue and digital techniques to evolve something new." Pixelgartens work isn't bound to any media, as you can see in their works. Illustrations on a wall in Berlin-Mitte with 1500 meters of electric cable could be the media of choice as well as classical black and white drawings for a posterbook about the Mount Everest.

B side – magazine – b side/route A66/city Offenbach – 2005

Interview with pixelgarten

1. What led to the formation of your studio?

We met while studying at the HfG Offenbach and started to work together on some projects, at first on some self-initiated projects and later on the first commissioned projects. Working together was a possibility to bring together our different talents in one project. Catrin was more into drawing and illustration – Adrian was working a lot with photography at that time. But we both were interested in installative works using real space. So a lot of works we do today are very close to the topics that we were interested in while studying.

2. How many staff people does your studio have and what are their main working fields?

Our studio is just the two of us – with a very good network of other creative people around. We do not have regular employees, but we do work with freelancers. There are lots of people with different abilities like musicians, texters or photographers that we involve in projects to form a team. We think it is quite important to work project-oriented in rather small groups in order to gain a more effective effective method of operation.

3. How does a regular working day at your studio look like, how is the day structured?

The day is structured by arriving at the studio and checking our mails. After that, its unstructured, and the next structure is coming home.

4. How much leisure time do you have during a year?

Very little at the moment – it is a luxury to us to have a free weekend.

5. Which business areas do your clients mainly come from?

Our clients come from various areas: culture, magazines, publishing houses, music, fashion, sport.

Is the number of your clients increasing or rather declining?

The number of clients is increasing at the moment.

6. Do you have a specific corporate philosophy or maybe a mission statement like other companies, which is reflected in the way you steer the studio's course?

No. We just do what we like to do – we really love our work. Every new project is challenging. And of course, we do the best for our clients.

Form - the making of design/50th anniversary – magazine cover and poster – form magazine/birkhäuser publishing – 2007

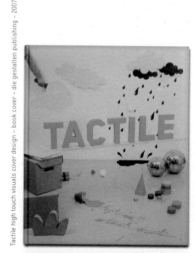

Tactile high touch visuals cover design – book cover – die gestalten publishing – 2007

7. What, from your point of view, makes the difference between a small studio and a big company?

A small studio has a lot more freedom to experiment. Many ideas we have come from self-initiated works we did before. Out of this freedom of creation, innovative ideas evolve. Small does also mean flexible. For each project we can reorganize our studio. How many people should work on this project? Is two enough? Who could strengthen our team? Which special abilities do we need for this job? A bigger studio works in more fixed structures, with less flexibility and less joy with experimenting.

8. What kind of advantages and disadvantages does a small studio have compared to a big company?

Flexibility and freedom are the biggest advantage of small studios. The disadvantage is that you do everything by yourself. Often these things also involve office work like written stuff or tax concerns.

9. What is your idea about the future of small studios? Do you think that small studios do not have any other choice but to expand in order to survive in these times of globalization?

Small Studios do not necessarily have to expand to survive. Keeping it small does also mean keeping the expenses small. Many interesting jobs are done by small studios – a lot of bigger agencies work together with small studios.

10. Please describe and elaborate on the goals or plans that you have for your studio for the next five years?

We do not make any plans at the moment. We just keep on going. There are lots of self-initiated projects we want to work on. There are still a lot of "to be done"-ideas in our minds.

Here in front – poster – hier vorne – 2006

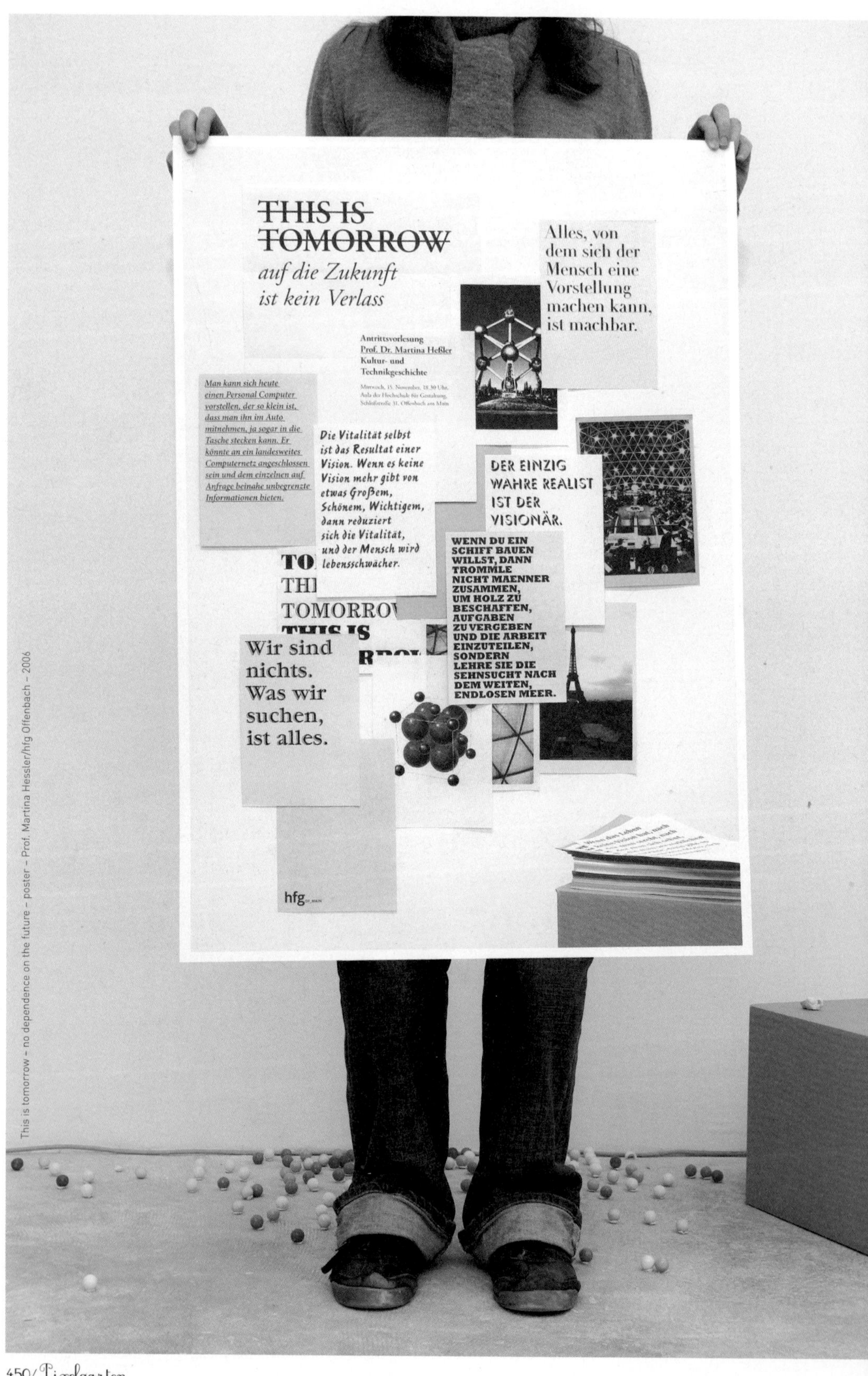

This is tomorrow – no dependence on the future – poster – Prof. Martina Hessler/hfg Offenbach – 2006

What it's not about – photography and installation – self Initiated – 2006

ONIONS
CLOVES
THYME
BREAD
CHESTNUTS
SAGE
GARLIC
PONYBOX.CO.UK
P
ON_OFF_ON_OFF_
O
NIALL&NIGEL
N
YEAR OF THE DOG
Y
Pony Ltd.
team:
Niall Sweeney
Nigel Truswell
Ollie
contact:
Unit 34, 1-13 Adler Street
London
E1 1EG
United Kingdom
T + 44 20 72477333
sugarcube@ponybox.co.uk
www.ponybox.com

Pony Ltd. is a graphic design studio founded at the beginning of the 21st Century. Based in London and producing work internationally, it is the partnership of Niall Sweeney (Dublin), Nigel Truswell (Sheffield) and Ollie (the studio dog). Pony promotes conflations of facts and fictions, is happy on screen, loves print, making music and running around the city at night with a loose collection of drag queens. The studio has a keen interest in words, pictures and the chance of a dance.

School of graphic design research newsletter – folded sheet – school of graphic design research, London college of communication – 2005

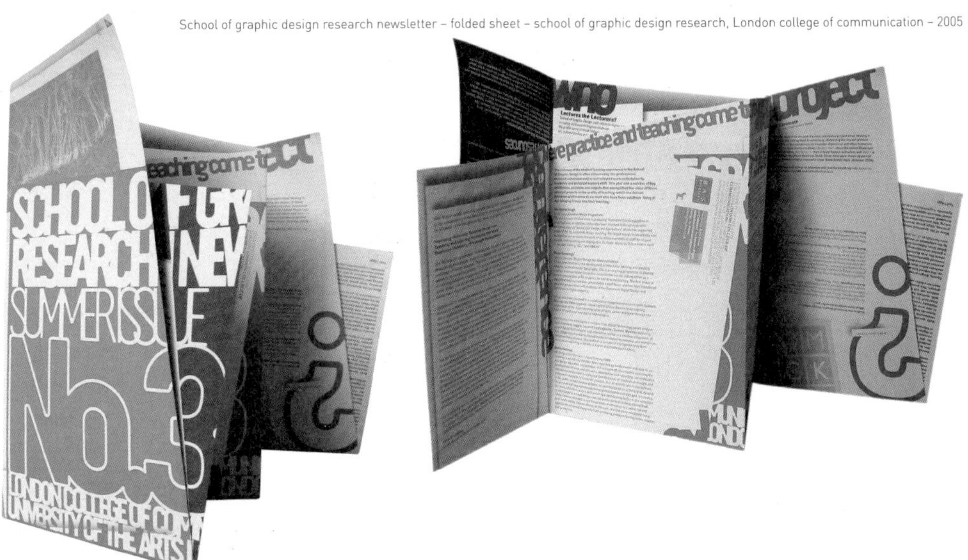

Dublin electronic arts festival – poster – DEAF – 2003

Interview with Pony Ltd.

1. What led to the formation of your studio?

A mutual desire.

2. How many staff people does your studio have and what are their main working fields?

Two men and a dog and the occasional drag queen as muse. Picture-taking, story-telling and music-making.

3. How does a regular working day at your studio look like, how is the day structured?

Think early – work late. And an afternoon nap after walking the dog always helps.

4. How much leisure time do you have during a year?

Anything between 0 and 365 days, depending.

5. Which business areas do your clients mainly come from?

Arts, education, social enterprise and cross-dressing.

Is the number of your clients increasing or rather declining?

Increasing.

6. Do you have a specific corporate philosophy or maybe a mission statement like other companies, which is reflected in the way you steer the studio's course?

Always be ready for the chance of a dance. Learn to read, write and look at pictures.

7. What, from your point of view, makes the difference between a small studio and a big company?

One is big and the other is small! Really, that makes all the difference.

DAY	TIME	VENUE	EVENT\ARTIST
SUN 20	1500-1700	IMMA	CRASH ENSEMBLE FEATURING DONNACHA DENNEHY[CRASH ENSEMBLE trace the history and development of electronic music and tape]
	2100-1230	INTERNATIONAL BAR	{LAZY BIRD PRESENTS}THE BLACK EGG & SCHROEDER'S CAT[LIVE]
MON 21	2000-1200	THOMAS HOUSE	{VIBRATOR PRESENTS}DUBTRONICA SOUND SYSTEM[DJs]
WED 23	2300-0200	PARNELL MOONEY'S	FIREHOUSE SKANK[MICHAEL KELLY, NEW ZEALAND ROOTS MAN selects for the FIREHOUSE SKANK MASSIVE]
THU 24	2000-1200	THOMAS HOUSE	{NEUROMANTEK PRESENTS}PILL HEARIN[ELECTRO & BREAKS SET]{ELECTRIX} / SKKATTER[LIVE PA] / PLUS RESIDENTS
	1930-2300	T.B. MUSIC CENTRE	UPTOWN RACQUET CLUB / CONNECT 4 ORCHESTRA / PLUS VERY SPECIAL GUEST
FRI 25	2300-0300	RI RA	{CHOICE CUTS PRESENTS}TU-KI / MAYHAEM / SPLYCE / OB / RIZM {UPSTAIRS}THE FEAR[LIVE]{DAVE CLEARY & DROID'N'SLUG}
	2200-0230	BODKINS	{BLEEP PRESENTS}DECAL / PLUS SPECIAL GUEST
	2100-1230	THOMAS HOUSE	THE LOFT SESSIONS[LIVE] DIRTY SANCHEZ{DUBLIN} / THE GAPPY FOUNDATION
	2300-0400	D1 AT CRYPT	DUBLIN/DETROIT KEITH TUCKER / OPTIC NERVE[LIVE] / UNDERGROUND RESISTANCE ASSAULT DJ / K1 DJs / SCOTT LOGAN{ASU} / PAUL SMITH

SIX STAGES OF ELECTRONIC MUSIC

SAT 26 2100-0230

GUINNESS STOREHOUSE SAT OCT 26

STARTS 2100 SHARP!
STRICTLY LIMITED CAPACITY
ADVANCE TICKETS ONLY
TICKETS 20euro
AVAILABLE FROM
TOWER RECORDS
BIG BROTHER RECORDS
SELECTA
ROAD RECORDS

{VISUAL ARTISTS}: PIXEL CORP / DELICIOUS NINE / DADDY / 3 MONKEYS / CLICK / FUSELAGE / VIBRATOR / DARKLIGHT / OPTIC NERVE / D1 / LUDLITES

1 {DEAF STAGE}:AUX MEN[LIVE](ex AUX88\DETROIT) / 4 HERO{REINFORCED\LONDON} / DECAL[LIVE]{ULTRAMACK\DUBLIN} / PLUS VERY SPECIAL GUESTS

2 {BASSBIN STAGE}:PARADOX[LIVE]{UK} / POLSKA[LIVE]{SOLAS} / NAPHTA & BREAKER{BASSBIN} / McWUZZA{BASSBIN} / DJ CON{BASSBIN}

3 {FRONTEND SYNTHETICS STAGE}:Mu-Ziq{MIKE PARADINAS\PLANET MU\UK} / AMBULANCE[LIVE]{F.E.S.\DUBLIN} / BURNING MAN[LIVE] / THE LAST SOUND[LIVE] / SOMADRONE[LIVE]

4 {HUSTLE STAGE}:MARK DIXON / BILLY SCURRY / SOULSAVER[LIVE]{JASON O'CALLAGHAN & FION HIGGINS}

5 {FIREHOUSE SKANK STAGE}:FIREHOUSE SKANK SOUNDSYSTEM INSTALLATION

6 {VIBRATOR STAGE}:COLOPHON[LIVE]{STATIC CARAVAN\TEMPORARY RESIDENT\USA} / MEJNFREJM[LIVE]{SNYGGLING\SWE} / STENDEC[LIVE]{EXPANDING RECORDS\UK} / HARD SLEEPER[LIVE]{SUB ROSA\EMIGRE\STATIC CARAVAN\IRL} / BENGE[LIVE]{EXPANDING RECORDS\UK} / KARL HIM[LIVE]{SPIT ROAST RECORDS\IRL} / VESSEL[LIVE] {EXPANDING RECORDS\UK} / PLUS VIBRATOR VISUALS & DJs

FREE CDS OF PARTICIPATING ACTS

DAY	TIME	VENUE	EVENT\ARTIST	
SAT 26 CONTINUED	2100-1230	THOMAS HOUSE	{CAPSULE PRESENTS}TRIPLE HORN & SIMALU[LIVE] / PLUS RESIDENT DJs	
	2200-0230	BODKINS	LET LOOSE[TOIRSE / ROB MCKEAN]	
SUN 27	2200-0230	BODKINS	EASY VINYL[DJs FROM POWER FM.ORG & PSYCHNAVIGATION RECORDS]	
	2000-	VICAR STREET	FLEADH ELECTRONIC{IRISH ELECTRONIC SESSIONS}:IRALA O'LIONAIRD[AFRO CELT SOUND SYSTEM] / ESOTERICA[LIVE] / PLUS VERY SPECIAL GUESTS	TICKETS 20euro WWW.TICKETMASTER.IE
	2000-0300	4 DAME LANE	DUBLIN/KÖLN/TALINN {LEVEL TWO}D1 RECORDINGS 100% LIVE SHOWCASE VISITOR[LIVE]{MARK BROOM & DAVE HILL} / ROB ROWLAND[LIVE] / JAYROD[LIVE] / DAVID DONOHOE[LIVE] / ACTIVE SERVICE UNIT[LIVE] / IKEABOY[LIVE] / DONAL TIERNEY[LIVE] / {VISUAL ARTISTS}FUSELAGE & PIXELCORPS {LEVEL ONE}CHOICE CUTS SOUNDCLASH / TRAUM / ULMAPLAADID TU-KI / MAYHEM / SPLYCE / OB / RIZM / IOUINN / RIELY REINHOLD{TRAUM\TRAPEZ \KOMPAKT\KOLN} / AIVAR TONSO{ULMAPLAADID\ESTONIA} / {VISUALS}TRAUM	TICKETS 5euro STRICTLYLIMITED TO 200 AVAILABLE FROM SELECTA BIG BROTHER RECORDS
MON 28	2000-1230	THE INTERNATIONAL BAR	{LAZY BIRD PRESENTS}EQUILIBRIUM RECORDINGS >VS< SPITROAST RECORDS AMOEBAZOID & DOUBLE ADAPTOR & KARL HIM >VS< TROUBLED SOUL & EXILE EYE & DC & MOONEYE	
	2000-1200	THOMAS HOUSE	{VIBRATOR PRESENTS}{ALL LIVE SETS} {DOWNSTAIRS}:COLOPHON[LIVE]{STATIC CARAVAN\TEMPORARY RESIDENT\USA} / KARL HIM[LIVE]{SPIT ROAST RECORDS\IRL} / MEJNFREJM[LIVE]{SNYGGLING\SWE} / BENGE[LIVE]{EXPANDING RECORDS\UK} {UPSTAIRS}:AMOEBAZOID[LIVE]{SPIT ROAST RECORDS\IRL} / VESSEL[LIVE]{EXPANDING RECORDS\UK} / STENDEC[LIVE]{EXPANDING RECORDS\UK} / VIBRATOR DJs & VISUALS	

{DEAF BARS}FRI 25-MON 28

{GLOBE}: MARK BROOM / DONAL / JIMMY BEHAN / DAVID KITT / DINEEN / EAMONN DOYLE / ROB / ROWLAND / IVAR TONSO / MARK CLARKE / EMMET / EDMONDS / SCOTT LOGAN / ALAN O'BOYLE / SHANE / SUTTON / PHIL BOYLE / PAUL / CHILLAGE / ALAN CARBERY / KILLIAN MURPHY / GOLDEN / MAVERICK / JAMES WALSHE / RICHARD BROPHY / CHRIS / ROONEY / SHANE O'SULLIVAN / CHRIS GOFF / BRIAN NEVIN / TRIPPLE A / GLEN DAVIS / MAD DOG / MARTIN MCKAY / SIMON CONWAY / JAMES / BOYLAN / DEREK CARR / SCOTT McNAUGHTON / PAT / McMELLOW / STEVE KEARNS

{HANDELS}: FRANCOIS / DON ROSCO / NAPHTA / GILES ARMSTRONG / CIARAN + MILLER / JOE MC GRATH / WARREN KIERNAN / RONS MOBILE / DISCO / ROCKY T DELGADO / ROHAN / CRIMINAL K / BRIAN CODY / ARAZEL / GMCD / ALI / KEEYO / GEOFF WALTERS / GEORGE / PETE LOOP / SUNIL / SHARP / ALAN SMITH / PAUL SMITH / JOHN HUSSY / PADDY GALLAGHER / JOHN FALLON / PHILIP RYAN / JOHN BRAINE / JAMIE BEHAN / NIALL POWER / KEV / K / KARL QUINN / PAT RYLAND / AZREAL / COSSY / BUTLER / BRENDAN GREGORY / DEREK F

{THOMAS HOUSE}: SPETAC / HERV / RICHIE EGAN / DROID + SLUG / CHILLAGE IDIOTS / DIGITAL WARFARE{GEDGE & GINT ON 3 DECKS AND EFX} / JOHN BRAINE / GRAHAM O'SULLIVAN / D-VANT / AMERICHOR / MIKE O'REILLY / ROSS CAREW / JAMES BOYLAN / SIMON CONWAY / CHRIS / ROONEY / ALAN SMITH / BRENDAN MURRAY / STEPHAN RENNICKS / PAUL WATTS / KROSSPHADER / SMAC / MIKE HARVEY

{MOLLOY'S BAR}: {LIVE ACTS}: T-WOC / MASCHINE / 2-BIT / THALAMUS / SI & LES / JON O'RIORDAN / EACH NIGHT / {DJS}: MICK O'REILLY / ROWAN / STEVE C / MICK DONOHUE / DEREK / AENGUS / & MORE

Dublin electronic arts festival – poster – DEAF – 2002

The margate exodus – promotional material for film production – artangel – 2006

3 commissions – recordings of collaborative performance by Mira Calix and London sinfonietta – warp records and Mira Calix – 2004

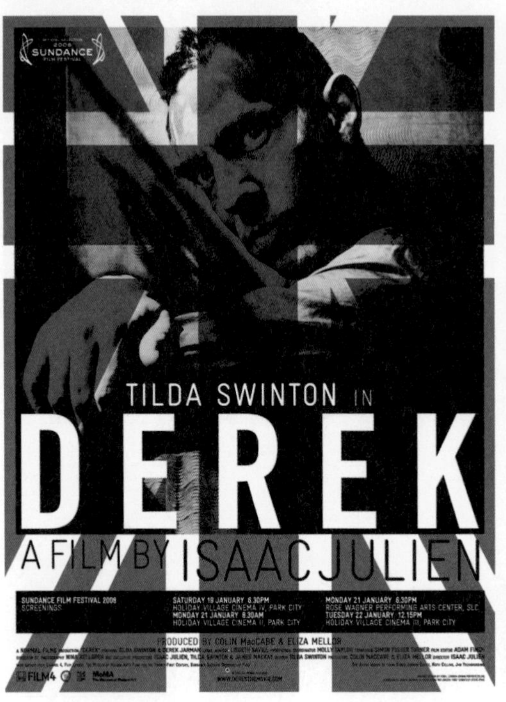

Derek Jarman, a film by Isaac Juien & Tilda Swinton – poster – Isaac Julien – 2008

Dublin electronic arts festival – poster – DEAF – 2008

Apprentice (a shoe collaboration between Doshi Levien design office andlobb shoes) – poster – Doshi Levien office London – 2007

A house in Cap-Martin – poster for filmwork – whitechapel project space and Laura Gannon – 2007

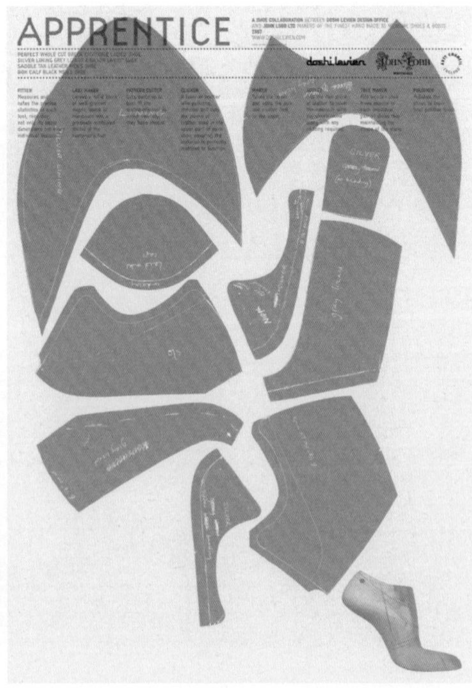

L'Esprit d'Escalier – book – Walther König, Thomas Demand (Berlin) and IMMA – 2007

8. What kind of advantages and disadvantages does a small studio have compared to a big company?

Big companies tend to be homogeneous. Small studios can be more diverse. But one can't exist without the other.

9. What is your idea about the future of small studios?

Small studios are the future. The more there are and the more diverse, the better. Collectively they make up a greater creative force.

Do you think that small studios do not have any other choice but to expand in order to survive in these times of globalization?

No, they do not have to expand at all. It's not always about getting bigger and bigger – it's about making more good work for more good people. And that may mean getting smaller.

10. Please describe and elaborate on the goals or plans that you have for your studio for the next five years?

To make more good work, more of our film Fata Morgana Travelogue, more music, and complete our pop-up book on "Early Christian Virgin Martyrs". And take the dog for some walks in-between.

Henry Wellcome portrait commission – collaged portraits – the Wellcome trust – 2007

Poor Designers

team:
Tassos Sapounakis
Demetris Tzavaras
Dimitris Kanellopoulos
George Yiakos
Kristine Fine

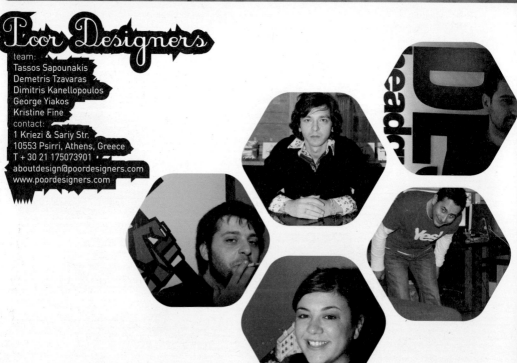

contact:
1 Kriezi & Sariy Str.
10553 Psirri, Athens, Greece
T + 30 21 175073901
aboutdesign@poordesigners.com
www.poordesigners.com

Poor Designers is a well-known and successful graphic design studio in Greece. The "poor designers" live and operate in downtown Athens. They work in all areas of graphic design including: the creation and implementation of corporate identity, illustrations in a wide range of styles and techniques, fashion graphics and print design, websites and multimedia, and large-scale print graphics for interior decoration. They offer fresh, challenging and effective solutions to meet the needs of even the most demanding project, driven by an unhealthy passion to do the best in everything they lay their hands and mouses on. But innovation for commercial communication purposes just isn't enough for some "poor designers" starving for creation! This studio was also set up to allow the production of experimental design work within the award-winning "Poor Designers Family". If you would like to know more about Poor Designers and enter the world of design, their headquarters are always. "Design or die" is their motto, because there is nothing else they would rather do.

Design walk 06 – various design artwork (mixed techniques) – design walk 06 – 2006/2007

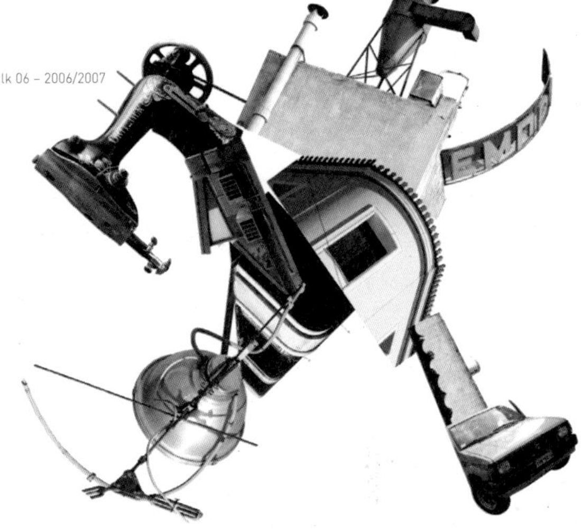

Interview with Poor Designers

1. What led to the formation of your studio?

Freedom of expressing our creativity was the main reason for setting up our small studio. Unfortunately, the Greek market does not allow creativity to be evolved.

2. How many staff people does your studio have and what are their main working fields?

We are a studio of five. The four of us are designers with different and broad illustration skills, and the fifth person is our organizer.

3. How does a regular working day at your studio look like, how is the day structured?

We have a Monday morning meeting where projects are analyzed and divided. Further, we have various small meetings throughout the week to check our progress. We try to remain punctual to our weekly schedule and the meetings are really helpful. During the day the 4 designers stick to what they know best – designing. Yet, at least 3 times per week we have meetings with clients to present our work or to talk about new projects. Loud music is the 6th person in our office. And we definitely have a small break for lunch every day.

4. How much leisure time do you have during a year?

Except for national holidays, Christmas, Easter, and of course the weekends, we usually have a month in August, which is a "dead" business period in Greece.

5. Which business areas do your clients mainly come from? Is the number of your clients increasing or rather declining?

Our clients include lifestyle-oriented companies and projects, the music industry (covers, posters & flyers for record labels), fashion, and corporate enterprises. The number of our clients is definitely increasing.

6. Do you have a specific corporate philosophy or maybe a mission statement like other companies, which is reflected in the way you steer the studio's course?

"Design or die" is our motto. We have to work constantly in order to reach beyond ourselves to produce better design – always with a really tight time schedule – and to become better designers, especially in terms of aesthetics.

Design walk 06 – various design artworks (mixed techniques) – design walk 06 – 2006/2007

7. What, from your point of view, makes the difference between a small studio and a big company?

Small studios are more flexible and efficient, and they contain a better team core as long as there are no intermediate levels involved in the process. This leads to a more direct and clear communication, too.

8. What kind of advantages and disadvantages does a small studio have compared to a big company?

The advantages of small studios in comparison to big companies are mentioned above. We do not believe that there are any severe disadvantages, at least not in our office since we always meet the demands for presenting a complete project in all of its aspects, from research and marketing to our main field of expertise, design.

9. What is your idea about the future of small studios? Do you think that small studios do not have any other choice but to expand in order to survive in these times of globalization?

Small studios can maintain their character without expanding or becoming a huge advertising agency. They have a specific position of their own in the market.

10. Please describe and elaborate on the goals or plans that you have for your studio for the next five years?

We are looking forward to doing business with clients abroad, and we currently consider hiring a few more designers as well as administrative personnel, since design management is something that does not exist in the Greek design industry.

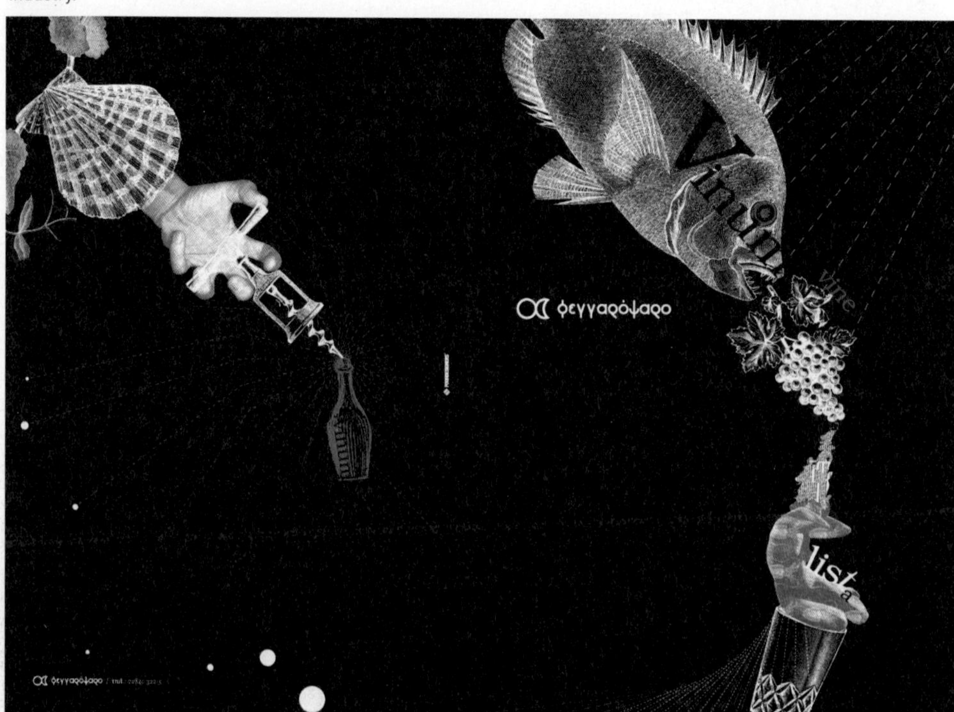

Various applications created for an elegant fish restaurant – business card/bill of fare/various applications – cyclادon choros, Fegaropsaro fish restaurant, sifnos island, Greece – 2007

Illustration for a magazine article – illustration – epsilon magazine, Athens, Greece – 2007

POORDESIGNERS

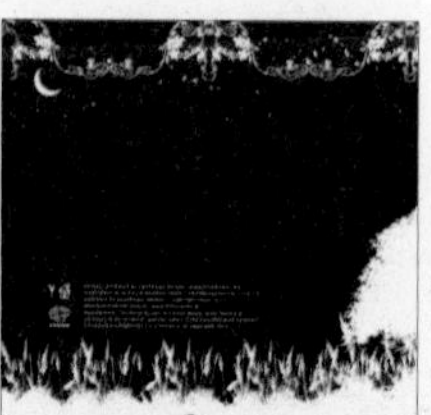

CD artwork – cd cover – klik records – 2006-07

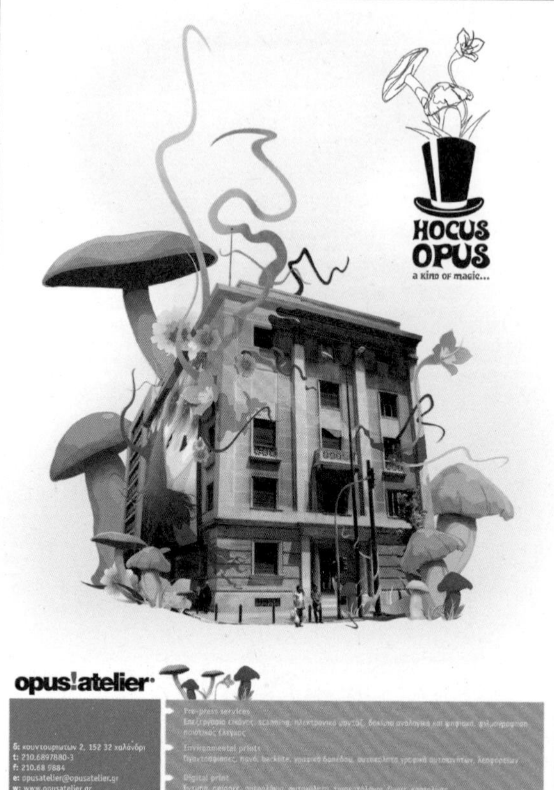

Illustrations created for magazine – magazine illustration – opus atelier – ditial printing studio – 2006

Golden egg – logo design – golden egg Sifnos island, Greece – 2007

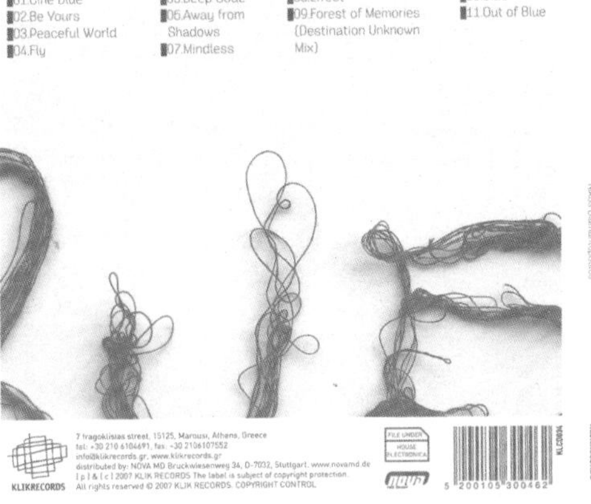

01.Cine Blue
02.Be Yours
03.Peaceful World
04.Fly
05.Deep Code
06.Away from Shadows
07.Mindless
08.Effect
09.Forest of Memories (Destination Unknown Mix)
10.Blue
11.Out of Blue
Nikos Diamantopoulos
KLIKRECORDS
7 fragoklisias street, 15125, Marousi, Athens, Greece
tel: +30 210 6104691, fax: +30 2106107552
info@klikrecords.gr, www.klikrecords.gr
distributed by: NOVA MD Bruckwiesenweg 34, D-7032, Stuttgart, www.novamd.de
[p] & [c] 2007 KLIK RECORDS The label is subject of copyright protection.
All rights reserved © 2007 KLIK RECORDS. COPYRIGHT CONTROL
FILE UNDER
HOUSE
ELECTRONICA
5 200105 300462
KLIKRECORDS

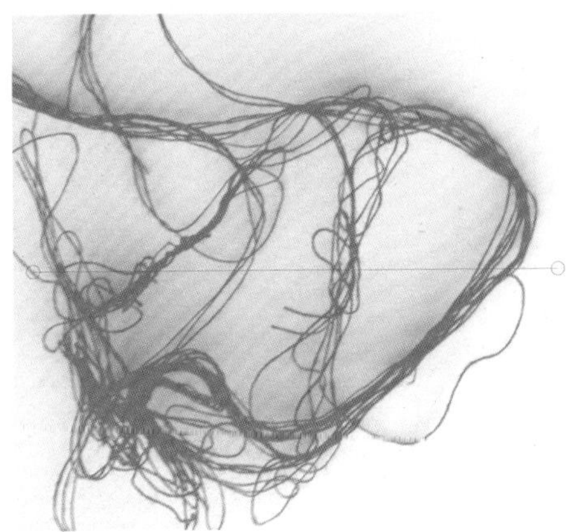

Cd artwork– cd cover – klik records – 2006-07

Design-art – exhibition posters – cycladon choros, Giomisti Kefali gallery, Sifnos Island, Greece – 2007

R2 Graphic Design

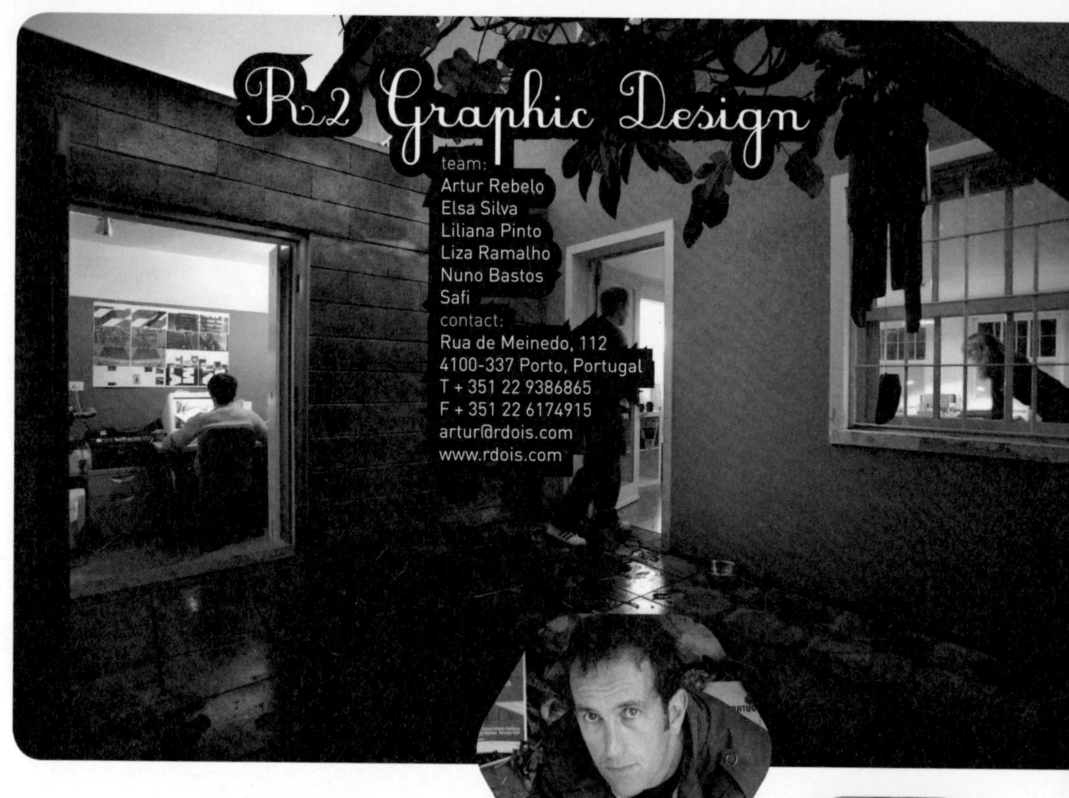

team:
Artur Rebelo
Elsa Silva
Liliana Pinto
Liza Ramalho
Nuno Bastos
Safi
contact:
Rua de Meinedo, 112
4100-337 Porto, Portugal
T + 351 22 9386865
F + 351 22 6174915
artur@rdois.com
www.rdois.com

R2 Graphic Design was formed by Lizá Defossez Ramalho and Artur Rebelo in 1996 while they were studying at the Faculty of Fine Art at the University of Porto. Both of them hold a DEA on design research from the Barcelona Fine Art University. Since then, they have also been working beyond their studio – e.g. teaching design at various Portuguese colleges or giving talks and coordinating workshops for many universities, schools and design events, such as the Basel School of Design, the École des Beaux Arts Besanon, Les Rencontres internationales de Lure, and the European Design Conference. Lizá and Artur have also been part of various judging panels, with a special mention to the international jury for the Chaumont Poster Festival in 2007 and Good 50x70 in 2008. R2 works for and with a wide range of cultural organizations, contemporary artists and architects. Their projects include visual identity as well as poster-, book- and exhibition design. Since 2007 the two designers are members of the Alliance Graphique Internationale (AGI).

Awards: Jury award, 9th Tehran International Poster Biennial Iran (2007); Grand Prix, 22nd International Biennale of Graphic Design in Brno, Czech Republic (2006); Judge special award, Taiwan International Poster Design Award, Taiwan (2005); 3rd price, Festival International de l'Affiche et des Arts Graphiques de Chaumont, France (2003); Gold Prize, International Poster Triennal of Toyama, Japan (2003); Certificate of Typographic Excellence, Type Directors Club of New York (2005, 2006 and 2007); 3rd prize, Europe 2020 Paneuropean Competition in Poster Design, Croatia (2002).

Meeting place, a place of all potential event – poster/leaflet – FIM/Cassiopeia – 2004

Interview with R2 Graphic Design

1. What led to the formation of your studio?

We started working together on design projects while still being students at the Faculty of Fine Arts in Oporto, in the wake of several commissions we received at that time. We thereby realized the advantages of working as a team, including discussion, exchange, sharing and capitalizing on our joint resources. The studio began to take off when a young theater company in Oporto – the Teatro Bruto – invited us to design their visual communications. These early projects were particularly important because they gave us room for experimentation and provided visibility for our work, above all via street posters. By the time we'd finished our studies, we'd already established a reasonable portfolio of clients, which led us to believe that we would be able to set up our own studio. We therefore decided to take the plunge.

2. How many staff people does your studio have and what are their main working fields?

We originally established R2 as a duo (Lizá Ramalho and Artur Rebelo) in 1995, and we have both pursued art direction and design functions since then. In 2000, we hired our longest-serving assistant, Nuno Bastos, who carries out production control and design tasks. Six years later we invited Liliana Pinto to join the team, responsible for the same functions. Several months ago, Elsa Silva, an art history graduate, began working with us doing research, project management and administrative work.

3. How does a regular working day at your studio look like, how is the day structured?

We're lucky enough to have a studio located on a street running parallel to our house, so that we save on travel time and can walk to work. We start our working day at 9 a.m. and take a 1 1/2 hour lunch break at 1 p.m.. At 7 p.m. sharp, our female dog Safi gives us the sign to leave, but she normally has to wait for at least 30 minutes, before we can actually exit the studio (unless of course, we have an upcoming deadline which extends the day into the night). In terms of work organization we don't have a standard routine. Management of each day depends on the type, scale and duration of the projects in progress. The two of us often use the evenings and weekends in order to discuss concepts, do research and initiate new projects.

Series of catalogues – art catalogues – Museu Serralves– 2004-07

4. How much leisure time do you have during a year?
We make a point of taking the annual holidays – 22 working days – stipulated in Portuguese legislation.
5. Which business areas do your clients mainly come from?
We primarily work for clients in the fields of architecture, contemporary art, performing arts, and recently in social projects.
Is the number of your clients increasing or rather declining?
Increasing.
6. Do you have a specific corporate philosophy or maybe a mission statement like other companies, which is reflected in the way you steer the studio's course?
Our projects take shape from conversations that systematically reflect the other's critical view, and are built on successive layers of opinions. We invest a lot of time for gathering data, research and experimentation in order to lay the foundations for several approaches. We highlight the project's underlying concept by pursuing different processes aimed at capturing the essence of the subject in question and creating structured graphic solutions. We believe that the designer, together with the other specialists involved, should become an intense and active partner in the early stage of the design process. We believe that the designer has an important role in helping to shape a better society.
7. What, from your point of view, makes the difference between a small studio and a big company?
We have never worked in a large company, and therefore our perspective does not result from direct personal experience. However while still students, on a trip to London, we were received by Alan Fletcher in his studio. He was the one who opened the door and invited us to come in for a chat and a glass of wine. This meeting had a profound impact on us, and we always imagined working in a friendly environment with a small team. Scale is very important for us and we find that a family atmosphere is very comforting. It is very important for us to have a small team with extensive knowledge of the people working with us. We also strive to share this sense of proximity with our customers and suppliers. The human factor that links together the different members of the team is essential in order to attain good results.
8. What kind of advantages and disadvantages does a small studio have compared to a big company?
Since all projects are developed by us from scratch, we have in-depth knowledge of the various stages and of everything going on in the studio. One of the advantages for the client is that there are no intermediaries between him and the designer, thereby enabling him to establish a dialogue with the people who are actually responsible for the project. The disadvantage of a small studio is that most large-scale projects lie beyond our reach and that the designers waste time on other activities such as management. A small studio can compensate this fact and turn it to their advantage, through mechanisms created over many years of achieving a great deal from limited resources. In a small company, people have to be more polyvalent. Improvisation and speed of adaptation are stimuli for project development. Flexibility, a lighter financial structure, and the capacity to rapidly reorganize activities can make smaller structures more competitive.

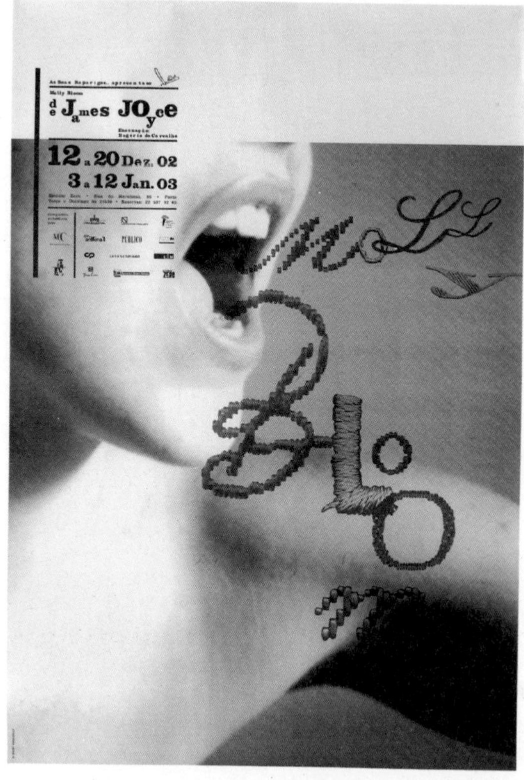

Molly Bloom – poster – as boasraparigas (theater company) – 2002
Bocca – poster – teatro bruto (theater company) – 2004

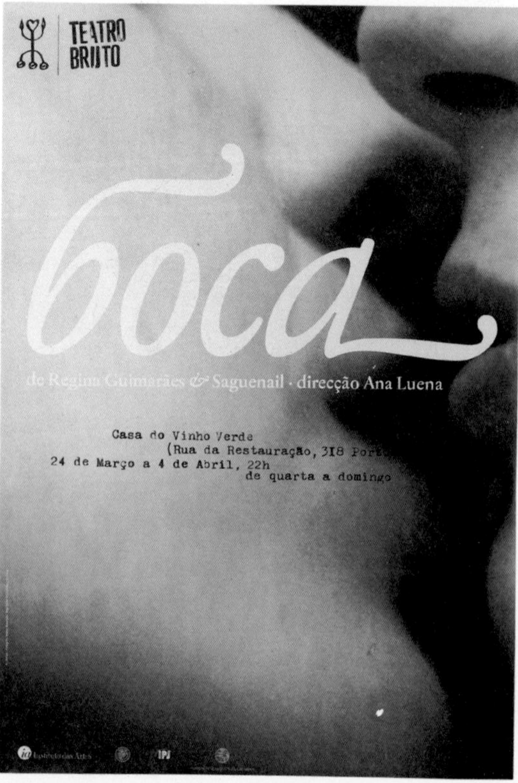

1. Prémio Fernando Távora
Apresentação / 20 Novembro
Salão Nobre da Faculdade de Ciências, UP / 21:30

2. Obra Pedagógica
Ciclo de conferências e vídeo + projecção de desenhos e fotografias de viagens lectivas 1980–1993
Salão Nobre e átrio da Faculdade de Ciências (Praça dos Leões), 21:30

Ciclo de Conferências
4ª feiras · 21:30

23 Nov: "A Viagem"
Alexandre Alves Costa, Joaquim Vieira

30 Nov: "Viajar / Coleccionar"
Eduardo Souto Moura

07 Dez: "Fernando Távora – Eu sou a Arquitectura Portuguesa"
Manuel Mendes

Ciclo de Vídeo
Reposição das "Aulas de Teoria Geral da Organização do Espaço, Fernando Távora, FAUP, 92/93" introduzidas por arquitectos e historiadores que com ele partilharam a docência
Domingos · 21:30

20 Nov: "A Aula"
Álvaro Siza Vieira

27 Nov
António Lousa

04 Dez
Manuel Graça Dias

11 Dez
Rui Lobo

15 Jan
Nuno Tasso de Sousa

08 Jan
João Mendes Ribeiro

22 Jan
Rui Tavares

29 Jan
Carlos Machado

05 Fev
Paulo Varela Gomes
(a confirmar)

3. Reunião de Obra – Exposição
Palácio do Freixo, Porto (1996–03)
Local Museus dos Transportes, Alfândega do Porto /15 Dezembro

4. Obra Aberta
Visitas guiadas a obras de arquitectura de Fernando Távora,
5 de Fev — 6 Maio (Sábados)

Mercado Municipal de Santa Maria da Feira /11 Fevereiro

Casa da Covilhã, Guimarães
25 de Fevereiro

Casa de Férias no Pinhal de Ofir
11 de Março

Pousada de Stª Marinha, Guimarães / 25 de Março

Centro Histórico de Guimarães
8 de Abril

Quinta da Conceição e Quinta de Santiago, Leça da Palmeira
6 de Maio

Casa dos 24, Porto / 22 de Abril

5. A Festa
I Love Távora
Quinta da Conceição,
Leça da Palmeira
06 de Maio, 22 horas

Entrada livre
em todos os eventos!

Comissariado:
Luís Tavares Pereira
Teresa Novais
Filipa Guerreiro

Beatriz Madureira (Ciclo de vídeo)
José Gigante (Festa)

Produção:
Ana Maio
Carlos Alberto Faustino

Comemorações do dia Mundial da Arquitectura

Ordem dos Arquitectos
Secção Regional do Norte
OASRN

I love Távora

20 Nov—06 Maio
2005/06

OASRN
Secção Regional Norte da Ordem dos Arquitectos
www.oasrn.org

Rua de D. Hugo, 5-7
4050-305 Porto – Portugal
T 222 074 250 · F 222 074 259
cultura@oasrn.org

faup · Banif · TUPAI · Miele · weber

I love távora – poster – OAS RN—northern regional branch of the Portuguese architects association – 2005

Ordem dos Arquitectos Secção Regional Norte
Museu dos Transportes e Comunicações Alfândega, Porto
30 Mar—21 Maio 2006
Reunião de Obra — Norte ➔ #002 Tema: Habitação Unifamiliar
Atelier:
José Paulo dos Santos
Projectos:
Casa Carlota / Porto
1998—2004
Casa Laranjeira / Miramar
1998—2004
Como se faz a coordenação das especialidades?
O que é um mapa de acabamentos?
Para que serve o projecto de execução?
Como se cota um projecto?
planta p1
A que correspondem os custos de um projecto?
Quais os tempos de um projecto?
Até onde vai o trabalho do arquitecto?
Qual é a vantagem de ter um arquitecto até ao final da obra?
REUNIÃO DE OBRA - NORTE / #002
COMISSARIADO: FILIPA GUERREIRO, LUÍS TAVARES PEREIRA E TERESA NOVAIS
PRODUÇÃO: PELOURO DA CULTURA: ANA MAIO E CARLOS FAUSTINO [cultura@oasrn.org / T 22 20 74 250]
+ ASSOCIAÇÃO PARA O MUSEU DOS TRANSPORTES E COMUNICAÇÕES - DRª SUZANA FARO
museu@amtc.pt / 222 074 250
PROGRAMA:
Inauguração e Conferência
com a presença da equipa projectista e outros intervenientes na obra
5ª Feira, 30 de Mar, 21:30h
Visita Guiada às Obras:
Arq. José Paulo dos Santos
•Casa Carlota
Sábado, 01 de Abr, 15h
•Casa Laranjeira
Sábado, 15 de Abr, 10h
[Inscrição Obrigatória]
HORÁRIO:
3ª a 6ª
10-12h e 14-18h
Sábado e Domingo
15-19h
MECENAS EXCLUSIVO
Somague
APOIOS
OSVALDO MATOS, LDA.

Site meeting #02 - poster - OAS RN, northern regional branch of the Portuguese architects association - 2005

9. What is your idea about the future of small studios? Do you think that small studios do not have any other choice but to expand in order to survive in these times of globalization?

We don't believe that globalization obliges small studios to close or to expand their activities. There is room for both small and large structures, each with their own specificities. We are happy that we've managed to maintain this dimension and aim to continue working this way.

10. Please describe and elaborate on the goals or plans that you have for your studio for the next five years?

Continue to work on stimulating design projects and have fun while working. Prepare our ground exhibition at Brno 2010, the International Biennale of Graphic Design. Keep the studio small!

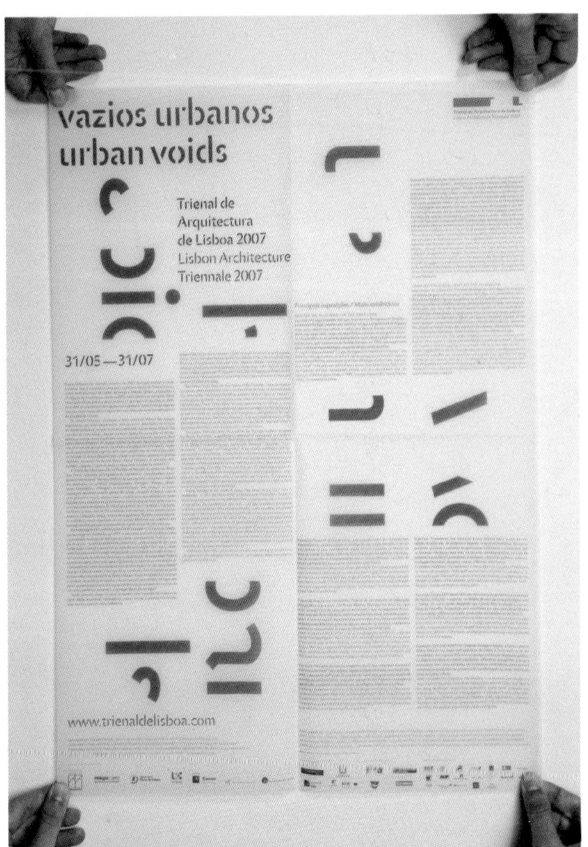

Urban voids – folder/poster – OAS RS, southern regional branch of the Portuguese architects association – 2006

ARX Portugal – visual identity – ARX Portugal architects – 2007

Slang International

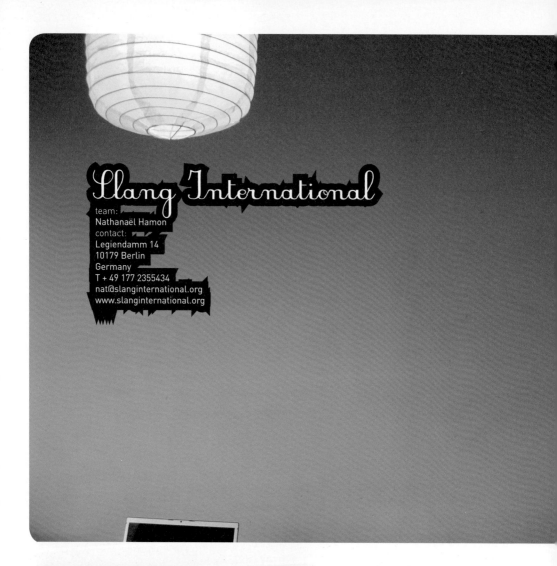

team:
Nathanaël Hamon
contact:
Legiendamm 14
10179 Berlin
Germany
T + 49 177 2355434
nat@slanginternational.org
www.slanginternational.org

Slang International – Nathanaël Hamon was born in France. When he was 10 years old, his family moved to the United States. He received a degree in art history but quickly changed direction and started working as a graphic designer. Since 2000, he has been living in Berlin. Why "Slang"? As a variant form of language, slang shares some characteristics with Hamon's sensibility and his approach to his work: being fresh, playful and constantly reinventing itself. Slang is a vivid and informal language, heartfelt and true to particular groups of people. So far, his work encompasses a lot of posters, record and CD covers, books, typefaces and illustrations, mainly for music, arts and culture. Examples of his work can be found in many books, magazines, and on walls.

Mélange – digitalprint – personal project – 2008

Interview with Slang International

1. What led to the formation of your studio?

Since my studio consists only of myself. In such a case the formation of a studio has to do primarily with developing a personal approach to work, and with setting up a space where to implement it. I've been working independently for many years, working at home in the beginning. At some point it became important for me to get out, to see more of my city on a daily basis, to be in a different neighborhood, to observe people and things happening around me. There's a basic fact about the connection between space and activity, it's easier to focus. I share a workspace with a few freelancers, having other people around you is very important. Design is about communication. You could even argue that it doesn't make sense to design in isolation. In terms of my work, that's something which is always developing. I try to form the output of my studio as a whole, not only meaning the way in which the work is produced but also what type of projects I take on, and the kind contexts I choose to be active in.

2. How many staff people does your studio have and what are their main working fields?

My studio consists only of myself. I collaborate with other designers from time to time. I want to form a group together with other designers, it's just a question of finding the right people.

3. How does a regular working day at your studio look like, how is the day structured?

It's not structured. But it also doesn't vary too much. I cycle to work and might run some errands along the way, or stop over somewhere for a meeting. Once I am at the studio, I just work on whatever is going on at that moment. At some point at the end of the day I turn off the lights and get back on my bike.

Vois plus loin avec un livre – screenprint – personal project – 2007

PSA – screenprint – personal project – 2008

Köpi – photocopy – personal project – 2007

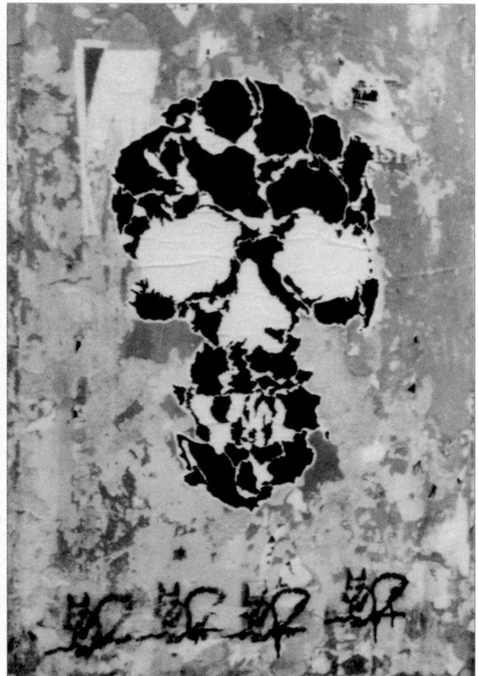

The world can´t wait – photocopy – personal project – 2006

4. How much leisure time do you have during a year?

It varies, but I make sure I take enough time to travel, seeing new places and people.

5. Which business areas do your clients mainly come from? Is the number of your clients increasing or rather declining?

I mainly work with people from the areas of music, arts and culture. I also work on a lot of self-initiated projects dealing with social issues. Most clients come and go. And then there are a few with whom I've worked several times or on a regular basis.

6. Do you have a specific corporate philosophy or maybe a mission statement like other companies, which is reflected in the way you steer the studio's course?

Slang. As a variant form of language, slang shares some characteristics with my sensibility and approach to design: being fresh, playful and constantly reinventing itself. Slang is a vivid and informal language, heartfelt and true to particular groups of people. I try to stick to interesting and worthwhile projects for myself and for society in general.

7. What, from your point of view, makes the difference between a small studio and a big company?

In a small studio, maybe there's more personal and emotional involvement in the work.

8. What kind of advantages and disadvantages does a small studio have compared to a big company?

A small studio can stay human and down to earth.

9. What is your idea about the future of small studios? Do you think that small studios do not have any other choice but to expand in order to survive in these times of globalization?

I think you can stay small and still continue to exist. It all depends on what you want to reach. A small studio can concentrate on producing quality work and become known for its output, or work within a specific field. It seems to me that a small studio has to have a focus.

10. Please describe and elaborate on the goals or plans that you have for your studio for the next five years?

To work, to have new experiences, and to collaborate with inspiring people.

Home – screenprint – Marek Claassen – 2007

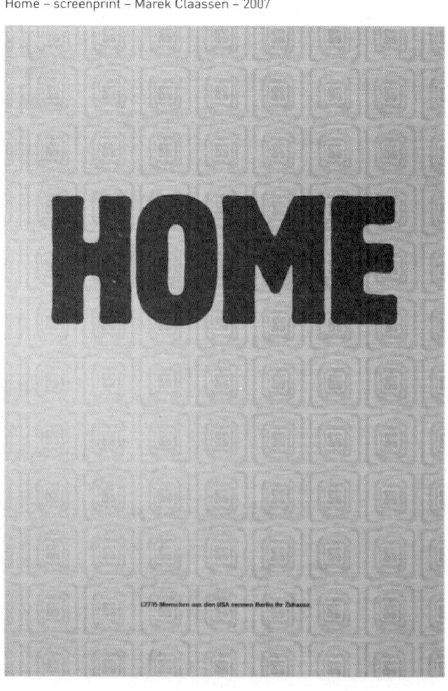

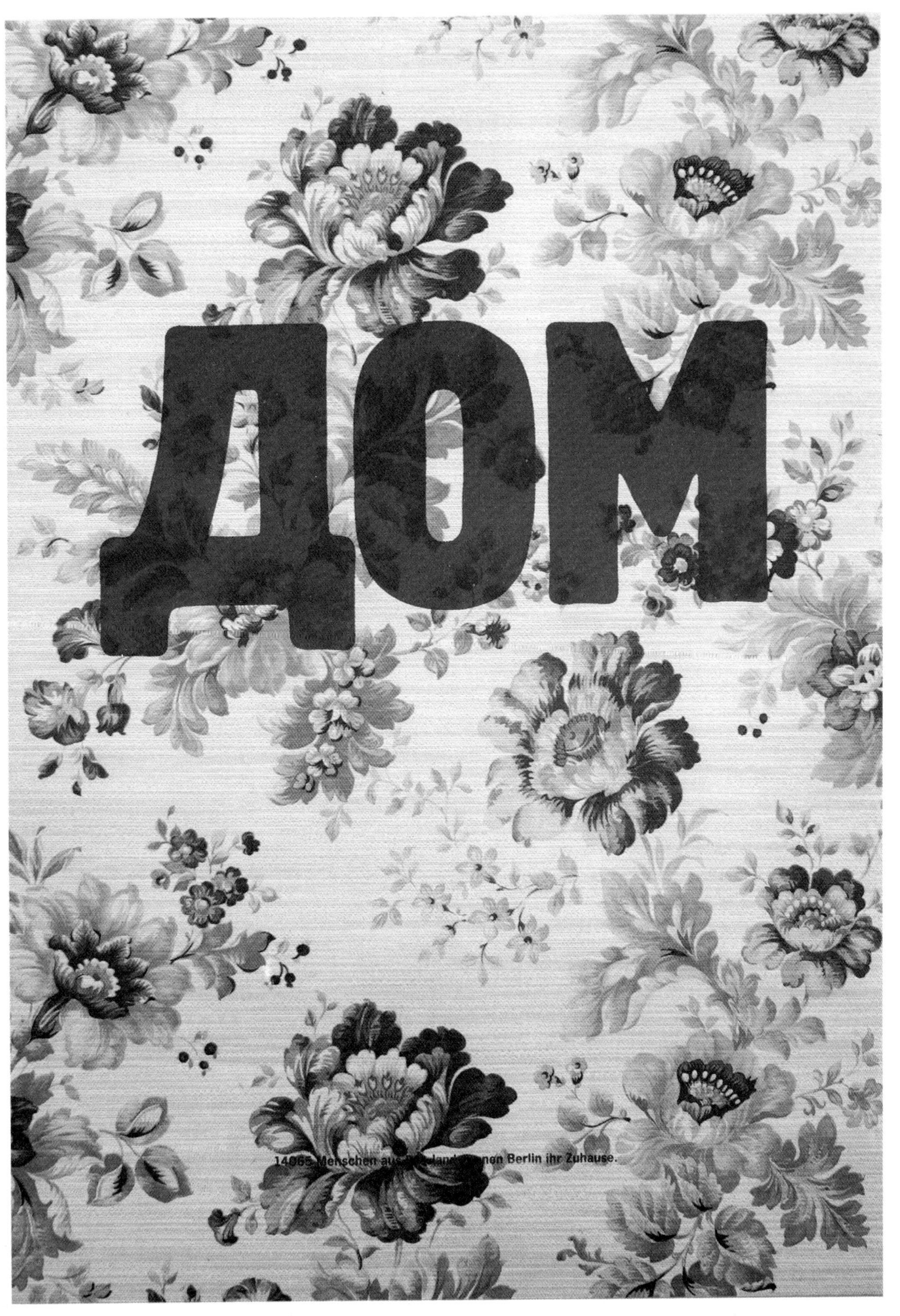

Home – screenprint – Marek Claassen – 2007

fueradeseriel presents:
snowdrop
a compilation by littleprettyautomatique

Snowdrop – screenprint – personal project – 2007

Buy Bye – digitalprint – personal project – 2008

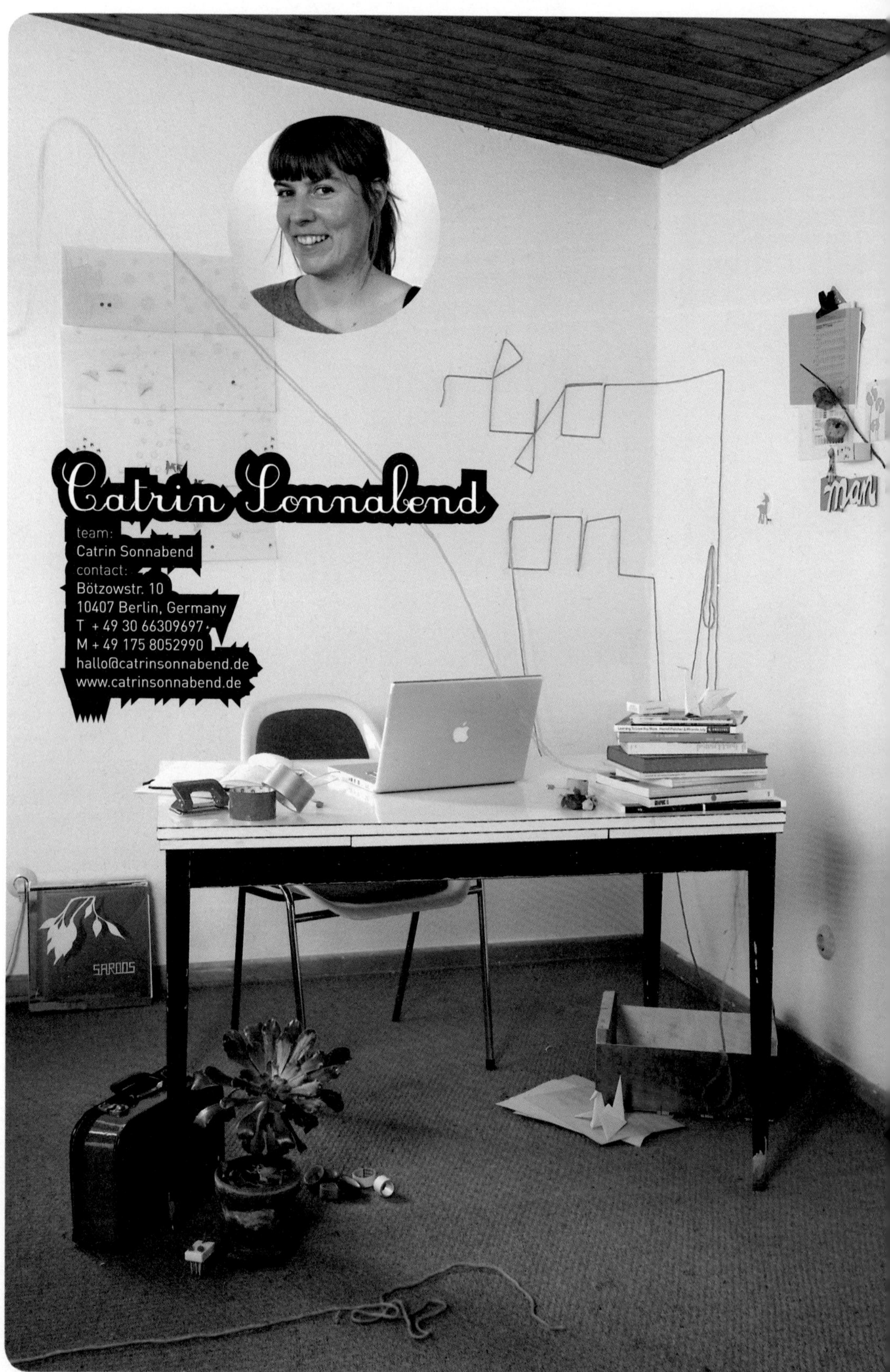
Catrin Sonnabend
team:
Catrin Sonnabend
contact:
Bötzowstr. 10
10407 Berlin, Germany
T + 49 30 66309697
M + 49 175 8052990
hallo@catrinsonnabend.de
www.catrinsonnabend.de
SARDOS

Catrin Sonnabend works as a graphic designer for various clients like, for example, the Verein fuer Kulturfoerderung Rhein Main e.V. and the label Alien Transistor, either on her own or in a team as she recently did at Stiletto, New York and now at Mario Lombardo, Berlin.

Interview with Catrin Sonnabend

1. What led to the formation of your studio?

When I left the university I got some offers to work on projects for interesting clients. So it just happened that I started to work on my own.

2. How many staff people does your studio have and what are their main working fields?

I don't have any staff people working for me. Sometimes I work together with other graphic designers.

3. How does a regular working day at your studio look like, how is the day structured?

There is not really a regular structure. Working hours and places depend on the projects.

4. How much leisure time do you have during a year?

That's hard to tell, because leisure time and working time are difficult to separate. I try to have some time off between projects. By now that is working out somehow.

5. Which business areas do your clients mainly come from?

Until now the focus was on clients from the cultural sector.

Is the number of your clients increasing or rather declining?

It remains constant.

6. Do you have a specific corporate philosophy or maybe a mission statement like other companies, which is reflected in the way you steer the studio's course?

7. What, from your point of view, makes the difference between a small studio and a big company?

8. What kind of advantages and disadvantages does a small studio have compared to a big company?

In the first place, I am just resposible for myself. I don't have to worry about keeping staff people busy or how to pay them. In some way that makes me more flexible regarding time, money and jobs. Another difference is that the whole work stays in one hand instead of being passed on. Information cannot get lost.

9. What is your idea about the future of small studios? Do you think that small studios do not have any other choice but to expand in order to survive in these times of globalization?

I think that might depend on whether you want to see it in the financial or artistic way. But anyway, I think there is always a chance for small studios with special ways of thinking and working.

10. Please describe and elaborate on the goals or plans that you have for your studio for the next five years?

I hope I will still enjoy being a graphic designer then. Have a steady client base, hopefully open-minded. Time and money for self-initiated projects from time to time. Have some people working with me at the studio.

Saroos – illustration – alien transistor – 2006

Saroos – cd cover – alien transistor – 2006

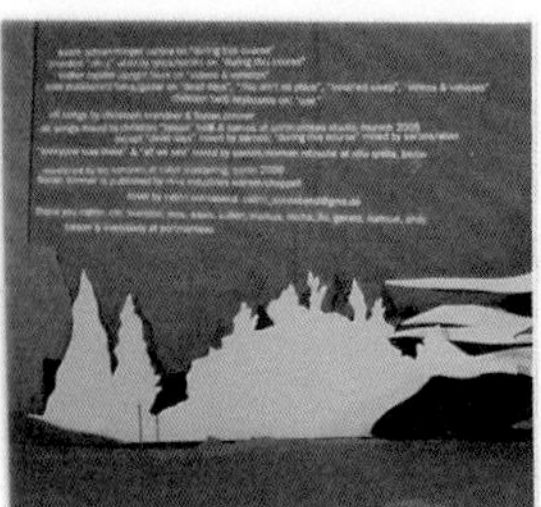

Here + Now. - 64 suggestions to waste of time – journal – self published – 2005

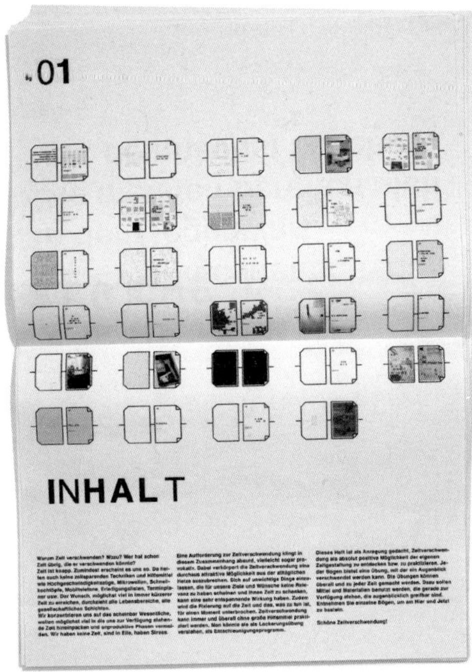

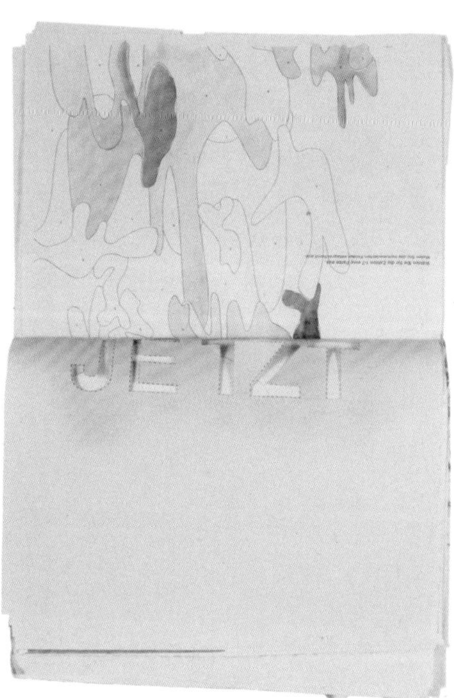

Here + Now. - 64 suggestions to waste time – journal – self published – 2005

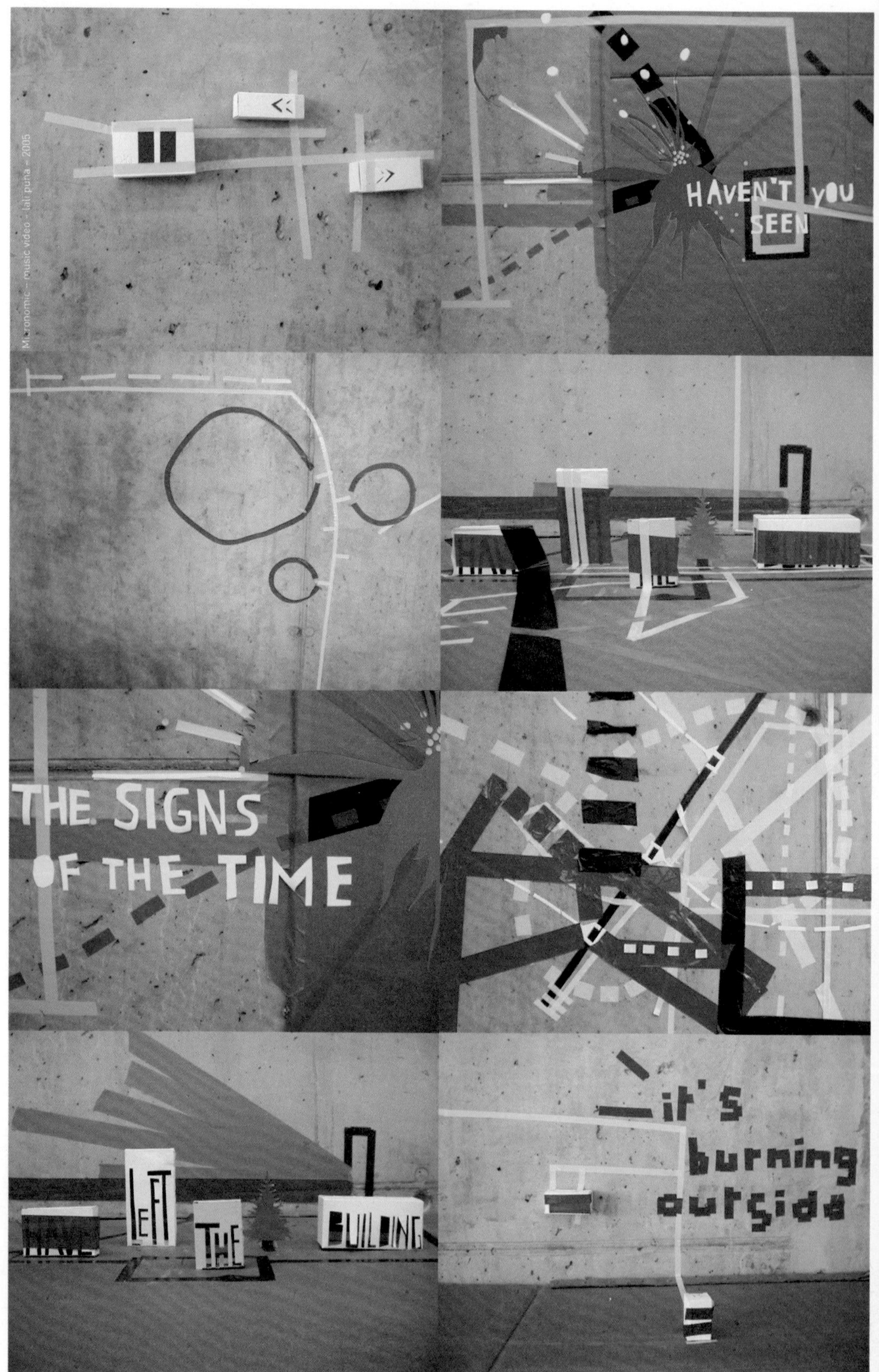
HAVEN'T you
SEEN
THE SIGNS
OF THE TIME
LEFT
THE
BUILDING
it's
burning
outside

Micronomic – music video – lali puna – 2005

Festival of young talents · poster · Verein für Kulturförderung, rhein-main e. V., Offenbach · 2006

St. Pierre & Miquelon

team:
Simon Elvins
contact:
21C Bradiston Road
London W9 3HN
United Kingdom
www.st-pierre-and-miquelon.com
mail@st-pierre-and-miquelon.com

St. Pierre & Miquelon interests and group practices are the ideas of process, communication and participation. They often, though not exclusively, create events and printed matter in order to find ways of forming connections between people and things. To a certain degree, the projects they realize are process-led, hence the primary focus is the activity of making, the act of doing, rather than the final result. It is essential to their work to communicate with people and to invite participation. The audience is often the completing part of their projects, bringing them into the public realm. Previous projects have taken the form of books, workshops, exhibitions and individual commissions.

Sexymachinery, issue a – magazine – 2008

Interview with St. Pierre & Miquelon

1. What led to the formation of your studio?

Previous to the formation of our studio we often worked individually, so the idea was to create a space in which we could begin to collaborate. In turn, this formed a new approach to how and where we worked. Parts of our new identity were created after visiting a psychic who amongst other things suggested that in the near future there would be five members at our studio instead of the current three. We then used a lecture we were holding at the Royal College of Art to conduct interviews, and invited the two new members to complete the line-up.

2. How many staff people does your studio have and what are their main working fields?

Five, and we are all designers.

3. How does a regular working day at your studio look like, how is the day structured?

Currently, there is no regular structure and each project creates different needs in terms of time and situation, so we try to be flexible and not to stick to a rigid routine.

4. How much leisure time do you have during a year?

We are interested in creating a subtler difference between our work and leisure time activities. We hope that using public spaces such as museums, pubs and parks (weather permitting) will help to facilitate this.

5. Which business areas do your clients mainly come from? Is the number of your clients increasing or rather declining?

The name client is not always an accurate word for describing the people we work with. Sometimes they are friends, collaborators or people that don't know (yet) that we are working for them. So far they are from the fields of politics, art, education, community services or even private individuals. We also work on self-initiated and independent projects.

6. Do you have a specific corporate philosophy or maybe a mission statement like other companies, which is reflected in the way you steer the studio's course?

To be defined by our work and actions rather than adhering to a strict set of principles defined at the outset.

7. What, from your point of view, makes the difference between a small studio and a big company?

For us it is probably the ability to remain flexible and adapt.

8. What kind of advantages and disadvantages does a small studio have compared to a big company?

Please see above.

9. What is your idea about the future of small studios? Do you think that small studios do not have any other choice but to expand in order to survive in these times of globalization?

We don't think globalization is a direct threat to the survival of a small studio. If anything, a small studio can have a much larger presence and influence today than it could in the past. The internet and cheaper communications has meant it is now much easier for a small studio to work and be seen internationally.

10. Please describe and elaborate on the goals or plans that you have for your studio for the next five years?

We don't really have long term plans or objectives as such. The formation of our studio is still new and develops quickly, so we are keen to be open to this rather than to try and dictate specifically what's next.

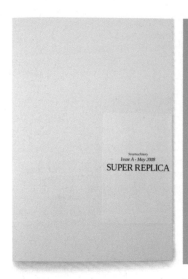

HAPPY BIRTHDAY
TO YOU

HAPPY BIRTHDAY
TO YOU

HAPPY BIRTHDAY
DEAR________

HAPPY BIRTHDAY
TO YOU

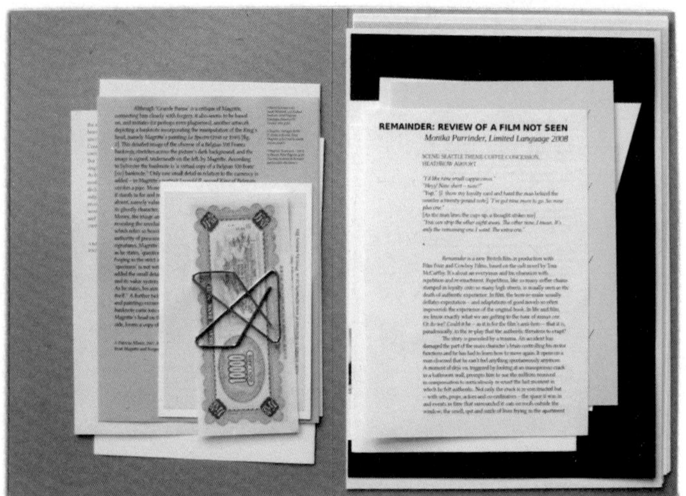

Sexymachinery, issue a – magazine – super replica-magazine – 2008

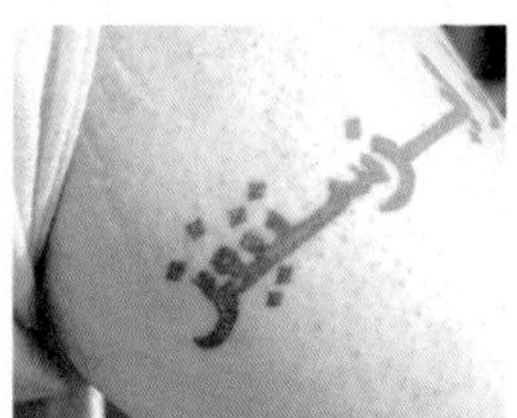

Cover-Up Design 1

Cover-Up Design 5

A dilemma: an enquiry into Steve Hater's Arabic tattoo – typography – self published project – 2008

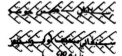

Cover-Up Design 3

Cover-Up Design 2

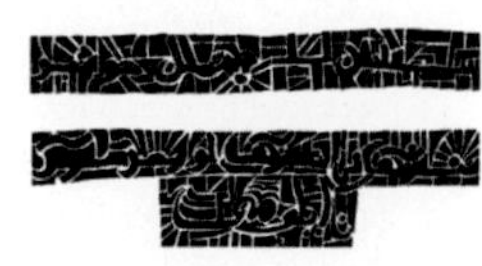

Cover-Up Design 4

PRINCIPLES OF TECHNOLOGICAL INDEPENDENCE 2025

- THE VALUE OF HUMAN ERROR AND INCONSISTENCY
- DIRECT HUMAN INTERACTION AND COMMUNICATION
- PRIVACY OVER CONNECTIVITY
- APPRECIATION OF THE BEAUTY IN AGEING AND DECAY
- BELIEF IN THE VITALITY OF THE PHYSICAL WORLD
- SELF HEALING AS CURE FOR ILLNESS
- AN ENVIRONMENT UNREGULATED BY TECHNOLOGY
- THE FALSE PROMISE OF TECHNOLOGICAL PROGRESS EFFICIENCY, ACCURACY AND SPEED
- NO TECHNOLOGICAL ENHANCEMENTS OR PRESERVATIONS OF LIFE
- THE VIRTUES OF MANUAL LABOUR AND PRODUCTION OF MAN MADE GOODS
- ELECTRONIC CURRENCY CAN BE OVERCOME THROUGH THE EXCHANGE OF GOODS AND SERVICES
- TO FULFILL OUR EMOTIONAL AND SPIRITUAL NEEDS THAT ARE RESTRICTED BY TECHNOLOGY
- TO RECOGNISE OUR POSITION WITHIN SOCIETY AS A RACE UNENHANCED BY TECHNOLOGY
- UPHOLD THE TRADITION OF REAL DAY: A CELEBRATION OF OUR INDEPENDENCE FROM THE VIRTUAL WORLD

Principles of technological independence 2025, exhibited at, stick stamp fly gasworks, London – poster – gasworks – 2007

EXHIBITION OF ODDITIES

ARNOLD CIRCUS

1st April 2007

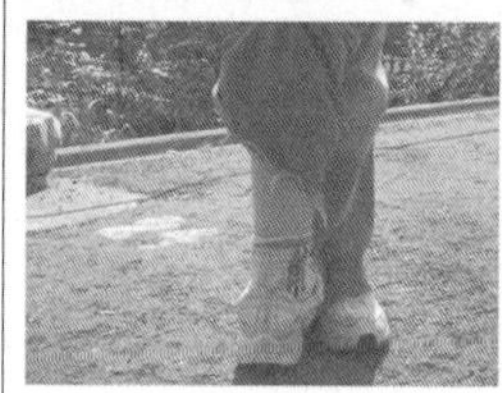

BACK TO FRONT BOY

FREDDY

ODDITY No.5

UNIMAGINABLE ARM

ALEX

ODDITY No.6

CIRCUS ON THE CIRCUS

EXHIBITION OF ODDITIES

Exhibition of oddities, one day event – friends of Arnold Circus – circus on the circus – 2007

WOULD YOU PASS THE TEST?
a. Thursday 27th September 2007
b. Doors open 7pm
c. The Old Queens Head, 44 Essex Road, Islington, London, N1 8LN
d. Test Cost £5
e. http://www.manifestoclub.com/citizenquiz
A project by Tom Mower, Julie Hill, Simon Elvins & www.manifestoclub.com
THE GREAT BRITISH CITIZENSHIP PUB QUIZ
45

The great British citizenship pub quiz – event – 2007

Answer Sheet

Team Name: Croydon United

1	A
2	D
3	B
4	D
5	A 10 %
6	D 50 %
7	A B B
8	C
9	B
10	B India, Pakistan
11	D 1/6
12	C 20 % Wiltshire
13	C
14	C
15	B 1/3
16	B not Protestant
17	B 15 million
18	D
19	B 1,000
20	C 1901
21	C £5.35
22	B 2.9 m
23	B
24	A True

1.2 2.9 3.4 5.3

TOTAL 12/24

50%

(C+)

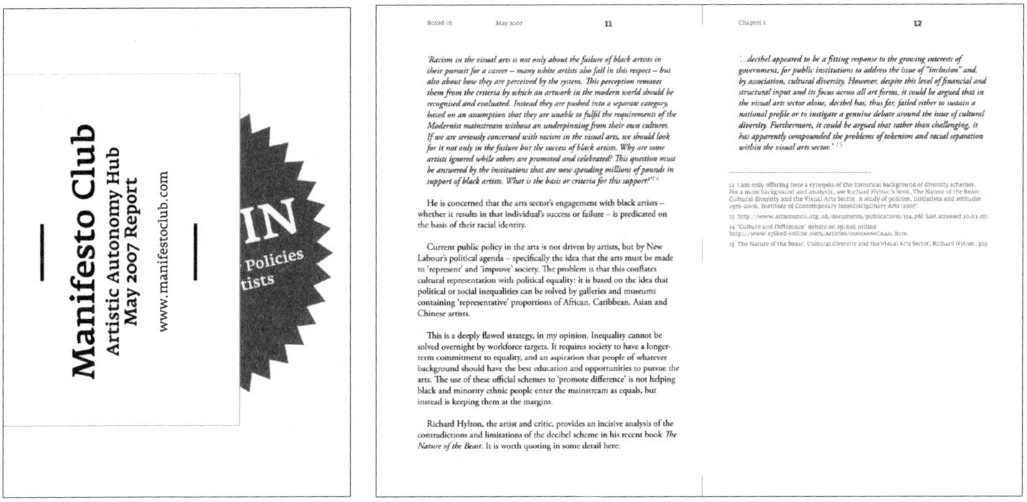

Boxed in May 2007 11

'Racism in the visual arts is not only about the failure of black artists in their pursuit for a career – many white artists also fail in this respect – but also about how they are perceived by the system. This perception removes them from the criteria by which an artwork in the modern world should be recognised and evaluated. Instead they are pushed into a separate category, based on an assumption that they are unable to fulfil the requirements of the Modernist mainstream without an underpinning from their own cultures. If we are seriously concerned with racism in the visual arts, we should look for it not only in the failure but the success of black artists. Why are some artists ignored while others are promoted and celebrated? This question must be answered by the institutions that are now spending millions of pounds in support of black artists. What is the basis or criteria for this support?'[14]

He is concerned that the arts sector's engagement with black artists – whether it results in that individual's success or failure – is predicated on the basis of their racial identity.

Current public policy in the arts is not driven by artists, but by New Labour's political agenda – specifically the idea that the arts must be made to 'represent' and 'improve' society. The problem is that this conflates cultural representation with political equality: it is based on the idea that political or social inequalities can be solved by galleries and museums containing 'representative' proportions of African, Caribbean, Asian and Chinese artists.

This is a deeply flawed strategy, in my opinion. Inequality cannot be solved overnight by workforce targets. It requires society to have a longer-term commitment to equality, and an aspiration that people of whatever background should have the best education and opportunities to pursue the arts. The use of these official schemes to 'promote difference' is not helping black and minority ethnic people enter the mainstream as equals, but instead is keeping them at the margins.

Richard Hylton, the artist and critic, provides an incisive analysis of the contradictions and limitations of the decibel scheme in his recent book *The Nature of the Beast*. It is worth quoting in some detail here:

Chapter 1 12

'...decibel appeared to be a fitting response to the growing interests of government, for public institutions to address the issue of "inclusion" and, by association, cultural diversity. However, despite this level of financial and structural input and its focus across all art forms, it could be argued that in the visual arts sector alone, decibel has, thus far, failed either to sustain a national profile or to instigate a genuine debate around the issue of cultural diversity. Furthermore, it could be argued that rather than challenging, it has apparently compounded the problems of tokenism and racial separation within the visual arts sector.'[15]

12 I am only offering here a synopsis of the historical background of diversity schemes. For a more background and analysis, see Richard Hylton's book, The Nature of the Beast: Cultural diversity and the Visual Arts Sector. A study of policies, initiatives and attitudes 1976–2006, Institute of Contemporary Interdisciplinary Arts (2007)

13 http://www.artscouncil.org.uk/documents/publications/354.pdf (last accessed 30.03.07)

14 'Culture and Difference' debate on spiked online http://www.spiked-online.com/Articles/0000000CA4a1.htm

15 The Nature of the Beast: Cultural diversity and the Visual Arts Sector, Richard Hylton, p19

Boxed in – online and printed report – manifesto club – 2007

Paper record player – 2006

Stripe
team:
Gail Swanlund
Jon Sueda
contact:
5051 Eagle Rock Boulevard ste. 212
Los Angeles, 90041, USA
T + 1 323 2551979
F + 1 323 2553545
jon@stripela.com
gail@stripela.com
www.stripela.com

Stripe is a full-service graphic design studio, with founding creatives Gail Swanlund and Jon Sueda, and an association of remarkable collaborators and experts: designers, photographers, illustrators, writers, thinkers, editors, researchers, and so forth. At the two headquarters in Los Angeles and San Francisco, they research, study, think, write, generate, eat, organize, calculate, assemble, discuss, dream, fool around with words, and then throw it all together to produce projects that communicate in a way speaking directly to the heart, by way of the brain. Working in the media range and for diverse industries, the common thread evident in all of their works is curiosity and an appreciation for the offbeat or strange, a love of smart ideas, and a pure exuberance of fabricating stuff. Each project they take on is considered and specific, its unique and particular requirements honored and cultivated. Collaboration is an essential part of their design process. The creative friction, discussion, energy generated by collaborating is a vital ingredient that opens up a place for the mysterious and unknowable to be made visible and physical. For Swanlund and Sueda, the design process is rarely a straight line from point A to B. It's intended to be a meandering journey of starts and stops, pauses, stubbed toes, fascinating discoveries, and finally a surprise destination. Above all, this process is a lot of fun and provides their clients with strong design solutions communicating in the best way imaginable. Their clients share Stripe's sense of adventure and exuberant affection for good form and communication.

Matt Greene: surrender – exhibition catalog – deitch projects – 2007
Jérôme Saint-Loubert Bié – poster – exhibiton curator: Jérôme Saint-Loubert Bié – 2007

Interview with Stripe

1. What led you to the formation of your studio?

We met in 2000 on a field trip to the Los Angeles cemetery to look at typography on grave stones. We already had a lot of friends in common: Martin Venezky, Geoff Kaplan, and Denise Gonzales Crisp, to name a few. A few years later we started to collaborate on a few projects and decided getting a shared workspace and working together on a more regular basis would be an exciting venture.

2. How many staff people does your studio have, and what are their working fields?

Two graphic designers and many collaborators.

3. How does a regular working day at your studio look like, what are your working schedules?

Both of us also teach, so an average day might start with teaching an early morning class for 2-3 hours, then rushing into the studio to work on a few different projects until sundown. We attempt to have lives outside the studio, so we try to get our work done and leave at a reasonable hour. Each day is fun here though, especially Fridays when we meet our friends for an Art&Design Lunch at Armon's Cafe across the street from the studio.

4. How much leisure time do you have during the year?

We take short breaks adding up to maybe 2 or 3 weeks a year, but teaching keeps us busy from September through May.

5. Which business areas do your clients mainly come from? Is the number of your clients increasing or declining?

We work with artists, museums, and art schools creating mainly books and other printed material. Recently we've been invited by a few curators to create graphic design to be displayed in the gallery exhibitions. Our number of clients is always growing and changing. Seems like the more books you do, the more people ask you to do them.

6. Do you have a specific corporate philosophy or maybe a mission statement like other companies, which is reflected in the way you steer your studio's course?

We have a mission statement on our website that fits the way we work pretty well: At STRIPE, we research, study, think, write, generate, eat, organize, calculate, assemble, discuss, dream, fool around with words, and then yank it all together to produce projects that communicate in a way that speaks directly to the heart, by way of the brain. Working in range of media and for diverse industries, the common thread that is evident in all our work is curiosity and an appreciation for the offbeat or strange, a love of smart ideas, and a pure exuberance for making stuff. Each project we take on is considered and specific, its unique and particular requirements honored and cultivated. Collaboration is an essential part of our design process. The creative friction, discussion, energy generated by collaborating is a vital ingredient that opens up a place for the mysterious and unknowable to be made visible and physical. For us the design process is rarely a straight line from point A to B. It's is intentionally a meandering journey of starts and stops, pauses, stubbed toes, fascinating discoveries, and finally a surprise destination. Above all, this process is a lot of fun and provides our clients with strong design solutions that communicate in the best way imaginable.

7. What, from your point of view, makes the difference between a small studio and a big company?

The idea of staying small seems to be about the freedom it affords you. You can work at your own pace, your own time schedule, in your own way. You can have personal relationships with your clients, and can work on all phases of the design process. I also think small studios are able to take a few more risks and experiment more freely. This is probably because the projects are smaller in scale and there isn't a whole lot of money at stake.

8. What kind of advantages and disadvantages does a small studio have compared to a big company?

Advantages: With a smaller studio, there is a possibility to have a more critical practice, where the work you make becomes a part of a personal investigation. It seems like in big studios, there is often a hierarchy built into the process of designing everything. You have creative directors, art directors, senior designers, junior designers, project managers... The "creatives" come up with ideas and the designers execute them. There is a detachment there. In a small studio, this big complex machine doesn't exist. We do everything from the research to execution and this is what makes it more fun and exciting. Disadvantages: We don't command huge salaries, and are forced to constantly multi-task (teach and work) in order to make a living.

Andrea Bowers: nothing is neutral – exhibiton catalog – REDCAT gallery – 2006

Tim Lee – exhibiton catalog – wattis institut for contemporary arts – 2008

Jennifer Steinkamp – exhibiton catalog – San Jose museum of art – 2006

Black clock poster – poster – black clock literary journal – 2007

9. What is your idea about the future of small studios?
In sympathetic design environments like the Netherlands for example, small studios are creating the most interesting and innovative new work. In countries like these, the government is very supportive of talented students coming out of school and help them to launch their practices once they graduate. This is a dream situation! For us Americans, the story is much different. Graphic design education here is extremely expensive, and most students are forced by necessity to look for jobs with bigger companies in order to payback their enormous student loans. As a result, there aren't many small young studios here in California and we don't see that trend changing very much in the future. So maybe the future is rough, yet we are encouraged by all the great work being done by the small American studios in existence.
10. Please describe and elaborate on the goals or plans that you have for your studio for the next five years?
We hope to self publish on a more frequent basis!

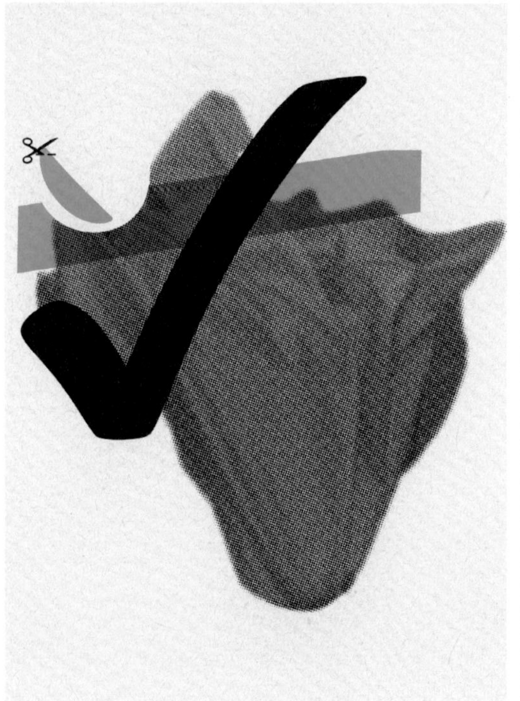

(result) (formed) (before) (receipt) (of) (client) (problem) – poster – Los Angeles contemporary exhibitions (lace gallery) – 2007

Earthquakes and aftershocks – exhibition catalog – école des beaux-arts de Rennes – 2006

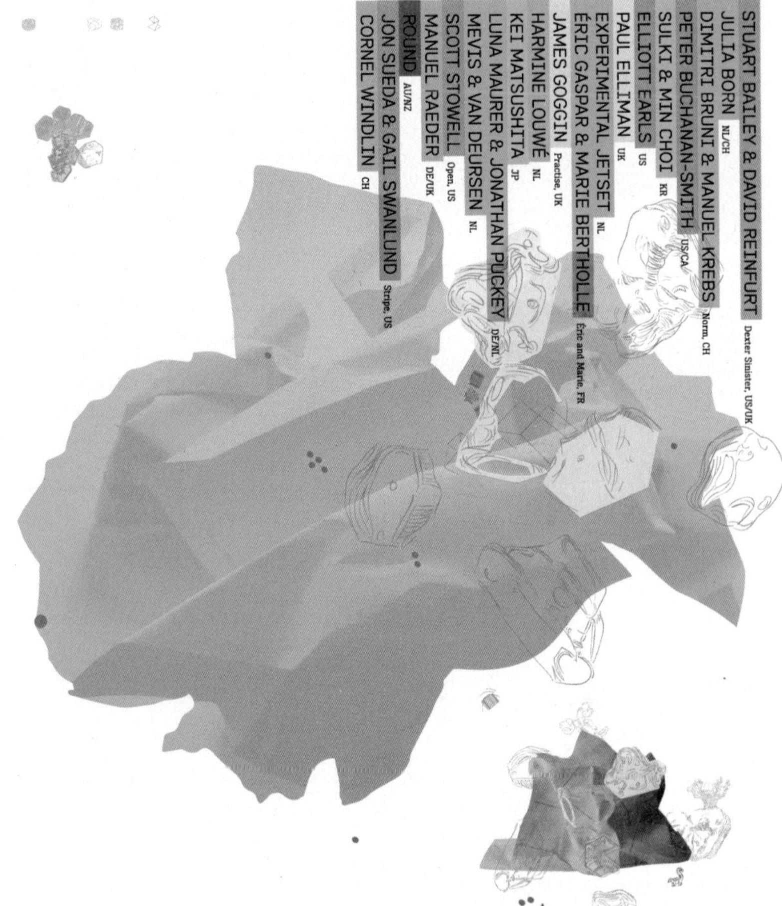

STUART BAILEY & DAVID REINFURT Dexter Sinister, US/UK
JULIA BORN NL/CH
DIMITRI BRUNI & MANUEL KREBS Norm, CH
PETER BUCHANAN-SMITH US/CA
SULKI & MIN CHOI KR
ELLIOTT EARLS US
PAUL ELLIMAN UK
EXPERIMENTAL JETSET NL
ÉRIC GASPAR & MARIE BERTHOLLE Éric and Marie, FR
JAMES GOGGIN Practise, UK
HARMINE LOUWÉ NL
KEI MATSUSHITA JP
LUNA MAURER & JONATHAN PUCKEY DE/NL
MEVIS & VAN DEURSEN NL
SCOTT STOWELL Open, US
MANUEL RAEDER DE/UK
ROUND AU/NZ
JON SUEDA & GAIL SWANLUND Stripe, US
CORNEL WINDLIN CH

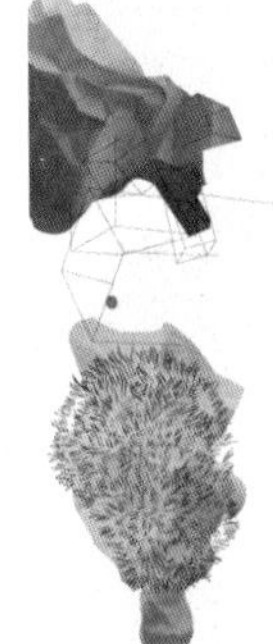

Grafický design v Graphic Design in the

BÍLÉ WHITE KRYCHLI CUBE

Vernisáž 13. 6. 2006 / Opening 13. 6. 2006

Otevřeno denně mimo pondělí a úterý od 10 do 18 hodin, ve čtvrtek do 19 hodin / Open daily except Monday and Tuesday from 10am to 6pm, Thursday until 7pm.

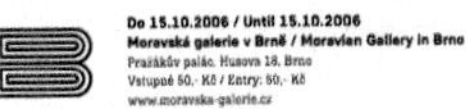

Do 15.10.2006 / Until 15.10.2006
Moravská galerie v Brně / Moravian Gallery in Brno
Pražákův palác, Husova 18, Brno
Vstupné 50,- Kč / Entry: 50,- Kč
www.moravska-galerie.cz

Graphic design in the white cube – poster – exhibiton curator: Peter Bilak – 2006

Studio Pip and Co.

team:
Ashton Andrew
Furzer Sarah
Lampe Elsie
Bennett Shelley
Band David

contact:
Suite 12/320 Carlisle Street
3183 Balaclava Victoria
Australia
T + 61 3 95259844
pipandco@peoplethings.com
www.peoplethings.com

Studio Pip and Co. was established in Melbourne, Australia in 2003. The studio works with no specific type of client or industry sector. It strives to help clients understand how they can communicate what it is they do and connect with their desired audiences with clarity. The studio's core activities include brand development, designs in print (brochures and catalogues), designs in environment (signing and events), and designs in digital (web and moving media). The studio's clients are its greatest collaborators. Fostering productive client relationships allows inspired and effective work to develop. The studio was founded Andrew Ashton. Ashton has over eighteen years of professional experience and is a member of Alliance Graphique Internationale. He has lectured in graphic design at Swinburne University and Hongki University, Korea. Ashton is focused on changing the perception of graphic design by the general public via initiatives such as industry service to maintaining a comprehensive internet based web log – www.peoplethings.com / and blog. Ashton's approach to graphic communication is a varied and unique journey incorporating inspiration from wayward sources found in contemporary culture, community and the media. Ashton employs conceptual themes, bespoke image making, writing, and unique product finishing. All the studio's work is a process that invites assessment, change, and reinvention. Ashton enjoys producing rigorous, diverse, unexpected and engaging outcomes.

No idea your idea: Stephen paper promotion – publication – spicers paper – 2007

Interview with Studio Pip and Co.

1. What led to the formation of your studio?

After three years of working in small design studios based in Sydney, I established a partnership with another designer and a design manager. At the time I was 24 years old, my business partners were at least ten years my senior and I found myself in an observing and learning role during the ten involvement years with the partnership. The partnership was a rich experience. I worked within a cheeky, well intended studio that grew into large design business. At the company's peak it employed 45 staff, and had offices in three cities across two continents in the Asia-Pacific region. In 2001 an Australian based media and communications company purchased the majority share holding from my partners and me. After this buy out I negotiated six months of leave. During this leave I planned my next move to a small, independent, and lively graphic design studio. It took twelve months to exit the partnership and start the current studio.

2. How many staff people does your studio have and what are their main working fields?

We have three full-time staffs. We also employ a student design intern on a regular basis on four to six week assignments. We are all graphic designers and image-makers.

3. What does a regular working day at your studio look like, how is the day structured?

As result of working in the larger studio environment we have very simple working structures. A weekly work in progress meeting determines the work flow. In the mornings we assess emails, project schedules and commence work. Project fees are estimated to time, schedule deadlines are identified, projects are split into a number of tasks and we block out parts of the week to execute these tasks. In the past the studio was too small to use formal time sheets effectively, as it was uncomplicated to track projects. However, the days of not working to timesheets are closing as we grow in clients and projects.

4. How much leisure time do you have during a year?

Our work in a small studio is exciting, diverse, hectic and demanding. On one hand designers are doing more, yet on the other hand they don't have enough leisure to compensate. The studio takes four weeks leave during the year as an extended break. We generally take time off over Christmas and New Year as most of Melbourne is on summer holiday in January. During the day we take what we need for lunch. Staff can determine their start and finishing times. We rarely work on weekends, as I feel that people cannot develop and positively contribute to the design process working indoors at a computer.

5. Which business areas do your clients mainly come from? Is the number of your clients increasing or rather declining? Our work comes to the studio from referral and maintaining good work relationships. At present we work in the cultural sector, hospitality, fine paper marketing, and event based sectors. Our client base tends to shift from sector to sector, rather than expand or contract. We started out doing a lot work for the design sector. We consistently work with around ten to fifteen clients, on projects as small as a website update to comprehensive programme running over six months.

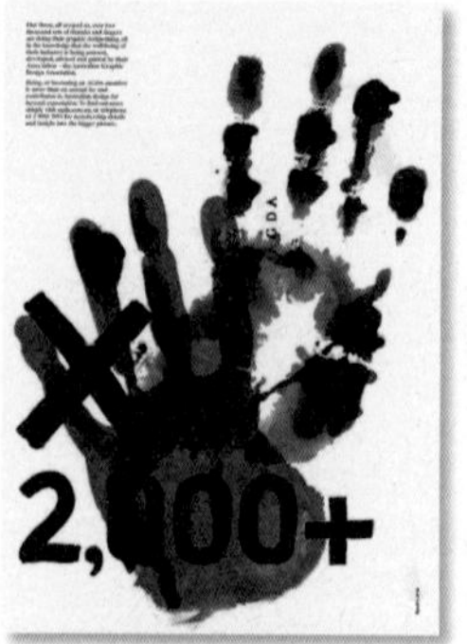

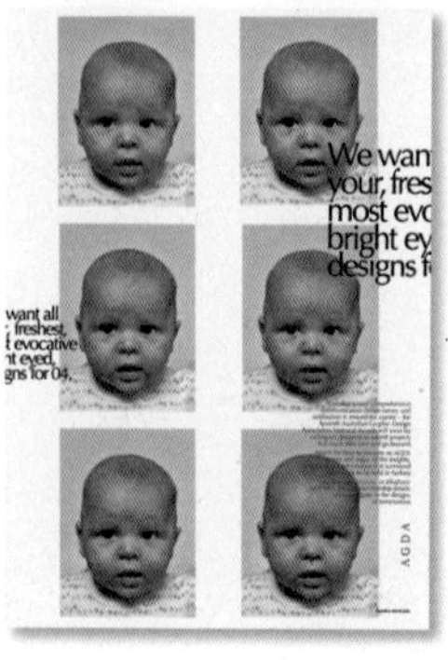

Australian graphic design association – print advertising campaign – chamber music Australia – 2007

Melbourne international chamber music competition – event identity – chamber music Australia – 2007

6. Do you have a specific corporate philosophy or maybe a mission statement like other companies, which is reflected in the way you steer the studio's course?

I generally refer to common sense principles where possible. When I feel the studio needs to develop a corporate philosophy or mission statement it is probably time to close the studio, have a break, and start something new. We work to a simple proposition – I believe that graphic design is a great vocation that allows one to experience many aspects of life. Though I contend that overall the profession is under-valued and under-paid. Within these opposing influences I try to foster an enriching, productive and enjoyable work place. In this space we work towards developing good work relationships and produce functional exciting work.

7. What, from your point of view, makes the difference between a small studio and a big company?

Graphic design ultimately serves commercial means. In this environment big studios require significant funds to operate as compared to small studios. In Australian, clients are inundated with design studios – from 1994 to 2004 studios Australia wide have doubled from 2500 to over 5500 studios. Large studios are typically well funded and better equipped. As a result big studios can market themselves comprehensively, offer structured working environments, and typically pay staff well. Yet big studios work tend to reduce designer contact with the client, offer clients work that is risk adverse and benchmarked. In contrast to large studios I see that there are two types of small studio – under funded and well funded. Under funded studios trade upon the good will, effort and resourcefulness of their founders and staff. Their projects often don't cover the actual time it takes to complete the work properly. Wittingly or unwittingly the studio sees that investing time and energy into project work as an investment in the development of compelling project case studies. This effort in turn, it is hoped, will attract well funded clients and projects. Within a few years of careful management and consistent delivery of effective and quality outcomes the small studio can become well funded while maintaining a list of quality ongoing clients and projects. At this point the studio can grow staff and clients or maintain staff and fine tune the quality of clients and projects.

Melbourne design festival image – digital rendering – national design centre – 2005

Sunday monday postcard series – postcards – self publisher – 2004

8. What kind of advantages and disadvantages does a small studio have compared to a big company?

As mentioned, big studios have the advantage of being better funded and consequently better resourced. In a small studio one can find them selves a little overwhelmed with range of tasks – from washing dishes to retouching, writing copy to invoicing or type design to client service. In busy times it would be great as a small studio to have a little more help.

9. What is your idea about the future of small studios?

Since the early 1990s, ongoing technology development has allowed individual designers to do more with less effort. Innovative equipment teamed with educated people make it unnecessary to have big studio and produce engaging and competent work. In recent times a number of my Australian peers have chosen to move from larger studios to set up and work in smaller studios. Having had experienced large studios, small studios by comparison are less complicated to operate and allowing more time to focus upon the quality of the designed outcomes. Many small studios, like my own, have opted to share larger workspaces with artists, project managers, architects, illustrators and writers. This shared practice has made it possible for small concerns to offer vibrant multi-skilled workplaces, to further reduce operational costs, and to make it possible for smaller studios to collaborate and execute larger projects. We share our studio with Australian fine artist David Band. David along with developing fine art is also commissioned to develop ideas for commercial graphic design contexts. We help David with executing the typography, layout and production management, we also assist him with the day to day runnings of projects, too. In return he pays us a percentage of the project's budget. We are also developing a fee incentive programme with our designers. A percentage of the design fees will be split a monthly basis with designers along with their base salary package for any projects they bring into the studio. It gives our designer the chance to contribute to the studio and be directly rewarded for their efforts.

Do you think that small studios do not have any other choice but to expand in order to survive in these times of globalization?

My initial response is to wonder if expansion and the current globalization model is one of the drivers for the current environmental imbalance. Growth without taking into account the effects is proving to be disastrous process to follow for all living things on planet Earth. So with this notion in mind I question whether to globalize and expand are the only options facing a successful studio. My first thought is to downplay the importance globalization in terms of human development and focus upon the emerging concept of localization. Current trends of over population, climate change and rapid reduction of carbon emissions are a global agenda that are best acted out at a local level. Localization is a proposition that humanity will undergo a process of shifting efforts back to local terms of reference – local production, local infrastructures servicing local communities. Under these circumstances the questions to ask are: Which studios will flourish in this environment?

The big, income focused and safe design businesses or, the small, prudent, and innovative design studios?

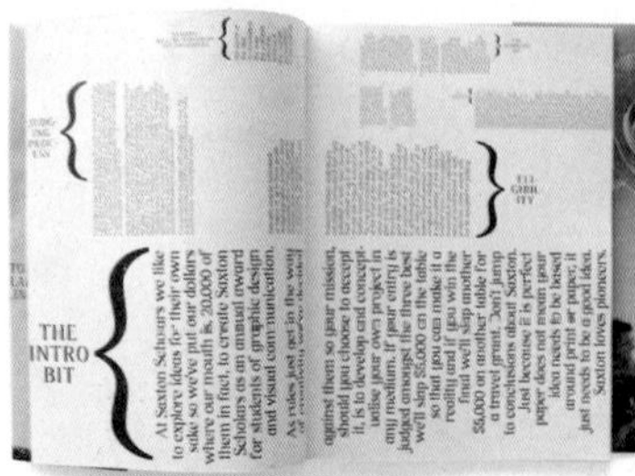

Ideas in the everyday: saxton scholars 2002 - student design competition – booklet with dust cover – Australien paper – 2002

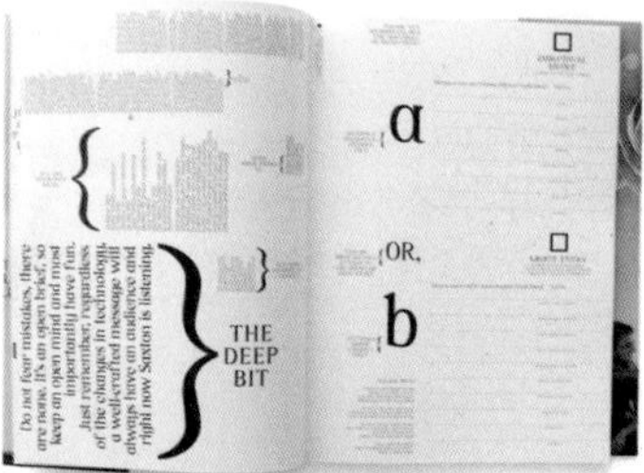

Will the big brands and the big design and marketing stories be the products we know today? Is expansion one several business tactics to chose from in terms of studio longevity? For these answers I am looking outside of business models to seek how entities develop in times of economic, technological and cultural prosperity. For example: there are lessons within family structure trends that can be applied to design studios. Is a large rural family of the early nineteenth century similar to a large studio of the 1980s, and a city based family two children similar to a small studio of the 2000's? It seems that as a structure like a family or a business enjoys better education, increased wealth and the benefits of better technology they have the options to determine the scale they want to operate at and develop a model that suits the lifestyle they aspire to. In the past people assumed critical mass to aid development. In the present people think through a situation, model outcomes to their means and choose a scenario that best suits their aspirations.

Faculty poster – poster – post graduate faculty of design research, Swinburne University – 2005

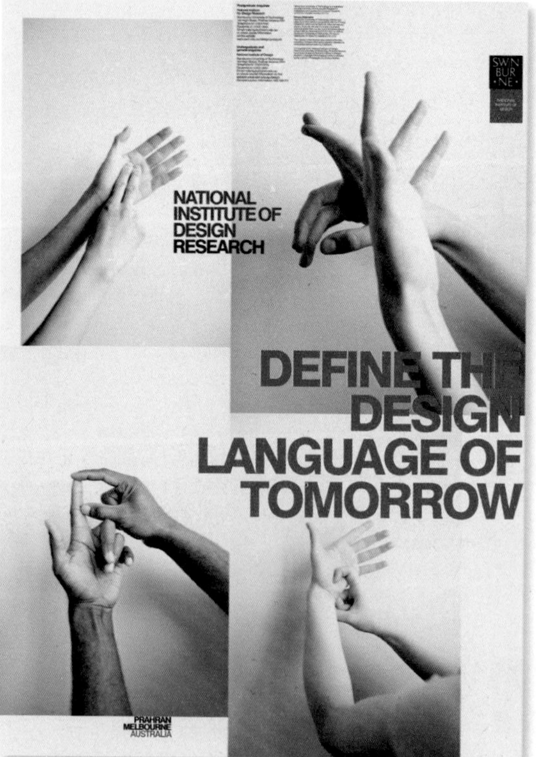

10. Please describe and elaborate on the goals or plans that you have for your studio for the next five years?

I have no desire to have a big studio. I would like to keep the studio small, work with a shared studio, continue to work on range of challenging and interesting projects, while strengthening the studio's financial position. I would like to amass staff viewing the studio as a place that they can develop their ideas for design and futures. Small studios offer its designers freedom and flexibility. I am open to the idea that a designer's roles and skill are required to change, revolve or evolves as history dictates. I am open to idea that today I am graphic designer, in five years I could be a writer, film maker, publisher, or the client.

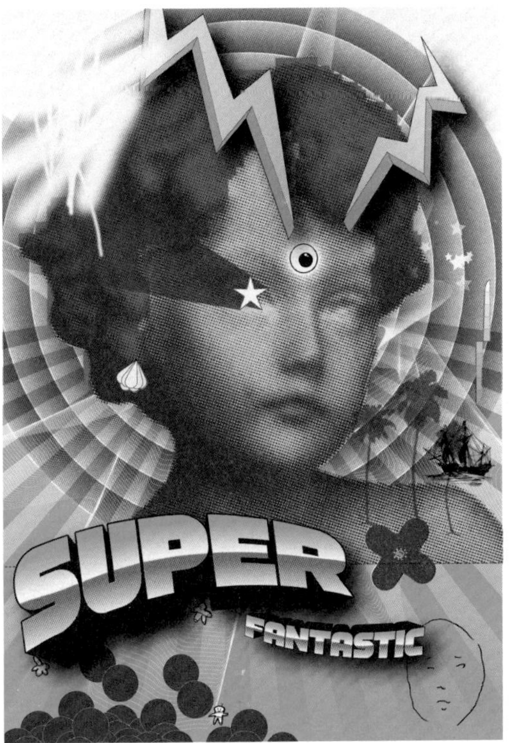

Super fantastic: saxton schloars 2006, student design competition, programme image – digital montage – Australian paper – 2006

Super fantastic: saxton schloars 2007, student design competition, programme image – digital montage – Australian paper – 2007

Australian graphic design association – print advertising campaign – chamber music Australia – 2007

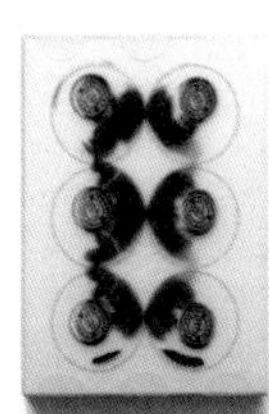

two years on design is...

Welcome to the Australian Graphic Design Association National Awards, 2002. It's been ten years since we rolled out the red carpet, and trod the boards in the name of graphic design in Melbourne Victoria.

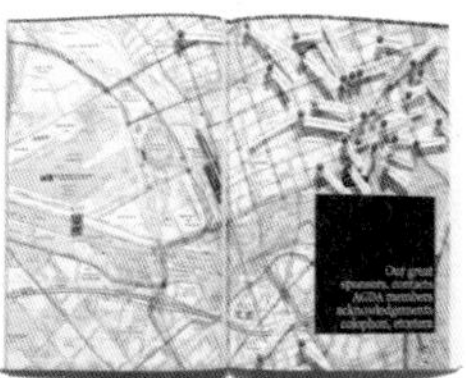

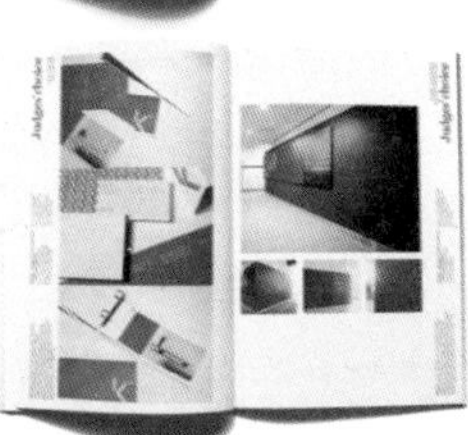

Studio-SM

team:
Sofia Leverbeck
Magnus Polbratt

contact:
20 Allen Road
Basement Flat
N16 8SD London
United Kingdom
T + 44 7 816062060
T + 44 7 817111809
hello@studio-sm.co.uk
www.studio-sm.co.uk

Studio-SM came about at the end of 2007, when Sofia and Magnus decided to start to work together rather than on their own. They both graduated from London College of communication in 2007, receiving a BA in Graphic Design. Originally they come from Sweden but Sofia has lived here in England for the last 3 years and Magnus for the last 5 years. They're still fairly new at a studio but they aim to grow more renowned within the next few years. They don't see themselves taking someone on in the near future. Clients that they work with have been mainly within the creative scene, but they would like to broaden the studio's client range. Their projects are mostly print- and type-based. Since they are so new they don't have an extensive range of projects to show but these are 4 that they would like to be featured.

Interview with Studio-SM

1. What led to the formation of your studio?

It came from when me (Sofia Leverbeck) and Magnus Polbratt decided that we wanted to do work together rather than on our own. We were/are both working full-time as graphic designers at other companies, so this is our way to do exactly what we want to do. The plan is that we eventually will do Studio-SM full-time.

2. How many staff people does your studio have and what are their main working fields?

Two people. We are both graphic designers and share all the other tasks that come up with running a studio.

3. How does a regular working day at your studio look like, how is the day structured?

A regular day for Magnus and me is that we go to our separate work places while the evenings and weekends consist of working for Studio-SM. We always try to go to meetings together. And the workload is split between the two of us.

4. How much leisure time do you have during a year?

That depends on the workload. But normally, about 20 days a year (the days we get from our separate work places).

5. Which business areas do your clients mainly come from? Is the number of your clients increasing or rather declining?

Our clients normally come from the art and culture sector. The number of clients is increasing.

6. Do you have a specific corporate philosophy or maybe a mission statement like other companies, which is reflected in the way you steer the studio's course?

We always want to produce great work.

7. What, from your point of view, makes the difference between a small studio and a big company?

Being a small studio means that we personally know all of our clients and can make all decisions ourselves.

The hardest thing to see is what is in front of your eyes – book – self initiated – 2007

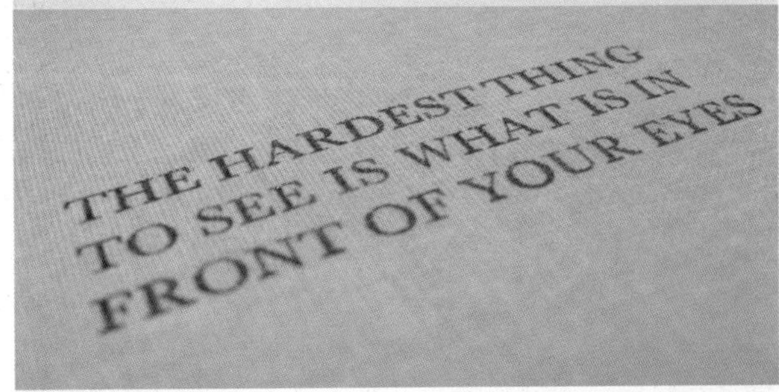

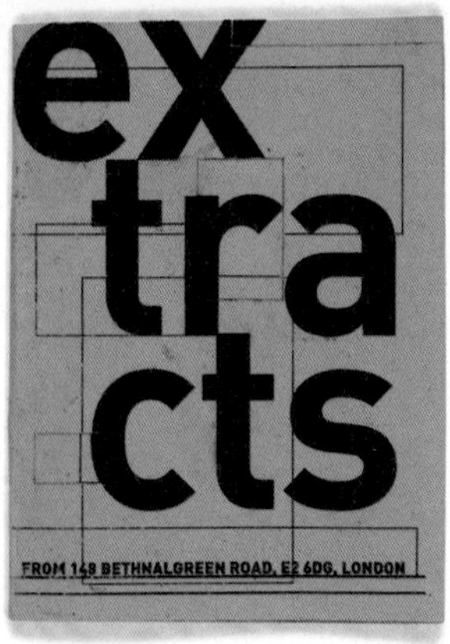

Extract – catalogue – self initiated – 2007

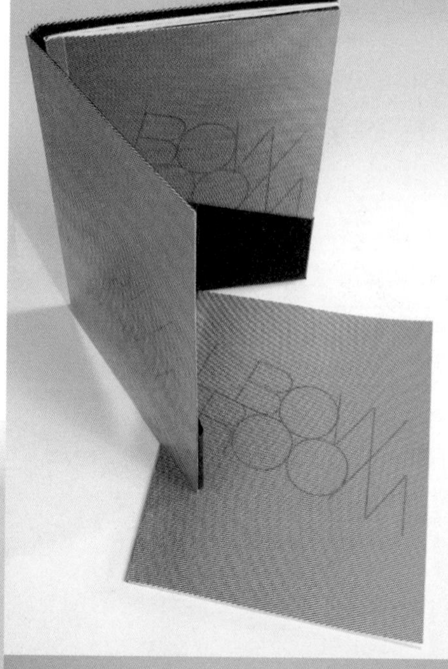

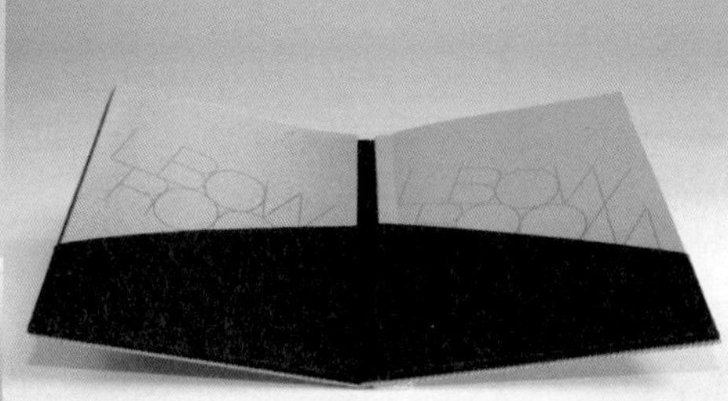

LBOWROOM – catalogue – LBOWROOM Sydney – 2005

LBOWROOM

PAUL PAPER

TINY PHOTOGRAPHS OF MELANCHOLY
PAUL PAPER

Tiny photographs of melancholy – print – Paul Paper – 2008

8. What kind of advantages and disadvantages does a small studio have compared to a big company?

An advantage is to be in control of everything relating to our studio. As a small studio we have little costs, and that means we can work on projects that have smaller budgets but might be more creative. A disadvantage is that we as a small studio cannot take on big projects.

9. What is your idea about the future of small studios? Do you think that small studios do not have any other choice but to expand in order to survive in these times of globalization?

I think that there is definitely room for smaller studios. The small studios need to be around to create more individual work.

10. Please describe and elaborate on the goals or plans that you have for your studio for the next five years?

The plan is that we eventually will do Studio SM full-time. In the future we will take someone on, and we want to grow. We want to expand our range of clients and keep challenging ourselves.

Paul Paper lives, day-dreams, sleeps, wonders and sometimes works in a strange city of Vilnius, Lithuania and has been shooting since the age of 16. He has been exhibited in France, Sweden, USA and Germany and published by Frankie, Afisha, The Quiet Life Camera Club and This is a Magazine in Australia, Russia, USA and Italy. Paul shoots spontaneously, capturing what he calls "the tiny tiny miracle in boring every day". See more of his work at www.itismyparty.org or just say hello at today@itismyparty.org

"Tiny photographs of melancholy" is a postcard gift-bundle. It is a collaboration between photographer Paul Paper and Studio-SM. It contains moods, places and feelings that you might want to share with your friends.

Design and Art Direction by Studio-SM which is a small design sudio based in London, run by Sofia Leverbeck & Magnus Polbratt. Feel free to get in contact if you like to work with them or just want to tell them you love them. Please visit their home: www.studio-sm.co.uk for further details.

© 2007 Paul Paper [A boring sea picture]
From the series "Tiny Photographs of Melancholy"
photographs of moods, places and feelings

www.itismyparty.org

Inside-out – book – self initiated – 2007

Magazine – magazine – self initiated – 2007

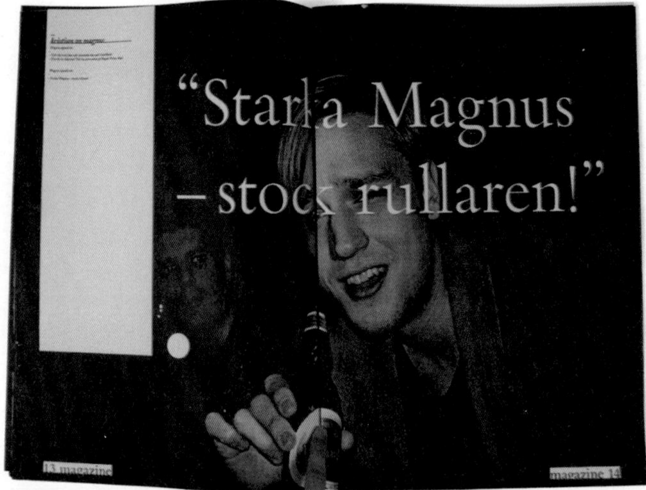

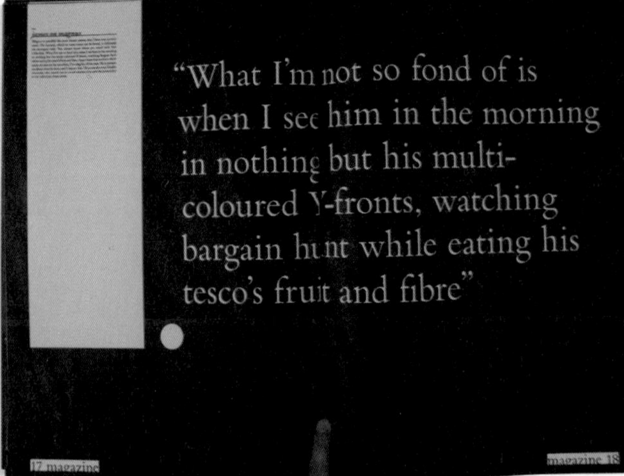

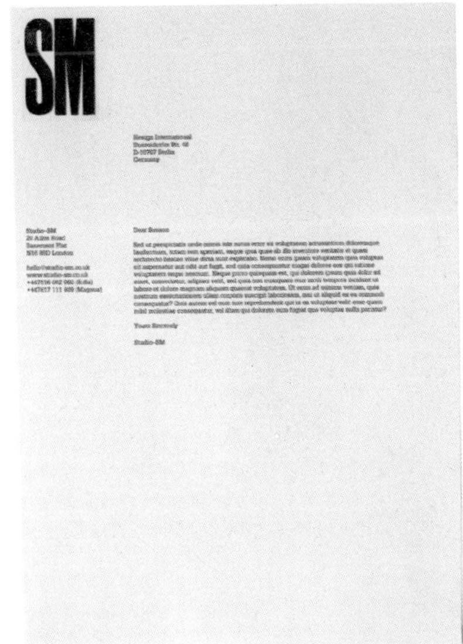

Studio-SM – identity – studio-SM – 2007

Proportions of a city – book – self initiated – 2007

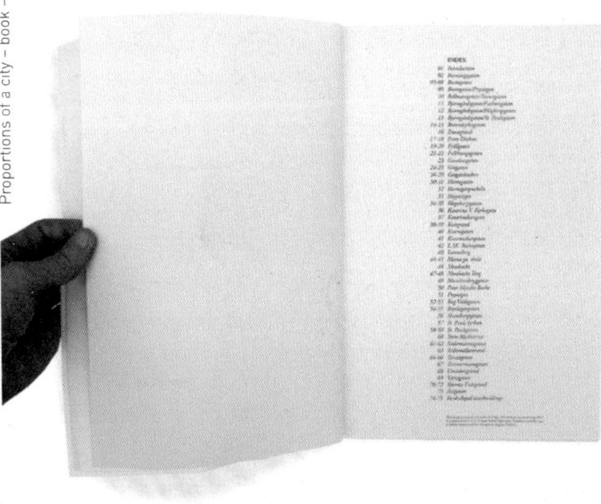

Superbüro

team:
Barbara Ehrbar
contact:
Mattenstr. 81
2503 Biel, Switzerland
T + 41 32 3232111
F + 41 32 3255122
info@superbuero.com
www.superbuero.ch

Photo by Alexander Jaquemet, CH-Erlach

Superbüro was founded in 2001 in Biel, Switzerland. The studio mainly works for cultural projects, architects and public institutions. Superbuero stands for graphic design with lots of passion and personal involvement. The joy of experimenting and a sense for adventure are the basics for a fresh visual product. Conception and functionality are important. Sex appeal as well.

Superbag – silkscreen on inflatable mattress – superbüro – 2006

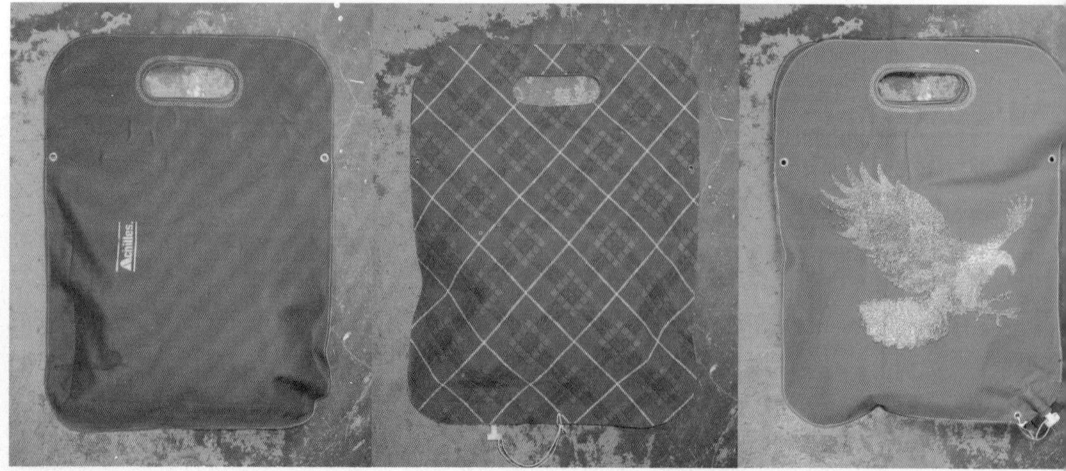

Disco-ver – cd cover – personal project – 2003

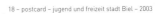

Interview with Superbüro

1. What led to the formation of your studio?

It was always my goal to run my own studio. I like to be my own boss.

2. How many staff people does your studio have and what are their main working fields?

My studio is a one-woman-show. I usually work with one intern.

3. How does a regular working day at your studio look like, how is the day structured?

I start working between 7 and 8 a.m.. I work in a big studio space which I share with other designers and architects, so we have a coffee break at 10 a.m. when we all meet at the bar, the same at 4 in the afternoon. I usually work until 6 or 8. I never do night shifts.

4. How much leisure time do you have during a year?

A lot. I just came back from a two-month biking trip to India.

5. Which business areas do your clients mainly come from?

From the fields of culture, architecture, science.

Is the number of your clients increasing or rather declining?

Increasing.

6. Do you have a specific corporate philosophy or maybe a mission statement like other companies, which is reflected in the way you steer the studio's course?

Superbuero means graphic design with lots of passion and personal involvement. The joy of experimenting and a sense for adventure are the basics for a fresh visual product. Conception and functionality are important. Sex appeal as well.

18 – postcard – jugend und freizeit stadt Biel – 2003

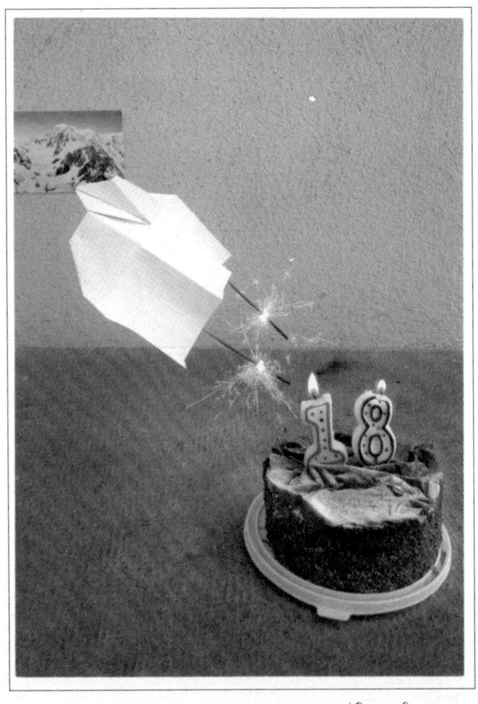

Commutications – book – kunstachse, Bern – 2005

Biel photo days 2007 – poster – Bieler fototage – 2007

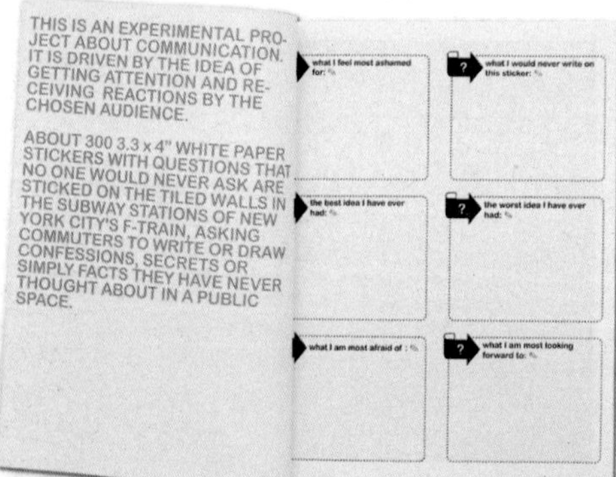

THIS IS AN EXPERIMENTAL PROJECT ABOUT COMMUNICATION. IT IS DRIVEN BY THE IDEA OF GETTING ATTENTION AND RECEIVING REACTIONS BY THE CHOSEN AUDIENCE.
ABOUT 300 3.3 x 4" WHITE PAPER STICKERS WITH QUESTIONS THAT NO ONE WOULD NEVER ASK ARE STICKED ON THE TILED WALLS IN THE SUBWAY STATIONS OF NEW YORK CITY'S F-TRAIN, ASKING COMMUTERS TO WRITE OR DRAW CONFESSIONS, SECRETS OR SIMPLY FACTS THEY HAVE NEVER THOUGHT ABOUT IN A PUBLIC SPACE.
what I feel most ashamed for:
what I would never write on this sticker:
the best idea I have ever had:
the worst idea I have ever had:
what I am most afraid of :
what I am most looking forward to:

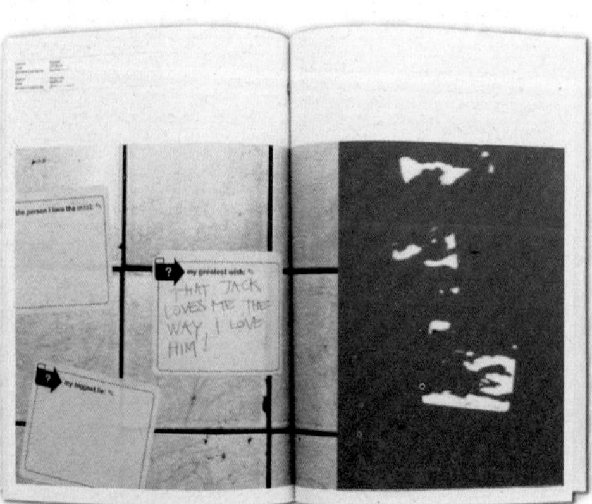

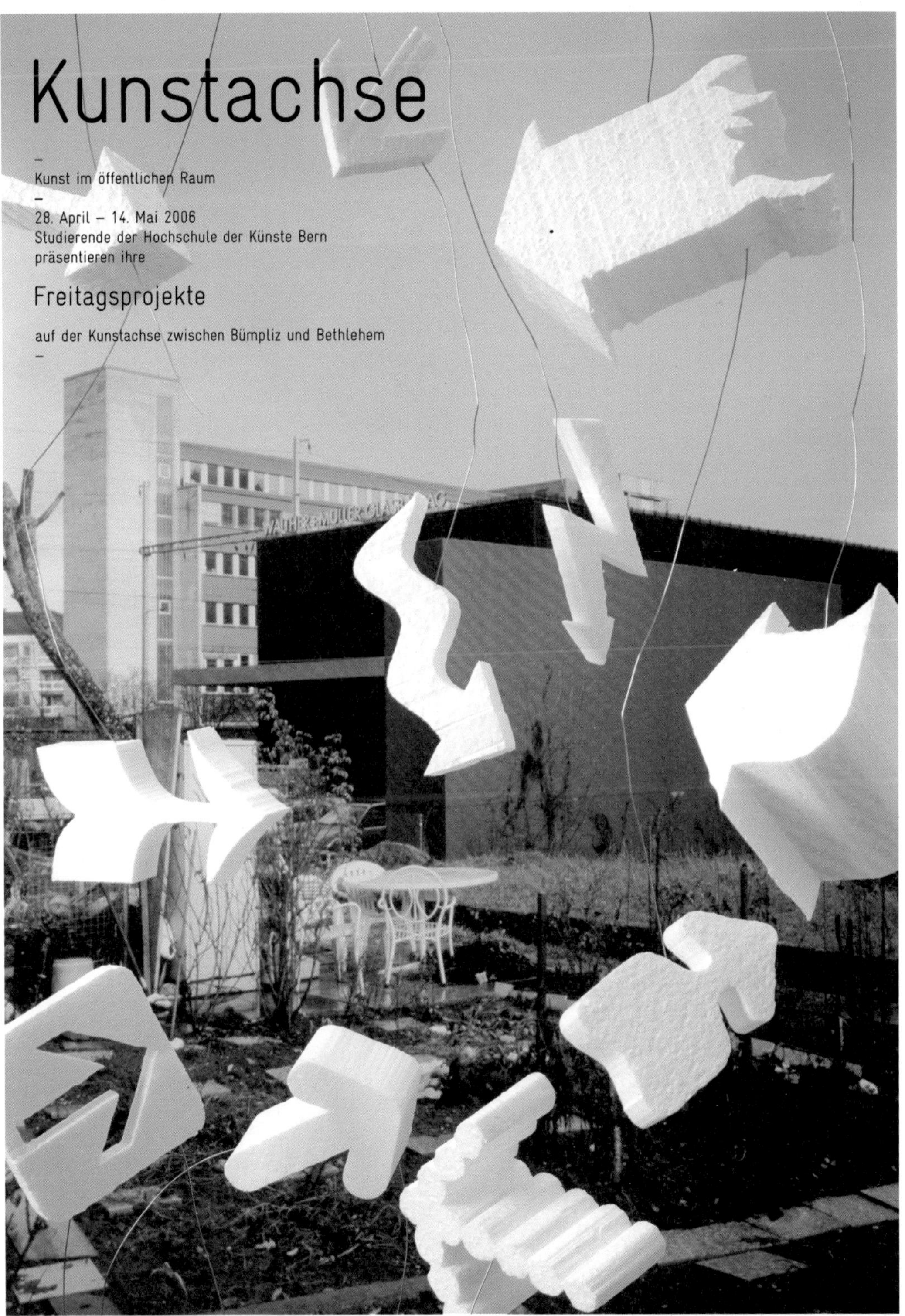

Kunstachse
–
Kunst im öffentlichen Raum
–
28. April – 14. Mai 2006
Studierende der Hochschule der Künste Bern
präsentieren ihre
Freitagsprojekte
auf der Kunstachse zwischen Bümpliz und Bethlehem
–

Art – poster – kunstachse, Bern – 2005

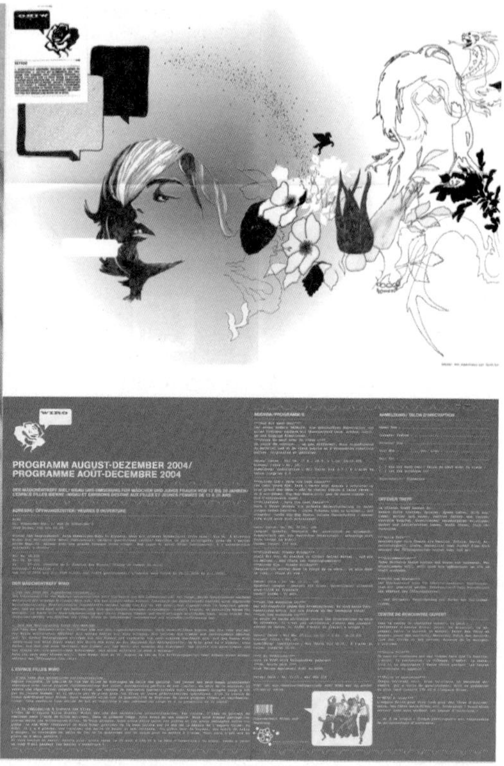

Wiro – agenda booklet, t-shirt – jugend und freizeit stadt Biel – 2003-08

USUS – poster – hochschule der künste, Bern – 2002 BOOKS + BOOM – poster – Berne university of the arts – 2002

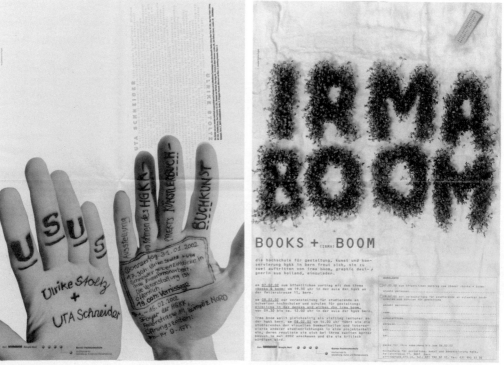

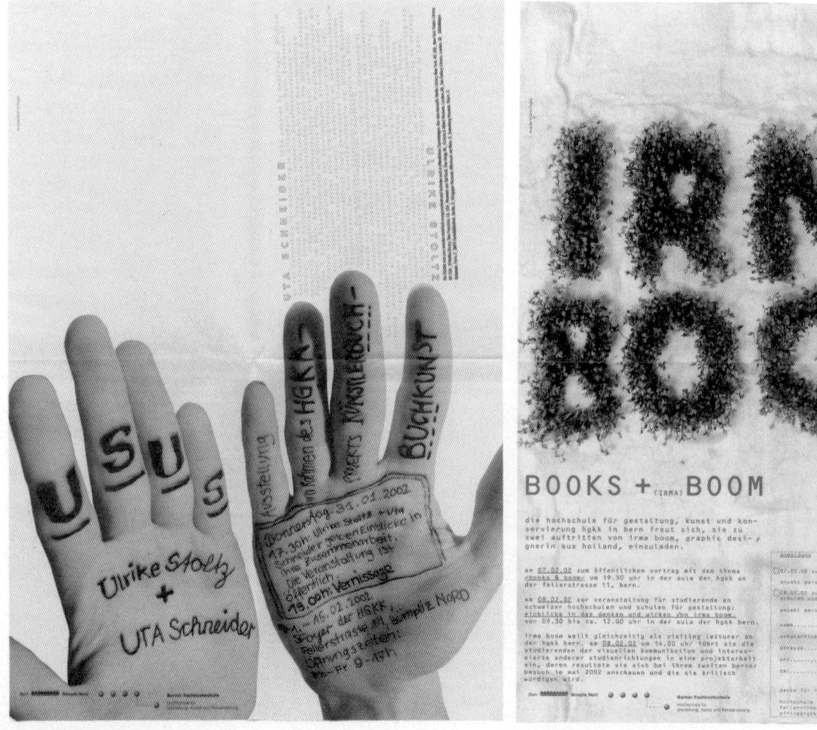

7. What, from your point of view, makes the difference between a small studio and a big company?

Small studios have a lot of freedom for experimentation.

8. What kind of advantages and disadvantages does a small studio have compared to a big company?

Advantages: freedom, room for experimentation, easy clients, clients often become friends

Disadvantages: some big clients have no confidence in small studios, a problem I have had once or twice.

9. What is your idea about the future of small studios?

I think the future belongs to small studios.

Do you think that small studios do not have any other choice but to expand in order to survive in these times of globalization?

Not at all. I want to stay small and flexible.

10. Please describe and elaborate on the goals or plans that you have for your studio for the next five years?

More cultural work, more books, more posters, learning how to make studio photography.

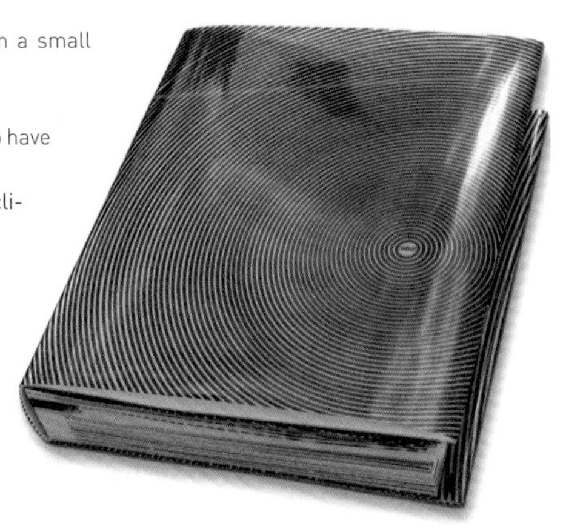

Mlzd - book - diploma project - 1999

Ten

team:
Masahiro Kakinokihara
Jun Ishiguro
contact:
Ten.Inc.
111 Shoto Raj Bldg.,
1-26-10, Shoto, Shibuya-ku,
150-0046 Tokyo, Japan
T + 81 3 57381030
kaki@tuba.ocn.ne.jp
www.10inc.jp

Ten was founded in August 2007 by Masahiro Kakinokihara, who is a managing director in the office. The studio does graphical works of widespread variety without dividing the graphic from the product, for example for films and museum exhibitions, corporate identities for companies as well as brand design management for companies and shops, and children's books and toys. However, they are principally involved in cultural art work. Masahiro won several prizes for his works. In 2003, he became New Art Director Award of Japanese Graphic Designers Association. Furthermore, he was awarded the Grand Prize of Art Directors Club for the direction of a museum exhibition in 2007. The exhibition named "Japanese Art is laughing" was shown by the MORI ART MUSEUM in Tokyo.

Interview with Ten

1. What led to the formation of your studio?

I established my studio "Ten" this autumn (2007), becoming independent of the design company "DRAFT", and assembled minimum staff. Small studio may have a brilliant future because they can be run with little funds and can realize challenging works. In big studio we can sometimes just do big business works to earn a lot of money.

2. How many staff people does your studio have and what are their main working fields?

Permanent staff: Masahiro KAKINOKIHARA (President) / Art Director & Designer
Jun ISHIGURO / Designer
Contracted staff: Arisa KAKUSUE / Producer
Sumika KOMORIYA / Package Designer
Trulie Okamocek / Game Designer

3. How does a regular working day at your studio look like, how is the day structured?

1/3 meetings, 1/3 thinking, 1/3 designing – from 10 a.m. to 10 p.m.

4. How much leisure time do you have during a year?

We started our studio only three months ago, so we haven't had a long vacation yet. But on a holiday, I drove to the green fields (Yatsugatake, Gotenba, Nasu) with my daughters and my wife.

5. Which business areas do your clients mainly come from? Is the number of your clients increasing or rather declining?

Clients come from credit card firms, art museums, fashion, and kindergartens. The number is increasing.

6. Do you have a specific corporate philosophy or maybe a mission statement like other companies, which is reflected in the way you steer the studio's course?

"Ten" - the name of our studio means "sky" and "dot" in Japanese. Either big or small, we'll take the same stance. Before starting with the actual design, we talk with our clients. We think that building a relationship of trust is most important.

7. What, from your point of view, makes the difference between a small studio and a big company?

They are not so different, we think. You ought to take the same stance dealing with both. But inside of a big company, people sometimes worry too much, because failure is attributed not to a single person but to the whole organization. In small studio, we can talk more obediently with clients. We are the persons who are responsible.

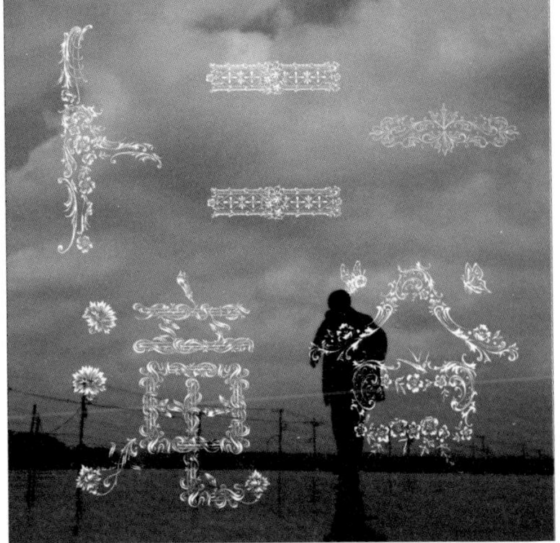

市川準（映画監督）
イッセー尾形（俳優）
宮沢りえ（女優）
村上春樹（小説家）
広川泰士（写真家）
坂本龍一（音楽家）

Tony Takitani – poster – wilcom – 2004

Dogora – poster – albatros-film – 2006

The smile in Japanese art – poster and board – mori art museum – 2007

Singing aeon – tagline and brandbook and visual on the street – aeon – 2004

Picnic2008 - calendar - d-bros - 2007

FUJI central dindergarden - logo and diploma and note and bus - FUJI central kindergarden - 2002

8. What kind of advantages and disadvantages does a small studio have compared to a big company?

Big companies always have to expand in terms of business. So sometimes, you have to turn down attractive jobs which are too risky or too small. In a small studio, you can take that risk and produce really creative works.

9. What is your idea about the future of small studios? Do you think that small studios do not have any other choice but to expand in order to survive in these times of globalization?

When I established my company, I didn't think about the financial superiority of small studios. I only wanted to improve the creative quality of our works, and small studio was the answer. We think our works must have structual power and beauty. Completing the surface layer is the next step. And we have to consider the influence of the work upon society. It must be effective, and above all, it must be "good". Strong structure and social goodness are not to be found in a stiff system. Good designs are flexible, pleasant and uplifting. Can we make that kind of good design? If we can, we will survive.

10. Please describe and elaborate on the goals or plans that you have for your studio for the next five years?

We want to produce good designs of lasting influence on our social fabric. In traditional Japanese architecture, we use Fusuma & Shoji (partition and sliding door made of paper). They are not only dividing space like concrete walls, but join people with each other and with nature. We hope our designs work can resemble these doors. A society needs ambiguity and torelance. Our goal is the same now or in five years, and making good designs is helping us with that.

Great ukioe masters – poster – the Shoto museum of art – 2007

Brazil body nostalgia – poster – the national museum of modern art, Tokyo – 2004

Charity exhibition would you like a cup of tea? – poster – recruit – 2007

Laforet autumn – poster – laforet harajuku – 2007

Sesson exhibition – poster – the shoto museum of art – 2003

Frédéric Teschner

team:
Frédéric Teschner
Olivier Lebrun

contact:
17 rue de la Révolution
93100 Montreuil, France
T + 33 1 48579894
f.teschner@wandadoo.fr
www.fredericteschner.com

Frédéric Teschner was born in 1972, and lives and works in Montreuil. He graduated from the Ecole Nationale Supérieure des Arts Décoratifs, Paris in 1997, and started working with Pierre Di Sciullo before joining the Atelier de Création Graphique (Pierre Bernard) in 1999. Since 2002, he has been developing his own style of work as an independent graphic designer by regulary working with architects (Pierre Jorge Gonzalez and Judith Haase AAS, Paris/Berlin, X'TU), designers (François Azambourg, Ronan + Erwan Bouroullec, Pierre Charpin, David Dubois, Martin Szekely), or choreographers (Compagnie Kataline Patkaï). Since 2003, he has been designing catalogues and signages for exhibitions at the Centre Pompidou, e.g. the new "Espace 315" exhibitions dedicated to contemporary creation (since 2004) or just recently, "Airs de Paris", celebrating the 30th anniversary of this institution (2007). During the last few years, the studio developed collaborations with several museums (Memorial de la Shoah, Paris, MAC/VAL – new Museum of Contemporary Art of the Val de Marne, Musée d'art moderne de la Ville de Paris and the Grand Palais), with art centers (Villa Noailles, Hyères, Cneai, Châtou and DCA, an association gathering most of the contemporary art centers in France), or with some main institutions of the Ministère de la Culture, such as the Centre national des arts plastiques (CNAP) or the DAP (Direction des arts plastiques). The close understanding of Teschner's artistic works and exhibition subjects, as well as the specific way he renders them can be observed in books like a set of twelve screen printed books called "Hors Commerce", published by the CNAP, the Grand Palais exhibition catalogue "La Force de l'art 1" (Réunion des musées nationaux, Paris, 2007), the monography "Martin Szekely" (Images Modernes / Kreo, Paris, 2003), and in "Le Guide des Maîtres d'art" (DAP / Ministère de la Culture, Paris, 2005). Frédéric Teschner has just been awarded by the 2007 Best French Art Book competition with "François Azambourg, 38 pièces" (Verlag der Buchhandlung Walther Koenig, Cologne, 2007). This year, the international poster & graphic design festival of Chaumont – the most famous French graphic design festival – invited him to create the poster and invitation for the event. Since 2007, he is a jury member of the art reasearch grantings awarded by the CNAP, as well as of the selection of the residents at the Villa Medicis in Rome. Frédéric Teschner is invited to different boards of examiners (École Estienne, Paris; ERG, Bruxelles), to give workshops in art schools (ESAD, Reims), and is currently teaching graphic design at the ESAD (Amiens).

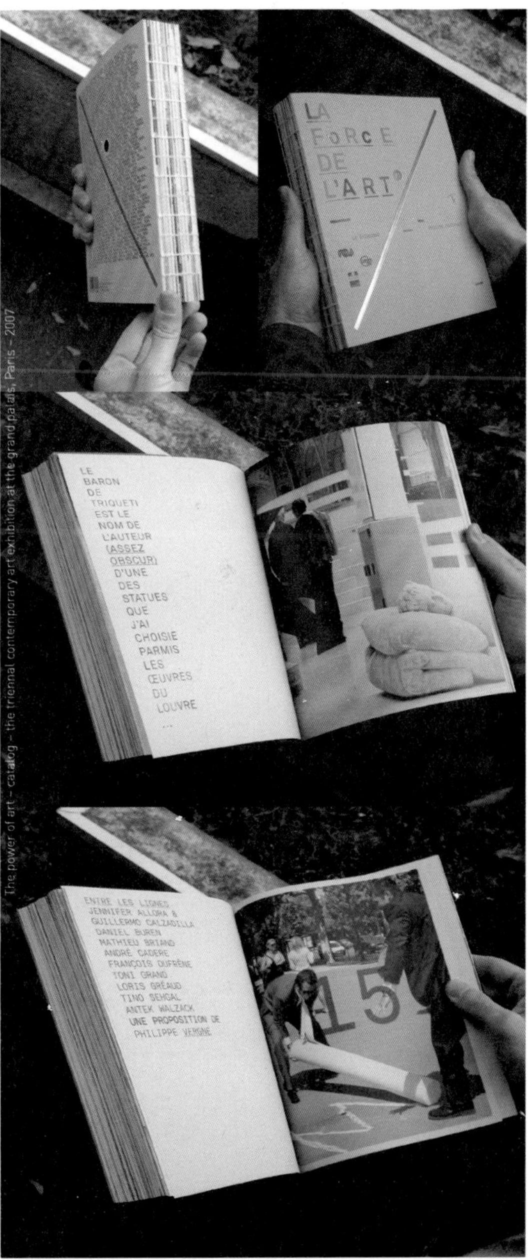

The power of art – catalog – the triennal contemporary art exhibition at the grand palais, Paris – 2007

Interview with Frédéric Teschner

1. What led to the formation of your studio?

After having practiced graphic design in studios in Paris (Atelier de création graphique/Pierre Bernard or Pierre DiSciullo) for about 4 years, I began to develop a personal portfolio for a few clients from the field of contemporary creation, e.g. new dance companies (Kataline Patkaï), young architects (Pierre-Jorge Gonzalez and Judith Haase/AAS Paris-Berlin), and other designers (Ronan and Erwan Bouroullec). Some were friends of mine from university, and some were people I was introduced to later. My own activities began in 2002. I was working alone at that time.

2. How many staff people does your studio have and what are their main working fields?

I have been working with a permanent assistant, Olivier Lebrun, for about two years, and since then also with one or two trainees. Each person is a graphic designer and can work on every type of project under my artistic direction, even though each stage is conceived together through a constant dialogue.

3. How does a regular working day at your studio look like, how is the day structured?

I think there is a very good and relaxed atmosphere in the studio. We all are very focused and busy. But we take care not to get stressed and never work at night. We often listen to music and quite regulary finish our days with a small drink.

Commissariat de la plaine-saint-denis – wallpainting and signage – police station – 2006

FRATERNITÉ

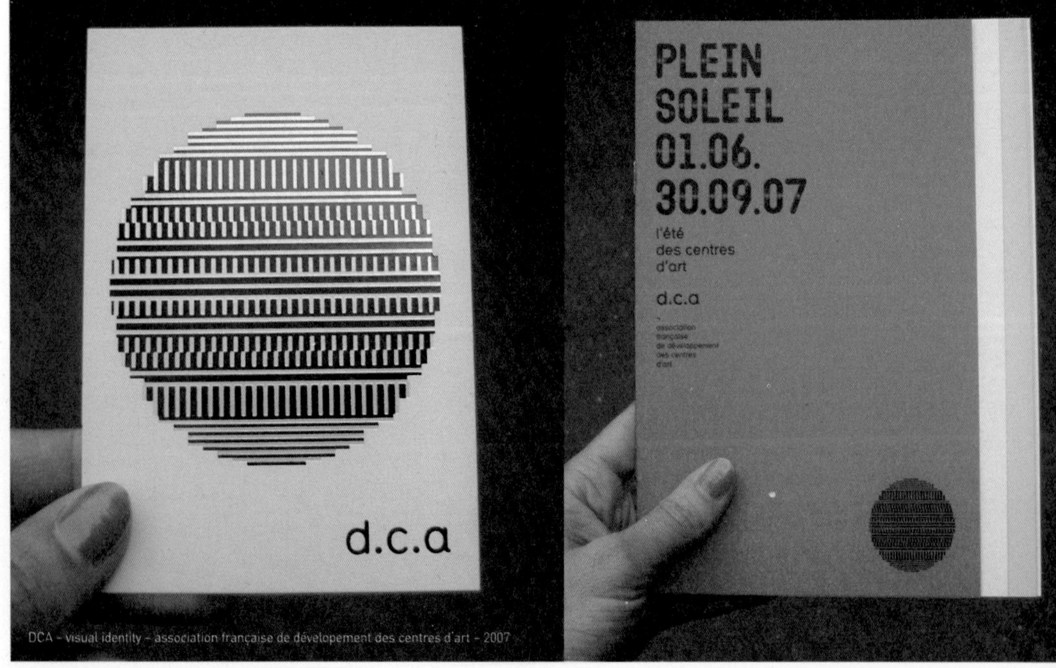

DCA – visual identity – association française de dévelopement des centres d'art – 2007

4. How much leisure time do you have during a year?

I'm generally working 50 hours a week, sometimes also on the weekend, and I take 2 or 3 weeks of holidays.

5. Which business areas do your clients mainly come from? Is the number of your clients increasing or rather declining?

The areas are in fact still the same as in the beginning (dance, design, contemporary art). But it is especially the field of contemporary art where my clients get more and more numerous. My activity is increasing year after year, in spite of the fact that I never really search new clients.

6. Do you have a specific corporate philosophy or maybe a mission statement like other companies, which is reflected in the way you steer the studio's course?

My philosophy is to produce for each subject things with maximal artistic ambition, aptness, significance, and a distinctive nature. For that purpose, I have the habit of long discussions on the project with the client in order to define or specify the most relevant answer. I always present only one proposal, the one I'm convinced of to be the best. Later, this proposal can be discussed with the client and sometime evolve, of course.

7. What, from your point of view, makes the difference between a small studio and a big company?

8. What kind of advantages and disadvantages does a small studio have compared to a big company?

The modest structure of the studio allows for the greatest freedom in the choice of my clients, the tarification of my work (notably for very young artists or associations). My work can be as experimental as suitable, and I feel really independant of all dogmatic theories or ready-made recipes of communication and marketing.

HOAC, RN 305 (in collaboration with Stefan Shankland) – billboard – HOAC, RN 305

Air de Paris – catalogue, poster and signage – exhibition of contemporary art at centre Pompidou – 2007

9. What is your idea about the future of small studios?

I think small studios provide a strong inspiration for contemporary artists. Most of them are working in small studios they have developed with a few assistants – more and more with success. This practice is principally based on the research of quality, not on profit. To persist, I think a small studio must afirm an author position to mark out their production. I further think that, for graphic design, the freedom of this small structure can easily be compromised when it grows up to more than 4-5 persons. This can lead to a financial pressure pushing to accept projects you would not have taken for different reasons.

10. Please describe and elaborate on the goals or plans that you have for your studio for the next five years?

I don't want to increase my team above 2 permanent assistants, and would like to work with the same pleasure, to meet more and more artists, curators, publishers, because those collaborations are so enriching for each one of us.

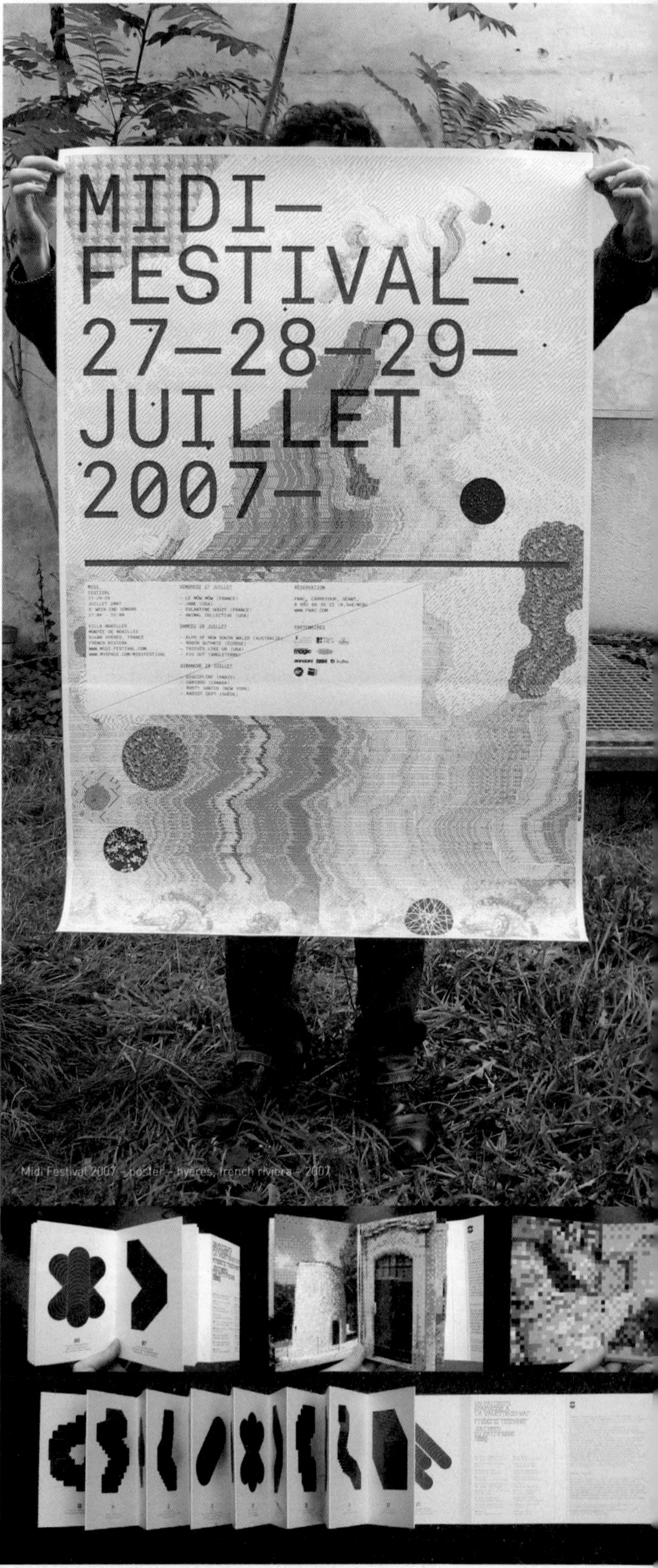

Midi Festival 2007 - poster - hyeres, french riviera - 2007

La Valette-du-Var - publication - journée des patrimoines at Valette-du-Var (France) - 2006

Frédéric Teschner studio - poster - studio - 2007

Timo Thurner

team:
Timo Thurner
contact:
Ateliergemeinschaft Gerwin Schmidt
Zenettistrasse 27 rgb
80337 Munich
Germany
T + 49 89 74689494
F + 49 89 74689495
hello@timothurner.com
www.timothurner.com

Timo Thurner was born 1976 in Traunstein, Bavaria. He studied visual communication in Paris, Melbourne, and Vorarlberg. Today, he lives and works in Munich as an independent graphic designer, being part of the Ateliergemeinschaft Gerwin Schmidt.

Logo – logodesign – Steiner kino festival – 2005

end of a journey – poster – mosaikfilm – 2005

Interview with Timo Thurner

1. What led to the formation of your studio?

During my studies at the FH Vorarlberg in Austria I met Gerwin Schmidt in a workshop. After an internship and my graduation, I continued to work with him. Later, Philipp von Keisenberg joined the studio. Over the last years it became clear that all three of us wanted to create an "Ateliergemeinschaft" where we could do projects together but also continue to work on our individual projects. At this point, we all have our own clients but do a lot of studio projects together as well.

2. How many staff people does your studio have and what are their main working fields?

We are three people in the Ateliergemeinschaft Gerwin Schmidt. We are all graphic designers working mainly in print design. The clients we are working for on joint projects mainly come from the cultural and corporate area. My main working field is corporate design, poster design and type design for film, nightlife, restaurants, and start-up clients.

3. How does a regular working day at your studio look like, how is the day structured?

A regular day begins around 9.30 a.m.. The structure of the day depends very much on the current projects. Normally, it is a mix of writing emails, talking on the phone, meeting clients, and working on the computer.

4. How much leisure time do you have during a year?

In one year, I have around 3 weeks of vacations, some weekend trips, and a few single days off during the week. I try not to work too much on weekends, but still I spent a lot of them in the office.

5. Which business areas do your clients mainly come from? Is the number of your clients increasing or rather declining?

Clients mainly come from the fields of film, nightlife/restaurants and start-up companies, but fortunately, there are also always new clients from very different areas such as photographers, lawyers, fashion designers, etc.

6. Do you have a specific corporate philosophy or maybe a mission statement like other companies, which is reflected in the way you steer the studio's course?

Something like a mission statement would be not to focus on a specific business area for the clients to come from, but to work for people from all kinds of areas, and try to understand their work and needs.

Thank you very much – poster – mars GmbH – 2007

Bombed out – poster – theater Erlangen – 2005

HEY LUIGI

spRing SumMer 2007

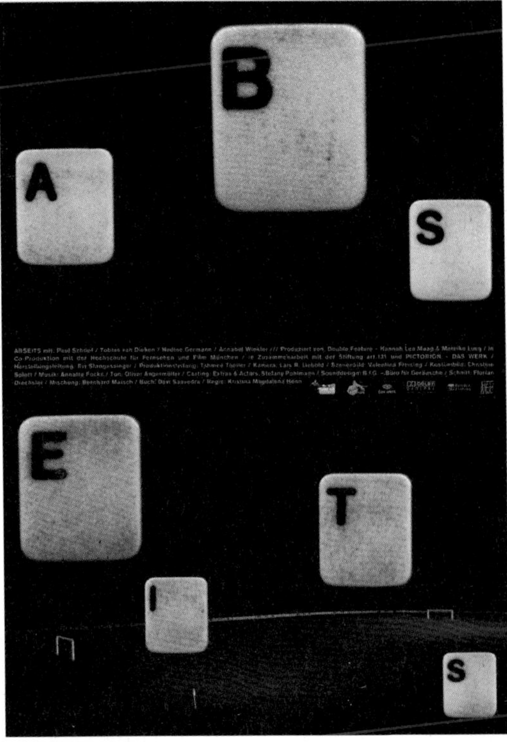

Hey Luigi spring summer 07 – poster – mars gmbh – 2007

Apart – poster – double feature – 2006

Mr. Zhu – poster –pellefilm – 2004

Open your mouth here comes the spoon – poster – baby entertainment gmbh – 2007

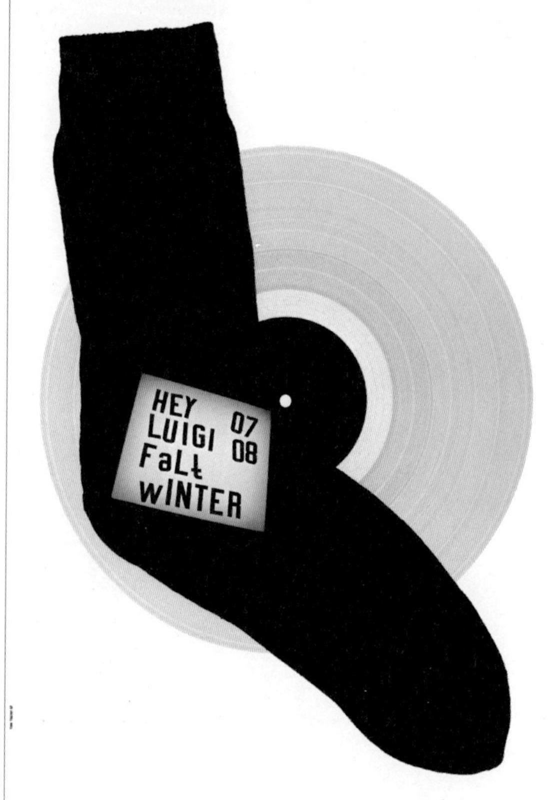

Hey Luigi fall winter 07 08 – poster – mars gmbh – 2007

A B C D a b c d
E F G H e f g h
I J K L i j k l
M N O P m n o p
Q R S T q r s t
U V W X u v w x
Y Z y z

Corporate font – font – mars gmbh – 2006

7. What, from your point of view, makes the difference between a small studio and a big company?

8. What kind of advantages and disadvantages does a small studio have compared to a big company?

I think the difference between a small studio and a big company lies mainly in the diversity of the work you do as a graphic designer. This can be the big advantage of the small studio. Here you are responsible for the whole process: getting clients, talking to clients, making concepts, doing layouts, doing presentations, talking and going to printers, keep the computers running, thinking about the studio, negotiating about money. All of that keeps the work as a designer interesting in my view. On the other hand, this can also be a disadvatage, because these tasks all take a lot of time, which might limit your "graphic-design-time".

sendsor
telemetric
personal
health
monitoring

Logo – logo design – sendsor telemetric personal health monitoring – 2004

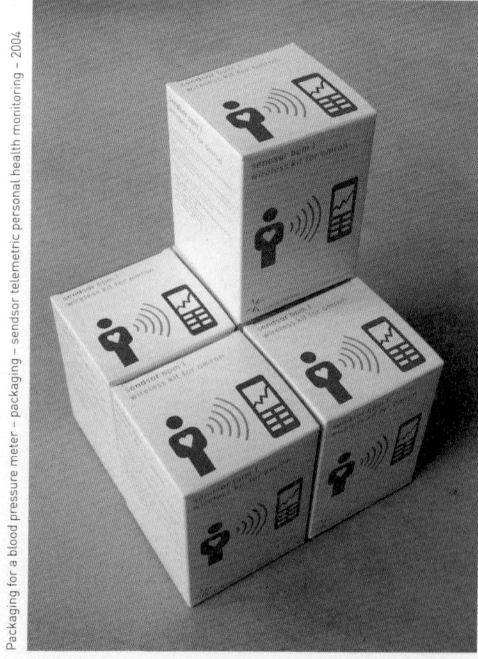

Packaging for a blood pressure meter – packaging – sendsor telemetric personal health monitoring – 2004

Party flyer – flyer – mojadeep – 2000-2002

PINGPONG

Pingpong logo – logodesign – pingpong production – 2004

9. What is your idea about the future of small studios? Do you think that small studios do not have any other choice but to expand in order to survive in these times of globalization?

I think that small studios will always have their place in our world. Like in all business areas there will be a few huge global companies and a lot of small companies. To expand to a certain extent might be necessary for most studios to earn a living. But I think good quality and good networks will secure the place of small studios in the future.

10. Please describe and elaborate on the goals or plans that you have for your studio for the next five years?

In the near future it is important for us to stabilize our concept of the "Ateliergemeinschaft". That means, it is important to have enough different clients, to expand a little bit, and to keep on learning. It's all about finding the right balance between money, office projects and personal work.

Rubybar logotype – flyer – mars gmbh – 2005

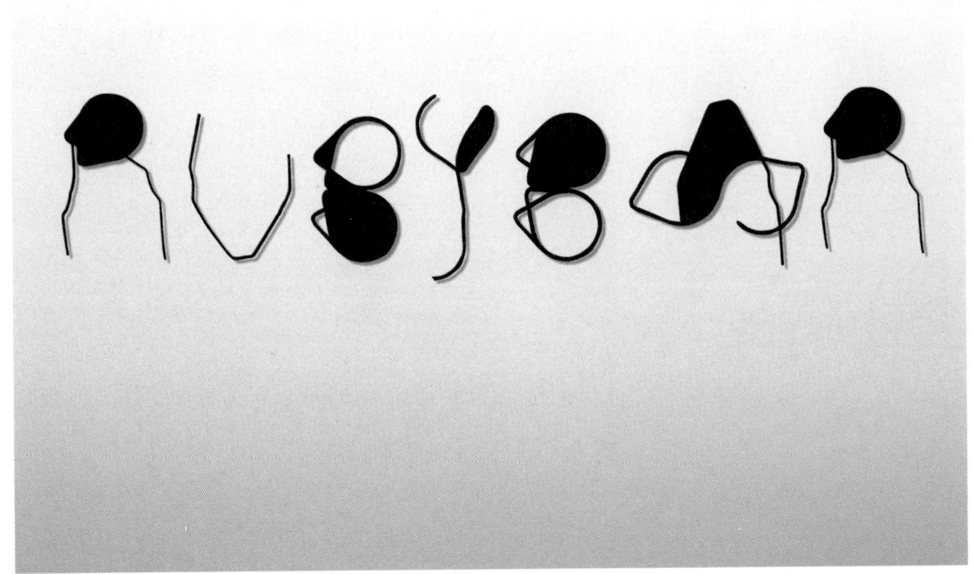

tin & ed

team:
Tin Nguyen
Ed Cutting
contact:
Level 8, Room 15
37 Swanston Street
Melbourne, Victoria
Australia 3000
T + 61 3 96713777
design@tinanded.com.an
www.tinanded.com.au

tin & ed officially took their positions on either side of the ampersand and became a studio on the 7th of August 2004. They remember the exact date because it was simultaneously the day they graduated from university and were offered their first major job. Previous to this time, Tin Nguyen and Ed Cutting were just two guys that were occasionally seen apart (although not very often). They met at Swinburne University of Technology in 2001, when they both volunteered to design a magazine about punk rock. When you meet them, it might seem to be kind of funny. Since they have both developed so incredible powers of intuition, it allows them to communicate without speaking to each other.

Interview with tin & ed

1. What led to the formation of your studio?

tin & ed formed in 2004. We had both completed a bachelor in visual communication at the the National School for Design at Swinburne University. We had worked together throughout university for a variety of clients, and when we left we won a big job to design the identity for an arts festival called Next Wave. This way the studio started, it was our first big job, and we worked for them for the next six months. Through this we were introduced to the art and design community of Melbourne, which helped us to get established as a studio, and the work just flew in from there. So, in many ways we became a studio by accident, pushed by the mere fact that we were being offered funny and interesting work. We didn't plan to start a studio when we finished university, it sort of just happened.

2. How many staff people does your studio have and what are their main working fields?

There are two people in our studio (Tin Nguyen and Edward Cutting). The studio had expanded to as many as 5 at some time, but we like to keep it small. Our process is very democratic, very collaborative. We work on almost all projects together from beginning to end, a symbiotic relationship, it is how we have always worked. We are quite different people, we have different ideas, different ways of seeing things. This really helps to balance out our work.

3. How does a regular working day at your studio look like, how is the day structured?

We are very unstructured, and we are quite relaxed on working days. We don't have a starting or ending time but usually work for around 8 hours a day though. Sometimes we start early and finish early, sometimes we start later and finish later. We allow ourselves breaks when we need to. It is not a traditional working environment, and we try and have as much fun as possible.

4. How much leisure time do you have during a year?

It has changed a lot. When we started, we had no leisure time at all, we worked day and night, weekdays and weekends. We worked really hard and maybe took a week off per year. Now that we are more established, we have a lot more time for play, we have weekends and holidays. Last year we took 3 months off and traveled for 2 months. Hopefully, we can do the same this year, it's very important to give yourself time off, to refresh and get inspired.

MINI International Melbourne issue – mixed media – MINI international – 2007

A-trak poster – poster – opulent & penny drop for atrak – 2007

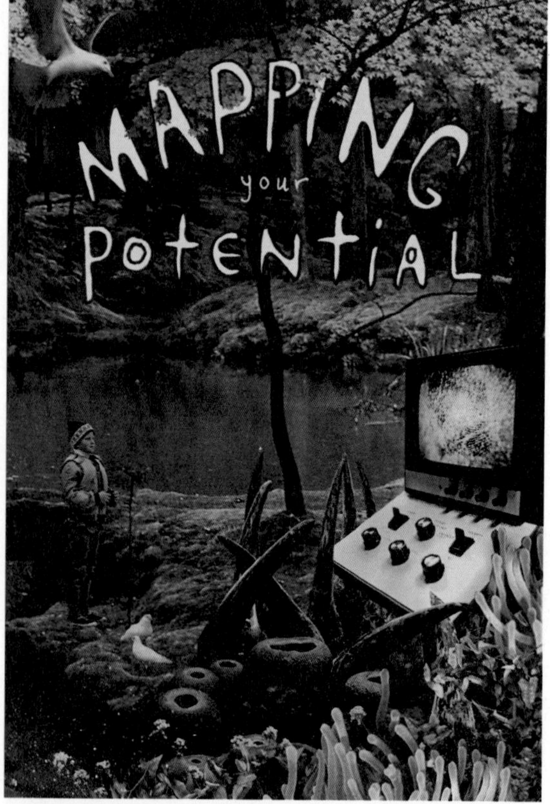

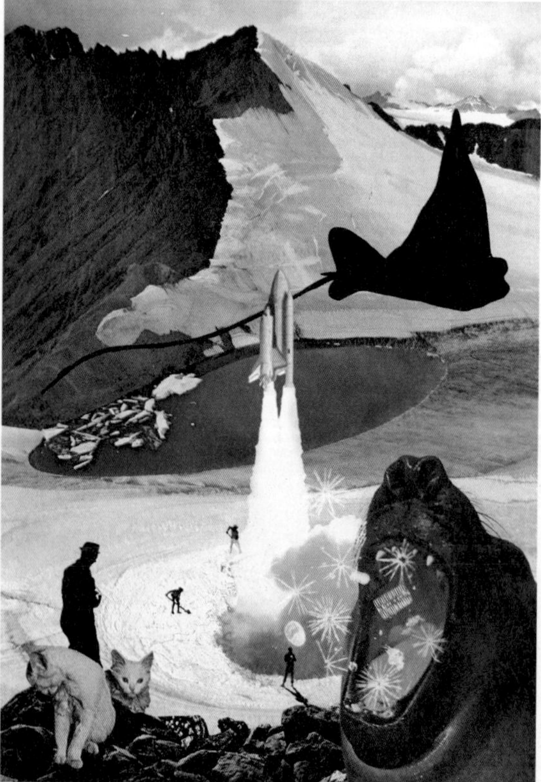

5. Which business areas do your clients mainly come from?

Most of our clients are from the cultural field, art, design, architecture, music. At the moment, we're working for the Australian Ballet and the Melbourne International design festival. Our clients are very varied though, some are very large, some are really small, we like that variety. We work for large advertising agencies like Publicis, we do album artwork for small bands. It's quite a mix, but we try to work with people who are open to new ideas, who want to have fun with a project.

Is the number of your clients increasing or rather declining?

We have always had a very stable amount of clients, we have always been quite busy, we've been very lucky in that way. We are lucky to be working with larger budgets now, but we still enjoy the smaller jobs too.

6. Do you have a specific corporate philosophy or maybe a mission statement like other companies, which is reflected in the way you steer the studio's course?

Our mission is to only take on jobs that we know we can enjoy, we can experiment and learn from, we are quite selective about who we will work for. The client is vitally important in the success of the work. We try to work with people who are open to ideas, open to new ways of doing things, collaboration is very important to us, and also trust, there has be trust on both sides. We try to work with people who are smarter then we are, people we can learn from.

7. What, from your point of view, makes the difference between a small studio and a big company?

I guess size is a very obvious one. There is a different mentality between a larger studio and a smaller one. I think there is more freedom in smaller studios. Obviously a larger studio produces a lot more work, smaller studios are more personal to work with though, a more intimate working relationship with the client.

8. What kind of advantages and disadvantages does a small studio have compared to a big company?

Smaller studios are more flexible. It allows us to do what we want to do, a lot more freedom. Larger studios can sometimes be a bit of a machine, but larger studios can handle much larger jobs, work on bigger projects. Our partnership has no hierarchy, people are often more equal in smaller studios, everyone's voice gets heard. The working process is more personal and intimate.

Mapping your potential – spreads – royal children's hospital – 2006

a is for anything goes – illustration – crumpler – 2007

MADC awards annual – book design, photography – Melbourne advertising and design club (MADC) – 2004

Crumpler catalogue – diorama, photography – crumpler – 2005

9. What is your idea about the future of small studios? Do you think that small studios do not have any other choice but to expand in order to survive in these times of globalization?

Not at all. With the internet, it doesn't matter how large or small, how new or established your studio is, it's about the work. In many ways we believe that smaller studios are more important now then ever. Anyone can start a studio out of their bedrooms, have a website and start working for clients on projects on the other side of the world. Smaller studios have the opportunity to create work that is more immediate, we don't like design by committee, this is less of a problem for a smaller studio. It is very hard to stay small though, its quite easy to expand, work comes in and you employ people to fill the jobs and before you know it you are running a large studio, you're no longer doing what you love, which is designing. We are very hands on with our work, we want to get our hands dirty, we don't want to stand back and direct, we want to create the work. For all this we need to remain small.

10. Please describe and elaborate on the goals or plans that you have for your studio for the next five years?

We want to work for more overseas clients, which it is becoming easier and easier to do. We plan to move to New York or Berlin next year. We want to continue working for cultural clients. We would like to collaborate more, to do more video clips, to work in film, to self-publish – the future is bright. We have no plans for expanding.

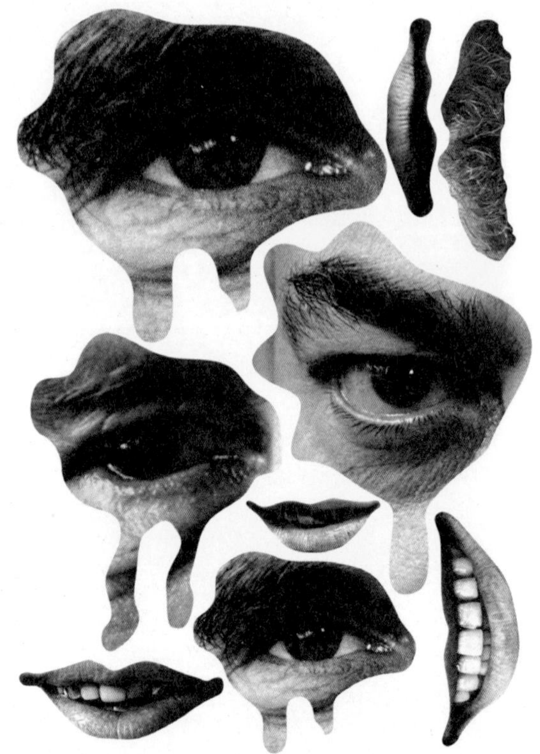

Crumpler catalogue – diorama, photography – crumpler – 2005

Private eyes – collage – self published – 2008

Next wave festival poster (unpopular culture) – pen drawing – next wave festival – 2004

Herman van Bostelen

team:
Herman van Bostelen
contact:
Breedstr. 9A
3512 TS Utrecht
The Netherlands
T + 31 30 2231424
info@hermanvanbostelen.nl
www.hermanvanbostelen.nl

Herman van Bostelen studied graphic design at the Utrecht School of the Arts. After his graduation in January 1996, he became an independent graphic designer working at his own small studio. Besides this work, he has been teaching typography and graphic design at the Utrecht School of the Arts (2001-2007), and was a member of the school's Gallery Committee (2005-2007). He is a current jury member and the chairman at the Art Directors Club Nederland/Graphic Design (2008), and writes about typography and graphic design.

CBKU – typeface/house style – CBKU – 2007

Interview with Herman van Bostelen

1. What led to the formation of your studio?

Most of my teachers at the Utrecht School of the Arts worked as independent graphic designers or had small studios. They set an example for us. Together with other students (e.g. Richard van der Laken and Pepijn Zurburg of the Designpolitie and Martijn Engelbregt of EGBG) I took up small assignments to compile a professional portfolio. By the time I was graduating, I had enough work to start my own studio. The little experience I had gained working for other designers or studios (mostly internships) convinced me that both artistically and financially I would be better off working by myself.

2. How many staff people does your studio have and what are their main working fields?

One, it's just me doing everything.

3. How does a regular working day at your studio look like, how is the day structured?

There's no real structure. The way I organize my work depends on deadlines, meetings and business in general. That means that often I'm working evenings and weekends. Since I have my studio at home, my personal and my professional life intertwine completely.

4. How much leisure time do you have during a year?

Not much. I try to get away for a few weeks during the year, sometimes in combination with a project I'm working on. Last month (March 2008), I spend a few days in Berlin with students from the Utrecht School of the Arts, where I have been teaching for the last seven years. The days were reserved for visiting exhibitions and design studios, the nighttime for leisure.

5. Which business areas do your clients mainly come from? Is the number of your clients increasing or rather declining?

Most of my clients are cultural organizations and publishers. When I was student, I was a volunteer at a small theater in Utrecht. I'm still working for the people I met in that period of time, or as I would rather put it, I'm still working with them. Until now the number of my clients is still increasing.

De snijzaal (the dissection room) – poster – 't barre land – 2007

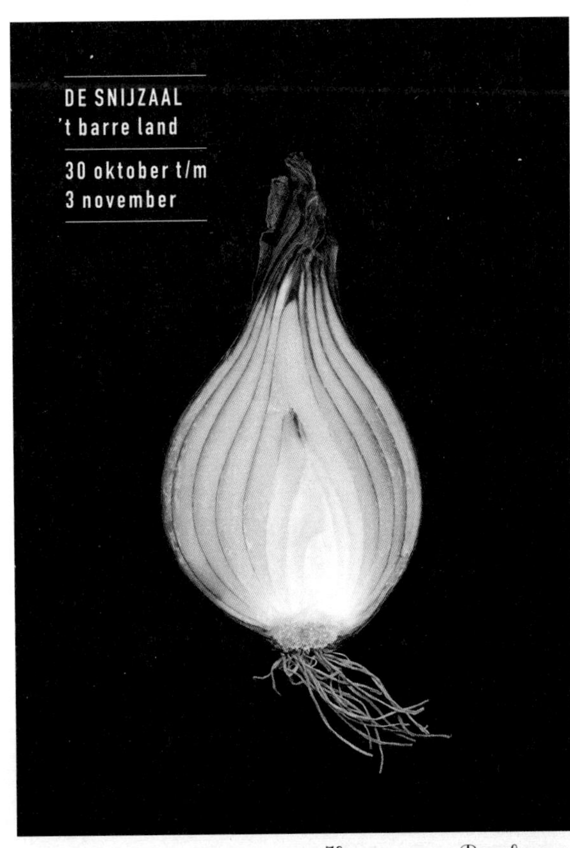

6. Do you have a specific corporate philosophy or maybe a mission statement like other companies, which is reflected in the way you steer the studio's course?

Although it is not possible, I try to work on each project as if it was the first project I'm working on. I depend very much on the information that a client is giving me and always search for a way to focus on the objectives of that client and the specific assignment. To come to quality, it's important for me to get to know the people and material I'm working with as good as I possibly can.

7. What, from your point of view, makes the difference between a small studio and a big company?

I think for a big company it's almost impossible to work in the way described above. Big companies often work for other big companies or organizations, which means that people have to direct other people on the contents and objectives of a project. By doing so, much of the information that I find important to a project gets lost. In my opinion big companies are able to work in a way that's more professional, but less personal.

8. What kind of advantages and disadvantages does a small studio have compared to a big company?

Small studios are often more innovative, more flexible and creatively distinctive than big companies. Big companies have to focus on income in order to pay for employees and facilities, but are also capacitated to work on projects of a much larger scale.

9. What is your idea about the future of small studios? Do you think that small studios do not have any other choice but to expand in order to survive in these times of globalization?

I don't think that globalization makes it harder for small studios to survive or that there is need for expanding. Big companies always create niches for small companies, because they cannot fulfill all economical, artistical and social needs. Globalization will lead to the expanding of companies, but will also create room for new small studios – maybe even more than before, because it also leads to a decrease in the costs of production.

10. Please describe and elaborate on the goals or plans that you have for your studio for the next five years?

In the next five years, I want to try to find a way to be more selective with regard to the projects I'm working on, and to find more room for my own initiatives.

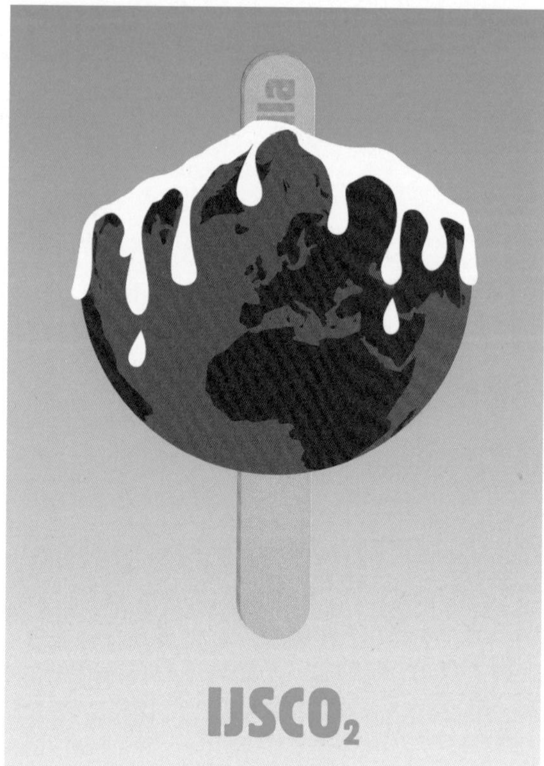

Gorilla – column – de volkskrant – 2007

gorilla – column – de volkskrant – 2007

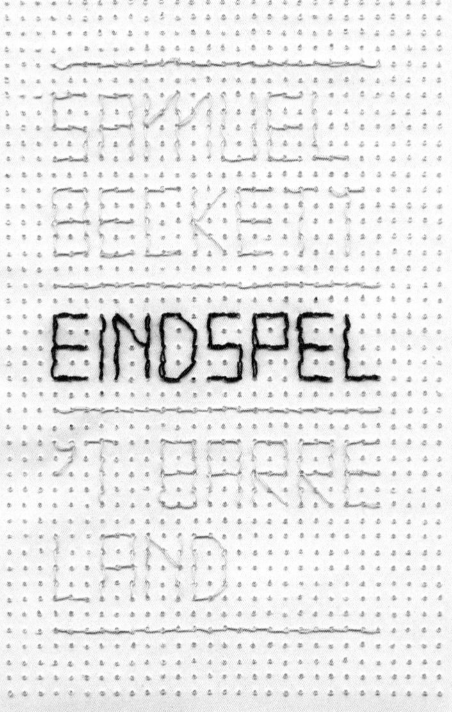

DAGELIJKS TOENEMEND LACHSUCCES

't Barre Land en De Onderneming } **brengen samen**

twee komedies van OSCAR **WILDE**

schitterend gemonteerd

De ideale ernst of het belang van een echtgenoot } *triviale komedie voor serieuze mensen*

met voorspel · *Een Florentijnse Tragedie*

vertaald, gerepeteerd, uitgevoerd, gekostumeerd en gedecoreerd door De Onderneming en 't Barre Land

VERRASSEND ALS HET LEVEN ZELF!

19 MAART T/M 17 MEI

IN DIVERSE STEDEN IN VERSCHILLENDE THEATERS

AANVANG 20U30 — PAUZE MET DRANKBUFFET 22U00 — EINDE 23U30 45?

BEKENDE PRIJZEN — KORTINGEN GELDIG — ZITPLAATS GEGARANDEERD — KLEDING GEWENST DOCH NIET VERPLICHT

Eindspel - poster - 't barre land - 2004

Klipdrift - bookcover -nieuw Amsterdam publishers - 2007

Focus - bookcover - nieuw Amsterdam publishers - 2006

WHL - poster - Utrecht school of the arts - 2002

Afscheidssymposium **21 juni 02**
Willem Henri Lucas 10u00

W H
L '

Lezingen van
Martijn Engelbregt
Ingmar Heytze
Loesje
Willem Henri Lucas

Hogeschool voor de Kunsten Utrecht
Faculteit Beeldende Kunst en Vormgeving

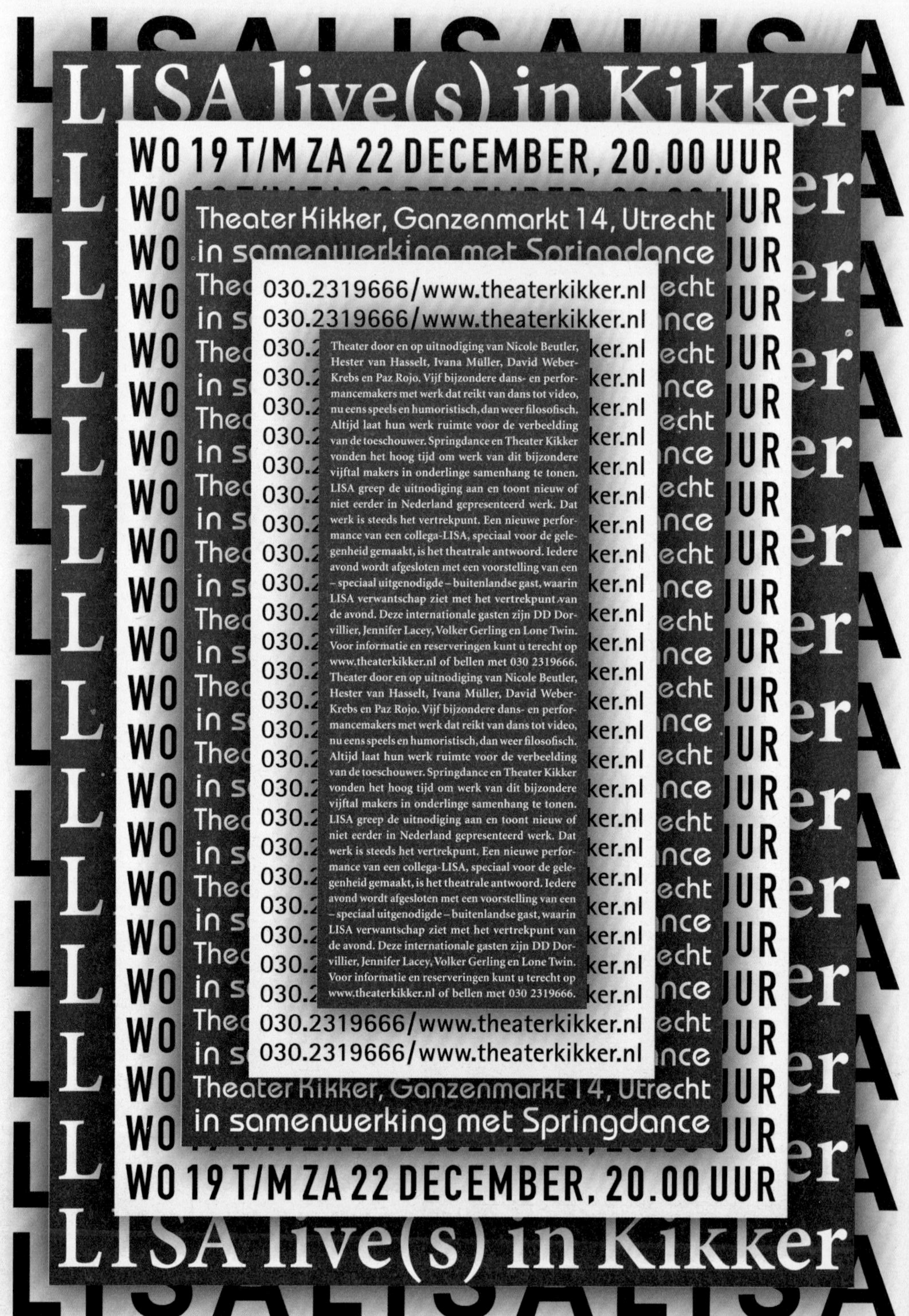

LISA – poster – theater kikker – 2007

van Georges Perec

Een brommertje met verchroomd stuur? Nee, absoluut niet. Hij had de legertrucks gezien, Pollak, met zijn eigen ogen had hij de fraaie legertrucks gezien die wachtten om geladen te worden en het hele stelletje naar het station te rijden.

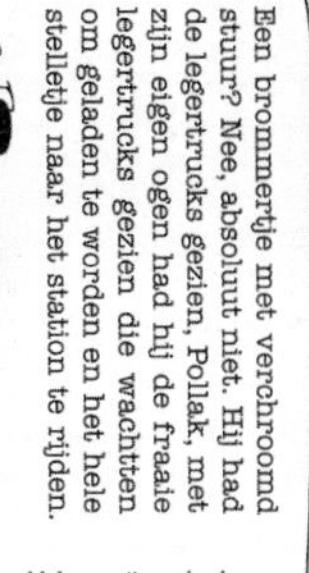

zacht

We hadden eerlijk gezegd lak aan zijn verhaal over een vent die vermankt wilde worden om Algerije te ontlopen en in de armen te blijven van het meisje waar hij smoorverliefd op was, totdat ondertussen de vrede zou worden getekend.
Maar omdat we enerzijds onze grote vriend Pollak Henri niet wilden teleurstellen en hij ons anderzijds heel vriendelijk had gevraagd na te denken en omdat zoals iedereen weet denken en leven hetzelfde is, sloegen we flink aan het piekeren.

BROMMERTJE MET VERCHROOMD STUUR ACHTER OP DE BINNENPLAATS?

WAT 'T VOOR

oulipo

'Ouwe jongen, we hebben erover nagedacht, over je geval. Het is bepaald niet leuk. Toch moeten we geen domme dingen doen. We zouden je arm best voorzichtig willen breken, maar dat is hartstikke gevaarlijk begrijp je, met die prik voel je niks en lopen we het risico je gewrichten te vernielen, je gewrichtskapsels kapot te maken, de gewrichtsbanden en pezen in je gewrichten te mollen. En verder ouwe jongen moet je niet denken dat die legerartsen achterlijk zijn snap je. Die neem je niet zo gauw in de maling. Je moet niet denken dat we achterlijk zijn zullen de legerartsen zeggen en dan zul je uiteindelijk toch moeten gaan vechten met zwachtel en al en een schop voor je achterste en als klap op de vuurpijl negentig dagen cel als het al geen krijgsraad wordt of kamp Foum Tatsouine of iets dergelijks, en wij de kastanjes eenmaal uit het vuur, wij hebben nog jarenlang de politie achter onze kont aan, snap je? Maar laten we vooral niet in paniek raken.

Teken de ontbrekende pijltjes !

Toen diezelfde ochtend onze allerbeste vriend Pollak Henri, wachtmeester, nog niet helemaal bijgekomen van de nachtelijke emoties en hartstikke misselijk van de vier verschillende soorten drank die hij zo onvoorzichtig was geweest door elkaar te drinken, melancholisch zijn karretje met opengewerkte pedalen had bestegen, het Montparnasse van zijn geboorte had verlaten, waar zijn verloofde, zijn bruidskamer, zijn bruidsjonkers en zijn huwelijksgeschenken hun permanente verblijf hadden, slaapdronken door de poorten van het Port Neuf was gegaan, de wacht en heel de ratsplan had gegroet, wat had hij, Pollak Henri toen gezien op de binnenplaats van de kazerne?

Het was een vent die Karamanlis heette of zoiets. Karawo? Karawasch? Karawiel? Affijn Karadinges. In elk geval een weinig alledaagse naam, een naam die je iets zei, die je niet makkelijk vergat. Hij zou heel goed een Armeense schilder van de Parijse school kunnen zijn, of een Bulgaarse worstelaar, een grote peer uit Macedonië, iemand uit die streken, een Balkanees, een Yoghurteter, een Slavofiel, een Turk. Maar voorlopig was hij dus militair, soldaat tweede klas bij een bevoorradingscompartiment gestationeerd in Vincennes. En een van zijn vrienden was een goede maat van ons, Henri Pollak zichzelf.

denk aan uw hoofd

Die arme Karalax! Hij dacht nog wel dat hij in de armen zou blijven van het meisje waar hij smoorverliefd op was en dat hij nooit de roestige bergtoppen op zou hoeven en warempel nu zat hij misschien wel in die trein, heel zielig en alleen. We dachten aan de oorlog daarginds, in de zon: het zand, de stenen en de ruïnes, het koude ontwaken in een tent, de geforceerde marsen, de gevechten van tien man tegen één, kortom, de oorlog. Oorlog is niet wat je noemt leuk, echt niet. Eerlijk waar, we hadden het liefst willen janken. En toen zeiden we zo van: 'We moeten toch maar eens gaan kijken.'

't Barre Land

Die Karadinges was een knappe soldaat, gekleed in een kaki tuniek met dito tressen, de pet kranig schuin op zijn bol en met grote bespijkerde strontstappers die krasten op ons vers in de was gezette parket. We maakten een plaatsje voor hem vrij en hij voelde de hartelijke blikken van de hele groep op zich rusten.

Vu-Huu Toan

team:
Vu-Huu Toan
contact:
17, boulevard de la Villette
75010 Paris, France
T + 33 9 53051610
M + 33 6 24170927
www.toanvuhuu.com
me@toanvuhuu.com

Vu-Huu Toan – Born and raised in Germany, where he graduated in visual communications, Vu-Huu Toan worked for five years at the design studio Intégral Ruedi Baur and Associates in Paris, specializing in the creation of visual identities and signage systems. At Intégral, Toan won several pitches and was in charge of high-profile projects, such as the Cologne Bonn Airport, La Cinémathèque Française and La Cité Internationale de Lyon. Aside from working on institutional projects, Toan Vu-Huu always kept his passion for music and designed album covers for different labels in England and Germany. In 2005, he opened his own design studio and also became a teacher at the École Supérieure d'Art et Design in Amiens, specialized in typography. To create and set up visual identities that are unique and perfectly tailored to clients is Toan's most important objective.

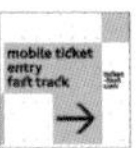

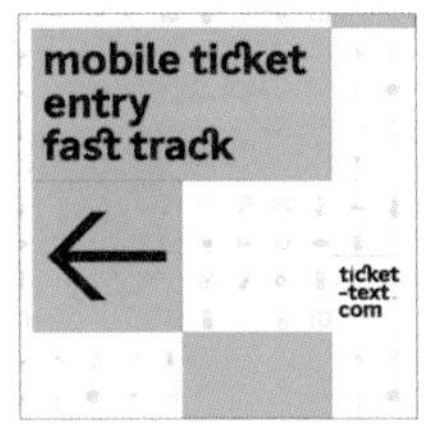

Ticket-text.com – signage/business card – ticket-text.com – 2007

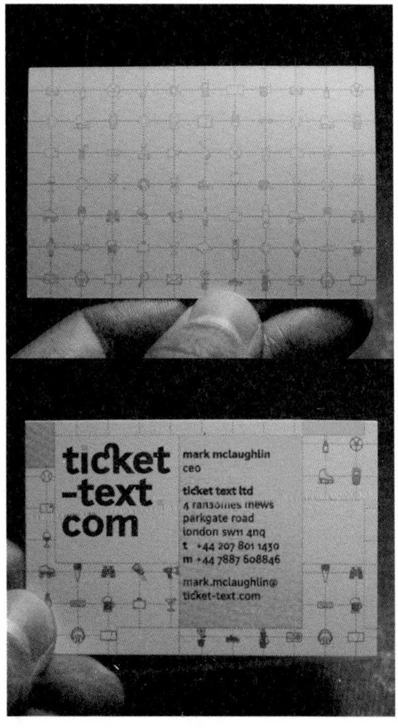

Interview with Vu-Huu Toan

1. What led to the formation of your studio?

The need to propose my own vision and chose my own clients.

2. How many staff people does your studio have and what are their main working fields?

There is only me. If I need help I ask some colleagues and maybe reinforce a bit more with specialists in order to cover a large field from print to web. The main fields are visual identities and editorial design.

3. How does a regular working day at your studio look like, how is the day structured?

I'm an early bird with coffee spread over the whole day. In the morning, I organize my projects, answer emails, write letters, and do all my administrative stuff. My brain is so much more efficient on those things in the morning. When all those things are done, I choose some good music and start on doing designs. For lunch time, there has to be a good restaurant meal with my studio mate. When there are no meetings with clients, I continue doing designs till very late.

4. How much leisure time do you have during a year?

Not enough, but once a year I try to take a big break, maybe for about four weeks, to travel the world.

5. Which business areas do your clients mainly come from?

From cultural institutions, the private sectors, and from the music business.

Is the number of your clients increasing or rather declining?

Helas, increasing.

6. Do you have a specific corporate philosophy or maybe a mission statement like other companies, which is reflected in the way you steer the studio's course?

Being creative by keeping flexible thoughts.

Ticket-text.com – website – ticket-text.com – 2007

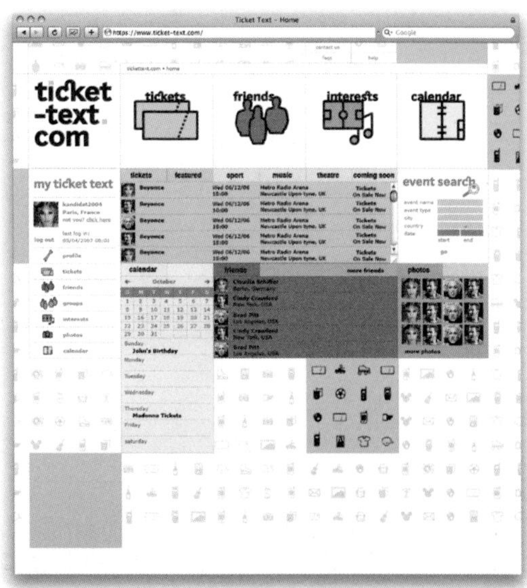

Iconofly #4 – magazine – iconofly – 2007

Magnum photo – invitation – la cinémathèque Française – 2006

7. What, from your point of view, makes the difference between a small studio and a big company?
A small studio is far more reactive.
8. What kind of advantages and disadvantages does a small studio have compared to a big company?
Advantage: A small studio is far more reactive. Disadvantage: The clients abuse your reactivity.
9. What is your idea about the future of small studios?
I think that the world needs small studios that are more unique and continuously re-invent themselves to compete in the market. It is about creating variety.
Do you think that small studios do not have any other choice but to expand in order to survive in these times of globalization?
I don't think so. The movement in music business has shown that with the liberation of communication structures on the internet, comes honor to small quality groups directly from the consumer. In times of globalization we find more and more of an opposite movement. Globalization needs individual movements and vice versa.
10. Please describe and elaborate on the goals or plans that you have for your studio for the next five years?
Stop trying to handle all jobs on my own, and stop being afraid of becoming a "bigger studio".

sniper – 12" cover – wordandsound – 2007

On air – lp cover – wordandsound – 2006

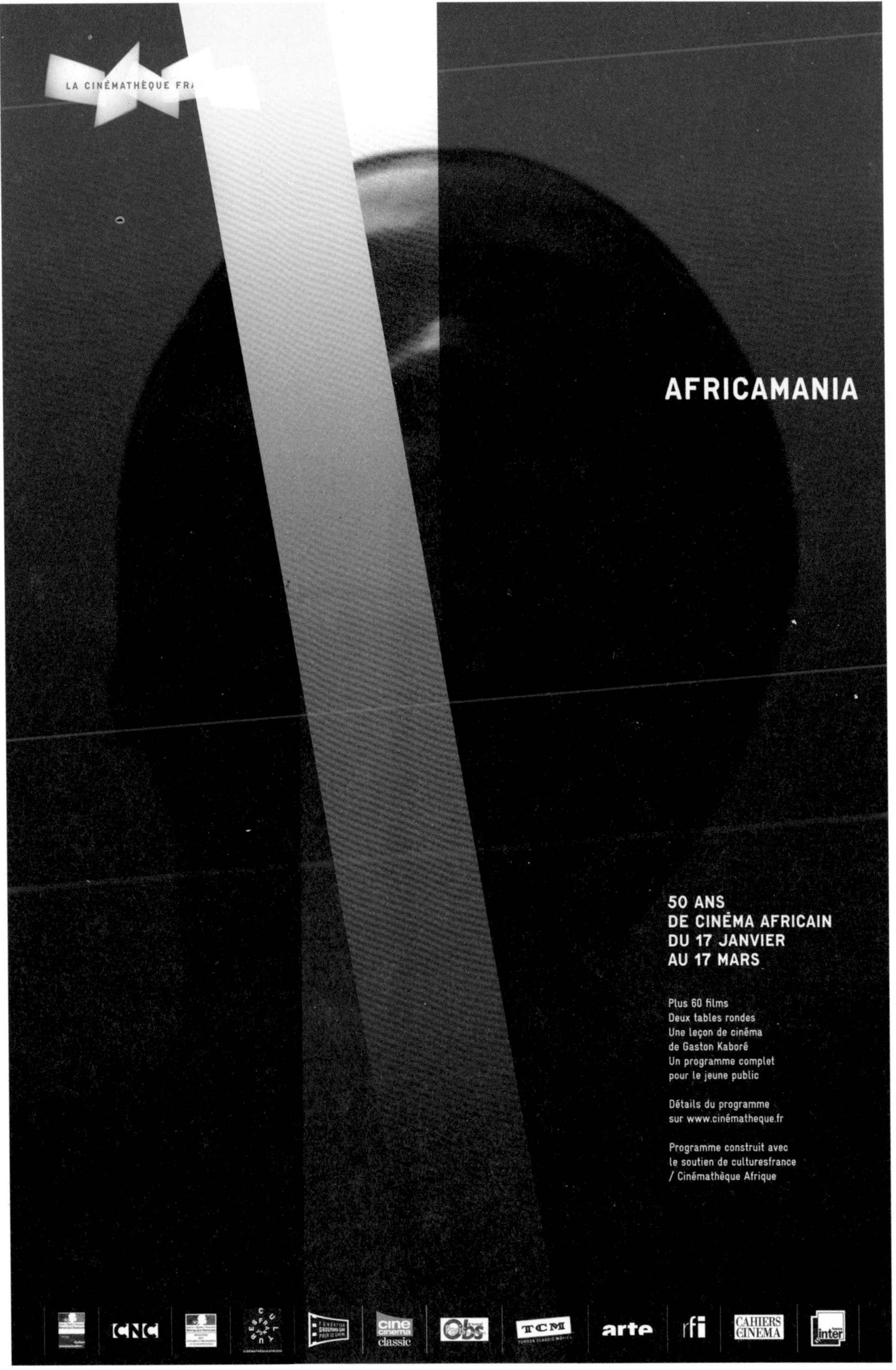

Africamania – poster – la cinémathèque Française – 2007

LA
CINÉMATHÈQUE
FRANÇAISE

AOÛT – SEPTEMBRE – OCTOBRE 2006

LES RENDEZ-VOUS CINÉMA

GEORGE CUKOR 23 AOÛT – 22 OCTOBRE
LA FÉMIS A 20 ANS 4 – 18 SEPTEMBRE
UNE INTRODUCTION AU CINÉMA THAÏLANDAIS 20 SEPTEMBRE – 2 OCTOBRE
JACQUES DOILLON (1ÈRE PARTIE) 4 – 23 OCTOBRE

www.cinematheque.fr
51, rue de Bercy
75012 Paris

Métro Bercy,
lignes 6 et 14
Bus n° 24, 62, 87

George Cukor – poster – la cinémathèque Française – 2006

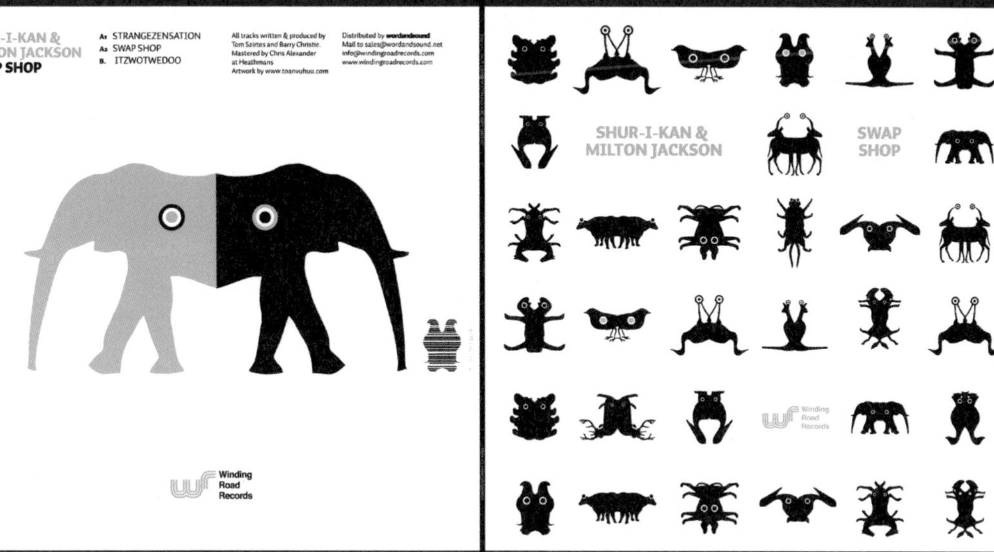

Swap shop – 12˝ cover – winding road records – 2007

George Cukor – poster – la cinémathèque française – 2006

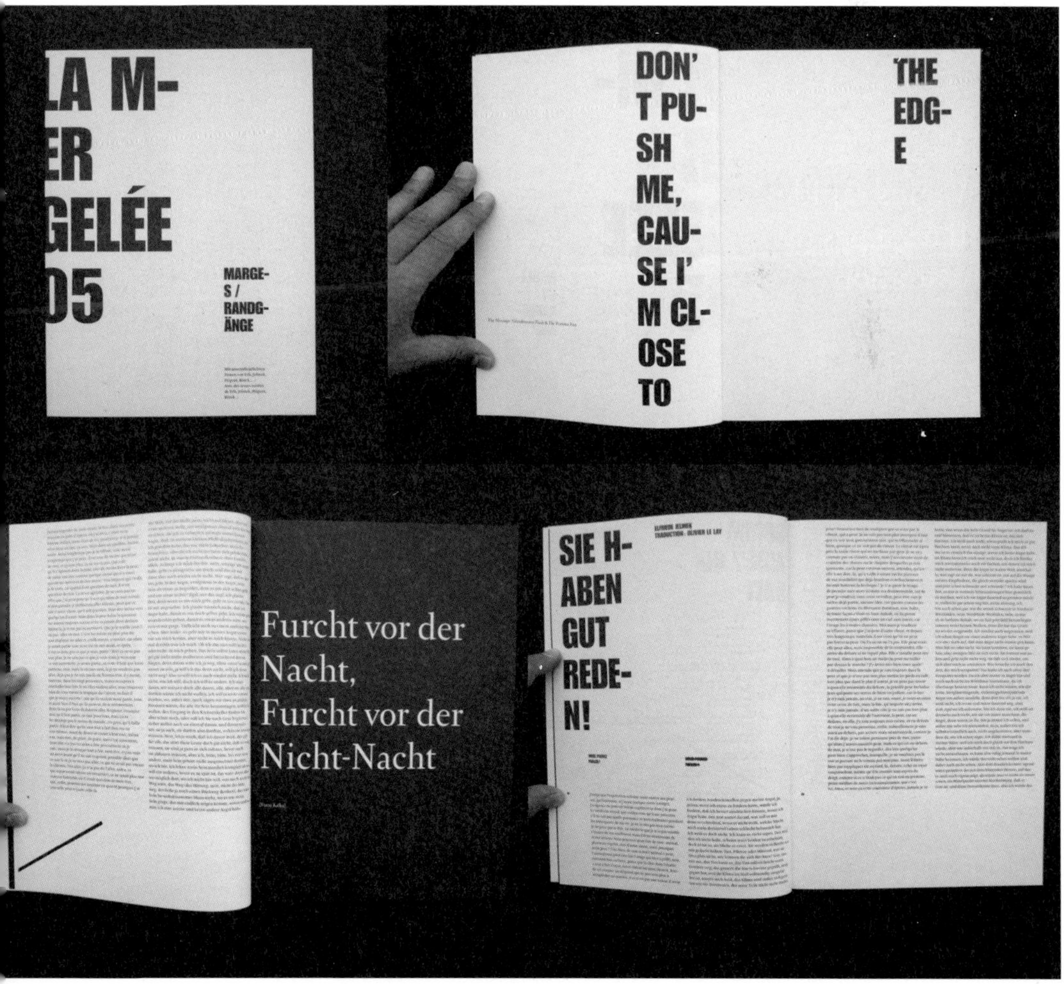

Annik Troxler first saw the light of day in Wolhusen, Switzerland, in 1979. She studied graphic design at the Cantonal School of Art of Lausanne (ECAL) and lives and works in Basel now. Her thesis "Vergissmeinnicht" was nominated for the Lucky Strike Design Award 2004, won among other things the Silver Award from Output'08 and the Swiss Federal Competition for Design 2005, which also gave her the opportunity to collaborate for six month with "Mevis & Van Deursen" in Amsterdam. Her posters were selected among the Type Directors Club, New York and Tokyo, Tehran Poster Biennale, International Poster Biennal Korea, Poster Biennale Brno, the Golden Bee Moskau, Chaumont Festival de l'Affiche, and 100 Best Posters of Germany, Switzerland and Austria. In 2004, Annik was also awarded a bronze prize in the group of poster promoting culture and art at the 19th Poster Biennale in Warsaw. In 2006, she won the Grand Prix of the International Poster Triennale of the Museum of Modern Art Toyama in Japan for her work "Intimities 2005".

Stedelijk museum bureau Amsterdam (at the studio Mevis & Van Deursen) – corporate identity – stedelijk museum bureau Amsterdam – 2006

Art book – book – comanicasino – 2006

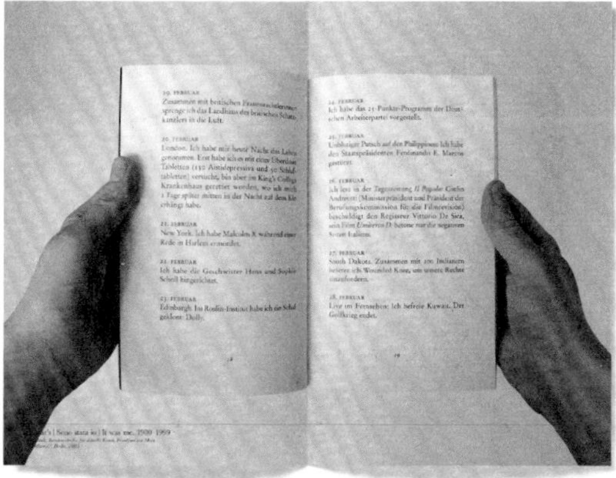

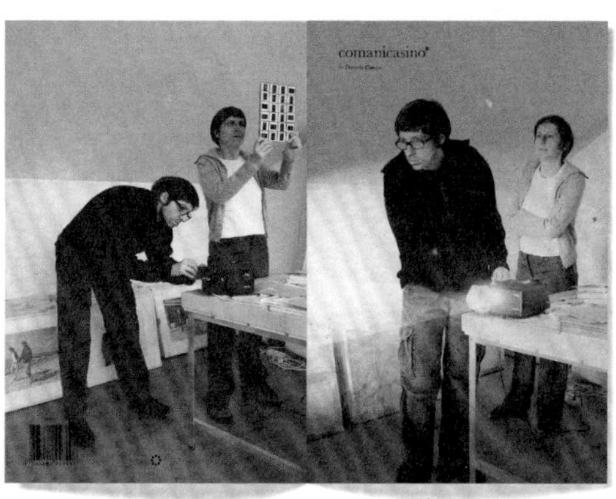

Interview with Annik Troxler

1. What led to the formation of your studio?

Nothing in particular. I just got some commissions and started to work on my own.

2. How many staff people does your studio have and what are their main working fields?

Just me – I do everything.

3. How does a regular working day at your studio look like, how is the day structured?

Since I have a little daughter, my independent work is not really structured anymore. Currently, I am working as an assistant at the Basel School of Design. At night and for one or two days a week, I have time to work on small projects.

4. How much leisure time do you have during a year?

I don't need any leisure time.

5. Which business areas do your clients mainly come from?

Mainly from the cultural field.

Is the number of your clients increasing or rather declining?

I don't know yet. But I am lucky that I always had as much work as I could do and as I wanted to have.

6. Do you have a specific corporate philosophy or maybe a mission statement like other companies, which is reflected in the way you steer the studio's course?

I always try to do something inventive, and I try to realize the best design solution for each challenge.

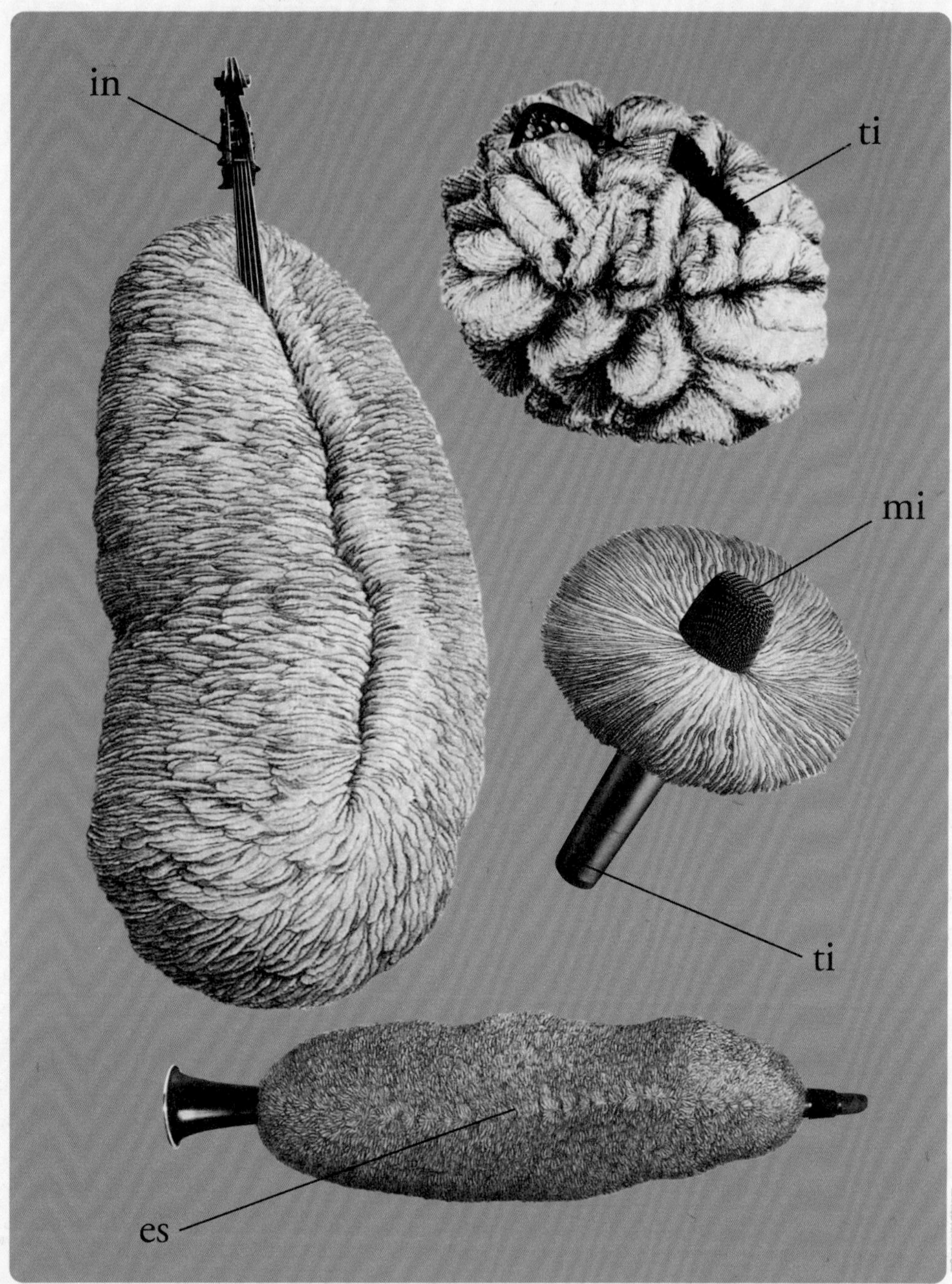

in
ti
mi
ti
es
intimities· jazz festival willisau 2005· stadtmühle
fr 1· sept· 18.00 uhr· erika stucky· suicidal yodels
sa 2· sept· 12.00 uhr· hans hassler· acc· cl
so 3· sept· 12.00 uhr· joëlle léandre· b· voice

Intimities 2005 – poster – jazz festival, series of concerts, stadtmühle Willisau – 2005

Fachhochschule Nordwestschweiz
Hochschule für Gestaltung und Kunst

Vortrag: Martin Woodtli / Mittwoch, 06. Juni / 17.00 / Aula
Hochschule für Gestaltung und Kunst / Vogelsangstrasse 15 / 4058 Basel
Eintritt frei / Veranstalter: FHNW/HGK Basel/Institut Visuelle Kommunikation
www.fhnw.ch/hgk/ivk

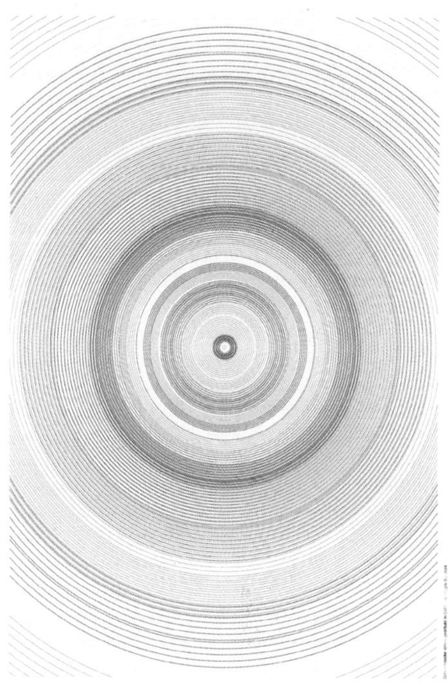

Lectures for designer – poster – FHNW HGK Basel – 2006-2007

Print-Test (at the studio Mevis & Van Deursen) – letterhead – print office, veenam in Rotterdam – 2006

Intimities 2003 – poster – jazz festival, series of concerts stadtmühle Willisau – 2003

Intimities 2004 – poster – jazz festival, series of concerts, stadtmühle Willisau – 2004

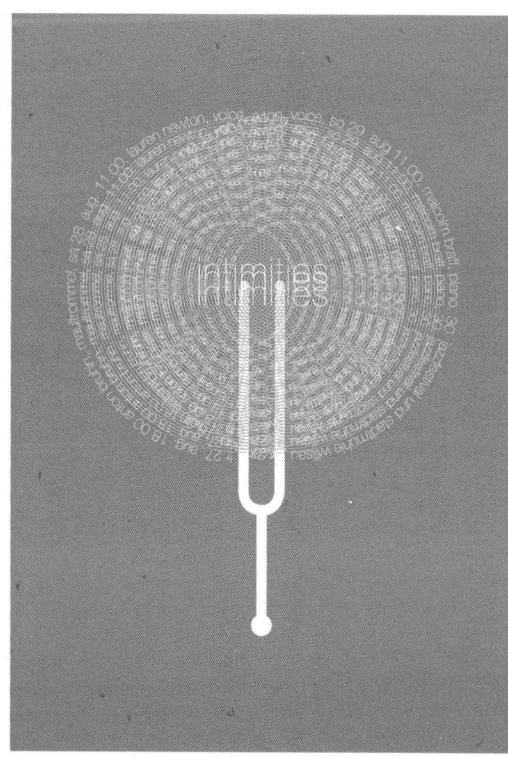

TIJDSCHRIFTEN MAKEN IS SAMENWERKEN

DESIGN IN NEDERLAND 1970-1980

avenue

AVENUE WORDT VIJF JAAR EEN "SLEEPING BEAUTY" GENOEMD

AVENUE IS TERUG. WAS AVENUE WEG DAN?

Avenue van a tot zero a retrospective of the magazine from 1965-2001 – book – Netherlands fotomuseum Rotterdam, veenman publishers Rotterdam – 2006

7. What, from your point of view, makes the difference between a small studio and a big company?

Small studios can act more creative, provocative and more self-determined.

8. What kind of advantages and disadvantages does a small studio have compared to a big company?

Advantages: More fun. Disadvantages: More stress.

9. What is your idea about the future of small studios?

It will be a big challenge for small studios to survive.

Do you think that small studios do not have any other choice but to expand in order to survive in these times of globalization?

I believe that small studios have to convince with highest quality.

10. Please describe and elaborate on the goals or plans that you have for your studio for the next five years?

When I will be able again to spend more time on graphic design, I'd like to collaborate with like minded people. Critical feedback and discussions on design are the conditions of my work.

Lectures for designer – poster – FHNW HGK Basel – 2006-07

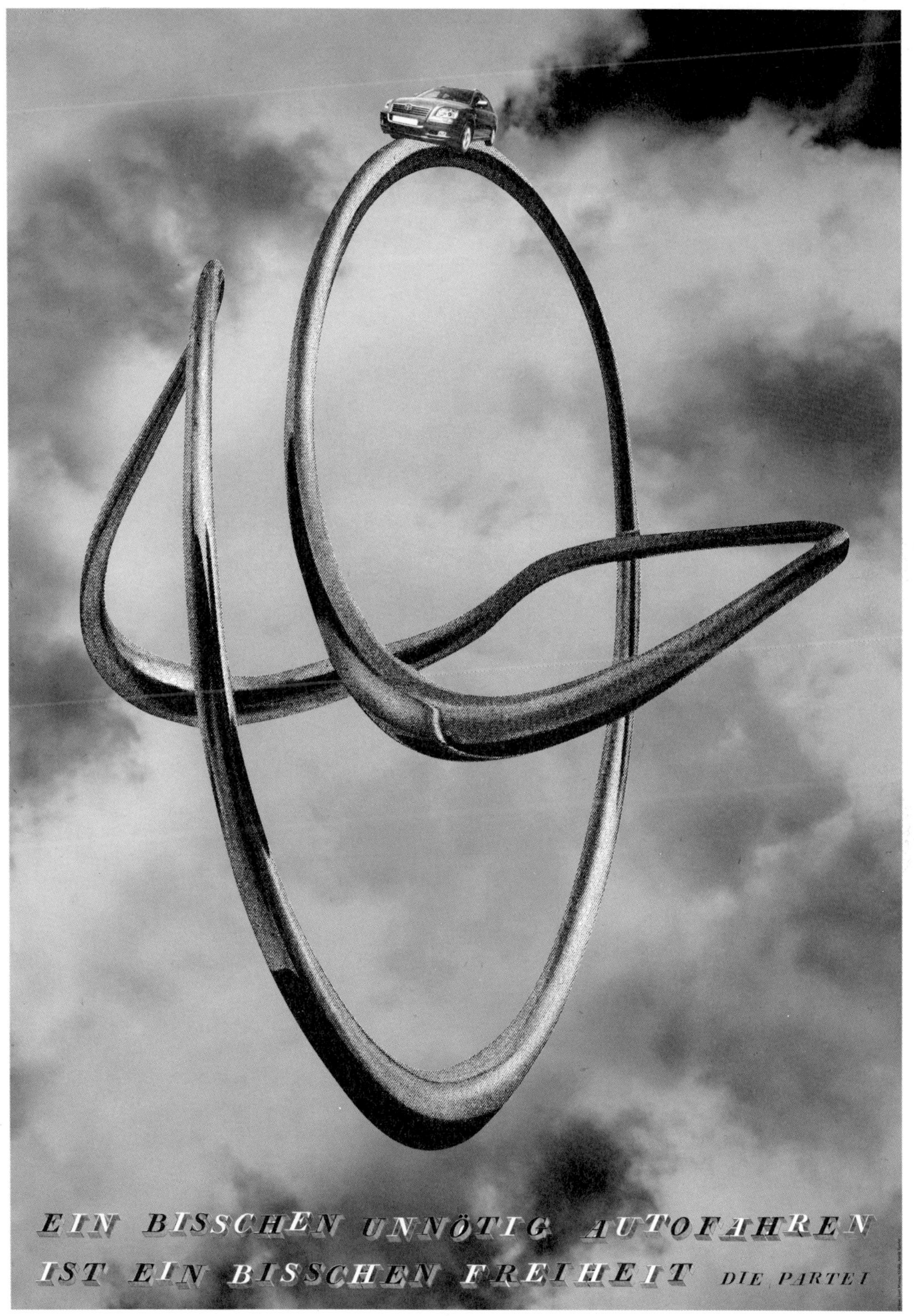
EIN BISSCHEN UNNÖTIG AUTOFAHREN
IST EIN BISSCHEN FREIHEIT DIE PARTEI

Ein bisschen unnötig autofahren ist ein bisschen freiheit – poster – exhibition of the Lucerne street artist Emil Manser – 2006

team:
Paula Troxler
contact:
Herbartstrasse 11
8004 Zurich
Switzerland
T + 41 79 59871 67
paula.troxler@gmail.com
www.paulatroxler.com

Paula Troxler

Paula Troxler was born in 1981 as the third daughter of Niklaus and Emma Troxler. She spends her childhood and schooldays in Willisau, a little village in Switzerland. In 2001, she began her studies in Visual Communication/Specification Illustration at the Artschool HGK in Lucerne, receiving a degree in July 2006. During the time of her studies, she had already worked on a lot of private projects, mostely posterwork for cultural places around Lucerne, and also illustrations for several magazines (e.g. Youth Theatre Willisau, PHZ Lucerne, Treibhaus Luzern/ Kraut Grafik). After her graduation, she continued to work in these fields at her own studio in Lucerne. Business is going well, in addition to establishing new contacts and creating works (Annabelle, Gessnerallee, Fantoche). In April 2007, Paula Troxler was offered to go to Ethiopia working on a book project for Caritas, an organization for development aid. She took that opportunity to leave her hometown and to give up her little studio in Lucerne. Altogether she spent 5 months in Ethiopia on two separate trips to do drawings. Since then, she doesn't have a permanent base. At the moment, she is staying in Berlin in a little studio, doing illustrations and poster works for different magazins (e.g. Campus Magazin, Die Zeit, Kulturmagazin), or working for other graphic design studios. The biggest part of her current work, however, is the design of the book on the Ethiopia project. After finishing this book, she wants to go back to Switzerland planning to start a new studio in the city of Zurich.

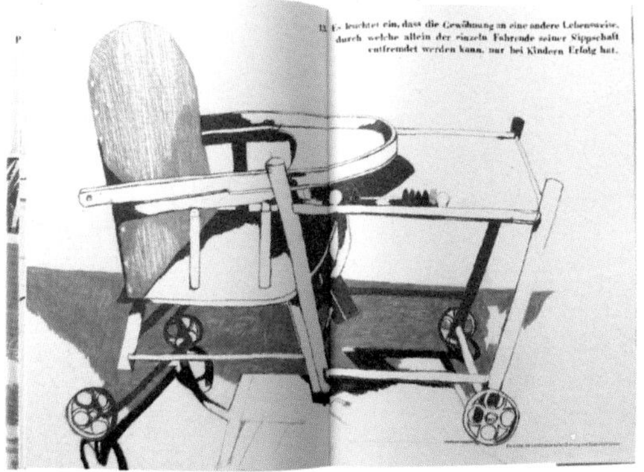

Hemvé/travels trough words and landscapes – book, limited edition – self published – 2006

Interview with Paula Troxler

1. What led to the formation of your studio?
I'm a single worker at my studio.

2. How many staff people does your studio have and what are their main working fields?
I'm the only member of the studio. I do work between illustration and graphic design.

3. How does a regular working day at your studio look like, how is the day structured?
I start to work around eight in the morning. First, I check my emails, and than I begin to work until around seven in the evening. I do a little break for lunch time each day, and sometimes I also work in the evening after 8 o'clock.

4. How much leisure time do you have during a year?
I'm working five to six days per week. Sometimes also in the evening, so I don't take much time for leisure during the week. For about six weeks per year I go for travelling, but most of the time this is somehow linked to my work, too. There is no clear line between work and leisure.

5. Which business areas do your clients mainly come from? Is the number of your clients increasing or rather declining?
I do illustrations for different magazines and posters for the cultural sector, e.g. for theaters and concerts. I also work as a freelancer for different graphic design studios. The number of clients is declining.

Seit je her ist die Schmuggelei eine mühsame Arbeit
und mit grossem Risiko verbunden.
22

Aufstieg und Einfall – cd cover – Integral – 2007

6. Do you have a specific corporate philosophy or maybe a mission statement like other companies, which is reflected in the way you steer the studio's course?

I work between illustration and graphic design. To create illustrations for magazines is only one part of my work. I also like to do bigger projects such as books. I have a personal resistance to the view of illustration as a form of decoration. In my opinion, there have to be a conceptual background and clear thoughts beyond that.

7. What, from your point of view, makes the difference between a small studio and a big company?

A small studio can work in more personal ways for clients. Further, the artist's style is more important. A small studio is more flexible and can work more freely.

8. What kind of advantages and disadvantages does a small studio have compared to a big company?

For a small studio is difficult to realize bigger jobs for companies like Nike or Coca Cola, which have more possibillities. A small studio can work with personal handwriting, and can change decisions more freely and faster. The client has a closer relationship with a small studio, and you can decide more on your own.

9. What is your idea about the future of small studios? Do you think that small studios do not have any other choice but to expand in order to survive in these times of globalization?

I think that small studios have a bright future. The client gets into direct contact with the artist and is offered more personality. Globalization has a negative impact for clients who wish to have such a personal approach and discussions about the creative work.

10. Please describe and elaborate on the goals or plans that you have for your studio for the next five years?

The plan is to go on with book projects and to build a studio with others designers from different fields who fit together.

Romeo and Juliet – a westside story von Paul Steinmann – poster – youth theater Willisau – 2005

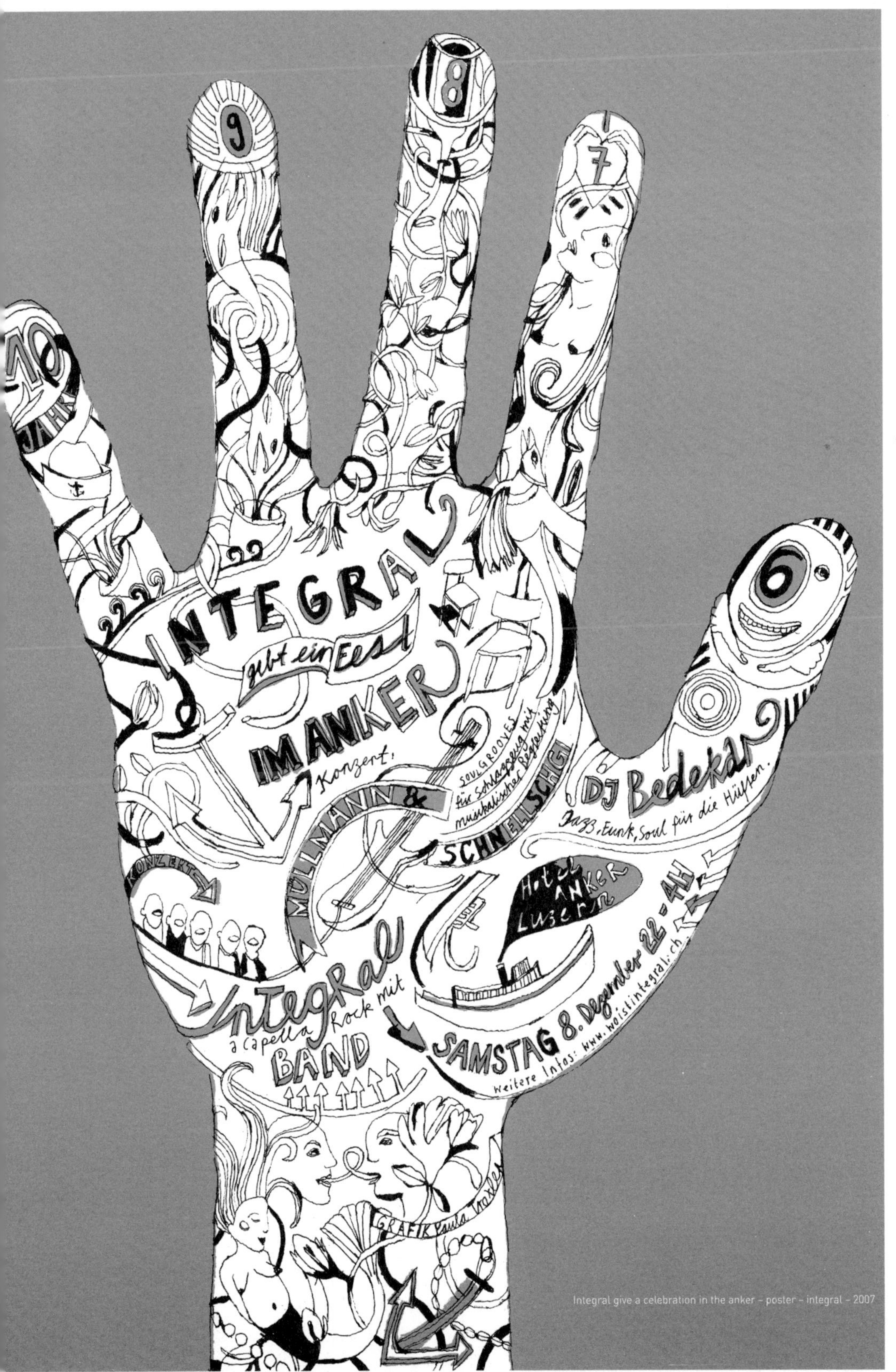

Integral give a celebration in the anker – poster – integral – 2007

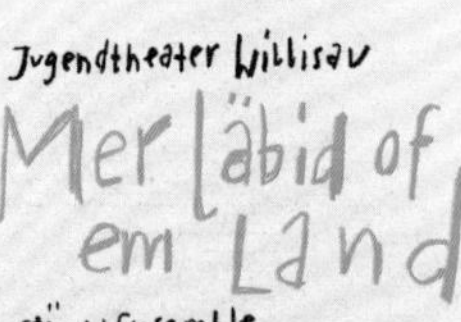

We live on the countryside – poster – youth theater Willisau – 2007

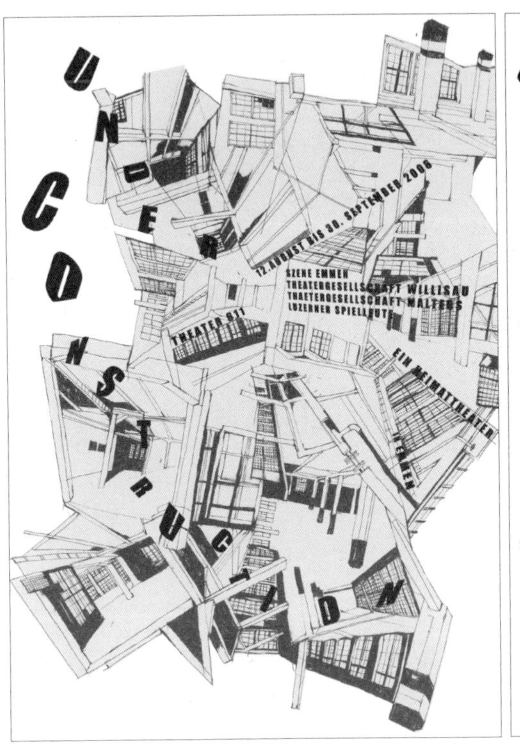

Under construction – poster – theater heimat 611 – 2006

Clash – frontpage of the program – theaterclub of PHZ, play of Kurt Schwitters – 2006

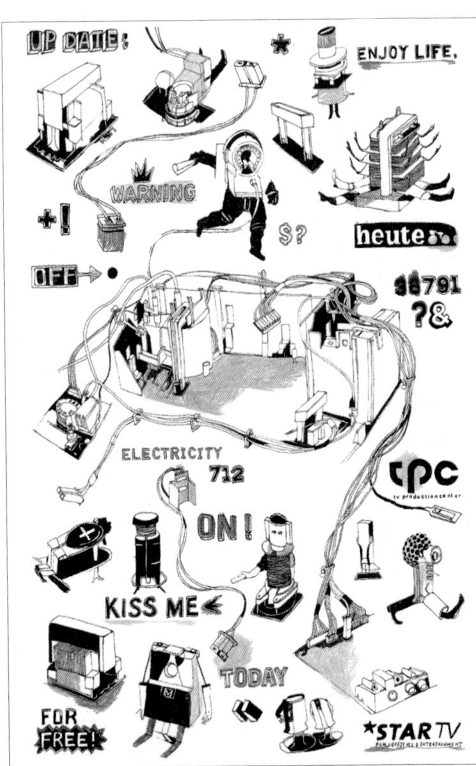

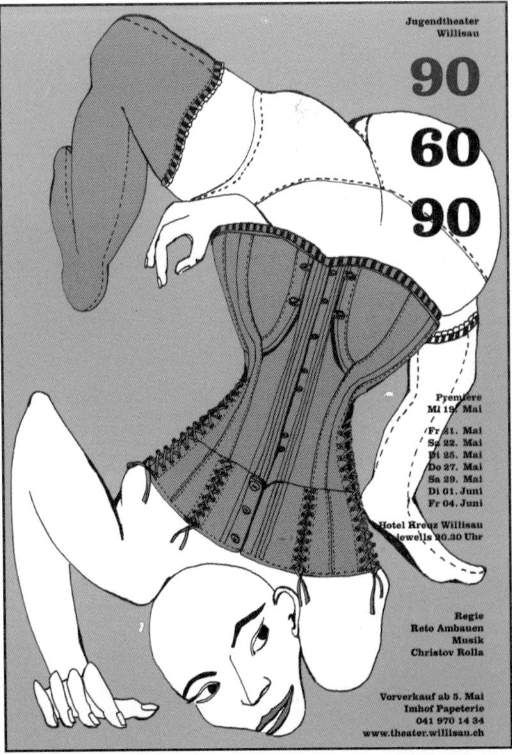

Sponsor illustration for fantoche – sponsor illustration – fantoche/published from bigrafik/Zürich – 2007

90-60-90 – poster – youth theater Willisau – 2004

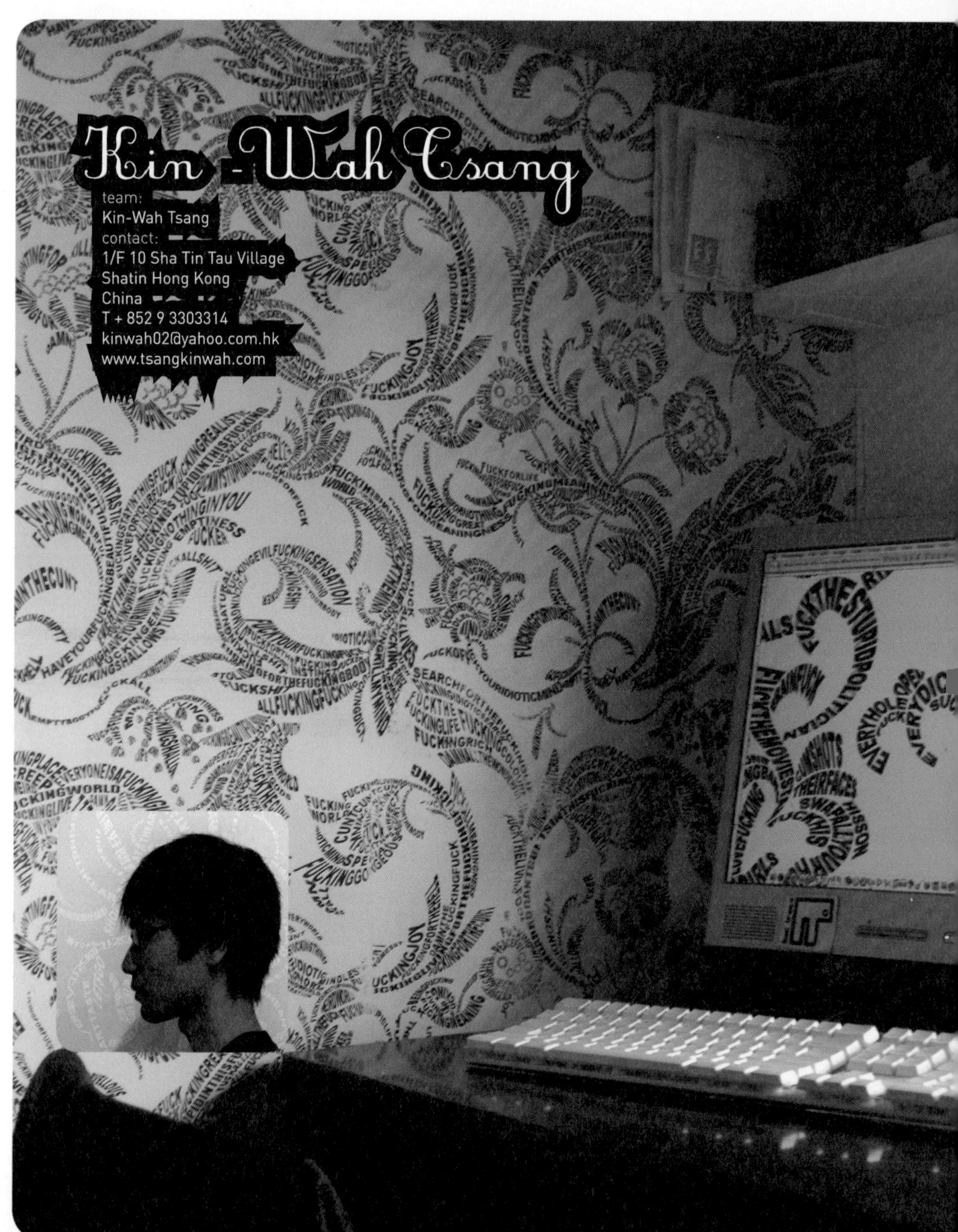

Kin-Wah Tsang

team:
Kin-Wah Tsang
contact:
1/F 10 Sha Tin Tau Village
Shatin Hong Kong
China
T + 852 9 3303314
kinwah02@yahoo.com.hk
www.tsangkinwah.com

Kin-Wah Tsang was born in China in 1976, and graduated from The Chinese University of Hong Kong and the Camberwell College of Arts, London Institute. Tsang has participated in various group exhibitions, such as ShContemporary 2007 (Shanghai), Art Fair Tokyo 2007 (Tokyo), Reversing Horizons (Museum of Contemporary Art Shanghai), Hobby Horse – Yeah Yeah Dada Asia (Avanthay Contemporary, Zurich), You Cannot Clone It, But You Can Buy It (ArtChina Gallery, Hamburg), The State of Things (National Museum of Art, Architecture and Design, Oslo), Dutch Design Week 2005 (Eindhoven), Hong Kong Art Biennial (2001, 2003, 2005), etc., and has been presented in the solo exhibitions White Cube, John Batten Gallery in Hong Kong (2005), Showcase: Tsang Kin Wah, at Art-U room in Tokyo (2006), Tsang Kin Wah, Yvon Lambert Gallery in New York (2007), and Paris (2008). He is the winner of the Hong Kong Art Biennial's Prize of Excellence (2001), the Sovereign Asian Art Prize (2005), the Tokyo TDC Prize (2007). His works are found in key collections worldwide, including the Sovereign Art Foundation, the Museum of Design in Zurich, the Camberwell College of Arts in London, the Hong Kong Museum of Art, and the Hong Kong Heritage Museum.

ragon/Jormungand/Serpent/Imperiality/Devil/Chinese/Norwegian/Satan/God/Overman ... – cold laminating film on windows – national museum of art, design and architecture, Oslo – 2006

Interview with Tsang Kin Wah

1. What led to the formation of your studio?

I'm an artist and always need space to make paintings, prints and other kinds of work. I used to live with my parents in the past working at their home, which I found somehow inconvenient and also made the place quite dirty and messy. So I rented a small flat as both my home and studio two years ago. It has become the place where I live and work.

2. How many staff people does your studio have and what are their main working fields?

I don't have any assistants, there's only me working in the studio.

3. How does a regular working day at your studio look like, how is the day structured?

Usually, I wake up around 9.30 or 10 in the morning and turn on my computer to check emails and news. While doing this, I have some bread for my breakfast. If there's something I need to do on the computer, I would stay in front of it for hours. Or if I have some other things to do like a painting or a print, I would start with this after breakfast. Generally, I won't stop to have lunch while I'm working. When I get tired or bored, I would have some snacks or play around with my cat, but most of the time I would turn on my hi-fi to listen to some music. When it's time for dinner, I stop by my parents' house, which is just a 15-minute walk, to have dinner with them or just by myself. After that, I would return to my home/studio to take a shower and get back to my desk, again checking my emails or continuing to work till midnight, and sometimes even later. Usually, I work like this almost everyday, and everyday is the same for me, no matter if it's the weekday or a holiday.

Chinese! It's Chinese... – dimensions variable – temporary art centre, Eindhoven – 2005

Di$trict Border$ – black tape on walls and floor – Shanghai street artspace, Hong Kong – 2006

mFDadFDaughterFTeacherFJesusFMaryFBillFMonicaFPoliticianFPastorFKidFMomFTeen ...– silkscreen, emulsion and acrylic on canavas & paper – Yvon Lambert gallery New York – 2007

4. How much leisure time do you have during a year?

It depends. Ideas usually don't come to me separated according to leisure or working time, they are all mixed together. Occasionally, however, I take a short holiday in other places just to relax. Sometimes there is also some leisure time after the end of an exhibition overseas, which can be at any time during the year.

5. Which business areas do your clients mainly come from? Is the number of your clients increasing or rather declining?

I usually create works for shows at art galleries and museums. Most of them are located in Europe, and some in Japan and the United States. The number has been increasing in the last few years.

6. Do you have a specific corporate philosophy or maybe a mission statement like other companies, which is reflected in the way you steer the studio's course?

No, I don't.

7. What, from your point of view, makes the difference between a small studio and a big company?

I think flexibility and efficiency make the difference between a small studio and a big company. In a small studio you can make or carry out a decision much quicker, without going to lots of people or several departments and having to wait for their ideas or decisions like it often happens in a big company. Once you have made a decision, you can carry it out just a few seconds later or any time you want it.

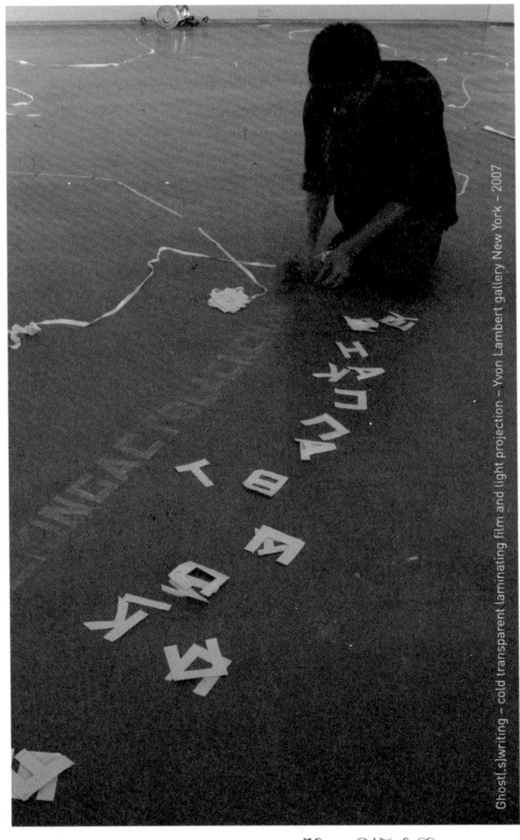
Ghost(.s)writing – cold transparent laminating film and light projection – Yvon Lambert gallery New York – 2007

Interior – silkscreen and acrylic on paper – camberwell college of art, London – 2003

Interior – silkscreen and acrylic on paper – Hong Kong arts centre – 2003

8. What kind of advantages and disadvantages does a small studio have compared to a big company?

As mentioned above, I think flexibility and efficiency make the difference, which obviously are the main advantages of a small studio. When your studio is getting more and more jobs or clients, on the other hand, you will find that a small studio may not be able to satisfy all of them or to handle a huge project because of its limited number of staff. And there may also be lack of capital. Sometimes these reasons really cause limitations and restrictions on the possibility of realizing a huge project. In this case, you have to find other people or companies to help you out a bit.

9. What is your idea about the future of small studios? Do you think that small studios do not have any other choice but to expand in order to survive in these times of globalization?

I don't know much about what is happening in other areas, but regarding the field of design I think small studios are getting more popular – in contrast to the field of arts, where in my view the big studios are preferred. Personally, I don't think small studios really need to expand in order to survive in these times of globalization. It really depends on the type of work the respective designers or artists are doing, and, of course, on their working habits. But this is not really related much to globalization, I think.

10. Please describe and elaborate on the goals or plans that you have for your studio for the next five years?

I think my studio won't change too much over the next five years. Maybe, I will try to find an assistant to help me with the paperwork or to give me a hand in setting up my works. I still haven't made that decision yet. If it's affordable, I may also try to find a bigger space to have sufficient space for making some bigger pieces of work.

I love u – silkscreen and acrylic on paper – GOD, Hong Kong – 2004

ISHOPYOUSHOPHESHOPSHESHOPITSHOPTHEYSHOPISHOPYOUSHOPHESHOPSHESHOPITSHOPTHEYSHOP... – video, lcd tv, speakers, silkscreen on paper and cushion, cold luminating film – Hong Kong heritage museum – 2006

Typecuts

team:
Andrea Tinnes
contact:
Das Deck
Schliemannstraße. 6
10437 Berlin, Germany
T + 49 30 61609554
F + 49 30 44031629
andrea@typecuts.com

Typecuts – Andrea Tinnes is a type and graphic designer based in Berlin. Her design practice is focused on client-based as well as self-initiated projects. Through her own label, Typecuts, she publishes as well as promotes all her type designs. In addition to her design practice, Andrea works both as Professor of Type and Typography at Burg Giebichenstein in Halle/Germany and as Adjunct Professor at Bergen National Academy of the Arts/Norway. Andrea's work has been featured in several publications, such as EYE Magazine, Area_2 and Graphic Design Now and in several exhibitions including the 22 annual 100 Show, the TDC53 exhibition and Chaumont 2007. She holds awards from the American Center for Design, red dot (2001/2002) as well as a Certificate of Typographic Excellence (TDC53 2007). She has a degree in communication design from the University of Applied Sciences Mainz and an MFA in graphic design from the California Institute of the Arts.

Interview with Typecuts

1. What led to the formation of your studio?

I have been working as an independent graphic and type designer since 1999. In 2004, I decided to start off my own label named typecuts, as a platform to promote and publish my type designs as well as my graphic work. I have made a conscious decision to be a one-woman studio, so I try to keep everything small and manageable and leave enough room for designing typefaces and my teaching commitments. The list of my clients is rather short. Luckily, this has put me in a position where I was able to establish a close and friendly working relation with my clients and collaborators and ultimately do only the kind of work I highly enjoy.

2. How many staff people does your studio have and what are their main working fields?

One single person with a special focus on type and typography.

3. How does a regular working day at your studio look like, how is the day structured?

A regular working day is divided into two blocks: email correspondence, office organization, type sales, teaching or course preparations on one side and practical design work on the other side.

4. How much leisure time do you have during a year?

Unfortunately, not as much as I actually need in order to rest and relax.

5. Which business areas do your clients mainly come from? Is the number of your clients increasing or rather declining?

I have a hybrid practice, dividing my time between client-based work, self-initiated projects, as well

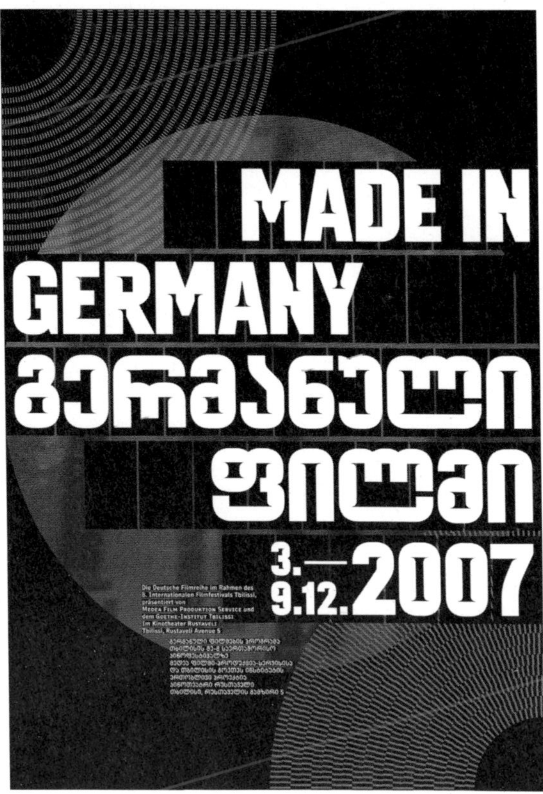

Made in Germany 2007 – double sided bilingual poster – medea: film/production/servcie – 2007

Made in Germany 2006 – double sided poster – medea: film/production/servcie – 2006

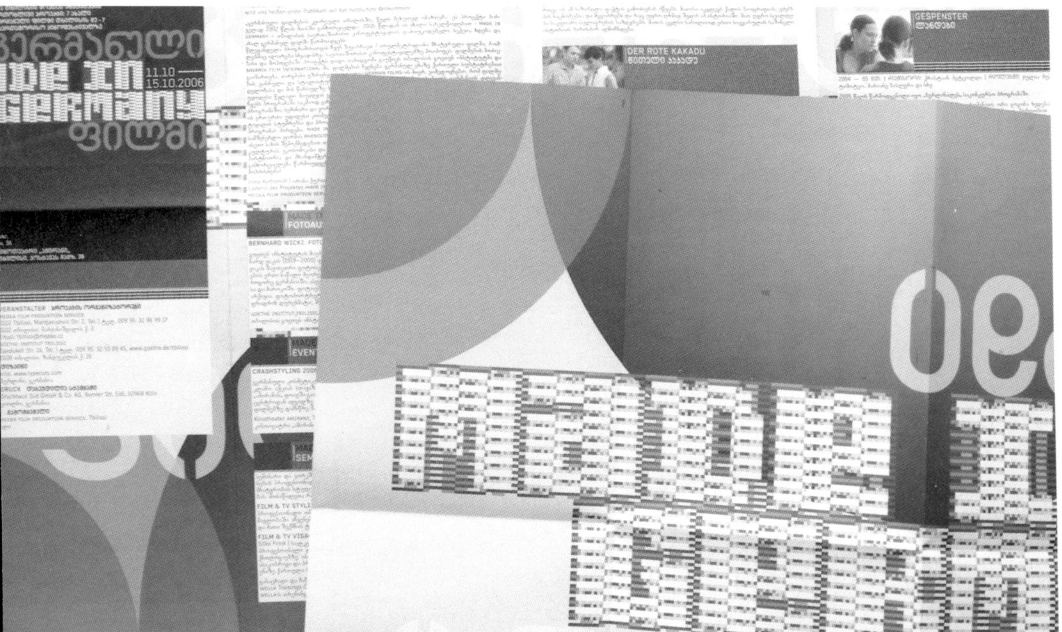

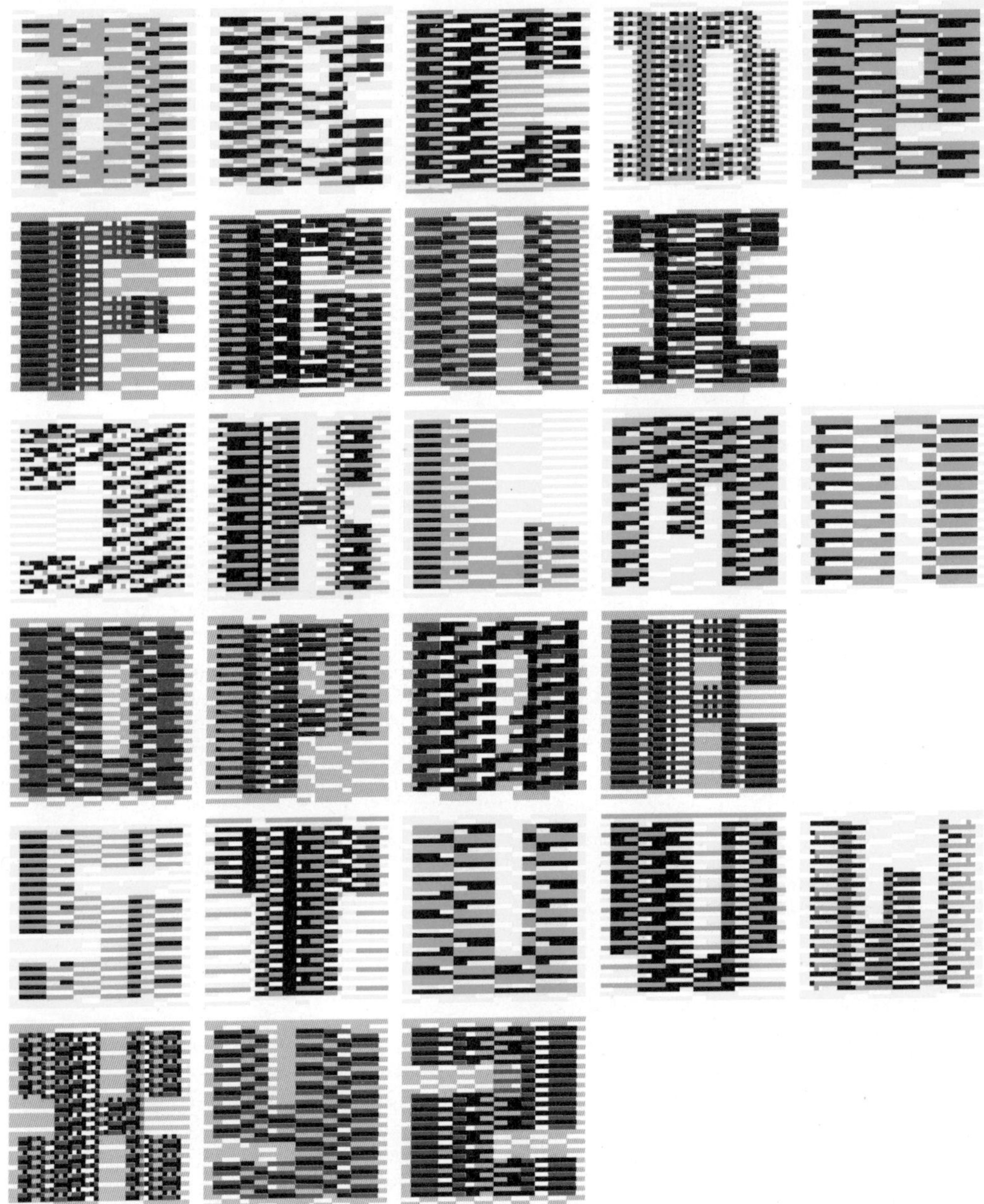

TJ – type jockey – set of alphabetic structures – the playground project – 2005

as teaching. There are two types of clients: cultural clients and design studios (with commissions such as custom fonts and logotypes). Although the number of clients has been constant, I have started to cut down commissions because of my teaching commitments as professor.

6. Do you have a specific corporate philosophy or maybe a mission statement like other companies, which is reflected in the way you steer the studio's course?

Enjoyment, excitement and pleasure. Self-criticism as well as faith in my own work. Curiosity. Courage to fail.

7. What, from your point of view, makes the difference between a small studio and a big company?

A small studio is more flexible because of shorter lines of decision making. A small studio can be more venturesome, because it's not responsible for a substructure of many employees; therefore a small studio doesn't have to sacrifice creativity and originality for the sake of profits. A small studio gives more control as well as responsibility to each single staff member over the entire design or work process, including close contact and direct communication with the client. A small studio can work more cost efficient. A small studio doesn't have to compromise stylistic authenticity and artistic expression

Made in Germany 2006 – double sided poster – medea: film/production/servcie – 2006

8. What kind of advantages and disadvantages does a small studio have compared to a big company?

A small studio often lacks relevant business and management skills. A small studio has less capacity and expertise to develop and manage complex extensive projects, requiring a big professional team of specialists. As small studio often lacks resources to face financial challenges.

9. What is your idea about the future of small studios? Do you think that small studios do not have any other choice but to expand in order to survive in these times of globalization?

It seems like there have never been as many small studios and independent designers as today. The democratization of technological tools, advanced software and means of distribution paired with an ambitious do-it-yourself attitude as well as a need to express one own's creative individuality while rejecting conventional business careers and commercial sell-off have let to a growing number of designers setting up their own business. However, the limitations are obvious when it comes to big corporate clients. Extensive big budget projects will often be beyond the reach of small sized studios. There has to be a clear choice between expanding or staying small, depending on the studio or the designer's very specific design approach. The real potential for small studios lies in developing specialist's skills while establishing an effective infrastructure of interdisciplinary team workers to cooperate on a project basis. And of course in creating idiosyncratic and innovative work for niche markets which aren't usually served by big firms.

10. Please describe and elaborate on the goals or plans that you have for your studio for the next five years?

As a matter of fact, I'm very happy with my current situation, having a hybrid practice of designing and teaching. My goal is just simply to continue my practice. At the same time, however, it has become more difficult for me to be available for extensive, yet short-term projects due to my teaching commitments. In this respect I hope to develop a good network of collaborators to individually work with, on a project-by-project basis.

Days of the German film in Tbilissi 2004 – double sided poster – medea: film/production/service – 2004

STEFAN TOLZ

AM RANDE DER ZEIT
MÄNNERWELTEN IM KAUKASUS

FRITZ PLEITGEN

DURCH DEN WILDEN KAUKASUS
ERSTER TEIL

ANDREAS DRESEN

FILMREIHE BERLIN

DIE LEGENDE DER FESTUNG SURAMI
AMBAWI SURAMIS ZIXISA

DIE REUE
MONANIEBA

DIE REISE DES JUNGEN KOMPONISTEN
AXALGASRDA KOMPOSITORIS MOGSAUROBA

HARUN FAROCKI

Trivium – interlocking icons – the offices of Anne Burdick – 2005

LOCATION

GEORGIEN

LOCATION:GEORGIEN
KRISE UND PERSPEKTIVE EINES FILMLANDES
FILMREIHE UND FOTOAUSSTELLUNG
KÖLN – BERLIN – TBILISSI
FILMFORUM NRW IM MUSEUM LUDWIG UND TRINITATISKIRCHE
08.03 – 31.03.2007

Location: Georgien – doublesided poster – medea, curator Kurtishvili – 2007

Institutions and Stations
AERIAL PHOTOGRAPHY
lambert conformal conic projection
globalization of rhetoric
[Roletta Serif & Sans]
environmental determinism
SUBTERRANEAN PRESSURES
CHUBBY
badlands result from the erosion
planets revolve in elliptical orbits
science of geostatistics
ocean zones

PTL roletta – type design and type specimen – primetype – 2006-08

Typotheque is a type foundry run by Peter and Johanna Bilak, based in The Hague, The Netherlands. Together, they develop and market original fonts for Mac and PC, continuing in the tradition of small independent type foundries, and contributing their part to the ongoing history of type development. They create quality typefaces to reflect our time and serve its needs.

Merkx+Girod – book design – frame publishers – 2002

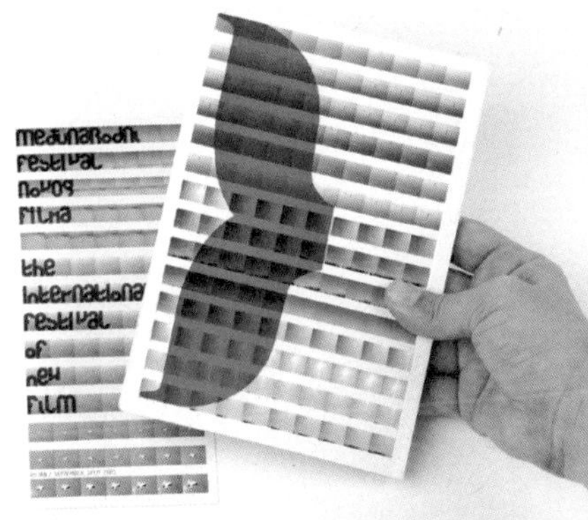

Split film festival – printed matter – split film festival – 2003

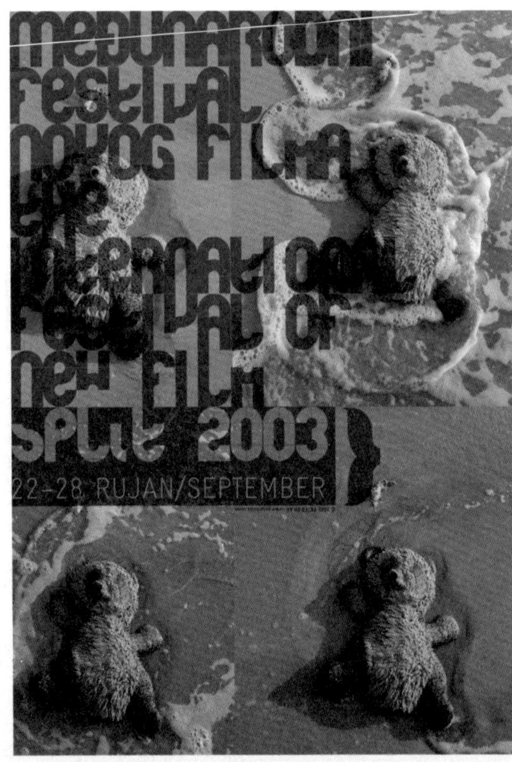

Interview with Typoteque

1. What led to the formation of your studio?

After completing my studies, and after having two design jobs (BBDO, Studio Dumbar), I felt confident enough to start on my own. It was still full of uncertainties and risks involved (I decided to do it in a foreign country). The Netherlands is a friendly place for starting businesses, and it worked out from the beginning. I suppose the main impetus was also that I was interested in areas of design which I couldn't practice in any existing job. I wanted to do type design, write about design, publish magazines, work on cultural projects or modern ballet concepts, organize events. I don't think any existing job could offer all this to me, it would be always about making compromises. A usual advice in such condition is: either accept what a job can offer, or create a job that offers it all. I decided or the latter. Three years later, my wife-to-be Johanna made a similar decision: after working for various design companies, she joined me in the studio, and we have continued working as a two-people-studio until today.

2. How many staff people does your studio have and what are their main working fields?

Typotheque is a two-people-studio, but we share a large studio space with other friends, so we are 6 in the space. The other people are also designers and programmers, so we sometimes end up working together. Such a setup makes our work very flexible, we can expand and shrink, depending on the project size. I regularly work with 1-2 assistants on type design projects, and recently Nikola Djurek, my ex-student, became important in many complex type design projects.

3. How does a regular working day at your studio look like, how is the day structured?

We start around 10, only after my morning yoga, slow breakfast and 30 minutes bicycle ride to the office. The rest of the morning is reserved for answering emails and phone calls. In the afternoon, depending on the work load, I personally tend to go "offline", to actually do some work. With emails coming in all the time (in ever increasing numbers), this is the only way to focus on the work. The way to relax is ping-pong, table-football, and wii-tennis with the colleagues in the studio. In the end of the afternoon I check my emails again, and finish around 7.

4. How much leisure time do you have during a year?

The first year, I had only a minimum of free time, it was all devoted to setting things up. Now, after creating an existing structure, we take a generous amount of time. We've been running the studio for 7 years now, so after setting up the practice, it is important to find the right working rhythm, to avoid the monotony, and to keep us inspired and motivated. Some people do it by taking a sabbatical every 5 or so years (the most well known example is Stefan Sagmeister, taking a year off every 6 years). We do it in a less dramatical fashion, but still take about 3 months off every year. After returning from travels/holidays, we really have the batteries recharged, and can't wait to begin working again.

5. Which business areas do your clients mainly come from?

We operate in a very wide area of design. We work a lot with text: all aspects of it – writing for various design periodicals, journals. In 2000, I co-founded a design/art magazine called DOT DOT DOT, and worked as editor for 7 years. This brings in writing assignments now, and book projects where we are involved also on an editorial level. Another aspect working with text is type design. We've been creating type families for 10 or so years, and by licensing them to end users, it finally pays for the time we spend on them. These are mainly self-commissioned projects with no deadline. And lastly, there are regular design projects such posters, books, exhibitions, stamp design, etc.

Is the number of your clients increasing or rather declining?

The number of clients is decreasing, but the number of projects has been increasing. We run a lot of self initiated projects, which we prioritize over the regular design commissions. We are developing new typefaces, organise research projects about non-Latin typography, publish books and catalogues, initiate exhibitions, conceive modern dance performances, and these projects pay off not immediately, but only much later. Nevertheless, because we act as both the client and the designer, we have the full control in such projects and prefer to work this way.

Experiment and typography posters – poster – self initiated – 2004

6. Do you have a specific corporate philosophy or maybe a mission statement like other companies, which is reflected in the way you steer the studio's course?

No we don't. We prefer to keep a degree of flexibility, and setting dogmas doesn't really help this. We feel responsible for what we do. Some design companies make their money on projects which they are not very proud of, and occasionally they do a project for free, which they put into books and magazines. We'd like to be able to welcome colleagues to our

Eilendenrijk – exhibition design – stroom Den Haag – 2007

The Slovak myth – identity, printed matter – moravian gallery in Brno – 2006

Irnava poster triennial – poster – Irnava poster triennial – 2003

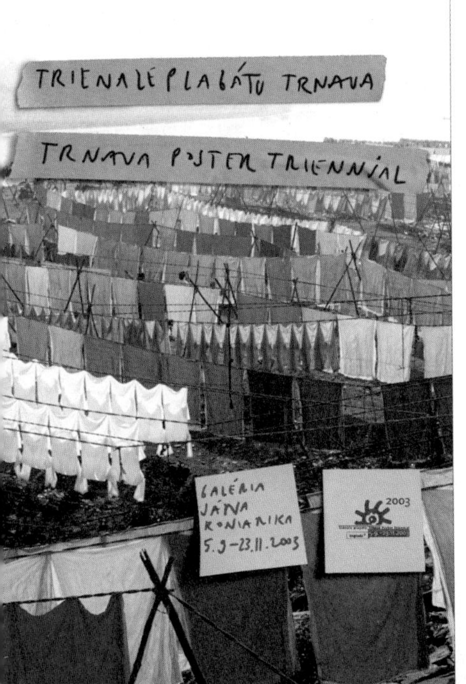

studio at any time, and be proud of all our projects on our desks and not only a selection of them. It is not easy, but keeping the consistency of our output also serves as a reference, and by now we never get offered projects which we don't want to work on. Interesting results attract other interesting projects. On the other hand, if we would accept doing some crappy work only for money, I am sure it would attract similarly crappy work in the future, and this is not a direction we want to go.

7. What, from your point of view, makes the difference between a small studio and a big company?

The big difference is of course the number of people in the company, which creates large overheads. Someone has to feed these people, and this means that well paid work is preferred over less paid, potentially more interesting work. That is a basic mechanics of the design company. Younger individuals don't have it easy in large existing structures, even more so, if the existing company is successful. Success is a tricky criterion of work, which forces people to repeat the work which became successful. If one comes to a successful company set up 20-30 years ago, it is likely that the company will try to keep something of the original success by replicating the work which they did a while ago, and an individual will have more troubles to find his/her own room in the structure. Of course, other people prefer the securities of the job, and a big company offers them a more stable position than a small studio.

8. What kind of advantages and disadvantages does a small studio have compared to a big company?

Size matters and determines what kinds of projects a studio gets or not. We can't receive projects that a company of 30 designers does. So basically. we very rarely do design identities projects, or work for multinationals. If someone is interested in these kind of projects, than it is important to find a studio of an appropriate size.

Peter Bilak: modular talk – poster – IED arti visive, Milano, Italy – 2006

On the other hand, large companies will never do a book project, or work on edition of stamps. Size is both an advantage and disadvantage. Because of the size, a company can acquire some clients. With increasing size, a company becomes less flexible to react to changes. Imagine a new technological breakthrough happens – this can bring a large company to its knees, if they can't adapt to changes. At the same time, operating individually or in a small team can also be risky, as a difference between the point of being busy or not, can be a single project. It is more complicated to plan work for a tiny studio like us.

9. What is your idea about the future of small studios?

They will always exist, and some of their outcome will be most inspiring.

Do you think that small studios do not have any other choice but to expand in order to survive in these times of globalization?

Absolutely. I see more studios now then ever before. It is true that many are simply contractors for large offices which prefer to outsource they work. But they are also many, which creates an important counterbalance to the globalising trends. Our small studio works with small local printers, small binders, and serves small local galleries or publishers. This is how it has always been, and I don't think it will change anytime soon.

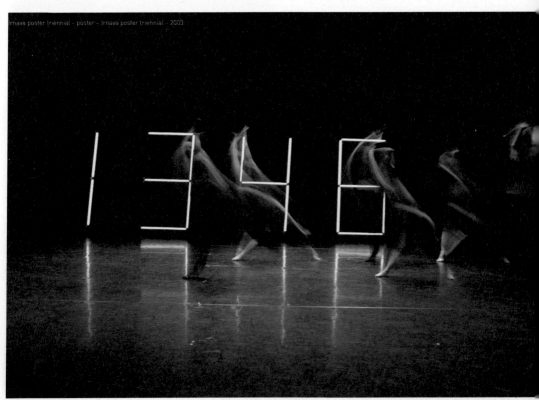

Irnava poster triennial – poster – Irnava poster triennial – 2003

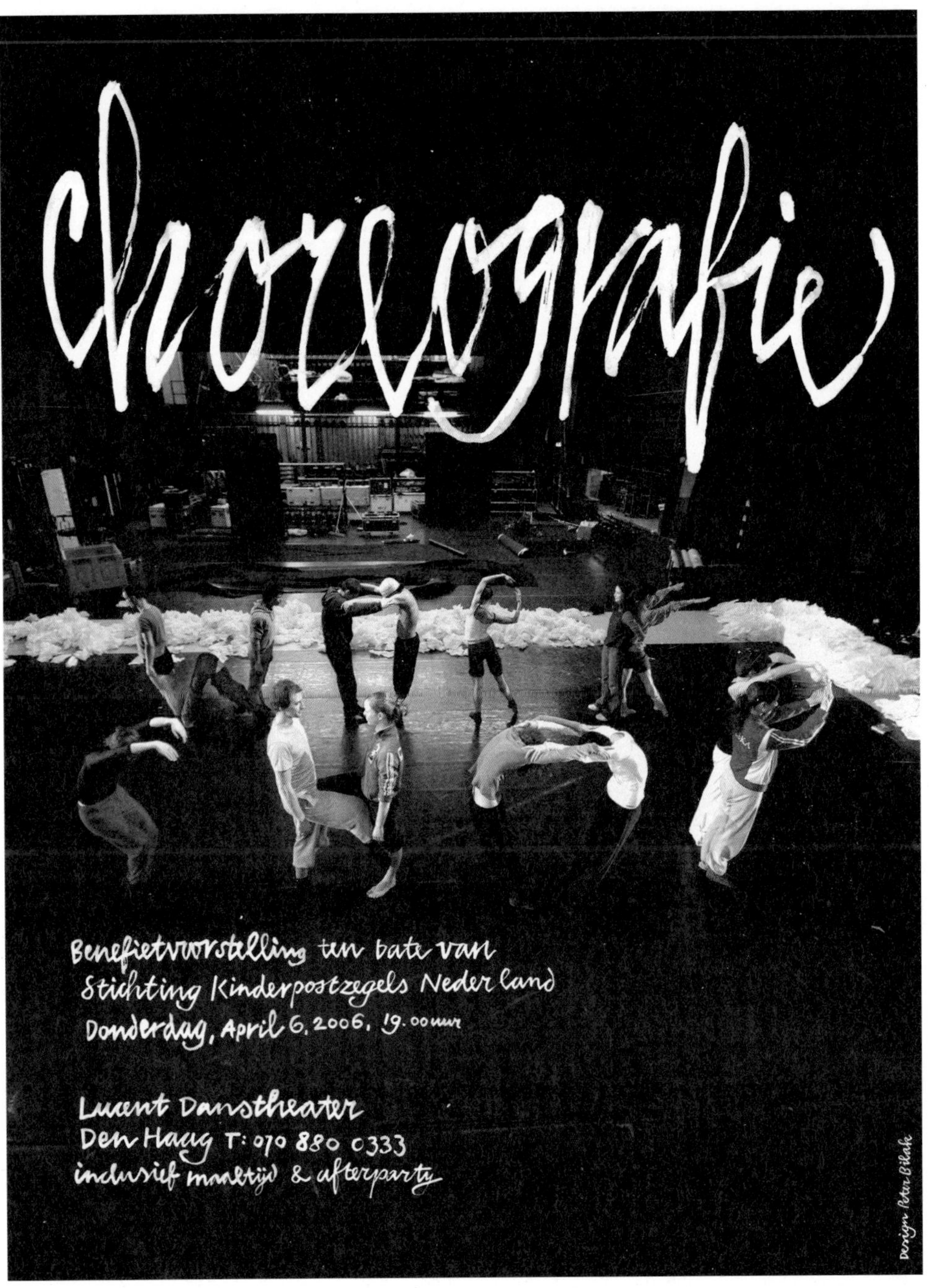

10. Please describe and elaborate on the goals or plans that you have for your studio for the next five years?

I already mentioned the difficulties of planning in small structures. I don't think it is realistic to describe the situation in 5 years. All fixed plans are doomed to fail, if one doesn't take into consideration possibilities of change. Plans usually work when one sees them in retrospect – but it is important to keep a certain flexibility to react to conditions as they unfold. Many of the things we do are results of chance, coincidences, random meetings, intuitive decisions, or even failures. It is exciting to be able to change premeditated plans when one feels that it needs to be changed.

NDT choreography workshop – poster – Netherlands dance theater – 2006

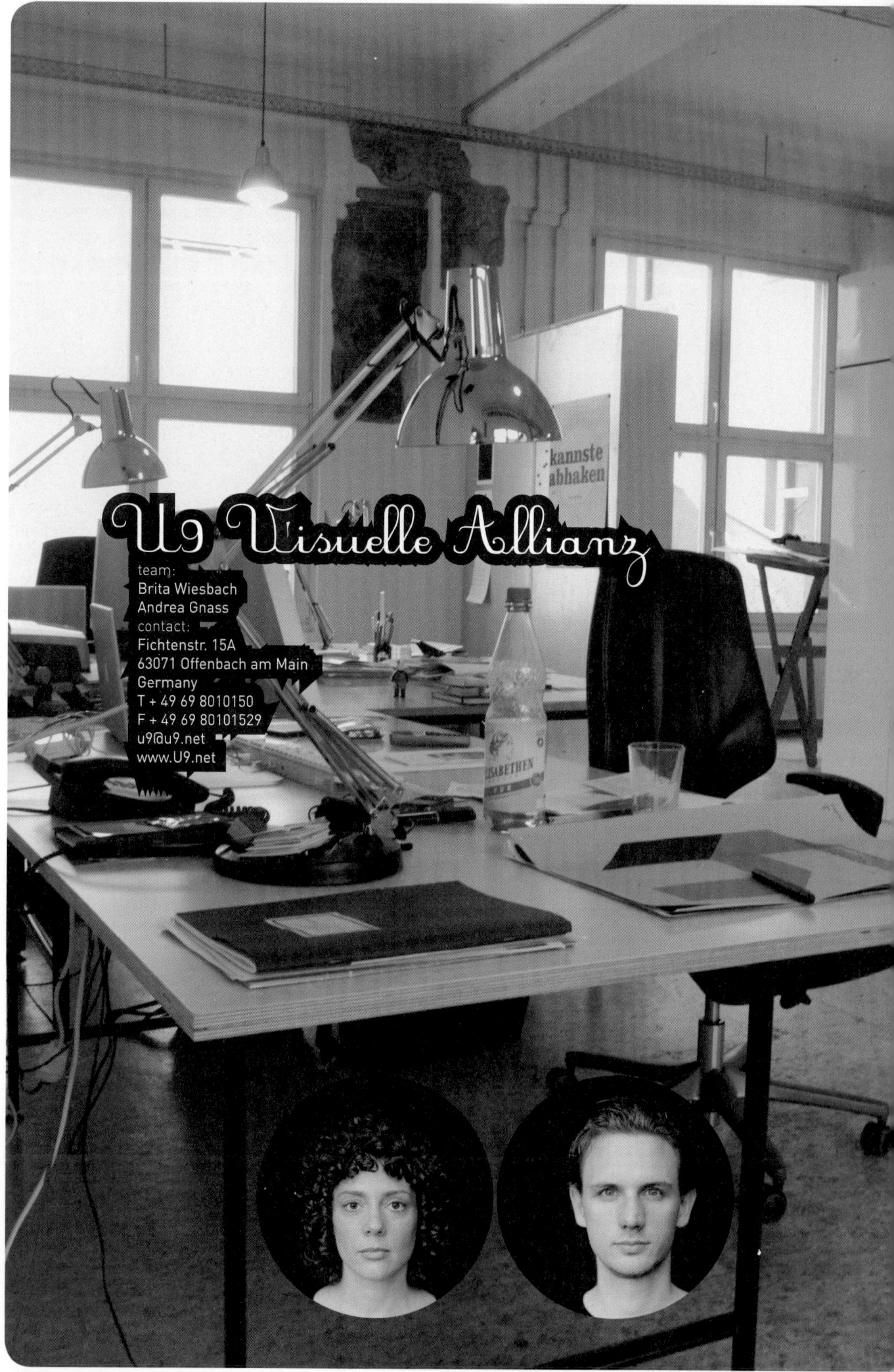
kannste
abhaken
U9 Visuelle Allianz
team:
Brita Wiesbach
Andrea Gnass
contact:
Fichtenstr. 15A
63071 Offenbach am Main
Germany
T + 49 69 8010150
F + 49 69 80101529
u9@u9.net
www.U9.net
ELISABETHEN

U9 Visuelle Allianz stands for designed communication. Interesting relations between text and image, form and letterpress are of great importance to them. Most of the time, they rather prefer the subtle notes over the visually loud ones. U9 visuelle Allianz was founded as a limited company by Brita Wiesbach and Andreas Gnass on the 1st of January, 2000.

AKH-public offer – folder – architekten- und stadtplanerkammer Hessen – 2008

Auslobung:
Auszeichnung vorbildlicher
Bauten im Land Hessen 2008
ARCHI–
TEKTUR
PREIS
Architekten- und
Stadtplanerkammer Hessen

Interview with Visuelle Allianz

1. What led to the formation of your studio?

Design is like love. If cooperation evolves into something more than just the duplication of manpower and becomes inspiring, you will get a precious commodity. This sums up in short why we have founded U9 visuelle Allianz.

2. How many staff people does your studio have and what are their main working fields?

Basically, there are the two of us as the founders and therefore significantly involved in all concept and creative activities. We work very closely with freelance graphic designers, writers and photographers. The teams are assembled according to the individual project requirements.

3. How does a regular working day at your studio look like, how is the day structured?

It is a sign of the times that working days are now heavily influenced by communication, besides our main activities of concept development and creative work. We therefore sympathize with ideas such as the attempt to declare an email-free Friday. The permanent and multi-channel flow of news entails many positive things but it also requires some effort to find the time when we can just concentrate on one subject.

4. How much leisure time do you have during a year?

Time felt: not enough. Real time: 3 weeks.

5. Which business areas do your clients mainly come from? Is the number of your clients increasing or rather declining?

We are time and again pleased with our diverse range of clients. Our various dealings with museums, start-up companies, established enterprises, universities and academies as well as public authorities open new perspectives and force us to look at things from different viewpoints. We are working with most of our clients on a long-term basis and can confirm that their number is steadily increasing.

6. Do you have a specific corporate philosophy or maybe a mission statement like other companies, which is reflected in the way you steer the studio's course?

"Be yourself, be real." (Benjamin Latimore, 1973)

7. What, from your point of view, makes the difference between a small studio and a big company?

Working with a small studio means direct contact – there are hardly any filters between the studio owner and the client.

8. What kind of advantages and disadvantages does a small studio have compared to a big company?

A big company must succeed in implementing "motivation", "quality assurance" and "identification" in each of its individual units. In small studios, however, these fundamentals come naturally. On the other-hand, small studios are more often challenged by new tasks without being able to rely on their company history and/or previous references due to the fact that the total amount of projects already executed is much lower.

GENAU
DEIN
DING.
23.
MAI
07
info messe der h_da, Hochschule Darmstadt:
25 Studiengänge stellen sich vor.
www.infomesse.org
h_da
HOCHSCHULE DARMSTADT
UNIVERSITY OF APPLIED SCIENCES

Info messe 2007 – poster – university of applied sciences Darmstadt, Germany – 2007

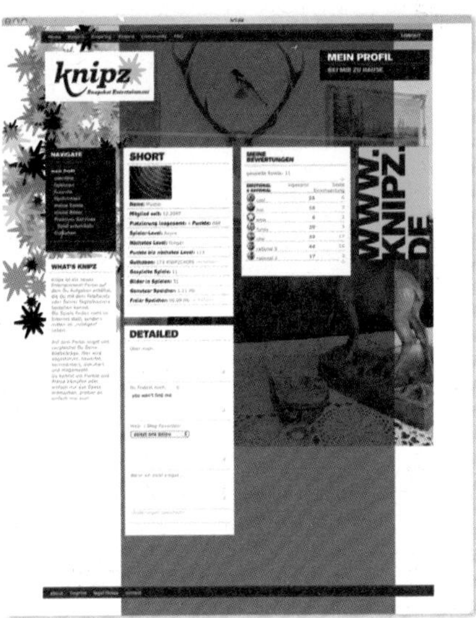

Knipz.de – screen – knipz.de – 2008

NIX DRIN, NIX DRAN

FONT T O, 2005
ABCDEFGHIJKLMN
OPQRSTUVWXYZ

Font T_O – font – 2005

9. What is your idea about the future of small studios? Do you think that small studios do not have any other choice but to expand in order to survive in these times of globalization?

You have to move and to connect, but you don't have to grow considerably.

10. Please describe and elaborate on the goals or plans that you have for your studio for the next five years?

The last time someone asked us this question, we were bold enough to claim that we would reside in Genua within five years. Genua was a synonym for a decisive step forward and away from where we were standing at this point. Geographically, this prediction did not become true, but figuratively, yes. A small studio resembles a small Pacific island. The world can survive without it, and if you are out of luck, some icebergs will melt somewhere and the sandy beach is gone. But still, you are happy this island exists, once you get to know it. And these are our goals: keep up the quality, increase the level of awareness of our studio and spread the risks.

NiO – corporate design – LNO, lokale nahverkehrsorganisation Offenbach am main – 2007

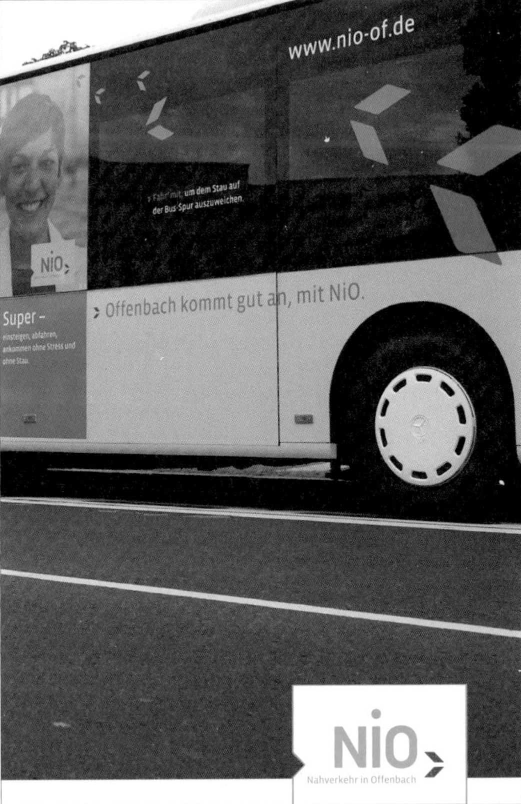

mitten ins Herz

Petra Herz – corporate design – Petra Herz – 2006

harbour 2 – anniversary poster – poster – hafen2 – 2008

Rock – poster – sheeg.com – 2005

Hobit 2008 – poster – university of applied sciences, Darmstadt – 2008

Hobit 2003 – poster – university of applied sciences, Darmstadt – 2003

Halle: Hafenküche. Sibel und Anny Öztürk — Modenschau. Tastbar.com — Film. Bernd Thiele
Saal: Konzert. LR Rockets (Art Goes Pop) (London) — Vinyl. Grrr! (lesypersound, silbergold) — Konzert. Ja, Panik
(schoenwetter, ZickZack) (Wien) — Lesung und Hörspiel. Kerstin Grether (Spex, Eichborn, Suhrkamp) (Berlin) —
Konzert. Doktorella feat. Jens Friebe, Sandra Grether (Berlin) — Vinyl. Jus-Ed (Underground Quality)
(Bridgeport, CT) — DJ Edits & Live Analog Drums. Jamal Moss a.k.a.
Hieroglyphic Being, The Sun God (Axis, Ghostly / Spectral, Klang Elektronik) (Chicago, IL)
Galerie: Ausstellungseröffnung. interim.projekte
Séparée: Musique. Julia Wahl, Geri, Frankie Patella
Kantine: Karaoke. E-sisters (Design und Sensationen)
Café: Vinyl und Live-Visuals. Indian Vibes (Asian Underground)
Hafen 2 wird vier Jubiläumsfestival
SA 23 02 2008 20 Uhr
VVK und AK 10 Euro
Hafen 2 Alter Lokschuppen der Hafenbahn, Offenbach
www.hafen2.net
HAFEN 2

Harbour 2 – poster – hafen2 – 2008

Unfolded

team:
Nadia Graf-Gisler
Friedrich-Wilhelm Graf
contact:
Weststr. 95
8003 Zurich
Switzerland
T + 41 44 4502582
F + 41 44 4610586
we@unfolded.ch
www.unfoldet.ch

Unfolded is a Zurich-based art and design office. They work in the range of print to digital. Nadia Graf née Gisler studied art education and computer art at the School of Art and Design Zurich (HGKZ) and at the School of Visual Art in New York (SVA). She did her diploma in 1999. Since then she has been a professor in interactive media and time-based art at the HGKZ. At the moment, she is enrolled in the master program z-node of the University of Plymouth, England, and HGK Zurich, researching on the topic of remembering and forgetting. Friedrich-Wilhelm Graf finished his studies as graphic designer at the HGK Zurich in 2003. Before that, a great interest in fashion took him to Antwerp for an internship at "design is dead", where he did his first commissioned work. After a few projects together with Nadia Gisler, they founded the design office: Unfolded. So instead of graduating as fashion designer, he is working now as an art director of Unfolded.

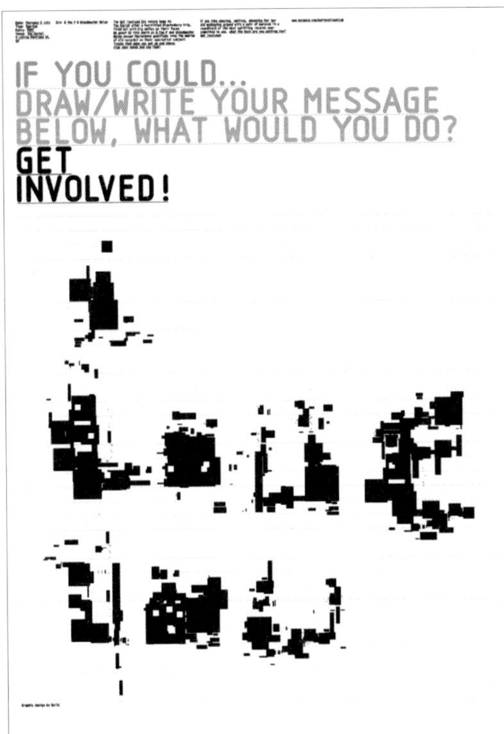

Get involded – poster – creative review & build – 2007

Interview with Unfolded

1. What led to the formation of your studio?

2. How many staff people does your studio have and what are their main working fields?

Our various backgrounds of fine art, graphics, design, new media and our cumulative apprenticeships influence our work. Nadia Gisler and Friedrich-Wilhelm Graf (the founding members) started to work together on some projects 4 years ago. We figured out that we liked working together and that we complemented each other perfectly. As we became more committed to the development of our projects, we founded Unfolded in winter 2003. Since then we work together with a small staple of patient freelancers. Depending on the project, they are trained photographers, media artists, programmers, editors, etc. Unfolded sometimes works as a pair or a group of three. We try to assess the needs of our clients. Depending on the size and nature of the project, we do work with specialists from a small network that is based not only in Zurich, but also worldwide. There are a couple of individuals we like a great deal, who we work often work with. To sum it up, the end result is more than what we started out with. 2 + 2 can sometimes equal more than 4. To define what kind of work we do a little more in two or three sentences? We are doing art: art direction, graphic and design. Analog and digital, time-based and timeless. Most importantly, no matter whether it is print or digital: interactive.

3. How does a regular working day at your studio look like, how is the day structured?

We wake up and we hope that we'll get the chance to go to sleep tonight.

4. How much leisure time do you have during a year?

Next question please.

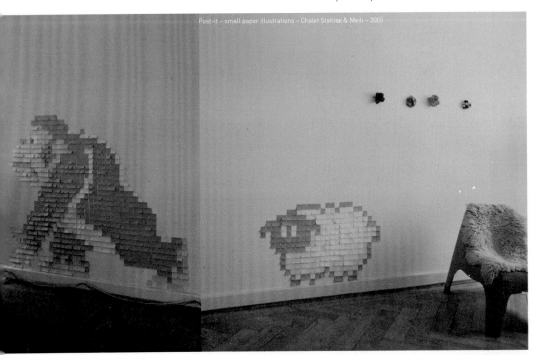

Post-it – small paper illustrations – Chalet Stahler & Meili – 2005

Theater blood 06 – diarybox, path and sticker – Swiss theater association – 2005

It-pool – programm poster – itz (it centre), school of art and design Zurich – 2007

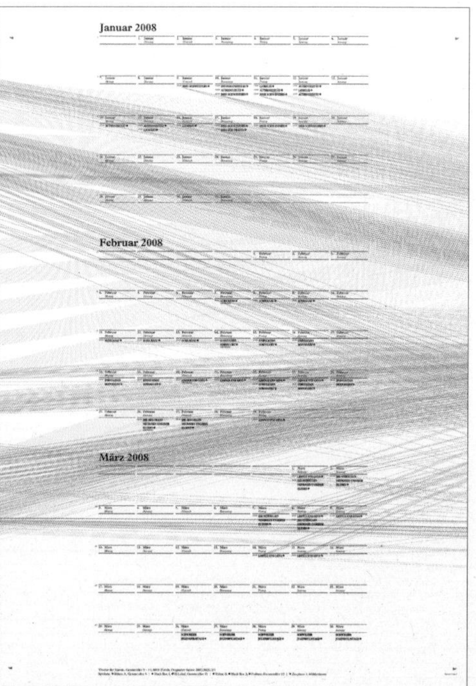

5. Which business areas do your clients mainly come from? Is the number of your clients increasing or rather declining?

Cultural/art clients, architecture, fashion, all and nothing. Not sure about declining or increasing, it is more important to develop a relationship which lives on after the first/initial project.

6. Do you have a specific corporate philosophy or maybe a mission statement like other companies, which is reflected in the way you steer the studio's course?

Passion, for work, process and output. Love for details and appreciation for the side stories, while always maintaining an eye for the big picture.

7. What, from your point of view, makes the difference between a small studio and a big company?

Process/discussions/making stuff and feedback are clearer, more direct and hopefully more sincere.

8. What kind of advantages and disadvantages does a small studio have compared to a big company?

As the Notorious B.I.G. said: "Mo Money, Mo Problems."

9. What is your idea about the future of small studios? Do you think that small studios do not have any other choice but to expand in order to survive in these times of globalization?

It appears that for the moment, structures tend to be developing in the direction of small units: well-networked, naturally global, better informed. Location isn't an issue anymore. Sometimes one knows more about the day-to-day life in Queens (NYC) than in their own city (district 4 in Zurich).

Spiilplätz – stamp and poster – design for a Swiss youth theatre festival – 2005

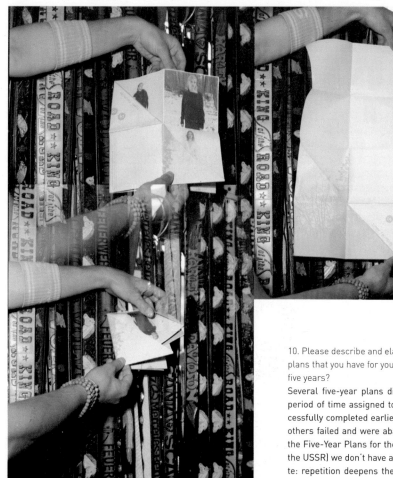

Winter 04|05 – fold-out poster-catalogue – Tommy Fjordside – 2004

10. Please describe and elaborate on the goals or plans that you have for your studio for the next five years?

Several five-year plans did not require the full period of time assigned to them (some were su cessfully completed earlier than expected, while others failed and were abandoned (for example, the Five-Year Plans for the National Economy of the USSR) we don't have any 5 year plans... Quote: repetition deepens the relationship between the different centers in the brain, which measures on brain activity waves. (Stefan Klein)

It-pool – programm poster – itz (it centre), school of art and design Zurich – 2007

it-pool
HERBST 2007

ALLGEMEINE INFOS IT-POOL

WANN STEHT DER KURS?

WER DARF TEILNEHMEN?

WAS KOSTET ES FÜR HGKZ-STUDIERENDE?

WAS BEZAHLEN HMT-STUDIERENDE?

UND DIPLOMANDEN?

WAS GILT FÜR EXTERN STUDIERENDE?

WIE BITTE?!

OS X FOR BEGINNERS

MACBOOK FITNESS

NEU: UBUNTU GNU/LINUX FOR BEGINNERS

VORAUSSETZUNGEN

UND TROTZDEM: MACOFFICE

NEU: UBUNTU STUDIO

DAS PROJEKT – GUT GEPLANT UND ORGANISIERT

DIGITALE FOTOGRAFIE

APPLE-ZERTIFIZIERUNGSKURS FÜR FINAL CUT PRO

ILLUSTRATION MIT ADOBE ILLUSTRATOR

TYPOGRAFIE UND LAYOUT (ADOBE INDESIGN)

TYPOGRAFIE-WORKSHOP FÜR FORTGESCHRITTENE

VISUALISIEREN IM VIRTUELLEN 3D-RAUM (CINEMA 4D)

ANIMIERTE 3D-WELTEN (CINEMA 4D)

NEU: ENTWERFEN UND KONSTRUIEREN IM 3D-RAUM (SOLID WORKS)

DIGITALER VIDEOSCHNITT (FINAL CUT PRO)

GRAFIK UND VIDEOANIMATION (AFTER EFFECTS)

BILDMONTAGE MIT ADOBE PHOTOSHOP

INTERAKTION UND ANIMATION MIT FLASH

PORTFOLIO ONLINE (WEB 0.5)

WEB HINTER DEN KULISSEN (WEB 1.0)

SMART CODE (WEB 2.0)

APPLE-ZERTIFIZIERUNGSKURS FÜR LOGIC PRO

INTERAKTION MIT MAX

EINSTIEG IN DIE DIGITALE MUSIKWELT

DVD PRODUZIEREN (DVD STUDIO PRO)

MUSIKPRODUKTION MIT DEM COMPUTER (LOGIC PRO)

MUSIKNOTATION MIT DEM COMPUTER (FINALE)

Visual Group Budapest

team:
David Barath
Aron Barath
Valentin Bajkov
contact:
Graphisoft Park
Apartmanház, fszt. 1.
Záhony u. 7.
1031 Budapest
Hungary
david@visualgroup.hu
www.visualgroup.hu

Visual Group is a Budapest-based creative consultancy specialized in art direction, graphic design and selective management of leading creative professionals in the field of photography and animation. They can offer you complete solutions from text to pictures and 3D for your ad campaign, or simply to make the best portrait of you ever made.

Interview with Visual Group Budapest

1. What led to the formation of your studio?

I have worked for years at advertising agencies and publishing houses, and in the meantime I was also working on my own projects. As time went by, I had more and more private assignments (logo and corporate identity, website and poster design) and I was more and more upset and bored by agencies' daily rush and poor quality work. In 2003, I founded Visual Group and since then I have been producing dozens of works I am proud of.

2. How many staff people does your studio have and what are their main working fields?

We are four alltogether. Valentin Bajkov is working on 3D designs and animations, my brother Aron Barath is a graphic designer and he's organizing pre-press and dtp works. Viktoria Vamosi is responsible for client service and photo productions' organizing, and I am the creative and managing director. I also do some designs, especially when a sophisticated logo is needed. We work with at least 20 freelancers: photographers, make-up artists, hair stylists, fashion stylists and copywriters.

3. How does a regular working day at your studio look like, how is the day structured?

There is no regular working day. We are generally quite busy and all sitting in the office, working on the computer and hanging on the phone. Shooting days are different, as me and Viktoria spend the whole day with the creative team in the photo studio or on locations. On these days, Valentin and Aron have some rest in the office.

4. How much leisure time do you have during a year?

August is quite calm, everybody is on holiday, I skip work at least for two weeks. At least 4-5 times a year I pack my suitcase and visit various European cities' design or art fairs and exhibitions. These trips usually take 4-5 days.

5. Which business areas do your clients mainly come from?

We work mostly for bigger agencies who need some fresh ideas. We act as an outsource company for them, in creating creative conceptions, producing photo shootings and 3D animations. We also work for magazines, producing fashion stories for fashion companies, producing catalogues and other pr materials. Our graphic design activity is focused around theatre and festival posters and smaller companies' logo, website and corporate identity works. The number of our clients is constantly growing, we usually have 6-8 projects at the same time, while last year this number was around 3-4. We have to confess that many of these works don't fit our creative standards, but we can not allow ourselves to refuse working for big agencies.

Romeo & Juliet – identity design/branding – Romeo & Juliet/fashion and design store – 2005

Thealter – poster – MASZK Szeged – 2005

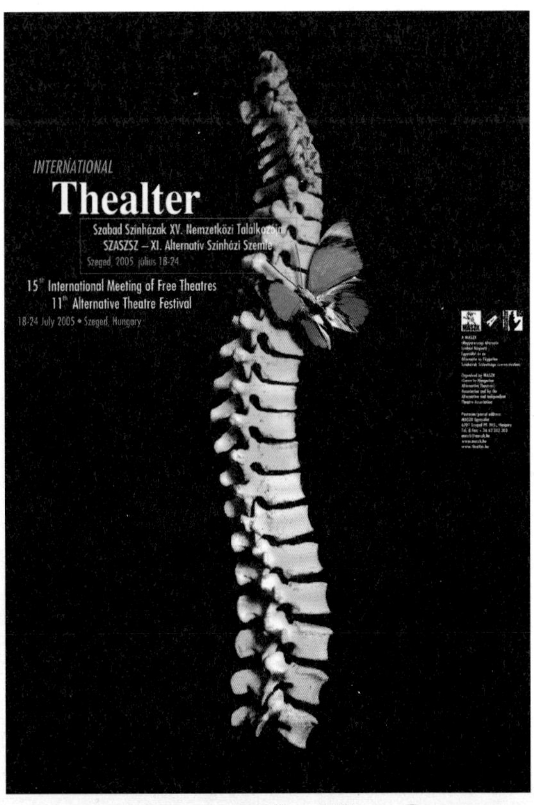

321 art of the sign – identity design/branding – 321 art of the sign – 2007

Free jazz festival – poster – free jazz festival – 2006

6. Do you have a specific corporate philosophy or maybe a mission statement like other companies, which is reflected in the way you steer the studio's course?

Less is more. Use Helvetica. Don't chat, work instead.

7. What, from your point of view, makes the difference between a small studio and a big company?

A small company is always more flexible and can offer more custom-made solutions than a big company. Our ideas are always fresh, while agency art directors' ones are often sear.

8. What kind of advantages and disadvantages does a small studio have compared to a big company?

Advantages are listed above. Disadvantages come from the missing financial background: we are often offered to enter a big competition or a tender, but to do that, we should rent a bigger studio, buy some new Macs and hire dozens of people. We cannot do that – maybe because we don't even want to.

9. What is your idea about the future of small studios?

None at all. I think the future of advertising and communication tends towards more personalized solutions. And a factory cannot always provide that. In the quality vs. quantity fight, the previous one will be winning.

10. Please describe and elaborate on the goals or plans that you have for your studio for the next five years?

We would like to have more foreign clients.

Our experience is that German, Serbian and Swedish clients are much more open-minded and don't want to tell us how to design a logo or a website. We also want to develop our photo production department by producing catalogues, ad campaigns and other materials for international fashion brands.

Free Jazz Festival
Regional Creative Atelier-Josef Nadj
18-22. Septembar 2006. • Kanjiza, Srbija i Crna Gora

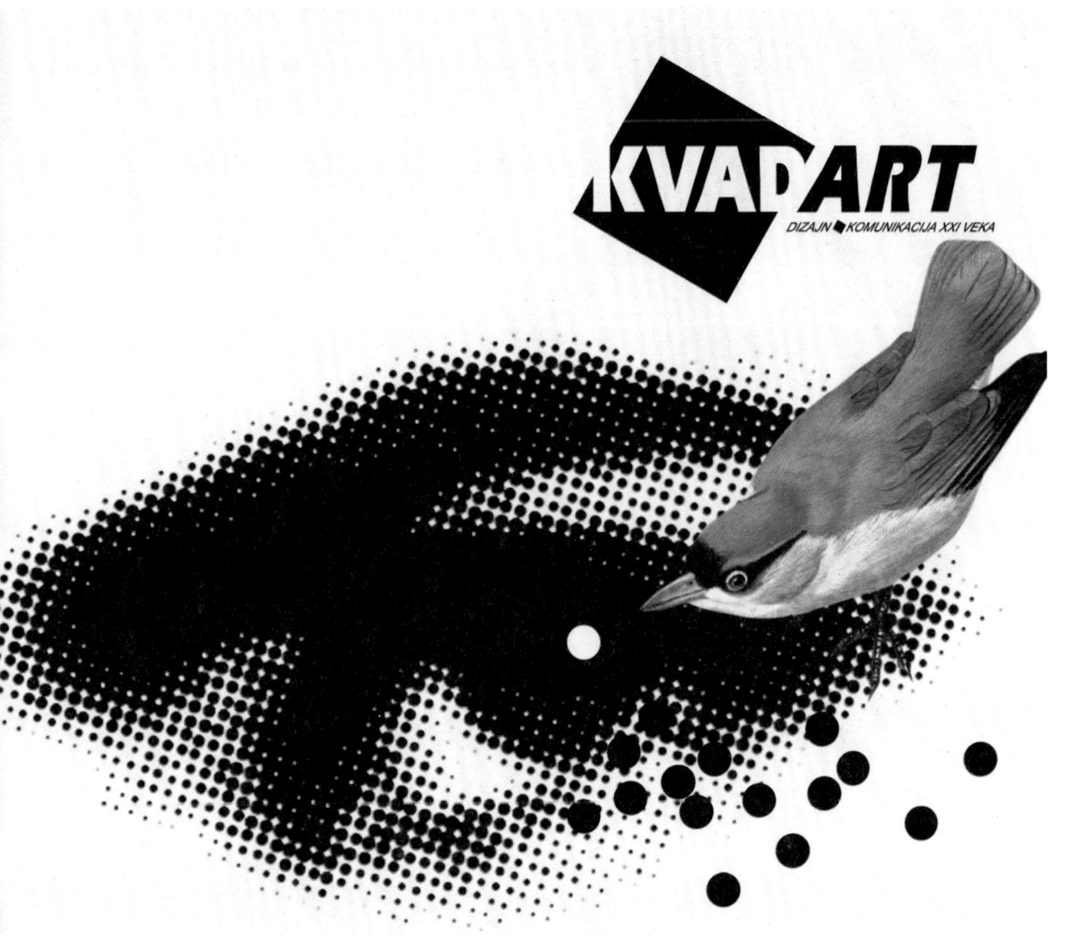

KVADART – cover design – KVADART magazine – 2003

Make love not war – poster – personal project – 2005

G13 art gallery – branding – G13 art gallery – 2007

Thealter – poster – MASZK Szeged – 2000

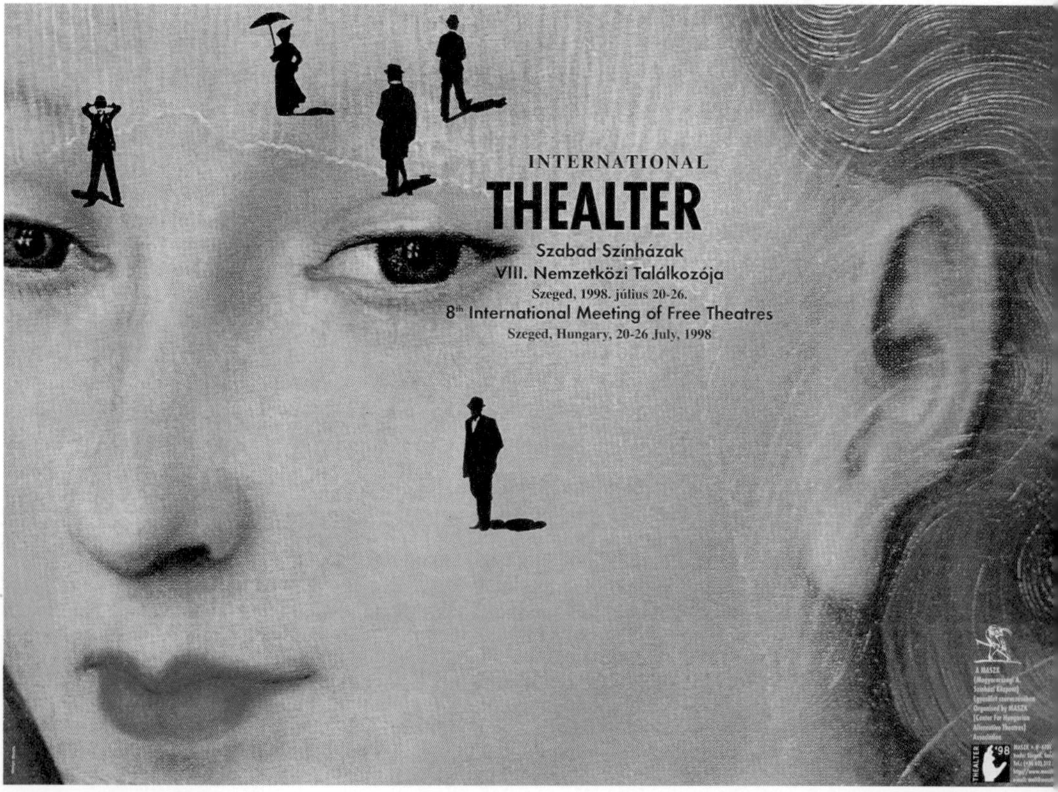

BLACK &
WHITE
FASHION
PHOTOGRAPHY
EXHIBITION AT
G13 ART GALLERY
29 NOVEMBER-15 DECEMBER 2007.
G13
G13 Art Gallery

Zhi-Hong Wang

team:
Zhi-Hong Wang
Yu-Wen Hsu
contact:
2F., No.5, Alley 3, Lane 359,
Fujin St., Songshan District,
10583 Taipei, Taiwan
T + 886 2 27635359
art.wzh@msa.hinet.net

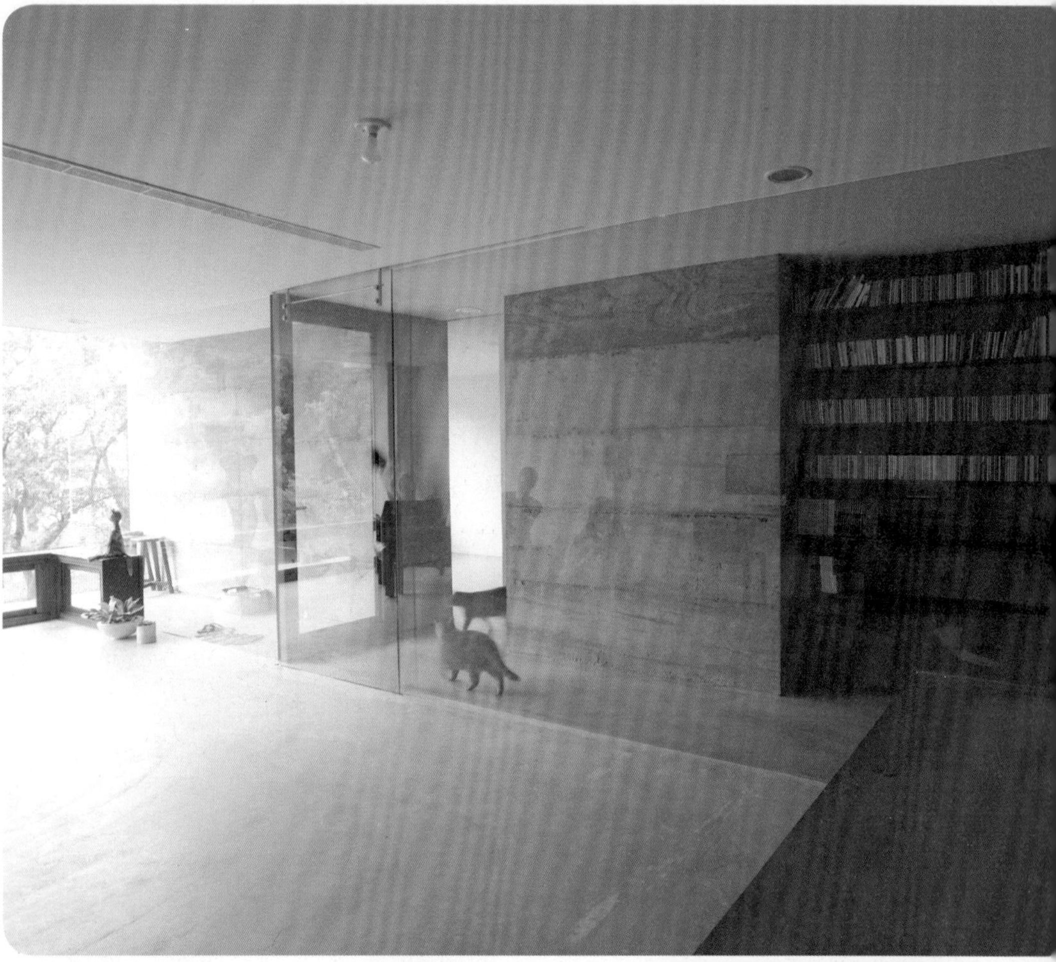

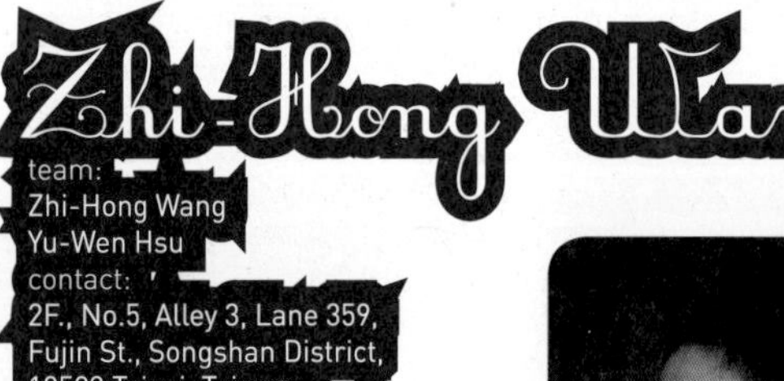

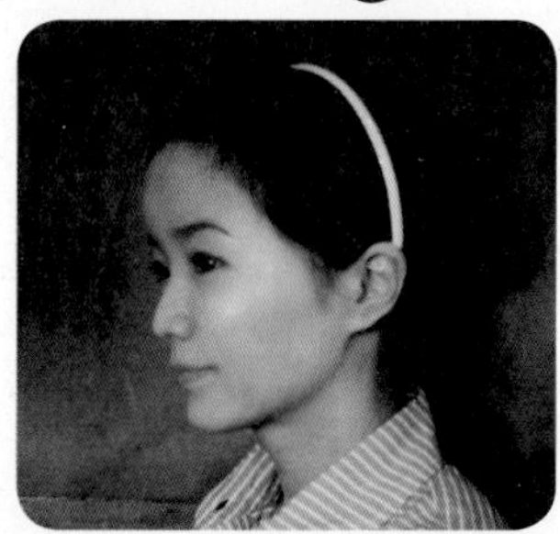

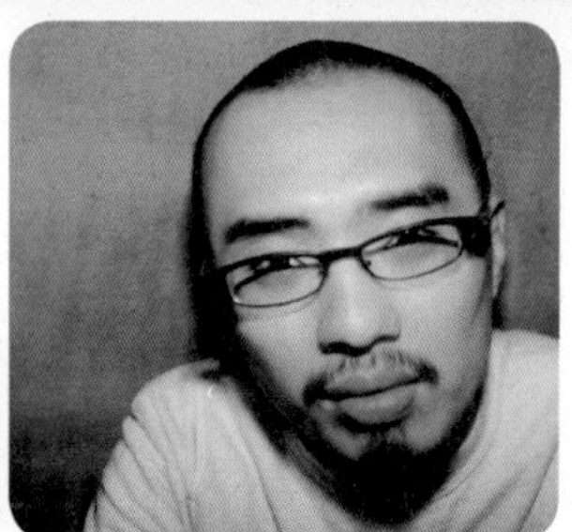

Zhi-Hong Wang, born in 1975 in Taipei, is a highly acclaimed graphic designer based in Taiwan. In 1995, he graduated from Department of Advertisement Design at Fu-Hsin Trade and Arts School. He started his own studio in 2000, and has been specializing in graphic design for books of various categories as well as fine art projects and events ranging from architecture, film, to music and dance. In 2008, Wang Zhi Hong launched his book publishing program "In-sight" with a trade publisher, featuring translated works on art and design. He is a multiple award-winner, including IdN Design Award Best 101 (2001) and four Gold Medals at the Golden Butterfly Award (2005, 2008), Taiwan's highest honor for excellence in book design.

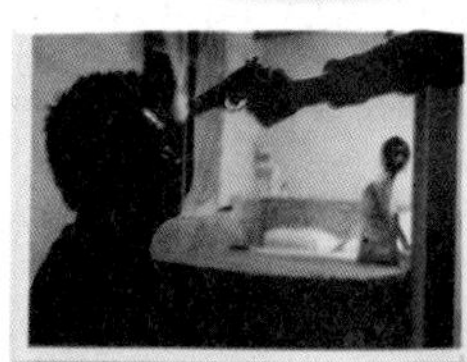

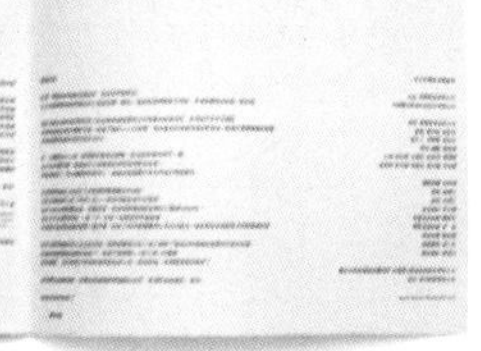

Do over- original soundtrack – CD – atom cinema – 2006

Tape-live in Taiwan – poster – node culture – 2006

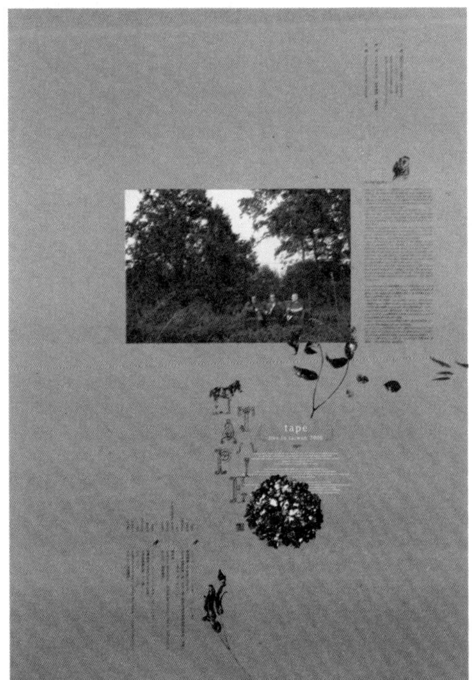

Interview with Zhi-Hong Wang

1. What led to the formation of your studio?

It was for having full control of my schedule and projects.

2. How many staff people does your studio have and what are their main working fields?

There are two of us. I am responsible for most of the projects. My partner shares some of my loads and sometimes helps on discussions and communications for certain projects.

3. How does a regular working day at your studio look like, how is the day structured?

Our workday usually lasts from noon until the next morning around 6. Most of our clients work during office hours, so the afternoon is the only time we can reach them by phone or have personal meetings inside and outside of our studio. At night we concentrate on work till dawn.

4. How much leisure time do you have during a year?

I work almost all year round.

5. Which business areas do your clients mainly come from?

My clients are mostly from the publishing industry. Some of them are from the fields of music and fine art, such as architecture, theater, dance and film. Their business areas sort of reflect my particular interests in the humanities. The projects with publishing houses, for instance, often deal with titles on architecture, literature, and cultural studies.

Is the number of your clients increasing or rather declining?

The number is increasing year by year.

HOLLOW

[adjective] 1: not solid; having a space or gap or cavity 2: deliberately deceptive 3: as if echoing in a hollow space [noun] 1: a cavity or space in something 2: a depression hollowed out of solid matter [verb] remove the inner part or the core of

HEART

bit everysound
number 001

featuring only electronic-folk

hello,
heart
!

August 28th of 2005
begins 5:00pm-11:00pm on Sunday evening
with Lim Giong J.j.j A-te Wang Zhi Hong Design
to enter: 200 NT dollars including 1 drink 2F, No.2, Lane 244, Sec 3, Roosevelt Rd, Taipei tel: 02-2364-1996

Hollow heart – poster –bit everysound – 2005

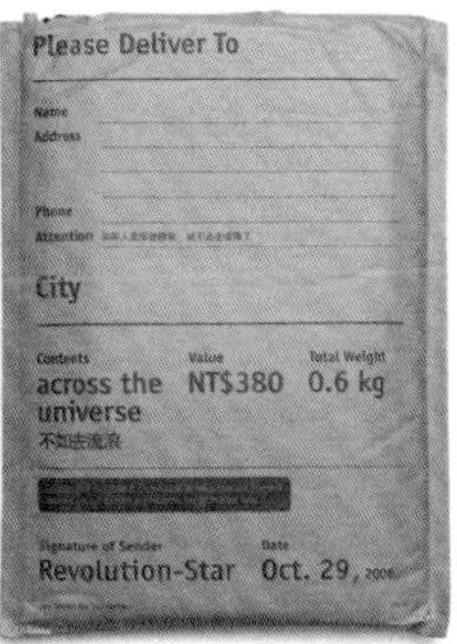

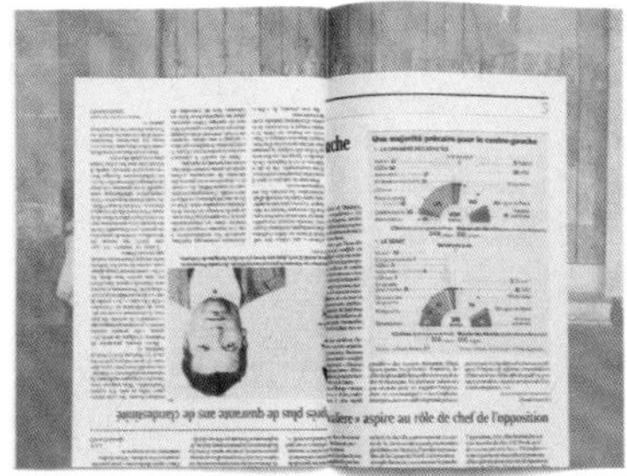

Across the universe - book - revolution-star - 2006

Across the universe - book - revolution-star - 2006

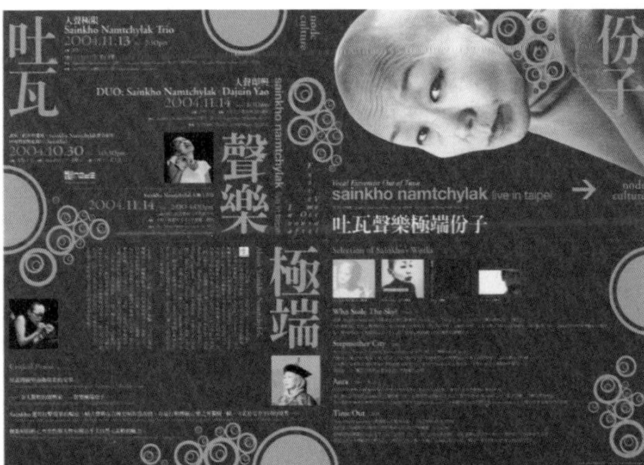

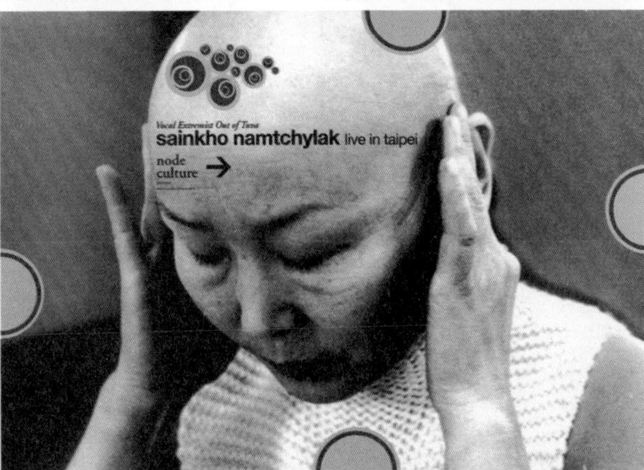

6. Do you have a specific corporate philosophy or maybe a mission statement like other companies, which is reflected in the way you steer the studio's course?

No.

7. What, from your point of view, makes the difference between a small studio and a big company?

The amount of resources.

8. What kind of advantages and disadvantages does a small studio have compared to a big company?

The advantage of big companies is to have more resources, so it is easier for them to take and execute bigger projects. Yet in return, they have more weights to bear, such as those of operation, finances, and personnel. As a result, it is harder for them to be consistent on the quality of their work or to pay attention to every detail. Very often they have to submit to clients' demands and to find a common ground when they disagree with each other. By contrast, small studios have less pressure on costs, which most likely means that we can stick to our original ideas; we can present our work as it is. This is the main reason I want my studio small and keep it small. Business success and artistic achievement are equally important to us. My goal is to find a balance between them and bring both of them to higher levels.

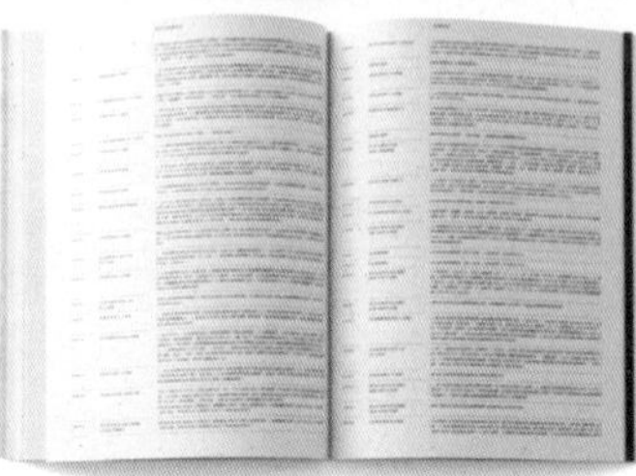
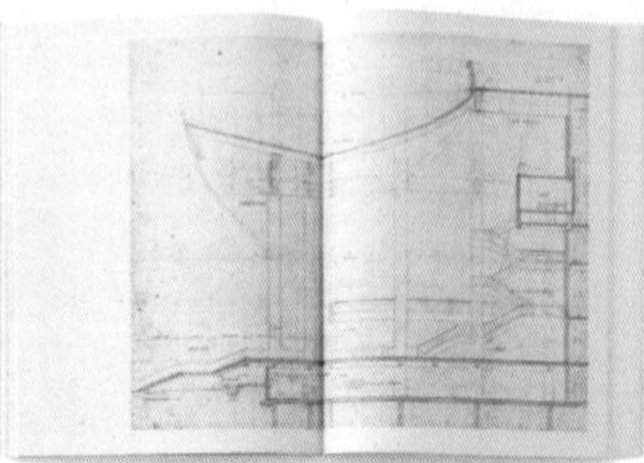

Insights of establishment of national Dr. Sun Yet Sen memorial hall – book – national Dr. Sun Yet Sen memorial hall – 2007

I'm a man: sex, gods and rock 'n' roll – book – business weekly publications – 2006

9. What is your idea about the future of small studios? Do you think that small studios do not have any other choice but to expand in order to survive in these times of globalization?

I think small studios will still be quite active in the future regarding their unique styles and operational models. In times of globalization, the strength of small studios is their flexibility. Expansion is not necessarily the right option for survival.

10. Please describe and elaborate on the goals or plans that you have for your studio for the next five years?

I have been thinking about publishing my own magazine, featuring subjects that I feel strongly about, for instance, architecture, cultural studies, and so on. My studio will be responsible for all the editorial work. In the face of commercialism this magazine would be so unique that it would tell people where my studio stands and what kind of impact I hope to make. This may be my five-year plan.

My blueberry nights – booklet – locus publishin – 2007

All I want is to speak simply
for this grace I pray.
For we have loaded down even the song
with so many kinds of music
That gradually it sinks.
And our art we so decorated
that beneath the gilt
Its face is eaten away.
And it is now time for us to say
the few words we have to say.
Because tomorrow our soul sets sail.

National Dr. Sun Yet Sen Memorial Hall

LONG TIME NO SEE

MR.DAHONG WANG! ARCHITECTURE EXHIBITION

久違了, 王大閎先生! 建築展

2007.11.17 (SAT) → 12.9 (SUN)

Exhibition Place: National Dr. Sun Yet Sen Memorial Hall 505, Jen-ai Rd. Sec. 4, Taipei
Inauguration: 2007.11.17 (SAT) 10:30 **Curator:** Ming-Song Shyu, Ching-Yueh Roan
Directive Organization: National Dr. Sun Yet Sen Memorial Hall
Executive Organization: Ming Chuan University
Sponsor Organization: Council for Cultural Affairs, Taiwan
Far Eastern Y. Z. Hsu Science and Technology Memorial Foundation

Long time no see, Mr. Dahong Wang! architecture exhibition – poster – national Dr. Sun Yet Sen memorial hall – 2007

Zhi-Hong Wang/601

Werkplaats Amsterdam

team:
Pieter Boddaert
Yolanda Huntelaar
contact:
Balistr. 43a
1094 JC Amsterdam
The Netherlands
T/F + 31 20 6630083
post@werkplaatsamsterdam.nl
www.werkplaatsamsterdam.nl

Illustrations for De Nicolaas Klei Wijnagenda 2009 (wine-diary 2009) – illustrations – podium and werkplaats Amsterdam – 2008

Werkplaats Amsterdam ("Workplace Amsterdam") was founded by the designers Pieter Boddaert and Yolanda Huntelaar in January 2007. After graduating in 1996 – both were in the same graduation-class at the Gerrit Retveld Academie Amsterdam – they had worked together for three years with Richard Niessen and Thomas Buxó as "OK-studio". Later, Pieter worked at two subsequent design studios in The Hague, while Yolanda became an independent designer in Amsterdam, sometimes cooperating with Roosje Klap and Esther de Vries. The former cooperation, however, was a good starting point for the professional reunion of the two in the end of 2006. The idea for Werkplaats Amsterdam was born while the long time friends Pieter and Yolanda were having diner one day. Pieter wanted to quit an unsatisfactory job, and Yolanda had lost the working space she shared with three other designers in Amsterdam. In March 2007, the studio was opened. Now, after one and a half year, Werkplaats Amsterdam has succeeded in acquiring different assignments in the field of publishing, history and culture, including the design of two books for the independent literary publisher Podium. Other assignments include the design of graphic identities, websites and typefaces, but also illustrations and three-dimensional work. Apart from that, they print more autonomous work on their own 1969-Korrex-Nuernberg printer. The "Wine-diary", a project initiated by the designers themselves, in which they are designers/illustrators as well as editors-in-chief, came to the stores in October 2008. Since 2006, Pieter also teaches typographic design at the Royal Academy of Arts in The Hague.

Interview with Werkplaats Amsterdam

1. What led to the formation of your studio?

Bad luck turned good. Yolanda lost the working space she shared with three other designers in Amsterdam. Pieter quit a job that he did not like anymore. One day, while the long time friends Pieter and Yolanda were having diner, the latter suggested they might possibly cooperate in the future. Soon after, Werkplaats Amsterdam ("Workplace Amsterdam") was formed.

2. How many staff people does your studio have and what are their main working fields?

Two: Yolanda Huntelaar and Pieter Boddaert. Like the duo Lennon-McCartney, there is no longer any individual work in our cooperation. Even when 95% of the work is done by just one of us, the result is still 100% Werkplaats Amsterdam. Our main working fields are, for the both of us: typography, book design and illustration, but also bookkeeping, website maintenance, and social networking.

3. How does a regular working day at your studio look like, how is the day structured?

We start at 9 a.m. and work until we are hungry. Then we have lunch at the studio and work again until 6. Since we both have children of our own, we are expected to be home on time most of the days. In busy times we sometimes work in the evenings, too. We have no planned internal meetings or strict schedules. We just do what has to be done and talk things over while doing this. We both work on the same projects, although not at the same time. So we are exchanging files and documents all the time, which gives us a fresh view our work. Whoever has time or the opportunity takes phone calls, pays visits to our clients, or goes shopping at the local supermarket.

4. How much leisure time do you have during a year?

We have granted ourselves five weeks of holidays each year. Sometimes we have to finish our work in the evenings, but not too often.

Guide for the modern woman – book – Uitgeverij podium, Amsterdam – 2008

Nice 2008/New Years greeting from werkplaats Amsterdam to realtions – hand-punched and hand-printed card – werkplaats Amsterdam – 2007

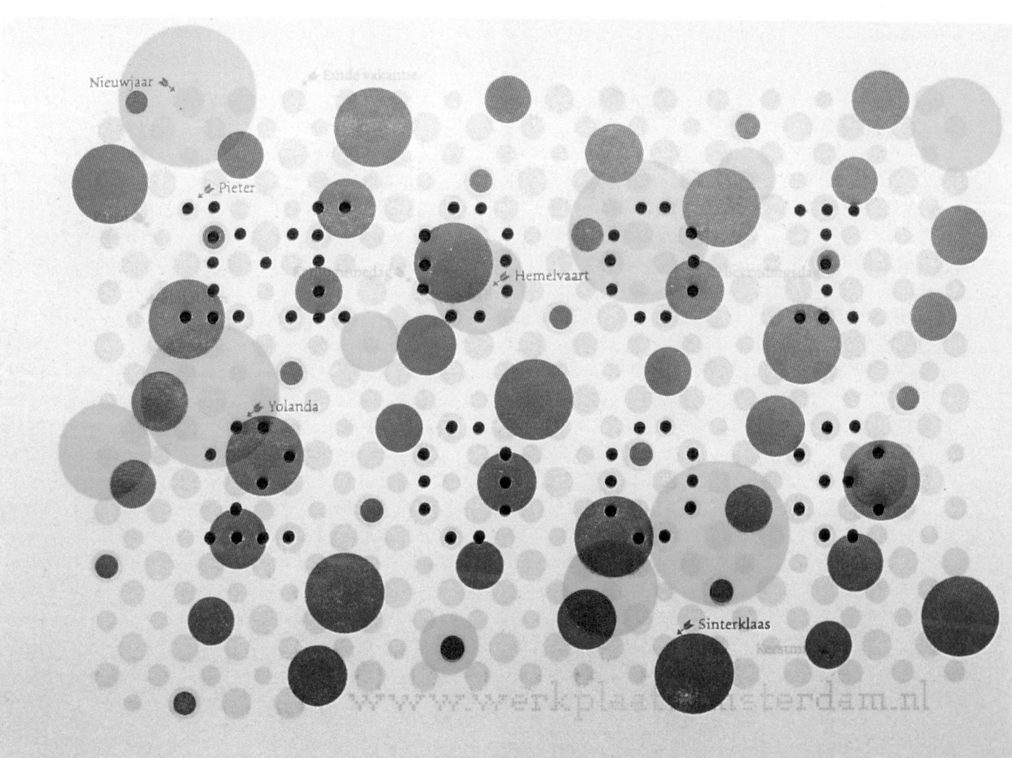

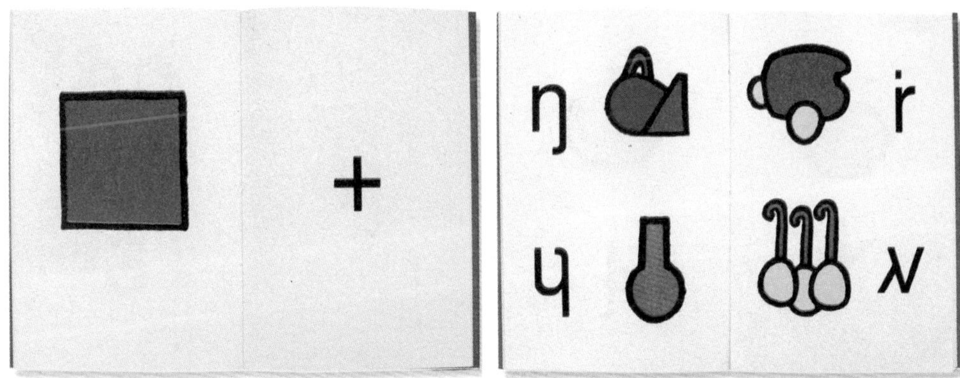
Unreadable alphabet – booklet – published by Uitgeverij de Buitenkant, Amsterdam – 1995

5. Which business areas do your clients mainly come from? Is the number of your clients increasing or rather declining?
Our (increasing) client base is coming mainly from the world of books, history and culture, but also, for instance, an elementary school and a communication agency. We are also responsible for creating our own projects. Like the project "Wijnagenda" (Wine-diary) in which we are designers and illustrators as well as authors and editors-in-chief.
6. Do you have a specific corporate philosophy or maybe a mission statement like other companies, which is reflected in the way you steer the studio's course?
One of Bruce Mau's statements describes it best: "Collaborate. The space between people working together is filled with conflict, friction, strife, exhilaration, delight, and vast creative potential." Furthermore, we think that every assignment and every budget deserves a solution of its own. By the use of the right techniques we give our designs an extra depth: use a punch instead of a color, mix two colors to create a free third one. The extra manual work involved is a welcome diversion from our work at the computer.
7. What, from your point of view, makes the difference between a small studio and a big company?
In a small studio a designer can be more autonomous and independent. However, this can only happen when the designer clearly chooses this way for himself/herself.
8. What kind of advantages and disadvantages does a small studio have compared to a big company?
Advantages: more freedom, less formality. Disadvantages: there is a lot of paperwork to be done, e.g. for taxes. But it's your own money, so you might as well control it yourself.

Home, history, costs, proofprinting – logo/icons for website – Uitgeverij Tienstuks (Tienstuks publishers) – 2008

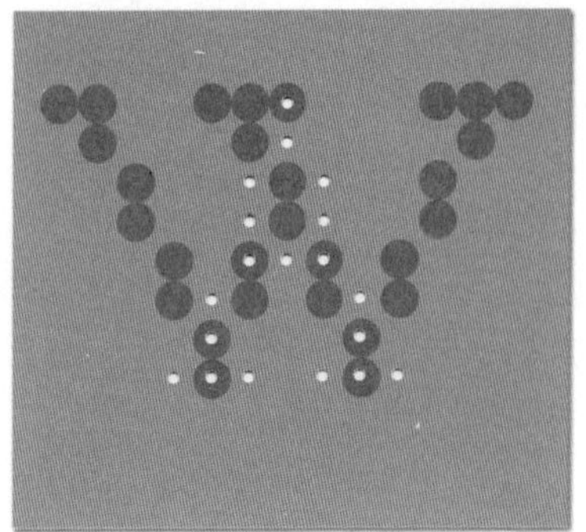

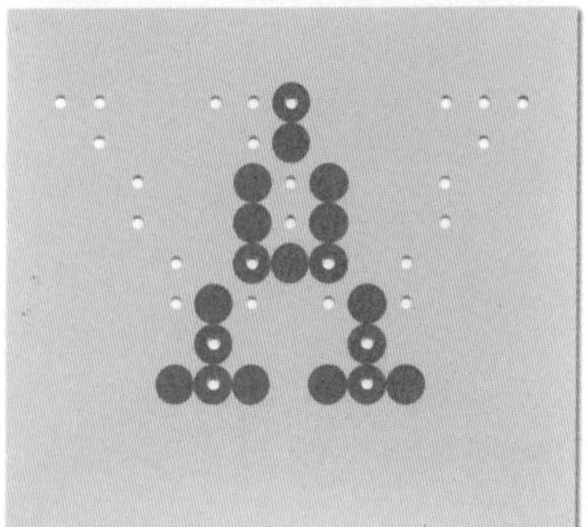

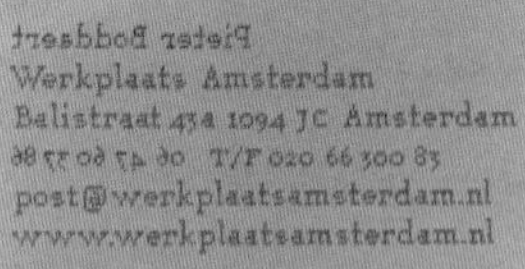

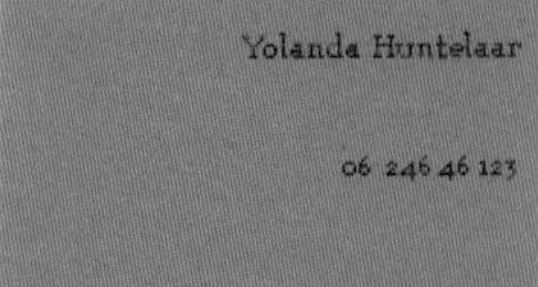

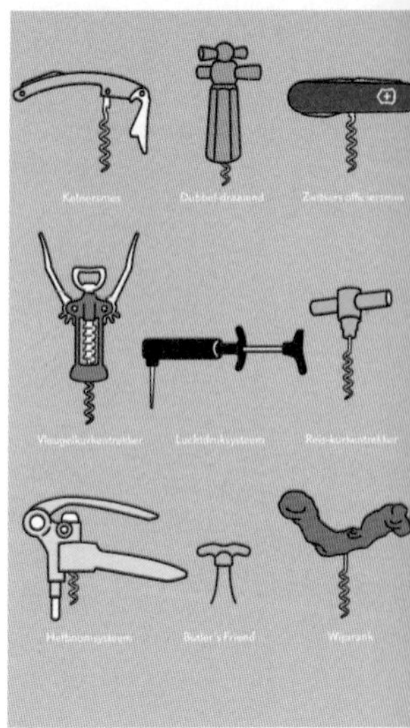

Illustrations for De Nicolaas Klei Wijnagenda 2009 (wine-diary 2009) – illustrations – Podium and Werkplaats Amsterdam – 2008

Insight into the studio - book - Ilona Herreiner - 20(

Back and Forth – proposal for a three-dimensional typographic installation at the roadside (in cooperation with Roosje Klap) – city of Breda – 2006

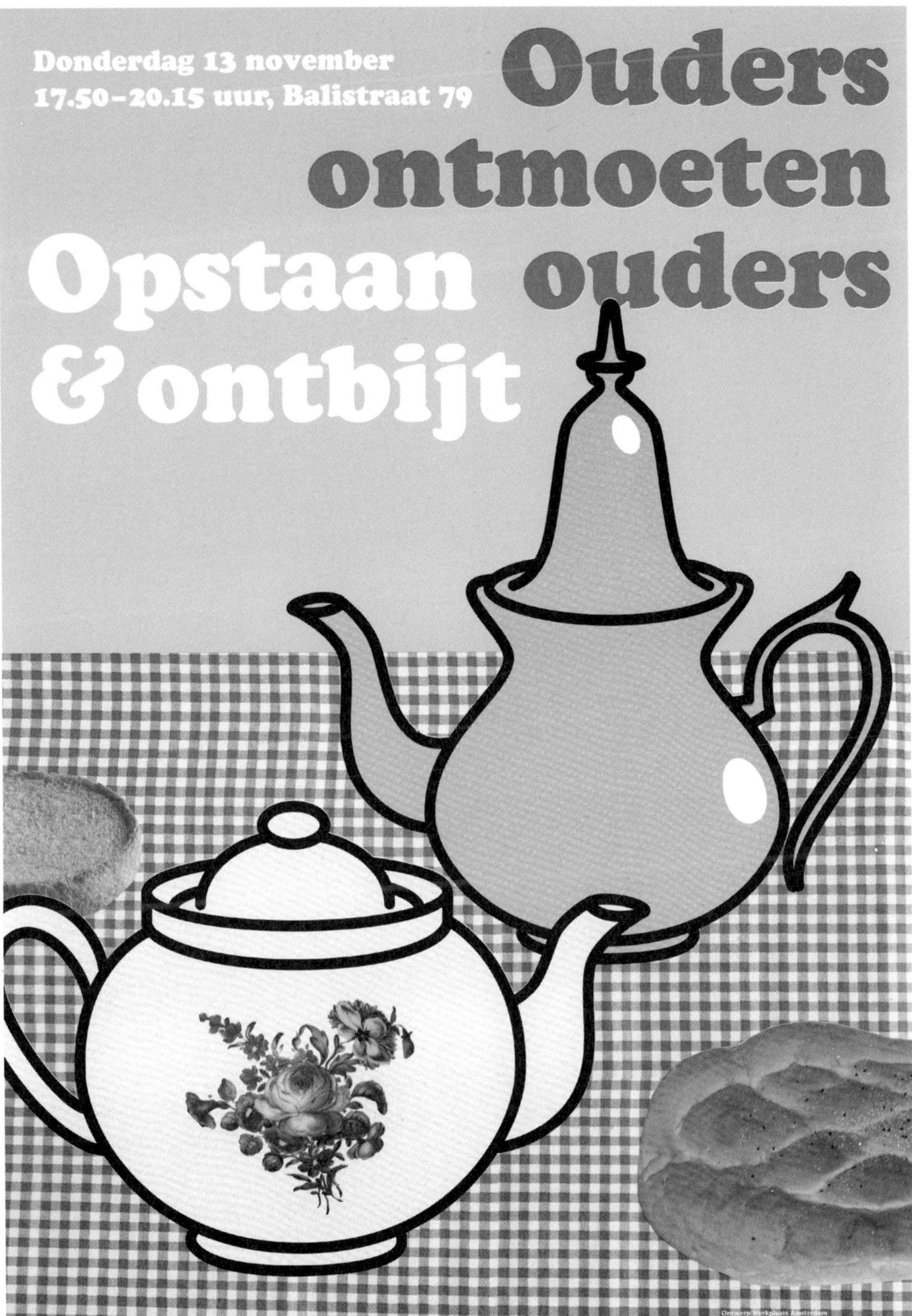

Parent meet with parents – flyer and poster – J.P. Coenschool Amsterdam – 2008

9. What is your idea about the future of small studios? Do you think that small studios do not have any other choice but to expand in order to survive in these times of globalization?

The rule of the big design factories is over. Small studios will become more and more influential. More clients discover that big design companies are less flexible (and sometimes less creative) than small studios. Even the big design companies know this and hire small studios to create designs for their big clients.

10. Please describe and elaborate on the goals or plans that you have for your studio for the next five years?

Stay independent. Stay true to ourselves.

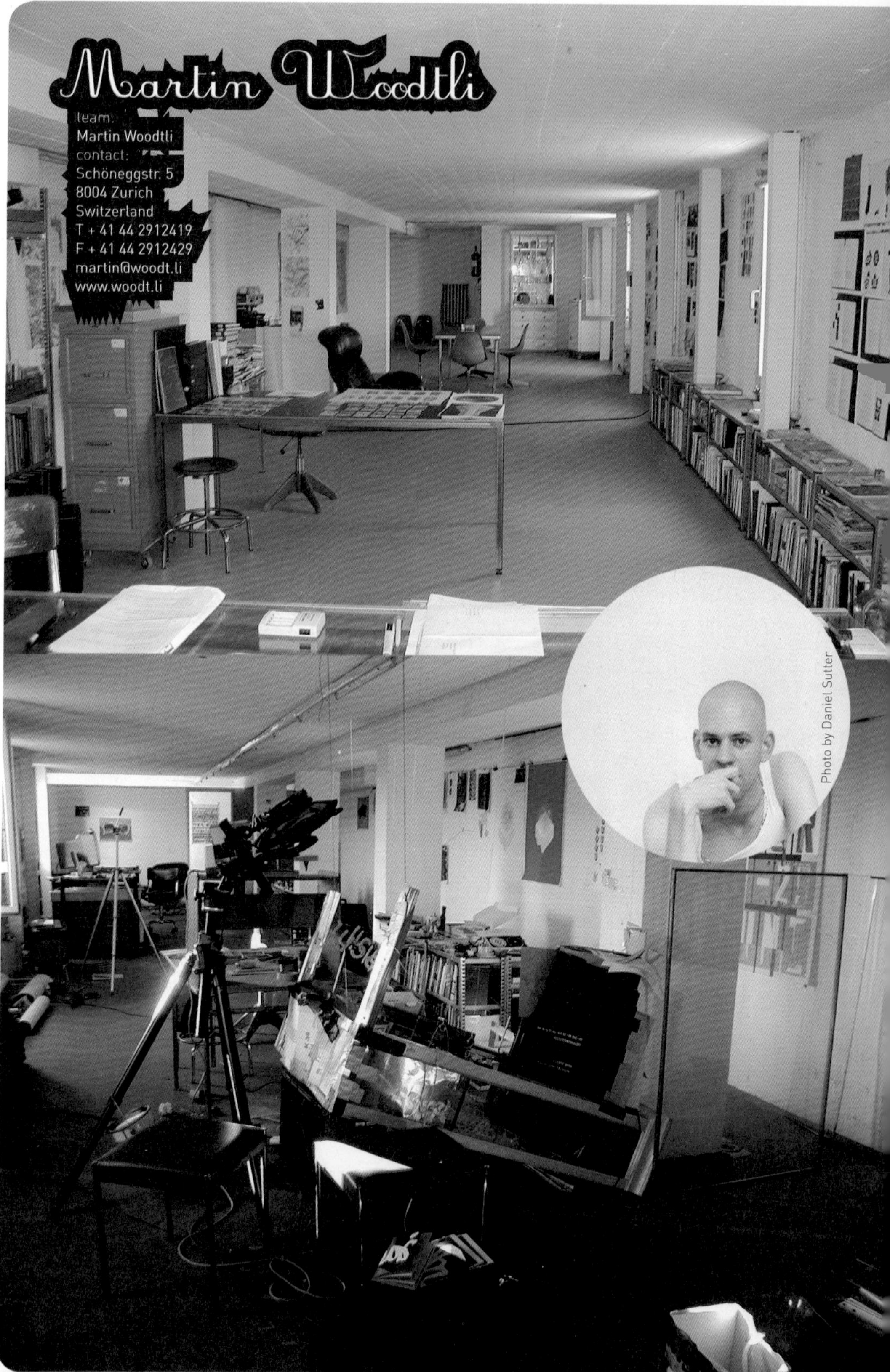
Martin Woodtli
team:
Martin Woodtli
contact:
Schöneggstr. 5
8004 Zurich
Switzerland
T + 41 44 2912419
F + 41 44 2912429
martin@woodt.li
www.woodt.li
Photo by Daniel Sutter

Martin Woodtli – born in 1971; graphic design apprenticeship in Bern; graduate studies at the University of Applied Sciences and Arts Zurich. Martin Woodtli has been working for David Carson and Stefan Sagmeister in New York and founded his own studio in Zurich in 1999. With idiosyncratic visual experiments and approaches he quickly made his mark within the international design scene and won several design awards. He is the author of the book "Woodtli" (Die Gestalten, Berlin 2002). Since 2001, he teaches at the Lucerne School of Art and Design and is a guest lecturer at diverse institutions in Switzerland and abroad. In a competition for the new Swiss banknote series he was nominated as second and received an invitation for the final round. In 2000 he became a member of the AGI. Martin Woodtli is associated with a young Swiss design scene, running their studios mainly with emphasis on passion and joy, rather than on monetary interests. Woodtli seems to live after a quote from the diary of Brian Eno: "to do something as persistently and sedulously as no one else would, is a good way of creating something unique." His work manifests itself in complex typographic arrangements and dense, manic-layered patterns of everyday objects.

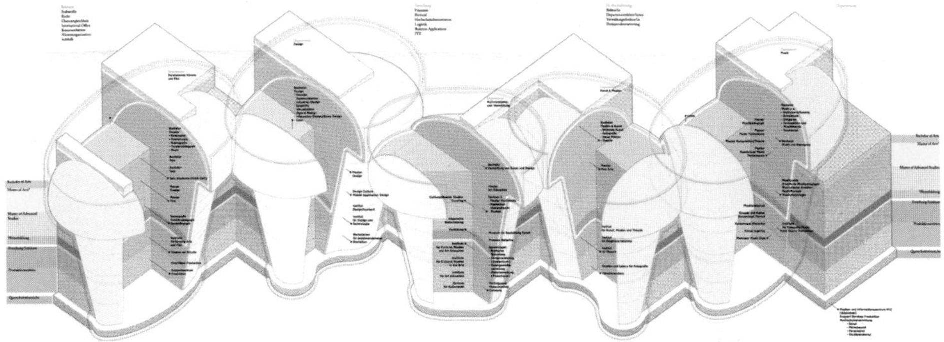

Organigram for founding the Zurich university of the arts – publication – ZHdK, Hans Peter Schwarz – 2007

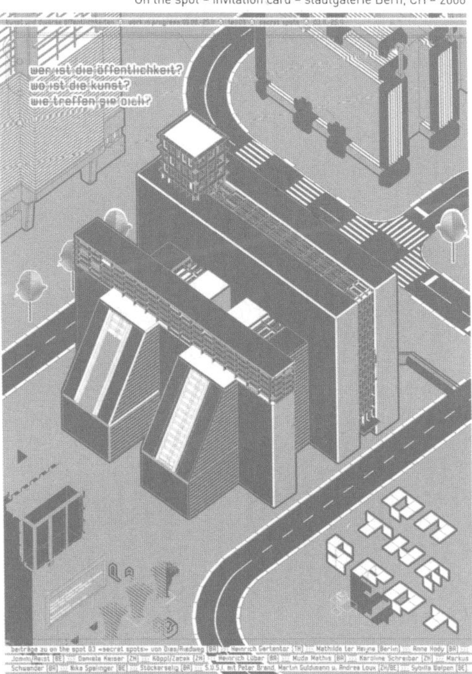

On the spot – invitation card – stadtgalerie Bern, CH – 2000

Interview with Martin Woodtli

1. What led to the formation of your studio?

The reasons for the studio's founding were the business demands in the cultural sector.

2. How many staff people does your studio have and what are their main working fields?

It is a one-person studio. The main focus is the domain of printing within the cultural sector.

3. How does a regular working day at your studio look like, how is the day structured?

The structure is to be arranged individually, as I usually work alone at the studio.

4. How much leisure time do you have during a year?

There are people running down the Amazon in their canoe, there are people that like bungee jumping off bridges, and there are people who design.

5. Which business areas do your clients mainly come from? Is the number of your clients increasing or rather declining?

Most of the customers come from the cultural domain. Additionally, there are customers from magazines and the commercial sector. The number of customers is always more or less the same.

6. Do you have a specific corporate philosophy or maybe a mission statement like other companies, which is reflected in the way you steer the studio's course?

Martin Woodtli belongs to a scene of young designers who keep their studios running by obsessions, by their enjoyment of designing – more than by monetary calculus. He seems to be re-living a line from the diary of Brian Eno: "to do something so persistently and sedulously like nobody else would be willing to take it upon oneself, is a good way to create unique things." Woodtli's work manifests in complex typographical arrangements, and in compact, wildly layered patterns of objects from everyday life.

7. What, from your point of view, makes the difference between a small studio and a big company?

See answer 6.

8. What kind of advantages and disadvantages does a small studio have compared to a big company?

Individuality and personal interests can be implemented more easily in a smaller environment. I do not see any disadvantages since I am not interested in short-dated profits.

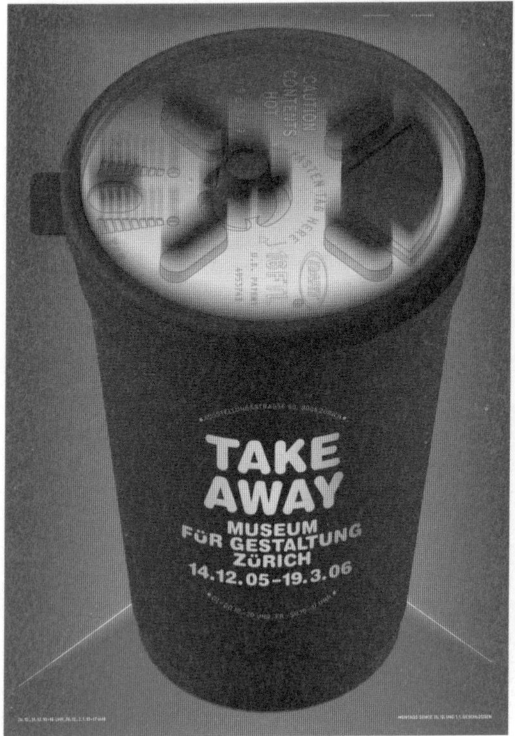

Take away – poster – museum of design Zurich – 2005

VideoEx – poster – international experimentalfilm & video festival – 2003

Play – poster – museum of design Zurich – 2005

Schaffhausen jazzfestival – poster – jazz festival Schaffhausen – 2003

Sportdesign – poster – museum of design Zurich – 2005

9. What is your idea about the future of small studios? Do you think that small studios do not have any other choice but to expand in order to survive in these times of globalization?

To my mind the crucial factor for being successful is not a studio's size but the cultivation of creative competence.

10. Please describe and elaborate on the goals or plans that you have for your studio for the next five years?

On the one hand, I want to carry on with my interests in graphics without repeating myself, and along the way remain in a permanent debate with my environment.

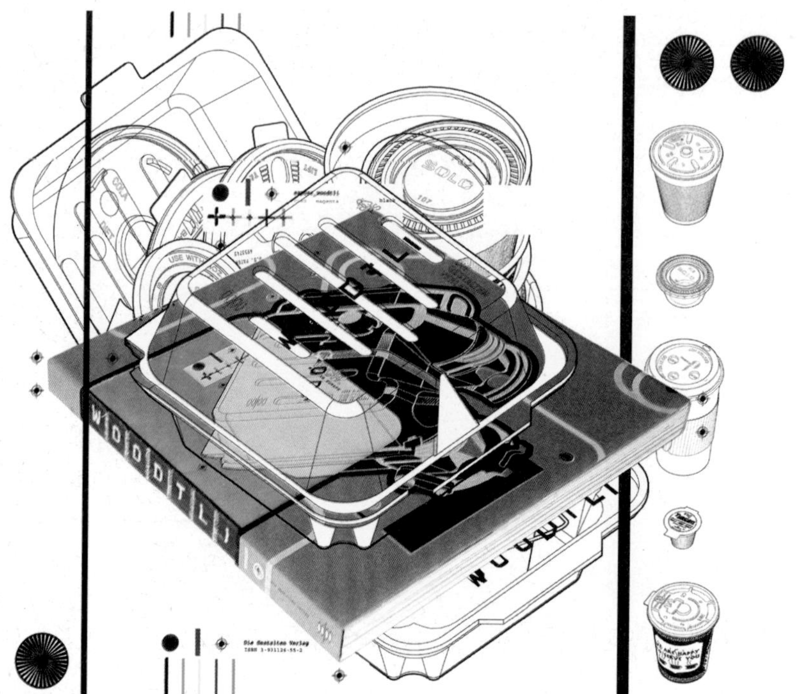

Woodtli– monograph about his work – die gestalten publisher, Berlin – 1996-2001

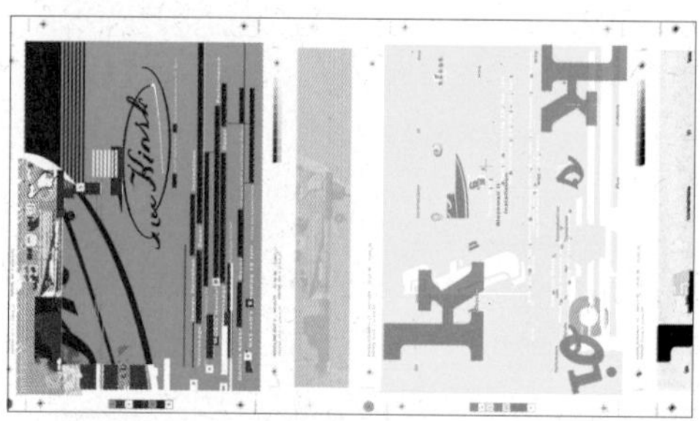

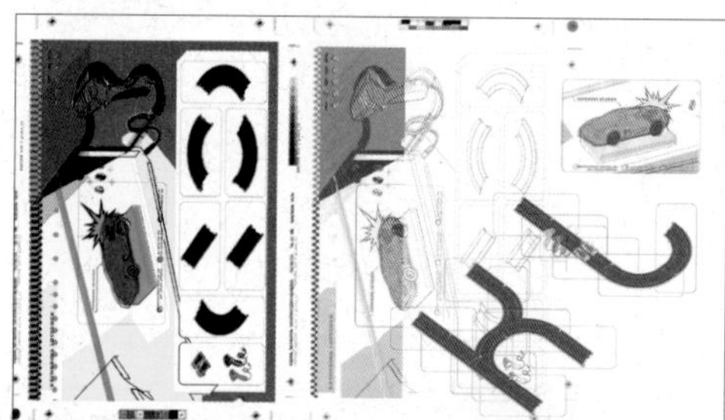

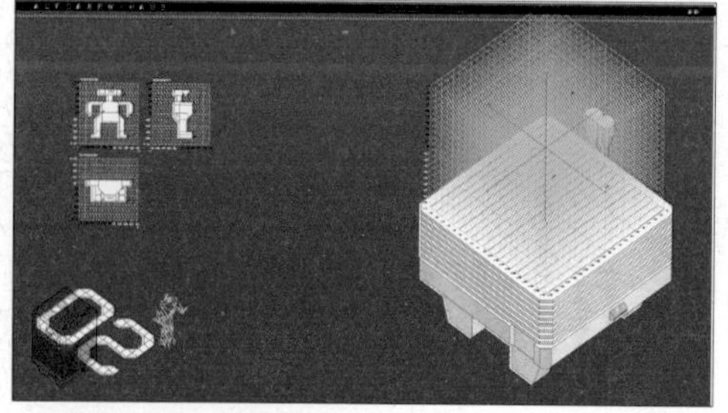

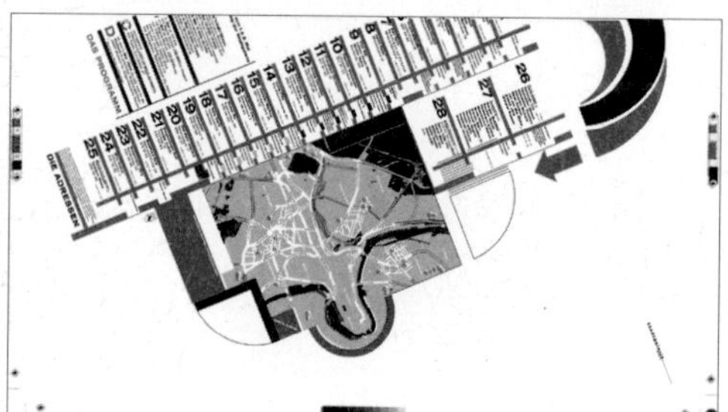

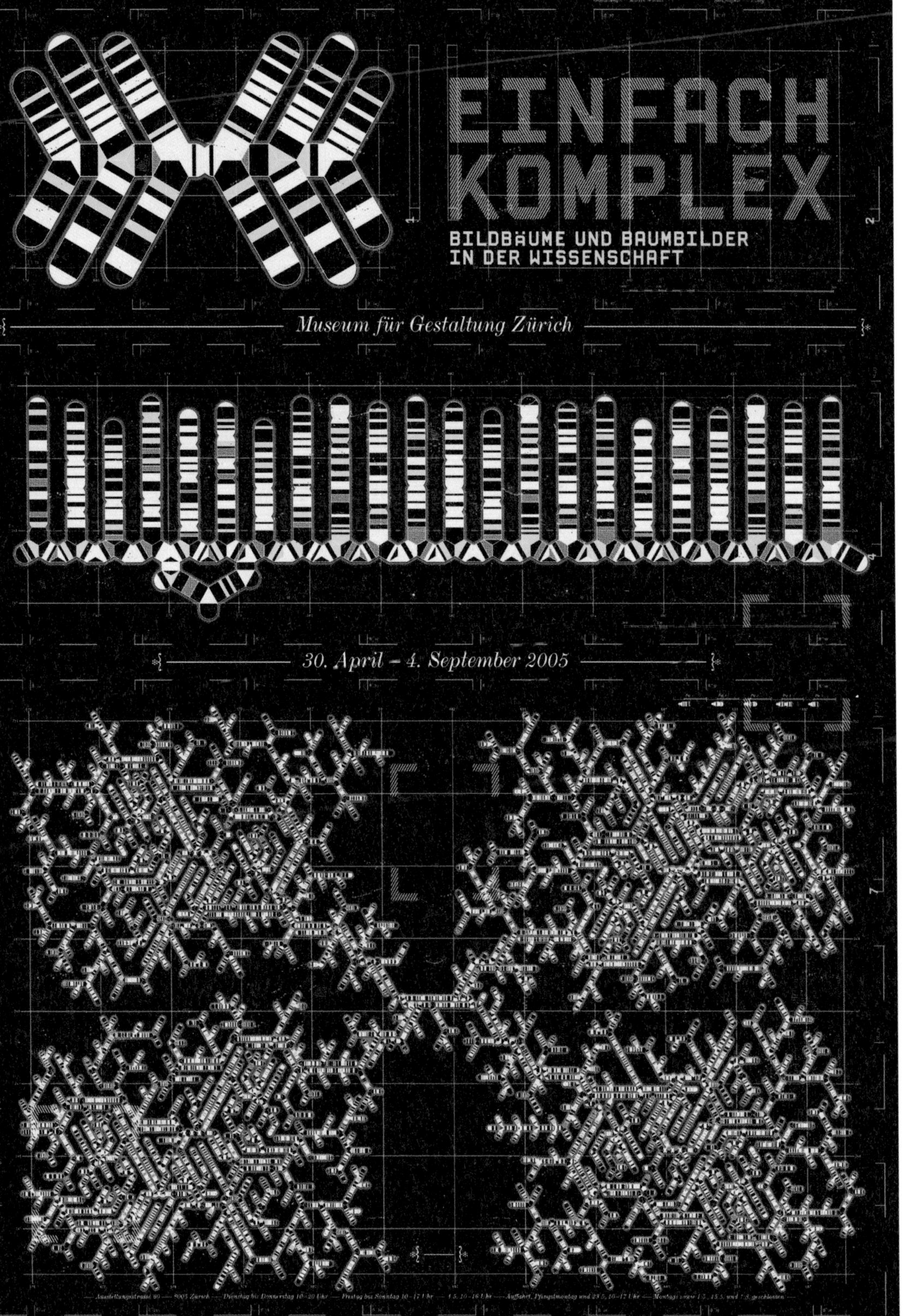

Simple-complex – poster – museum of design Zurich – 2005

Xiao Mage + Chengzi

team:
Xiao Mage
Chengzi
contact:
Dongsi 12 Tiao 21 Hao,
Room 402,
100708 Beijing, China
maggy2004@126.com

Xiao Mage + Chengzi graduated from the graphic design specialty, College of Fine Arts Tsinghua University in 2000, and jointly engaged in graphic design work from graduation to present. Works have obtained prizes for many times in domestic and foreign design competitions, including the silver cube of the ADC 87th Annual Award, the 07GDC biennial exhibition gold prize, the grand prize of the whole, the title of "The Beauty of Books in China" for four consecutive years in 2004, 2005, 2006 and 2007, and won gold prize of the 6th National Book Design Exhibition, in the exhibitions of "Get it Louder 2007", X Exbitors, 40 Contemporary Chinese Book Designers Exhibition and 70/80 New Hong Kong Designers Exhibition, etc..

Interview with Xiao Mage + Chengzi

1. What led to the formation of your studio?

In fact, there are not any reasons, one works as an editor of literature and art at a publishing house, the other has no job at present. What should we do ?

2. How many staff people does your studio have and what are their main working fields?

We both have to do all the work because we have no other staff members.

3. How does a regular working day at your studio look like, how is the day structured?

We devoted our efforts to work if we have assignments. We spend our time on going to the exhibitions, surfing the internet or sleeping while we have no tasks.

4. How much leisure time do you have during a year?

It depends. Sometimes we have leisure time, but probably we have to get into work at any moment.

5. Which business areas do your clients mainly come from? Is the number of your clients increasing or rather declining?

Museums, international art fairs, galleries, housing and land organizations, also environmental planning offices. Some are increasing, some are decreasing. It keeps a stable workload of us two.

6. Do you have a specific corporate philosophy or maybe a mission statement like other companies, which is reflected in the way you steer the studio's course?

As for designing work it is beyond people's energy (only describing us two).

7. What, from your point of view, makes the difference between a small studio and a big company?

Each staff member of the studio must be a hero, presenting heroic design. It is not easy that a small studio and a big company can succeed, they cannot replace each other.

8. What kind of advantages and disadvantages does a small studio have, compared to a big company?

The customers they serve are different, contents are also different. Sometimes we even feel we do not take on the same trade.

9. What is your idea about the future of small studios? Do you think that small studios do not have any other choice but to expand in order to survive in these times of globalization?

Small studios close the doors when their master cannot work. As for small studios, they will have to change in terms of quality if they expand.

10. Please describe and elaborate on the goals or plans that you have for your studio for the next five years?

We are trying to have a qualitative change if possible, and it means we will change our trade if a qualitative change takes place.

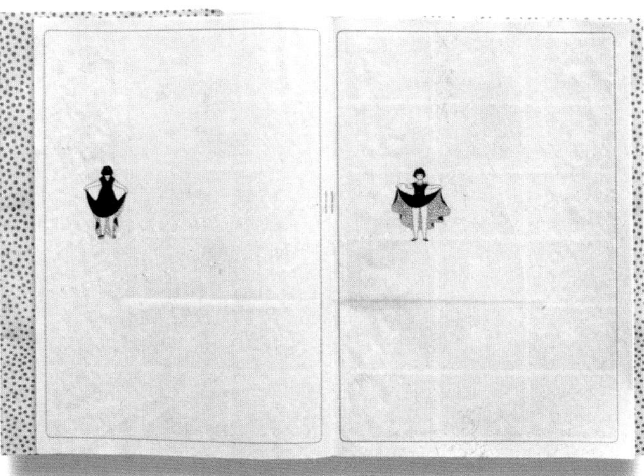

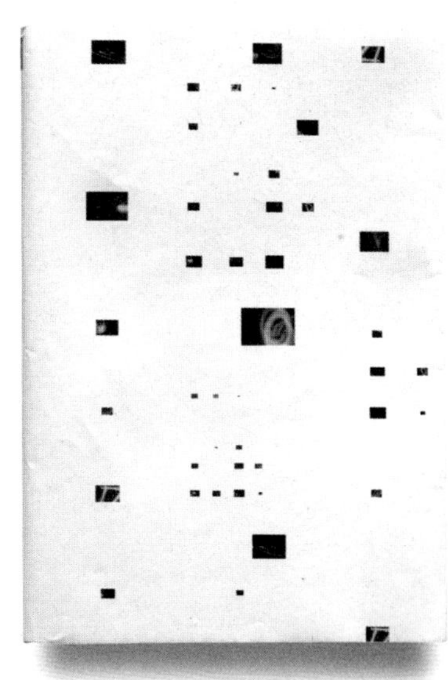

Quiet radical voice – catalog – 2007

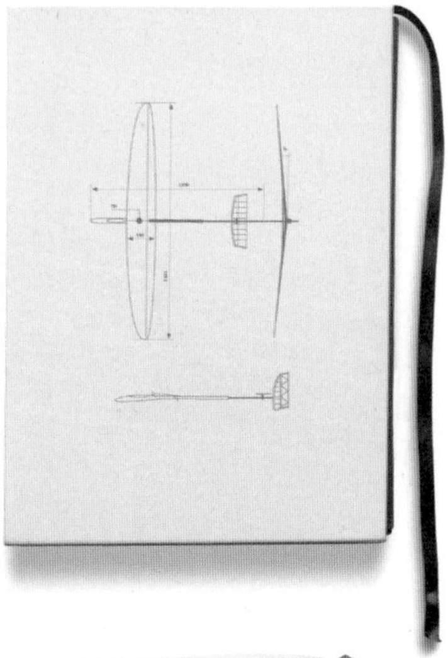

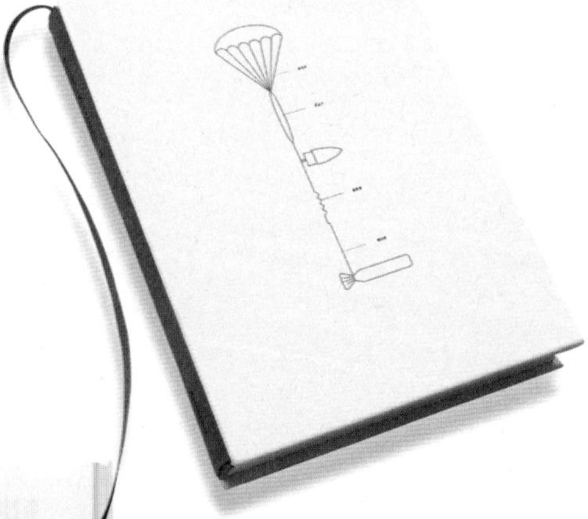

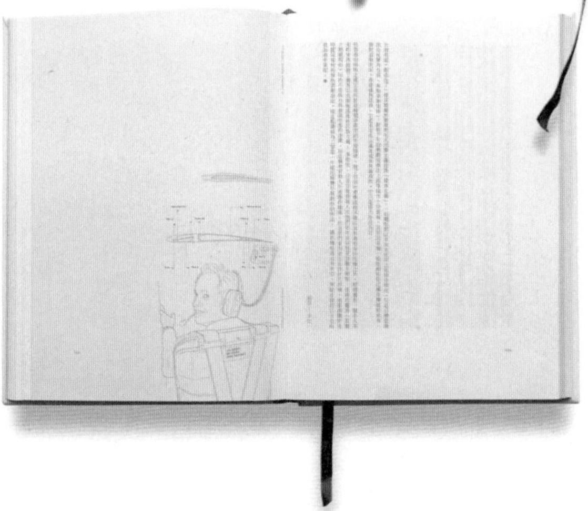

Airplanes and parachutes – booklet – 2008

40 contemporary Chinese book designers – catalog – 2008

Downtown production – catalog – 2007

Everything material, something immaterial/get it louder 2007 – catalog – 2007

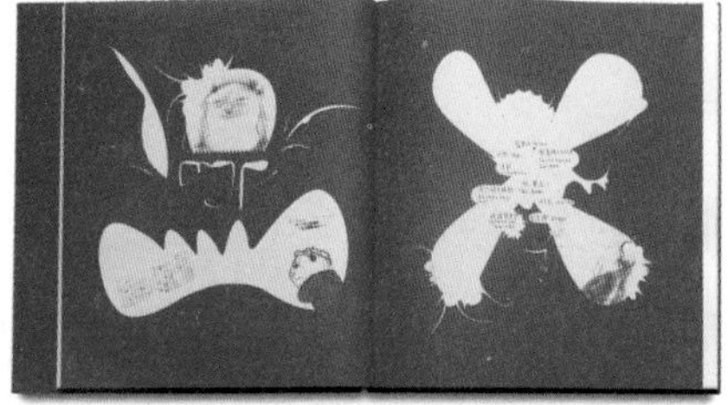

Comedy of youth – booklet – 2007

Invitation of book design exhibition – VI – 2007

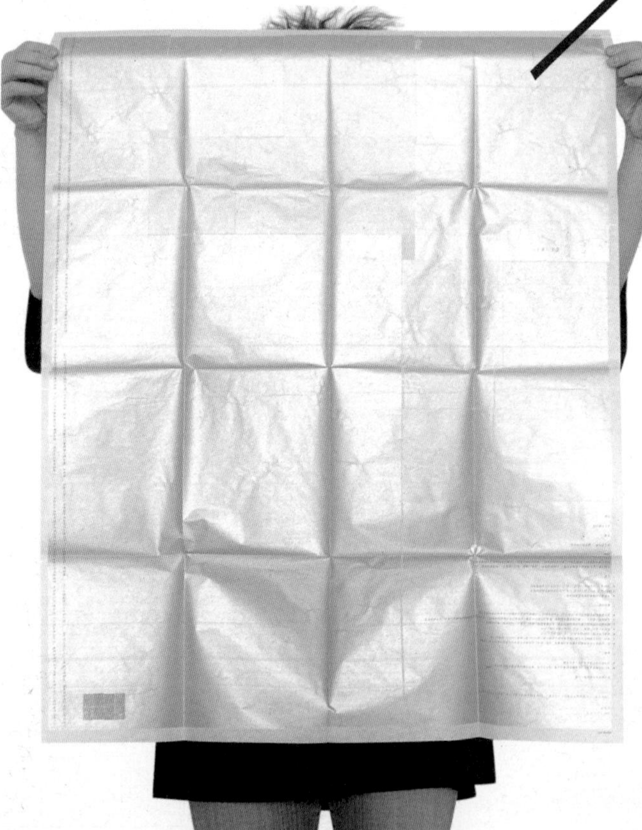

Comedy of youth – poster – 2007

Xiao Mage + Chengzi/619

team:
Colin Henderson
Daniel Brereton
contact:
Studio 101F,
203 Mare Street,
Hackney, London E8 3QE
United Kingdom
T + 44 7921135125
heyo@yofest.co.uk
www.colin-henderson.co.uk
www.yofest.co.uk

Yo!Fest was born in 2007 from an egg. From the egg hatched two eyes that went out to look for food. Yo!Fest enjoy making, playing football and eating. The town Yo! Ville is currently under construction, come and visit one day.

Yo!go – digital – Yo!Fest – 2007

Interview with Yo!Fest

1. What led to the formation of your studio?

Luck and good timing mainly. I graduated in 2006 and was working from home. It was by chance that when I moved to London and met Daniel Brereton, we found we had a mutual appreciation of each other's work and we ended up playing for the same football team. Daniel moved into a studio and I moved in a few months later.

2. How many staff people does your studio have and what are their main working fields?

The studio is occupied by myself and Daniel. We work independently but also collaborate. Daniel draws and directs music videos. I draw, design and provide art direction, although we both art direct and give guidance on each other's work.

3. How does a regular working day at your studio look like, how is the day structured?

Depending on how much work I/we have on, the day starts around 9 - 10 a.m., I check and reply emails, maybe do a bit of administration and paperwork for the first hour or so, and then work til lunch. The day finishes around 7 p.m.. There are also intermittent breaks of tea and table tennis.

4. How much leisure time do you have during a year?

I don't think I could give an exact figure! I work Monday to Friday, sometimes Saturday, but make sure that I have enough time off to get away from work. A break around December/January and a break around July/August is a necessity!

5. Which business areas do your clients mainly come from?

A high proportion of my client base is editorial. As Yo!Fest is quite young, so far a lot of our clients have come from all sorts of areas such as music, editorial, retail.

Is the number of your clients increasing or rather declining?

Myself and Yo!Fest seem to be getting busier, it's been a steady increase.

The void – hand drawn – Yo!Fest – 2007

Ego – hand drawn – crossfields – 2007

G&D – hand cut paper – G&D – 2007

149 magic carpet – hand drawn – Yo!Fest – 2007

Radio ladio – promo directed by Daniel Brereton – metronomy – 2007

6. Do you have a specific corporate philosophy or maybe a mission statement like other companies, which is reflected in the way you steer the studio's course?

I don't have a mission statement with which I aim to steer my work towards, but a Yo!Fest philosophy or outlook would be: "Good stuff, keep it nice".

7. What, from your point of view, makes the difference between a small studio and a big company?

A big company appears faceless because of the large number of employees, whereas a small studio is approachable and has personality.

8. What kind of advantages and disadvantages does a small studio have compared to a big company?

Advantages: Ease of communication. Independence and clarity of thought and vision. Autonomy over the work and business.

Disadvantages: None. I'm not envious of a big company or feel disadvantaged of my position.

Scorpion tail – digital – nylon x urban outfitters – 2007

9. What is your idea about the future of small studios?

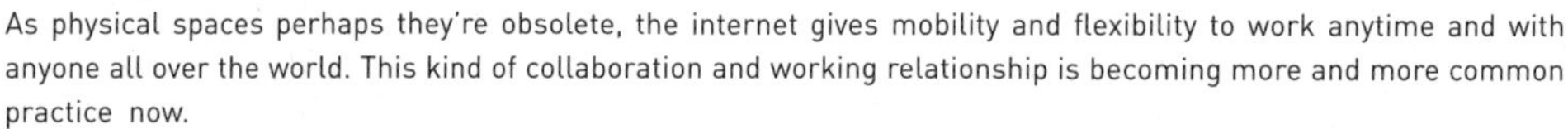

As physical spaces perhaps they're obsolete, the internet gives mobility and flexibility to work anytime and with anyone all over the world. This kind of collaboration and working relationship is becoming more and more common practice now.

Do you think that small studios do not have any other choice but to expand in order to survive in these times of globalization?

Growth is inevitable, but I don't think that this type of expansion necessarily means taking on more people and moving into bigger spaces. Studios are more multi-disciplinary today and are able to take on a greater variety of work from more diverse sectors, by growth I mean that studios and freelancers are learning to become more self-sufficient by acquiring more skills in areas that they had little or no knowledge of before.

10. Please describe and elaborate on the goals or plans that you have for your studio for the next five years?

I hope to keep enjoying what I do along with the work produced with Daniel. It's important to be open to change and open to collaboration. In the near future myself and Daniel would like Yo!Fest to become a real place, Yo!Ville. We will eventually buy an island where we will build an outdoor market, a bowling alley, a dentist's and a Turkish restaurant. It will be bigger and better than Richard Branson's island. Everyone will be welcome to visit.

Yo Jungle – hand drawn – Yo!Fest – 2007

Mouth – hand drawn – Yo!Fest – 2007

Yo!Tile – digital – Yo!Fest – 2007

1
2 x Goldstein
team:
Andrew Goldstein
Jeffrey Goldstein
contact:
Kriegsstr. 89
76133 Karlsruhe
Germany
T + 49 721 2016757
M + 49 175 1662709
F + 49 721 2016758
mail@2xgoldstein.de
www.2xgoldstein.de

2
"Nabi
team:
Sung Min Park
Bo Bae Kim
Chang Gun Kim
Se Young Lee
contact:
1f, Hyehwa Castle,
8-10 Hyehwa-dong,
Chongro-gu
110-530 Seoul
Korea
T + 82 2 7428742
F + 82 2 7423742
nabiooo@empal.com

3
Aaron Nieh Workshop
team:
Aaron Nieh
Yung-mei Nieh
contact:
3F, No.145, Sec. 2, Anhe Rd.
106 Taipei
Taiwan
T + 886 2 27358735
F + 886 2 27321550
somekidding@mac.com

4
Airdesign
| Stavitsky Design
team:
Vitaly Stavitsky
contact:
Razanskiy prospect 8a, build 1,
office 519
109428, Moskow
Russia
T + 7 495 2320433
F + 7 495 2320433
M + 7 495 5047969
vitaly@airdesign.ru
www.airdesign.ru

5
Alfalfa Studio
team:
Rafael Esquer
Jessica Covi
contact:
247 Centre Street, 6th Floor
10 013 New York
USA
T + 1 212 6299550
F + 1 212 3431343
raf@rafaelesquer.com
www.rafaelesquer.com

6
Amen
team:
Michaela Mansch
Claudio Prisco
contact:
Klenzestr. 99
80469 Munich
Germany
T + 49 89 20206501
F + 49 89 20206502
amen@soseies.com
www.soseies.com

7
Andersen M studio
team:
Martin Andersen
Line Andersen
contact:
10 Aylesbury Suite
City View House
463 Bethnal Green Road
E2 9QY London
United Kingdom
T + 44 20 77393918
martin@andersenm.com
www.andersenm.com

8
Apfel Zet
team:
Roman Bittner
Jarek Sierpinski
Julia Bittner
contact:
Brunnenstr. 7d
10119 Berlin
Germany
T + 49 30 68224853
F + 49 1805 996262953
contact@apfelzet.de
www.apfelzet.de

9
Appetite Engineers
team:
Martin Venezky
contact:
165 Jessie Street
2nd Floor
94105 California
USA
T + 1 650 4155380059
martin@appetiteengineers.com
www.appetiteengineers.com

10
B&J
team:
Brigitte Speich
Jaques Magiera
contact:
Prinzessinnenstr. 16
10969 Berlin
Germany
T + 49 30 65705231
F + 49 30 65705230
ja@materia.li
info@brigittespeich.com
www. materia.li
www.brigittespeich.com

11
Andreu Balius
team:
Andreu Balius
contact:
Milà i Fontanals 14-26
08012 Barcelona
Spain
T + 34 93 4591652
mail@andreubalius.com
www.andreubalius.com

12
Banana Moon Studio
team:
Hiroshi Maeda
contact:
312 Odori-Heim, Nishi-15,
Kita-1
Chuo-ku, Sapporo 060-0001
Japan
T + 81 11 6418776
F + 81 11 6416443
maeda@bananamoon.jp
www.bananamoon.jp

13
BANK™
team:
Sebastian Bissinger
Laure Boer
contact:
Rungestr. 22-24
10179 Berlin
Germany
T + 49 30 24047570
F + 49 30 24047571
tellme@bankassociates.de
www.bankassociates.de

14
Alex Bec
team:
Alex Bec
contact:
1 Pavan Court
114-116 Sceptre Road
E2 0JS London
United Kingdom
T + 44 77 09105590
hello@alexbec.com
www.alexbec.com

15
Better New World
team:
Kleon Medugorac
contact:
Mozartstr. 52
70180 Stuttgart
Germany
T + 49 711 2637443
kleon@gmx.net
www.better-new-world.com

16
Büro Weiss
team:
Christoph Bebermeier
Jan Pauls
contact:
Gabriel-Max-Str. 4
10245 Berlin
Germany
T + 49 30 78083780
F + 49 30 78083781
post@bueroweiss.de
www.bueroweiss.de

17
bueronardin
team:
Christof Nardin
contact:
Mariahilferstr. 9/7
1060 Wien
Austria
T + 43 699 19432298
cn@christofnardin.com
www.bueronardin.com

18
C2F Cybu Richli & Fabienne Burri
team:
Cybu Richli
Fabienne Burri
contact:
Kasimir-Pfyffer-Strasse 18a
CH-6003 Luzern
Switzerland
T + 41 41 240 44 24
to@c2f.to
www.c2f.to

19
Bouwe van der Molen
graphic design
team:
Bouwe van der Molen
contact:
Kramatweg 90-2
1095 KD, Amsterdam
The Netherlands
M + 31 6 49309255
info@bouwevandermolen.com
www.bouwevandermolen.com

20
Remo Caminada
team:
Donat Caduff
Remo Caminada
contact:
Puoz 229
7152 Sagogn
Switzerland
M + 31 654 948555
M + 41 78 8503322
info@remocaminada.com
www.remocaminada.com

21
Catalogtree
team:
Daniel Gross
Joris Maltha
contact:
Schoolstr. 35
6828 GT Arnhem
The Netherlands
T + 31 26 3895655
F + 31 26 3637252
mail@catalogtree.net
www.catalogtree.net

22
Savas Cekric
team:
Savas Cekic
Sendogan Yazici
contact:
Havyar Sk. No: 27/4
Cihangir 34433
Beyoglu Istanbul
Turkey
T + 21 224 96918
F + 21 224 55009
info@savascekric.com
www.savascekric.om

23
Change is good
team:
Rik Bas Baker
José Albergaria
contact:
20 rue Rochechouart
75009 Paris
France
T + 33 1 42213119
pleasewriteus@changeisgood.fr
www.changeisgood.fr

24
Stefan Claudius
team:
Stefan Claudius
contact:
Savignystr. 59
45147 Essen, Germany
T + 49 201 7268210
stefan@claudius-design.de
www.claudius-design.de

25
Collerette Coco Fill Lsd.
team:
Constant Mathieu
Laurent Baudoux
Fabrizio Terranova
contact:
98 rue du Coq
1180 Brussels, Belgium
F + 32 2 3721710
M + 32 485433146
constant@collerettecocofilllsd.com
www.collerettecocofilllsd.com

26
coup
team:
Peter van Denhoogen
Erica Terpstra
contact:
Zeeburgerpad 51bg
1019 Ab Amsterdam
The Netherlands
T + 31 20 4272584
hello@coup.nl
www.coup.nl/hello.html

27
De Desingpolitie
team:
Richard van der Laken
Pepijn Zurburg
contact:
Graaf Florisstr. 1a
1091 TD Amsterdam
The Netherlands
T + 31 20 4686720
F + 31 20 4686721
info@designpolitie.nl
www.designpolitie.nl

28
Dog Design
team:
Ilona Ilottu
Petri Salmela
Eeva Sivula
contact:
Tallberginkatu 1 C 145
00180 Helsinki
Finland
T + 358 9 6932343
M + 358 50 3545910
dog@dogdesign.fi
www.dogdesign.fi

29
Drop
team:
João Faria
João Guedes
contact:
Rua de Pedro Hispano 1271, 1º
4250-368 Porto, Portugal
T + 351 228300678
jfaria@drop.pt
www.drop.pt

30
Vladimir Dubko
team:
Vladimir Dubko
contact:
Room 502, 100/1, Chang Shu Rd.
200031 Shanghai (Jing An)
China
M + 86 15800468357 (Shanghai)
M + 85 267429870 (Hong Kong)
mailbox@vladimirdubko.com
www.vladimirdubko.com

31
Boris Dworschak
team:
Boris Dworschak
contact:
Theaterstr. 9a
75175 Pforzheim
Germany
T + 49 7231 1398778
F + 49 7231 1398776
info@borisdworschak.de
www.borisdworschak.de

32
Eboy
team:
Steffen Sauerteig
Svend Smital
Kai Vermehr
contact:
Gerichtstr. 12-13
Aufgang 2
13347 Berlin
Germany
T + 49 30 44008715
eboy@eboy.com
www.eboy.com

33
Eric and Marie
team:
Éric Gaspar
Marie Bertholle
contact:
45 Avenue Montaigne
75008 Paris
France
T + 33 1 47235127
info@ericandmarie.com
www.ericandmarie.com

34
Oded Ezer
team:
Oded Ezer
contact:
35a Gordon Street
Givatayim 53229, Israel
T + 972 542288042
F + 972 36725489
oded@ezerdesign.com
www.ezerdesign.com

35
Floor 5
team:
Marek Polewski
Jens Pieper
contact:
Friedrichstr. 127
10117 Berlin, Germany
T + 49 30 39747021
F + 49 30 39747010
info@floor5.de
www.floor5.de

36
Christina Föllmer
team:
Christina Föllmer
contact:
Bernardstraße 47-49
63067 Offenbach
Germany
T + 49 69 17511792
M + 49 179 5267515
hallo@christinafoellmer.de
www.christinafoellmer.de

37
Fontef
team:
Lahav Iontef
Yanek Halevy
contact:
31 Rothschild Blvd.
Room 35
66883 Tel Aviv
Israel
T + 972 3 5605801
F + 972 3 5602501
info@fontef.com
www.fontef.com

38
Futro ICB
team:
Slavimir Stojanovic
Melisa Antic, Nevena Petrovic
Aleksandar Milic
Marko Samardzija
Nebojsa Knezevic
contact:
Bul. Mihajla Pupina 6
11070 Novi Beograd
Serbia
T + 38 111 2200801 office@
futro-icb.com
www.futro-icb.com

39
General Working Group
team:
Geoff Kaplan
contact:
178 Amber Drive
94131 San Francisco, USA
T + 1 415 5581745
geoff@generalworkinggroup.com
www.generalworkinggroup.com

40
Gluekit
team:
Christopher Sleboda
Kathleen Burns
contact:
3331 Town Walk Drive
Hamden CT 06518, USA
T + 1 203 2872071
gluekit@comcast.net
www.gluekit.com

41
Grain Studio
team:
Imaya Wong
Hsueh-Yin Lin
contact:
33-1 Bangsar Heights
59100 Kuala. Lumpur,
Malaysia
T + 60 3 22872208
imaya.wong@gmail.com

42
Götz Gramlich
team:
Götz Gramlich
contact:
Treitschkestr. 3
69117 Heidelberg
Germany
T + 49 6221 8901656
F + 49 6221 8901666
M + 49 177 8654784
gg@gggrafik.de
www.gggrafik.de

43
Hi
team:
Megi Zumstein
Claudio Barandun
contact:
Neustadtstrasse 28
6003 Luzern
Switzerland
T + 41 41 3604366
megi.zumstein@hi-mail.ch
claudio.barandun@hi-mail.ch
www.hi-web.ch

44
Homework
team:
Joanna Górska
Jerzy Skakun
contact:
01-991 Warszawa
Poland
ul. Heroldów 21B/26
T + 48 600 941234
homework@hot.pl
www.homework.com.pl

45
Ice Cream for Free
team:
Oliver Wiegner
contact:
Anklamerstr. 13
10115 Berlin
Germany
T + 49 177 6283161
hello@icecreamforfree.com
www.icecreamforfree.com

46
Hiroshi Iguchi
team:
Hiroshi Iguchi
contact:
1-38-11, Chateau Yoyogi
Uehara #103,
Uehara, Shibuya-Ku,
151-0064 Tokyo
Japan
T/F + 81 3 34816481
info@thebwoy.com

47
Zsuzsanna Ilijin
team:
Zsuzsanna Ilijin
contact:
Kramatweg 90-2
1095 KD Amsterdam
The Netherlands
T + 31 0 648195426
www.ilijin.com
mail@ilijin.com

48
Jan en Randoald
team:
Randoald Sabbe
Jan W. Hespeel
contact:
Randoald Sabbe
S. de Mirabellostr. 28
9000 Gent
Belgium
T + 32 4 79296733
Jan W. Hespeel
Wezestr. 30a
8850 Ardooie
Belgium
T + 32 4 86756857
www.janenrandoald.be
info@janenrandoald.be

49
John Morgan Studio
team:
John Morgan
Michael Evidon
Catarina Pereira
Daniel Chehade
contact:
Room B.128
MacMillan House
Platform 1
Paddington Station
London W2 1FT
United Kingdom
F + 44 20 74026622
info@morganstudio.co.uk
www.morganstudio.co.uk

50
Jung und Wenig
team:
Christopher Jung
Tobias Wenig
contact:
Naumburgerstr. 44
Haus E
04229 Leipzig, Germany
info@jungundwenig.com
www.jungundwenig.com

51
Karlsonwilker
team:
Hjalti Karlsson
Jan Wilker
contact:
karlssonwilker inc
536 6th avenue
New York City 10011
USA
T + 1 212 9298064
F + 1 212 9298063
tellmewhy@karlssonwilker.com
www.karlssonwilker.com

52
Oliver Kartak
team:
Oliver Kartak
contact:
Gersthoferstr. 126/10
1180 Wien
Austria
T + 43 195 77127
M + 43 699 10410690
office@oliverkartak.com
www.oliverkartak.com

53
Kawakong Designworks
team:
Ong Chung Ping
Ng Ai Beng (Ming)
contact:
sunwaymas commercial
centre
92-A-3B, Jalan PJU1/3B
47301 Petaling Jaya
Selangor
Malaysia
T /F + 603 78809971
info@kawakong.com
www.kawakong.com

54
Harmen Liemburg
team:
Harmen Liemburg
contact:
Elandsstraat 201 B
1016 SC Amsterdam
The Netherlands
F + 31 20 4199456
mail@harmenliemburg.nl
www.harmenliemburg.nl

55
Lighthouse Media
team:
Dimitris Karaiskos
contact:
115 Zoodohou Pigis Str,
Athens 11473
Greece
T + 30 6948084263
dkaraisk@gmail.com

56
Lo Siento
team:
Borja Martinez Perez
Carolina Rodriguez
contact:
Comunicación gráfica
Palo Alto
Pellaires 30-38
08019 Barcelona
Spain
T + 34 933036492
www.losiento.net
borja@losiento.net

57
Matusiak
team:
Paulina Matusiak
contact:
Frans de Wollantstr. 12
1018 SC Amsterdam
The Netherlands
T + 31 20 3317797
M + 31 6 16508765
studio@matusiak.nl
www.matusiak.nl

58
merkwürdig
team:
Nadine Häfner
Jennifer Staudacher
Kai Staudacher
contact:
merkwürdig GmbH
Hanauer Landstr. 161-173
60314 Frankfurt am Main
Germany
T + 49 69 94943315
F + 48 69 94943309
www.merkwuerdig.com
info@merkwuerdig.com

59
Milkshake
team:
Javin Mo
Wilson Tang
contact:
3/F, B, Lam Shan Bldg,
113-119 Belcher's St.,
Kennedy Town,
Hong Kong
China
www.milkxhake.org
mix@aa.org

60
Mischen
team:
Barbara Bättig
Harri Kuhn
Vera Rammelmeyer
contact:
Erkelenzdamm 11-13
10999 Berlin
Germany
T + 49 30 44042082
F + 49 30 44042083
studio@mischen-berlin.de
www.mischen-berlin.de

61
Mixer
team:
Erich Brechbühl
Marco Sieber
Maurus Domeisen
Remko van Hoof
contact:
Löwenplatz 5
6004 Luzern,
Switzerland
T + 41 41 4103535
F + 41 41 4601504
erich@mixer.ch
www.mixer.ch

62
Monsters
team:
Pavel Frič
Lukáš Müller/lumír
Michaela Labudová/mlsa
Bery/dog
contact:
Michaela Labudová
U Blaženky 14
150 00 Prague 5
Czech Republic
T + 420 605 973498
pavelfricz@yahoo.co.uk
www.monsters.cz

63
Lesley Moore
team:
Alex Clay
Karin van den Brandt
contact:
Graphic Designers
Tweede Atjehstraat 60hs
1094 LK Amsterdam
The Netherlands
T + 31 20 6635110
mail@lesley-moore.nl
www.lesley-moore.nl

64
Julia Müller
team:
Julia Müller
Arjan Groot
contact:
Donker Curtiusstr. 25c
1051 JM Amsterdam
The Netherlands
M + 31 630047753
M + 49 163278874
jule@gmx.de
www.hellojulia.com

65
Niessen & de Vries
team:
Richard Niessen
Esther de Vries
contact:
Florijn 34
1102 BA Amsterdam
The Netherlands
T + 31 20 6633323
richard@tm-online.nl
www.niessendevries.nl

66
NLXL
team:
Bob van Dijk
Oscar Smeulders
Joost Roozekrans
contact:
Paviljoensgracht 70
2512 BR The Hague
The Netherlands
T + 31 70 3601770
F + 31 70 3469557
info@nlxl.com
www.nlxl.com

67
Node
team:
Anders Hofgaard
Llovet Casademont
Serge Rompza
contact:
Schwedterstr. 36a
10435 Berlin
Germany
T + 49 30 44049749
F + 49 30 44039332
mail@nodeberlin.com
----
c/o Supertanker
Pløensgate 4
0181 Oslo
Norway
T + 47 21 985777
mail@nodeoslo.com
www.nodeberlin.com

68
Nonameshop
team:
Gun-tae Kim
Jong-bum Kim
Jee-hyang Jun
Kyung-ok Park
Shin-hye Lee
Hye-yeon Lee
contact:
2F, 365-3, Seokyo-dong
KR-Mapo-gu, Seoul,
Korea
T + 82 2 3343556
nonamenoshop@nonameno-shop.com
rheomode@hanmail.net
www.nonamenoshop.com

69
Parallax Design PTY LTd
team:
Matthew Remphrey
Kellie Campbell
Sam Barrat
Lucy Fox
contact:
447 Pulteney Street
Adelaide SA 5000
Australia
T + 61 8 82328066
F + 61 8 82328055
matt@parallaxdesign.com.au
hello@parallaxdesign.com.au
www.parallaxdesign.com.au

70
Rose Pistola
team:
Karin Höfling
Holger Felten
Frank von Grafenstein
Beate Pietrek
Helene Kargruber
contact:
Neureutherstraße 19
80799 München
Germany
T +49 89 28701314
F +49 89 28701305
Lippmannstraße 53
22769 Hamburg
Germany
T +49 40 23517646
F +49 40 23517649
kh@rosepistola.de
www.rosepistola.de

71
Pixelgarten
team:
Adrian Nießler
Catrin Altenbrandt
contact:
c/o basis frankfurt
Elbestrasse 10 HH
60329 Frankfurt
Germany
T + 49 69 80087940/34
M + 49 160 7257997
info@pixelgarten.de
www.pixelgarten.de

72
Pony Ltd.
team:
Niall Sweeney
Nigel Truswell
Ollie
contact:
Unit 34, 1-13 Adler Street
London
E1 1EG
United Kingdom
T + 44 20 72477333
sugarcube@ponybox.co.uk
www.ponybox.com

73
Poor Designers
team:
Tassos Sapounakis
Demetris Tzavaras
Dimitris Kanellopoulos
George Yiakos
Kristine Fine
contact:
1 Kriezi & Sariy Str.
10553 Psirri, Athens
Greece
T + 30 21 175073901
aboutdesign@poordesigners.com
www.poordesigners.com

74
R2 Graphic Design
team:
Artur Rebelo
Elsa Silva
Liliana Pinto
Lıza Ramalho
Nuno Bastos
Safi
contact:
Rua de Meinedo, 112
4100-337 Porto
Portugal
T + 351 22 9386865
F + 351 22 6174915
artur@rdois.com
www.rdois.com

75
Slang International
team:
Nathanaël Hamon
contact:
Legiendamm 14
10179 Berlin
Germany
T + 49 177 2355434
nat@slanginternational.org
www.slanginternational.org

76
Catrin Sonnabend
team:
Catrin Sonnabend
contact:
Bötzowstr. 10
10407 Berlin
Germany
T + 49 30 66309697
M + 49 175 8052990
hallo@catrinsonnabend.de
www.catrinsonnabend.de

77
St. Pierre and Miquellon
team:
Simon Elvins
contact:
21C Bradiston Road
London W9 3HN
United Kingdom
www.st-pierre-and-miquelon.com
mail@st-pierre-and-miquelon.com

78
Stripe
team:
Gail Swanlund
Jon Sueda
contact:
5051 Eagle Rock
Boulevard ste. 212
Los Angeles, 90041
USA
T + 1 323 2551979
F + 1 323 2553545
jon@stripela.com
gail@stripela.com
www.stripela.com

79
Studio Pip and co.
team:
Ashton Andrew
Furzer Sarah
Lampe Elsie
Bennett Shelley
Band David
contact:
Suite 12/320 Carlisle Street
3183 Balaclava Victoria
Australia
T + 61 3 95259844
pipandco@peoplethings.com
www.peoplethings.com

80
Studio SM
team:
Sofia Leverbeck
Magnus Polbratt
contact:
20 Allen Road
Basement Flat
N16 8SD London
United Kingdom
T + 44 7 816062060
T + 44 7 817111809
hello@studio-sm.co.uk
www.studio-sm.co.uk

81
Superbüro
team:
Barbara Ehrbar
contact:
Mattenstr. 81
2503 Biel
Switzerland
T + 41 32 3232111
F + 41 32 3255122
info@superbuero.com
www.superbuero.ch

82
Ten
team:
Masahiro Kakinokihara
Jun Ishiguro
contact:
Ten.Inc.
111 Shoto Raj Bldg.,
1-26-10, Shoto, Shibuya-ku,
150-0046 Tokyo
Japan
T + 81 3 57381030
kaki@tuba.ocn.ne.jp
www.10inc.jp

83
Frédéric Teschner
team:
Frédéric Teschner
Olivier Lebrun
contact:
17 rue de la Révolution
93100 Montreuil
France
T + 33 1 48579894
f.teschner@wandadoo.fr
www.fredericteschner.com

84
Timo Thurner
team:
Timo Thurner
contact:
Ateliergemeinschaft Gerwin Schmidt
Zenettistrasse 27 rgb
80337 Munich
Germany
T + 49 89 74689494
F + 49 89 74689495
hello@timothurner.com
www.timothurner.com

85
Tin and Ed
team:
Tin Nguyen
Ed Cutting
contact:
Level 8, Room 15
37 Swanston Street
Melbourne, Victoria
Australia 3000
T + 61 3 96713777
design@tinanded.com.an
www.tinanded.com.au

86
Hermann van Bostelen
team:
Herman van Bostelen
contact:
Breedstr. 9A
3512 TS Utrecht
The Netherlands
T + 31 30 2231424
info@hermanvanbostelen.nl
www.hermanvanbostelen.nl

87
Vu-Huu Toan
team:
Vu-Huu Toan
contact:
17, boulevard de la Villette
75010 Paris
France
T + 33 9 53051610
M + 33 6 24170927
me@toanvuhuu.com
www.toanvuhuu.com

88
Annik Troxler
team:
Annik Troxler
contact:
Baldeggerstr. 54
4052 Basel
Switzerland
T + 41 61 3113919
info@anniktroxler.ch
www.anniktroxler.ch

89
Paula Troxler
team:
Paula Troxler
contact:
Herbartstrasse 11
8004 Zurich
Switzerland
T + 41 79 59871 67
paula.troxler@gmail.com
www.paulatroxler.com

90
Kin-Wah-Tsang
team:
Kin-Wah Tsang
contact:
1/F 10 Sha Tin Tau Village
Shatin Hong Kong
China
T + 852 9 3303314
kinwah02@yahoo.com.hk
www.tsangkinwah.com

91
Typecuts
team:
Andrea Tinnes
contact:
Das Deck
Schliemannstraße. 6
10437 Berlin, Germany
T + 49 30 61609554
F + 49 30 44031629
andrea@typecuts.com

92
Typotheque
team:
Peter Bilak
Johanna Bilak
contact:
Zwaardstraat 16
2584 TX The Hague
The Netherlands
T + 31 70 3226119
F + 31 84 8316741
info@typotheque.com
www.typotheque.com

93
U9 Visuelle Allianz
team:
Brita Wiesbach
Andrea Gnass
contact:
Fichtenstr. 15A
63071 Offenbach am Main
Germany
T + 49 69 8010150
F + 49 69 80101529
u9@u9.net
www.U9.net

94
Unolded
team:
Nadia Graf-Gisler
Friedrich-Wilhelm Graf
contact:
Weststr. 95
8003 Zurich
Switzerland
T + 41 44 4502582
F + 41 44 4610586
we@unfolded.ch
www.unfoldet.ch

95
Visual Group Budapest
team:
David Barath
Aron Barath
Valentin Bajkov
contact:
Graphisoft Park
Apartmanház, fszt. 1.
Záhony u. 7.
1031 Budapest
Hungary
david@visualgroup.hu
www.visualgroup.hu

96
Zhi-Hong Wang
team:
Zhi-Hong Wang
Yu-Wen Hsu
contact:
2F., No.5, Alley 3, Lane 359,
Fujin St., Songshan District,
10583 Taipei, Taiwan
T + 886 2 27635359
art.wzh@msa.hinet.net

97
Werkplaats Amsterdam
team:
Pieter Boddaert
Yolanda Huntelaar
contact:
Balistr. 43a
1094 JC Amsterdam
The Netherlands
T/F + 31 20 6630083
post@werkplaatsamsterdam.nl
www.werkplaatsamsterdam.nl

98
Martin Woodtli
team:
Martin Woodtli
contact:
Schöneggstr. 5
8004 Zurich
Switzerland
T + 41 44 2912419
F + 41 44 2912429
martin@woodt.li
www.woodt.li

99
Xiao Mage + Chengzi
team:
Xiao Mage
Chengzi
contact:
Dongsi 12 Tiao 21 Hao,
Room 402,
100708 Beijing
China
maggy2004@126.com

100
Yo! Fest
team:
Colin Henderson
Daniel Brereton
contact:
Studio 101F,
203 Mare Street,
Hackney, London E8 3QE
United Kingdom
T + 44 7921135125
heyo@yofest.co.uk
www.colin-henderson.co.uk
www.yofest.co.uk

Book Concept by hesign

Hesign was established in 2002. The Hesign team is dedicated to bringing about cooperation between European and Asian publishing institutes. In accordance with its expertise in art and graphic design, Hesign has focused itself on two types of publications, namely graphic design and fine art. Since 2005, Hesign has begun independent work on investment, publication and distribution. It continues to place emphasis on exploring professional art and design works from different countries while distributing publications in markets around Asia and Europe. (www.hesign.com)

All Man are Brothers - Designer's Edition / 25 x 18 cm / Berlin / 2006 / Hesign Publishing (Shanghai, Berlin)/ ISBN: 7-80142-734-3 / A luxurious book asking 108 leading contemporary graphic designers eight basic questions on life and design, and showing their recent work. The title refers to a famous Chinese classical novel about 108 heros fighting for freedom, for the poor and against the rich, and for mutual respect of each other.

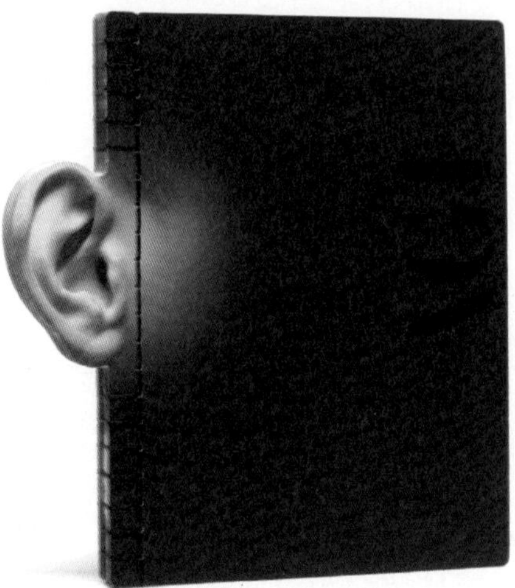

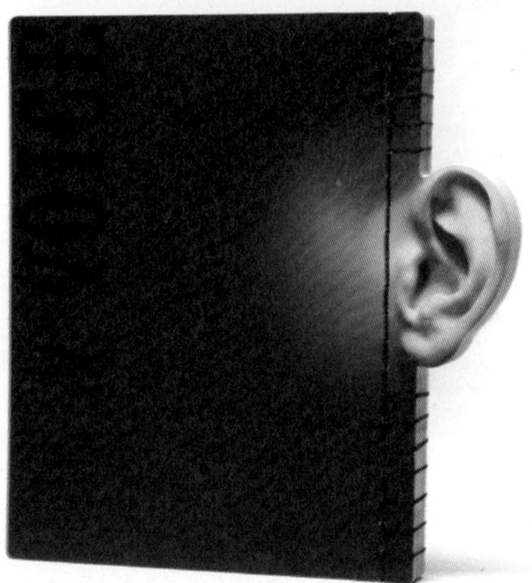

AGI - New Voice / 21 x 15 / Berlin / 2006 / Hesign Publishing Berlin, Germany / ISBN: 3-9810544-5-8 / 280 pages with more than 343 color illustrations, featuring the AGI New members 2004/2005 with their work and reports about AGI Congress in Beijing (2004) and Berlin (2005).

AGI - To Kyo To / 21 x 16 cm / Berlin / July 2007 / ISBN: 978-3-9810544-6-0 / Hesign Publishing (Berlin/Shanghai) / The book includes reports about the AGI Congress "To Kyo To" in Tokyo and Kyoto,2006, Japan, which international leading graphic designers under the theme "Diversity of Japanese Culture" participated in. The congress "To Kyo To" showed the opposites in Japanese Culture, more specifically directed to graphic design, in relation to the characteristic flatness of Japanese Graphic Design. The book consists of 276 pages with more than 407 color illustrations, featuring the work of the new AGI members 2006.

Designer Portraits / 22 x 29,7 cm / Berlin / Sept. 2007 / Hesign Publishing (Shanghai, Berlin) / ISBN: 978-3-9810544-8-4 / Portraits of graphic designers and a 500-page publication. This was the point of departure for the exhibition of Kunst zone D4 2007. The motivation for Melchior Imboden and the D4 Business Center Luzern in taking on such a daunting project was to combine in perfect harmony the fascination for photography and poster design . World stars in graphic design tookpart .

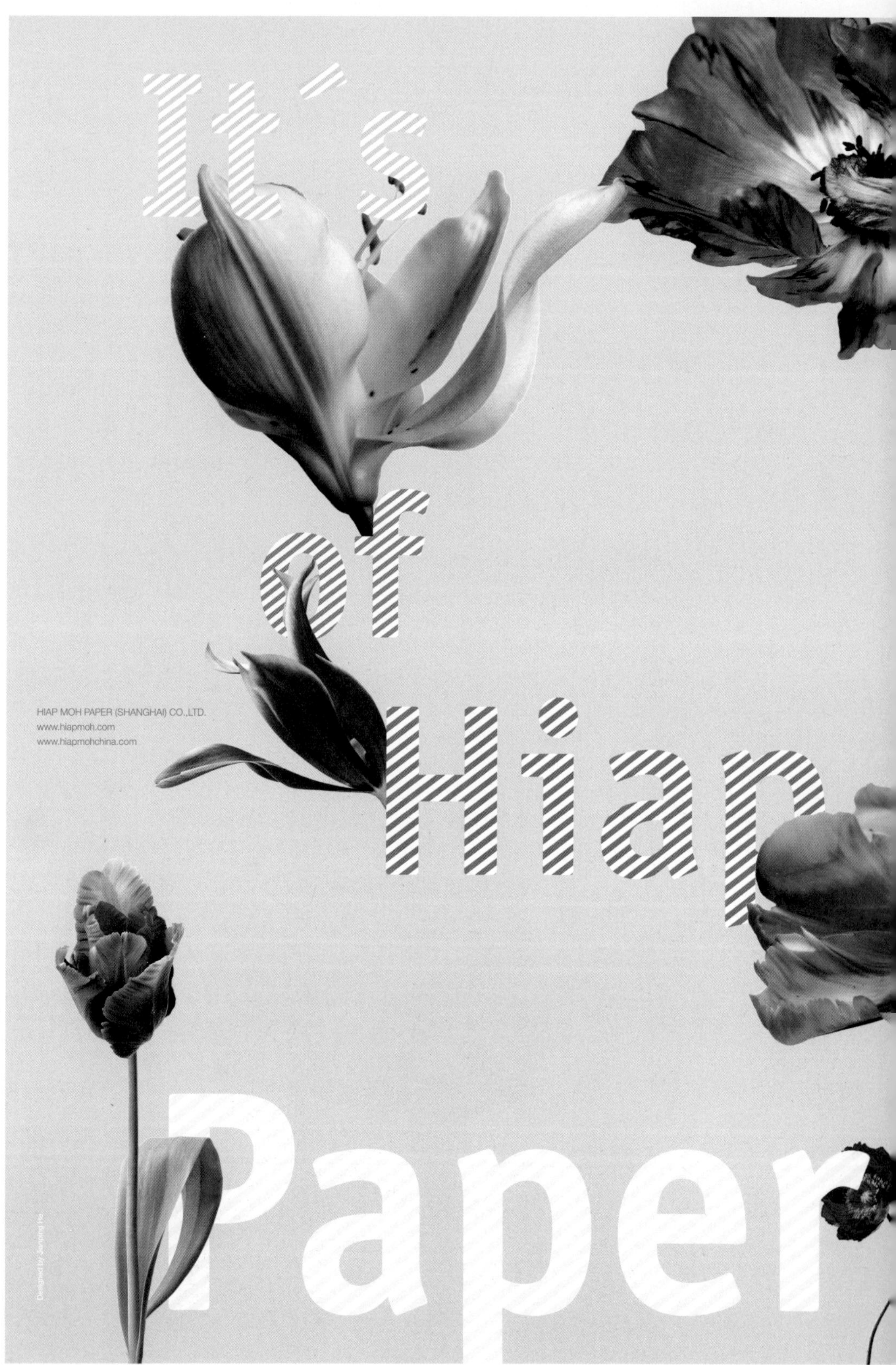
It's
of
Hiap
Paper
HIAP MOH PAPER (SHANGHAI) CO.,LTD.
www.hiapmoh.com
www.hiapmohchina.com
Designed by Janping He

the
World
Moh
HM

Small Studios Imprint

ISBN 978-981-245-823-0

Printed in China

Published in 2010 by:
Page One Publishing Pte Ltd
20 Kaki Bukit View
Kaki Bukit Techpark II
Singapore 415956
Tel: (65) 6742-2088
Fax: (65) 6744-2088
enquiries@pageonegroup.com
www.pageonegroup.com

Editor: Jianping He
Design & Layout: Jianping He
Staff: Katharina Wanner (10.2007 - 12.2007)
Annika Wolfzettel (09.2007 - 09.2008)
Susann Szilágyi (03.2008 - 08.2008)
Simone Amrein (05.2008 - 09.2008)
Magdalena Leupold (09.2008 - 12.2008)
Translation & Proofreading: Michael Funk
Paper: Hiap Moh Paper (Shanghai)

hesign (Publishing & Design)
Germany
Düsseldorfer Str. 48
D-10707 Berlin, Germany
Tel.: +49-30-88676915; Fax: +49-30-88676915
China
hesign International (Hangzhou)
No. 1 Chuangyi Rd. Zhuantang Town
West Lake District, 310024 Hangzhou
PR. China
Tel: + 86-571-8709 8605
info@hesign.com
www.hesign.com
www.hesignchina.com

hesign special thank to:
Majid Abbasi, Sang-Soo Ahn, Dimitris Arvanitis, Pierre Bernard, Michel Bouvet, Erik Brandt, Francois Caspar, Anke Feuchtenberger, Joseph Foo, Piet Gerards, Catherine Griffits, Klaus Hesse, Fons Hickmann, Andreas Homann, Yossi Lemel, Tommy Li, Susan Liang, Pekka Loiri, Junyi Lu, Lech Majewski, Shin Matsunaga, Hideki Nakajima, Istvan Orosz, Kari Piippo, Stefan Sagmeister, U.G. Sato, Clemens Theobert Schedler, Ralph Schraivogel, Leonardo Sonnoli, Bernard Stein, Henry Steiner, David Tartakover, Niklaus Troxler and all participating designers.

small studios

PAGE ONE

small
studios

PAGE ONE

small studios

PAGEONE